W9-CBH-395

DATE DUE

JUL 2 9 2010	

DEMCO, INC. 38-2931

200 Best Jobs® for Introverts

Part of JIST's Best Jobs® Series

The Editors @ JIST **and Laurence Shatkin, Ph.D.**

Also in JIST's Best Jobs® Series

- Best Jobs for the 21st Century
- 200 Best Jobs for College Graduates
- 300 Best Jobs Without a Four-Year Degree
- 250 Best Jobs Through Apprenticeships
- 50 Best Jobs for Your Personality
- 40 Best Fields for Your Career

- 225 Best Jobs for Baby Boomers
- 250 Best-Paying Jobs
- 175 Best Jobs Not Behind a Desk
- 150 Best Jobs for Your Skills
- 150 Best Jobs Through Military Training
- 150 Best Jobs for a Better World

200 Best Jobs for Introverts

© 2008 by JIST Publishing

Published by JIST Works, an imprint of JIST Publishing
7321 Shadeland Station, Suite 200
Indianapolis, IN 46256-3923

Phone: 800-648-JIST   Fax: 877-454-7839
E-mail: info@jist.com   Web site: www.jist.com

Some Other Books by the Authors

The Editors at JIST

EZ Occupational Outlook Handbook

Salary Facts Handbook

Enhanced Occupational Outlook Handbook

Guide to America's Federal Jobs

Health-Care CareerVision Book and DVD

Laurence Shatkin

90-Minute College Major Matcher

Quantity discounts are available for JIST products. Have future editions of JIST books automatically delivered to you on publication through our convenient standing order program. Please call 800-648-JIST or visit www.jist.com for a free catalog and more information.

Visit www.jist.com for information on JIST, free job search information, book excerpts, and ordering information on our many products.

Acquisitions Editor: Susan Pines
Development Editor: Stephanie Koutek
Cover and Interior Designer: Aleata Halbig
Cover Image: Photodisc Red/Getty Images
Interior Layout: Aleata Halbig
Proofreaders: Paula Lowell, Jeanne Clark
Indexer: Cheryl Lenser

Printed in the United States of America

12 11 10 09 08 07   9 8 7 6 5 4 3 2 1

   Library of Congress Cataloging-in-Publication Data
200 best jobs for introverts / the editors at JIST and Laurence Shatkin.
        p. cm. -- (JIST's best jobs series)
   Includes index.
   ISBN 978-1-59357-477-2 (alk. paper)
   1. Introverts--Vocational guidance--United States. 2. Introverts--Employment--United States. 3. Vocational qualifications--United States. 4. Job hunting--United States. 5. Occupations--United States--Classification. I. Shatkin, Laurence. II. JIST Publishing. III. Title: Two hundred best jobs for introverts.
   HF5382.694.U6A15 2008
   331.7020973--dc22

                                                                                                                2007035436

We have been careful to provide accurate information throughout this book, but it is possible that errors and omissions have been introduced. Please consider this in making any career plans or other important decisions. Trust your own judgment above all else and in all things.

ISBN 978-1-59357-477-2

This Is a Big Book, But It Is Very Easy to Use

Do you like working by yourself, quietly focusing on the task at hand? Do you dislike having your concentration interrupted by the telephone or by people who drop by for idle chit-chat? You may be an introvert.

Introverts sometimes get frustrated working in today's service-based economy, with so many jobs that emphasize serving the public or working in teams. But this book lists lots of good jobs that let you work by yourself and without interruptions. The jobs on the lists are selected and ordered to emphasize those with the highest earnings and the highest demand for workers. Specialized lists arrange these jobs by the level of education or training required and by interest fields. You can also see lists of jobs that have high percentages of part-time or self-employed workers.

Every job is described in detail later in the book, so you can explore the jobs that interest you the most. You'll learn the major work tasks, all the important skills, educational programs, and many other informative facts.

Using this book, you'll be surprised how quickly you'll get new ideas for career goals that can let you work in the solitary style you prefer and can suit you in many other ways.

Some Things You Can Do with This Book

- Identify introvert-friendly jobs that don't require you to get additional training or education.
- Develop long-term career plans that may require additional training, education, or experience.
- Explore and select a training or educational program that relates to a career objective that suits your personality.
- Prepare for interviews by learning how to connect your work preferences to your career goal.

These are a few of the many ways you can use this book. We hope you find it as interesting to browse as we did to put together. We have tried to make it easy to use and as interesting as occupational information can be.

When you are done with this book, pass it along or tell someone else about it. We wish you well in your career and in your life.

Credits and Acknowledgments: While the authors created this book, it is based on the work of many others. The occupational information is based on data obtained from the U.S. Department of Labor and the U.S. Census Bureau. These sources provide the most authoritative occupational information available. The job titles and their related descriptions are from the O*NET database, which was developed by researchers and developers under the direction of the U.S. Department of Labor. They, in turn, were assisted by thousands of employers who provided details on the nature of work in the many thousands of job samplings used in the database's development. We used the most recent version of the O*NET database, release 11.0. We appreciate and thank the staff of the U.S. Department of Labor for their efforts and expertise in providing such a rich source of data.

Table of Contents

Summary of Major Sections

Introduction. A short overview to help you better understand and use the book. *Starts on page 1.*

Part I. Overview of Introversion and Careers. Explains what introversion is and how it relates to career choice. This section includes a discussion of the workplace advantages of introversion and how these can be useful in a career. *Starts on page 13.*

Part II. The Best Jobs Lists. Very useful for exploring career options! The first group of lists presents the 200 best introvert-friendly jobs overall. These jobs are selected to have a high level of working alone; have a low level of interruptions from other people; and be outstanding in terms of earnings, job growth, and job openings. Another series of lists gives the 50 best-paying introvert-friendly jobs, the 50 fastest-growing introvert-friendly jobs, and the 50 introvert-friendly jobs with the most openings. More-specialized lists follow, presenting jobs with particular features attractive to introverts. You can also see lists of the best jobs that have a high concentration of certain kinds of workers (for example, workers in certain age brackets, part-time workers, or female workers) and lists with the jobs organized by level of education or training and by interest area. The column starting at right presents all the list titles. *Starts on page 21.*

Part III. Descriptions of the Best Jobs for Introverts. Provides complete descriptions of the jobs that appear on the lists in Part II. Each description contains information on work tasks, skills, education and training required, earnings, projected growth, job duties, related knowledge and courses, and many other details. *Starts on page 107.*

Appendix A. Resources for Further Exploration. A helpful list of resources to learn more about careers, career decision making and planning, and searching for a job. *Starts on page 407.*

Appendix B. The GOE Interest Areas and Work Groups. This list of the 16 GOE Interest Areas and their related Work Groups can help you narrow down your career interests. *Starts on page 409.*

Detailed Table of Contents

Introduction

Not everybody will want to read this introduction. You may want to skip this background information and go directly to Part I, which discusses introversion and its relationship to careers, or Part II, which lists the best jobs for introverts.

But if you want to understand how (and why) we put this book together, where the information comes from, and what makes a job "introvert-friendly" and "best," this introduction can answer a lot of questions.

Where the Information Came From

The information we used in creating this book came mostly from databases created by the U.S. Department of Labor:

⊚ We started with the job information included in the Department of Labor's O*NET (Occupational Information Network) database, which is now the primary source of detailed information on occupations. The Labor Department updates the O*NET on a regular basis, and we used the most recent one available—O*NET release 11. Data from the O*NET allowed us to determine the amount of solitary work that characterizes each job, among other topics.

⊚ We linked the information from the O*NET to several other kinds of data that the U.S. Bureau of Labor Statistics collects: on earnings, projected growth, number of openings, part-time workers, and self-employed workers. For data on these topics, the BLS uses a slightly different set of job titles than the O*NET uses, so we had to match similar titles. In a few cases, we could not obtain data about each of these topics for every occupation. Nevertheless, the information we report here is the most reliable data we could obtain.

⊚ We used the Classification of Instructional Programs, a system developed by the U.S. Department of Education, to cross-reference the education or training programs related to each job.

Of course, information in a database format can be boring and even confusing, so we did many things to help make the data useful and present it to you in a form that is easy to understand.

1

How the Best Jobs for Introverts Were Selected

Here is the procedure we followed to select the 200 jobs we included in the lists in this book:

1. We began with the 949 job titles in the O*NET database. Of these, 741 have the full range of information—economic topics, work tasks, skills, and work conditions—needed for a reasonably complete description in this book. We eliminated 13 jobs that are expected to employ fewer than 500 workers per year and to shrink rather than grow in workforce size and that therefore cannot be considered best jobs.

2. Next we eliminated 62 jobs with annual median earnings of less than $20,000. These jobs are held by roughly the lowest 25 percent of wage-earners. Some introvert-friendly jobs that were eliminated were Nonfarm Animal Caretakers; Maids and Housekeeping Cleaners; Packers and Packagers, Hand; and Dishwashers. Although these jobs have characteristics that are appealing to introverts and some employ a lot of workers, their low pay makes them unlikely to be of interest to the readers of this book. Admittedly, some of the jobs that do appear in this book—such as Slaughterers and Meat Packers—may not appeal to you for other reasons, but we'll leave it to you to decide how you feel about other aspects of jobs.

3. We combined several O*NET jobs because information on job openings is available only at a higher level of aggregation. For example, we combined three inspecting jobs in the field of transportation because the Department of Labor reports the job openings only for a combined occupation called Transportation Inspectors. The list at this point included 583 jobs.

4. For each job, we looked at two measures in the O*NET database that indicate characteristics that are important to introverts. One is a work-related value called Independence, which is defined as doing work alone. Every job has a rating between 1 and 5 on this measure. The other measure is a work-context feature called Contact with Others, which represents how much the job requires workers to be in contact with others—whether that contact is face-to-face, by telephone, or otherwise. This measure also uses a rating scale between 1 and 5, so we subtracted each job's rating from 5 to determine the amount to which the job *does not* involve contact with others. We then took the average of these two measures to get an overall score indicating how friendly the job is to introverts.

5. We ordered all 583 jobs by this introversion score, from highest to lowest, and then cut this list in half by removing the least-introverted half of the jobs and keeping the most-introverted half.

6. We ranked the 291 remaining introverted jobs three times, based on these major criteria: median annual earnings, projected growth through 2014, and number of job openings projected per year.

7. We then added the three numerical rankings for each job to calculate its overall score.

8. To emphasize jobs that tend to pay more, are likely to grow more rapidly, and have more job openings, we selected the 200 job titles with the best total overall scores.

For example, the introverted job with the best combined score for earnings, growth, and number of job openings is Computer Software Engineers, Applications, so this job is listed first even though it is not the best-paying job (which is Astronomers), the fastest-growing job (which is Network Systems and Data Communications Analysts), or the job with the most openings (which is Stock Clerks and Order Fillers).

Why This Book Has More Than 200 Job Descriptions

We didn't think you would mind that this book actually provides information on more than 200 jobs. We combined several jobs to create the lists in Part II, as mentioned earlier, but in Part III we describe these jobs separately. This means that although we used 200 job titles to construct the lists, Part III actually has a total of 225 job descriptions.

Understand the Limits of the Data in This Book

In this book we use the most reliable and up-to-date information available on earnings, projected growth, number of openings, and other topics. The earnings data came from the U.S. Department of Labor's Bureau of Labor Statistics. As you look at the figures, keep in mind that they are estimates. They give you a general idea about the number of workers employed, annual earnings, rate of job growth, and annual job openings.

Understand that a problem with such data is that it describes an average. Just as there is no precisely average person, there is no such thing as a statistically average example of a particular job. We say this because data, while helpful, can also be misleading.

Take, for example, the yearly earnings information in this book. This is highly reliable data obtained from a very large U.S. working population sample by the Bureau of Labor Statistics. It tells us the average annual pay received as of May 2005 by people in various job titles (actually, it is the median annual pay, which means that half earned more and half less).

This sounds great, except that half of all people in that occupation earned less than that amount. For example, people who are new to the occupation or with only a few years of work experience often earn much less than the median amount. People who live in rural areas or who work for smaller employers typically earn less than those who do similar work in cities (where the cost of living is higher) or for bigger employers. People in certain areas of the country earn less than those in others. Other factors also influence how much you are likely to earn in a given job in your area. For example, Aircraft Mechanics and Service Technicians in the Detroit–Warren–Livonia, Michigan, metropolitan area have median earnings of $73,070, probably because Northwest Airlines has a hub at Detroit and their mechanics are unionized. By comparison, the New Haven, Connecticut, metropolitan area has no major airline hub and only a small aircraft service facility with nonunionized workers; Aircraft Mechanics and Service Technicians there earn only a median of $26,280.

Also keep in mind that the figures for job growth and number of openings are projections by labor economists—their best guesses about what we can expect between now and 2014. They are not guarantees. A major economic downturn, war, or technological breakthrough could change the actual outcome.

Finally, don't forget that the job market consists of both job openings and job *seekers*. The figures on job growth and openings don't tell you how many people will be competing with you to be hired. The Department of Labor does not publish figures on the supply of job candidates, so we are unable to tell you about the level of competition you can expect. Competition is an important issue that you should research for any tentative career goal. The *Occupational Outlook Handbook* provides informative statements for many occupations. You should speak to people who educate or train tomorrow's workers; they probably have a good idea of how many graduates find rewarding employment and how quickly. People in the workforce also can provide insights into this issue. Use your critical thinking skills to evaluate what people tell you. For example, educators or trainers may be trying to recruit you, whereas people in the workforce may be trying to discourage you from competing. Get a variety of opinions to balance out possible biases.

So, in reviewing the information in this book, please understand the limitations of the data. You need to use common sense in career decision making as in most other things in life. We hope that, using that approach, you find the information helpful and interesting.

The Data Complexities

For those of you who like details (and introverts often do), we present some of the complexities inherent in our sources of information and what we did to make sense of them here. You don't need to know this to use the book, so jump to the next section of the introduction if you are bored with details.

We include information on earnings, projected growth, and number of job openings for each job throughout this book.

Earnings

The employment security agency of each state gathers information on earnings for various jobs and forwards it to the U.S. Bureau of Labor Statistics. This information is organized in standardized ways by a BLS program called Occupational Employment Statistics, or OES. To keep the earnings for the various jobs and regions comparable, the OES screens out certain types of earnings and includes others, so the OES earnings we use in this book represent straight-time gross pay exclusive of premium pay. More specifically, the OES earnings include the job's base rate; cost-of-living allowances; guaranteed pay; hazardous-duty pay; incentive pay, including commissions and production bonuses; on-call pay; and tips but do not include back pay, jury duty pay, overtime pay, severance pay, shift differentials, nonproduction bonuses, or tuition reimbursements. Also, self-employed workers are not included in the estimates, and they can be a significant segment in certain occupations. When data on annual earnings for an occupation is highly unreliable, OES does not report a figure, which meant that we reluctantly had to exclude from this book a few occupations such as Hunters and Trappers. The median earnings for all workers in all occupations were $30,400 in May 2006. The 200 introvert-friendly jobs in this book were chosen partly on the basis of good earnings, so their average is a respectable $39,281.

The data from the OES survey is reported under a system of job titles called the Standard Occupational Classification system, or SOC. These are the job titles we use in the lists in Part II, but in Part III we cross-reference these titles to O*NET job titles so we can provide O*NET-derived information on many useful topics. In some cases, an SOC title cross-references to more than one O*NET job title. For example, the SOC title Architectural and Civil Drafters, which we use in Part II, is linked to two jobs described in Part III: Architectural Drafters and Civil Drafters. Because earnings data is available only for the combined job title Architectural and Civil Drafters, in Part III you will find the same earnings figure, $40,390, reported for both kinds of drafters. In reality there probably is a difference in what the two kinds of drafters earn, but this is the best information that is available.

Projected Growth and Number of Job Openings

This information comes from the Office of Occupational Statistics and Employment Projections, a program within the Bureau of Labor Statistics that develops information about projected trends in the nation's labor market for the next ten years. The most recent projections available cover the years from 2004 to 2014. The projections are based on information about people moving into and out of occupations. The BLS uses data from various sources in projecting the growth and number of openings for each job title—some data comes from the Census Bureau's Current Population Survey and some comes from an OES survey. The projections assume that there will be no major war, depression, or other economic upheaval.

Like the earnings figures, the figures on projected growth and job openings are reported according to the SOC classification, so again you will find that some of the SOC jobs that we use in Part II crosswalk to more than one O*NET job in Part III. To continue the example we used earlier, SOC reports growth (4.6 percent) and openings (9,000) for one occupation called Architectural and Civil Drafters, but in Part III of this book we report these figures separately for the occupation Architectural Drafters and for the occupation Civil Drafters. In Part III, when you see that Architectural Drafters is described as having 4.6 percent projected growth and 9,000 projected job openings and Civil Drafters is described with the same two numbers, you should realize that the 4.6-percent rate of projected growth represents the *average* of these two occupations—one may actually experience higher growth than the other—and that these two occupations will *share* the 9,000 projected openings.

While salary figures are fairly straightforward, you may not know what to make of job-growth figures. For example, is projected growth of 15 percent good or bad? Keep in mind that the average (mean) growth projected for all occupations by the Bureau of Labor Statistics is 13.0 percent. One-quarter of the SOC occupations have a growth projection of 3.2 percent or lower. Growth of 11.6 percent is the median, meaning that half of the occupations have more, half less. Only one-quarter of the occupations have growth projected at more than 17.4 percent.

You're probably already aware that much of the job growth in our economy is happening for jobs with a lot of interpersonal contact—for example, jobs in health care. As a result, many of the fastest-growing jobs are not attractive to introverts and are not included in this book. Therefore, even though the jobs in this book were selected as "best" partly on the basis of job growth, their mean growth is 11.7 percent, which is slightly lower than the mean for all jobs. Among these 200 jobs, the job ranked 50th by projected growth has a figure of 15.6 percent, the job ranked 100th (the median) has a projected growth of 10.6 percent, and the job ranked 150th has a projected growth of 4.7 percent.

The number of job openings for introvert-friendly jobs is similar to the rate of job growth: lower than the national average for all occupations. The Bureau of Labor statistics projects an average of about 35,000 job openings per year for the 750 occupations that it studies, but for the 200 occupations included in this book, the average is slightly more than 20,000 openings. The job ranked 50th for job openings has a figure of 18,000 annual openings, the job ranked 50th (the median) has 7,000 openings projected, and the job ranked 150th has 2,000 openings projected.

Perhaps you're wondering why we present figures on both job growth *and* number of openings. Aren't these two ways of saying the same thing? Actually, you need to know both. Consider the occupation Hydrologists, which is projected to grow at the outstanding rate of 31.6 percent. There should be lots of opportunities in such a fast-growing job, right? Not exactly. This is a tiny occupation, with only about 8,000 people currently employed, so even though it is growing rapidly, it will not create many new jobs (about 1,000 per year). Now consider Bookkeeping, Accounting, and Auditing Clerks. This occupation is growing at the sluggish rate of 5.9 percent, held back by computer programs that automate many routine clerical tasks. Nevertheless, this is a huge occupation that employs more than two million workers, so even though its growth rate is unimpressive, it is expected to take on 291,000 new workers each year as existing workers retire, die, or move on to other jobs. That's why we base our selection of the best jobs on both of these economic indicators and why you should pay attention to both when you scan our lists of best jobs.

How This Book Is Organized

The information in this book about best introvert-friendly jobs moves from the general to the highly specific.

Part I. Overview of Introversion and Careers

What exactly is an introvert? Part I defines the term and explains how this aspect of your personality interacts with certain aspects of the work environment and thus can have a great effect on your overall satisfaction with your job. You'll also see the strengths introverts bring to the workplace and how these strengths can compensate for some of the challenges that introverts face.

Part II. The Best Jobs Lists

For many people, the 76 lists in Part II are the most interesting feature of the book. Here you can see titles of the 200 introvert-friendly jobs that have the best combination of high salaries, fast growth, and plentiful job openings. You can see which jobs are best in terms of each of these factors combined and considered separately. Additional lists highlight jobs with a high percentage of female, male, part-time, and self-employed workers. Look in the Table of Contents for a complete list of lists. Although there are a lot of lists, they are not difficult to understand because they have clear titles and are organized into groupings of related lists.

Depending on your situation, some of the lists in Part II will interest you more than others. For example, if you are young, you may be interested in the best-paying introverted jobs that employ high percentages of people age 16–24. Other lists show jobs within interest groupings, personality types, levels of education, or other ways that you might find helpful in exploring your career options.

Whatever your situation, we suggest you use the lists that make sense for you to help explore career options. Following are the names of each group of lists along with short comments on each group. You will find additional information in a brief introduction provided at the beginning of each group of lists in Part II.

Best Jobs Overall: Best Jobs for Introverts with the Highest Pay, Fastest Growth, and Most Openings

Four lists are in this group, and they are the ones that most people want to see first. The first list presents the top 200 introverted job titles in order of their combined scores for earnings, growth, and number of job openings. Three more lists in this group are extracted from the 200 best and present the 50 jobs with the highest earnings, the 50 jobs projected to grow most rapidly, and the 50 jobs with the most openings.

Best Jobs with Particular Features Attractive to Introverts

Each of these lists shows the 20 jobs that have the greatest amount of a feature that appeals to introverts: solitary work, little contact with others, independent decision making, lack of exposure to the public, and quiet.

Best Jobs Lists by Demographic

This group of lists presents interesting information for a variety of types of people based on data from the U.S. Census Bureau. The lists are arranged into groups for workers age 16–24, workers 55 and older, part-time workers, self-employed workers, women, and men. We created five lists for each group, basing the last four on the information in the first list:

- The jobs for introverts having the highest percentage of people of each type
- The 25 jobs with the highest combined scores for earnings, growth, and number of openings
- The 25 jobs with the highest earnings
- The 25 jobs with the highest growth rates
- The 25 jobs with the largest number of openings

Best Jobs for Introverts Sorted by Education or Training Required

We created separate lists for each level of education, training, and experience as defined by the U.S. Department of Labor. We put each of the top 200 job titles into one of the lists based on the kind of preparation required for entry. Jobs within these lists are presented in order of their total combined scores for earnings, growth, and number of openings. The lists include introvert-friendly jobs in these groupings:

- Short-term on-the-job training
- Moderate-term on-the-job training
- Long-term on-the-job training
- Work experience in a related job
- Postsecondary vocational training
- Associate degree
- Bachelor's degree
- Work experience plus degree
- Master's degree
- Doctoral degree
- First professional degree

Best Jobs for Introverts Sorted by Interests

These lists organize the 200 best jobs into groups based on interests. Within each list, jobs are presented in order of their total scores for earnings, growth, and number of openings. Here are the 16 interest areas used in these lists: Agriculture and Natural Resources; Architecture and Construction; Arts and Communication; Business and Administration; Education and Training; Finance and Insurance; Government and Public Administration; Health Science; Hospitality, Tourism, and Recreation; Human Service; Information

Technology; Law and Public Safety; Manufacturing; Retail and Wholesale Sales and Service; Scientific Research, Engineering, and Mathematics; and Transportation, Distribution, and Logistics.

Best Jobs for Introverts Sorted by Personality Types

These lists organize the 200 best jobs into six personality types described in the introduction to the lists: Realistic, Investigative, Artistic, Social, Enterprising, and Conventional. The jobs within each list are presented in order of their total scores for earnings, growth, and number of openings.

Part III: Descriptions of the Best Jobs for Introverts

This part contains 225 job descriptions and covers each of the 200 best jobs for introverts, using a format that is informative yet compact and easy to read. The descriptions contain statistics such as earnings and projected percent of growth; ratings of solitary work and contact with others; lists such as major skills and work tasks; and key descriptors such as personality type and interest field. Because the jobs in this section are arranged in alphabetical order, you can easily find a job that you've identified from Part II and that you want to learn more about.

In some cases, a job title in Part II cross-references to two or more job titles in Part III. For example, if you look up Nuclear Technicians in Part III, you'll find a note telling you to look at the descriptions for Nuclear Equipment Operation Technicians and Nuclear Monitoring Technicians. That's why there are 225 descriptions in Part III rather than 200.

We used the most current information from a variety of government sources to create the descriptions. Although we've tried to make the descriptions easy to understand, the sample that follows—with an explanation of each of its parts—may help you better understand and use the descriptions.

Here are some details on each of the major parts of the job descriptions you will find in Part III:

- **Job Title:** This is the job title for the job as defined by the U.S. Department of Labor and used in its O*NET database.

- **Data Elements:** The information comes from various U.S. Department of Labor and Census Bureau databases, as explained elsewhere in this Introduction. The Level of Solitary Work is based on the value Independence in the O*NET database. The Level of Contact with Others is based on the work-context factor Contact with Others in the same database. These two "level" ratings use a scale in which 0 is the lowest level and 100 is the highest. These ratings are not percentages and represent the amount of the feature that *characterizes* the job, not the amount of *time* spent working a certain way.

◎ **Summary Description and Tasks:** The bold sentence provides a summary description of the occupation. It is followed by a listing of tasks that are generally performed by people who work in this job. This information comes from the O*NET database but where necessary has been edited to avoid exceeding 2,200 characters.

◎ **Personality Type:** The O*NET database assigns each job to its most closely related personality type. Our job descriptions include the name of the related personality type as well as a brief definition of this personality type.

Job Title →

Data Entry Keyers

◎ Education/Training Required: Moderate-term on-the-job training

Data Elements →
◎ Annual Earnings: $23,810
◎ Growth: –0.7%
◎ Annual Job Openings: 85,000
◎ Self-Employed: 1.0%
◎ Part-Time: 20.9%

Level of Solitary Work: 81.2 (out of 100)

Level of Contact with Others: 83.5 (out of 100)

Summary Description and Tasks →
Operate data entry device, such as keyboard or photo-composing perforator. Duties may include verifying data and preparing materials for printing. Read source documents such as canceled checks, sales reports, or bills and enter data in specific data fields or onto tapes or disks for subsequent entry, using keyboards or scanners. Compile, sort, and verify the accuracy of data before it is entered. Compare data with source documents or re-enter data in verification format to detect errors. Store completed documents in appropriate locations. Locate and correct data entry errors or report them to supervisors. Maintain logs of activities and completed work. Select materials needed to complete work assignments. Load machines with required input or output media such as paper, cards, disks, tape, or Braille media. Resolve garbled or indecipherable messages, using cryptographic procedures and equipment.

Personality Type →
Personality Type: Conventional. Conventional occupations frequently involve following set procedures and routines. These occupations can include working with data and details more than with ideas. Usually there is a clear line of authority to follow.

GOE Information →
GOE—**Interest Area:** 04. Business and Administration. **Work Group:** 04.08. Clerical Machine Operation. **Other Jobs in This Work**

Group: Billing, Posting, and Calculating Machine Operators; Mail Clerks and Mail Machine Operators, Except Postal Service; Office Machine Operators, Except Computer; Switchboard Operators, Including Answering Service; Word Processors and Typists.

Skills—Service Orientation: Actively looking for ← **Skills** ways to help people. **Social Perceptiveness:** Being aware of others' reactions and understanding why they react as they do.

Education and Training Programs: Business/Office ← Automation/Technology/Data Entry; Data Entry/ Microcomputer Applications, General; Graphic and Printing Equipment Operator, General Production. **Education and Training Program(s)** **Related Knowledge/Courses: Clerical Practices:** Administrative and clerical procedures and systems such as word processing, managing files and records, stenography and transcription, designing forms, and other office procedures and terminology. **Economics** ← **Related Knowledge/Courses** **and Accounting:** Economic and accounting principles and practices, the financial markets, banking, and the analysis and reporting of financial data. **Computers and Electronics:** Circuit boards, processors, chips, electronic equipment, and computer hardware and software, including applications and programming. **Customer and Personal Service:** Principles and processes for providing customer and personal services. This includes customer needs assessment, meeting quality standards for services, and evaluation of customer satisfaction. **Personnel and Human Resources:** Principles and procedures for personnel recruitment, selection, training, compensation and benefits, labor relations and negotiation, and personnel information systems. **Administration and Management:** Business and management principles involved in strategic planning, resource allocation, human resources modeling, leadership technique, production methods, and coordination of people and resources.

Work Environment: Indoors; noisy; sitting; using ← **Work Environment** hands on objects, tools, or controls; repetitive motions.

⊚ **GOE Information:** This information cross-references the Guide for Occupational Exploration (or the GOE), a system developed by the U.S. Department of Labor that organizes jobs based on interests. We use the groups from the *New Guide for Occupational Exploration*, Fourth Edition, as published by JIST. That book uses a set of interest areas based on the 16 career clusters developed by the U.S. Department of Education and used in a variety of career information systems. Here we include the major Interest Area the job fits into, its more-specific Work Group, and a list of related O*NET job titles that are in this same GOE Work Group. This information will help you identify other job titles that have similar interests or require similar skills, but note that not all jobs in a work group are equally friendly to introverts. You can find a list of the GOE Interest Areas and Work Groups in Appendix B.

⊚ **Skills:** For each job, we included the skills whose level-of-performance scores exceeded the average for all jobs by the greatest amount and whose ratings on the importance scale were higher than very low. We included as many as 6 such skills for each job, and we ranked them by the extent to which their rating exceeds the average.

⊚ **Education and Training Program(s):** This part of the job description provides the name of the educational or training program or programs for the job. It will help you identify sources of formal or informal training for a job that interests you. To get this information, we adapted a crosswalk created by the National Center for O*NET Development to connect information in the Classification of Instructional Programs (CIP) to the O*NET job titles we use in this book. We made various changes to connect the O*NET job titles to the education or training programs related to them and also modified the names of some education and training programs so they would be more easily understood. In three cases, we abbreviated the listing of related programs for the sake of space; such entries end with "others."

⊚ **Related Knowledge/Courses:** This entry can help you understand the most important knowledge areas that are required for a job and the types of courses or programs you will likely need to take to prepare for it. We used information in the Department of Labor's O*NET database for this entry. For each job, we identified any knowledge area with a rating that was higher than the average rating for that knowledge area for all jobs; then we listed as many as six in descending order.

⊚ **Work Environment:** We included any work condition with a rating that exceeds the midpoint of the rating scale. The order does not indicate their frequency on the job. Consider whether you like these conditions and whether any of these conditions would make you uncomfortable. Keep in mind that when hazards are present (for example, contaminants), protective equipment and procedures are provided to keep you safe.

Getting all the information we used in the job descriptions was not a simple process, and it is not always perfect. Even so, we used the best and most recent sources of data we could find, and we think that our efforts will be helpful to many people.

PART I

Overview of Introversion and Careers

You probably consider yourself an introvert—that's why you're reading this book. In this section of the book we look at what an introvert is and is not. We consider why you need to consider your introversion when you make a career choice, the strengths your personality brings to the job, and the workplace disadvantages of introversion, together with suggestions for how to overcome these by using your strengths.

Although introverts make up only 25 percent of the population (estimates vary), they make up a majority of the gifted population. Many highly successful people are thought to be introverts—even some presidents of the United States. So start feeling good about your introversion (if you don't already) and learn how to make the most of it in your career.

What Is an Introvert?

The psychologist Carl Jung described two kinds of people: **extroverts,** whose psychic energy flows inward, gained from other people; and **introverts,** whose psychic energy flows outward, gained from solitude. Nowadays the concept of psychic energy is not taken literally, but psychologists continue to recognize that some people are stimulated by social settings and feel most comfortable there, whereas others are more energetic and productive when they can escape distractions caused by other people. So psychologists still speak of introverts and extroverts, and it can be helpful to understand whether your personality leans toward one of these types.

Do you seek out social occasions, or do you treasure the time you get to spend alone? When you're traveling on a plane or bus, do you like to strike up a conversation with the person sitting next to you, or do you prefer to keep your thoughts to yourself? When you're alone in a public place, do you tend to take out your cell phone and call up a friend, or do you leave the cell phone alone? When you're alone at home, do you usually turn on the television or curl up with a good book or crossword puzzle? When you're working, do you like to have music or talk radio playing in the background, or do you prefer a quiet environment? Do you check your e-mail constantly or only as often as necessary? Do you work best collaboratively or solo? Depending on how you answered these questions, you may be showing some of the behaviors of an extrovert or an introvert.

If your answers showed a strong preference for solitude and quiet, *200 Best Jobs for Introverts* is going to be very useful to you. This book will help you identify good jobs that are well suited to introverted people. The unfortunate fact is that introvert-friendly jobs are harder to find than they used to be. The U.S. economy has shifted toward service industries such as health care and hospitality. As a result, more and more opportunities will be found in jobs that involve a lot of interpersonal contact, and chances to work alone will become more scarce. Even jobs in manufacturing are increasingly being done by teams of workers.

Fortunately, there are still plenty of well-paid introvert-friendly jobs for people who prefer them and who are willing to make the effort to seek them out. That's where this book can help you. We identified 200 jobs that tend to be done alone; that are rarely interrupted by visitors and phone calls; and that offer a good combination of earnings, job growth, and job openings. So browse the lists in Part II to find introverted jobs that match your interests, your age group, your work preferences (for example, for self-employment), and your plans for education or training. Then read the job descriptions in Part III to get more detailed facts and narrow down your choices.

What Does Introversion Have to Do with Career Choice?

One of the cornerstones of modern career development theory is the idea of *person-environment fit,* sometimes called *congruence.* The idea is that people will be most satisfied with their work and most productive if the work environment fits their personality. You've probably heard a clichéd version of this idea expressed in terms of "fitting round pegs into round holes."

So psychologists try to understand the "shapes" of people's personalities, and one very conspicuous dimension is the tendency toward introversion or extroversion. Not everybody tends toward one extreme or the other, but for many people the presence or absence of social contact and distractions can be a very important factor that determines whether a job will be satisfying or frustrating. Research has shown that this factor can contribute more to job satisfaction than a 10 percent raise in pay. Therefore many career counselors encourage their clients to consider whether they are introverted or extroverted as part of the process of career exploration and choice.

One resource that career counselors sometimes use, the Myers-Briggs Type Indicator (MBTI), is a personality test that includes a measure of extroversion (spelled *extraversion*) and introversion. MBTI uses this measure along with three other dimensions to suggest careers that might be suitable.

The extroversion-introversion dimension also can be applied to the personality types theorized by John L. Holland. During the 1950s, Holland was trying to find a meaningful new way to arrange the output of an interest inventory and relate it to occupations. He devised a set of six personality types and called them Realistic, Investigative, Artistic, Social, Enterprising, and Conventional. (The acronym RIASEC is a convenient way to remember them.)

If you're unfamiliar with these terms, they may be a little hard to understand, and you'll find the following descriptions useful. They define the personality types in terms of the occupations that fit well:

- **Realistic:** These occupations frequently involve work activities that include practical, hands-on problems and solutions. They often deal with plants; animals; and real-world materials such as wood, tools, and machinery. Many of the occupations require working outside and do not involve a lot of paperwork or working closely with others.

- **Investigative:** These occupations frequently involve working with ideas and require an extensive amount of thinking. These occupations can involve searching for facts and figuring out problems mentally.

- **Artistic:** These occupations frequently involve working with forms, designs, and patterns. They often require self-expression, and the work can be done without following a clear set of rules.

- **Social:** These occupations frequently involve working with, communicating with, and teaching people. These occupations often involve helping or providing service to others.

- **Enterprising:** These occupations frequently involve starting up and carrying out projects. These occupations can involve leading people and making many decisions. They sometimes require risk taking and often deal with business.

- **Conventional:** These occupations frequently involve following set procedures and routines. These occupations can include working with data and details more than with ideas. Usually there is a clear line of authority to follow.

From these definitions, you can see that the Realistic and Social types characterize the opposite extremes of the introverted and extroverted personality types.

Holland arranged his six types on a hexagon to show their relationships with one another, and the diagram also serves to illustrate how all six personality types align on the introversion-extroversion axis. As you'll see in Part II, introvert-friendly jobs tend to be associated with the Realistic, Conventional, and Investigative types.

If you use an assessment, such as the *Self-Directed Search,* that uses Holland personality types in its score report, you may want to consider what your output reveals about your tendency toward introversion or extroversion. Use Figure 1 as a map to help you find your tendency. For example, if your score report produces the code RI (indicating that your personality borders between Realistic and Investigative), you probably lean toward introversion.

Researchers have found that people who show introverted behavior off the job are more likely to be working where social interaction is also low on the job. So it appears that people are naturally gravitating toward jobs that suit their personalities. With the help of this book, you can identify good jobs that are likely to suit your tendency toward introversion.

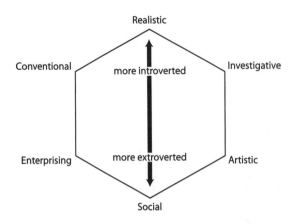

Figure 1: Holland's hexagon of personality types. (Modified from Holland, A Theory of Vocational Choice, *1959.)*

What Strengths Do Introverts Bring to the Job?

Extroverts often misunderstand introverts and think there's something wrong with being introverted. But introversion can be a useful personality trait that helps get the job done, especially if you understand what introversion is and organize your job to take advantage of its strengths.

Introversion is not the same thing as shyness; it does not mean being afraid of or anxious about social situations. In fact, some introverts are highly skilled at social interaction. But introverts *prefer* to work without a lot of social contact, or perhaps only in contact with a familiar group, because they find the presence of other people distracting and energy-draining.

When introverts are able to focus on the task at hand without interruptions, they often are able to provide very thoughtful solutions to problems. Their patience and persistence enable them to solve problems that take a long time to complete and that require mastery of both the big picture and the details. By avoiding a herd mentality, introverts can produce highly original ideas. The volume of their work output also may be very high, because they don't have to adjust their work pace to fit other people's schedules or preferences. Introverts tend to be good writers, because they prefer to give a thoughtful response rather than work out their ideas in conversation. Research shows that multitasking tends to lower productivity, so the introverted workers' tendency to turn off their cell phones and ignore e-mail arrivals probably makes them more efficient.

What Challenges Do Introverts Face on the Job?

Today's workplace has embraced the notion that communication should be instantaneous, thus increasing opportunities for introverts to be interrupted by questions, suggestions, and minor problems that demand to be treated like emergencies. In some offices e-mail is not considered fast enough; workers are expected to respond to instant-messaging programs that flash impossible-to-ignore alerts each time a communication arrives. Workers are assigned to cubicles, where there is no door that can be closed to fend off interruptions, and workers are often asked to multitask—for example, talking to a client on the phone while making corrections to a spreadsheet. This environment can make introverts feel as if they cannot achieve the focus they need to do their work well.

The team-oriented workplace is another environment that is not friendly to introverts. A popular management theory says that workers are more productive and turn out work of higher quality when they are organized into teams. This may be true for extroverts, but introverts may rightly feel that this environment prevents them from doing the kind of thoughtful problem solving that is their particular strength.

If you know you're introverted, you may be able to make arrangements that diminish some of the unfriendly aspects of your work environment. With your skills for analytical thinking, you should be able to identify the aspects of your job that most trouble you, set priorities among them, and prepare a thoughtful set of suggestions to take to your boss or co-workers. Try to negotiate arrangements with co-workers so that you'll have times when you're not interrupted except for emergencies. Perhaps you can get your boss to allow you to work at home for one or more days in the week. But in any such arrangement, accept the fact that at other times, when you are easy to access, you will have to make accommodations for people who interrupt your work. In meetings, ask for ground rules that allow everyone to be heard and try to schedule time-outs that will allow you to gather your thoughts.

In some jobs it may be impossible to shape the work environment into one where you feel comfortable. A nurse, a fitness trainer, a classroom teacher, or a movie director has to work in constant contact with other people, often in highly distracting situations. That's why this book can be helpful: as a guide to occupations where your introversion can help you do the job well.

Perhaps the biggest challenge of all is not doing the job well, but *getting* the job. The most effective way of finding a job—networking—is a technique that introverts may resist using because it involves so much social contact. Introverts can network successfully by concentrating on the strengths that they bring to the task: their understanding of themselves, their ability to articulate their skills, and their ability to cultivate relationships over time.

Finding a job opening is only half the battle; you still need to convince the employer to hire you. Introverts may be highly effective at crafting the perfect resume and cover letter, but they run the risk of being misunderstood in job interviews, especially if the person interviewing them is an extrovert. The interviewer may perceive them as "guarded," "reserved," "standoffish," "private," or "too serious."

Again, introverts can compensate by using their strengths, especially their ability to prepare for the interview. A good book about interviewing techniques, such as *The Career Coward's Guide to Interviewing* (JIST Publishing), can help you anticipate many standard interview questions and prepare a thoughtful answer. Apply your research skills and do a thorough job of finding out whatever you can about the employer—and, if possible, the interviewer. Jot down some notes that will suggest intelligent questions you can ask about the business and your future role there. Assemble a portfolio that will provide examples of your best work. Your thorough knowledge of the business, your pointed questions, and your specific examples of your work will help dispel the notion that you are "aloof."

It also helps to apply for jobs where introversion is common or even the norm and where the odds are better that your employment interviewer will be used to working with introverts. The reverse situation can create problems: For jobs where extroversion is an advantage, employers sometimes administer personality tests to weed out introverts. That's okay—you probably wouldn't like those jobs anyway! Focus your efforts on the jobs where your personality will be appealing to the interviewer. Here again this book can be helpful.

How Can I Use the Information About Jobs in This Book?

This book focuses on 200 introvert-friendly jobs that also have good income and job opportunities. As you look over the jobs listed in Part II and described in Part III, keep in mind that the job should suit your *whole* personality—not just your introversion. Don't assume that the more introvert-friendly the job is, the happier you'll be doing that job.

Take another look at the hexagonal diagram of Holland personality types (Figure 1) that you saw earlier in this section. The most introverted personality type of the six is the Realistic type, but many highly introverted people are not interested in work activities that involve practical, hands-on problems and solutions. For example, these people may prefer searching for facts and figuring out problems mentally—activities that characterize the Investigative type. Or they may prefer the set procedures and routines that characterize Conventional jobs. You can identify the introvert-friendly jobs associated with all six Holland types in Part II under the heading "Best Jobs for Introverts Sorted by Personality Types."

These large personality issues are not the only considerations you should bear in mind as you evaluate possible career goals. You'll want to read the job descriptions in Part III to learn whether the specific tasks, skills, and other requirements of the job meet your interests and abilities; whether the context of the work (for example, an outdoor setting) suits you; and whether the level and type of education or training required are consistent with your aspirations and resources.

Because you're an introvert, these words of caution may not be necessary. Introverts tend to research their options and weigh them carefully before making a choice. But remember that research in books or on the Web is not thorough enough for a decision of this importance. When you have identified a job that looks promising, you should visit a workplace and observe the workers, their tasks, and their surroundings. Prepare some questions to ask workers or the people who educate and train workers. They probably won't mind if—in true introverted style—you cut through the chit-chat and move quickly to your specific questions. You'll save them time from their workday and you'll find out what you need to know about the job.

PART II

The Best Jobs Lists

This part contains a lot of interesting lists, and it's a good place for you to start using the book. Here are some suggestions for using the lists to explore career options that introverts may find satisfying:

◎ The table of contents at the beginning of this book presents a complete listing of the list titles in this section. You can browse the lists or use the table of contents to find those that interest you most.

◎ We gave the lists clear titles, so most require little explanation. We provide comments for each group of lists.

◎ As you review the lists of jobs, one or more of the jobs may appeal to you enough that you want to seek additional information. As this happens, mark that job (or, if someone else will be using this book, write it on a separate sheet of paper) so that you can look up the description of the job in Part III.

◎ Keep in mind that all jobs in these lists meet our basic criteria for being included in this book, as explained in the introduction. All lists, therefore, contain jobs that offer lots of opportunities for solitary and focused work, with emphasis on occupations that have high pay, high growth, or large numbers of openings. These economic measures are easily quantified and are often presented in lists of best jobs in the newspapers and other media. While earnings, growth, and openings are important, there are other factors to consider in your career planning. Obviously you are considering the amount of solitary, undistracted work that characterizes the job; that's why you're reading this book. Other examples of factors to consider are location, liking the people you work with, and having opportunities to be creative. Many other factors that may help define the ideal job for you are difficult or impossible to quantify and thus are not used in this book, so you will need to consider the importance of these issues yourself.

◎ All data used to create these lists comes from the U.S. Department of Labor and the Census Bureau. The earnings figures are based on the average annual pay received by full-time workers. Because the earnings represent the national averages, actual pay rates can vary greatly by location, amount of previous work experience, and other factors.

Some Details on the Lists

The sources of the information we used in constructing these lists are presented in this book's introduction. Here are some additional details on how we created the lists:

- Some jobs have the same scores for one or more data elements. For example, in the category of growth, two jobs (Pest Control Workers and Sound Engineering Technicians) are expected to grow at the same rate, 18.4 percent. Therefore we ordered these two jobs alphabetically, and their order has no other significance. There was no way to avoid these ties, so simply understand that the difference of several positions on a list may not mean as much as it seems.

- Some job titles represent combinations of two or more closely related jobs. For example, here in Part II you will find a job called Architectural and Civil Drafters. The U.S. Department of Labor provides data on earnings, job growth, and job openings for Architectural and Civil Drafters, so this job title is useful for the purposes of these lists. In Part III, however, where you'll turn to find more detailed information about the jobs on these lists, you can find *separate* descriptions of the jobs Architectural Drafters and Civil Drafters. That level of detail is more appropriate for that section of the book.

Best Jobs Overall: Best Jobs for Introverts with the Highest Pay, Fastest Growth, and Most Openings

The four sets of lists that follow are the most important lists in this book. The first set of lists presents the jobs meeting the criteria for this book with the highest combined scores for pay, growth, and number of openings. These are very appealing lists because they represent introvert-friendly jobs with the very highest quantifiable measures from our labor market. The 200 jobs in the first list are the basis for all the job lists in Part II and are described in detail in Part III.

The three additional sets of lists present 50 jobs with the highest scores on each of three measures: annual earnings, projected percentage growth, and largest number of openings.

The 200 Best Jobs Overall for Introverts

This is the list that most people want to see first. You can see the introverted jobs that have the highest overall combined ratings for earnings, projected growth, and number of openings. (The section in the introduction called "How the Best Jobs for Introverts Were Selected" explains in detail how we rated jobs to assemble this list.)

You'll notice a wide variety of jobs on the list. For example, although the top 10 jobs are dominated by the computer and business fields, among the top 50 you'll also find jobs in scientific research, mechanical repair, construction, and the arts. Some fields are not well represented, however, because jobs in these fields tend to require working closely with other people. Thus you'll find few jobs in education, social service, and health care.

A look at the list will clarify how we ordered the jobs. The occupation with the best total score was Computer Software Engineers, Applications, so it tops the list. Coming in at second place is the related job Computer Software Engineers, Systems Software. Although it offers better earnings than the top-ranked job, it is expected to offer slightly slower growth and considerably fewer job openings—and therefore had a lower total score. The other occupations follow in descending order based on their total scores. Many jobs had tied scores and were simply listed one after another, so there are often only very small or even no differences between the scores of jobs that are near each other on the list. All other jobs lists in this book use these jobs as their source list. You can find descriptions for each of these jobs in Part III, beginning on page 107. If a job appeals to you, or if you're not sure what it is, find it alphabetically in Part III and read the description.

The 200 Best Jobs Overall for Introverts

Job	Annual Earnings	Percent Growth	Annual Openings
1. Computer Software Engineers, Applications	$77,090	48.4%	54,000
2. Computer Software Engineers, Systems Software	$82,120	43.0%	37,000
3. Computer Systems Analysts	$68,300	31.4%	56,000
4. Network Systems and Data Communications Analysts	$61,750	54.6%	43,000
5. Accountants and Auditors	$52,210	22.4%	157,000
6. Lawyers	$98,930	15.0%	40,000
7. Financial Analysts	$63,860	17.3%	28,000
8. Personal Financial Advisors	$63,500	25.9%	17,000
9. Medical Scientists, Except Epidemiologists	$61,730	34.1%	15,000
10. Market Research Analysts	$57,300	19.6%	20,000
11. Civil Engineers	$66,190	16.5%	19,000
12. Database Administrators	$63,250	38.2%	9,000
13. Cost Estimators	$52,020	18.2%	15,000
14. Plumbers, Pipefitters, and Steamfitters	$42,160	15.7%	61,000
15. Writers and Authors	$46,420	17.7%	14,000
16. Heating, Air Conditioning, and Refrigeration Mechanics and Installers	$37,040	19.0%	33,000
17. Environmental Scientists and Specialists, Including Health	$52,630	17.1%	8,000
18. Electrical Engineers	$73,510	11.8%	12,000
19. Graphic Designers	$38,390	15.2%	35,000
20. Actuaries	$81,640	23.2%	3,000
21. Technical Writers	$55,160	23.2%	5,000
22. Appraisers and Assessors of Real Estate	$43,440	22.8%	9,000
23. Electronics Engineers, Except Computer	$78,030	9.7%	11,000

(continued)

(continued)

The 200 Best Jobs Overall for Introverts

Job	Annual Earnings	Percent Growth	Annual Openings
24. Editors	$45,510	14.8%	16,000
25. Automotive Service Technicians and Mechanics	$33,050	15.7%	93,000
26. Bus and Truck Mechanics and Diesel Engine Specialists	$36,620	14.4%	32,000
27. Bus Drivers, Transit and Intercity	$31,010	21.7%	34,000
28. Tile and Marble Setters	$36,530	22.9%	9,000
29. Payroll and Timekeeping Clerks	$31,360	17.3%	36,000
30. Truck Drivers, Heavy and Tractor-Trailer	$34,280	12.9%	274,000
31. Aircraft Mechanics and Service Technicians	$47,310	13.4%	11,000
32. Hazardous Materials Removal Workers	$33,690	31.2%	11,000
33. Electrical and Electronic Engineering Technicians	$48,040	9.8%	18,000
34. Maintenance and Repair Workers, General	$31,210	15.2%	154,000
35. Roofers	$31,230	16.8%	38,000
36. Interior Designers	$41,350	15.5%	10,000
37. Clergy	$38,540	12.4%	26,000
38. Telecommunications Line Installers and Repairers	$42,410	10.8%	23,000
39. Cement Masons and Concrete Finishers	$32,030	15.9%	32,000
40. Brickmasons and Blockmasons	$41,860	12.0%	17,000
41. Operating Engineers and Other Construction Equipment Operators	$35,830	11.6%	37,000
42. Aerospace Engineers	$84,090	8.3%	6,000
43. Commercial and Industrial Designers	$52,200	10.8%	7,000
44. Hydrologists	$63,820	31.6%	1,000
45. Computer Programmers	$63,420	2.0%	28,000
46. Operations Research Analysts	$62,180	8.4%	7,000
47. Desktop Publishers	$32,800	23.2%	8,000
48. Biochemists and Biophysicists	$71,000	21.0%	1,000
49. Elevator Installers and Repairers	$59,190	14.8%	3,000
50. Painters, Construction and Maintenance	$30,800	12.6%	102,000
51. Atmospheric and Space Scientists	$73,940	16.5%	1,000
52. Painters, Transportation Equipment	$34,840	14.1%	10,000
53. Environmental Science and Protection Technicians, ncluding Health	$36,260	16.3%	6,000
54. Epidemiologists	$52,170	26.2%	1,000
55. Automotive Body and Related Repairers	$34,810	10.3%	18,000
56. Mobile Heavy Equipment Mechanics, Except Engines	$39,410	8.8%	14,000

The 200 Best Jobs Overall for Introverts

Job	Annual Earnings	Percent Growth	Annual Openings
57. Health and Safety Engineers, Except Mining Safety Engineers and Inspectors	$65,210	13.4%	2,000
58. Water and Liquid Waste Treatment Plant and System Operators	$34,930	16.2%	6,000
59. Private Detectives and Investigators	$32,650	17.7%	7,000
60. Materials Engineers	$69,660	12.2%	2,000
61. Truck Drivers, Light or Delivery Services	$24,790	15.7%	169,000
62. Microbiologists	$56,870	17.2%	1,000
63. Drywall and Ceiling Tile Installers	$34,740	9.0%	17,000
64. Mechanical Engineering Technicians	$44,830	12.3%	5,000
65. Financial Examiners	$63,090	9.5%	3,000
66. Landscaping and Groundskeeping Workers	$20,670	19.5%	243,000
67. Music Directors and Composers	$34,810	10.4%	11,000
68. Medical Equipment Repairers	$39,570	14.8%	4,000
69. Chemists	$57,890	7.3%	5,000
70. Reinforcing Iron and Rebar Workers	$34,910	14.1%	6,000
71. Sound Engineering Technicians	$38,390	18.4%	2,000
72. Motorboat Mechanics	$32,780	15.1%	7,000
73. Electrical Power-Line Installers and Repairers	$50,150	2.5%	11,000
74. Geoscientists, Except Hydrologists and Geographers	$71,640	8.3%	2,000
75. Computer, Automated Teller, and Office Machine Repairers	$36,060	3.8%	31,000
76. Tree Trimmers and Pruners	$27,920	16.5%	11,000
77. Machinists	$34,350	4.3%	33,000
78. Postal Service Mail Carriers	$46,330	0.0%	19,000
79. Nuclear Technicians	$61,120	13.7%	1,000
80. Telecommunications Equipment Installers and Repairers, Except Line Installers	$50,620	–4.9%	21,000
81. Bookkeeping, Accounting, and Auditing Clerks	$29,490	5.9%	291,000
82. Soil and Plant Scientists	$54,530	13.9%	1,000
83. Paving, Surfacing, and Tamping Equipment Operators	$30,320	15.6%	7,000
84. Fashion Designers	$60,860	8.4%	2,000
85. Cartographers and Photogrammetrists	$48,250	15.2%	1,000
86. Transportation Inspectors	$49,490	11.4%	2,000
87. Bus Drivers, School	$24,070	13.6%	76,000
88. Embalmers	$36,960	15.7%	2,000
89. Architectural and Civil Drafters	$40,390	4.6%	9,000
90. Mechanical Drafters	$43,350	5.5%	7,000

(continued)

(continued)

The 200 Best Jobs Overall for Introverts

Job	Annual Earnings	Percent Growth	Annual Openings
91. Crossing Guards	$20,050	19.7%	26,000
92. Fine Artists, Including Painters, Sculptors, and Illustrators	$41,280	10.2%	4,000
93. Bakers	$21,520	15.2%	37,000
94. Welders, Cutters, Solderers, and Brazers	$30,990	5.0%	52,000
95. Excavating and Loading Machine and Dragline Operators	$32,380	8.0%	11,000
96. Locksmiths and Safe Repairers	$30,880	16.1%	5,000
97. Ship Engineers	$52,780	12.7%	1,000
98. Arbitrators, Mediators, and Conciliators	$54,360	15.5%	fewer than 500
99. Zoologists and Wildlife Biologists	$52,050	13.0%	1,000
100. Medical Equipment Preparers	$24,880	20.0%	8,000
101. Millwrights	$44,780	5.9%	5,000
102. Aircraft Structure, Surfaces, Rigging, and Systems Assemblers	$43,990	7.8%	4,000
103. Subway and Streetcar Operators	$47,500	13.7%	1,000
104. Boilermakers	$48,050	8.7%	2,000
105. Recreational Vehicle Service Technicians	$30,480	19.5%	3,000
106. Riggers	$37,010	13.9%	2,000
107. Surveying and Mapping Technicians	$31,290	9.6%	9,000
108. Avionics Technicians	$46,630	9.1%	2,000
109. Gas Plant Operators	$51,920	7.7%	2,000
110. Physicists	$89,810	7.0%	1,000
111. Astronomers	$104,670	10.5%	fewer than 500
112. Driver/Sales Workers	$20,120	13.8%	72,000
113. Anthropologists and Archeologists	$45,910	17.0%	fewer than 500
114. Conservation Scientists	$53,350	6.3%	2,000
115. Helpers—Brickmasons, Blockmasons, Stonemasons, and Tile and Marble Setters	$24,600	14.9%	14,000
116. Statisticians	$62,450	4.6%	2,000
117. Electro-Mechanical Technicians	$43,880	9.7%	2,000
118. Food Scientists and Technologists	$51,440	10.9%	1,000
119. Industrial Machinery Mechanics	$39,740	−0.2%	13,000
120. Tapers	$39,870	5.9%	5,000
121. Motorcycle Mechanics	$29,450	13.7%	6,000
122. Control and Valve Installers and Repairers, Except Mechanical Door	$44,120	4.9%	4,000
123. Museum Technicians and Conservators	$34,090	14.1%	2,000
124. Pesticide Handlers, Sprayers, and Applicators, Vegetation	$26,120	16.6%	6,000

The 200 Best Jobs Overall for Introverts

Job	Annual Earnings	Percent Growth	Annual Openings
125. Economists	$73,690	5.6%	1,000
126. Outdoor Power Equipment and Other Small Engine Mechanics	$25,810	14.0%	10,000
127. Stationary Engineers and Boiler Operators	$44,600	3.4%	5,000
128. Purchasing Agents and Buyers, Farm Products	$46,680	7.0%	2,000
129. Credit Analysts	$50,370	3.6%	3,000
130. Slaughterers and Meat Packers	$21,220	13.8%	22,000
131. Captains, Mates, and Pilots of Water Vessels	$50,940	4.8%	2,000
132. Pest Control Workers	$27,170	18.4%	4,000
133. Printing Machine Operators	$30,730	2.9%	26,000
134. Stonemasons	$34,640	13.0%	2,000
135. Marine Engineers and Naval Architects	$72,920	8.5%	fewer than 500
136. Traffic Technicians	$37,070	14.1%	1,000
137. Billing and Posting Clerks and Machine Operators	$27,780	3.4%	70,000
138. Butchers and Meat Cutters	$26,590	7.9%	20,000
139. Farmers and Ranchers	$34,140	–14.5%	96,000
140. Set and Exhibit Designers	$37,390	9.3%	2,000
141. Materials Scientists	$71,450	8.0%	fewer than 500
142. Political Scientists	$84,100	7.3%	fewer than 500
143. Tax Preparers	$25,700	10.6%	11,000
144. Tool and Die Makers	$43,580	–2.6%	7,000
145. Earth Drillers, Except Oil and Gas	$33,770	7.9%	4,000
146. Helpers—Production Workers	$20,390	7.9%	107,000
147. Petroleum Pump System Operators, Refinery Operators, and Gaugers	$51,060	–8.6%	6,000
148. Structural Metal Fabricators and Fitters	$30,290	2.9%	18,000
149. Paper Goods Machine Setters, Operators, and Tenders	$31,160	2.4%	15,000
150. Pile-Driver Operators	$48,900	11.9%	fewer than 500
151. Title Examiners, Abstractors, and Searchers	$35,120	0.9%	8,000
152. Inspectors, Testers, Sorters, Samplers, and Weighers	$29,200	–2.6%	85,000
153. Animal Trainers	$24,800	20.3%	3,000
154. Foresters	$48,670	6.7%	1,000
155. Terrazzo Workers and Finishers	$32,030	15.2%	1,000
156. Geographers	$63,550	6.8%	fewer than 500
157. Electrical and Electronics Repairers, Powerhouse, Substation, and Relay	$54,970	–0.4%	2,000
158. Electrical and Electronics Drafters	$45,550	1.2%	3,000

(continued)

(continued)

The 200 Best Jobs Overall for Introverts

Job	Annual Earnings	Percent Growth	Annual Openings
159. Animal Scientists	$43,170	12.9%	fewer than 500
160. Merchandise Displayers and Window Trimmers	$22,590	10.3%	13,000
161. Maintenance Workers, Machinery	$33,650	2.8%	6,000
162. Chemical Equipment Operators and Tenders	$39,030	−4.5%	6,000
163. Job Printers	$31,920	1.8%	8,000
164. Mechanical Door Repairers	$30,310	15.8%	1,000
165. Mixing and Blending Machine Setters, Operators, and Tenders	$28,890	2.0%	16,000
166. Agricultural Inspectors	$32,840	6.8%	3,000
167. Dental Laboratory Technicians	$32,240	7.6%	3,000
168. Computer-Controlled Machine Tool Operators, Metal and Plastic	$31,010	−1.2%	13,000
169. Logging Equipment Operators	$28,920	3.4%	9,000
170. Packaging and Filling Machine Operators and Tenders	$22,930	2.3%	80,000
171. Separating, Filtering, Clarifying, Precipitating, and Still Machine Setters, Operators, and Tenders	$34,650	1.6%	5,000
172. Sociologists	$52,760	4.7%	fewer than 500
173. Cabinetmakers and Bench Carpenters	$26,020	4.1%	12,000
174. Electric Motor, Power Tool, and Related Repairers	$33,460	4.1%	3,000
175. Prepress Technicians and Workers	$32,840	−8.4%	10,000
176. Signal and Track Switch Repairers	$49,200	2.3%	1,000
177. Data Entry Keyers	$23,810	−0.7%	85,000
178. Parking Enforcement Workers	$29,070	15.1%	1,000
179. Electronic Home Entertainment Equipment Installers and Repairers	$28,940	4.7%	6,000
180. Commercial Divers	$37,960	9.4%	fewer than 500
181. Paperhangers	$33,450	3.2%	3,000
182. Fence Erectors	$24,930	9.9%	5,000
183. Rail Car Repairers	$42,530	−1.2%	2,000
184. Insulation Workers, Floor, Ceiling, and Wall	$31,360	3.0%	4,000
185. Numerical Tool and Process Control Programmers	$41,830	−1.1%	2,000
186. Sailors and Marine Oilers	$29,360	5.2%	4,000
187. Welding, Soldering, and Brazing Machine Setters, Operators, and Tenders	$30,430	0.4%	7,000
188. Home Appliance Repairers	$32,980	2.6%	3,000
189. Tire Repairers and Changers	$20,960	4.5%	17,000
190. Word Processors and Typists	$29,020	−15.3%	30,000

The 200 Best Jobs Overall for Introverts

Job	Annual Earnings	Percent Growth	Annual Openings
191. Helpers—Painters, Paperhangers, Plasterers, and Stucco Masons	$20,560	11.5%	6,000
192. Medical Appliance Technicians	$29,080	13.3%	1,000
193. Coin, Vending, and Amusement Machine Servicers and Repairers	$28,200	2.4%	7,000
194. Insulation Workers, Mechanical	$35,510	1.0%	2,000
195. Historians	$44,400	4.3%	fewer than 500
196. Bridge and Lock Tenders	$37,980	7.2%	fewer than 500
197. Lathe and Turning Machine Tool Setters, Operators, and Tenders, Metal and Plastic	$31,750	–9.0%	7,000
198. Coating, Painting, and Spraying Machine Setters, Operators, and Tenders	$26,670	–3.4%	16,000
199. Multiple Machine Tool Setters, Operators, and Tenders, Metal and Plastic	$29,780	0.3%	6,000
200. Semiconductor Processors	$31,030	–7.5%	7,000

The 50 Best-Paying Jobs for Introverts

In the following list you'll find the 50 best-paying jobs that met our criteria for this book. This is a popular list, for obvious reasons.

It shouldn't be a big surprise to learn that most of the highest-paying jobs require advanced levels of education, training, or experience. For example, all of the top 20 jobs require at least a bachelor's degree to qualify. Although the top 20 jobs may not appeal to you for a variety of reasons, you are likely to find others that will among the top 50 jobs with the highest earnings.

Keep in mind that the earnings reflect the national average for all workers in the occupation. This is an important consideration because starting pay in the job is usually a lot less than the pay that workers can earn with several years of experience. Earnings also vary significantly by region of the country, so actual pay in your area could be substantially different.

The 50 Best-Paying Jobs for Introverts

Job	Annual Earnings
1. Astronomers	$104,670
2. Lawyers	$98,930
3. Physicists	$89,810

(continued)

(continued)

The 50 Best-Paying Jobs for Introverts

Job	Annual Earnings
4. Political Scientists	$84,100
5. Aerospace Engineers	$84,090
6. Computer Software Engineers, Systems Software	$82,120
7. Actuaries	$81,640
8. Electronics Engineers, Except Computer	$78,030
9. Computer Software Engineers, Applications	$77,090
10. Atmospheric and Space Scientists	$73,940
11. Economists	$73,690
12. Electrical Engineers	$73,510
13. Marine Engineers and Naval Architects	$72,920
14. Geoscientists, Except Hydrologists and Geographers	$71,640
15. Materials Scientists	$71,450
16. Biochemists and Biophysicists	$71,000
17. Materials Engineers	$69,660
18. Computer Systems Analysts	$68,300
19. Civil Engineers	$66,190
20. Health and Safety Engineers, Except Mining Safety Engineers and Inspectors	$65,210
21. Financial Analysts	$63,860
22. Hydrologists	$63,820
23. Geographers	$63,550
24. Personal Financial Advisors	$63,500
25. Computer Programmers	$63,420
26. Database Administrators	$63,250
27. Financial Examiners	$63,090
28. Statisticians	$62,450
29. Operations Research Analysts	$62,180
30. Network Systems and Data Communications Analysts	$61,750
31. Medical Scientists, Except Epidemiologists	$61,730
32. Nuclear Technicians	$61,120
33. Fashion Designers	$60,860
34. Elevator Installers and Repairers	$59,190
35. Chemists	$57,890
36. Market Research Analysts	$57,300
37. Microbiologists	$56,870
38. Technical Writers	$55,160
39. Electrical and Electronics Repairers, Powerhouse, Substation, and Relay	$54,970

The 50 Best-Paying Jobs for Introverts

Job	Annual Earnings
40. Soil and Plant Scientists	$54,530
41. Arbitrators, Mediators, and Conciliators	$54,360
42. Conservation Scientists	$53,350
43. Ship Engineers	$52,780
44. Sociologists	$52,760
45. Environmental Scientists and Specialists, Including Health	$52,630
46. Accountants and Auditors	$52,210
47. Commercial and Industrial Designers	$52,200
48. Epidemiologists	$52,170
49. Zoologists and Wildlife Biologists	$52,050
50. Cost Estimators	$52,020

The 50 Fastest-Growing Jobs for Introverts

From the list of the 200 best jobs for introverts, this list shows the 50 jobs that are projected to have the highest percentage increase in the numbers of people employed through 2014.

You'll find a wide variety of fields represented by the top 20 fastest-growing jobs, including high tech, health care, and construction. Most require at least a bachelor's degree, but some require less. You can find a wide range of rapidly growing jobs in a variety of fields and at different levels of training and education among the 50 fastest-growing jobs.

The 50 Fastest-Growing Jobs for Introverts

Job	Percent Growth
1. Network Systems and Data Communications Analysts	54.6%
2. Computer Software Engineers, Applications	48.4%
3. Computer Software Engineers, Systems Software	43.0%
4. Database Administrators	38.2%
5. Medical Scientists, Except Epidemiologists	34.1%
6. Hydrologists	31.6%
7. Computer Systems Analysts	31.4%
8. Hazardous Materials Removal Workers	31.2%
9. Epidemiologists	26.2%
10. Personal Financial Advisors	25.9%
11. Actuaries	23.2%
12. Desktop Publishers	23.2%
13. Technical Writers	23.2%

(continued)

(continued)

The 50 Fastest-Growing Jobs for Introverts

Job	Percent Growth
14. Tile and Marble Setters	22.9%
15. Appraisers and Assessors of Real Estate	22.8%
16. Accountants and Auditors	22.4%
17. Bus Drivers, Transit and Intercity	21.7%
18. Biochemists and Biophysicists	21.0%
19. Animal Trainers	20.3%
20. Medical Equipment Preparers	20.0%
21. Crossing Guards	19.7%
22. Market Research Analysts	19.6%
23. Landscaping and Groundskeeping Workers	19.5%
24. Recreational Vehicle Service Technicians	19.5%
25. Heating, Air Conditioning, and Refrigeration Mechanics and Installers	19.0%
26. Pest Control Workers	18.4%
27. Sound Engineering Technicians	18.4%
28. Cost Estimators	18.2%
29. Private Detectives and Investigators	17.7%
30. Writers and Authors	17.7%
31. Financial Analysts	17.3%
32. Payroll and Timekeeping Clerks	17.3%
33. Microbiologists	17.2%
34. Environmental Scientists and Specialists, Including Health	17.1%
35. Anthropologists and Archeologists	17.0%
36. Roofers	16.8%
37. Pesticide Handlers, Sprayers, and Applicators, Vegetation	16.6%
38. Atmospheric and Space Scientists	16.5%
39. Civil Engineers	16.5%
40. Tree Trimmers and Pruners	16.5%
41. Environmental Science and Protection Technicians, Including Health	16.3%
42. Water and Liquid Waste Treatment Plant and System Operators	16.2%
43. Locksmiths and Safe Repairers	16.1%
44. Cement Masons and Concrete Finishers	15.9%
45. Mechanical Door Repairers	15.8%
46. Automotive Service Technicians and Mechanics	15.7%
47. Embalmers	15.7%
48. Plumbers, Pipefitters, and Steamfitters	15.7%
49. Truck Drivers, Light or Delivery Services	15.7%
50. Paving, Surfacing, and Tamping Equipment Operators	15.6%

The 50 Jobs for Introverts with the Most Openings

From the list of best jobs for introverts, this list shows the 50 jobs that are projected to have the largest number of job openings per year through 2014.

Jobs with many openings present several advantages that may be attractive to you. Because there are many openings, these jobs can be easier to obtain, particularly for those just entering the job market. These jobs may also offer more opportunities to move from one employer to another with relative ease. Though some of these jobs have average or below-average pay, some also pay quite well and can provide good long-term career opportunities or the ability to move up to more responsible roles. This list is especially noteworthy because most of the highest-ranked jobs require only on-the-job training.

The 50 Jobs for Introverts with the Most Openings

Job	Annual Openings
1. Bookkeeping, Accounting, and Auditing Clerks	291,000
2. Truck Drivers, Heavy and Tractor-Trailer	274,000
3. Landscaping and Groundskeeping Workers	243,000
4. Truck Drivers, Light or Delivery Services	169,000
5. Accountants and Auditors	157,000
6. Maintenance and Repair Workers, General	154,000
7. Helpers—Production Workers	107,000
8. Painters, Construction and Maintenance	102,000
9. Farmers and Ranchers	96,000
10. Automotive Service Technicians and Mechanics	93,000
11. Data Entry Keyers	85,000
12. Inspectors, Testers, Sorters, Samplers, and Weighers	85,000
13. Packaging and Filling Machine Operators and Tenders	80,000
14. Bus Drivers, School	76,000
15. Driver/Sales Workers	72,000
16. Billing and Posting Clerks and Machine Operators	70,000
17. Plumbers, Pipefitters, and Steamfitters	61,000
18. Computer Systems Analysts	56,000
19. Computer Software Engineers, Applications	54,000
20. Welders, Cutters, Solderers, and Brazers	52,000
21. Network Systems and Data Communications Analysts	43,000
22. Lawyers	40,000
23. Roofers	38,000
24. Bakers	37,000
25. Computer Software Engineers, Systems Software	37,000
26. Operating Engineers and Other Construction Equipment Operators	37,000

(continued)

(continued)

The 50 Jobs for Introverts with the Most Openings

Job	Annual Openings
27. Payroll and Timekeeping Clerks	36,000
28. Graphic Designers	35,000
29. Bus Drivers, Transit and Intercity	34,000
30. Heating, Air Conditioning, and Refrigeration Mechanics and Installers	33,000
31. Machinists	33,000
32. Bus and Truck Mechanics and Diesel Engine Specialists	32,000
33. Cement Masons and Concrete Finishers	32,000
34. Computer, Automated Teller, and Office Machine Repairers	31,000
35. Word Processors and Typists	30,000
36. Computer Programmers	28,000
37. Financial Analysts	28,000
38. Clergy	26,000
39. Crossing Guards	26,000
40. Printing Machine Operators	26,000
41. Telecommunications Line Installers and Repairers	23,000
42. Slaughterers and Meat Packers	22,000
43. Telecommunications Equipment Installers and Repairers, Except Line Installers	21,000
44. Butchers and Meat Cutters	20,000
45. Market Research Analysts	20,000
46. Civil Engineers	19,000
47. Postal Service Mail Carriers	19,000
48. Automotive Body and Related Repairers	18,000
49. Electrical and Electronic Engineering Technicians	18,000
50. Structural Metal Fabricators and Fitters	18,000

Best Jobs with Particular Features Attractive to Introverts

Because you enjoy working alone, without interruptions and distractions, we thought you would be interested in jobs that have particular types of introvert-friendly characteristics. The lists that follow consist of subsets of the 200 best jobs and are selected to highlight work conditions that you might appreciate.

The 20 Jobs with the Most Solitary Work

The 200 best jobs all rank high on the O*NET work value Independence, which is defined as working alone. We created the following list by identifying the 20 jobs with the highest ratings on Independence. The jobs are ordered with the most solitary at the top, and for each job we show the O*NET rating on Independence. The scale we use represents the rating on a scale with 0 as the lowest level and 100 as the highest. Although this rating resembles a percentage, it does not represent the percentage of *time* that people work alone. Rather, it measures the amount that solitary work *characterizes* the job.

The 20 Jobs with the Most Solitary Work

Job	Rating for Working Alone
1. Postal Service Mail Carriers	100.0
2. Astronomers	90.5
3. Fine Artists, Including Painters, Sculptors, and Illustrators	83.5
4. Biochemists and Biophysicists	81.2
5. Data Entry Keyers	81.2
6. Locksmiths and Safe Repairers	81.2
7. Statisticians	81.2
8. Truck Drivers, Light or Delivery Services	81.2
9. Soil and Plant Scientists	79.8
10. Animal Scientists	78.0
11. Bus Drivers, School	78.0
12. Control and Valve Installers and Repairers, Except Mechanical Door	76.0
13. Animal Trainers	75.0
14. Bookkeeping, Accounting, and Auditing Clerks	75.0
15. Bridge and Lock Tenders	75.0
16. Bus Drivers, Transit and Intercity	75.0
17. Chemists	75.0
18. Dental Laboratory Technicians	75.0
19. Electro-Mechanical Technicians	75.0
20. Embalmers	75.0

The 20 Jobs with the Least Contact with Others

If you're an introvert, working mostly alone isn't enough. You also want to avoid interruptions from other people: the ringing phone, the instant message begging for your attention, the people appearing at your door at random intervals with questions or suggestions. These kinds of interruptions, which you dislike so much, are described in O*NET by a feature called Contact with Others. Using the O*NET ratings on this feature, we created the following list, which highlights those jobs that allow workers to get through the day without many interruptions. The 20 jobs ranked *lowest* on Contact with Others are listed next, and we represent the rating as a number on a scale in which 0 is the lowest rating and 100 the highest.

The 20 Jobs with the Least Contact with Others

Job	Rating for Contact with Others
1. Drywall and Ceiling Tile Installers	9.5
2. Fence Erectors	10.5
3. Pile-Driver Operators	10.5
4. Signal and Track Switch Repairers	10.5
5. Tapers	10.5
6. Tree Trimmers and Pruners	10.5
7. Slaughterers and Meat Packers	11.0
8. Biochemists and Biophysicists	11.5
9. Coin, Vending, and Amusement Machine Servicers and Repairers	11.8
10. Motorboat Mechanics	11.8
11. Outdoor Power Equipment and Other Small Engine Mechanics	11.8
12. Paperhangers	11.8
13. Roofers	11.8
14. Aircraft Structure, Surfaces, Rigging, and Systems Assemblers	12.3
15. Gas Plant Operators	12.5
16. Reinforcing Iron and Rebar Workers	12.5
17. Earth Drillers, Except Oil and Gas	15.5
18. Insulation Workers, Floor, Ceiling, and Wall	16.5
19. Insulation Workers, Mechanical	16.5
20. Petroleum Pump System Operators, Refinery Operators, and Gaugers	19.0

The 20 Jobs with the Most Independent Decision Making

Introverts prefer to make work decisions independently. Doing so has two aspects: Introverts try to avoid collaborative work situations, where decisions are shared by a group, and also hierarchical work situations, where most decisions must be cleared with the boss. Two closely related work values in the O*NET database enable us to identify jobs that avoid these two kinds of situations and that encourage independent decision making. The value Responsibility is defined as making decisions on your own, and the value Autonomy is defined as making plans with little supervision. To create the following list, we looked at how each of the 200 best jobs is rated on these two values and computed the average of the two ratings. We then used that combined score to rank all the jobs and listed the top 20 jobs we found. For each job, we show the average rating as a number on a scale in which 0 is the lowest rating and 100 is the highest.

The 20 Jobs with the Most Independent Decision Making

Job	Rating for Independent Decision Making
1. Farmers and Ranchers	84.4
2. Operations Research Analysts	84.4
3. Statisticians	82.7
4. Cartographers and Photogrammetrists	81.1
5. Computer Software Engineers, Applications	81.1
6. Computer Software Engineers, Systems Software	81.1
7. Financial Analysts	78.1
8. Computer Systems Analysts	78.0
9. Appraisers and Assessors of Real Estate	72.6
10. Actuaries	70.2
11. Financial Examiners	68.8
12. Computer Programmers	68.6
13. Database Administrators	68.6
14. Purchasing Agents and Buyers, Farm Products	67.1
15. Network Systems and Data Communications Analysts	65.5
16. Accountants and Auditors	64.8
17. Personal Financial Advisors	62.5
18. Cost Estimators	60.9
19. Credit Analysts	60.9
20. Tax Preparers	48.4

The 20 Jobs Most Removed from the Public

Some introverts don't mind dealing with a familiar cast of characters in an office, lab, construction site, or other work setting, but they really want to avoid dealing constantly with strangers. The O*NET database rates each job on a work activity called Performing for or Working Directly with the Public, so we were able to assemble a list of the 20 jobs out of the 200 best that are rated *lowest* on this activity. In other words, these jobs are the most removed from the public. We express their rating on this activity by using a number on a scale from 0 (lowest) to 100 (highest).

The 20 Jobs Most Removed from the Public

Job	Rating for Performing or Working Directly with the Public
1. Commercial Divers	0.0
2. Petroleum Pump System Operators, Refinery Operators, and Gaugers	0.0
3. Pile-Driver Operators	0.0
4. Reinforcing Iron and Rebar Workers	0.0
5. Signal and Track Switch Repairers	0.0
6. Slaughterers and Meat Packers	0.0
7. Electro-Mechanical Technicians	0.6
8. Aircraft Structure, Surfaces, Rigging, and Systems Assemblers	1.9
9. Credit Analysts	2.3
10. Tapers	2.3
11. Gas Plant Operators	3.6
12. Aerospace Engineers	4.7
13. Insulation Workers, Floor, Ceiling, and Wall	4.7
14. Insulation Workers, Mechanical	4.7
15. Ship Engineers	4.7
16. Multiple Machine Tool Setters, Operators, and Tenders, Metal and Plastic	5.0
17. Electrical Engineers	5.9
18. Maintenance Workers, Machinery	5.9
19. Biochemists and Biophysicists	6.0
20. Drywall and Ceiling Tile Installers	6.0

The 20 Quietest Jobs

Introverts crave peace and quiet where they work. Noise interferes with their ability to focus on the tasks at hand. To identify the quietest jobs, we used an O*NET rating called Sounds, Noise Levels Are Distracting or Uncomfortable. We ordered the 200 best jobs according to their rating on this measure of noise and put the 20 *lowest*-rated jobs on the following list. The rating for each job is shown on a scale in which 0 is the lowest rating and 100 the highest.

The 20 Quietest Jobs

Job	Rating for Sounds, Noise Levels Are Distracting or Uncomfortable
1. Arbitrators, Mediators, and Conciliators	5.0
2. Biochemists and Biophysicists	5.0
3. Personal Financial Advisors	5.0
4. Private Detectives and Investigators	15.0
5. Interior Designers	17.5
6. Political Scientists	18.5
7. Music Directors and Composers	18.8
8. Sociologists	19.0
9. Title Examiners, Abstractors, and Searchers	19.0
10. Fashion Designers	20.0
11. Helpers—Painters, Paperhangers, Plasterers, and Stucco Masons	20.0
12. Paperhangers	20.0
13. Purchasing Agents and Buyers, Farm Products	20.0
14. Operations Research Analysts	20.8
15. Geographers	22.7
16. Economists	23.0
17. Hydrologists	23.2
18. Astronomers	23.5
19. Lawyers	23.8
20. Embalmers	24.3

Best Jobs Lists by Demographic

We decided it would be interesting to include lists in this section that show what sorts of jobs different types of people are most likely to have. For example, what introvert-friendly jobs have the highest percentage of men or young workers? We're not saying that men or young people should consider these jobs over others, but it is interesting information to know.

In some cases, the lists can give you ideas for jobs to consider that you might otherwise over-look. For example, perhaps women should consider some jobs that traditionally have high percentages of men in them. Or older workers might consider some jobs typically held by young people. Although these are not obvious ways of using these lists, the lists may give you some good ideas on jobs to consider. The lists may also help you identify jobs that work well for others in your situation—for example, jobs with plentiful opportunities for part-time work, if that is something you want to do.

All of the lists in this section were created using a similar process. We began with the 200 best jobs for introverts. Next, we sorted those jobs in order of the primary criterion for each set of lists. For example, we sorted the 200 jobs based on the percentage of workers age 16 to 24 from highest to lowest percentage and then selected the jobs with a high percentage (the 64 jobs with a percentage greater than 10 percent). From this initial list of jobs with a high percentage of each type of worker, we created four more-specialized lists:

- 25 Best Jobs Overall (the subset of jobs that have the highest combined scores for earnings, growth rate, and number of openings)
- 25 Best-Paying Jobs
- 25 Fastest-Growing Jobs
- 25 Jobs with the Most Openings

Again, each of these four lists includes only jobs that have high percentages of different types of workers. The same basic process was used to create all the lists in this section. The lists are very interesting, and we hope you find them helpful.

Best Jobs for Introverts with the Highest Percentage of Workers Age 16–24

These jobs have higher percentages (more than 10 percent) of workers between the ages of 16 and 24. Young people are found in all jobs, but those with higher percentages of young people may present more opportunities for initial entry or upward mobility. Many jobs with the highest percentages of young people are those that are learned through on-the-job training, such as construction jobs, but there is a wide variety of jobs in different fields among the top 64.

Best Jobs for Introverts with the Highest Percentage of Workers Age 16–24	
Job	Percent Age 16–24
1. Helpers—Brickmasons, Blockmasons, Stonemasons, and Tile and Marble Setters	43.0%
2. Helpers—Painters, Paperhangers, Plasterers, and Stucco Masons	43.0%
3. Mechanical Door Repairers	39.6%
4. Tire Repairers and Changers	39.6%
5. Helpers—Production Workers	35.9%
6. Aircraft Structure, Surfaces, Rigging, and Systems Assemblers	27.3%
7. Environmental Science and Protection Technicians, Including Health	26.7%
8. Landscaping and Groundskeeping Workers	25.2%
9. Pesticide Handlers, Sprayers, and Applicators, Vegetation	25.2%
10. Tree Trimmers and Pruners	25.2%

Best Jobs for Introverts with the Highest Percentage of Workers Age 16–24

Job	Percent Age 16–24
11. Fence Erectors	24.2%
12. Roofers	23.0%
13. Logging Equipment Operators	20.7%
14. Medical Equipment Preparers	19.8%
15. Sailors and Marine Oilers	18.8%
16. Data Entry Keyers	18.7%
17. Prepress Technicians and Workers	18.2%
18. Traffic Technicians	18.2%
19. Hazardous Materials Removal Workers	17.9%
20. Butchers and Meat Cutters	17.8%
21. Drywall and Ceiling Tile Installers	17.8%
22. Slaughterers and Meat Packers	17.8%
23. Tapers	17.8%
24. Automotive Service Technicians and Mechanics	17.5%
25. Surveying and Mapping Technicians	17.5%
26. Tile and Marble Setters	17.5%
27. Word Processors and Typists	16.3%
28. Packaging and Filling Machine Operators and Tenders	15.7%
29. Insulation Workers, Floor, Ceiling, and Wall	15.6%
30. Insulation Workers, Mechanical	15.6%
31. Painters, Construction and Maintenance	15.6%
32. Electronic Home Entertainment Equipment Installers and Repairers	14.7%
33. Riggers	14.3%
34. Automotive Body and Related Repairers	14.2%
35. Computer, Automated Teller, and Office Machine Repairers	14.1%
36. Music Directors and Composers	14.0%
37. Cement Masons and Concrete Finishers	13.9%
38. Terrazzo Workers and Finishers	13.9%
39. Brickmasons and Blockmasons	13.8%
40. Earth Drillers, Except Oil and Gas	13.8%
41. Stonemasons	13.8%
42. Coating, Painting, and Spraying Machine Setters, Operators, and Tenders	13.1%
43. Painters, Transportation Equipment	13.1%
44. Bakers	12.8%
45. Cabinetmakers and Bench Carpenters	12.8%

(continued)

(continued)

Best Jobs for Introverts with the Highest Percentage of Workers Age 16–24

Job	Percent Age 16–24
46. Motorboat Mechanics	12.1%
47. Motorcycle Mechanics	12.1%
48. Outdoor Power Equipment and Other Small Engine Mechanics	12.1%
49. Recreational Vehicle Service Technicians	12.1%
50. Heating, Air Conditioning, and Refrigeration Mechanics and Installers	12.0%
51. Sound Engineering Technicians	12.0%
52. Payroll and Timekeeping Clerks	11.8%
53. Architectural and Civil Drafters	11.7%
54. Electrical and Electronics Drafters	11.7%
55. Mechanical Drafters	11.7%
56. Editors	11.6%
57. Paving, Surfacing, and Tamping Equipment Operators	11.5%
58. Welders, Cutters, Solderers, and Brazers	11.5%
59. Welding, Soldering, and Brazing Machine Setters, Operators, and Tenders	11.5%
60. Animal Trainers	11.4%
61. Plumbers, Pipefitters, and Steamfitters	11.2%
62. Billing and Posting Clerks and Machine Operators	10.9%
63. Inspectors, Testers, Sorters, Samplers, and Weighers	10.4%
64. Home Appliance Repairers	10.2%

The jobs in the following four lists are derived from the preceding list of the introvert-friendly jobs with the highest percentage of workers age 16–24.

Best Jobs for Introverts Overall with a High Percentage of Workers Age 16–24

Job	Percent Age 16–24	Annual Earnings	Percent Growth	Annual Openings
1. Plumbers, Pipefitters, and Steamfitters	11.2%	$42,160	15.7%	61,000
2. Heating, Air Conditioning, and Refrigeration Mechanics and Installers	12.0%	$37,040	19.0%	33,000
3. Automotive Service Technicians and Mechanics	17.5%	$33,050	15.7%	93,000
4. Editors	11.6%	$45,510	14.8%	16,000

Best Jobs for Introverts Overall with a High Percentage of Workers Age 16–24

Job	Percent Age 16–24	Annual Earnings	Percent Growth	Annual Openings
5. Tile and Marble Setters	17.5%	$36,530	22.9%	9,000
6. Hazardous Materials Removal Workers	17.9%	$33,690	31.2%	11,000
7. Payroll and Timekeeping Clerks	11.8%	$31,360	17.3%	36,000
8. Roofers	23.0%	$31,230	16.8%	38,000
9. Cement Masons and Concrete Finishers	13.9%	$32,030	15.9%	32,000
10. Brickmasons and Blockmasons	13.8%	$41,860	12.0%	17,000
11. Landscaping and Groundskeeping Workers	25.2%	$20,670	19.5%	243,000
12. Painters, Construction and Maintenance	15.6%	$30,800	12.6%	102,000
13. Environmental Science and Protection Technicians, Including Health	26.7%	$36,260	16.3%	6,000
14. Painters, Transportation Equipment	13.1%	$34,840	14.1%	10,000
15. Automotive Body and Related Repairers	14.2%	$34,810	10.3%	18,000
16. Sound Engineering Technicians	12.0%	$38,390	18.4%	2,000
17. Drywall and Ceiling Tile Installers	17.8%	$34,740	9.0%	17,000
18. Music Directors and Composers	14.0%	$34,810	10.4%	11,000
19. Computer, Automated Teller, and Office Machine Repairers	14.1%	$36,060	3.8%	31,000
20. Tree Trimmers and Pruners	25.2%	$27,920	16.5%	11,000
21. Mechanical Drafters	11.7%	$43,350	5.5%	7,000
22. Motorboat Mechanics	12.1%	$32,780	15.1%	7,000
23. Architectural and Civil Drafters	11.7%	$40,390	4.6%	9,000
24. Bakers	12.8%	$21,520	15.2%	37,000
25. Welders, Cutters, Solderers, and Brazers	11.5%	$30,990	5.0%	52,000

Best-Paying Jobs for Introverts with a High Percentage of Workers Age 16–24

Job	Percent Age 16–24	Annual Earnings
1. Electrical and Electronics Drafters	11.7%	$45,550
2. Editors	11.6%	$45,510
3. Aircraft Structure, Surfaces, Rigging, and Systems Assemblers	27.3%	$43,990
4. Mechanical Drafters	11.7%	$43,350
5. Plumbers, Pipefitters, and Steamfitters	11.2%	$42,160

(continued)

(continued)

Best-Paying Jobs for Introverts with a High Percentage of Workers Age 16–24

Job	Percent Age 16–24	Annual Earnings
6. Brickmasons and Blockmasons	13.8%	$41,860
7. Architectural and Civil Drafters	11.7%	$40,390
8. Tapers	17.8%	$39,870
9. Sound Engineering Technicians	12.0%	$38,390
10. Traffic Technicians	18.2%	$37,070
11. Heating, Air Conditioning, and Refrigeration Mechanics and Installers	12.0%	$37,040
12. Riggers	14.3%	$37,010
13. Tile and Marble Setters	17.5%	$36,530
14. Environmental Science and Protection Technicians, Including Health	26.7%	$36,260
15. Computer, Automated Teller, and Office Machine Repairers	14.1%	$36,060
16. Insulation Workers, Mechanical	15.6%	$35,510
17. Painters, Transportation Equipment	13.1%	$34,840
18. Automotive Body and Related Repairers	14.2%	$34,810
19. Music Directors and Composers	14.0%	$34,810
20. Drywall and Ceiling Tile Installers	17.8%	$34,740
21. Stonemasons	13.8%	$34,640
22. Earth Drillers, Except Oil and Gas	13.8%	$33,770
23. Hazardous Materials Removal Workers	17.9%	$33,690
24. Automotive Service Technicians and Mechanics	17.5%	$33,050
25. Home Appliance Repairers	10.2%	$32,980

Fastest-Growing Jobs for Introverts with a High Percentage of Workers Age 16–24

Job	Percent Age 16–24	Percent Growth
1. Hazardous Materials Removal Workers	17.9%	31.2%
2. Tile and Marble Setters	17.5%	22.9%
3. Animal Trainers	11.4%	20.3%
4. Medical Equipment Preparers	19.8%	20.0%
5. Landscaping and Groundskeeping Workers	25.2%	19.5%
6. Recreational Vehicle Service Technicians	12.1%	19.5%
7. Heating, Air Conditioning, and Refrigeration Mechanics and Installers	12.0%	19.0%

Fastest-Growing Jobs for Introverts with a High Percentage of Workers Age 16–24

Job	Percent Age 16–24	Percent Growth
8. Sound Engineering Technicians	12.0%	18.4%
9. Payroll and Timekeeping Clerks	11.8%	17.3%
10. Roofers	23.0%	16.8%
11. Pesticide Handlers, Sprayers, and Applicators, Vegetation	25.2%	16.6%
12. Tree Trimmers and Pruners	25.2%	16.5%
13. Environmental Science and Protection Technicians, Including Health	26.7%	16.3%
14. Cement Masons and Concrete Finishers	13.9%	15.9%
15. Mechanical Door Repairers	39.6%	15.8%
16. Automotive Service Technicians and Mechanics	17.5%	15.7%
17. Plumbers, Pipefitters, and Steamfitters	11.2%	15.7%
18. Paving, Surfacing, and Tamping Equipment Operators	11.5%	15.6%
19. Bakers	12.8%	15.2%
20. Terrazzo Workers and Finishers	13.9%	15.2%
21. Motorboat Mechanics	12.1%	15.1%
22. Helpers—Brickmasons, Blockmasons, Stonemasons, and Tile and Marble Setters	43.0%	14.9%
23. Editors	11.6%	14.8%
24. Painters, Transportation Equipment	13.1%	14.1%
25. Traffic Technicians	18.2%	14.1%

Jobs for Introverts with the Most Openings with a High Percentage of Workers Age 16–24

Job	Percent Age 16–24	Annual Openings
1. Landscaping and Groundskeeping Workers	25.2%	243,000
2. Helpers—Production Workers	35.9%	107,000
3. Painters, Construction and Maintenance	15.6%	102,000
4. Automotive Service Technicians and Mechanics	17.5%	93,000
5. Data Entry Keyers	18.7%	85,000
6. Inspectors, Testers, Sorters, Samplers, and Weighers	10.4%	85,000
7. Packaging and Filling Machine Operators and Tenders	15.7%	80,000
8. Billing and Posting Clerks and Machine Operators	10.9%	70,000
9. Plumbers, Pipefitters, and Steamfitters	11.2%	61,000

(continued)

(continued)

Jobs for Introverts with the Most Openings with a High Percentage of Workers Age 16–24		
Job	Percent Age 16–24	Annual Openings
10. Welders, Cutters, Solderers, and Brazers	11.5%	52,000
11. Roofers	23.0%	38,000
12. Bakers	12.8%	37,000
13. Payroll and Timekeeping Clerks	11.8%	36,000
14. Heating, Air Conditioning, and Refrigeration Mechanics and Installers	12.0%	33,000
15. Cement Masons and Concrete Finishers	13.9%	32,000
16. Computer, Automated Teller, and Office Machine Repairers	14.1%	31,000
17. Word Processors and Typists	16.3%	30,000
18. Slaughterers and Meat Packers	17.8%	22,000
19. Butchers and Meat Cutters	17.8%	20,000
20. Automotive Body and Related Repairers	14.2%	18,000
21. Brickmasons and Blockmasons	13.8%	17,000
22. Drywall and Ceiling Tile Installers	17.8%	17,000
23. Tire Repairers and Changers	39.6%	17,000
24. Coating, Painting, and Spraying Machine Setters, Operators, and Tenders	13.1%	16,000
25. Editors	11.6%	16,000

Best Jobs for Introverts with a High Percentage of Workers Age 55 and Over

We created the following list by identifying the best jobs for introverts that employ a high percentage (more than 10 percent) of workers age 55 and over.

You may be surprised to note that 149 of the best 200 jobs meet this cutoff, whereas only 64 employ the same percentage of people age 16–24. You may be wondering, why are so many jobs with a high percentage of older workers well suited to introverts?

There are a number of reasons for this situation. First of all, we selected our 200 best jobs partly by eliminating all jobs with annual earnings of less than $20,000, and a lot of entry-level jobs with high concentrations of young people were among those removed. In addition, much of the growth in our economy is in industries that involve a lot of personal contact, such as health care and hospitality. That means a lot of young people who are entering the workforce are finding the best employment opportunities in jobs that are not well suited to introverts. Some of the introverted jobs have high concentrations of older workers who established themselves in those careers several decades ago, when those jobs held more promise than they do now. A good example is Farmers and Ranchers. Other introvert-friendly jobs are not physically demanding and therefore permit workers to postpone retirement. Finally, many of the jobs on the following list require workers to spend many years of preparation (for example, completing college and law school to become a lawyer), and therefore these workers tend to stay in the workforce longer so that they may better profit from their earlier investments of time and money.

Best Jobs for Introverts with the Highest Percentage of Workers Age 55 and Over

Job	Percent Age 55 and Over
1. Farmers and Ranchers	51.3%
2. Bridge and Lock Tenders	50.0%
3. Embalmers	50.0%
4. Tax Preparers	39.8%
5. Crossing Guards	34.7%
6. Arbitrators, Mediators, and Conciliators	34.4%
7. Millwrights	32.2%
8. Agricultural Inspectors	31.6%
9. Clergy	30.8%
10. Astronomers	30.4%
11. Physicists	30.4%
12. Bus Drivers, School	30.2%
13. Bus Drivers, Transit and Intercity	30.2%
14. Paperhangers	26.7%
15. Technical Writers	26.5%
16. Tool and Die Makers	25.6%
17. Writers and Authors	25.3%
18. Economists	24.0%
19. Fine Artists, Including Painters, Sculptors, and Illustrators	23.9%
20. Bookkeeping, Accounting, and Auditing Clerks	23.4%
21. Anthropologists and Archeologists	23.3%
22. Geographers	23.3%
23. Historians	23.3%
24. Lawyers	23.3%
25. Political Scientists	23.3%
26. Water and Liquid Waste Treatment Plant and System Operators	23.2%
27. Medical Equipment Repairers	22.6%
28. Private Detectives and Investigators	22.2%
29. Music Directors and Composers	21.8%

(continued)

(continued)

Best Jobs for Introverts with the Highest Percentage of Workers Age 55 and Over

Job	Percent Age 55 and Over
30. Appraisers and Assessors of Real Estate	21.0%
31. Payroll and Timekeeping Clerks	20.9%
32. Cost Estimators	20.4%
33. Commercial Divers	20.0%
34. Locksmiths and Safe Repairers	20.0%
35. Parking Enforcement Workers	20.0%
36. Structural Metal Fabricators and Fitters	20.0%
37. Civil Engineers	19.8%
38. Postal Service Mail Carriers	19.6%
39. Museum Technicians and Conservators	19.4%
40. Paving, Surfacing, and Tamping Equipment Operators	19.2%
41. Motorboat Mechanics	19.0%
42. Motorcycle Mechanics	19.0%
43. Outdoor Power Equipment and Other Small Engine Mechanics	19.0%
44. Recreational Vehicle Service Technicians	19.0%
45. Lathe and Turning Machine Tool Setters, Operators, and Tenders, Metal and Plastic	18.8%
46. Environmental Scientists and Specialists, Including Health	18.6%
47. Geoscientists, Except Hydrologists and Geographers	18.6%
48. Hydrologists	18.6%
49. Transportation Inspectors	18.4%
50. Industrial Machinery Mechanics	18.2%
51. Subway and Streetcar Operators	18.2%
52. Driver/Sales Workers	18.1%
53. Truck Drivers, Heavy and Tractor-Trailer	18.1%
54. Truck Drivers, Light or Delivery Services	18.1%
55. Captains, Mates, and Pilots of Water Vessels	17.9%
56. Bakers	17.6%
57. Personal Financial Advisors	16.9%
58. Conservation Scientists	16.7%
59. Epidemiologists	16.7%
60. Foresters	16.7%
61. Semiconductor Processors	16.7%
62. Mobile Heavy Equipment Mechanics, Except Engines	16.6%
63. Rail Car Repairers	16.6%

Best Jobs for Introverts with the Highest Percentage of Workers Age 55 and Over

Job	Percent Age 55 and Over
64. Aircraft Mechanics and Service Technicians	16.3%
65. Excavating and Loading Machine and Dragline Operators	16.3%
66. Surveying and Mapping Technicians	16.3%
67. Mixing and Blending Machine Setters, Operators, and Tenders	16.2%
68. Butchers and Meat Cutters	16.1%
69. Electric Motor, Power Tool, and Related Repairers	16.1%
70. Slaughterers and Meat Packers	16.1%
71. Machinists	16.0%
72. Statisticians	16.0%
73. Accountants and Auditors	15.9%
74. Aerospace Engineers	15.9%
75. Animal Trainers	15.9%
76. Bus and Truck Mechanics and Diesel Engine Specialists	15.7%
77. Operating Engineers and Other Construction Equipment Operators	15.5%
78. Billing and Posting Clerks and Machine Operators	15.4%
79. Financial Examiners	15.4%
80. Cabinetmakers and Bench Carpenters	15.1%
81. Paper Goods Machine Setters, Operators, and Tenders	15.1%
82. Commercial and Industrial Designers	14.9%
83. Fashion Designers	14.9%
84. Graphic Designers	14.9%
85. Interior Designers	14.9%
86. Merchandise Displayers and Window Trimmers	14.9%
87. Set and Exhibit Designers	14.9%
88. Market Research Analysts	14.5%
89. Animal Scientists	14.3%
90. Desktop Publishers	14.3%
91. Electrical and Electronics Repairers, Powerhouse, Substation, and Relay	14.3%
92. Food Scientists and Technologists	14.3%
93. Ship Engineers	14.3%
94. Soil and Plant Scientists	14.3%
95. Electrical and Electronic Engineering Technicians	14.2%
96. Electro-Mechanical Technicians	14.2%
97. Mechanical Engineering Technicians	14.2%

(continued)

(continued)

Best Jobs for Introverts with the Highest Percentage of Workers Age 55 and Over

Job	Percent Age 55 and Over
98. Data Entry Keyers	14.1%
99. Health and Safety Engineers, Except Mining Safety Engineers and Inspectors	14.1%
100. Helpers—Production Workers	14.1%
101. Editors	14.0%
102. Electrical Engineers	14.0%
103. Electronics Engineers, Except Computer	14.0%
104. Maintenance and Repair Workers, General	13.9%
105. Maintenance Workers, Machinery	13.9%
106. Earth Drillers, Except Oil and Gas	13.8%
107. Inspectors, Testers, Sorters, Samplers, and Weighers	13.8%
108. Word Processors and Typists	13.8%
109. Automotive Body and Related Repairers	13.6%
110. Boilermakers	13.6%
111. Welders, Cutters, Solderers, and Brazers	13.5%
112. Welding, Soldering, and Brazing Machine Setters, Operators, and Tenders	13.5%
113. Environmental Science and Protection Technicians, Including Health	13.3%
114. Brickmasons and Blockmasons	13.0%
115. Dental Laboratory Technicians	13.0%
116. Medical Appliance Technicians	13.0%
117. Stonemasons	13.0%
118. Chemists	12.8%
119. Materials Scientists	12.8%
120. Telecommunications Equipment Installers and Repairers, Except Line Installers	12.8%
121. Chemical Equipment Operators and Tenders	12.7%
122. Separating, Filtering, Clarifying, Precipitating, and Still Machine Setters, Operators, and Tenders	12.7%
123. Title Examiners, Abstractors, and Searchers	12.6%
124. Cartographers and Photogrammetrists	12.5%
125. Control and Valve Installers and Repairers, Except Mechanical Door	12.5%
126. Plumbers, Pipefitters, and Steamfitters	12.4%
127. Stationary Engineers and Boiler Operators	12.4%
128. Job Printers	12.3%
129. Medical Equipment Preparers	12.3%
130. Biochemists and Biophysicists	12.2%
131. Home Appliance Repairers	12.2%

Best Jobs for Introverts with the Highest Percentage of Workers Age 55 and Over

Job	Percent Age 55 and Over
132. Microbiologists	12.2%
133. Zoologists and Wildlife Biologists	12.2%
134. Computer Systems Analysts	12.0%
135. Landscaping and Groundskeeping Workers	12.0%
136. Logging Equipment Operators	12.0%
137. Pesticide Handlers, Sprayers, and Applicators, Vegetation	12.0%
138. Tree Trimmers and Pruners	12.0%
139. Computer-Controlled Machine Tool Operators, Metal and Plastic	11.9%
140. Numerical Tool and Process Control Programmers	11.9%
141. Packaging and Filling Machine Operators and Tenders	11.9%
142. Architectural and Civil Drafters	11.2%
143. Electrical and Electronics Drafters	11.2%
144. Mechanical Drafters	11.2%
145. Computer, Automated Teller, and Office Machine Repairers	11.1%
146. Heating, Air Conditioning, and Refrigeration Mechanics and Installers	11.1%
147. Insulation Workers, Floor, Ceiling, and Wall	11.1%
148. Insulation Workers, Mechanical	11.1%
149. Electronic Home Entertainment Equipment Installers and Repairers	10.3%

The jobs in the following four lists are derived from the preceding list of the introvert-friendly jobs with the highest percentage of workers age 55 and over.

Best Jobs for Introverts Overall with a High Percentage of Workers Age 55 and Over

Job	Percent Age 55 and Over	Annual Earnings	Percent Growth	Annual Openings
1. Computer Systems Analysts	12.0%	$68,300	31.4%	56,000
2. Accountants and Auditors	15.9%	$52,210	22.4%	157,000
3. Personal Financial Advisors	16.9%	$63,500	25.9%	17,000
4. Lawyers	23.3%	$98,930	15.0%	40,000
5. Market Research Analysts	14.5%	$57,300	19.6%	20,000
6. Civil Engineers	19.8%	$66,190	16.5%	19,000

(continued)

(continued)

Best Jobs for Introverts Overall with a High Percentage of Workers Age 55 and Over

Job	Percent Age 55 and Over	Annual Earnings	Percent Growth	Annual Openings
7. Cost Estimators	20.4%	$52,020	18.2%	15,000
8. Plumbers, Pipefitters, and Steamfitters	12.4%	$42,160	15.7%	61,000
9. Writers and Authors	25.3%	$46,420	17.7%	14,000
10. Technical Writers	26.5%	$55,160	23.2%	5,000
11. Environmental Scientists and Specialists, Including Health	18.6%	$52,630	17.1%	8,000
12. Heating, Air Conditioning, and Refrigeration Mechanics and Installers	11.1%	$37,040	19.0%	33,000
13. Electrical Engineers	14.0%	$73,510	11.8%	12,000
14. Appraisers and Assessors of Real Estate	21.0%	$43,440	22.8%	9,000
15. Graphic Designers	14.9%	$38,390	15.2%	35,000
16. Editors	14.0%	$45,510	14.8%	16,000
17. Electronics Engineers, Except Computer	14.0%	$78,030	9.7%	11,000
18. Hydrologists	18.6%	$63,820	31.6%	1,000
19. Bus Drivers, Transit and Intercity	30.2%	$31,010	21.7%	34,000
20. Biochemists and Biophysicists	12.2%	$71,000	21.0%	1,000
21. Payroll and Timekeeping Clerks	20.9%	$31,360	17.3%	36,000
22. Bus and Truck Mechanics and Diesel Engine Specialists	15.7%	$36,620	14.4%	32,000
23. Aircraft Mechanics and Service Technicians	16.3%	$47,310	13.4%	11,000
24. Maintenance and Repair Workers, General	13.9%	$31,210	15.2%	154,000
25. Truck Drivers, Heavy and Tractor-Trailer	18.1%	$34,280	12.9%	274,000

Best-Paying Jobs for Introverts with a High Percentage of Workers Age 55 and Over

Job	Percent Age 55 and Over	Annual Earnings
1. Astronomers	30.4%	$104,670
2. Lawyers	23.3%	$98,930
3. Physicists	30.4%	$89,810
4. Political Scientists	23.3%	$84,100
5. Aerospace Engineers	15.9%	$84,090

Best-Paying Jobs for Introverts with a High Percentage of Workers Age 55 and Over

Job	Percent Age 55 and Over	Annual Earnings
6. Electronics Engineers, Except Computer	14.0%	$78,030
7. Economists	24.0%	$73,690
8. Electrical Engineers	14.0%	$73,510
9. Geoscientists, Except Hydrologists and Geographers	18.6%	$71,640
10. Materials Scientists	12.8%	$71,450
11. Biochemists and Biophysicists	12.2%	$71,000
12. Computer Systems Analysts	12.0%	$68,300
13. Civil Engineers	19.8%	$66,190
14. Health and Safety Engineers, Except Mining Safety Engineers and Inspectors	14.1%	$65,210
15. Hydrologists	18.6%	$63,820
16. Geographers	23.3%	$63,550
17. Personal Financial Advisors	16.9%	$63,500
18. Financial Examiners	15.4%	$63,090
19. Statisticians	16.0%	$62,450
20. Fashion Designers	14.9%	$60,860
21. Chemists	12.8%	$57,890
22. Market Research Analysts	14.5%	$57,300
23. Microbiologists	12.2%	$56,870
24. Technical Writers	26.5%	$55,160
25. Electrical and Electronics Repairers, Powerhouse, Substation, and Relay	14.3%	$54,970

Fastest-Growing Jobs for Introverts with a High Percentage of Workers Age 55 and Over

Job	Percent Age 55 and Over	Percent Growth
1. Hydrologists	18.6%	31.6%
2. Computer Systems Analysts	12.0%	31.4%
3. Epidemiologists	16.7%	26.2%
4. Personal Financial Advisors	16.9%	25.9%
5. Desktop Publishers	14.3%	23.2%
6. Technical Writers	26.5%	23.2%

(continued)

(continued)

Fastest-Growing Jobs for Introverts with a High Percentage of Workers Age 55 and Over

Job	Percent Age 55 and Over	Percent Growth
7. Appraisers and Assessors of Real Estate	21.0%	22.8%
8. Accountants and Auditors	15.9%	22.4%
9. Bus Drivers, Transit and Intercity	30.2%	21.7%
10. Biochemists and Biophysicists	12.2%	21.0%
11. Animal Trainers	15.9%	20.3%
12. Medical Equipment Preparers	12.3%	20.0%
13. Crossing Guards	34.7%	19.7%
14. Market Research Analysts	14.5%	19.6%
15. Landscaping and Groundskeeping Workers	12.0%	19.5%
16. Recreational Vehicle Service Technicians	19.0%	19.5%
17. Heating, Air Conditioning, and Refrigeration Mechanics and Installers	11.1%	19.0%
18. Cost Estimators	20.4%	18.2%
19. Private Detectives and Investigators	22.2%	17.7%
20. Writers and Authors	25.3%	17.7%
21. Payroll and Timekeeping Clerks	20.9%	17.3%
22. Microbiologists	12.2%	17.2%
23. Environmental Scientists and Specialists, Including Health	18.6%	17.1%
24. Anthropologists and Archeologists	23.3%	17.0%
25. Pesticide Handlers, Sprayers, and Applicators, Vegetation	12.0%	16.6%

Jobs for Introverts with the Most Openings with a High Percentage of Workers Age 55 and Over

Job	Percent Age 55 and Over	Annual Openings
1. Bookkeeping, Accounting, and Auditing Clerks	23.4%	291,000
2. Truck Drivers, Heavy and Tractor-Trailer	18.1%	274,000
3. Landscaping and Groundskeeping Workers	12.0%	243,000
4. Truck Drivers, Light or Delivery Services	18.1%	169,000
5. Accountants and Auditors	15.9%	157,000
6. Maintenance and Repair Workers, General	13.9%	154,000
7. Helpers—Production Workers	14.1%	107,000

Jobs for Introverts with the Most Openings with a High Percentage of Workers Age 55 and Over

Job	Percent Age 55 and Over	Annual Openings
8. Farmers and Ranchers	51.3%	96,000
9. Data Entry Keyers	14.1%	85,000
10. Inspectors, Testers, Sorters, Samplers, and Weighers	13.8%	85,000
11. Packaging and Filling Machine Operators and Tenders	11.9%	80,000
12. Bus Drivers, School	30.2%	76,000
13. Driver/Sales Workers	18.1%	72,000
14. Billing and Posting Clerks and Machine Operators	15.4%	70,000
15. Plumbers, Pipefitters, and Steamfitters	12.4%	61,000
16. Computer Systems Analysts	12.0%	56,000
17. Welders, Cutters, Solderers, and Brazers	13.5%	52,000
18. Lawyers	23.3%	40,000
19. Bakers	17.6%	37,000
20. Operating Engineers and Other Construction Equipment Operators	15.5%	37,000
21. Payroll and Timekeeping Clerks	20.9%	36,000
22. Graphic Designers	14.9%	35,000
23. Bus Drivers, Transit and Intercity	30.2%	34,000
24. Heating, Air Conditioning, and Refrigeration Mechanics and Installers	11.1%	33,000
25. Machinists	16.0%	33,000

Best Jobs for Introverts with a High Percentage of Part-Time Workers

Look over the list of the introverted jobs with high percentages (more than 20 percent) of part-time workers and you will find some interesting things. For example, almost one-third of the jobs involve the arts or design, which leads one to think that many people working in these fields do so less than full time. (That is certainly true for performing artists such as actors and dancers, but those jobs are not well suited to introverts and are not included in this book.) But a wide variety of other industries—including agriculture, business, and manufacturing—are also represented in this list.

In some cases, people work part time because they want the freedom of time this arrangement can provide, but others may do so because they can't find full-time employment in these jobs. These folks may work in other full- or part-time jobs to make ends meet. If you want to work part time now or in the future, these lists will help you identify introvert-friendly jobs that are more likely to provide that opportunity. If you want full-time work, the lists may also help you identify introverted jobs for which such opportunities are more difficult to find. In either case, it's good information to know in advance.

Best Jobs for Introverts with the Highest Percentage of Part-Time Workers

Job	Percent Part-Time Workers
1. Crossing Guards	53.9%
2. Music Directors and Composers	46.1%
3. Embalmers	44.0%
4. Bus Drivers, Transit and Intercity	38.4%
5. Bus Drivers, School	38.4%
6. Tax Preparers	31.2%
7. Semiconductor Processors	31.2%
8. Fine Artists, Including Painters, Sculptors, and Illustrators	30.9%
9. Writers and Authors	30.7%
10. Bookkeeping, Accounting, and Auditing Clerks	29.5%
11. Parking Enforcement Workers	27.6%
12. Medical Equipment Preparers	27.5%
13. Bakers	26.8%
14. Word Processors and Typists	26.0%
15. Landscaping and Groundskeeping Workers	24.4%
16. Pesticide Handlers, Sprayers, and Applicators, Vegetation	24.4%
17. Tree Trimmers and Pruners	24.4%
18. Farmers and Ranchers	23.6%
19. Helpers—Production Workers	23.3%
20. Animal Trainers	23.1%
21. Nuclear Technicians	22.7%
22. Environmental Science and Protection Technicians, Including Health	22.7%
23. Commercial and Industrial Designers	21.3%
24. Fashion Designers	21.3%
25. Graphic Designers	21.3%
26. Interior Designers	21.3%
27. Merchandise Displayers and Window Trimmers	21.3%
28. Set and Exhibit Designers	21.3%
29. Bridge and Lock Tenders	21.2%
30. Data Entry Keyers	20.9%

The jobs in the following four lists are derived from the preceding list of the introvert-friendly jobs with the highest percentage of part-time workers.

Best Jobs Overall for Introverts with a High Percentage of Part-Time Workers

Job	Percent Part-Time Workers	Annual Earnings	Percent Growth	Annual Openings
1. Writers and Authors	30.7%	$46,420	17.7%	14,000
2. Bus Drivers, Transit and Intercity	38.4%	$31,010	21.7%	34,000
3. Graphic Designers	21.3%	$38,390	15.2%	35,000
4. Interior Designers	21.3%	$41,350	15.5%	10,000
5. Landscaping and Groundskeeping Workers	24.4%	$20,670	19.5%	243,000
6. Commercial and Industrial Designers	21.3%	$52,200	10.8%	7,000
7. Environmental Science and Protection Technicians, Including Health	22.7%	$36,260	16.3%	6,000
8. Tree Trimmers and Pruners	24.4%	$27,920	16.5%	11,000
9. Bookkeeping, Accounting, and Auditing Clerks	29.5%	$29,490	5.9%	291,000
10. Medical Equipment Preparers	27.5%	$24,880	20.0%	8,000
11. Nuclear Technicians	22.7%	$61,120	13.7%	1,000
12. Crossing Guards	53.9%	$20,050	19.7%	26,000
13. Embalmers	44.0%	$36,960	15.7%	2,000
14. Music Directors and Composers	46.1%	$34,810	10.4%	11,000
15. Bakers	26.8%	$21,520	15.2%	37,000
16. Bus Drivers, School	38.4%	$24,070	13.6%	76,000
17. Farmers and Ranchers	23.6%	$34,140	–14.5%	96,000
18. Pesticide Handlers, Sprayers, and Applicators, Vegetation	24.4%	$26,120	16.6%	6,000
19. Animal Trainers	23.1%	$24,800	20.3%	3,000
20. Fashion Designers	21.3%	$60,860	8.4%	2,000
21. Fine Artists, Including Painters, Sculptors, and Illustrators	30.9%	$41,280	10.2%	4,000
22. Tax Preparers	31.2%	$25,700	10.6%	11,000
23. Helpers—Production Workers	23.3%	$20,390	7.9%	107,000
24. Set and Exhibit Designers	21.3%	$37,390	9.3%	2,000
25. Data Entry Keyers	20.9%	$23,810	–0.7%	85,000

Best-Paying Jobs for Introverts with a High Percentage of Part-Time Workers

Job	Percent Part-Time Workers	Annual Earnings
1. Nuclear Technicians	22.7%	$61,120
2. Fashion Designers	21.3%	$60,860
3. Commercial and Industrial Designers	21.3%	$52,200
4. Writers and Authors	30.7%	$46,420
5. Interior Designers	21.3%	$41,350
6. Fine Artists, Including Painters, Sculptors, and Illustrators	30.9%	$41,280
7. Graphic Designers	21.3%	$38,390
8. Bridge and Lock Tenders	21.2%	$37,980
9. Set and Exhibit Designers	21.3%	$37,390
10. Embalmers	44.0%	$36,960
11. Environmental Science and Protection Technicians, Including Health	22.7%	$36,260
12. Music Directors and Composers	46.1%	$34,810
13. Farmers and Ranchers	23.6%	$34,140
14. Semiconductor Processors	31.2%	$31,030
15. Bus Drivers, Transit and Intercity	38.4%	$31,010
16. Bookkeeping, Accounting, and Auditing Clerks	29.5%	$29,490
17. Parking Enforcement Workers	27.6%	$29,070
18. Word Processors and Typists	26.0%	$29,020
19. Tree Trimmers and Pruners	24.4%	$27,920
20. Pesticide Handlers, Sprayers, and Applicators, Vegetation	24.4%	$26,120
21. Tax Preparers	31.2%	$25,700
22. Medical Equipment Preparers	27.5%	$24,880
23. Animal Trainers	23.1%	$24,800
24. Bus Drivers, School	38.4%	$24,070
25. Data Entry Keyers	20.9%	$23,810

Fastest-Growing Jobs for Introverts with a High Percentage of Part-Time Workers

Job	Percent Part-Time Workers	Percent Growth
1. Bus Drivers, Transit and Intercity	38.4%	21.7%
2. Animal Trainers	23.1%	20.3%
3. Medical Equipment Preparers	27.5%	20.0%
4. Crossing Guards	53.9%	19.7%
5. Landscaping and Groundskeeping Workers	24.4%	19.5%
6. Writers and Authors	30.7%	17.7%
7. Pesticide Handlers, Sprayers, and Applicators, Vegetation	24.4%	16.6%
8. Tree Trimmers and Pruners	24.4%	16.5%
9. Environmental Science and Protection Technicians, Including Health	22.7%	16.3%
10. Embalmers	44.0%	15.7%
11. Interior Designers	21.3%	15.5%
12. Bakers	26.8%	15.2%
13. Graphic Designers	21.3%	15.2%
14. Parking Enforcement Workers	27.6%	15.1%
15. Nuclear Technicians	22.7%	13.7%
16. Bus Drivers, School	38.4%	13.6%
17. Commercial and Industrial Designers	21.3%	10.8%
18. Tax Preparers	31.2%	10.6%
19. Music Directors and Composers	46.1%	10.4%
20. Merchandise Displayers and Window Trimmers	21.3%	10.3%
21. Fine Artists, Including Painters, Sculptors, and Illustrators	30.9%	10.2%
22. Set and Exhibit Designers	21.3%	9.3%
23. Fashion Designers	21.3%	8.4%
24. Helpers—Production Workers	23.3%	7.9%
25. Bridge and Lock Tenders	21.2%	7.2%

Jobs for Introverts with the Most Openings with a High Percentage of Part-Time Workers

Job	Percent Part-Time Workers	Annual Openings
1. Bookkeeping, Accounting, and Auditing Clerks	29.5%	291,000
2. Landscaping and Groundskeeping Workers	24.4%	243,000
3. Helpers—Production Workers	23.3%	107,000
4. Farmers and Ranchers	23.6%	96,000
5. Data Entry Keyers	20.9%	85,000
6. Bus Drivers, School	38.4%	76,000
7. Bakers	26.8%	37,000
8. Graphic Designers	21.3%	35,000
9. Bus Drivers, Transit and Intercity	38.4%	34,000
10. Word Processors and Typists	26.0%	30,000
11. Crossing Guards	53.9%	26,000
12. Writers and Authors	30.7%	14,000
13. Merchandise Displayers and Window Trimmers	21.3%	13,000
14. Music Directors and Composers	46.1%	11,000
15. Tax Preparers	31.2%	11,000
16. Tree Trimmers and Pruners	24.4%	11,000
17. Interior Designers	21.3%	10,000
18. Medical Equipment Preparers	27.5%	8,000
19. Commercial and Industrial Designers	21.3%	7,000
20. Semiconductor Processors	31.2%	7,000
21. Environmental Science and Protection Technicians, Including Health	22.7%	6,000
22. Pesticide Handlers, Sprayers, and Applicators, Vegetation	24.4%	6,000
23. Fine Artists, Including Painters, Sculptors, and Illustrators	30.9%	4,000
24. Animal Trainers	23.1%	3,000
25. Embalmers	44.0%	2,000

Best Jobs for Introverts with a High Percentage of Self-Employed Workers

About 8 percent of all working people are self-employed. Although you may think of the self-employed as having similar jobs, they actually work in an enormous range of situations, fields, and work environments that you may not have considered.

Among the self-employed are people who own small or large businesses, as many animal trainers and locksmiths do; professionals such as lawyers and accountants; part-time workers;

people working on a contract basis for one or more employers; people running home consulting or other businesses; and people in many other situations. They may go to the same worksite every day, as commercial and industrial designers do; visit multiple employers during the course of a week, as personal financial advisors do; or do most of their work from home, as many writers and authors do. Some work part time, others full time, some as a way to have fun, some so they can spend time with their kids or go to school.

The point is that there is an enormous range of situations, and one of them could make sense for you now or in the future.

The following list contains introvert-friendly jobs in which more than 10 percent of the workers are self-employed.

Best Jobs for Introverts with the Highest Percentage of Self-Employed Workers

Job	Percent Self-Employed Workers
1. Farmers and Ranchers	100.0%
2. Writers and Authors	67.7%
3. Fine Artists, Including Painters, Sculptors, and Illustrators	61.9%
4. Animal Trainers	58.2%
5. Music Directors and Composers	44.8%
6. Painters, Construction and Maintenance	44.6%
7. Paperhangers	43.9%
8. Personal Financial Advisors	38.9%
9. Locksmiths and Safe Repairers	37.6%
10. Appraisers and Assessors of Real Estate	37.2%
11. Soil and Plant Scientists	35.9%
12. Tax Preparers	35.6%
13. Fence Erectors	34.6%
14. Logging Equipment Operators	31.7%
15. Animal Scientists	31.3%
16. Electronic Home Entertainment Equipment Installers and Repairers	30.7%
17. Commercial and Industrial Designers	30.1%
18. Food Scientists and Technologists	28.8%
19. Brickmasons and Blockmasons	28.6%
20. Set and Exhibit Designers	27.6%
21. Fashion Designers	26.5%
22. Merchandise Displayers and Window Trimmers	25.9%

Best Jobs for Introverts with the Highest Percentage of Self-Employed Workers

Job	Percent Self-Employed Workers
23. Graphic Designers	25.6%
24. Interior Designers	25.3%
25. Tile and Marble Setters	24.4%
26. Lawyers	24.1%
27. Roofers	23.8%
28. Private Detectives and Investigators	23.7%
29. Drywall and Ceiling Tile Installers	23.4%
30. Stonemasons	23.1%
31. Tree Trimmers and Pruners	22.2%
32. Electric Motor, Power Tool, and Related Repairers	21.2%
33. Tapers	21.0%
34. Landscaping and Groundskeeping Workers	20.5%
35. Network Systems and Data Communications Analysts	19.9%
36. Pesticide Handlers, Sprayers, and Applicators, Vegetation	19.6%
37. Outdoor Power Equipment and Other Small Engine Mechanics	19.2%
38. Excavating and Loading Machine and Dragline Operators	19.1%
39. Motorboat Mechanics	18.9%
40. Home Appliance Repairers	18.0%
41. Automotive Body and Related Repairers	17.6%
42. Coin, Vending, and Amusement Machine Servicers and Repairers	17.5%
43. Medical Equipment Repairers	16.2%
44. Motorcycle Mechanics	15.7%
45. Cabinetmakers and Bench Carpenters	15.7%
46. Editors	14.8%
47. Automotive Service Technicians and Mechanics	14.8%
48. Computer, Automated Teller, and Office Machine Repairers	13.7%
49. Plumbers, Pipefitters, and Steamfitters	13.3%
50. Heating, Air Conditioning, and Refrigeration Mechanics and Installers	13.1%
51. Sociologists	11.7%
52. Insulation Workers, Floor, Ceiling, and Wall	11.0%
53. Accountants and Auditors	10.9%
54. Title Examiners, Abstractors, and Searchers	10.7%
55. Earth Drillers, Except Oil and Gas	10.5%
56. Dental Laboratory Technicians	10.2%

The jobs in the following four lists are derived from the preceding list of the introvert-friendly jobs with the highest percentage of self-employed workers. Where the following lists give earnings estimates, keep in mind that these figures are based on a survey that *does not include self-employed workers*. The median earnings for self-employed workers may be significantly higher or lower.

Best Jobs Overall for Introverts with a High Percentage of Self-Employed Workers

Job	Percent Self-Employed Workers	Annual Earnings	Percent Growth	Annual Openings
1. Network Systems and Data Communications Analysts	19.9%	$61,750	54.6%	43,000
2. Accountants and Auditors	10.9%	$52,210	22.4%	157,000
3. Personal Financial Advisors	38.9%	$63,500	25.9%	17,000
4. Lawyers	24.1%	$98,930	15.0%	40,000
5. Plumbers, Pipefitters, and Steamfitters	13.3%	$42,160	15.7%	61,000
6. Writers and Authors	67.7%	$46,420	17.7%	14,000
7. Heating, Air Conditioning, and Refrigeration Mechanics and Installers	13.1%	$37,040	19.0%	33,000
8. Appraisers and Assessors of Real Estate	37.2%	$43,440	22.8%	9,000
9. Graphic Designers	25.6%	$38,390	15.2%	35,000
10. Editors	14.8%	$45,510	14.8%	16,000
11. Tile and Marble Setters	24.4%	$36,530	22.9%	9,000
12. Automotive Service Technicians and Mechanics	14.8%	$33,050	15.7%	93,000
13. Brickmasons and Blockmasons	28.6%	$41,860	12.0%	17,000
14. Interior Designers	25.3%	$41,350	15.5%	10,000
15. Roofers	23.8%	$31,230	16.8%	38,000
16. Landscaping and Groundskeeping Workers	20.5%	$20,670	19.5%	243,000
17. Commercial and Industrial Designers	30.1%	$52,200	10.8%	7,000
18. Automotive Body and Related Repairers	17.6%	$34,810	10.3%	18,000
19. Painters, Construction and Maintenance	44.6%	$30,800	12.6%	102,000
20. Private Detectives and Investigators	23.7%	$32,650	17.7%	7,000
21. Music Directors and Composers	44.8%	$34,810	10.4%	11,000
22. Drywall and Ceiling Tile Installers	23.4%	$34,740	9.0%	17,000
23. Medical Equipment Repairers	16.2%	$39,570	14.8%	4,000
24. Soil and Plant Scientists	35.9%	$54,530	13.9%	1,000
25. Tree Trimmers and Pruners	22.2%	$27,920	16.5%	11,000

Best-Paying Jobs for Introverts with a High Percentage of Self-Employed Workers

Job	Percent Self-Employed Workers	Annual Earnings
1. Lawyers	24.1%	$98,930
2. Personal Financial Advisors	38.9%	$63,500
3. Network Systems and Data Communications Analysts	19.9%	$61,750
4. Fashion Designers	26.5%	$60,860
5. Soil and Plant Scientists	35.9%	$54,530
6. Sociologists	11.7%	$52,760
7. Accountants and Auditors	10.9%	$52,210
8. Commercial and Industrial Designers	30.1%	$52,200
9. Food Scientists and Technologists	28.8%	$51,440
10. Writers and Authors	67.7%	$46,420
11. Editors	14.8%	$45,510
12. Appraisers and Assessors of Real Estate	37.2%	$43,440
13. Animal Scientists	31.3%	$43,170
14. Plumbers, Pipefitters, and Steamfitters	13.3%	$42,160
15. Brickmasons and Blockmasons	28.6%	$41,860
16. Interior Designers	25.3%	$41,350
17. Fine Artists, Including Painters, Sculptors, and Illustrators	61.9%	$41,280
18. Tapers	21.0%	$39,870
19. Medical Equipment Repairers	16.2%	$39,570
20. Graphic Designers	25.6%	$38,390
21. Set and Exhibit Designers	27.6%	$37,390
22. Heating, Air Conditioning, and Refrigeration Mechanics and Installers	13.1%	$37,040
23. Tile and Marble Setters	24.4%	$36,530
24. Computer, Automated Teller, and Office Machine Repairers	13.7%	$36,060
25. Title Examiners, Abstractors, and Searchers	10.7%	$35,120

Fastest-Growing Jobs for Introverts with a High Percentage of Self-Employed Workers

Job	Percent Self-Employed Workers	Percent Growth
1. Network Systems and Data Communications Analysts	19.9%	54.6%
2. Personal Financial Advisors	38.9%	25.9%
3. Tile and Marble Setters	24.4%	22.9%
4. Appraisers and Assessors of Real Estate	37.2%	22.8%
5. Accountants and Auditors	10.9%	22.4%
6. Animal Trainers	58.2%	20.3%
7. Landscaping and Groundskeeping Workers	20.5%	19.5%
8. Heating, Air Conditioning, and Refrigeration Mechanics and Installers	13.1%	19.0%
9. Private Detectives and Investigators	23.7%	17.7%
10. Writers and Authors	67.7%	17.7%
11. Roofers	23.8%	16.8%
12. Pesticide Handlers, Sprayers, and Applicators, Vegetation	19.6%	16.6%
13. Tree Trimmers and Pruners	22.2%	16.5%
14. Locksmiths and Safe Repairers	37.6%	16.1%
15. Automotive Service Technicians and Mechanics	14.8%	15.7%
16. Plumbers, Pipefitters, and Steamfitters	13.3%	15.7%
17. Interior Designers	25.3%	15.5%
18. Graphic Designers	25.6%	15.2%
19. Motorboat Mechanics	18.9%	15.1%
20. Lawyers	24.1%	15.0%
21. Editors	14.8%	14.8%
22. Medical Equipment Repairers	16.2%	14.8%
23. Outdoor Power Equipment and Other Small Engine Mechanics	19.2%	14.0%
24. Soil and Plant Scientists	35.9%	13.9%
25. Motorcycle Mechanics	15.7%	13.7%

Jobs for Introverts with the Most Openings with a High Percentage of Self-Employed Workers

Job	Percent Self-Employed Workers	Annual Openings
1. Landscaping and Groundskeeping Workers	20.5%	243,000
2. Accountants and Auditors	10.9%	157,000
3. Painters, Construction and Maintenance	44.6%	102,000
4. Farmers and Ranchers	100.0%	96,000
5. Automotive Service Technicians and Mechanics	14.8%	93,000
6. Plumbers, Pipefitters, and Steamfitters	13.3%	61,000
7. Network Systems and Data Communications Analysts	19.9%	43,000
8. Lawyers	24.1%	40,000
9. Roofers	23.8%	38,000
10. Graphic Designers	25.6%	35,000
11. Heating, Air Conditioning, and Refrigeration Mechanics and Installers	13.1%	33,000
12. Computer, Automated Teller, and Office Machine Repairers	13.7%	31,000
13. Automotive Body and Related Repairers	17.6%	18,000
14. Brickmasons and Blockmasons	28.6%	17,000
15. Drywall and Ceiling Tile Installers	23.4%	17,000
16. Personal Financial Advisors	38.9%	17,000
17. Editors	14.8%	16,000
18. Writers and Authors	67.7%	14,000
19. Merchandise Displayers and Window Trimmers	25.9%	13,000
20. Cabinetmakers and Bench Carpenters	15.7%	12,000
21. Excavating and Loading Machine and Dragline Operators	19.1%	11,000
22. Music Directors and Composers	44.8%	11,000
23. Tax Preparers	35.6%	11,000
24. Tree Trimmers and Pruners	22.2%	11,000
25. Interior Designers	25.3%	10,000

Best Jobs for Introverts Employing a High Percentage of Women

To create the eight lists that follow, we sorted the 200 best jobs for introverts according to the percentages of women and men in the workforce. These are our most controversial lists, and we knew we would create some controversy when we first included the best jobs lists with high percentages (more than 70 percent) of men and women in earlier *Best Jobs* books. But these lists are not meant to restrict women or men from considering job options—our reason for including these lists is exactly the opposite. We hope the lists help people see possibilities that they might not otherwise have considered.

The fact is that jobs with high percentages of women or high percentages of men offer good opportunities for both men and women if they want to do one of these jobs. So we suggest that women browse the lists of introvert-friendly jobs that employ high percentages of men and that men browse the lists of introvert-friendly jobs with high percentages of women. There are jobs among both lists that pay well, and women or men who are interested in them and who have or can obtain the necessary education and training should consider them.

It is interesting to compare the two sets of introvert-friendly jobs—those with the highest percentage of men and those with the highest percentage of women—in terms of the economic measures that we use to rank these lists. The male-dominated jobs have higher average earnings ($39,105) than the female-dominated jobs ($28,817). This is unfortunate but consistent with most other books in the *Best Jobs* series where we look at jobs by the sex of the workers. What is unusual, however, is that the female-dominated jobs also average slower growth than the male-dominated jobs—4.5 percent versus 12.2 percent. Current growth patterns of the U.S. economy generally are friendly to women, but the fast-growing, female-dominated segments of the economy—especially health care and many office-based industries—are not friendly to introverts. Because in this book we look only at the introvert-friendly jobs dominated by women, we find comparatively slow job growth for them. On the other hand, among the female-dominated jobs we find more job openings than among the male-dominated jobs—an average of 75,000 openings compared to 19,000 openings. Although the male-dominated jobs are growing faster and are better paid, they tend to have smaller workforces. Over one-third of the male-dominated introverted occupations have a workforce of fewer than 30,000 people, whereas the smallest female-dominated occupation listed here has a workforce of 43,000 people. Therefore the male-dominated introverted occupations tend to provide fewer job openings.

Best Jobs for Introverts Employing the Highest Percentage of Women

Job	Percent Women
1. Word Processors and Typists	95.0%
2. Payroll and Timekeeping Clerks	91.4%
3. Bookkeeping, Accounting, and Auditing Clerks	91.3%
4. Billing and Posting Clerks and Machine Operators	89.0%
5. Medical Equipment Preparers	89.0%
6. Data Entry Keyers	82.2%
7. Title Examiners, Abstractors, and Searchers	75.3%

The jobs in the following four lists are derived from the preceding list of the introvert-friendly jobs employing the highest percentage of women.

Best Jobs Overall for Introverts Employing a High Percentage of Women

Job	Percent Women	Annual Earnings	Percent Growth	Annual Openings
1. Bookkeeping, Accounting, and Auditing Clerks	91.3%	$29,490	5.9%	291,000
2. Payroll and Timekeeping Clerks	91.4%	$31,360	17.3%	36,000
3. Billing and Posting Clerks and Machine Operators	89.0%	$27,780	3.4%	70,000
4. Title Examiners, Abstractors, and Searchers	75.3%	$35,120	0.9%	8,000
5. Medical Equipment Preparers	89.0%	$24,880	20.0%	8,000
6. Data Entry Keyers	82.2%	$23,810	−0.7%	85,000
7. Word Processors and Typists	95.0%	$29,020	−15.3%	30,000

Best-Paying Jobs for Introverts Employing a High Percentage of Women

Job	Percent Women	Annual Earnings
1. Title Examiners, Abstractors, and Searchers	75.3%	$35,120
2. Payroll and Timekeeping Clerks	91.4%	$31,360
3. Bookkeeping, Accounting, and Auditing Clerks	91.3%	$29,490
4. Word Processors and Typists	95.0%	$29,020
5. Billing and Posting Clerks and Machine Operators	89.0%	$27,780
6. Medical Equipment Preparers	89.0%	$24,880
7. Data Entry Keyers	82.2%	$23,810

Fastest-Growing Jobs for Introverts Employing a High Percentage of Women

Job	Percent Women	Percent Growth
1. Medical Equipment Preparers	89.0%	20.0%
2. Payroll and Timekeeping Clerks	91.4%	17.3%
3. Bookkeeping, Accounting, and Auditing Clerks	91.3%	5.9%
4. Billing and Posting Clerks and Machine Operators	89.0%	3.4%
5. Title Examiners, Abstractors, and Searchers	75.3%	0.9%
6. Data Entry Keyers	82.2%	−0.7%
7. Word Processors and Typists	95.0%	−15.3%

Jobs for Introverts with the Most Openings Employing a High Percentage of Women

Job	Percent Women	Annual Openings
1. Bookkeeping, Accounting, and Auditing Clerks	91.3%	291,000
2. Data Entry Keyers	82.2%	85,000
3. Billing and Posting Clerks and Machine Operators	89.0%	70,000
4. Payroll and Timekeeping Clerks	91.4%	36,000
5. Word Processors and Typists	95.0%	30,000
6. Medical Equipment Preparers	89.0%	8,000
7. Title Examiners, Abstractors, and Searchers	75.3%	8,000

Best Jobs for Introverts Employing a High Percentage of Men

If you have not already read the intro to the previous group of lists, "Best Jobs for Introverts Employing a High Percentages of Women," consider doing so. Much of the content there applies to these lists as well.

We did not include these groups of lists with the assumption that men should consider introverted jobs with high percentages of men or that women should consider introverted jobs with high percentages of women. Instead, these lists are here because we think they are interesting and perhaps helpful in considering nontraditional career options. For example, some men would do very well in and enjoy some of the jobs with high percentages of women but may not have considered them seriously. In a similar way, some women would very much enjoy and do well in some jobs that traditionally have been held by high percentages of men. We hope that these lists help you consider options that you simply did not seriously consider because of gender stereotypes.

In the jobs on the following lists, more than 70 percent of the workers are men. Note that 132 jobs meet this cutoff, whereas only 7 female-dominated jobs do. This huge imbalance should not be surprising, because solitary jobs have traditionally had high concentrations of men, whereas women have traditionally been concentrated in jobs that have a lot of personal contact. Nevertheless, increasing numbers of women are entering many of these jobs.

Best Jobs for Introverts Employing the Highest Percentage of Men

Job	Percent Men
1. Excavating and Loading Machine and Dragline Operators	99.8%
2. Bus and Truck Mechanics and Diesel Engine Specialists	99.5%
3. Drywall and Ceiling Tile Installers	99.2%
4. Tapers	99.2%
5. Brickmasons and Blockmasons	99.1%
6. Stonemasons	99.1%
7. Tool and Die Makers	98.9%
8. Plumbers, Pipefitters, and Steamfitters	98.8%
9. Earth Drillers, Except Oil and Gas	98.6%
10. Elevator Installers and Repairers	98.6%
11. Heating, Air Conditioning, and Refrigeration Mechanics and Installers	98.6%
12. Ship Engineers	98.5%
13. Control and Valve Installers and Repairers, Except Mechanical Door	98.4%
14. Mechanical Door Repairers	98.4%
15. Mobile Heavy Equipment Mechanics, Except Engines	98.4%
16. Rail Car Repairers	98.4%
17. Tire Repairers and Changers	98.4%
18. Cement Masons and Concrete Finishers	98.3%
19. Riggers	98.3%
20. Terrazzo Workers and Finishers	98.3%
21. Automotive Service Technicians and Mechanics	98.2%
22. Motorboat Mechanics	98.2%
23. Motorcycle Mechanics	98.2%
24. Outdoor Power Equipment and Other Small Engine Mechanics	98.2%
25. Recreational Vehicle Service Technicians	98.2%
26. Automotive Body and Related Repairers	98.1%
27. Millwrights	98.0%
28. Electronic Home Entertainment Equipment Installers and Repairers	97.9%
29. Tile and Marble Setters	97.7%
30. Reinforcing Iron and Rebar Workers	97.6%
31. Roofers	97.6%
32. Fence Erectors	97.4%
33. Industrial Machinery Mechanics	97.4%
34. Pest Control Workers	97.4%
35. Operating Engineers and Other Construction Equipment Operators	97.3%
36. Surveying and Mapping Technicians	97.3%

Best Jobs for Introverts Employing the Highest Percentage of Men

Job	Percent Men
37. Logging Equipment Operators	97.2%
38. Captains, Mates, and Pilots of Water Vessels	97.1%
39. Home Appliance Repairers	97.0%
40. Stationary Engineers and Boiler Operators	97.0%
41. Boilermakers	96.8%
42. Helpers—Brickmasons, Blockmasons, Stonemasons, and Tile and Marble Setters	96.8%
43. Helpers—Painters, Paperhangers, Plasterers, and Stucco Masons	96.8%
44. Electrical Power-Line Installers and Repairers	96.5%
45. Insulation Workers, Floor, Ceiling, and Wall	95.9%
46. Insulation Workers, Mechanical	95.9%
47. Maintenance and Repair Workers, General	95.9%
48. Maintenance Workers, Machinery	95.9%
49. Signal and Track Switch Repairers	95.9%
50. Commercial Divers	95.8%
51. Locksmiths and Safe Repairers	95.8%
52. Aircraft Mechanics and Service Technicians	95.5%
53. Electric Motor, Power Tool, and Related Repairers	95.5%
54. Electrical and Electronics Repairers, Powerhouse, Substation, and Relay	95.5%
55. Truck Drivers, Heavy and Tractor-Trailer	95.5%
56. Truck Drivers, Light or Delivery Services	95.5%
57. Paving, Surfacing, and Tamping Equipment Operators	95.4%
58. Pile-Driver Operators	95.4%
59. Water and Liquid Waste Treatment Plant and System Operators	95.4%
60. Cabinetmakers and Bench Carpenters	95.1%
61. Marine Engineers and Naval Architects	94.9%
62. Sailors and Marine Oilers	94.5%
63. Welders, Cutters, Solderers, and Brazers	94.2%
64. Welding, Soldering, and Brazing Machine Setters, Operators, and Tenders	94.2%
65. Telecommunications Line Installers and Repairers	94.0%
66. Machinists	93.2%
67. Electrical Engineers	92.9%
68. Electronics Engineers, Except Computer	92.9%
69. Landscaping and Groundskeeping Workers	92.5%
70. Painters, Construction and Maintenance	92.5%
71. Pesticide Handlers, Sprayers, and Applicators, Vegetation	92.5%
72. Tree Trimmers and Pruners	92.5%

(continued)

(*continued*)

Best Jobs for Introverts Employing the Highest Percentage of Men

Job	Percent Men
73. Medical Equipment Repairers	92.3%
74. Subway and Streetcar Operators	91.1%
75. Hazardous Materials Removal Workers	90.8%
76. Health and Safety Engineers, Except Mining Safety Engineers and Inspectors	89.2%
77. Mixing and Blending Machine Setters, Operators, and Tenders	89.2%
78. Avionics Technicians	88.8%
79. Computer-Controlled Machine Tool Operators, Metal and Plastic	88.8%
80. Numerical Tool and Process Control Programmers	88.8%
81. Materials Engineers	88.0%
82. Lathe and Turning Machine Tool Setters, Operators, and Tenders, Metal and Plastic	87.6%
83. Atmospheric and Space Scientists	87.1%
84. Civil Engineers	86.8%
85. Aerospace Engineers	86.7%
86. Telecommunications Equipment Installers and Repairers, Except Line Installers	86.5%
87. Sound Engineering Technicians	86.4%
88. Coin, Vending, and Amusement Machine Servicers and Repairers	86.3%
89. Computer, Automated Teller, and Office Machine Repairers	86.3%
90. Bridge and Lock Tenders	86.2%
91. Traffic Technicians	86.2%
92. Astronomers	86.1%
93. Physicists	86.1%
94. Parking Enforcement Workers	85.7%
95. Conservation Scientists	85.3%
96. Foresters	85.3%
97. Coating, Painting, and Spraying Machine Setters, Operators, and Tenders	85.0%
98. Painters, Transportation Equipment	85.0%
99. Chemical Equipment Operators and Tenders	84.8%
100. Gas Plant Operators	84.8%
101. Petroleum Pump System Operators, Refinery Operators, and Gaugers	84.8%
102. Separating, Filtering, Clarifying, Precipitating, and Still Machine Setters, Operators, and Tenders	84.8%
103. Clergy	84.5%
104. Printing Machine Operators	84.4%
105. Helpers—Production Workers	83.8%
106. Transportation Inspectors	83.8%

Best Jobs for Introverts Employing the Highest Percentage of Men

Job	Percent Men
107. Cost Estimators	82.6%
108. Cartographers and Photogrammetrists	82.0%
109. Job Printers	79.9%
110. Electrical and Electronic Engineering Technicians	79.8%
111. Electro-Mechanical Technicians	79.8%
112. Mechanical Engineering Technicians	79.8%
113. Multiple Machine Tool Setters, Operators, and Tenders, Metal and Plastic	79.7%
114. Architectural and Civil Drafters	78.4%
115. Electrical and Electronics Drafters	78.4%
116. Mechanical Drafters	78.4%
117. Computer Software Engineers, Applications	78.1%
118. Computer Software Engineers, Systems Software	78.1%
119. Computer Systems Analysts	78.1%
120. Embalmers	78.0%
121. Butchers and Meat Cutters	77.7%
122. Slaughterers and Meat Packers	77.7%
123. Environmental Scientists and Specialists, Including Health	77.5%
124. Geoscientists, Except Hydrologists and Geographers	77.5%
125. Hydrologists	77.5%
126. Network Systems and Data Communications Analysts	75.4%
127. Farmers and Ranchers	74.4%
128. Computer Programmers	74.0%
129. Animal Scientists	73.9%
130. Food Scientists and Technologists	73.9%
131. Soil and Plant Scientists	73.9%
132. Paperhangers	70.3%

The jobs in the following four lists are derived from the preceding list of the introvert-friendly jobs employing the highest percentage of men.

Best Jobs Overall for Introverts Employing a High Percentage of Men

Job	Percent Men	Annual Earnings	Percent Growth	Annual Openings
1. Computer Software Engineers, Applications	78.1%	$77,090	48.4%	54,000
2. Computer Software Engineers, Systems Software	78.1%	$82,120	43.0%	37,000
3. Computer Systems Analysts	78.1%	$68,300	31.4%	56,000
4. Network Systems and Data Communications Analysts	75.4%	$61,750	54.6%	43,000
5. Civil Engineers	86.8%	$66,190	16.5%	19,000
6. Cost Estimators	82.6%	$52,020	18.2%	15,000
7. Plumbers, Pipefitters, and Steamfitters	98.8%	$42,160	15.7%	61,000
8. Environmental Scientists and Specialists, Including Health	77.5%	$52,630	17.1%	8,000
9. Heating, Air Conditioning, and Refrigeration Mechanics and Installers	98.6%	$37,040	19.0%	33,000
10. Electrical Engineers	92.9%	$73,510	11.8%	12,000
11. Electronics Engineers, Except Computer	92.9%	$78,030	9.7%	11,000
12. Automotive Service Technicians and Mechanics	98.2%	$33,050	15.7%	93,000
13. Bus and Truck Mechanics and Diesel Engine Specialists	99.5%	$36,620	14.4%	32,000
14. Roofers	97.6%	$31,230	16.8%	38,000
15. Tile and Marble Setters	97.7%	$36,530	22.9%	9,000
16. Aircraft Mechanics and Service Technicians	95.5%	$47,310	13.4%	11,000
17. Hydrologists	77.5%	$63,820	31.6%	1,000
18. Maintenance and Repair Workers, General	95.9%	$31,210	15.2%	154,000
19. Truck Drivers, Heavy and Tractor-Trailer	95.5%	$34,280	12.9%	274,000
20. Cement Masons and Concrete Finishers	98.3%	$32,030	15.9%	32,000
21. Electrical and Electronic Engineering Technicians	79.8%	$48,040	9.8%	18,000
22. Hazardous Materials Removal Workers	90.8%	$33,690	31.2%	11,000
23. Atmospheric and Space Scientists	87.1%	$73,940	16.5%	1,000
24. Clergy	84.5%	$38,540	12.4%	26,000
25. Landscaping and Groundskeeping Workers	92.5%	$20,670	19.5%	243,000

Best-Paying Jobs for Introverts Employing a High Percentage of Men

Job	Percent Men	Annual Earnings
1. Astronomers	86.1%	$104,670
2. Physicists	86.1%	$89,810
3. Aerospace Engineers	86.7%	$84,090
4. Computer Software Engineers, Systems Software	78.1%	$82,120

Best-Paying Jobs for Introverts Employing a High Percentage of Men

Job	Percent Men	Annual Earnings
5. Electronics Engineers, Except Computer	92.9%	$78,030
6. Computer Software Engineers, Applications	78.1%	$77,090
7. Atmospheric and Space Scientists	87.1%	$73,940
8. Electrical Engineers	92.9%	$73,510
9. Marine Engineers and Naval Architects	94.9%	$72,920
10. Geoscientists, Except Hydrologists and Geographers	77.5%	$71,640
11. Materials Engineers	88.0%	$69,660
12. Computer Systems Analysts	78.1%	$68,300
13. Civil Engineers	86.8%	$66,190
14. Health and Safety Engineers, Except Mining Safety Engineers and Inspectors	89.2%	$65,210
15. Hydrologists	77.5%	$63,820
16. Computer Programmers	74.0%	$63,420
17. Network Systems and Data Communications Analysts	75.4%	$61,750
18. Elevator Installers and Repairers	98.6%	$59,190
19. Electrical and Electronics Repairers, Powerhouse, Substation, and Relay	95.5%	$54,970
20. Soil and Plant Scientists	73.9%	$54,530
21. Conservation Scientists	85.3%	$53,350
22. Ship Engineers	98.5%	$52,780
23. Environmental Scientists and Specialists, Including Health	77.5%	$52,630
24. Cost Estimators	82.6%	$52,020
25. Gas Plant Operators	84.8%	$51,920

Fastest-Growing Jobs for Introverts Employing a High Percentage of Men

Job	Percent Men	Percent Growth
1. Network Systems and Data Communications Analysts	75.4%	54.6%
2. Computer Software Engineers, Applications	78.1%	48.4%
3. Computer Software Engineers, Systems Software	78.1%	43.0%
4. Hydrologists	77.5%	31.6%
5. Computer Systems Analysts	78.1%	31.4%
6. Hazardous Materials Removal Workers	90.8%	31.2%
7. Tile and Marble Setters	97.7%	22.9%
8. Landscaping and Groundskeeping Workers	92.5%	19.5%
9. Recreational Vehicle Service Technicians	98.2%	19.5%

(continued)

(continued)

Fastest-Growing Jobs for Introverts Employing a High Percentage of Men

Job	Percent Men	Percent Growth
10. Heating, Air Conditioning, and Refrigeration Mechanics and Installers	98.6%	19.0%
11. Pest Control Workers	97.4%	18.4%
12. Sound Engineering Technicians	86.4%	18.4%
13. Cost Estimators	82.6%	18.2%
14. Environmental Scientists and Specialists, Including Health	77.5%	17.1%
15. Roofers	97.6%	16.8%
16. Pesticide Handlers, Sprayers, and Applicators, Vegetation	92.5%	16.6%
17. Atmospheric and Space Scientists	87.1%	16.5%
18. Civil Engineers	86.8%	16.5%
19. Tree Trimmers and Pruners	92.5%	16.5%
20. Water and Liquid Waste Treatment Plant and System Operators	95.4%	16.2%
21. Locksmiths and Safe Repairers	95.8%	16.1%
22. Cement Masons and Concrete Finishers	98.3%	15.9%
23. Mechanical Door Repairers	98.4%	15.8%
24. Automotive Service Technicians and Mechanics	98.2%	15.7%
25. Embalmers	78.0%	15.7%

Jobs for Introverts with the Most Openings Employing a High Percentage of Men

Job	Percent Men	Annual Openings
1. Truck Drivers, Heavy and Tractor-Trailer	95.5%	274,000
2. Landscaping and Groundskeeping Workers	92.5%	243,000
3. Truck Drivers, Light or Delivery Services	95.5%	169,000
4. Maintenance and Repair Workers, General	95.9%	154,000
5. Helpers—Production Workers	83.8%	107,000
6. Painters, Construction and Maintenance	92.5%	102,000
7. Farmers and Ranchers	74.4%	96,000
8. Automotive Service Technicians and Mechanics	98.2%	93,000
9. Plumbers, Pipefitters, and Steamfitters	98.8%	61,000
10. Computer Systems Analysts	78.1%	56,000
11. Computer Software Engineers, Applications	78.1%	54,000
12. Welders, Cutters, Solderers, and Brazers	94.2%	52,000
13. Network Systems and Data Communications Analysts	75.4%	43,000

Jobs for Introverts with the Most Openings Employing a High Percentage of Men

Job	Percent Men	Annual Openings
14. Roofers	97.6%	38,000
15. Computer Software Engineers, Systems Software	78.1%	37,000
16. Operating Engineers and Other Construction Equipment Operators	97.3%	37,000
17. Heating, Air Conditioning, and Refrigeration Mechanics and Installers	98.6%	33,000
18. Machinists	93.2%	33,000
19. Bus and Truck Mechanics and Diesel Engine Specialists	99.5%	32,000
20. Cement Masons and Concrete Finishers	98.3%	32,000
21. Computer, Automated Teller, and Office Machine Repairers	86.3%	31,000
22. Computer Programmers	74.0%	28,000
23. Clergy	84.5%	26,000
24. Printing Machine Operators	84.4%	26,000
25. Telecommunications Line Installers and Repairers	94.0%	23,000

Best Jobs for Introverts Sorted by Education or Training Required

The lists in this section organize the 200 best jobs for introverts into groups based on the education or training typically required for entry. Unlike in many of the previous sections, here we do not include separate lists for highest pay, growth, or number of openings. Instead, we provide one list that includes all the best introvert-friendly jobs that fit into each of the education levels and ranks them by their total combined score for earnings, growth, and number of openings.

These lists can help you identify a job with higher earnings or upward mobility but with a similar level of education to the job you now hold. For example, you will find jobs within the same level of education that require similar skills, yet one pays significantly better than the other, is projected to grow more rapidly, or has significantly more job openings per year. This information can help you leverage your present skills and experience into jobs that might provide better long-term career opportunities.

You can also use these lists to explore possible job options if you were to get additional training, education, or work experience. For example, you can use these lists to identify introverted occupations that offer high potential and then look into the education or training required to get the jobs that interest you most.

The lists can also help you when you plan your education. For example, you might be thinking about a construction job but you aren't sure what kind of work you want to do. The lists show that drywall and ceiling tile installers need moderate-term on-the-job training and earn $34,740, whereas terrazzo workers and finishers need long-term on-the-job training but earn an average of $32,030. If you want higher earnings without lengthy training, this information might make a difference in your choice.

The Education Levels

Here are brief descriptions used by the U.S. Department of Labor for the training and education levels used in the lists that follow:

- **Short-term on-the-job training.** It is possible to work in these occupations and achieve an average level of performance within a few days or weeks through on-the-job training.
- **Moderate-term on-the-job training.** Occupations that require this type of training can be performed adequately after a one- to 12-month period of combined on-the-job and informal training. Typically, untrained workers observe experienced workers performing tasks and are gradually moved into progressively more difficult assignments.
- **Long-term on-the-job training.** This training requires more than 12 months of on-the-job training or combined work experience and formal classroom instruction. This includes occupations that use formal apprenticeships for training workers that may take up to four years. It also includes intensive occupation-specific, employer-sponsored training such as police academies. Furthermore, it includes occupations that require natural talent that must be developed over many years.
- **Work experience in a related occupation.** This type of job requires experience in a related occupation. For example, police detectives are selected based on their experience as police patrol officers.
- **Postsecondary vocational training.** This training requirement can vary in length; training usually lasts from a few months up to one year. In a few instances, there may be as many as four years of training.
- **Associate degree.** This degree usually requires two years of full-time academic work beyond high school.
- **Bachelor's degree.** This degree requires approximately four to five years of full-time academic work beyond high school.
- **Work experience plus degree.** Jobs in this category are often management-related and require some experience in a related nonmanagerial position.
- **Master's degree.** Completion of a master's degree usually requires one to two years of full-time study beyond the bachelor's degree.
- **Doctoral degree.** This degree normally requires two or more years of full-time academic work beyond the bachelor's degree.
- **First professional degree.** This type of degree normally requires a minimum of two years of education beyond the bachelor's degree and frequently requires three years.

Another Warning About the Data

We warned you in the introduction to use caution in interpreting the data we use, and we want to do it again here. The occupational data we use is the most accurate available anywhere, but it has its limitations. For example, the education or training requirements for entry into a job are those typically required as a minimum—but some people working in those jobs may have considerably more or different credentials. For example, although an associate degree is considered the usual requirement for semiconductor processors, two-thirds of the people working in this occupation have no formal education beyond high school. On the other hand, appraisers and assessors of real estate usually need to have completed only post-secondary vocational training, but more than half of these workers are college graduates.

In a similar way, you need to be cautious about assuming that more education or training always leads to higher income. It is true that people with jobs that require long-term on-the-job training typically earn more than people with jobs that require short-term on-the-job training. (For the jobs in this book, the difference is an average of $37,445 versus an average of $24,564.) However, some people with short-term on-the-job training do earn more than the average for the highest-paying occupations listed in this book; furthermore, some people with long-term on-the-job training earn much less than the average shown in this book—this is particularly true early in a person's career.

So as you browse the lists that follow, please use them as a way to be encouraged rather than discouraged. Education and training are very important for success in the labor market of the future, but so are ability, drive, initiative, and, yes, luck.

Having said this, we encourage you to get as much education and training as you can. An old saying goes, "The harder you work, the luckier you get." It is just as true now as it ever was.

Best Jobs for Introverts Requiring Short-Term On-the-Job Training

Job	Annual Earnings	Percent Growth	Annual Openings
1. Truck Drivers, Light or Delivery Services	$24,790	15.7%	169,000
2. Landscaping and Groundskeeping Workers	$20,670	19.5%	243,000
3. Medical Equipment Preparers	$24,880	20.0%	8,000
4. Tree Trimmers and Pruners	$27,920	16.5%	11,000
5. Bus Drivers, School	$24,070	13.6%	76,000
6. Crossing Guards	$20,050	19.7%	26,000
7. Helpers—Brickmasons, Blockmasons, Stonemasons, and Tile and Marble Setters	$24,600	14.9%	14,000
8. Postal Service Mail Carriers	$46,330	0.0%	19,000
9. Traffic Technicians	$37,070	14.1%	1,000
10. Riggers	$37,010	13.9%	2,000
11. Parking Enforcement Workers	$29,070	15.1%	1,000
12. Helpers—Production Workers	$20,390	7.9%	107,000
13. Driver/Sales Workers	$20,120	13.8%	72,000
14. Bridge and Lock Tenders	$37,980	7.2%	fewer than 500

(continued)

(continued)

Best Jobs for Introverts Requiring Short-Term On-the-Job Training

Job	Annual Earnings	Percent Growth	Annual Openings
15. Maintenance Workers, Machinery	$33,650	2.8%	6,000
16. Packaging and Filling Machine Operators and Tenders	$22,930	2.3%	80,000
17. Sailors and Marine Oilers	$29,360	5.2%	4,000
18. Tire Repairers and Changers	$20,960	4.5%	17,000
19. Helpers—Painters, Paperhangers, Plasterers, and Stucco Masons	$20,560	11.5%	6,000

Best Jobs for Introverts Requiring Moderate-Term On-the-Job Training

Job	Annual Earnings	Percent Growth	Annual Openings
1. Truck Drivers, Heavy and Tractor-Trailer	$34,280	12.9%	274,000
2. Payroll and Timekeeping Clerks	$31,360	17.3%	36,000
3. Operating Engineers and Other Construction Equipment Operators	$35,830	11.6%	37,000
4. Roofers	$31,230	16.8%	38,000
5. Bus Drivers, Transit and Intercity	$31,010	21.7%	34,000
6. Cement Masons and Concrete Finishers	$32,030	15.9%	32,000
7. Hazardous Materials Removal Workers	$33,690	31.2%	11,000
8. Maintenance and Repair Workers, General	$31,210	15.2%	154,000
9. Painters, Construction and Maintenance	$30,800	12.6%	102,000
10. Drywall and Ceiling Tile Installers	$34,740	9.0%	17,000
11. Bookkeeping, Accounting, and Auditing Clerks	$29,490	5.9%	291,000
12. Excavating and Loading Machine and Dragline Operators	$32,380	8.0%	11,000
13. Subway and Streetcar Operators	$47,500	13.7%	1,000
14. Tapers	$39,870	5.9%	5,000
15. Pile-Driver Operators	$48,900	11.9%	fewer than 500
16. Surveying and Mapping Technicians	$31,290	9.6%	9,000
17. Locksmiths and Safe Repairers	$30,880	16.1%	5,000
18. Paving, Surfacing, and Tamping Equipment Operators	$30,320	15.6%	7,000
19. Control and Valve Installers and Repairers, Except Mechanical Door	$44,120	4.9%	4,000
20. Printing Machine Operators	$30,730	2.9%	26,000
21. Billing and Posting Clerks and Machine Operators	$27,780	3.4%	70,000
22. Slaughterers and Meat Packers	$21,220	13.8%	22,000

Best Jobs for Introverts Requiring Moderate-Term On-the-Job Training

Job	Annual Earnings	Percent Growth	Annual Openings
23. Commercial Divers	$37,960	9.4%	fewer than 500
24. Earth Drillers, Except Oil and Gas	$33,770	7.9%	4,000
25. Paper Goods Machine Setters, Operators, and Tenders	$31,160	2.4%	15,000
26. Title Examiners, Abstractors, and Searchers	$35,120	0.9%	8,000
27. Outdoor Power Equipment and Other Small Engine Mechanics	$25,810	14.0%	10,000
28. Structural Metal Fabricators and Fitters	$30,290	2.9%	18,000
29. Pesticide Handlers, Sprayers, and Applicators, Vegetation	$26,120	16.6%	6,000
30. Pest Control Workers	$27,170	18.4%	4,000
31. Signal and Track Switch Repairers	$49,200	2.3%	1,000
32. Chemical Equipment Operators and Tenders	$39,030	–4.5%	6,000
33. Inspectors, Testers, Sorters, Samplers, and Weighers	$29,200	–2.6%	85,000
34. Separating, Filtering, Clarifying, Precipitating, and Still Machine Setters, Operators, and Tenders	$34,650	1.6%	5,000
35. Tax Preparers	$25,700	10.6%	11,000
36. Mechanical Door Repairers	$30,310	15.8%	1,000
37. Merchandise Displayers and Window Trimmers	$22,590	10.3%	13,000
38. Computer-Controlled Machine Tool Operators, Metal and Plastic	$31,010	–1.2%	13,000
39. Paperhangers	$33,450	3.2%	3,000
40. Insulation Workers, Floor, Ceiling, and Wall	$31,360	3.0%	4,000
41. Animal Trainers	$24,800	20.3%	3,000
42. Logging Equipment Operators	$28,920	3.4%	9,000
43. Insulation Workers, Mechanical	$35,510	1.0%	2,000
44. Mixing and Blending Machine Setters, Operators, and Tenders	$28,890	2.0%	16,000
45. Lathe and Turning Machine Tool Setters, Operators, and Tenders, Metal and Plastic	$31,750	–9.0%	7,000
46. Data Entry Keyers	$23,810	–0.7%	85,000
47. Word Processors and Typists	$29,020	–15.3%	30,000
48. Welding, Soldering, and Brazing Machine Setters, Operators, and Tenders	$30,430	0.4%	7,000
49. Fence Erectors	$24,930	9.9%	5,000
50. Coin, Vending, and Amusement Machine Servicers and Repairers	$28,200	2.4%	7,000
51. Coating, Painting, and Spraying Machine Setters, Operators, and Tenders	$26,670	–3.4%	16,000
52. Multiple Machine Tool Setters, Operators, and Tenders, Metal and Plastic	$29,780	0.3%	6,000

Best Jobs for Introverts Requiring Long-Term On-the-Job Training

Job	Annual Earnings	Percent Growth	Annual Openings
1. Plumbers, Pipefitters, and Steamfitters	$42,160	15.7%	61,000
2. Heating, Air Conditioning, and Refrigeration Mechanics and Installers	$37,040	19.0%	33,000
3. Telecommunications Line Installers and Repairers	$42,410	10.8%	23,000
4. Tile and Marble Setters	$36,530	22.9%	9,000
5. Elevator Installers and Repairers	$59,190	14.8%	3,000
6. Brickmasons and Blockmasons	$41,860	12.0%	17,000
7. Water and Liquid Waste Treatment Plant and System Operators	$34,930	16.2%	6,000
8. Painters, Transportation Equipment	$34,840	14.1%	10,000
9. Bakers	$21,520	15.2%	37,000
10. Telecommunications Equipment Installers and Repairers, Except Line Installers	$50,620	–4.9%	21,000
11. Electrical Power-Line Installers and Repairers	$50,150	2.5%	11,000
12. Automotive Body and Related Repairers	$34,810	10.3%	18,000
13. Reinforcing Iron and Rebar Workers	$34,910	14.1%	6,000
14. Motorboat Mechanics	$32,780	15.1%	7,000
15. Millwrights	$44,780	5.9%	5,000
16. Aircraft Structure, Surfaces, Rigging, and Systems Assemblers	$43,990	7.8%	4,000
17. Gas Plant Operators	$51,920	7.7%	2,000
18. Machinists	$34,350	4.3%	33,000
19. Boilermakers	$48,050	8.7%	2,000
20. Fine Artists, Including Painters, Sculptors, and Illustrators	$41,280	10.2%	4,000
21. Petroleum Pump System Operators, Refinery Operators, and Gaugers	$51,060	–8.6%	6,000
22. Stationary Engineers and Boiler Operators	$44,600	3.4%	5,000
23. Welders, Cutters, Solderers, and Brazers	$30,990	5.0%	52,000
24. Industrial Machinery Mechanics	$39,740	–0.2%	13,000
25. Recreational Vehicle Service Technicians	$30,480	19.5%	3,000
26. Tool and Die Makers	$43,580	–2.6%	7,000
27. Butchers and Meat Cutters	$26,590	7.9%	20,000
28. Farmers and Ranchers	$34,140	–14.5%	96,000
29. Motorcycle Mechanics	$29,450	13.7%	6,000
30. Stonemasons	$34,640	13.0%	2,000
31. Terrazzo Workers and Finishers	$32,030	15.2%	1,000
32. Cabinetmakers and Bench Carpenters	$26,020	4.1%	12,000
33. Rail Car Repairers	$42,530	–1.2%	2,000
34. Job Printers	$31,920	1.8%	8,000

Best Jobs for Introverts Requiring Long-Term On-the-Job Training

Job	Annual Earnings	Percent Growth	Annual Openings
35. Dental Laboratory Technicians	$32,240	7.6%	3,000
36. Numerical Tool and Process Control Programmers	$41,830	–1.1%	2,000
37. Home Appliance Repairers	$32,980	2.6%	3,000
38. Medical Appliance Technicians	$29,080	13.3%	1,000

Best Jobs for Introverts Requiring Work Experience in a Related Occupation

Job	Annual Earnings	Percent Growth	Annual Openings
1. Cost Estimators	$52,020	18.2%	15,000
2. Private Detectives and Investigators	$32,650	17.7%	7,000
3. Transportation Inspectors	$49,490	11.4%	2,000
4. Captains, Mates, and Pilots of Water Vessels	$50,940	4.8%	2,000
5. Purchasing Agents and Buyers, Farm Products	$46,680	7.0%	2,000
6. Agricultural Inspectors	$32,840	6.8%	3,000

Best Jobs for Introverts Requiring Postsecondary Vocational Training

Job	Annual Earnings	Percent Growth	Annual Openings
1. Aircraft Mechanics and Service Technicians	$47,310	13.4%	11,000
2. Appraisers and Assessors of Real Estate	$43,440	22.8%	9,000
3. Automotive Service Technicians and Mechanics	$33,050	15.7%	93,000
4. Bus and Truck Mechanics and Diesel Engine Specialists	$36,620	14.4%	32,000
5. Mobile Heavy Equipment Mechanics, Except Engines	$39,410	8.8%	14,000
6. Avionics Technicians	$46,630	9.1%	2,000
7. Desktop Publishers	$32,800	23.2%	8,000
8. Sound Engineering Technicians	$38,390	18.4%	2,000
9. Architectural and Civil Drafters	$40,390	4.6%	9,000
10. Mechanical Drafters	$43,350	5.5%	7,000
11. Ship Engineers	$52,780	12.7%	1,000

(continued)

(continued)

Best Jobs for Introverts Requiring Postsecondary Vocational Training

Job	Annual Earnings	Percent Growth	Annual Openings
12. Embalmers	$36,960	15.7%	2,000
13. Computer, Automated Teller, and Office Machine Repairers	$36,060	3.8%	31,000
14. Electrical and Electronics Repairers, Powerhouse, Substation, and Relay	$54,970	−0.4%	2,000
15. Electrical and Electronics Drafters	$45,550	1.2%	3,000
16. Electric Motor, Power Tool, and Related Repairers	$33,460	4.1%	3,000
17. Prepress Technicians and Workers	$32,840	−8.4%	10,000
18. Electronic Home Entertainment Equipment Installers and Repairers	$28,940	4.7%	6,000

Best Jobs for Introverts Requiring an Associate Degree

Job	Annual Earnings	Percent Growth	Annual Openings
1. Electrical and Electronic Engineering Technicians	$48,040	9.8%	18,000
2. Interior Designers	$41,350	15.5%	10,000
3. Environmental Science and Protection Technicians, Including Health	$36,260	16.3%	6,000
4. Mechanical Engineering Technicians	$44,830	12.3%	5,000
5. Nuclear Technicians	$61,120	13.7%	1,000
6. Medical Equipment Repairers	$39,570	14.8%	4,000
7. Fashion Designers	$60,860	8.4%	2,000
8. Electro-Mechanical Technicians	$43,880	9.7%	2,000
9. Semiconductor Processors	$31,030	−7.5%	7,000

Best Jobs for Introverts Requiring a Bachelor's Degree

Job	Annual Earnings	Percent Growth	Annual Openings
1. Computer Software Engineers, Applications	$77,090	48.4%	54,000
2. Computer Software Engineers, Systems Software	$82,120	43.0%	37,000
3. Computer Systems Analysts	$68,300	31.4%	56,000
4. Network Systems and Data Communications Analysts	$61,750	54.6%	43,000
5. Financial Analysts	$63,860	17.3%	28,000

Best Jobs for Introverts Requiring a Bachelor's Degree

Job	Annual Earnings	Percent Growth	Annual Openings
6. Personal Financial Advisors	$63,500	25.9%	17,000
7. Accountants and Auditors	$52,210	22.4%	157,000
8. Civil Engineers	$66,190	16.5%	19,000
9. Database Administrators	$63,250	38.2%	9,000
10. Market Research Analysts	$57,300	19.6%	20,000
11. Electrical Engineers	$73,510	11.8%	12,000
12. Electronics Engineers, Except Computer	$78,030	9.7%	11,000
13. Atmospheric and Space Scientists	$73,940	16.5%	1,000
14. Technical Writers	$55,160	23.2%	5,000
15. Aerospace Engineers	$84,090	8.3%	6,000
16. Health and Safety Engineers, Except Mining Safety Engineers and Inspectors	$65,210	13.4%	2,000
17. Materials Engineers	$69,660	12.2%	2,000
18. Graphic Designers	$38,390	15.2%	35,000
19. Writers and Authors	$46,420	17.7%	14,000
20. Computer Programmers	$63,420	2.0%	28,000
21. Editors	$45,510	14.8%	16,000
22. Financial Examiners	$63,090	9.5%	3,000
23. Commercial and Industrial Designers	$52,200	10.8%	7,000
24. Soil and Plant Scientists	$54,530	13.9%	1,000
25. Marine Engineers and Naval Architects	$72,920	8.5%	fewer than 500
26. Chemists	$57,890	7.3%	5,000
27. Cartographers and Photogrammetrists	$48,250	15.2%	1,000
28. Materials Scientists	$71,450	8.0%	fewer than 500
29. Zoologists and Wildlife Biologists	$52,050	13.0%	1,000
30. Food Scientists and Technologists	$51,440	10.9%	1,000
31. Conservation Scientists	$53,350	6.3%	2,000
32. Credit Analysts	$50,370	3.6%	3,000
33. Set and Exhibit Designers	$37,390	9.3%	2,000
34. Animal Scientists	$43,170	12.9%	fewer than 500
35. Foresters	$48,670	6.7%	1,000

Best Jobs for Introverts Requiring Work Experience Plus Degree

Job	Annual Earnings	Percent Growth	Annual Openings
1. Actuaries	$81,640	23.2%	3,000
2. Arbitrators, Mediators, and Conciliators	$54,360	15.5%	fewer than 500
3. Music Directors and Composers	$34,810	10.4%	11,000

Best Jobs for Introverts Requiring a Master's Degree

Job	Annual Earnings	Percent Growth	Annual Openings
1. Hydrologists	$63,820	31.6%	1,000
2. Environmental Scientists and Specialists, Including Health	$52,630	17.1%	8,000
3. Geoscientists, Except Hydrologists and Geographers	$71,640	8.3%	2,000
4. Operations Research Analysts	$62,180	8.4%	7,000
5. Epidemiologists	$52,170	26.2%	1,000
6. Clergy	$38,540	12.4%	26,000
7. Economists	$73,690	5.6%	1,000
8. Political Scientists	$84,100	7.3%	fewer than 500
9. Museum Technicians and Conservators	$34,090	14.1%	2,000
10. Statisticians	$62,450	4.6%	2,000
11. Anthropologists and Archeologists	$45,910	17.0%	fewer than 500
12. Geographers	$63,550	6.8%	fewer than 500
13. Sociologists	$52,760	4.7%	fewer than 500
14. Historians	$44,400	4.3%	fewer than 500

Best Jobs for Introverts Requiring a Doctoral Degree

Job	Annual Earnings	Percent Growth	Annual Openings
1. Medical Scientists, Except Epidemiologists	$61,730	34.1%	15,000
2. Biochemists and Biophysicists	$71,000	21.0%	1,000
3. Physicists	$89,810	7.0%	1,000
4. Astronomers	$104,670	10.5%	fewer than 500
5. Microbiologists	$56,870	17.2%	1,000

Best Jobs for Introverts Requiring a First Professional Degree			
Job	Annual Earnings	Percent Growth	Annual Openings
1. Lawyers	$98,930	15.0%	40,000

Best Jobs for Introverts Sorted by Interests

This group of lists organizes the 200 best jobs for introverts into 16 interest areas. You can use these lists to identify jobs quickly based on your interests. Within each interest area, jobs are listed in order of their combined score on earnings, job growth, and job openings, from highest to lowest.

Find the interest area or areas that appeal to you most and review the introvert-friendly jobs in those areas. When you find jobs you want to explore in more detail, look up their descriptions in Part III. You can also review interest areas where you have had past experience, education, or training to see if other jobs in those areas would meet your current requirements.

As you scan the following lists, you may notice that one of the interest areas has *no* jobs listed—Retail and Wholesale Sales and Service—and three others include only one job each—Education and Training; Hospitality, Tourism, and Recreation; and Human Service. These interest areas are dominated by human contact, and any introverted jobs they may include tend not to have sufficient economic rewards to earn a place in this book. But keep in mind that this book is based on averages. If you have the right skills and are really motivated, you may be able to find an introvert-friendly and rewarding position in the education, human service, or hospitality industry. That's one reason we describe all 16 interest areas here. Another reason is that you can more easily decide on your most important interests in the context of the complete classification scheme.

Note: The 16 interest areas used in these lists are those used in the *New Guide for Occupational Exploration,* Fourth Edition, published by JIST. The original GOE was developed by the U.S. Department of Labor as an intuitive way to assist in career exploration. The 16 interest areas used in the *New GOE* are based on the 16 career clusters that were developed by the U.S. Department of Education's Office of Vocational and Adult Education around 1999 and that presently are being used by many states to organize their career-oriented programs and career information.

Descriptions for the 16 Interest Areas

Brief descriptions for the 16 interest areas we use in the lists follow. The descriptions are from the *New Guide for Occupational Exploration,* Fourth Edition. Some of them refer to jobs (as examples) that aren't included in this book.

Also note that we put each of the 200 best jobs into only one interest area list, the one it fit into best. However, many jobs could be included in more than one list, so consider reviewing a variety of these interest areas to find jobs that you might otherwise overlook.

For a detailed outline of the interest areas that shows the work groups classified into each interest area, see Appendix B.

- **Agriculture and Natural Resources:** *An interest in working with plants, animals, forests, or mineral resources for agriculture, horticulture, conservation, extraction, and other purposes.* You can satisfy this interest by working in farming, landscaping, forestry, fishing, mining, and related fields. You may like doing physical work outdoors, such as on a farm or ranch, in a forest, or on a drilling rig. If you have scientific curiosity, you could study plants and animals or analyze biological or rock samples in a lab. If you have management ability, you could own, operate, or manage a fish hatchery, a landscaping business, or a greenhouse.

- **Architecture and Construction:** *An interest in designing, assembling, and maintaining components of buildings and other structures.* You may want to be part of the team of architects, drafters, and others who design buildings and render the plans. If construction interests you, you can find fulfillment in the many building projects that are being undertaken at all times. If you like to organize and plan, you can find careers in managing these projects. Or you can play a more direct role in putting up and finishing buildings by doing jobs such as plumbing, carpentry, masonry, painting, or roofing, either as a skilled craftsworker or as a helper. You can prepare the building site by operating heavy equipment or install, maintain, and repair vital building equipment and systems such as electricity and heating.

- **Arts and Communication:** *An interest in creatively expressing feelings or ideas, in communicating news or information, or in performing.* You can satisfy this interest in creative, verbal, or performing activities. For example, if you enjoy literature, perhaps writing or editing would appeal to you. Journalism and public relations are other fields for people who like to use their writing or speaking skills. Do you prefer to work in the performing arts? If so, you could direct or perform in drama, music, or dance. If you especially enjoy the visual arts, you could create paintings, sculpture, or ceramics or design products or visual displays. A flair for technology might lead you to specialize in photography, broadcast production, or dispatching.

- **Business and Administration:** *An interest in making a business organization or function run smoothly.* You can satisfy this interest by working in a position of leadership or by specializing in a function that contributes to the overall effort in a business, a nonprofit organization, or a government agency. If you especially enjoy working with people, you may find fulfillment from working in human resources. An interest in numbers may lead you to consider accounting, finance, budgeting, billing, or financial record-keeping. A job as an administrative assistant may interest you if you like a variety of work in a busy environment. If you are good with details and word processing, you may enjoy a job as a secretary or data entry keyer. Or perhaps you would do well as the manager of a business.

◎ **Education and Training:** *An interest in helping people learn.* You can satisfy this interest by teaching students, who may be preschoolers, retirees, or any age in between. You may specialize in a particular academic field or work with learners of a particular age, with a particular interest, or with a particular learning problem. Working in a library or museum may give you an opportunity to expand people's understanding of the world.

◎ **Finance and Insurance:** *An interest in helping businesses and people be assured of a financially secure future.* You can satisfy this interest by working in a financial or insurance business in a leadership or support role. If you like gathering and analyzing information, you may find fulfillment as an insurance adjuster or financial analyst. Or you may deal with information at the clerical level as a banking or insurance clerk or in person-to-person situations providing customer service. Another way to interact with people is to sell financial or insurance services that will meet their needs.

◎ **Government and Public Administration:** *An interest in helping a government agency serve the needs of the public.* You can satisfy this interest by working in a position of leadership or by specializing in a function that contributes to the role of government. You may help protect the public by working as an inspector or examiner to enforce standards. If you enjoy using clerical skills, you may work as a clerk in a law court or government office. Or perhaps you prefer the top-down perspective of a government executive or urban planner.

◎ **Health Science:** *An interest in helping people and animals be healthy.* You can satisfy this interest by working in a health care team as a doctor, therapist, or nurse. You might specialize in one of the many different parts of the body (such as the teeth or eyes) or in one of the many different types of care. Or you may wish to be a generalist who deals with the whole patient. If you like technology, you might find satisfaction working with X rays or new methods of diagnosis. You might work with healthy people, helping them eat right. If you enjoy working with animals, you might care for them and keep them healthy.

◎ **Hospitality, Tourism, and Recreation:** *An interest in catering to the personal wishes and needs of others so that they may enjoy a clean environment, good food and drink, comfortable lodging away from home, and recreation.* You can satisfy this interest by providing services for the convenience, care, and pampering of others in hotels, restaurants, airplanes, beauty parlors, and so on. You may wish to use your love of cooking as a chef. If you like working with people, you may wish to provide personal services by being a travel guide, a flight attendant, a concierge, a hairdresser, or a waiter. You may wish to work in cleaning and building services if you like a clean environment. If you enjoy sports or games, you may work for an athletic team or casino.

◎ **Human Service:** *An interest in improving people's social, mental, emotional, or spiritual well-being.* You can satisfy this interest as a counselor, social worker, or religious worker who helps people sort out their complicated lives or solve personal problems. You may work as a caretaker for very young people or the elderly. Or you may interview people to help identify the social services they need.

◎ **Information Technology:** *An interest in designing, developing, managing, and supporting information systems.* You can satisfy this interest by working with hardware, software, multimedia, or integrated systems. If you like to use your organizational skills, you might work as an administrator of a system or database. Or you can solve complex problems as a software engineer or systems analyst. If you enjoy getting your hands on the hardware, you might find work servicing computers, peripherals, and information-intense machines such as cash registers and ATMs.

🔘 **Law and Public Safety:** *An interest in upholding people's rights or in protecting people and property by using authority, inspecting, or investigating.* You can satisfy this interest by working in law, law enforcement, fire fighting, the military, and related fields. For example, if you enjoy mental challenge and intrigue, you could investigate crimes or fires for a living. If you enjoy working with verbal skills and research skills, you may want to defend citizens in court or research deeds, wills, and other legal documents. If you want to help people in critical situations, you may want to fight fires, work as a police officer, or become a paramedic. Or, if you want more routine work in public safety, perhaps a job in guarding, patrolling, or inspecting would appeal to you. If you have management ability, you could seek a leadership position in law enforcement and the protective services. Work in the military gives you a chance to use technical and leadership skills while serving your country.

🔘 **Manufacturing:** *An interest in processing materials into intermediate or final products or maintaining and repairing products by using machines or hand tools.* You can satisfy this interest by working in one of many industries that mass-produce goods or by working for a utility that distributes electric power or other resources. You may enjoy manual work, using your hands or hand tools in highly skilled jobs such as assembling engines or electronic equipment. If you enjoy making machines run efficiently or fixing them when they break down, you could seek a job installing or repairing such devices as copiers, aircraft engines, cars, or watches. Perhaps you prefer to set up or operate machines that are used to manufacture products made of food, glass, or paper. You may enjoy cutting and grinding metal and plastic parts to desired shapes and measurements. Or you may wish to operate equipment in systems that provide water and process wastewater. You may like inspecting, sorting, counting, or weighing products. Another option is to work with your hands and machinery to move boxes and freight in a warehouse. If leadership appeals to you, you could manage people engaged in production and repair.

🔘 **Retail and Wholesale Sales and Service:** *An interest in bringing others to a particular point of view by personal persuasion and by sales and promotional techniques.* You can satisfy this interest in a variety of jobs that involve persuasion and selling. If you like using knowledge of science, you may enjoy selling pharmaceutical, medical, or electronic products or services. Real estate offers several kinds of sales jobs as well. If you like speaking on the phone, you could work as a telemarketer. Or you may enjoy selling apparel and other merchandise in a retail setting. If you prefer to help people, you may want a job in customer service.

🔘 **Scientific Research, Engineering, and Mathematics:** *An interest in discovering, collecting, and analyzing information about the natural world; in applying scientific research findings to problems in medicine, the life sciences, human behavior, and the natural sciences; in imagining and manipulating quantitative data; and in applying technology to manufacturing,* *transportation, and other economic activities.* You can satisfy this interest by working with the knowledge and processes of the sciences. You may enjoy researching and developing new knowledge in mathematics, or perhaps solving problems in the physical, life, or social sciences would appeal to you. You may wish to study engineering and help create new machines, processes, and structures. If you want to work with scientific equipment and procedures, you could seek a job in a research or testing laboratory.

◉ **Transportation, Distribution, and Logistics:** *An interest in operations that move people or materials.* You can satisfy this interest by managing a transportation service, by helping vehicles keep on their assigned schedules and routes, or by driving or piloting a vehicle. If you enjoy taking responsibility, perhaps managing a rail line would appeal to you. Or would you rather get out on the highway, on the water, or up in the air? If so, then you could drive a truck from state to state, be employed on a ship, or fly a crop duster over a cornfield. If you prefer to stay closer to home, you could drive a delivery van, taxi, or school bus. You can use your physical strength to load freight and arrange it so it gets to its destination in one piece.

Best Jobs for Introverts Interested in Agriculture and Natural Resources

Job	Annual Earnings	Percent Growth	Annual Openings
1. Landscaping and Groundskeeping Workers	$20,670	19.5%	243,000
2. Environmental Science and Protection Technicians, Including Health	$36,260	16.3%	6,000
3. Soil and Plant Scientists	$54,530	13.9%	1,000
4. Tree Trimmers and Pruners	$27,920	16.5%	11,000
5. Zoologists and Wildlife Biologists	$52,050	13.0%	1,000
6. Excavating and Loading Machine and Dragline Operators	$32,380	8.0%	11,000
7. Pest Control Workers	$27,170	18.4%	4,000
8. Pesticide Handlers, Sprayers, and Applicators, Vegetation	$26,120	16.6%	6,000
9. Food Scientists and Technologists	$51,440	10.9%	1,000
10. Conservation Scientists	$53,350	6.3%	2,000
11. Farmers and Ranchers	$34,140	–14.5%	96,000
12. Purchasing Agents and Buyers, Farm Products	$46,680	7.0%	2,000
13. Earth Drillers, Except Oil and Gas	$33,770	7.9%	4,000
14. Foresters	$48,670	6.7%	1,000
15. Animal Scientists	$43,170	12.9%	fewer than 500
16. Logging Equipment Operators	$28,920	3.4%	9,000

Best Jobs for Introverts Interested in Architecture and Construction

Job	Annual Earnings	Percent Growth	Annual Openings
1. Plumbers, Pipefitters, and Steamfitters	$42,160	15.7%	61,000
2. Heating, Air Conditioning, and Refrigeration Mechanics and Installers	$37,040	19.0%	33,000
3. Tile and Marble Setters	$36,530	22.9%	9,000
4. Roofers	$31,230	16.8%	38,000
5. Brickmasons and Blockmasons	$41,860	12.0%	17,000
6. Cement Masons and Concrete Finishers	$32,030	15.9%	32,000
7. Elevator Installers and Repairers	$59,190	14.8%	3,000
8. Hazardous Materials Removal Workers	$33,690	31.2%	11,000
9. Telecommunications Line Installers and Repairers	$42,410	10.8%	23,000
10. Maintenance and Repair Workers, General	$31,210	15.2%	154,000
11. Operating Engineers and Other Construction Equipment Operators	$35,830	11.6%	37,000
12. Telecommunications Equipment Installers and Repairers, Except Line Installers	$50,620	–4.9%	21,000
13. Painters, Construction and Maintenance	$30,800	12.6%	102,000
14. Electrical Power-Line Installers and Repairers	$50,150	2.5%	11,000
15. Reinforcing Iron and Rebar Workers	$34,910	14.1%	6,000
16. Architectural and Civil Drafters	$40,390	4.6%	9,000
17. Drywall and Ceiling Tile Installers	$34,740	9.0%	17,000
18. Riggers	$37,010	13.9%	2,000
19. Helpers—Brickmasons, Blockmasons, Stonemasons, and Tile and Marble Setters	$24,600	14.9%	14,000
20. Paving, Surfacing, and Tamping Equipment Operators	$30,320	15.6%	7,000
21. Pile-Driver Operators	$48,900	11.9%	fewer than 500
22. Boilermakers	$48,050	8.7%	2,000
23. Tapers	$39,870	5.9%	5,000
24. Electrical and Electronics Repairers, Powerhouse, Substation, and Relay	$54,970	–0.4%	2,000
25. Stonemasons	$34,640	13.0%	2,000
26. Terrazzo Workers and Finishers	$32,030	15.2%	1,000
27. Commercial Divers	$37,960	9.4%	fewer than 500
28. Helpers—Painters, Paperhangers, Plasterers, and Stucco Masons	$20,560	11.5%	6,000
29. Fence Erectors	$24,930	9.9%	5,000
30. Insulation Workers, Mechanical	$35,510	1.0%	2,000
31. Paperhangers	$33,450	3.2%	3,000
32. Insulation Workers, Floor, Ceiling, and Wall	$31,360	3.0%	4,000

Best Jobs for Introverts Interested in Arts and Communication

Job	Annual Earnings	Percent Growth	Annual Openings
1. Writers and Authors	$46,420	17.7%	14,000
2. Technical Writers	$55,160	23.2%	5,000
3. Editors	$45,510	14.8%	16,000
4. Graphic Designers	$38,390	15.2%	35,000
5. Interior Designers	$41,350	15.5%	10,000
6. Commercial and Industrial Designers	$52,200	10.8%	7,000
7. Sound Engineering Technicians	$38,390	18.4%	2,000
8. Fashion Designers	$60,860	8.4%	2,000
9. Music Directors and Composers	$34,810	10.4%	11,000
10. Merchandise Displayers and Window Trimmers	$22,590	10.3%	13,000
11. Fine Artists, Including Painters, Sculptors, and Illustrators	$41,280	10.2%	4,000
12. Set and Exhibit Designers	$37,390	9.3%	2,000

Best Jobs for Introverts Interested in Business and Administration

Job	Annual Earnings	Percent Growth	Annual Openings
1. Accountants and Auditors	$52,210	22.4%	157,000
2. Bookkeeping, Accounting, and Auditing Clerks	$29,490	5.9%	291,000
3. Payroll and Timekeeping Clerks	$31,360	17.3%	36,000
4. Operations Research Analysts	$62,180	8.4%	7,000
5. Billing and Posting Clerks and Machine Operators	$27,780	3.4%	70,000
6. Tax Preparers	$25,700	10.6%	11,000
7. Data Entry Keyers	$23,810	–0.7%	85,000
8. Word Processors and Typists	$29,020	–15.3%	30,000

Best Jobs for Introverts Interested in Education and Training

Job	Annual Earnings	Percent Growth	Annual Openings
1. Museum Technicians and Conservators	$34,090	14.1%	2,000

Best Jobs for Introverts Interested in Finance and Insurance

Job	Annual Earnings	Percent Growth	Annual Openings
1. Personal Financial Advisors	$63,500	25.9%	17,000
2. Financial Analysts	$63,860	17.3%	28,000
3. Market Research Analysts	$57,300	19.6%	20,000
4. Cost Estimators	$52,020	18.2%	15,000
5. Appraisers and Assessors of Real Estate	$43,440	22.8%	9,000
6. Credit Analysts	$50,370	3.6%	3,000

Best Jobs for Introverts Interested in Government and Public Administration

Job	Annual Earnings	Percent Growth	Annual Openings
1. Transportation Inspectors	$49,490	11.4%	2,000
2. Financial Examiners	$63,090	9.5%	3,000
3. Agricultural Inspectors	$32,840	6.8%	3,000

Best Jobs for Introverts Interested in Health Science

Job	Annual Earnings	Percent Growth	Annual Openings
1. Medical Equipment Preparers	$24,880	20.0%	8,000
2. Animal Trainers	$24,800	20.3%	3,000
3. Embalmers	$36,960	15.7%	2,000

Best Jobs for Introverts Interested in Hospitality, Tourism, and Recreation

Job	Annual Earnings	Percent Growth	Annual Openings
1. Butchers and Meat Cutters	$26,590	7.9%	20,000

Best Jobs for Introverts Interested in Human Service

Job	Annual Earnings	Percent Growth	Annual Openings
1. Clergy	$38,540	12.4%	26,000

Best Jobs for Introverts Interested in Information Technology

Job	Annual Earnings	Percent Growth	Annual Openings
1. Computer Software Engineers, Applications	$77,090	48.4%	54,000
2. Computer Software Engineers, Systems Software	$82,120	43.0%	37,000
3. Computer Systems Analysts	$68,300	31.4%	56,000
4. Network Systems and Data Communications Analysts	$61,750	54.6%	43,000
5. Database Administrators	$63,250	38.2%	9,000
6. Computer Programmers	$63,420	2.0%	28,000
7. Computer, Automated Teller, and Office Machine Repairers	$36,060	3.8%	31,000
8. Coin, Vending, and Amusement Machine Servicers and Repairers	$28,200	2.4%	7,000

Best Jobs for Introverts Interested in Law and Public Safety

Job	Annual Earnings	Percent Growth	Annual Openings
1. Lawyers	$98,930	15.0%	40,000
2. Crossing Guards	$20,050	19.7%	26,000
3. Private Detectives and Investigators	$32,650	17.7%	7,000
4. Arbitrators, Mediators, and Conciliators	$54,360	15.5%	fewer than 500
5. Title Examiners, Abstractors, and Searchers	$35,120	0.9%	8,000
6. Parking Enforcement Workers	$29,070	15.1%	1,000

Best Jobs for Introverts Interested in Manufacturing

Job	Annual Earnings	Percent Growth	Annual Openings
1. Automotive Service Technicians and Mechanics	$33,050	15.7%	93,000
2. Bus and Truck Mechanics and Diesel Engine Specialists	$36,620	14.4%	32,000
3. Aircraft Mechanics and Service Technicians	$47,310	13.4%	11,000

(continued)

(continued)

Best Jobs for Introverts Interested in Manufacturing

Job	Annual Earnings	Percent Growth	Annual Openings
4. Automotive Body and Related Repairers	$34,810	10.3%	18,000
5. Mobile Heavy Equipment Mechanics, Except Engines	$39,410	8.8%	14,000
6. Painters, Transportation Equipment	$34,840	14.1%	10,000
7. Water and Liquid Waste Treatment Plant and System Operators	$34,930	16.2%	6,000
8. Desktop Publishers	$32,800	23.2%	8,000
9. Machinists	$34,350	4.3%	33,000
10. Motorboat Mechanics	$32,780	15.1%	7,000
11. Bakers	$21,520	15.2%	37,000
12. Medical Equipment Repairers	$39,570	14.8%	4,000
13. Welders, Cutters, Solderers, and Brazers	$30,990	5.0%	52,000
14. Millwrights	$44,780	5.9%	5,000
15. Ship Engineers	$52,780	12.7%	1,000
16. Aircraft Structure, Surfaces, Rigging, and Systems Assemblers	$43,990	7.8%	4,000
17. Avionics Technicians	$46,630	9.1%	2,000
18. Gas Plant Operators	$51,920	7.7%	2,000
19. Industrial Machinery Mechanics	$39,740	–0.2%	13,000
20. Slaughterers and Meat Packers	$21,220	13.8%	22,000
21. Control and Valve Installers and Repairers, Except Mechanical Door	$44,120	4.9%	4,000
22. Helpers—Production Workers	$20,390	7.9%	107,000
23. Stationary Engineers and Boiler Operators	$44,600	3.4%	5,000
24. Locksmiths and Safe Repairers	$30,880	16.1%	5,000
25. Printing Machine Operators	$30,730	2.9%	26,000
26. Outdoor Power Equipment and Other Small Engine Mechanics	$25,810	14.0%	10,000
27. Paper Goods Machine Setters, Operators, and Tenders	$31,160	2.4%	15,000
28. Recreational Vehicle Service Technicians	$30,480	19.5%	3,000
29. Structural Metal Fabricators and Fitters	$30,290	2.9%	18,000
30. Tool and Die Makers	$43,580	–2.6%	7,000
31. Motorcycle Mechanics	$29,450	13.7%	6,000
32. Petroleum Pump System Operators, Refinery Operators, and Gaugers	$51,060	–8.6%	6,000
33. Maintenance Workers, Machinery	$33,650	2.8%	6,000
34. Packaging and Filling Machine Operators and Tenders	$22,930	2.3%	80,000
35. Signal and Track Switch Repairers	$49,200	2.3%	1,000
36. Tire Repairers and Changers	$20,960	4.5%	17,000
37. Inspectors, Testers, Sorters, Samplers, and Weighers	$29,200	–2.6%	85,000

Best Jobs for Introverts Interested in Manufacturing

Job	Annual Earnings	Percent Growth	Annual Openings
38. Job Printers	$31,920	1.8%	8,000
39. Dental Laboratory Technicians	$32,240	7.6%	3,000
40. Mechanical Door Repairers	$30,310	15.8%	1,000
41. Cabinetmakers and Bench Carpenters	$26,020	4.1%	12,000
42. Chemical Equipment Operators and Tenders	$39,030	–4.5%	6,000
43. Computer-Controlled Machine Tool Operators, Metal and Plastic	$31,010	–1.2%	13,000
44. Electric Motor, Power Tool, and Related Repairers	$33,460	4.1%	3,000
45. Mixing and Blending Machine Setters, Operators, and Tenders	$28,890	2.0%	16,000
46. Separating, Filtering, Clarifying, Precipitating, and Still Machine Setters, Operators, and Tenders	$34,650	1.6%	5,000
47. Prepress Technicians and Workers	$32,840	–8.4%	10,000
48. Electronic Home Entertainment Equipment Installers and Repairers	$28,940	4.7%	6,000
49. Home Appliance Repairers	$32,980	2.6%	3,000
50. Numerical Tool and Process Control Programmers	$41,830	–1.1%	2,000
51. Rail Car Repairers	$42,530	–1.2%	2,000
52. Welding, Soldering, and Brazing Machine Setters, Operators, and Tenders	$30,430	0.4%	7,000
53. Coating, Painting, and Spraying Machine Setters, Operators, and Tenders	$26,670	–3.4%	16,000
54. Semiconductor Processors	$31,030	–7.5%	7,000
55. Lathe and Turning Machine Tool Setters, Operators, and Tenders, Metal and Plastic	$31,750	–9.0%	7,000
56. Medical Appliance Technicians	$29,080	13.3%	1,000
57. Multiple Machine Tool Setters, Operators, and Tenders, Metal and Plastic	$29,780	0.3%	6,000

None of the best jobs for introverts is associated with the interest area Retail and Wholesale Sales and Service.

Best Jobs for Introverts Interested in Scientific Research, Engineering, and Mathematics

Job	Annual Earnings	Percent Growth	Annual Openings
1. Actuaries	$81,640	23.2%	3,000
2. Medical Scientists, Except Epidemiologists	$61,730	34.1%	15,000

(continued)

(continued)

Best Jobs for Introverts Interested in Scientific Research, Engineering, and Mathematics

Job	Annual Earnings	Percent Growth	Annual Openings
3. Civil Engineers	$66,190	16.5%	19,000
4. Electrical Engineers	$73,510	11.8%	12,000
5. Electronics Engineers, Except Computer	$78,030	9.7%	11,000
6. Atmospheric and Space Scientists	$73,940	16.5%	1,000
7. Aerospace Engineers	$84,090	8.3%	6,000
8. Biochemists and Biophysicists	$71,000	21.0%	1,000
9. Hydrologists	$63,820	31.6%	1,000
10. Environmental Scientists and Specialists, Including Health	$52,630	17.1%	8,000
11. Health and Safety Engineers, Except Mining Safety Engineers and Inspectors	$65,210	13.4%	2,000
12. Materials Engineers	$69,660	12.2%	2,000
13. Astronomers	$104,670	10.5%	fewer than 500
14. Electrical and Electronic Engineering Technicians	$48,040	9.8%	18,000
15. Epidemiologists	$52,170	26.2%	1,000
16. Geoscientists, Except Hydrologists and Geographers	$71,640	8.3%	2,000
17. Microbiologists	$56,870	17.2%	1,000
18. Physicists	$89,810	7.0%	1,000
19. Nuclear Technicians	$61,120	13.7%	1,000
20. Mechanical Engineering Technicians	$44,830	12.3%	5,000
21. Cartographers and Photogrammetrists	$48,250	15.2%	1,000
22. Economists	$73,690	5.6%	1,000
23. Political Scientists	$84,100	7.3%	fewer than 500
24. Chemists	$57,890	7.3%	5,000
25. Marine Engineers and Naval Architects	$72,920	8.5%	fewer than 500
26. Surveying and Mapping Technicians	$31,290	9.6%	9,000
27. Anthropologists and Archeologists	$45,910	17.0%	fewer than 500
28. Materials Scientists	$71,450	8.0%	fewer than 500
29. Electro-Mechanical Technicians	$43,880	9.7%	2,000
30. Statisticians	$62,450	4.6%	2,000
31. Mechanical Drafters	$43,350	5.5%	7,000
32. Geographers	$63,550	6.8%	fewer than 500
33. Electrical and Electronics Drafters	$45,550	1.2%	3,000
34. Sociologists	$52,760	4.7%	fewer than 500
35. Historians	$44,400	4.3%	fewer than 500

Best Jobs for Introverts Interested in Transportation, Distribution, and Logistics

Job	Annual Earnings	Percent Growth	Annual Openings
1. Bus Drivers, Transit and Intercity	$31,010	21.7%	34,000
2. Truck Drivers, Light or Delivery Services	$24,790	15.7%	169,000
3. Truck Drivers, Heavy and Tractor-Trailer	$34,280	12.9%	274,000
4. Subway and Streetcar Operators	$47,500	13.7%	1,000
5. Traffic Technicians	$37,070	14.1%	1,000
6. Bus Drivers, School	$24,070	13.6%	76,000
7. Captains, Mates, and Pilots of Water Vessels	$50,940	4.8%	2,000
8. Driver/Sales Workers	$20,120	13.8%	72,000
9. Postal Service Mail Carriers	$46,330	0.0%	19,000
10. Bridge and Lock Tenders	$37,980	7.2%	fewer than 500
11. Sailors and Marine Oilers	$29,360	5.2%	4,000

Best Jobs for Introverts Sorted by Personality Types

These lists organize the 200 best jobs for introverts into groups matching six personality types. The personality types are Realistic, Investigative, Artistic, Social, Enterprising, and Conventional. This system was developed by John Holland and is used in the _Self-Directed Search (SDS)_ and other career assessment inventories and information systems.

If you have used one of these career inventories or systems, the lists will help you identify jobs that most closely match these personality types. Even if you have not used one of these systems, the concept of personality types and the jobs that are related to them can help you identify introverted jobs that most closely match the type of person you are.

Review the descriptions of the six personality types in Part I. Select the two or three descriptions that most closely describe you and then use the following lists to identify introverted jobs that best fit these personality types.

We've ranked the introvert-friendly jobs within each personality type based on their total combined scores for earnings, growth, and annual job openings. Like the job lists for education levels, there is only one list for each personality type. Note that each job is listed in the one personality type it most closely matches, even though it might also fit into others. Consider reviewing the jobs for more than one personality type so you don't overlook possible jobs that would interest you.

It should come as no surprise that the smallest list in this set, with only four jobs, is the list for the Social personality type. Because Social jobs tend to involve a lot of human contact, few of them are attractive to introverted people. It is also significant that the second- and third-smallest lists in this set are for the Enterprising and Artistic personality types, which are adjacent to Social on the hexagonal diagram that Holland uses to show the relationships between the types. Conversely, the most heavily populated list, Realistic, is located on the opposite side of the hexagon from Social. (The Holland hexagon is shown in Figure 1 in Part I.)

Best Jobs for Introverts with a Realistic Personality Type

Job	Annual Earnings	Percent Growth	Annual Openings
1. Civil Engineers	$66,190	16.5%	19,000
2. Plumbers, Pipefitters, and Steamfitters	$42,160	15.7%	61,000
3. Heating, Air Conditioning, and Refrigeration Mechanics and Installers	$37,040	19.0%	33,000
4. Automotive Service Technicians and Mechanics	$33,050	15.7%	93,000
5. Bus and Truck Mechanics and Diesel Engine Specialists	$36,620	14.4%	32,000
6. Tile and Marble Setters	$36,530	22.9%	9,000
7. Electrical and Electronic Engineering Technicians	$48,040	9.8%	18,000
8. Aircraft Mechanics and Service Technicians	$47,310	13.4%	11,000
9. Bus Drivers, Transit and Intercity	$31,010	21.7%	34,000
10. Roofers	$31,230	16.8%	38,000
11. Truck Drivers, Heavy and Tractor-Trailer	$34,280	12.9%	274,000
12. Hazardous Materials Removal Workers	$33,690	31.2%	11,000
13. Telecommunications Line Installers and Repairers	$42,410	10.8%	23,000
14. Maintenance and Repair Workers, General	$31,210	15.2%	154,000
15. Cement Masons and Concrete Finishers	$32,030	15.9%	32,000
16. Brickmasons and Blockmasons	$41,860	12.0%	17,000
17. Operating Engineers and Other Construction Equipment Operators	$35,830	11.6%	37,000
18. Elevator Installers and Repairers	$59,190	14.8%	3,000
19. Desktop Publishers	$32,800	23.2%	8,000
20. Landscaping and Groundskeeping Workers	$20,670	19.5%	243,000
21. Water and Liquid Waste Treatment Plant and System Operators	$34,930	16.2%	6,000
22. Painters, Transportation Equipment	$34,840	14.1%	10,000
23. Truck Drivers, Light or Delivery Services	$24,790	15.7%	169,000
24. Mobile Heavy Equipment Mechanics, Except Engines	$39,410	8.8%	14,000
25. Automotive Body and Related Repairers	$34,810	10.3%	18,000
26. Painters, Construction and Maintenance	$30,800	12.6%	102,000

Best Jobs for Introverts with a Realistic Personality Type

Job	Annual Earnings	Percent Growth	Annual Openings
27. Mechanical Engineering Technicians	$44,830	12.3%	5,000
28. Sound Engineering Technicians	$38,390	18.4%	2,000
29. Medical Equipment Repairers	$39,570	14.8%	4,000
30. Drywall and Ceiling Tile Installers	$34,740	9.0%	17,000
31. Reinforcing Iron and Rebar Workers	$34,910	14.1%	6,000
32. Electrical Power-Line Installers and Repairers	$50,150	2.5%	11,000
33. Nuclear Technicians	$61,120	13.7%	1,000
34. Telecommunications Equipment Installers and Repairers, Except Line Installers	$50,620	–4.9%	21,000
35. Bakers	$21,520	15.2%	37,000
36. Motorboat Mechanics	$32,780	15.1%	7,000
37. Computer, Automated Teller, and Office Machine Repairers	$36,060	3.8%	31,000
38. Tree Trimmers and Pruners	$27,920	16.5%	11,000
39. Embalmers	$36,960	15.7%	2,000
40. Transportation Inspectors	$49,490	11.4%	2,000
41. Machinists	$34,350	4.3%	33,000
42. Mechanical Drafters	$43,350	5.5%	7,000
43. Ship Engineers	$52,780	12.7%	1,000
44. Subway and Streetcar Operators	$47,500	13.7%	1,000
45. Bus Drivers, School	$24,070	13.6%	76,000
46. Architectural and Civil Drafters	$40,390	4.6%	9,000
47. Medical Equipment Preparers	$24,880	20.0%	8,000
48. Millwrights	$44,780	5.9%	5,000
49. Paving, Surfacing, and Tamping Equipment Operators	$30,320	15.6%	7,000
50. Gas Plant Operators	$51,920	7.7%	2,000
51. Boilermakers	$48,050	8.7%	2,000
52. Aircraft Structure, Surfaces, Rigging, and Systems Assemblers	$43,990	7.8%	4,000
53. Avionics Technicians	$46,630	9.1%	2,000
54. Riggers	$37,010	13.9%	2,000
55. Locksmiths and Safe Repairers	$30,880	16.1%	5,000
56. Welders, Cutters, Solderers, and Brazers	$30,990	5.0%	52,000
57. Electro-Mechanical Technicians	$43,880	9.7%	2,000
58. Helpers—Brickmasons, Blockmasons, Stonemasons, and Tile and Marble Setters	$24,600	14.9%	14,000
59. Slaughterers and Meat Packers	$21,220	13.8%	22,000
60. Excavating and Loading Machine and Dragline Operators	$32,380	8.0%	11,000

(continued)

(continued)

Best Jobs for Introverts with a Realistic Personality Type

Job	Annual Earnings	Percent Growth	Annual Openings
61. Pile-Driver Operators	$48,900	11.9%	fewer than 500
62. Industrial Machinery Mechanics	$39,740	–0.2%	13,000
63. Marine Engineers and Naval Architects	$72,920	8.5%	fewer than 500
64. Pesticide Handlers, Sprayers, and Applicators, Vegetation	$26,120	16.6%	6,000
65. Recreational Vehicle Service Technicians	$30,480	19.5%	3,000
66. Tapers	$39,870	5.9%	5,000
67. Traffic Technicians	$37,070	14.1%	1,000
68. Captains, Mates, and Pilots of Water Vessels	$50,940	4.8%	2,000
69. Control and Valve Installers and Repairers, Except Mechanical Door	$44,120	4.9%	4,000
70. Stationary Engineers and Boiler Operators	$44,600	3.4%	5,000
71. Farmers and Ranchers	$34,140	–14.5%	96,000
72. Helpers—Production Workers	$20,390	7.9%	107,000
73. Outdoor Power Equipment and Other Small Engine Mechanics	$25,810	14.0%	10,000
74. Petroleum Pump System Operators, Refinery Operators, and Gaugers	$51,060	–8.6%	6,000
75. Pest Control Workers	$27,170	18.4%	4,000
76. Tool and Die Makers	$43,580	–2.6%	7,000
77. Stonemasons	$34,640	13.0%	2,000
78. Foresters	$48,670	6.7%	1,000
79. Motorcycle Mechanics	$29,450	13.7%	6,000
80. Butchers and Meat Cutters	$26,590	7.9%	20,000
81. Printing Machine Operators	$30,730	2.9%	26,000
82. Terrazzo Workers and Finishers	$32,030	15.2%	1,000
83. Earth Drillers, Except Oil and Gas	$33,770	7.9%	4,000
84. Electrical and Electronics Repairers, Powerhouse, Substation, and Relay	$54,970	–0.4%	2,000
85. Structural Metal Fabricators and Fitters	$30,290	2.9%	18,000
86. Paper Goods Machine Setters, Operators, and Tenders	$31,160	2.4%	15,000
87. Chemical Equipment Operators and Tenders	$39,030	–4.5%	6,000
88. Commercial Divers	$37,960	9.4%	fewer than 500
89. Inspectors, Testers, Sorters, Samplers, and Weighers	$29,200	–2.6%	85,000
90. Mechanical Door Repairers	$30,310	15.8%	1,000
91. Signal and Track Switch Repairers	$49,200	2.3%	1,000
92. Maintenance Workers, Machinery	$33,650	2.8%	6,000
93. Packaging and Filling Machine Operators and Tenders	$22,930	2.3%	80,000

Best Jobs for Introverts with a Realistic Personality Type

Job	Annual Earnings	Percent Growth	Annual Openings
94. Agricultural Inspectors	$32,840	6.8%	3,000
95. Bridge and Lock Tenders	$37,980	7.2%	fewer than 500
96. Dental Laboratory Technicians	$32,240	7.6%	3,000
97. Job Printers	$31,920	1.8%	8,000
98. Computer-Controlled Machine Tool Operators, Metal and Plastic	$31,010	–1.2%	13,000
99. Tire Repairers and Changers	$20,960	4.5%	17,000
100. Prepress Technicians and Workers	$32,840	–8.4%	10,000
101. Rail Car Repairers	$42,530	–1.2%	2,000
102. Separating, Filtering, Clarifying, Precipitating, and Still Machine Setters, Operators, and Tenders	$34,650	1.6%	5,000
103. Cabinetmakers and Bench Carpenters	$26,020	4.1%	12,000
104. Helpers—Painters, Paperhangers, Plasterers, and Stucco Masons	$20,560	11.5%	6,000
105. Mixing and Blending Machine Setters, Operators, and Tenders	$28,890	2.0%	16,000
106. Numerical Tool and Process Control Programmers	$41,830	–1.1%	2,000
107. Electric Motor, Power Tool, and Related Repairers	$33,460	4.1%	3,000
108. Logging Equipment Operators	$28,920	3.4%	9,000
109. Fence Erectors	$24,930	9.9%	5,000
110. Paperhangers	$33,450	3.2%	3,000
111. Electronic Home Entertainment Equipment Installers and Repairers	$28,940	4.7%	6,000
112. Insulation Workers, Mechanical	$35,510	1.0%	2,000
113. Medical Appliance Technicians	$29,080	13.3%	1,000
114. Home Appliance Repairers	$32,980	2.6%	3,000
115. Insulation Workers, Floor, Ceiling, and Wall	$31,360	3.0%	4,000
116. Welding, Soldering, and Brazing Machine Setters, Operators, and Tenders	$30,430	0.4%	7,000
117. Coating, Painting, and Spraying Machine Setters, Operators, and Tenders	$26,670	–3.4%	16,000
118. Lathe and Turning Machine Tool Setters, Operators, and Tenders, Metal and Plastic	$31,750	–9.0%	7,000
119. Sailors and Marine Oilers	$29,360	5.2%	4,000
120. Coin, Vending, and Amusement Machine Servicers and Repairers	$28,200	2.4%	7,000
121. Semiconductor Processors	$31,030	–7.5%	7,000
122. Multiple Machine Tool Setters, Operators, and Tenders, Metal and Plastic	$29,780	0.3%	6,000

Best Jobs for Introverts with an Investigative Personality Type

Job	Annual Earnings	Percent Growth	Annual Openings
1. Computer Software Engineers, Applications	$77,090	48.4%	54,000
2. Computer Software Engineers, Systems Software	$82,120	43.0%	37,000
3. Computer Systems Analysts	$68,300	31.4%	56,000
4. Network Systems and Data Communications Analysts	$61,750	54.6%	43,000
5. Financial Analysts	$63,860	17.3%	28,000
6. Database Administrators	$63,250	38.2%	9,000
7. Medical Scientists, Except Epidemiologists	$61,730	34.1%	15,000
8. Electrical Engineers	$73,510	11.8%	12,000
9. Electronics Engineers, Except Computer	$78,030	9.7%	11,000
10. Biochemists and Biophysicists	$71,000	21.0%	1,000
11. Market Research Analysts	$57,300	19.6%	20,000
12. Aerospace Engineers	$84,090	8.3%	6,000
13. Atmospheric and Space Scientists	$73,940	16.5%	1,000
14. Hydrologists	$63,820	31.6%	1,000
15. Health and Safety Engineers, Except Mining Safety Engineers and Inspectors	$65,210	13.4%	2,000
16. Materials Engineers	$69,660	12.2%	2,000
17. Geoscientists, Except Hydrologists and Geographers	$71,640	8.3%	2,000
18. Physicists	$89,810	7.0%	1,000
19. Astronomers	$104,670	10.5%	fewer than 500
20. Environmental Scientists and Specialists, Including Health	$52,630	17.1%	8,000
21. Microbiologists	$56,870	17.2%	1,000
22. Operations Research Analysts	$62,180	8.4%	7,000
23. Epidemiologists	$52,170	26.2%	1,000
24. Computer Programmers	$63,420	2.0%	28,000
25. Political Scientists	$84,100	7.3%	fewer than 500
26. Economists	$73,690	5.6%	1,000
27. Soil and Plant Scientists	$54,530	13.9%	1,000
28. Environmental Science and Protection Technicians, Including Health	$36,260	16.3%	6,000
29. Chemists	$57,890	7.3%	5,000
30. Materials Scientists	$71,450	8.0%	fewer than 500
31. Zoologists and Wildlife Biologists	$52,050	13.0%	1,000
32. Statisticians	$62,450	4.6%	2,000
33. Food Scientists and Technologists	$51,440	10.9%	1,000
34. Conservation Scientists	$53,350	6.3%	2,000
35. Anthropologists and Archeologists	$45,910	17.0%	fewer than 500

Best Jobs for Introverts with an Investigative Personality Type

Job	Annual Earnings	Percent Growth	Annual Openings
36. Geographers	$63,550	6.8%	fewer than 500
37. Animal Scientists	$43,170	12.9%	fewer than 500
38. Sociologists	$52,760	4.7%	fewer than 500
39. Historians	$44,400	4.3%	fewer than 500

Best Jobs for Introverts with an Artistic Personality Type

Job	Annual Earnings	Percent Growth	Annual Openings
1. Writers and Authors	$46,420	17.7%	14,000
2. Technical Writers	$55,160	23.2%	5,000
3. Editors	$45,510	14.8%	16,000
4. Graphic Designers	$38,390	15.2%	35,000
5. Interior Designers	$41,350	15.5%	10,000
6. Commercial and Industrial Designers	$52,200	10.8%	7,000
7. Fashion Designers	$60,860	8.4%	2,000
8. Music Directors and Composers	$34,810	10.4%	11,000
9. Merchandise Displayers and Window Trimmers	$22,590	10.3%	13,000
10. Fine Artists, Including Painters, Sculptors, and Illustrators	$41,280	10.2%	4,000
11. Museum Technicians and Conservators	$34,090	14.1%	2,000
12. Set and Exhibit Designers	$37,390	9.3%	2,000

Best Jobs for Introverts with a Social Personality Type

Job	Annual Earnings	Percent Growth	Annual Openings
1. Personal Financial Advisors	$63,500	25.9%	17,000
2. Clergy	$38,540	12.4%	26,000
3. Crossing Guards	$20,050	19.7%	26,000
4. Animal Trainers	$24,800	20.3%	3,000

Best Jobs for Introverts with an Enterprising Personality Type

Job	Annual Earnings	Percent Growth	Annual Openings
1. Lawyers	$98,930	15.0%	40,000
2. Appraisers and Assessors of Real Estate	$43,440	22.8%	9,000
3. Private Detectives and Investigators	$32,650	17.7%	7,000
4. Arbitrators, Mediators, and Conciliators	$54,360	15.5%	fewer than 500
5. Driver/Sales Workers	$20,120	13.8%	72,000
6. Financial Examiners	$63,090	9.5%	3,000
7. Purchasing Agents and Buyers, Farm Products	$46,680	7.0%	2,000

Best Jobs for Introverts with a Conventional Personality Type

Job	Annual Earnings	Percent Growth	Annual Openings
1. Accountants and Auditors	$52,210	22.4%	157,000
2. Actuaries	$81,640	23.2%	3,000
3. Cost Estimators	$52,020	18.2%	15,000
4. Payroll and Timekeeping Clerks	$31,360	17.3%	36,000
5. Bookkeeping, Accounting, and Auditing Clerks	$29,490	5.9%	291,000
6. Cartographers and Photogrammetrists	$48,250	15.2%	1,000
7. Credit Analysts	$50,370	3.6%	3,000
8. Postal Service Mail Carriers	$46,330	0.0%	19,000
9. Surveying and Mapping Technicians	$31,290	9.6%	9,000
10. Billing and Posting Clerks and Machine Operators	$27,780	3.4%	70,000
11. Electrical and Electronics Drafters	$45,550	1.2%	3,000
12. Tax Preparers	$25,700	10.6%	11,000
13. Title Examiners, Abstractors, and Searchers	$35,120	0.9%	8,000
14. Parking Enforcement Workers	$29,070	15.1%	1,000
15. Data Entry Keyers	$23,810	–0.7%	85,000
16. Word Processors and Typists	$29,020	–15.3%	30,000

PART III

Descriptions of the Best Jobs for Introverts

This part provides descriptions for all the jobs included in one or more of the lists in Part II. The introduction gives more details on how to use and interpret the job descriptions, but here is some additional information:

- Job descriptions are arranged in alphabetical order by job title. This approach allows you to find a description quickly if you know its correct title from one of the lists in Part II.

- In some cases a job title that appears in Part II is linked to two or more different job titles in Part III. For example, if you look for the job title Nuclear Technicians, you will find it listed here alphabetically, but a note will tell you to see the descriptions for Nuclear Equipment Operation Technicians and Nuclear Monitoring Technicians. These job titles are also listed alphabetically, so you can find the descriptions easily.

- Consider the job descriptions in this section as a first step in career exploration. When you find a job that interests you, turn to the appendix for suggestions about resources for further exploration.

- If you are using this section to browse for interesting options, we suggest you begin with the table of contents. Part II features many interesting lists that will help you identify job titles to explore in more detail. If you have not browsed the lists in Part II, consider spending some time there. The lists are interesting and will help you identify job titles you can find described in the material that follows. The job titles in Part III are also listed in the table of contents.

Accountants

This job can be found in the Part II lists under the title Accountants and Auditors.

- Education/Training Required: Bachelor's degree
- Annual Earnings: $52,210
- Growth: 22.4%
- Annual Job Openings: 157,000
- Self-Employed: 10.9%
- Part-Time: 10.2%

The job openings listed here are shared with Auditors.

Level of Solitary Work: 60.9 (out of 100)

Level of Contact with Others: 80.5 (out of 100)

Analyze financial information and prepare financial reports to determine or maintain record of assets, liabilities, profit and loss, tax liability, or other financial activities within an organization. Prepare, examine, or analyze accounting records, financial statements, or other financial reports to assess accuracy, completeness, and conformance to reporting and procedural standards. Compute taxes owed and prepare tax returns, ensuring compliance with payment, reporting, or other tax requirements. Analyze business operations, trends, costs, revenues, financial commitments, and obligations to project future revenues and expenses or to provide advice. Report to management regarding the finances of establishment. Establish tables of accounts and assign entries to proper accounts. Develop, maintain, and analyze budgets, preparing periodic reports that compare budgeted costs to actual costs. Develop, implement, modify, and document recordkeeping and accounting systems, making use of current computer technology. Prepare forms and manuals for accounting and bookkeeping personnel and direct their work activities. Survey operations to ascertain accounting needs and to recommend, develop, or maintain solutions to business and financial problems. Work as Internal Revenue Service (IRS) agents. Advise management about issues such as resource utilization, tax strategies, and the assumptions underlying budget forecasts. Provide internal and external auditing services for businesses or individuals. Advise clients in areas such as compensation, employee health-care benefits, the design of accounting or data processing systems, or long-range tax or estate plans. Investigate bankruptcies and other complex financial transactions and prepare reports summarizing the findings. Represent clients before taxing authorities and provide support during litigation involving financial issues. Appraise, evaluate, and inventory real property and equipment, recording information such as the description, value, and location of property. Maintain or examine the records of government agencies. Serve as bankruptcy trustees or business valuators.

Personality Type: Conventional. Conventional occupations frequently involve following set procedures and routines. These occupations can include working with data and details more than with ideas. Usually there is a clear line of authority to follow.

GOE—Interest Area: 04. Business and Administration. **Work Group:** 04.05. Accounting, Auditing, and Analytical Support. **Other Jobs in This Work Group:** Accountants and Auditors; Auditors; Budget Analysts; Industrial Engineering Technicians; Logisticians; Management Analysts; Operations Research Analysts.

Skills—Management of Financial Resources: Determining how money will be spent to get the work done and accounting for these expenditures. **Systems Analysis:** Determining how a system should work and how changes in conditions, operations, and the environment will affect outcomes. **Systems Evaluation:** Identifying measures or indicators of system performance and the actions needed to improve or correct performance relative to the goals of the system. **Operations Analysis:** Analyzing needs and product requirements to create a design. **Judgment and Decision Making:** Considering the relative costs and benefits of potential actions to choose the most appropriate one. **Programming:** Writing computer programs for various purposes.

Education and Training Programs: Accounting; Accounting and Business/Management; Accounting and Computer Science; Accounting and Finance. **Related Knowledge/Courses: Economics and Accounting:** Economic and accounting principles and practices, the financial markets, banking, and the analysis and reporting of financial data. **Clerical Practices:** Administrative and clerical procedures and systems such as word processing, managing files and records, stenography and transcription, designing forms, and other office procedures and terminology. **Mathematics:** Arithmetic, algebra, geometry, calculus, and statistics and their applications. **Law and Government:** Laws, legal codes, court procedures, precedents, government regulations, executive orders, agency rules, and the democratic political process. **Computers and Electronics:** Circuit boards, processors, chips, electronic equipment, and computer hardware and software, including applications and programming. **Personnel and Human Resources:** Principles and procedures for personnel recruitment, selection, training, compensation and benefits, labor relations and negotiation, and personnel information systems.

Work Environment: Indoors; sitting.

Accountants and Auditors

See the descriptions of these jobs:

- ◎ **Accountants**
- ◎ **Auditors**

Actuaries

- ◎ Education/Training Required: Work experience plus degree
- ◎ Annual Earnings: $81,640
- ◎ Growth: 23.2%
- ◎ Annual Job Openings: 3,000
- ◎ Self-Employed: 0.0%
- ◎ Part-Time: 3.8%

Level of Solitary Work: 68.8 (out of 100)

Level of Contact with Others: 64.7 (out of 100)

Analyze statistical data, such as mortality, accident, sickness, disability, and retirement rates, and construct probability tables to forecast risk and liability for payment of future benefits. May ascertain premium rates required and cash reserves necessary to ensure payment of future benefits. Ascertain premium rates required and cash reserves and liabilities necessary to ensure payment of future benefits. Analyze statistical information to estimate mortality, accident, sickness, disability, and retirement rates. Design, review, and help administer insurance, annuity, and pension plans, determining financial soundness and calculating premiums. Collaborate with programmers, underwriters, accounts, claims experts, and senior management to help companies develop plans for new lines of business or improving existing business. Determine or help determine company policy and explain complex technical matters to company executives, government officials, shareholders, policyholders, or the public. Testify before public agencies on proposed legislation affecting businesses. Provide advice to clients on a contract basis, working as a consultant. Testify in court as expert witness or to provide legal evidence on matters such as the value of potential lifetime earnings of a person who is disabled or killed in an accident. Construct probability tables for events such as fires, natural disasters, and unemployment, based on analysis of statistical data and other pertinent information. Determine policy contract provisions for each type of insurance. Manage credit and help price corporate security offerings. Provide expertise to help financial institutions manage risks and maximize returns associated with investment products or credit offerings. Determine equitable basis for distributing surplus earnings under participating insurance and annuity contracts in mutual companies. Explain changes in contract provisions to customers.

Personality Type: Conventional. Conventional occupations frequently involve following set procedures and routines. These occupations can include working with data and details more than with ideas. Usually there is a clear line of authority to follow.

GOE—Interest Area: 15. Scientific Research, Engineering, and Mathematics. **Work Group:** 15.06. Mathematics and Data Analysis. **Other Jobs in This Work Group:** Mathematical Technicians; Mathematicians; Social Science Research Assistants; Statistical Assistants; Statisticians.

Skills—Programming: Writing computer programs for various purposes. **Mathematics:** Using mathematics to solve problems. **Active Learning:** Understanding the implications of new information for both current and future problem solving and decision making. **Complex Problem Solving:** Identifying complex problems and reviewing related information to develop and evaluate options and implement solutions. **Operations Analysis:** Analyzing needs and product requirements to create a design. **Quality Control Analysis:** Conducting tests and inspections of products, services, or processes to evaluate quality or performance.

Education and Training Program: Actuarial Science. **Related Knowledge/Courses: Mathematics:** Arithmetic, algebra, geometry, calculus, and statistics and their applications. **Economics and Accounting:** Economic and accounting principles and practices, the financial markets, banking, and the analysis and reporting of financial data. **Sales and Marketing:** Principles and methods for showing, promoting, and selling products or services. This includes marketing strategy and tactics, product demonstration, sales

techniques, and sales control systems. **Computers and Electronics:** Circuit boards, processors, chips, electronic equipment, and computer hardware and software, including applications and programming. **Personnel and Human Resources:** Principles and procedures for personnel recruitment, selection, training, compensation and benefits, labor relations and negotiation, and personnel information systems. **English Language:** The structure and content of the English language, including the meaning and spelling of words, rules of composition, and grammar.

Work Environment: Indoors; sitting; using hands on objects, tools, or controls; repetitive motions.

Aerospace Engineers

- ◎ Education/Training Required: Bachelor's degree
- ◎ Annual Earnings: $84,090
- ◎ Growth: 8.3%
- ◎ Annual Job Openings: 6,000
- ◎ Self-Employed: 0.0%
- ◎ Part-Time: 2.4%

Level of Solitary Work: 46.7 (out of 100)

Level of Contact with Others: 63.0 (out of 100)

Perform a variety of engineering work in designing, constructing, and testing aircraft, missiles, and spacecraft. May conduct basic and applied research to evaluate adaptability of materials and equipment to aircraft design and manufacture. May recommend improvements in testing equipment and techniques. Formulate conceptual design of aeronautical or aerospace products or systems to meet customer requirements. Direct and coordinate activities of engineering or technical personnel designing, fabricating, modifying, or testing aircraft or aerospace products. Develop design criteria for aeronautical or aerospace products or systems, including testing methods, production costs, quality standards, and completion dates. Plan and conduct experimental, environmental, operational, and stress tests on models and prototypes of aircraft and aerospace systems and equipment. Evaluate product data and design from inspections and reports for conformance to engineering principles, customer requirements, and quality standards. Formulate mathematical models or other methods of computer analysis to develop, evaluate, or modify design according to customer engineering requirements. Write technical reports and other documentation, such as handbooks and bulletins, for use by engineering staff, management, and customers. Analyze project requests and proposals and engineering data to determine feasibility, productibility, cost, and production time of aerospace or aeronautical product. Review performance reports and documentation from customers and field engineers and inspect malfunctioning or damaged products to determine problem. Direct research and development programs. Evaluate and approve selection of vendors by study of past performance and new advertisements. Plan and coordinate activities concerned with investigating and resolving customers' reports of technical problems with aircraft or aerospace vehicles. Maintain records of performance reports for future reference.

Personality Type: Investigative. Investigative occupations frequently involve working with ideas and require an extensive amount of thinking. These occupations can involve searching for facts and figuring out problems mentally.

GOE—Interest Area: 15. Scientific Research, Engineering, and Mathematics. **Work Group:** 15.07. Research and Design Engineering. **Other Jobs in This Work Group:** Biomedical Engineers; Chemical Engineers; Civil Engineers; Computer Hardware Engineers; Electrical Engineers; Electronics Engineers, Except Computer; Marine Architects; Marine Engineers; Marine Engineers and Naval Architects; Materials Engineers; Mechanical Engineers; Nuclear Engineers.

Skills—Systems Evaluation: Identifying measures or indicators of system performance and the actions needed to improve or correct performance relative to the goals of the system. **Systems Analysis:** Determining how a system should work and how changes in conditions, operations, and the environment will affect outcomes. **Science:** Using scientific rules and methods to solve problems. **Judgment and Decision Making:** Considering the relative costs and benefits of potential actions to choose the most appropriate one. **Persuasion:** Persuading others to change their minds or behavior. **Technology Design:** Generating or adapting equipment and technology to serve user needs.

Education and Training Program: Aerospace, Aeronautical, and Astronautical Engineering. **Related Knowledge/Courses: Engineering and Technology:** The practical application of engineering science and technology. This includes applying principles, techniques, procedures, and equipment to the design and production of various goods and services. **Physics:** Physical principles and laws and their interrelationships and applications to understanding fluid, material, and atmospheric dynamics and mechanical, electrical, atomic, and subatomic structures and processes. **Design:** Design techniques, tools, and principles involved in production of precision technical plans, blueprints, drawings, and models. **Mechanical Devices:** Machines and tools, including their designs, uses, repair, and maintenance. **Production and Processing:** Raw materials, production processes, quality control, costs, and other techniques for maximizing the effective manufacture and distribution of goods. **Mathematics:** Arithmetic, algebra, geometry, calculus, and statistics and their applications.

Work Environment: Indoors; sitting; repetitive motions.

Agricultural Inspectors

- Education/Training Required: Work experience in a related occupation
- Annual Earnings: $32,840
- Growth: 6.8%
- Annual Job Openings: 3,000
- Self-Employed: 0.0%
- Part-Time: 7.1%

Level of Solitary Work: 62.5 (out of 100)

Level of Contact with Others: 36.8 (out of 100)

Inspect agricultural commodities, processing equipment, and facilities, and fish and logging operations to ensure compliance with regulations and laws governing health, quality, and safety. Set standards for the production of meat and poultry products and for food ingredients, additives, and compounds used to prepare and package products. Direct and monitor the quarantine and treatment or destruction of plants and plant products. Monitor the operations and sanitary conditions of slaughtering and meat processing plants. Verify that transportation and handling procedures meet regulatory requirements. Take emergency actions such as closing production facilities if product safety is compromised. Set labeling standards and approve labels for meat and poultry products. Review and monitor foreign product inspection systems in countries of origin to ensure equivalence to the U.S. system. Inspect the cleanliness and practices of establishment employees. Advise farmers and growers of development programs or new equipment and techniques to aid in quality production. Inspect livestock to determine effectiveness of medication and feeding programs. Provide consultative services in areas such as equipment and product evaluation, plant construction and layout, and food safety systems. Monitor the grading performed by company employees to verify conformance to standards. Write reports of findings and recommendations and advise farmers, growers, or processors of corrective action to be taken. Inspect and test horticultural products or livestock to detect harmful diseases, chemical residues, and infestations and to determine the quality of products or animals. Examine, weigh, and measure commodities such as poultry, eggs, meat, and seafood to certify qualities, grades, and weights. Label and seal graded products and issue official grading certificates. Interpret and enforce government acts and regulations and explain required standards to agricultural workers. Inspect food products and processing procedures to determine whether products are safe to eat. Inspect agricultural commodities and related operations, as well as fish and logging operations, for compliance with laws and regulations governing health, quality, and safety. Testify in legal proceedings. Collect samples from animals, plants, or products and route them to laboratories for microbiological assessment, ingredient verification, and other testing.

Personality Type: Realistic. Realistic occupations frequently involve work activities that include practical, hands-on problems and solutions. They often deal with plants; animals; and real-world materials such as wood, tools, and machinery. Many of the occupations require working outside and do not involve a lot of paperwork or working closely with others.

GOE—Interest Area: 07. Government and Public Administration. **Work Group:** 07.03. Regulations Enforcement. **Other Jobs in This Work Group:** Aviation Inspectors; Compliance Officers, Except Agriculture, Construction, Health and Safety, and Transportation; Construction and Building Inspectors; Environmental Compliance Inspectors; Equal Opportunity Representatives and Officers; Financial Examiners; Fire Inspectors; Fish and Game Wardens; Forest Fire Inspectors and Prevention Specialists; Freight and Cargo Inspectors; Government Property Inspectors and Investigators; Immigration and Customs Inspectors; Licensing Examiners and Inspectors; Nuclear Monitoring Technicians; Occupational Health and Safety Specialists; Occupational Health and Safety

Technicians; Tax Examiners, Collectors, and Revenue Agents; Transportation Vehicle, Equipment, and Systems Inspectors, Except Aviation.

Skills—Quality Control Analysis: Conducting tests and inspections of products, services, or processes to evaluate quality or performance. **Science:** Using scientific rules and methods to solve problems. **Operation Monitoring:** Watching gauges, dials, or other indicators to make sure a machine is working properly. **Systems Evaluation:** Identifying measures or indicators of system performance and the actions needed to improve or correct performance relative to the goals of the system.

Education and Training Program: Agricultural and Food Products Processing. **Related Knowledge/ Courses: Food Production:** Techniques and equipment for planting, growing, and harvesting food products (both plant and animal) for consumption, including storage/handling techniques. **Biology:** Plant and animal organisms and their tissues, cells, functions, interdependencies, and interactions with each other and the environment. **Production and Processing:** Raw materials, production processes, quality control, costs, and other techniques for maximizing the effective manufacture and distribution of goods. **Law and Government:** Laws, legal codes, court procedures, precedents, government regulations, executive orders, agency rules, and the democratic political process.

Work Environment: More often outdoors than indoors; standing; walking and running; using hands on objects, tools, or controls.

Aircraft Mechanics and Service Technicians

- Education/Training Required: Postsecondary vocational training
- Annual Earnings: $47,310
- Growth: 13.4%
- Annual Job Openings: 11,000
- Self-Employed: 3.0%
- Part-Time: 1.8%

Level of Solitary Work: 54.3 (out of 100)

Level of Contact with Others: 80.8 (out of 100)

Diagnose, adjust, repair, or overhaul aircraft engines and assemblies, such as hydraulic and pneumatic systems. Read and interpret maintenance manuals, service bulletins, and other specifications to determine the feasibility and method of repairing or replacing malfunctioning or damaged components. Inspect completed work to certify that maintenance meets standards and that aircraft are ready for operation. Maintain repair logs, documenting all preventive and corrective aircraft maintenance. Conduct routine and special inspections as required by regulations. Examine and inspect aircraft components, including landing gear, hydraulic systems, and de-icers, to locate cracks, breaks, leaks, or other problem. Inspect airframes for wear or other defects. Maintain, repair, and rebuild aircraft structures; functional components; and parts such as wings and fuselage, rigging, hydraulic units, oxygen systems, fuel systems, electrical systems, gaskets, and seals. Measure the tension of control cables. Replace or repair worn, defective, or damaged components, using hand tools, gauges, and testing equipment. Measure parts for wear, using precision instruments. Assemble and install electrical, plumbing, mechanical, hydraulic, and structural components and accessories, using hand tools and power tools. Test operation of engines and other systems, using test equipment such as ignition analyzers, compression checkers, distributor timers, and ammeters. Obtain fuel and oil samples and check them for contamination. Reassemble engines following repair or inspection and re-install engines in aircraft. Read and interpret pilots' descriptions of problems to diagnose causes. Modify aircraft structures, space vehicles, systems, or components, following drawings, schematics, charts, engineering orders, and technical publications. Install and align repaired or replacement parts for subsequent riveting or welding, using clamps and wrenches. Locate and mark dimensions and reference lines on defective or replacement parts, using templates, scribes, compasses, and steel rules. Clean, strip, prime, and sand structural surfaces and materials to prepare them for bonding. Service and maintain aircraft and related apparatus by performing activities such as flushing crankcases, cleaning screens, and lubricating moving parts.

Personality Type: Realistic. Realistic occupations frequently involve work activities that include practical, hands-on problems and solutions. They often deal with plants; animals; and real-world materials such as wood, tools, and machinery. Many of the occupations require working outside and do not involve a lot of paperwork or working closely with others.

GOE—Interest Area: 13. Manufacturing. **Work Group:** 13.14. Vehicle and Facility Mechanical Work. **Other Jobs in This Work Group:** Aircraft Structure, Surfaces, Rigging, and Systems Assemblers; Automotive Body and Related Repairers; Automotive Glass Installers and Repairers; Automotive Master Mechanics; Automotive Service Technicians and Mechanics; Automotive Specialty Technicians; Bus and Truck Mechanics and Diesel Engine Specialists; Farm Equipment Mechanics; Fiberglass Laminators and Fabricators; Mobile Heavy Equipment Mechanics, Except Engines; Motorboat Mechanics; Motorcycle Mechanics; Outdoor Power Equipment and Other Small Engine Mechanics; Rail Car Repairers; Recreational Vehicle Service Technicians; Tire Repairers and Changers.

Skills—Repairing: Repairing machines or systems by using the needed tools. **Equipment Maintenance:** Performing routine maintenance on equipment and determining when and what kind of maintenance is needed. **Operation Monitoring:** Watching gauges, dials, or other indicators to make sure a machine is working properly. **Installation:** Installing equipment, machines, wiring, or programs to meet specifications. **Troubleshooting:** Determining causes of operating errors and deciding what to do about them. **Operation and Control:** Controlling operations of equipment or systems.

Education and Training Programs: Agricultural Mechanics and Equipment/Machine Technology; Aircraft Powerplant Technology/Technician Training; Airframe Mechanics and Aircraft Maintenance Technology/Technician Training. **Related Knowledge/Courses: Mechanical Devices:** Machines and tools, including their designs, uses, repair, and maintenance. **Design:** Design techniques, tools, and principles involved in production of precision technical plans, blueprints, drawings, and models. **Physics:** Physical principles and laws and their interrelationships and applications to understanding fluid, material, and atmospheric dynamics and mechanical, electrical, atomic, and subatomic structures and processes. **Chemistry:** The chemical composition, structure, and properties of substances and of the chemical processes and transformations that they undergo. This includes uses of chemicals and their danger signs, production techniques, and disposal methods. **Engineering and Technology:** The practical application of engineering science and technology. This includes applying principles, techniques, procedures, and equipment to the design and production of various goods and services. **Transportation:** Principles and methods for moving people or goods by air, rail, sea, or road, including the relative costs and benefits.

Work Environment: Noisy; contaminants; cramped work space, awkward positions; standing; using hands on objects, tools, or controls; bending or twisting the body.

Aircraft Structure, Surfaces, Rigging, and Systems Assemblers

- ◎ Education/Training Required: Long-term on-the-job training
- ◎ Annual Earnings: $43,990
- ◎ Growth: 7.8%
- ◎ Annual Job Openings: 4,000
- ◎ Self-Employed: 0.0%
- ◎ Part-Time: 1.7%

Level of Solitary Work: 67.8 (out of 100)

Level of Contact with Others: 12.3 (out of 100)

Assemble, fit, fasten, and install parts of airplanes, space vehicles, or missiles, such as tails, wings, fuselage, bulkheads, stabilizers, landing gear, rigging and control equipment, or heating and ventilating systems. Form loops or splices in cables, using clamps and fittings, or reweave cable strands. Align and fit structural assemblies manually or signal crane operators to position assemblies for joining. Align, fit, assemble, connect, and install system components, using jigs, fixtures, measuring instruments, hand tools, and power tools. Assemble and fit prefabricated parts to form subassemblies. Assemble, install, and connect parts, fittings, and assemblies on aircraft, using layout tools; hand tools; power tools; and fasteners such as bolts, screws, rivets, and clamps. Attach brackets, hinges, or clips to secure or support components and subassemblies, using bolts, screws, rivets, chemical bonding, or welding. Select and install accessories in swaging machines, using hand tools. Fit and fasten sheet metal coverings to surface areas and other sections of aircraft prior to welding or riveting. Lay out and mark reference points and locations for installation of parts and components, using jigs, templates, and measuring and marking instruments. Inspect and test installed units, parts, systems, and assemblies for fit, alignment, performance, defects,

and compliance with standards, using measuring instruments and test equipment. Install mechanical linkages and actuators and verify tension of cables, using tensiometers. Join structural assemblies such as wings, tails, and fuselage. Measure and cut cables and tubing, using master templates, measuring instruments, and cable cutters or saws. Read and interpret blueprints, illustrations, and specifications to determine layouts, sequences of operations, or identities and relationships of parts. Prepare and load live ammunition, missiles, and bombs onto aircraft according to established procedures. Adjust, repair, rework, or replace parts and assemblies to eliminate malfunctions and to ensure proper operation. Cut, trim, file, bend, and smooth parts and verify sizes and fitting tolerances to ensure proper fit and clearance of parts. Install and connect control cables to electronically controlled units, using hand tools, ring locks, cotter keys, threaded connectors, turnbuckles, and related devices.

Personality Type: Realistic. Realistic occupations frequently involve work activities that include practical, hands-on problems and solutions. They often deal with plants; animals; and real-world materials such as wood, tools, and machinery. Many of the occupations require working outside and do not involve a lot of paperwork or working closely with others.

GOE—Interest Area: 13. Manufacturing. **Work Group:** 13.14. Vehicle and Facility Mechanical Work. **Other Jobs in This Work Group:** Aircraft Mechanics and Service Technicians; Automotive Body and Related Repairers; Automotive Glass Installers and Repairers; Automotive Master Mechanics; Automotive Service Technicians and Mechanics; Automotive Specialty Technicians; Bus and Truck Mechanics and Diesel Engine Specialists; Farm Equipment Mechanics; Fiberglass Laminators and Fabricators; Mobile Heavy Equipment Mechanics, Except Engines; Motorboat Mechanics; Motorcycle Mechanics; Outdoor Power Equipment and Other Small Engine Mechanics; Rail Car Repairers; Recreational Vehicle Service Technicians; Tire Repairers and Changers.

Skills—**Installation:** Installing equipment, machines, wiring, or programs to meet specifications. **Repairing:** Repairing machines or systems by using the needed tools. **Quality Control Analysis:** Conducting tests and inspections of products, services, or processes to evaluate quality or performance. **Equipment Maintenance:** Performing routine maintenance on equipment and determining when and what kind of maintenance is needed. **Operation and Control:** Controlling operations of equipment or systems. **Troubleshooting:** Determining causes of operating errors and deciding what to do about them.

Education and Training Programs: Aircraft Powerplant Technology/Technician Training; Airframe Mechanics and Aircraft Maintenance Technology/Technician Training; Avionics Maintenance Technology/Technician Training. **Related Knowledge/Courses: Mechanical Devices:** Machines and tools, including their designs, uses, repair, and maintenance. **Production and Processing:** Raw materials, production processes, quality control, costs, and other techniques for maximizing the effective manufacture and distribution of goods. **Design:** Design techniques, tools, and principles involved in production of precision technical plans, blueprints, drawings, and models. **Building and Construction:** The materials, methods, and tools involved in the construction or repair of houses, buildings, or other structures such as highways and roads. **Engineering and Technology:** The practical application of engineering science and technology. This includes applying principles, techniques, procedures, and equipment to the design and production of various goods and services. **Physics:** Physical principles and laws and their interrelationships and applications to understanding fluid, material, and atmospheric dynamics and mechanical, electrical, atomic, and subatomic structures and processes.

Work Environment: More often indoors than outdoors; hazardous equipment; standing; using hands on objects, tools, or controls; repetitive motions.

Animal Scientists

- Education/Training Required: Bachelor's degree
- Annual Earnings: $43,170
- Growth: 12.9%
- Annual Job Openings: Fewer than 500
- Self-Employed: 31.3%
- Part-Time: No data available

Level of Solitary Work: 78.0 (out of 100)

Level of Contact with Others: 73.3 (out of 100)

Conduct research in the genetics, nutrition, reproduction, growth, and development of domestic farm animals. Conduct research concerning animal nutrition, breeding, or management to improve products or processes. Advise producers about improved products and techniques that could enhance their animal production efforts. Study nutritional requirements of animals and nutritive values of animal feed materials. Study effects of management practices, processing methods, feed, or environmental conditions on quality and quantity of animal products, such as eggs and milk. Develop improved practices in feeding, housing, sanitation, or parasite and disease control of animals. Research and control animal selection and breeding practices to increase production efficiency and improve animal quality. Determine genetic composition of animal populations and heritability of traits, utilizing principles of genetics. Crossbreed animals with existing strains or cross strains to obtain new combinations of desirable characteristics.

Personality Type: Investigative. Investigative occupations frequently involve working with ideas and require an extensive amount of thinking. These occupations can involve searching for facts and figuring out problems mentally.

GOE—Interest Area: 01. Agriculture and Natural Resources. **Work Group:** 01.02. Resource Science/Engineering for Plants, Animals, and the

Environment. **Other Jobs in This Work Group:** Agricultural Engineers; Conservation Scientists; Environmental Engineers; Foresters; Mining and Geological Engineers, Including Mining Safety Engineers; Petroleum Engineers; Range Managers; Soil and Plant Scientists; Soil and Water Conservationists; Zoologists and Wildlife Biologists.

Skills—Science: Using scientific rules and methods to solve problems. **Management of Financial Resources:** Determining how money will be spent to get the work done and accounting for these expenditures. **Systems Analysis:** Determining how a system should work and how changes in conditions, operations, and the environment will affect outcomes. **Writing:** Communicating effectively in writing as appropriate for the needs of the audience. **Complex Problem Solving:** Identifying complex problems and reviewing related information to develop and evaluate options and implement solutions. **Reading Comprehension:** Understanding written sentences and paragraphs in work-related documents.

Education and Training Programs: Agricultural Animal Breeding; Agriculture, General; Animal Health; Animal Nutrition; Animal Sciences, General; Animal Sciences, Other; Dairy Science; Poultry Science; Range Science and Management. **Related Knowledge/Courses: Food Production:** Techniques and equipment for planting, growing, and harvesting food products (both plant and animal) for consumption, including storage/handling techniques. **Biology:** Plant and animal organisms and their tissues, cells, functions, interdependencies, and interactions with each other and the environment. **Chemistry:** The chemical composition, structure, and properties of substances and of the chemical processes and transformations that they undergo. This includes uses of chemicals and their danger signs, production techniques, and disposal methods. **Education and Training:** Principles and methods for curriculum and training design, teaching and instruction for individuals and groups, and the measurement of training effects. **Mathematics:** Arithmetic, algebra, geometry, calculus, and statistics and their

applications. **Physics:** Physical principles and laws and their interrelationships and applications to understanding fluid, material, and atmospheric dynamics and mechanical, electrical, atomic, and subatomic structures and processes.

Work Environment: More often indoors than outdoors; sitting.

Animal Trainers

- Education/Training Required: Moderate-term on-the-job training
- Annual Earnings: $24,800
- Growth: 20.3%
- Annual Job Openings: 3,000
- Self-Employed: 58.2%
- Part-Time: 23.1%

Level of Solitary Work: 75.0 (out of 100)

Level of Contact with Others: 74.5 (out of 100)

Train animals for riding, harness, security, performance, or obedience or assisting persons with disabilities. Accustom animals to human voice and contact and condition animals to respond to commands. Train animals according to prescribed standards for show or competition. May train animals to carry pack loads or work as part of pack team. Observe animals' physical conditions to detect illness or unhealthy conditions requiring medical care. Cue or signal animals during performances. Administer prescribed medications to animals. Evaluate animals to determine their temperaments, abilities, and aptitude for training. Feed and exercise animals and provide other general care such as cleaning and maintaining holding and performance areas. Talk to and interact with animals in order to familiarize them to human voices and contact. Conduct training programs to develop and maintain desired animal behaviors for competition, entertainment, obedience, security, riding, and related areas. Keep records documenting animal health, diet, and behavior. Advise animal owners regarding the purchase of specific animals. Instruct jockeys in handling specific horses during races. Train horses or other equines for riding, harness, show, racing, or other work, using knowledge of breed characteristics, training methods, performance standards, and the peculiarities of each animal. Use oral, spur, rein, and hand commands to condition horses to carry riders or to pull horse-drawn equipment. Place tack or harnesses on horses to accustom horses to the feel of equipment. Train dogs in human-assistance or property protection duties. Retrain horses to break bad habits, such as kicking, bolting, and resisting bridling and grooming. Train and rehearse animals, according to scripts, for motion picture, television, film, stage, or circus performances. Organize and conduct animal shows. Arrange for mating of stallions and mares and assist mares during foaling.

Personality Type: Social. Social occupations frequently involve working with, communicating with, and teaching people. These occupations often involve helping or providing service to others.

GOE—Interest Area: 08. Health Science. **Work Group:** 08.05. Animal Care. **Other Jobs in This Work Group:** Animal Breeders; Nonfarm Animal Caretakers; Veterinarians; Veterinary Assistants and Laboratory Animal Caretakers; Veterinary Technologists and Technicians.

Skills—Management of Financial Resources: Determining how money will be spent to get the work done and accounting for these expenditures. **Persuasion:** Persuading others to change their minds or behavior. **Instructing:** Teaching others how to do something. **Service Orientation:** Actively looking for ways to help people. **Learning Strategies:** Selecting and using training or instructional methods and procedures appropriate for the situation when learning or teaching new things. **Monitoring:** Monitoring or assessing your own performance or that of other individuals or organizations to make improvements or take corrective action.

Education and Training Programs: Animal Training; Equestrian/Equine Studies. **Related Knowledge/ Courses: Sales and Marketing:** Principles and methods for showing, promoting, and selling products or services. This includes marketing strategy and tactics, product demonstration, sales techniques, and sales control systems. **Biology:** Plant and animal organisms and their tissues, cells, functions, interdependencies, and interactions with each other and the environment. **Customer and Personal Service:** Principles and processes for providing customer and personal services. This includes customer needs assessment, meeting quality standards for services, and evaluation of customer satisfaction. **Economics and Accounting:** Economic and accounting principles and practices, the financial markets, banking, and the analysis and reporting of financial data. **Communications and Media:** Media production, communication, and dissemination techniques and methods. This includes alternative ways to inform and entertain via written, oral, and visual media. **Clerical Practices:** Administrative and clerical procedures and systems such as word processing, managing files and records, stenography and transcription, designing forms, and other office procedures and terminology.

Work Environment: Outdoors; noisy; standing; walking and running; using hands on objects, tools, or controls; repetitive motions.

Anthropologists and Archeologists

See the descriptions of these jobs:

- Anthropologists
- Archeologists

Anthropologists

This job can be found in the Part II lists under the title Anthropologists and Archeologists.

- Education/Training Required: Master's degree
- Annual Earnings: $45,910
- Growth: 17.0%
- Annual Job Openings: Fewer than 500
- Self-Employed: 3.8%
- Part-Time: 14.8%

The job openings listed here are shared with Archeologists.

Level of Solitary Work: 51.5 (out of 100)

Level of Contact with Others: 76.0 (out of 100)

Research, evaluate, and establish public policy concerning the origins of humans; their physical, social, linguistic, and cultural development; and their behavior, as well as the cultures, organizations, and institutions they have created. Collect information and make judgments through observation, interviews, and the review of documents. Plan and direct research to characterize and compare the economic, demographic, health-care, social, political, linguistic, and religious institutions of distinct cultural groups, communities, and organizations. Write about and present research findings for a variety of specialized and general audiences. Advise government agencies, private organizations, and communities regarding proposed programs, plans, and policies and their potential impacts on cultural institutions, organizations, and communities. Identify culturally specific beliefs and practices affecting health status and access to services for distinct populations and communities in collaboration with medical and public health officials. Build and use text-based database management systems to support the analysis of detailed firsthand observational records, or "field notes." Develop intervention procedures, utilizing techniques such as individual and focus group interviews, consultations, and participant observation of social interaction. Construct and test data collection methods. Explain the origins and physical, social, or cultural development of humans, including physical attributes, cultural traditions, beliefs, languages, resource management practices, and settlement patterns. Conduct participatory action research in communities and organizations to assess how work is done and to design work systems, technologies, and environments. Train others in the application of ethnographic research methods to solve problems in organizational effectiveness, communications, technology development, policy-making, and program planning. Formulate general rules that describe and predict the development and behavior of cultures and social institutions. Collaborate with economic development planners to decide on the implementation of proposed development policies, plans, and programs based on culturally institutionalized barriers and facilitating circumstances. Create data records for use in describing and analyzing social patterns and processes, using photography, videography, and audio recordings.

Personality Type: Investigative. Investigative occupations frequently involve working with ideas and require an extensive amount of thinking. These occupations can involve searching for facts and figuring out problems mentally.

GOE—Interest Area: 15. Scientific Research, Engineering, and Mathematics. **Work Group:** 15.04. Social Sciences. **Other Jobs in This Work Group:** Anthropologists and Archeologists; Archeologists; Economists; Historians; Industrial-Organizational Psychologists; Political Scientists; School Psychologists; Sociologists.

Skills—Writing: Communicating effectively in writing as appropriate for the needs of the audience. **Social Perceptiveness:** Being aware of others' reactions and understanding why they react as they do. **Complex Problem Solving:** Identifying complex problems and reviewing related information to develop and evaluate options and implement solutions. **Science:** Using scientific rules and methods to solve problems. **Systems Evaluation:** Identifying measures or indicators of system performance and the actions needed to improve or correct performance relative to the goals of the system. **Reading Comprehension:** Understanding written sentences and paragraphs in work-related documents.

Education and Training Programs: Anthropology; Physical Anthropology. **Related Knowledge/ Courses: Sociology and Anthropology:** Group behavior and dynamics, societal trends and influences, human migrations, ethnicity, and cultures and their history and origins. **History and Archeology:** Historical events and their causes, indicators, and effects on civilizations and cultures. **Foreign Language:** The structure and content of a foreign (non-English) language, including the meaning and spelling of words, rules of composition and grammar, and pronunciation. **Philosophy and Theology:** Different philosophical systems and religions. This includes their basic principles, values, ethics, ways of thinking, customs, and practices and their impact on human culture. **Geography:** Principles and methods for describing the features of land, sea, and air masses, including their physical characteristics; locations; interrelationships; and distribution of plant, animal, and human life. **Biology:** Plant and animal organisms and their tissues, cells, functions, interdependencies, and interactions with each other and the environment.

Work Environment: Indoors; sitting.

Appraisers and Assessors of Real Estate

See the descriptions of these jobs:

- Appraisers, Real Estate
- Assessors

Appraisers, Real Estate

This job can be found in the Part II lists under the title Appraisers and Assessors of Real Estate.

- Education/Training Required: Postsecondary vocational training
- Annual Earnings: $43,440
- Growth: 22.8%
- Annual Job Openings: 9,000
- Self-Employed: 37.2%
- Part-Time: 10.9%

The job openings listed here are shared with Assessors.

Level of Solitary Work: 71.9 (out of 100)

Level of Contact with Others: 88.7 (out of 100)

Appraise real property to determine its value for purchase, sales, investment, mortgage, or loan purposes. Prepare written reports that estimate property values, outline methods by which the estimations were made, and meet appraisal standards. Compute final estimation of property values, taking into account such factors as depreciation, replacement costs, value comparisons of similar properties, and income potential. Search public records for transactions such as sales, leases, and assessments. Inspect properties to evaluate construction, condition, special features, and functional design and to take property measurements. Photograph interiors and exteriors of properties in order to assist in estimating property value, substantiate findings, and complete appraisal reports. Evaluate land and neighborhoods where properties are situated, considering locations and trends or impending changes that could influence future values. Obtain county land values and sales information about nearby properties in order to aid in establishment of property values. Verify legal descriptions of properties by comparing them to county records. Check building codes and zoning bylaws in order to determine any effects on the properties being appraised. Estimate building replacement costs, using building valuation manuals and professional cost estimators. Examine income records and operating costs of income properties. Interview persons familiar with properties and immediate surroundings, such as contractors, homeowners, and realtors, in order to obtain pertinent information. Examine the type and location of nearby services such as shopping centers, schools, parks, and other neighborhood features in order to evaluate their impact on property values. Draw land diagrams that will be used in appraisal reports to support findings. Testify in court as to the value of a piece of real estate property.

Personality Type: Enterprising. Enterprising occupations frequently involve starting up and carrying out projects. These occupations can involve leading people and making many decisions. They sometimes require risk taking and often deal with business.

GOE—Interest Area: 06. Finance and Insurance. **Work Group:** 06.02. Finance/Insurance Investigation and Analysis. **Other Jobs in This Work Group:** Appraisers and Assessors of Real Estate; Assessors; Claims Adjusters, Examiners, and Investigators; Claims Examiners, Property and Casualty Insurance; Cost Estimators; Credit Analysts; Financial Analysts; Insurance Adjusters, Examiners, and Investigators; Insurance Appraisers, Auto Damage; Insurance Underwriters; Loan Counselors; Loan Officers; Market Research Analysts; Survey Researchers.

Skills—Mathematics: Using mathematics to solve problems. **Writing:** Communicating effectively in writing as appropriate for the needs of the audience. **Critical Thinking:** Using logic and reasoning to identify the strengths and weaknesses of alternative solutions, conclusions, or approaches to problems. **Management of Financial Resources:** Determining how money will be spent to get the work done and accounting for these expenditures. **Complex Problem Solving:** Identifying complex problems and reviewing related information to develop and evaluate options and implement solutions. **Speaking:** Talking to others to convey information effectively.

Education and Training Program: Real Estate. **Related Knowledge/Courses: Building and Construction:** The materials, methods, and tools involved in the construction or repair of houses, buildings, or other structures such as highways and roads. **Economics and Accounting:** Economic and accounting principles and practices, the financial markets, banking, and the analysis and reporting of financial data. **Geography:** Principles and methods for describing the features of land, sea, and air masses, including their physical characteristics; locations; interrelationships; and distribution of plant, animal, and human life. **Clerical Practices:** Administrative and clerical procedures and systems such as word processing, managing files and records, stenography and transcription, designing forms, and other office procedures and terminology. **Law and Government:** Laws, legal codes, court procedures, precedents, government regulations, executive orders, agency rules, and the democratic political process. **Customer and Personal Service:** Principles and processes for providing customer and personal services. This includes customer needs assessment, meeting quality standards for services, and evaluation of customer satisfaction.

Work Environment: More often outdoors than indoors; sitting.

Arbitrators, Mediators, and Conciliators

- Education/Training Required: Work experience plus degree
- Annual Earnings: $54,360
- Growth: 15.5%
- Annual Job Openings: Fewer than 500
- Self-Employed: 0.0%
- Part-Time: No data available

Level of Solitary Work: 56.3 (out of 100)

Level of Contact with Others: 60.0 (out of 100)

Facilitate negotiation and conflict resolution through dialogue. Resolve conflicts outside of the court system by mutual consent of parties involved. Use mediation techniques to facilitate communication between disputants, to further parties' understanding of different perspectives, and to guide parties toward mutual agreement. Set up appointments for parties to meet for mediation. Rule on exceptions, motions, and admissibility of evidence. Prepare written opinions and decisions regarding cases. Notify claimants of denied claims and appeal rights. Issue subpoenas and administer oaths to prepare for formal hearings. Authorize payment of valid claims. Organize and deliver public presentations about mediation to organizations such as community agencies and schools. Conduct studies of appeals procedures to ensure adherence to legal requirements and to facilitate disposition of cases. Arrange and conduct hearings to obtain information and evidence relative to disposition of claims. Determine existence and amount of liability according to evidence, laws, and administrative and judicial precedents. Review and evaluate information from documents such as claim applications, birth or death certificates, and physician or employer records. Analyze evidence and apply relevant laws, regulations, policies, and precedents to reach conclusions. Conduct initial meetings with disputants to outline the arbitration process, settle procedural matters such as fees, and determine details such as witness numbers and time requirements. Confer with disputants to clarify issues, identify underlying concerns, and develop an understanding of their respective needs and interests. Interview claimants, agents, or witnesses to obtain information about disputed issues. Participate in court proceedings. Prepare settlement agreements for disputants to sign. Recommend acceptance or rejection of compromise settlement offers. Research laws, regulations, policies, and precedent decisions to prepare for hearings.

Personality Type: Enterprising. Enterprising occupations frequently involve starting up and carrying out

projects. These occupations can involve leading people and making many decisions. They sometimes require risk taking and often deal with business.

GOE—Interest Area: 12. Law and Public Safety. **Work Group:** 12.02. Legal Practice and Justice Administration. **Other Jobs in This Work Group:** Administrative Law Judges, Adjudicators, and Hearing Officers; Judges, Magistrate Judges, and Magistrates; Lawyers.

Skills—Judgment and Decision Making: Considering the relative costs and benefits of potential actions to choose the most appropriate one. **Active Listening:** Giving full attention to what other people are saying, taking time to understand the points being made, asking questions as appropriate, and not interrupting at inappropriate times. **Critical Thinking:** Using logic and reasoning to identify the strengths and weaknesses of alternative solutions, conclusions, or approaches to problems. **Writing:** Communicating effectively in writing as appropriate for the needs of the audience. **Reading Comprehension:** Understanding written sentences and paragraphs in work-related documents. **Speaking:** Talking to others to convey information effectively.

Education and Training Programs: Law (LL.B., J.D.); Legal Professions and Studies, Other. **Related Knowledge/Courses: Law and Government:** Laws, legal codes, court procedures, precedents, government regulations, executive orders, agency rules, and the democratic political process. **Psychology:** Human behavior and performance; individual differences in ability, personality, and interests; learning and motivation; psychological research methods; and the assessment and treatment of behavioral and affective disorders. **English Language:** The structure and content of the English language, including the meaning and spelling of words, rules of composition, and grammar. **Administration and Management:** Business and management principles involved in strategic planning, resource allocation, human resources modeling, leadership technique, production methods, and coordination of people and resources.

Work Environment: Indoors; sitting.

Archeologists

This job can be found in the Part II lists under the title Anthropologists and Archeologists.

- Education/Training Required: Master's degree
- Annual Earnings: $45,910
- Growth: 17.0%
- Annual Job Openings: Fewer than 500
- Self-Employed: 3.8%
- Part-Time: 14.8%

The job openings listed here are shared with Anthropologists.

Level of Solitary Work: 51.5 (out of 100)

Level of Contact with Others: 76.0 (out of 100)

Conduct research to reconstruct record of past human life and culture from human remains, artifacts, architectural features, and structures recovered through excavation, underwater recovery, or other means of discovery. Write, present, and publish reports that record site history, methodology, and artifact analysis results, along with recommendations for conserving and interpreting findings. Compare findings from one site with archeological data from other sites to find similarities or differences. Research, survey, or assess sites of past societies and cultures in search of answers to specific research questions. Study objects and structures recovered by excavation to identify, date, and authenticate them and to interpret their significance. Develop and test theories concerning the origin and development of past cultures. Consult site reports, existing artifacts, and topographic maps to identify archeological sites. Create a grid of each site and draw and update maps of unit profiles, stratum surfaces, features, and findings. Record the exact locations and conditions of artifacts uncovered in diggings or surveys, using drawings and photographs as necessary. Assess archeological sites for resource management, development, or conservation purposes and recommend methods for site protection. Describe artifacts' physical properties or attributes, such as the materials from which artifacts are made and their size, shape, function, and decoration. Teach archeology at colleges and universities. Collect artifacts made of stone, bone, metal, and other materials, placing them in bags and marking them to show where they were found. Create artifact typologies to organize and make sense of past material cultures. Lead field training sites and train field staff, students, and volunteers in excavation methods. Clean, restore, and preserve artifacts.

Personality Type: Investigative. Investigative occupations frequently involve working with ideas and require an extensive amount of thinking. These occupations can involve searching for facts and figuring out problems mentally.

GOE—Interest Area: 15. Scientific Research, Engineering, and Mathematics. **Work Group:** 15.04. Social Sciences. **Other Jobs in This Work Group:** Anthropologists; Anthropologists and Archeologists; Economists; Historians; Industrial-Organizational Psychologists; Political Scientists; School Psychologists; Sociologists.

Skills—Management of Financial Resources: Determining how money will be spent to get the work done and accounting for these expenditures. **Science:** Using scientific rules and methods to solve problems. **Writing:** Communicating effectively in writing as appropriate for the needs of the audience. **Management of Personnel Resources:** Motivating, developing, and directing people as they work; identifying the best people for the job. **Active Learning:** Understanding the implications of new information for both current and future problem solving and decision making. **Reading Comprehension:** Understanding written sentences and paragraphs in work-related documents.

Education and Training Program: Archeology. **Related Knowledge/Courses:** History and Archeology: Historical events and their causes, indicators, and effects on civilizations and cultures. **Sociology and Anthropology:** Group behavior and dynamics, societal trends and influences, human migrations, ethnicity, and cultures and their history and origins. **Geography:** Principles and methods for describing the features of land, sea, and air masses, including their physical characteristics; locations; interrelationships; and distribution of plant, animal, and human life. **Philosophy and Theology:** Different philosophical systems and religions. This includes their basic principles, values, ethics, ways of thinking, customs, and practices and their impact on human culture. **Foreign Language:** The structure and content of a foreign (non-English) language, including the meaning and spelling of words, rules of composition and grammar, and pronunciation. **English Language:** The structure and content of the English language, including the meaning and spelling of words, rules of composition, and grammar.

Work Environment: More often indoors than outdoors; sitting; using hands on objects, tools, or controls.

Architectural and Civil Drafters

See the descriptions of these jobs:

- Architectural Drafters
- Civil Drafters

Architectural Drafters

This job can be found in the Part II lists under the title Architectural and Civil Drafters.

- Education/Training Required: Postsecondary vocational training
- Annual Earnings: $40,390
- Growth: 4.6%
- Annual Job Openings: 9,000
- Self-Employed: 6.1%
- Part-Time: 8.4%

The job openings listed here are shared with Civil Drafters.

Level of Solitary Work: 70.2 (out of 100)

Level of Contact with Others: 73.8 (out of 100)

Prepare detailed drawings of architectural designs and plans for buildings and structures according to specifications provided by architect. Analyze building codes, by-laws, space and site requirements, and other technical documents and reports to determine their effect on architectural designs. Operate computer-aided drafting (CAD) equipment or conventional drafting station to produce designs, working drawings, charts, forms, and records. Coordinate structural, electrical, and mechanical designs and determine a method of presentation to graphically represent building plans. Obtain and assemble data to complete architectural designs, visiting job sites to compile measurements as necessary. Lay out and plan interior room arrangements for commercial buildings, using computer-assisted drafting (CAD) equipment and software. Draw rough and detailed scale plans for foundations, buildings, and structures based on preliminary concepts, sketches, engineering calculations, specification sheets, and other data. Supervise, coordinate, and inspect the work of draftspersons, technicians, and technologists on construction projects. Represent architect on construction site, ensuring builder compliance with design specifications and advising on design corrections under architect's supervision. Check dimensions of materials to be used and assign numbers to lists of materials. Determine procedures and instructions to be followed according to design specifications and quantity of required materials. Analyze technical implications of architect's design concept, calculating weights, volumes, and stress factors. Create freehand drawings and lettering to accompany drawings. Prepare colored drawings of landscape and interior designs for presentation to client. Reproduce drawings on copy machines or trace copies of plans and drawings, using transparent paper or cloth, ink, pencil, and standard drafting instruments. Prepare cost estimates, contracts, bidding documents, and technical reports for specific projects under an architect's supervision. Calculate heat loss and gain of buildings and structures to determine required equipment specifications, following standard procedures. Build landscape, architectural, and display models.

Personality Type: Realistic. Realistic occupations frequently involve work activities that include practical, hands-on problems and solutions. They often deal with plants; animals; and real-world materials such as wood, tools, and machinery. Many of the occupations require working outside and do not involve a lot of paperwork or working closely with others.

GOE—Interest Area: 02. Architecture and Construc-tion. **Work Group:** 02.03. Architecture/Construction Engineering Technologies. **Other Jobs in This Work Group:** Architectural and Civil Drafters; Civil Drafters; Surveyors.

Skills—Operations Analysis: Analyzing needs and product requirements to create a design. **Coordination:** Adjusting actions in relation to others' actions. **Active Learning:** Understanding the implications of new information for both current and future

problem solving and decision making. **Technology Design:** Generating or adapting equipment and technology to serve user needs. **Mathematics:** Using mathematics to solve problems. **Complex Problem Solving:** Identifying complex problems and reviewing related information to develop and evaluate options and implement solutions.

Education and Training Programs: Architectural Drafting and Architectural CAD/CADD; Architectural Technology/Technician Training; CAD/CADD Drafting or Design Technology/Technician Training; Civil Drafting and Civil Engineering CAD/CADD; Drafting and Design Technology/Technician Training, General. **Related Knowledge/Courses:** **Design:** Design techniques, tools, and principles involved in production of precision technical plans, blueprints, drawings, and models. **Building and Construction:** The materials, methods, and tools involved in the construction or repair of houses, buildings, or other structures such as highways and roads. **Engineering and Technology:** The practical application of engineering science and technology. This includes applying principles, techniques, procedures, and equipment to the design and production of various goods and services. **Computers and Electronics:** Circuit boards, processors, chips, electronic equipment, and computer hardware and software, including applications and programming. **Mathematics:** Arithmetic, algebra, geometry, calculus, and statistics and their applications. **Public Safety and Security:** Relevant equipment, policies, procedures, and strategies to promote effective local, state, or national security operations for the protection of people, data, property, and institutions.

Work Environment: Indoors; noisy; sitting; using hands on objects, tools, or controls; repetitive motions.

Assessors

This job can be found in the Part II lists under the title Appraisers and Assessors of Real Estate.

- ◎ Education/Training Required:
  Postsecondary vocational training
- ◎ Annual Earnings: $43,440
- ◎ Growth: 22.8%
- ◎ Annual Job Openings: 9,000
- ◎ Self-Employed: 37.2%
- ◎ Part-Time: 10.9%

The job openings listed here are shared with Appraisers, Real Estate.

Level of Solitary Work: 71.9 (out of 100)

Level of Contact with Others: 88.7 (out of 100)

Appraise real and personal property to determine its fair value. May assess taxes in accordance with prescribed schedules. Determine taxability and value of properties, using methods such as field inspection, structural measurement, calculation, sales analysis, market trend studies, and income and expense analysis. Inspect new construction and major improvements to existing structures to determine values. Explain assessed values to property owners and defend appealed assessments at public hearings. Inspect properties, considering factors such as market value, location, and building or replacement costs to determine appraisal value. Prepare and maintain current data on each parcel assessed, including maps of boundaries, inventories of land and structures, property characteristics, and any applicable exemptions. Identify the ownership of each piece of taxable property. Conduct regular reviews of property within jurisdictions to determine changes in property due to construction or demolition. Complete and maintain assessment rolls that show the assessed values and status of all property in a municipality. Issue notices of assessments and taxes. Review information about transfers of property to ensure its accuracy, checking basic information on buyers, sellers, and sales prices and making corrections as necessary. Maintain familiarity with aspects of local real estate markets. Analyze trends in sales prices, construction costs, and rents to assess property values or determine the accuracy of assessments. Approve applications for property tax exemptions or deductions. Establish uniform and equitable systems for assessing all classes and kinds of property. Write and submit appraisal and tax reports for public record. Serve on assessment review boards. Hire staff members. Provide sales analyses to be used for equalization of school aid. Calculate tax bills for properties by multiplying assessed values by jurisdiction tax rates.

Personality Type: Conventional. Conventional occupations frequently involve following set procedures and routines. These occupations can include working with data and details more than with ideas. Usually there is a clear line of authority to follow.

GOE—Interest Area: 06. Finance and Insurance. **Work Group:** 06.02. Finance/Insurance Investigation and Analysis. **Other Jobs in This Work Group:** Appraisers and Assessors of Real Estate; Appraisers, Real Estate; Claims Adjusters, Examiners, and Investigators; Claims Examiners, Property and Casualty Insurance; Cost Estimators; Credit Analysts; Financial Analysts; Insurance Adjusters, Examiners, and Investigators; Insurance Appraisers, Auto Damage; Insurance Underwriters; Loan Counselors; Loan Officers; Market Research Analysts; Survey Researchers.

Skills—Mathematics: Using mathematics to solve problems. **Systems Analysis:** Determining how a system should work and how changes in conditions, operations, and the environment will affect outcomes. **Negotiation:** Bringing others together and trying to reconcile differences. **Speaking:** Talking to others to convey information effectively. **Persuasion:** Persuading others to change their minds or behavior. **Systems Evaluation:** Identifying measures or indicators of system performance and the actions needed to improve or correct performance relative to the goals of the system.

Education and Training Program: Real Estate. **Related Knowledge/Courses: Building and Construction:** The materials, methods, and tools involved in the construction or repair of houses, buildings, or other structures such as highways and roads. **Clerical Practices:** Administrative and clerical procedures and systems such as word processing, managing files and records, stenography and transcription, designing forms, and other office procedures and terminology. **Law and Government:** Laws, legal codes, court procedures, precedents, government regulations, executive orders, agency rules, and the democratic political process. **Mathematics:** Arithmetic, algebra, geometry, calculus, and statistics and their applications. **Computers and Electronics:** Circuit boards, processors, chips, electronic equipment, and computer hardware and software, including applications and programming. **Economics and Accounting:** Economic and accounting principles and practices, the financial markets, banking, and the analysis and reporting of financial data.

Work Environment: More often indoors than outdoors; sitting; using hands on objects, tools, or controls; repetitive motions.

Astronomers

- ◉ Education/Training Required: Doctoral degree
- ◉ Annual Earnings: $104,670
- ◉ Growth: 10.5%
- ◉ Annual Job Openings: Fewer than 500
- ◉ Self-Employed: 0.0%
- ◉ Part-Time: 8.0%

Level of Solitary Work: 90.5 (out of 100)

Level of Contact with Others: 61.8 (out of 100)

Observe, research, and interpret celestial and astronomical phenomena to increase basic knowledge and apply such information to practical problems.

Study celestial phenomena, using a variety of ground-based and space-borne telescopes and scientific instruments. Analyze research data to determine its significance, using computers. Present research findings at scientific conferences and in papers written for scientific journals. Measure radio, infrared, gamma, and X-ray emissions from extraterrestrial sources. Develop theories based on personal observations or on observations and theories of other astronomers. Raise funds for scientific research. Collaborate with other astronomers to carry out research projects. Develop instrumentation and software for astronomical observation and analysis. Teach astronomy or astrophysics. Develop and modify astronomy-related programs for public presentation. Calculate orbits and determine sizes, shapes, brightness, and motions of different celestial bodies. Direct the operations of a planetarium.

Personality Type: Investigative. Investigative occupations frequently involve working with ideas and require an extensive amount of thinking. These occupations can involve searching for facts and figuring out problems mentally.

GOE—Interest Area: 15. Scientific Research, Engineering, and Mathematics. **Work Group:** 15.02. Physical Sciences. **Other Jobs in This Work Group:** Atmospheric and Space Scientists; Chemists; Geographers; Geoscientists, Except Hydrologists and Geographers; Hydrologists; Materials Scientists; Physicists.

Skills—Science: Using scientific rules and methods to solve problems. **Programming:** Writing computer programs for various purposes. **Mathematics:** Using mathematics to solve problems. **Complex Problem Solving:** Identifying complex problems and reviewing related information to develop and evaluate options and implement solutions. **Active Learning:** Understanding the implications of new information for both current and future problem solving and decision making. **Critical Thinking:** Using logic and reasoning to identify the strengths and weaknesses of alternative solutions, conclusions, or approaches to problems.

Education and Training Programs: Astronomy; Astronomy and Astrophysics, Other; Astrophysics; Planetary Astronomy and Science. **Related Knowledge/Courses: Physics:** Physical principles and laws and their interrelationships and applications to understanding fluid, material, and atmospheric dynamics and mechanical, electrical, atomic, and subatomic structures and processes. **Mathematics:** Arithmetic, algebra, geometry, calculus, and statistics and their applications. **Engineering and Technology:** The practical application of engineering science and technology. This includes applying principles, techniques, procedures, and equipment to the design and production of various goods and services. **Chemistry:** The chemical composition, structure, and properties of substances and of the chemical processes and transformations that they undergo. This includes uses of chemicals and their danger signs, production techniques, and disposal methods. **Computers and Electronics:** Circuit boards, processors, chips, electronic equipment, and computer hardware and software, including applications and programming. **Education and Training:** Principles and methods for curriculum and training design, teaching and instruction for individuals and groups, and the measurement of training effects.

Work Environment: Indoors; sitting.

Atmospheric and Space Scientists

- ◉ Education/Training Required: Bachelor's degree
- ◉ Annual Earnings: $73,940
- ◉ Growth: 16.5%
- ◉ Annual Job Openings: 1,000
- ◉ Self-Employed: 0.0%
- ◉ Part-Time: 4.3%

Level of Solitary Work: 65.5 (out of 100)

Level of Contact with Others: 90.8 (out of 100)

Investigate atmospheric phenomena and interpret meteorological data gathered by surface and air stations, satellites, and radar to prepare reports and forecasts for public and other uses. Study and interpret data, reports, maps, photographs, and charts to predict long- and short-range weather conditions, using computer models and knowledge of climate theory, physics, and mathematics. Broadcast weather conditions, forecasts, and severe weather warnings to the public via television, radio, and the Internet or provide this information to the news media. Gather data from sources such as surface and upper air stations, satellites, weather bureaus, and radar for use in meteorological reports and forecasts. Prepare forecasts and briefings to meet the needs of industry, business, government, and other groups. Apply meteorological knowledge to problems in areas including agriculture, pollution control, and water management and to issues such as global warming or ozone depletion. Conduct basic or applied meteorological research into the processes and determinants of atmospheric phenomena, weather, and climate. Operate computer graphic equipment to produce weather reports and maps for analysis, distribution, or use in weather broadcasts. Measure wind, temperature, and humidity in the upper atmosphere, using weather balloons. Develop and use weather forecasting tools such as mathematical and computer models. Direct forecasting services at weather stations or at radio or television broadcasting facilities. Research and analyze the impact of industrial projects and pollution on climate, air quality, and weather phenomena. Collect air samples from planes and ships over land and sea to study atmospheric composition. Conduct numerical simulations of climate conditions to understand and predict global and regional weather patterns. Collect and analyze historical climate information such as precipitation and temperature records help predict future weather and climate trends. Consult with agencies, professionals, or researchers regarding the use and interpretation of climatological information. Design and develop new equipment and methods for meteorological data collection, remote sensing, or related applications. Make scientific presentations and publish reports, articles, or texts.

Personality Type: Investigative. Investigative occupations frequently involve working with ideas and require an extensive amount of thinking. These occupations can involve searching for facts and figuring out problems mentally.

GOE—Interest Area: 15. Scientific Research, Engineering, and Mathematics. **Work Group:** 15.02. Physical Sciences. **Other Jobs in This Work Group:** Astronomers; Chemists; Geographers; Geoscientists, Except Hydrologists and Geographers; Hydrologists; Materials Scientists; Physicists.

Skills—Science: Using scientific rules and methods to solve problems. **Programming:** Writing computer programs for various purposes. **Judgment and Decision Making:** Considering the relative costs and benefits of potential actions to choose the most appropriate one. **Operation Monitoring:** Watching gauges, dials, or other indicators to make sure a machine is working properly. **Technology Design:** Generating or adapting equipment and technology to serve user needs. **Operations Analysis:** Analyzing needs and product requirements to create a design.

Education and Training Programs: Atmospheric Chemistry and Climatology; Atmospheric Physics and Dynamics; Atmospheric Sciences and Meteorology, General; Atmospheric Sciences and Meteorology, Other; Meteorology. **Related Knowledge/Courses: Geography:** Principles and methods for describing the features of land, sea, and air masses, including their physical characteristics; locations; interrelationships; and distribution of plant, animal, and human life. **Physics:** Physical principles and laws and their interrelationships and applications to understanding fluid, material, and atmospheric dynamics and mechanical, electrical, atomic, and subatomic structures and processes. **Computers and Electronics:** Circuit boards, processors, chips, electronic equipment, and computer

hardware and software, including applications and programming. **Mathematics:** Arithmetic, algebra, geometry, calculus, and statistics and their applications. **Communications and Media:** Media production, communication, and dissemination techniques and methods. This includes alternative ways to inform and entertain via written, oral, and visual media. **Customer and Personal Service:** Principles and processes for providing customer and personal services. This includes customer needs assessment, meeting quality standards for services, and evaluation of customer satisfaction.

Work Environment: Indoors; noisy; sitting; repetitive motions.

Auditors

This job can be found in the Part II lists under the title Accountants and Auditors.

- Education/Training Required: Bachelor's degree
- Annual Earnings: $52,210
- Growth: 22.4%
- Annual Job Openings: 157,000
- Self-Employed: 10.9%
- Part-Time: 10.2%

The job openings listed here are shared with Accountants.

Level of Solitary Work: 60.9 (out of 100)

Level of Contact with Others: 80.5 (out of 100)

Examine and analyze accounting records to determine financial status of establishment and prepare financial reports concerning operating procedures. Collect and analyze data to detect deficient controls; duplicated effort; extravagance; fraud; or non-compliance with laws, regulations, and management policies. Report to management about asset utilization and audit results and recommend changes in operations and financial activities. Prepare detailed reports on audit findings. Review data about material assets, net worth, liabilities, capital stock, surplus, income, and expenditures. Inspect account books and accounting systems for efficiency, effectiveness, and use of accepted accounting procedures to record transactions. Examine and evaluate financial and information systems, recommending controls to ensure system reliability and data integrity. Supervise auditing of establishments and determine scope of investigation required. Prepare, analyze, and verify annual reports, financial statements, and other records, using accepted accounting and statistical procedures to assess financial condition and facilitate financial planning. Confer with company officials about financial and regulatory matters. Inspect cash on hand, notes receivable and payable, negotiable securities, and canceled checks to confirm that records are accurate. Examine inventory to verify journal and ledger entries. Examine whether the organization's objectives are reflected in its management activities and whether employees understand the objectives. Examine records and interview workers to ensure recording of transactions and compliance with laws and regulations. Direct activities of personnel engaged in filing, recording, compiling, and transmitting financial records. Produce up-to-the-minute information, using internal computer systems, to allow management to base decisions on actual, not historical, data. Conduct pre-implementation audits to determine if systems and programs under development will work as planned. Review taxpayer accounts and conduct audits on site, by correspondence, or by summoning taxpayer to office. Evaluate taxpayer finances to determine tax liability, using knowledge of interest and discount rates, annuities, valuation of stocks and bonds, and amortization valuation of depletable assets.

Personality Type: Conventional. Conventional occupations frequently involve following set procedures and routines. These occupations can include working with data and details more than with ideas. Usually there is a clear line of authority to follow.

GOE—Interest Area: 04. Business and Administration. **Work Group:** 04.05. Accounting, Auditing, and Analytical Support. **Other Jobs in This Work Group:** Accountants; Accountants and Auditors; Budget Analysts; Industrial Engineering Technicians; Logisticians; Management Analysts; Operations Research Analysts.

Skills—Management of Financial Resources: Determining how money will be spent to get the work done and accounting for these expenditures. **Writing:** Communicating effectively in writing as appropriate for the needs of the audience. **Mathematics:** Using mathematics to solve problems. **Time Management:** Managing one's own time and the time of others. **Negotiation:** Bringing others together and trying to reconcile differences. **Service Orientation:** Actively looking for ways to help people.

Education and Training Programs: Accounting; Accounting and Business/Management; Accounting and Computer Science; Accounting and Finance; Auditing. **Related Knowledge/Courses: Economics and Accounting:** Economic and accounting principles and practices, the financial markets, banking, and the analysis and reporting of financial data. **Sales and Marketing:** Principles and methods for showing, promoting, and selling products or services. This includes marketing strategy and tactics, product demonstration, sales techniques, and sales control systems. **Mathematics:** Arithmetic, algebra, geometry, calculus, and statistics and their applications. **Law and Government:** Laws, legal codes, court procedures, precedents, government regulations, executive orders, agency rules, and the democratic political process. **Computers and Electronics:** Circuit boards, processors, chips, electronic equipment, and computer hardware and software, including applications and programming. **Personnel and Human Resources:** Principles and procedures for personnel recruitment, selection, training, compensation and benefits, labor relations and negotiation, and personnel information systems.

Work Environment: Indoors; noisy; sitting; using hands on objects, tools, or controls; repetitive motions.

Automotive Body and Related Repairers

- ◎ Education/Training Required: Long-term on-the-job training
- ◎ Annual Earnings: $34,810
- ◎ Growth: 10.3%
- ◎ Annual Job Openings: 18,000
- ◎ Self-Employed: 17.6%
- ◎ Part-Time: 6.7%

Level of Solitary Work: 59.2 (out of 100)

Level of Contact with Others: 66.3 (out of 100)

Repair and refinish automotive vehicle bodies and straighten vehicle frames. File, grind, sand, and smooth filled or repaired surfaces, using power tools and hand tools. Sand body areas to be painted and cover bumpers, windows, and trim with masking tape or paper to protect them from the paint. Follow supervisors' instructions as to which parts to restore or replace and how much time the job should take. Remove damaged sections of vehicles, using metal-cutting guns, air grinders, and wrenches, and install replacement parts, using wrenches or welding equipment. Cut and tape plastic separating film to outside repair areas to avoid damaging surrounding surfaces during repair procedure and remove tape and wash surfaces after repairs are complete. Prime and paint repaired surfaces, using paint spray guns and motorized sanders. Inspect repaired vehicles for dimensional accuracy and test drive them to ensure proper alignment and handling. Mix polyester resins and hardeners to be used in restoring damaged areas. Chain or clamp frames and sections to alignment machines that use hydraulic pressure to align damaged components. Fill small dents that cannot be worked out with plastic or solder. Fit and weld replacement parts into place, using wrenches and welding equipment, and grind down welds to smooth them, using power grinders and other tools. Position dolly blocks against surfaces of dented areas and beat opposite surfaces to remove dents, using hammers. Remove damaged panels and identify the family and properties of the plastic used on a vehicle. Review damage reports, prepare or review repair cost estimates, and plan work to be performed. Remove small pits and dimples in body metal, using pick hammers and punches. Remove upholstery, accessories, electrical window-and-seat-operating equipment, and trim to gain access to vehicle bodies and fenders. Clean work areas, using air hoses, to remove damaged material and discarded fiberglass strips used in repair procedures. Adjust or align headlights, wheels, and brake systems. Apply heat to plastic panels, using hot-air welding guns or immersion in hot water, and press the softened panels back into shape by hand. Soak fiberglass matting in resin mixtures and apply layers of matting over repair areas to specified thickness.

Personality Type: Realistic. Realistic occupations frequently involve work activities that include practical, hands-on problems and solutions. They often deal with plants; animals; and real-world materials such as wood, tools, and machinery. Many of the occupations require working outside and do not involve a lot of paperwork or working closely with others.

GOE—Interest Area: 13. Manufacturing. **Work Group:** 13.14. Vehicle and Facility Mechanical Work. **Other Jobs in This Work Group:** Aircraft Mechanics and Service Technicians; Aircraft Structure, Surfaces, Rigging, and Systems Assemblers; Automotive Glass Installers and Repairers; Automotive Master Mechanics; Automotive Service Technicians and Mechanics; Automotive Specialty Technicians; Bus and Truck Mechanics and Diesel Engine Specialists; Farm Equipment Mechanics; Fiberglass Laminators and Fabricators; Mobile Heavy Equipment Mechanics, Except Engines; Motorboat Mechanics; Motorcycle Mechanics; Outdoor Power Equipment and Other Small Engine Mechanics; Rail

Car Repairers; Recreational Vehicle Service Technicians; Tire Repairers and Changers.

Skills—Repairing: Repairing machines or systems by using the needed tools. **Installation:** Installing equipment, machines, wiring, or programs to meet specifications. **Equipment Maintenance:** Performing routine maintenance on equipment and determining when and what kind of maintenance is needed. **Troubleshooting:** Determining causes of operating errors and deciding what to do about them. **Equipment Selection:** Determining the kind of tools and equipment needed to do a job. **Management of Financial Resources:** Determining how money will be spent to get the work done and accounting for these expenditures.

Education and Training Program: Autobody/ Collision and Repair Technology/Technician Training. **Related Knowledge/Courses: Mechanical Devices:** Machines and tools, including their designs, uses, repair, and maintenance. **Building and Construction:** The materials, methods, and tools involved in the construction or repair of houses, buildings, or other structures such as highways and roads. **Chemistry:** The chemical composition, structure, and properties of substances and of the chemical processes and transformations that they undergo. This includes uses of chemicals and their danger signs, production techniques, and disposal methods. **Administration and Management:** Business and management principles involved in strategic planning, resource allocation, human resources modeling, leadership technique, production methods, and coordination of people and resources. **Production and Processing:** Raw materials, production processes, quality control, costs, and other techniques for maximizing the effective manufacture and distribution of goods. **Transportation:** Principles and methods for moving people or goods by air, rail, sea, or road, including the relative costs and benefits.

Work Environment: Noisy; contaminants; hazardous equipment; standing; using hands on objects, tools, or controls; repetitive motions.

Automotive Master Mechanics

This job can be found in the Part II lists under the title Automotive Service Technicians and Mechanics.

- Education/Training Required: Postsecondary vocational training
- Annual Earnings: $33,050
- Growth: 15.7%
- Annual Job Openings: 93,000
- Self-Employed: 14.8%
- Part-Time: 7.0%

The job openings listed here are shared with Automotive Specialty Technicians.

Level of Solitary Work: 62.5 (out of 100)

Level of Contact with Others: 86.6 (out of 100)

Repair automobiles, trucks, buses, and other vehicles. Master mechanics repair virtually any part on the vehicle or specialize in the transmission system. Examine vehicles to determine extent of damage or malfunctions. Test drive vehicles and test components and systems, using equipment such as infrared engine analyzers, compression gauges, and computerized diagnostic devices. Repair, reline, replace, and adjust brakes. Review work orders and discuss work with supervisors. Follow checklists to ensure all important parts are examined, including belts, hoses, steering systems, spark plugs, brake and fuel systems, wheel bearings, and other potentially troublesome areas. Plan work procedures, using charts, technical manuals, and experience. Test and adjust repaired systems to meet manufacturers' performance specifications. Confer with customers to obtain descriptions of vehicle problems and to discuss work to be performed and future repair requirements. Perform routine and scheduled maintenance services such as oil changes, lubrications, and tune-ups. Disassemble units and inspect parts for wear, using micrometers, calipers, and gauges. Overhaul or replace carburetors, blowers, generators, distributors, starters, and pumps. Repair and service air conditioning, heating, engine-cooling, and electrical systems. Repair or replace parts such as pistons, rods, gears, valves, and bearings. Tear down, repair, and rebuild faulty assemblies such as power systems, steering systems, and linkages. Rewire ignition systems, lights, and instrument panels. Repair radiator leaks. Install and repair accessories such as radios, heaters, mirrors, and windshield wipers. Repair manual and automatic transmissions. Repair or replace shock absorbers. Align vehicles' front ends. Rebuild parts such as crankshafts and cylinder blocks. Repair damaged automobile bodies. Replace and adjust headlights.

Personality Type: Realistic. Realistic occupations frequently involve work activities that include practical, hands-on problems and solutions. They often deal with plants; animals; and real-world materials such as wood, tools, and machinery. Many of the occupations require working outside and do not involve a lot of paperwork or working closely with others.

GOE—Interest Area: 13. Manufacturing. **Work Group:** 13.14. Vehicle and Facility Mechanical Work. **Other Jobs in This Work Group:** Aircraft Mechanics and Service Technicians; Aircraft Structure, Surfaces, Rigging, and Systems Assemblers; Automotive Body and Related Repairers; Automotive Glass Installers and Repairers; Automotive Service Technicians and Mechanics; Automotive Specialty Technicians; Bus and Truck Mechanics and Diesel Engine Specialists; Farm Equipment Mechanics; Fiberglass Laminators and Fabricators; Mobile Heavy Equipment Mechanics, Except Engines; Motorboat Mechanics; Motorcycle Mechanics; Outdoor Power Equipment and Other Small Engine Mechanics; Rail Car Repairers; Recreational Vehicle Service Technicians; Tire Repairers and Changers.

Skills—Repairing: Repairing machines or systems by using the needed tools. **Troubleshooting:** Determining causes of operating errors and deciding what to do about them. **Installation:** Installing equipment, machines, wiring, or programs to meet specifications. **Equipment Maintenance:** Performing routine maintenance on equipment and determining when and what kind of maintenance is needed. **Operation Monitoring:** Watching gauges, dials, or other indicators to make sure a machine is working properly. **Complex Problem Solving:** Identifying complex problems and reviewing related information to develop and evaluate options and implement solutions.

Education and Training Programs: Automobile/Automotive Mechanics Technology/Technician Training; Automotive Engineering Technology/Technician Training; Medium/Heavy Vehicle and Truck Technology/Technician Training. **Related Knowledge/Courses: Mechanical Devices:** Machines and tools, including their designs, uses, repair, and maintenance. **Physics:** Physical principles and laws and their interrelationships and applications to understanding fluid, material, and atmospheric dynamics and mechanical, electrical, atomic, and subatomic structures and processes. **Computers and Electronics:** Circuit boards, processors, chips, electronic equipment, and computer hardware and software, including applications and programming. **Engineering and Technology:** The practical application of engineering science and technology. This includes applying principles, techniques, procedures, and equipment to the design and production of various goods and services. **Chemistry:** The chemical composition, structure, and properties of substances and of the chemical processes and transformations that they undergo. This includes uses of chemicals and their danger signs, production techniques, and disposal methods. **Public Safety and Security:** Relevant equipment, policies, procedures, and strategies to promote effective local, state, or national security operations for the protection of people, data, property, and institutions.

Work Environment: Noisy; contaminants; hazardous equipment; minor burns, cuts, bites, or stings; standing; using hands on objects, tools, or controls.

Automotive Service Technicians and Mechanics

See the descriptions of these jobs:

- Automotive Master Mechanics
- Automotive Specialty Technicians

Automotive Specialty Technicians

This job can be found in the Part II lists under the title Automotive Service Technicians and Mechanics.

- Education/Training Required: Postsecondary vocational training
- Annual Earnings: $33,050
- Growth: 15.7%
- Annual Job Openings: 93,000
- Self-Employed: 14.8%
- Part-Time: 7.0%

The job openings listed here are shared with Automotive Master Mechanics.

Level of Solitary Work: 62.5 (out of 100)

Level of Contact with Others: 86.6 (out of 100)

Repair only one system or component on a vehicle, such as brakes, suspension, or radiator. Examine vehicles, compile estimates of repair costs, and secure customers' approval to perform repairs. Repair, overhaul, and adjust automobile brake systems. Use electronic test equipment to locate and correct malfunctions in fuel, ignition, and emissions control systems. Repair and replace defective ball joint suspensions, brake shoes, and wheel bearings. Inspect and test new vehicles for damage; then record find-

ings so that necessary repairs can be made. Test electronic computer components in automobiles to ensure that they are working properly. Tune automobile engines to ensure proper and efficient functioning. Install and repair air conditioners and service components such as compressors, condensers, and controls. Repair, replace, and adjust defective carburetor parts and gasoline filters. Remove and replace defective mufflers and tailpipes. Repair and replace automobile leaf springs. Rebuild, repair, and test automotive fuel injection units. Align and repair wheels, axles, frames, torsion bars, and steering mechanisms of automobiles, using special alignment equipment and wheel-balancing machines. Repair, install, and adjust hydraulic and electromagnetic automatic lift mechanisms used to raise and lower automobile windows, seats, and tops. Repair and rebuild clutch systems. Convert vehicle fuel systems from gasoline to butane gas operations and repair and service operating butane fuel units.

Personality Type: Realistic. Realistic occupations frequently involve work activities that include practical, hands-on problems and solutions. They often deal with plants; animals; and real-world materials such as wood, tools, and machinery. Many of the occupations require working outside and do not involve a lot of paperwork or working closely with others.

GOE—Interest Area: 13. Manufacturing. **Work Group:** 13.14. Vehicle and Facility Mechanical Work. **Other Jobs in This Work Group:** Aircraft Mechanics and Service Technicians; Aircraft Structure, Surfaces, Rigging, and Systems Assemblers; Automotive Body and Related Repairers; Automotive Glass Installers and Repairers; Automotive Master Mechanics; Automotive Service Technicians and Mechanics; Bus and Truck Mechanics and Diesel Engine Specialists; Farm Equipment Mechanics; Fiberglass Laminators and Fabricators; Mobile Heavy Equipment Mechanics, Except Engines; Motorboat Mechanics; Motorcycle Mechanics; Outdoor Power Equipment and Other Small Engine Mechanics; Rail Car Repairers; Recreational Vehicle Service Technicians; Tire Repairers and Changers.

Skills—Repairing: Repairing machines or systems by using the needed tools. **Troubleshooting:** Determining causes of operating errors and deciding what to do about them. **Operation Monitoring:** Watching gauges, dials, or other indicators to make sure a machine is working properly. **Equipment Maintenance:** Performing routine maintenance on equipment and determining when and what kind of maintenance is needed. **Installation:** Installing equipment, machines, wiring, or programs to meet specifications. **Equipment Selection:** Determining the kind of tools and equipment needed to do a job.

Education and Training Programs: Alternative Fuel Vehicle Technology/Technician Training; Automotive Engineering Technology/Technician Training; Vehicle Emissions Inspection and Maintenance Technology/Technician Training. **Related Knowledge/Courses: Mechanical Devices:** Machines and tools, including their designs, uses, repair, and maintenance. **Physics:** Physical principles and laws and their interrelationships and applications to understanding fluid, material, and atmospheric dynamics and mechanical, electrical, atomic, and subatomic structures and processes. **Engineering and Technology:** The practical application of engineering science and technology. This includes applying principles, techniques, procedures, and equipment to the design and production of various goods and services. **Customer and Personal Service:** Principles and processes for providing customer and personal services. This includes customer needs assessment, meeting quality standards for services, and evaluation of customer satisfaction. **Sales and Marketing:** Principles and methods for showing, promoting, and selling products or services. This includes marketing strategy and tactics, product demonstration, sales techniques, and sales control systems. **Administration and Management:** Business and management principles involved in strategic planning, resource allocation, human resources modeling, leadership technique, production methods, and coordination of people and resources.

Work Environment: Contaminants; cramped work space, awkward positions; minor burns, cuts, bites, or stings; standing; using hands on objects, tools, or controls; bending or twisting the body.

Aviation Inspectors

This job can be found in the Part II lists under the title Transportation Inspectors.

- Education/Training Required: Work experience in a related occupation
- Annual Earnings: $49,490
- Growth: 11.4%
- Annual Job Openings: 2,000
- Self-Employed: 1.9%
- Part-Time: 2.3%

The job openings listed here are shared with Freight and Cargo Inspectors and with Transportation Vehicle, Equipment, and Systems Inspectors, Except Aviation.

Level of Solitary Work: 58.9 (out of 100)

Level of Contact with Others: 57.6 (out of 100)

Inspect aircraft, maintenance procedures, air navigational aids, air traffic controls, and communications equipment to ensure conformance with federal safety regulations. Inspect work of aircraft mechanics performing maintenance, modification, or repair and overhaul of aircraft and aircraft mechanical systems to ensure adherence to standards and procedures. Start aircraft and observe gauges, meters, and other instruments to detect evidence of malfunctions. Examine aircraft access plates and doors for security. Examine landing gear, tires, and exteriors of fuselage, wings, and engines for evidence of damage or corrosion and to determine whether repairs are needed. Prepare and maintain detailed repair, inspection, investigation, and certification records and reports. Inspect new, repaired, or modified aircraft to identify damage or defects and to assess airworthiness and conformance to standards, using checklists, hand tools, and test instruments. Examine maintenance records and flight logs to determine if service and maintenance checks and overhauls were performed at prescribed intervals. Recommend replacement, repair, or modification of aircraft equipment. Recommend changes in rules, policies, standards, and regulations based on knowledge of operating conditions, aircraft improvements, and other factors. Issue pilots' licenses to individuals meeting standards. Investigate air accidents and complaints to determine causes. Observe flight activities of pilots to assess flying skills and to ensure conformance to flight and safety regulations. Conduct flight test programs to test equipment, instruments, and systems under a variety of conditions, using both manual and automatic controls. Approve or deny issuance of certificates of airworthiness. Analyze training programs and conduct oral and written examinations to ensure the competency of persons operating, installing, and repairing aircraft equipment. Schedule and coordinate in-flight testing programs with ground crews and air traffic control to ensure availability of ground tracking, equipment monitoring, and related services.

Personality Type: Realistic. Realistic occupations frequently involve work activities that include practical, hands-on problems and solutions. They often deal with plants; animals; and real-world materials such as wood, tools, and machinery. Many of the occupations require working outside and do not involve a lot of paperwork or working closely with others.

GOE—Interest Area: 07. Government and Public Administration. **Work Group:** 07.03. Regulations Enforcement. **Other Jobs in This Work Group:** Agricultural Inspectors; Compliance Officers, Except Agriculture, Construction, Health and Safety, and Transportation; Construction and Building Inspectors; Environmental Compliance Inspectors; Equal Opportunity Representatives and Officers; Financial Examiners; Fire Inspectors; Fish and Game Wardens; Forest Fire Inspectors and Prevention Specialists; Freight and Cargo Inspectors; Government Property Inspectors and Investigators; Immigration and Customs Inspectors; Licensing Examiners and Inspectors; Nuclear Monitoring Technicians;

Occupational Health and Safety Specialists; Occupational Health and Safety Technicians; Tax Examiners, Collectors, and Revenue Agents; Transportation Vehicle, Equipment, and Systems Inspectors, Except Aviation.

Skills—Systems Analysis: Determining how a system should work and how changes in conditions, operations, and the environment will affect outcomes. **Systems Evaluation:** Identifying measures or indicators of system performance and the actions needed to improve or correct performance relative to the goals of the system. **Quality Control Analysis:** Conducting tests and inspections of products, services, or processes to evaluate quality or performance. **Operation Monitoring:** Watching gauges, dials, or other indicators to make sure a machine is working properly. **Troubleshooting:** Determining causes of operating errors and deciding what to do about them. **Reading Comprehension:** Understanding written sentences and paragraphs in work-related documents.

Education and Training Program: Avionics Maintenance Technology/Technician Training. **Related Knowledge/Courses: Mechanical Devices:** Machines and tools, including their designs, uses, repair, and maintenance. **Physics:** Physical principles and laws and their interrelationships and applications to understanding fluid, material, and atmospheric dynamics and mechanical, electrical, atomic, and subatomic structures and processes. **Transportation:** Principles and methods for moving people or goods by air, rail, sea, or road, including the relative costs and benefits. **Design:** Design techniques, tools, and principles involved in production of precision technical plans, blueprints, drawings, and models. **Chemistry:** The chemical composition, structure, and properties of substances and of the chemical processes and transformations that they undergo. This includes uses of chemicals and their danger signs, production techniques, and disposal methods. **Law and Government:** Laws, legal codes, court procedures, precedents, government regulations, executive orders, agency rules, and the democratic political process.

Work Environment: More often indoors than outdoors; noisy; sitting.

Avionics Technicians

- ◎ Education/Training Required:
  Postsecondary vocational training
- ◎ Annual Earnings: $46,630
- ◎ Growth: 9.1%
- ◎ Annual Job Openings: 2,000
- ◎ Self-Employed: 0.0%
- ◎ Part-Time: 4.9%

Level of Solitary Work: 65.5 (out of 100)

Level of Contact with Others: 72.5 (out of 100)

Install, inspect, test, adjust, or repair avionics equipment, such as radar, radio, navigation, and missile control systems in aircraft or space vehicles. Set up and operate ground support and test equipment to perform functional flight tests of electrical and electronic systems. Test and troubleshoot instruments, components, and assemblies, using circuit testers, oscilloscopes, and voltmeters. Keep records of maintenance and repair work. Coordinate work with that of engineers, technicians, and other aircraft maintenance personnel. Interpret flight test data to diagnose malfunctions and systemic performance problems. Install electrical and electronic components, assemblies, and systems in aircraft, using hand tools, power tools, and soldering irons. Adjust, repair, or replace malfunctioning components or assemblies, using hand tools and soldering irons. Connect components to assemblies such as radio systems, instruments, magnetos, inverters, and in-flight refueling systems, using hand tools and soldering irons. Assemble components such as switches, electrical controls, and junction boxes, using hand tools and soldering irons. Fabricate parts and test aids as required. Lay out installation of aircraft assemblies and systems, following documentation such as blueprints, manuals, and wiring diagrams. Assemble prototypes or models of circuits, instruments, and systems so that they can be used for testing. Operate computer-aided drafting and design applications to design avionics system modifications.

Personality Type: Realistic. Realistic occupations frequently involve work activities that include practical, hands-on problems and solutions. They often deal with plants; animals; and real-world materials such as wood, tools, and machinery. Many of the occupations require working outside and do not involve a lot of paperwork or working closely with others.

GOE—Interest Area: 13. Manufacturing. **Work Group:** 13.12. Electrical and Electronic Repair. **Other Jobs in This Work Group:** Electric Motor, Power Tool, and Related Repairers; Electrical and Electronics Installers and Repairers, Transportation Equipment; Electrical and Electronics Repairers, Commercial and Industrial Equipment; Electronic Equipment Installers and Repairers, Motor Vehicles; Electronic Home Entertainment Equipment Installers and Repairers; Radio Mechanics.

Skills—Installation: Installing equipment, machines, wiring, or programs to meet specifications. **Repairing:** Repairing machines or systems by using the needed tools. **Equipment Maintenance:** Performing routine maintenance on equipment and determining when and what kind of maintenance is needed. **Troubleshooting:** Determining causes of operating errors and deciding what to do about them. **Operation Monitoring:** Watching gauges, dials, or other indicators to make sure a machine is working properly. **Operation and Control:** Controlling operations of equipment or systems.

Education and Training Programs: Airframe Mechanics and Aircraft Maintenance Technology/Technician Training; Avionics Maintenance Technology/Technician Training. **Related Knowledge/Courses: Engineering and Technology:** The practical application of engineering science and technology. This includes applying principles, techniques, procedures, and equipment to the design and production of various goods and services. **Mechanical Devices:** Machines and tools, including their designs, uses, repair, and maintenance. **Computers and Electronics:** Circuit boards, processors, chips, electronic equipment, and computer hardware and software, including applications and programming. **Telecommunications:** Transmission, broadcasting, switching, control, and operation of telecommunications systems. **Production and Processing:** Raw materials, production processes, quality control, costs, and other techniques for maximizing the effective manufacture and distribution of goods. **Design:** Design techniques, tools, and principles involved in production of precision technical plans, blueprints, drawings, and models.

Work Environment: Indoors; noisy; contaminants; hazardous conditions; sitting; using hands on objects, tools, or controls.

Bakers

- ◉ Education/Training Required: Long-term on-the-job training
- ◉ Annual Earnings: $21,520
- ◉ Growth: 15.2%
- ◉ Annual Job Openings: 37,000
- ◉ Self-Employed: 8.1%
- ◉ Part-Time: 26.8%

Level of Solitary Work: 59.2 (out of 100)

Level of Contact with Others: 74.8 (out of 100)

Mix and bake ingredients according to recipes to produce breads, rolls, cookies, cakes, pies, pastries, or other baked goods. Observe color of products being baked and adjust oven temperatures, humidity, and conveyor speeds accordingly. Set oven temperatures and place items into hot ovens for baking. Combine measured ingredients in bowls of mixing, blending, or cooking machinery. Measure and weigh flour and other ingredients to prepare batters, doughs, fillings, and icings, using scales and graduated containers. Roll, knead, cut, and shape dough to form sweet rolls, pie crusts, tarts, cookies, and other products. Place dough in pans, in molds, or on sheets and bake in production ovens or on grills. Check the quality of raw materials to ensure that standards and specifications are met. Adapt the quantity of ingredients to match the amount of items to be baked. Apply glazes, icings, or other toppings to baked goods, using spatulas or brushes. Check equipment to ensure that it meets health and safety regulations and perform maintenance or cleaning as necessary. Decorate baked goods such as cakes and pastries. Set time and speed controls for mixing machines, blending machines, or steam kettles so that ingredients will be mixed or cooked according to instructions. Prepare and maintain inventory and production records. Direct and coordinate bakery deliveries. Order and receive supplies and equipment. Operate slicing and wrapping machines. Develop new recipes for baked goods.

Personality Type: Realistic. Realistic occupations frequently involve work activities that include practical, hands-on problems and solutions. They often deal with plants; animals; and real-world materials such as wood, tools, and machinery. Many of the occupations require working outside and do not involve a lot of paperwork or working closely with others.

GOE—Interest Area: 13. Manufacturing. **Work Group:** 13.03. Production Work, Assorted Materials Processing. **Other Jobs in This Work Group:** Cementing and Gluing Machine Operators and Tenders; Chemical Equipment Operators and Tenders; Cleaning, Washing, and Metal Pickling Equipment Operators and Tenders; Coating, Painting, and Spraying Machine Setters, Operators, and Tenders; Cooling and Freezing Equipment Operators and Tenders; Cutting and Slicing Machine Setters, Operators, and Tenders; Extruding and Forming Machine Setters, Operators, and Tenders, Synthetic and Glass Fibers; Extruding, Forming, Pressing, and Compacting Machine Setters, Operators, and Tenders; Food and Tobacco Roasting, Baking, and Drying Machine Operators and Tenders; Food Batchmakers; Food Cooking Machine Operators and Tenders; Furnace, Kiln, Oven, Drier, and Kettle Operators and Tenders; Heat Treating Equipment Setters, Operators, and Tenders, Metal and Plastic; Helpers—Production Workers; Meat, Poultry, and Fish Cutters and Trimmers; Metal-Refining Furnace Operators and Tenders; Mixing and Blending Machine Setters, Operators, and Tenders; Packaging and Filling Machine Operators and Tenders; Plating and Coating Machine Setters, Operators, and Tenders, Metal and Plastic; Pourers and Casters, Metal; Sawing Machine Setters, Operators, and Tenders, Wood; Separating, Filtering, Clarifying, Precipitating, and Still Machine Setters, Operators, and Tenders; Sewing Machine Operators; Shoe Machine Operators and Tenders; Slaughterers and Meat Packers; Team Assemblers; Textile Bleaching and Dyeing Machine Operators and Tenders; Tire Builders; Woodworking Machine Setters, Operators, and Tenders, Except Sawing.

Skills—Systems Evaluation: Identifying measures or indicators of system performance and the actions needed to improve or correct performance relative to the goals of the system. **Quality Control Analysis:** Conducting tests and inspections of products, services, or processes to evaluate quality or performance. **Equipment Maintenance:** Performing routine maintenance on equipment and determining when and what kind of maintenance is needed. **Operation and Control:** Controlling operations of equipment or systems. **Management of Personnel Resources:** Motivating, developing, and directing people as they work; identifying the best people for the job. **Systems Analysis:** Determining how a system should work and how changes in conditions, operations, and the environment will affect outcomes.

Education and Training Program: Baking and Pastry Arts/Baker/Pastry Chef Training. **Related Knowledge/Courses: Food Production:** Techniques and equipment for planting, growing, and harvesting food products (both plant and animal) for consumption, including storage/handling techniques. **Production and Processing:** Raw materials, production processes, quality control, costs, and other techniques for maximizing the effective manufacture and

distribution of goods. **Personnel and Human Resources:** Principles and procedures for personnel recruitment, selection, training, compensation and benefits, labor relations and negotiation, and personnel information systems. **Mathematics:** Arithmetic, algebra, geometry, calculus, and statistics and their applications. **Administration and Management:** Business and management principles involved in strategic planning, resource allocation, human resources modeling, leadership technique, production methods, and coordination of people and resources. **Sales and Marketing:** Principles and methods for showing, promoting, and selling products or services. This includes marketing strategy and tactics, product demonstration, sales techniques, and sales control systems.

Work Environment: Indoors; very hot or cold; minor burns, cuts, bites, or stings; standing; walking and running; using hands on objects, tools, or controls.

Billing and Posting Clerks and Machine Operators

See the descriptions of these jobs:

- Billing, Cost, and Rate Clerks
- Billing, Posting, and Calculating Machine Operators
- Statement Clerks

Billing, Cost, and Rate Clerks

This job can be found in the Part II lists under the title Billing and Posting Clerks and Machine Operators.

- ◉ Education/Training Required: Moderate-term on-the-job training
- ◉ Annual Earnings: $27,780
- ◉ Growth: 3.4%
- ◉ Annual Job Openings: 70,000
- ◉ Self-Employed: 2.6%
- ◉ Part-Time: 14.5%

The job openings listed here are shared with Billing, Posting, and Calculating Machine Operators and with Statement Clerks.

Level of Solitary Work: 67.7 (out of 100)

Level of Contact with Others: 89.4 (out of 100)

Compile data, compute fees and charges, and prepare invoices for billing purposes. Duties include computing costs and calculating rates for goods, services, and shipment of goods; posting data; and keeping other relevant records. May involve use of computer or typewriter, calculator, and adding and bookkeeping machines. Verify accuracy of billing data and revise any errors. Operate typing, adding, calculating, and billing machines. Prepare itemized statements, bills, or invoices and record amounts due for items purchased or services rendered. Review documents such as purchase orders, sales tickets, charge slips, or hospital records to compute fees and charges due. Perform bookkeeping work, including posting data and keeping other records concerning costs of goods and services and the shipment of goods. Keep records of invoices and support documents. Resolve discrepancies in accounting records. Type billing documents, shipping labels, credit memorandums, and credit forms, using typewriters or computers.

Contact customers to obtain or relay account information. Compute credit terms, discounts, shipment charges, and rates for goods and services to complete billing documents. Answer mail and telephone inquiries regarding rates, routing, and procedures. Track accumulated hours and dollar amounts charged to each client job to calculate client fees for professional services such as legal and accounting services. Review compiled data on operating costs and revenues to set rates. Compile reports of cost factors, such as labor, production, storage, and equipment. Consult sources such as rate books, manuals, and insurance company representatives to determine specific charges and information such as rules, regulations, and government tax and tariff information. Update manuals when rates, rules, or regulations are amended. Estimate market value of products or services.

Personality Type: Conventional. Conventional occupations frequently involve following set procedures and routines. These occupations can include working with data and details more than with ideas. Usually there is a clear line of authority to follow.

GOE—Interest Area: 04. Business and Administration. **Work Group:** 04.06. Mathematical Clerical Support. **Other Jobs in This Work Group:** Billing and Posting Clerks and Machine Operators; Bookkeeping, Accounting, and Auditing Clerks; Brokerage Clerks; Payroll and Timekeeping Clerks; Statement Clerks; Tax Preparers.

Skills—Writing: Communicating effectively in writing as appropriate for the needs of the audience. **Active Listening:** Giving full attention to what other people are saying, taking time to understand the points being made, asking questions as appropriate, and not interrupting at inappropriate times. **Service Orientation:** Actively looking for ways to help people. **Reading Comprehension:** Understanding written sentences and paragraphs in work-related documents. **Instructing:** Teaching others how to do something. **Social Perceptiveness:** Being aware of others' reactions and understanding why they react as they do.

Education and Training Program: Accounting Technology/Technician Training and Bookkeeping. **Related Knowledge/Courses: Clerical Practices:** Administrative and clerical procedures and systems such as word processing, managing files and records, stenography and transcription, designing forms, and other office procedures and terminology. **Economics and Accounting:** Economic and accounting principles and practices, the financial markets, banking, and the analysis and reporting of financial data. **Computers and Electronics:** Circuit boards, processors, chips, electronic equipment, and computer hardware and software, including applications and programming. **Customer and Personal Service:** Principles and processes for providing customer and personal services. This includes customer needs assessment, meeting quality standards for services, and evaluation of customer satisfaction. **Mathematics:** Arithmetic, algebra, geometry, calculus, and statistics and their applications. **English Language:** The structure and content of the English language, including the meaning and spelling of words, rules of composition, and grammar.

Work Environment: Indoors; sitting.

Billing, Posting, and Calculating Machine Operators

This job can be found in the Part II lists under the title Billing and Posting Clerks and Machine Operators.

- Education/Training Required: Moderate-term on-the-job training
- Annual Earnings: $27,780
- Growth: 3.4%
- Annual Job Openings: 70,000
- Self-Employed: 2.6%
- Part-Time: 14.5%

The job openings listed here are shared with Billing, Cost, and Rate Clerks and with Statement Clerks.

Level of Solitary Work: 67.7 (out of 100)

Level of Contact with Others: 89.4 (out of 100)

Operate machines that automatically perform mathematical processes, such as addition, subtraction, multiplication, and division, to calculate and record billing, accounting, statistical, and other numerical data. Duties include operating special billing machines to prepare statements, bills, and invoices and operating bookkeeping machines to copy and post data, make computations, and compile records of transactions. Enter into machines all information needed for bill generation. Train other calculating machine operators and review their work. Operate special billing machines to prepare statements, bills, and invoices. Operate bookkeeping machines to copy and post data, make computations, and compile records of transactions. Reconcile and post receipts for cash received by various departments. Prepare transmittal reports for changes to assessment and tax rolls; redemption file changes; and warrants, deposits, and invoices. Encode and add amounts of transaction documents, such as checks or money orders, using encoding machines. Balance and reconcile batch control totals with source documents or computer listings to locate errors, encode correct amounts, or prepare correction records. Compute payroll and retirement amounts, applying knowledge of payroll deductions, actuarial tables, disability factors, and survivor allowances. Maintain ledgers and registers, posting charges and refunds to individual funds and computing and verifying balances. Compute monies due on personal and real property, inventories, redemption payments, and other amounts, applying specialized knowledge of tax rates, formulas, interest rates, and other relevant information. Verify and post to ledgers purchase orders, reports of goods received, invoices, paid vouchers, and other information. Assign purchase order numbers to invoices, requisitions, and formal and informal bids. Verify completeness and accuracy of original documents such as business property statements, tax rolls, invoices, bonds and coupons, and redemption certificates. Bundle sorted documents to prepare those drawn on other banks for collection. Transcribe data from office records, using specified forms, billing machines, and transcribing machines. Sort and list items for proof or collection. Send completed bills to billing clerks for information verification. Transfer data from machines, such as encoding machines, to computers. Sort and microfilm transaction documents, such as checks, using sorting machines. Observe operation of sorters to locate documents that machines cannot read and manually record amounts of these documents.

Personality Type: Conventional. Conventional occupations frequently involve following set procedures and routines. These occupations can include working with data and details more than with ideas. Usually there is a clear line of authority to follow.

GOE—Interest Area: 04. Business and Administration. **Work Group:** 04.08. Clerical Machine Operation. **Other Jobs in This Work Group:** Data Entry Keyers; Mail Clerks and Mail Machine Operators, Except Postal Service; Office Machine Operators, Except Computer; Switchboard Operators, Including Answering Service; Word Processors and Typists.

Skills—Speaking: Talking to others to convey information effectively. **Active Listening:** Giving full attention to what other people are saying, taking time to understand the points being made, asking questions as appropriate, and not interrupting at inappropriate times. **Writing:** Communicating effectively in writing as appropriate for the needs of the audience.

Education and Training Program: Accounting Technology/Technician Training and Bookkeeping. **Related Knowledge/Courses: Economics and Accounting:** Economic and accounting principles and practices, the financial markets, banking, and the analysis and reporting of financial data. **Clerical Practices:** Administrative and clerical procedures and systems such as word processing, managing files and records, stenography and transcription, designing

forms, and other office procedures and terminology. **Personnel and Human Resources:** Principles and procedures for personnel recruitment, selection, training, compensation and benefits, labor relations and negotiation, and personnel information systems.

Work Environment: Indoors; noisy; contaminants; sitting; using hands on objects, tools, or controls; repetitive motions.

Biochemists and Biophysicists

- ◎ Education/Training Required: Doctoral degree
- ◎ Annual Earnings: $71,000
- ◎ Growth: 21.0%
- ◎ Annual Job Openings: 1,000
- ◎ Self-Employed: 2.7%
- ◎ Part-Time: 8.2%

Level of Solitary Work: 81.2 (out of 100)

Level of Contact with Others: 11.5 (out of 100)

Study the chemical composition and physical principles of living cells and organisms and their electrical and mechanical energy and related phenomena. May conduct research to further understanding of the complex chemical combinations and reactions involved in metabolism, reproduction, growth, and heredity. May determine the effects of foods, drugs, serums, hormones, and other substances on tissues and vital processes of living organisms. Investigate damage to cells and tissues caused by X rays and nuclear particles. Research how characteristics of plants and animals are carried through successive generations. Research the chemical effects of substances such as drugs, serums, hormones, and food on tissues and vital processes. Share research findings by writing scientific articles and by making presentations at scientific conferences. Study physical principles of living cells and organisms and their electrical and mechanical energy, applying methods and knowledge of mathematics, physics, chemistry, and biology. Study the chemistry of living processes, such as cell development, breathing, and digestion, and living energy changes such as growth, aging, and death. Study the mutations in organisms that lead to cancer and other diseases. Design and build laboratory equipment needed for special research projects. Prepare reports and recommendations based upon research outcomes. Develop and execute tests to detect diseases, genetic disorders, or other abnormalities. Develop methods to process, store, and use foods, drugs, and chemical compounds. Investigate the transmission of electrical impulses along nerves and muscles. Manage laboratory teams and monitor the quality of a team's work. Research cancer treatment, using radiation and nuclear particles. Research transformations of substances in cells, using atomic isotopes. Study how light is absorbed in processes such as photosynthesis or vision. Study spatial configurations of submicroscopic molecules such as proteins, using X rays and electron microscopes. Determine the three-dimensional structure of biological macromolecules. Investigate the nature, composition, and expression of genes and research how genetic engineering can impact these processes. Develop new methods to study the mechanisms of biological processes. Develop and test new drugs and medications intended for commercial distribution. Design and perform experiments with equipment such as lasers, accelerators, and mass spectrometers. Analyze brain functions such as learning, thinking, and memory and the dynamics of seeing and hearing.

Personality Type: Investigative. Investigative occupations frequently involve working with ideas and require an extensive amount of thinking. These occupations can involve searching for facts and figuring out problems mentally.

GOE—Interest Area: 15. Scientific Research, Engineering, and Mathematics. **Work Group:** 15.03. Life Sciences. **Other Jobs in This Work Group:** Biologists; Environmental Scientists and Specialists,

Including Health; Epidemiologists; Medical Scientists, Except Epidemiologists; Microbiologists.

Skills—Science: Using scientific rules and methods to solve problems. **Programming:** Writing computer programs for various purposes. **Mathematics:** Using mathematics to solve problems. **Reading Comprehension:** Understanding written sentences and paragraphs in work-related documents. **Writing:** Communicating effectively in writing as appropriate for the needs of the audience. **Active Learning:** Understanding the implications of new information for both current and future problem solving and decision making.

Education and Training Programs: Biochemistry/Biophysics and Molecular Biology; Biophysics; Cell/Cellular Biology and Anatomical Sciences, Other; Molecular Biophysics; Soil Chemistry and Physics; Soil Microbiology. **Related Knowledge/Courses: Biology:** Plant and animal organisms and their tissues, cells, functions, interdependencies, and interactions with each other and the environment. **Chemistry:** The chemical composition, structure, and properties of substances and of the chemical processes and transformations that they undergo. This includes uses of chemicals and their danger signs, production techniques, and disposal methods. **Physics:** Physical principles and laws and their interrelationships and applications to understanding fluid, material, and atmospheric dynamics and mechanical, electrical, atomic, and subatomic structures and processes. **Mathematics:** Arithmetic, algebra, geometry, calculus, and statistics and their applications.

Work Environment: Indoors; sitting; using hands on objects, tools, or controls.

Boilermakers

- Education/Training Required: Long-term on-the-job training
- Annual Earnings: $48,050
- Growth: 8.7%
- Annual Job Openings: 2,000
- Self-Employed: 0.0%
- Part-Time: No data available

Level of Solitary Work: 53.0 (out of 100)

Level of Contact with Others: 79.8 (out of 100)

Construct, assemble, maintain, and repair stationary steam boilers and boiler house auxiliaries. Align structures or plate sections to assemble boiler frame tanks or vats, following blueprints. Work involves use of hand and power tools, plumb bobs, levels, wedges, dogs, or turnbuckles. Assist in testing assembled vessels. Direct cleaning of boilers and boiler furnaces. Inspect and repair boiler fittings, such as safety valves, regulators, automatic-control mechanisms, water columns, and auxiliary machines. Bolt or arc-weld pressure vessel structures and parts together, using wrenches and welding equipment. Examine boilers, pressure vessels, tanks, and vats to locate defects such as leaks, weak spots, and defective sections so that they can be repaired. Repair or replace defective pressure vessel parts, such as safety valves and regulators, using torches, jacks, caulking hammers, power saws, threading dies, welding equipment, and metalworking machinery. Inspect assembled vessels and individual components, such as tubes, fittings, valves, controls, and auxiliary mechanisms, to locate any defects. Attach rigging and signal crane or hoist operators to lift heavy frame and plate sections and other parts into place. Bell, bead with power hammers, or weld pressure vessel tube ends to ensure leakproof joints. Lay out plate, sheet steel, or other heavy metal and locate and mark bending and cutting lines, using protrac-tors, compasses, and drawing instruments or templates. Install manholes, handholes, taps, tubes, valves, gauges, and feedwater connections in drums of water tube boilers, using hand tools. Study blueprints to determine locations, relationships, and dimensions of parts. Straighten or reshape bent pressure vessel plates and structure parts, using hammers, jacks, and torches. Shape seams, joints, and irregular edges of pressure vessel sections and structural parts to attain specified fit of parts, using cutting torches, hammers, files, and metalworking machines. Position, align, and secure structural parts and related assemblies to boiler frames, tanks, or vats of pressure vessels, following blueprints. Locate and mark reference points for columns or plates on boiler foundations, following blueprints and using straightedges, squares, transits, and measuring instruments. Shape and fabricate parts, such as stacks, uptakes, and chutes, to adapt pressure vessels, heat exchangers, and piping to premises, using heavy-metalworking machines such as brakes, rolls, and drill presses. Clean pressure vessel equipment, using scrapers, wire brushes, and cleaning solvents.

Personality Type: Realistic. Realistic occupations frequently involve work activities that include practical, hands-on problems and solutions. They often deal with plants; animals; and real-world materials such as wood, tools, and machinery. Many of the occupations require working outside and do not involve a lot of paperwork or working closely with others.

GOE—Interest Area: 02. Architecture and Construction. **Work Group:** 02.04. Construction Crafts. **Other Jobs in This Work Group:** Brickmasons and Blockmasons; Carpet Installers; Cement Masons and Concrete Finishers; Commercial Divers; Construction Carpenters; Crane and Tower Operators; Drywall and Ceiling Tile Installers; Electricians; Fence Erectors; Floor Layers, Except Carpet, Wood, and Hard Tiles; Floor Sanders and Finishers; Glaziers; Hazardous Materials Removal Workers; Insulation Workers, Floor, Ceiling, and Wall; Insulation Workers, Mechanical; Manufactured Building and Mobile Home Installers; Operating Engineers and

Other Construction Equipment Operators; Painters, Construction and Maintenance; Paperhangers; Paving, Surfacing, and Tamping Equipment Operators; Pile-Driver Operators; Pipe Fitters and Steamfitters; Pipelayers; Plasterers and Stucco Masons; Plumbers; Plumbers, Pipefitters, and Steamfitters; Rail-Track Laying and Maintenance Equipment Operators; Refractory Materials Repairers, Except Brickmasons; Reinforcing Iron and Rebar Workers; Riggers; Roofers; Rough Carpenters; Security and Fire Alarm Systems Installers; Segmental Pavers; Sheet Metal Workers; Stone Cutters and Carvers, Manufacturing; Stonemasons; Structural Iron and Steel Workers; Tapers; Terrazzo Workers and Finishers; Tile and Marble Setters.

Skills—Repairing: Repairing machines or systems by using the needed tools. **Installation:** Installing equipment, machines, wiring, or programs to meet specifications. **Equipment Maintenance:** Performing routine maintenance on equipment and determining when and what kind of maintenance is needed. **Operation Monitoring:** Watching gauges, dials, or other indicators to make sure a machine is working properly. **Troubleshooting:** Determining causes of operating errors and deciding what to do about them. **Mathematics:** Using mathematics to solve problems.

Education and Training Program: Boilermaking/ Boilermaker Training. **Related Knowledge/Courses: Building and Construction:** The materials, methods, and tools involved in the construction or repair of houses, buildings, or other structures such as highways and roads. **Mechanical Devices:** Machines and tools, including their designs, uses, repair, and maintenance. **Engineering and Technology:** The practical application of engineering science and technology. This includes applying principles, techniques, procedures, and equipment to the design and production of various goods and services. **Design:** Design techniques, tools, and principles involved in production of precision technical plans, blueprints, drawings, and models. **Physics:** Physical principles and laws and their interrelationships and applications to understanding fluid, material, and atmospheric

dynamics and mechanical, electrical, atomic, and subatomic structures and processes. **Transportation:** Principles and methods for moving people or goods by air, rail, sea, or road, including the relative costs and benefits.

Work Environment: Noisy; very hot or cold; contaminants; minor burns, cuts, bites, or stings; standing; using hands on objects, tools, or controls.

Bookkeeping, Accounting, and Auditing Clerks

- Education/Training Required: Moderate-term on-the-job training
- Annual Earnings: $29,490
- Growth: 5.9%
- Annual Job Openings: 291,000
- Self-Employed: 7.0%
- Part-Time: 29.5%

Level of Solitary Work: 75.0 (out of 100)

Level of Contact with Others: 86.7 (out of 100)

Compute, classify, and record numerical data to keep financial records complete. Perform any combination of routine calculating, posting, and verifying duties to obtain primary financial data for use in maintaining accounting records. May also check the accuracy of figures, calculations, and postings pertaining to business transactions recorded by other workers. Operate computers programmed with accounting software to record, store, and analyze information. Check figures, postings, and documents for correct entry, mathematical accuracy, and proper codes. Comply with federal, state, and company policies, procedures, and regulations. Debit, credit, and total accounts on computer spreadsheets and databases, using specialized accounting software. Classify, record, and summarize numerical and financial data to compile and keep financial records, using journals and ledgers or computers. Calculate, prepare, and issue bills, invoices, account statements, and other financial statements according to established procedures. Code documents according to company procedures. Compile statistical, financial, accounting, or auditing reports and tables pertaining to such matters as cash receipts, expenditures, accounts payable and receivable, and profits and losses. Operate 10-key calculators, typewriters, and copy machines to perform calculations and produce documents. Access computerized financial information to answer general questions as well as those related to specific accounts. Reconcile or note and report discrepancies found in records. Perform financial calculations such as amounts due, interest charges, balances, discounts, equity, and principal. Perform general office duties such as filing, answering telephones, and handling routine correspondence. Prepare bank deposits by compiling data from cashiers; verifying and balancing receipts; and sending cash, checks, or other forms of payment to banks. Receive, record, and bank cash, checks, and vouchers. Calculate and prepare checks for utilities, taxes, and other payments. Compare computer printouts to manually maintained journals to determine if they match. Reconcile records of bank transactions. Prepare trial balances of books. Monitor status of loans and accounts to ensure that payments are up to date. Transfer details from separate journals to general ledgers or data-processing sheets. Compile budget data and documents based on estimated revenues and expenses and previous budgets. Calculate costs of materials, overhead, and other expenses, based on estimates, quotations, and price lists.

Personality Type: Conventional. Conventional occupations frequently involve following set procedures and routines. These occupations can include working with data and details more than with ideas. Usually there is a clear line of authority to follow.

GOE—Interest Area: 04. Business and Administration. **Work Group:** 04.06. Mathematical Clerical Support. **Other Jobs in This Work Group:** Billing and Posting Clerks and Machine Operators; Billing, Cost, and Rate Clerks; Brokerage Clerks; Payroll and Timekeeping Clerks; Statement Clerks; Tax Preparers.

Skills—Management of Financial Resources: Determining how money will be spent to get the work done and accounting for these expenditures. **Mathematics:** Using mathematics to solve problems. **Time Management:** Managing one's own time and the time of others. **Critical Thinking:** Using logic and reasoning to identify the strengths and weaknesses of alternative solutions, conclusions, or approaches to problems. **Active Learning:** Understanding the implications of new information for both current and future problem solving and decision making. **Instructing:** Teaching others how to do something.

Education and Training Programs: Accounting and Related Services, Other; Accounting Technology/ Technician Training and Bookkeeping. **Related Knowledge/Courses: Clerical Practices:** Administrative and clerical procedures and systems such as word processing, managing files and records, stenography and transcription, designing forms, and other office procedures and terminology. **Economics and Accounting:** Economic and accounting principles and practices, the financial markets, banking, and the analysis and reporting of financial data. **Mathematics:** Arithmetic, algebra, geometry, calculus, and statistics and their applications. **Computers and Electronics:** Circuit boards, processors, chips, electronic equipment, and computer hardware and software, including applications and programming.

Work Environment: Indoors; sitting; repetitive motions.

Brickmasons and Blockmasons

- ◎ Education/Training Required: Long-term on-the-job training
- ◎ Annual Earnings: $41,860
- ◎ Growth: 12.0%
- ◎ Annual Job Openings: 17,000
- ◎ Self-Employed: 28.6%
- ◎ Part-Time: No data available

Level of Solitary Work: 59.2 (out of 100)

Level of Contact with Others: 78.8 (out of 100)

Lay and bind building materials, such as brick, structural tile, concrete block, cinderblock, glass block, and terra-cotta block, with mortar and other substances to construct or repair walls, partitions, arches, sewers, and other structures. Construct corners by fastening in plumb position a corner pole or building a corner pyramid of bricks and filling in between the corners, using a line from corner to corner to guide each course, or layer, of brick. Measure distance from reference points and mark guidelines to lay out work, using plumb bobs and levels. Fasten or fuse brick or other building material to structure with wire clamps, anchor holes, torch, or cement. Calculate angles and courses and determine vertical and horizontal alignment of courses. Break or cut bricks, tiles, or blocks to size, using trowel edge, hammer, or power saw. Remove excess mortar with trowels and hand tools and finish mortar joints with jointing tools for a sealed, uniform appearance. Interpret blueprints and drawings to determine specifications and to calculate the materials required. Apply and smooth mortar or other mixture over work surface. Mix specified amounts of sand, clay, dirt, or mortar powder with water to form refractory mixtures. Examine brickwork or structure to determine need for repair. Clean working surface to remove scale, dust, soot, or chips of brick and mortar, using broom, wire brush, or scraper. Lay and align bricks, blocks, or tiles to build or repair structures or high-temperature equipment, such as cupola, kilns, ovens, or furnaces. Remove burned or damaged brick or mortar, using sledgehammer, crowbar, chipping gun, or chisel. Spray or spread refractory material over brickwork to protect against deterioration.

Personality Type: Realistic. Realistic occupations frequently involve work activities that include practical, hands-on problems and solutions. They often deal with plants; animals; and real-world materials such as wood, tools, and machinery. Many of the occupations require working outside and do not involve a lot of paperwork or working closely with others.

GOE—Interest Area: 02. Architecture and Construction. **Work Group:** 02.04. Construction Crafts. **Other Jobs in This Work Group:** Boilermakers; Carpet Installers; Cement Masons and Concrete Finishers; Commercial Divers; Construction Carpenters; Crane and Tower Operators; Drywall and Ceiling Tile Installers; Electricians; Fence Erectors; Floor Layers, Except Carpet, Wood, and Hard Tiles; Floor Sanders and Finishers; Glaziers; Hazardous Materials Removal Workers; Insulation Workers, Floor, Ceiling, and Wall; Insulation Workers, Mechanical; Manufactured Building and Mobile Home Installers; Operating Engineers and Other Construction Equipment Operators; Painters, Construction and Maintenance; Paperhangers; Paving, Surfacing, and Tamping Equipment Operators; Pile-Driver Operators; Pipe Fitters and Steamfitters; Pipelayers; Plasterers and Stucco Masons; Plumbers; Plumbers, Pipefitters, and Steamfitters; Rail-Track Laying and Maintenance Equipment Operators; Refractory Materials Repairers, Except Brickmasons; Reinforcing Iron and Rebar Workers; Riggers; Roofers; Rough Carpenters; Security and Fire Alarm Systems Installers; Segmental Pavers; Sheet Metal Workers; Stone Cutters and Carvers, Manufacturing; Stonemasons; Structural Iron and Steel Workers; Tapers; Terrazzo Workers and Finishers; Tile and Marble Setters.

Skills—Equipment Maintenance: Performing routine maintenance on equipment and determining when and what kind of maintenance is needed. Mathematics: Using mathematics to solve problems. Installation: Installing equipment, machines, wiring, or programs to meet specifications. Management of Financial Resources: Determining how money will be spent to get the work done and accounting for these expenditures. Repairing: Repairing machines or systems by using the needed tools. Technology Design: Generating or adapting equipment and technology to serve user needs.

Education and Training Program: Mason Training/Masonry. Related Knowledge/Courses: Building and Construction: The materials, methods, and tools involved in the construction or repair of houses, buildings, or other structures such as highways and roads. Design: Design techniques, tools, and principles involved in production of precision technical plans, blueprints, drawings, and models. Production and Processing: Raw materials, production processes, quality control, costs, and other techniques for maximizing the effective manufacture and distribution of goods. Mechanical Devices: Machines and tools, including their designs, uses, repair, and maintenance. Public Safety and Security: Relevant equipment, policies, procedures, and strategies to promote effective local, state, or national security operations for the protection of people, data, property, and institutions. Mathematics: Arithmetic, algebra, geometry, calculus, and statistics and their applications.

Work Environment: Outdoors; very hot or cold; hazardous equipment; standing; using hands on objects, tools, or controls; bending or twisting the body.

Bridge and Lock Tenders

- Education/Training Required: Short-term on-the-job training
- Annual Earnings: $37,980
- Growth: 7.2%
- Annual Job Openings: Fewer than 500
- Self-Employed: 0.0%
- Part-Time: 21.2%

Level of Solitary Work: 75.0 (out of 100)

Level of Contact with Others: 73.3 (out of 100)

Operate and tend bridges, canal locks, and lighthouses to permit marine passage on inland waterways, near shores, and at danger points in waterway passages. May supervise such operations. Includes drawbridge operators, lock tenders and operators, and slip bridge operators. Move levers to activate traffic signals, navigation lights, and alarms. Record names, types, and destinations of vessels passing through bridge openings or locks and numbers of trains or vehicles crossing bridges. Control machinery to open and close canal locks and dams, railroad or highway drawbridges, or horizontally or vertically adjustable bridges. Direct movements of vessels in locks or bridge areas, using signals, telecommunication equipment, or loudspeakers. Prepare accident reports. Observe approaching vessels to determine size and speed and listen for whistle signals indicating desire to pass. Observe position and progress of vessels to ensure best utilization of lock spaces or bridge opening spaces. Maintain and guard stations in bridges to check waterways for boat traffic. Inspect canal and bridge equipment and areas such as roadbeds for damage or defects, reporting problems to supervisors as necessary. Clean and lubricate equipment and make minor repairs and adjustments. Log data such as water levels and weather conditions. Write and submit maintenance work requisitions. Perform maintenance duties such as sweeping, painting, and yard work to keep facilities clean and in order. Check that bridges are clear of vehicles and pedestrians prior to opening. Turn valves to increase or decrease water levels in locks. Stop automobile and pedestrian traffic on bridges and lower automobile gates prior to moving bridges. Raise drawbridges and observe passage of water traffic; then lower drawbridges and raise automobile gates. Operate lighthouses to assist marine passage near shores and dangerous waters. Add and remove balance weights to bridge mechanisms as necessary. Attach ropes or cable lines to bitts on lock decks or wharfs to secure vessels.

Personality Type: Realistic. Realistic occupations frequently involve work activities that include practical, hands-on problems and solutions. They often deal with plants; animals; and real-world materials such as wood, tools, and machinery. Many of the occupations require working outside and do not involve a lot of paperwork or working closely with others.

GOE—Interest Area: 16. Transportation, Distribution, and Logistics. **Work Group:** 16.07. Transportation Support Work. **Other Jobs in This Work Group:** Cargo and Freight Agents; Cleaners of Vehicles and Equipment; Laborers and Freight, Stock, and Material Movers, Hand; Railroad Brake, Signal, and Switch Operators; Traffic Technicians.

Skills—Operation and Control: Controlling operations of equipment or systems. **Operation Monitoring:** Watching gauges, dials, or other indicators to make sure a machine is working properly. **Equipment Maintenance:** Performing routine maintenance on equipment and determining when and what kind of maintenance is needed. **Troubleshooting:** Determining causes of operating errors and deciding what to do about them.

Education and Training Program: No related CIP programs; this job is learned through informal short-term on-the-job training. **Related Knowledge/Courses: Public Safety and Security:** Relevant equipment, policies, procedures, and strategies to promote effective local, state, or national security operations for the protection of people, data, property, and institutions. **Transportation:** Principles and methods for

moving people or goods by air, rail, sea, or road, including the relative costs and benefits. **Personnel and Human Resources:** Principles and procedures for personnel recruitment, selection, training, compensation and benefits, labor relations and negotiation, and personnel information systems. **Psychology:** Human behavior and performance; individual differences in ability, personality, and interests; learning and motivation; psychological research methods; and the assessment and treatment of behavioral and affective disorders. **Education and Training:** Principles and methods for curriculum and training design, teaching and instruction for individuals and groups, and the measurement of training effects. **Communications and Media:** Media production, communication, and dissemination techniques and methods. This includes alternative ways to inform and entertain via written, oral, and visual media.

Work Environment: More often indoors than outdoors; noisy; standing; using hands on objects, tools, or controls.

Bus and Truck Mechanics and Diesel Engine Specialists

- Education/Training Required: Postsecondary vocational training
- Annual Earnings: $36,620
- Growth: 14.4%
- Annual Job Openings: 32,000
- Self-Employed: 5.3%
- Part-Time: 2.8%

Level of Solitary Work: 59.2 (out of 100)

Level of Contact with Others: 83.0 (out of 100)

Diagnose, adjust, repair, or overhaul trucks, buses, and all types of diesel engines. Includes mechanics

working primarily with automobile diesel engines.
Use hand tools such as screwdrivers, pliers, wrenches,
pressure gauges, and precision instruments, as well as
power tools such as pneumatic wrenches, lathes,
welding equipment, and jacks and hoists. Inspect
brake systems, steering mechanisms, wheel bearings,
and other important parts to ensure that they are in
proper operating condition. Perform routine maintenance such as changing oil, checking batteries, and
lubricating equipment and machinery. Adjust and
reline brakes, align wheels, tighten bolts and screws,
and reassemble equipment. Raise trucks, buses, and
heavy parts or equipment, using hydraulic jacks or
hoists. Test drive trucks and buses to diagnose malfunctions or to ensure that they are working properly. Inspect, test, and listen to defective equipment to
diagnose malfunctions, using test instruments such as
handheld computers, motor analyzers, chassis charts,
and pressure gauges. Examine and adjust protective
guards, loose bolts, and specified safety devices.
Inspect and verify dimensions and clearances of parts
to ensure conformance to factory specifications.
Specialize in repairing and maintaining parts of the
engine, such as fuel injection systems. Attach test
instruments to equipment and read dials and gauges
to diagnose malfunctions. Rewire ignition systems,
lights, and instrument panels. Recondition and
replace parts, pistons, bearings, gears, and valves.
Repair and adjust seats, doors, and windows and
install and repair accessories. Inspect, repair, and
maintain automotive and mechanical equipment and
machinery such as pumps and compressors.
Disassemble and overhaul internal combustion
engines, pumps, generators, transmissions, clutches,
and differential units. Rebuild gas or diesel engines.
Align front ends and suspension systems. Operate
valve-grinding machines to grind and reset valves.

Personality Type: Realistic. Realistic occupations frequently involve work activities that include practical,
hands-on problems and solutions. They often deal
with plants; animals; and real-world materials such as
wood, tools, and machinery. Many of the occupations require working outside and do not involve a lot
of paperwork or working closely with others.

GOE—Interest Area: 13. Manufacturing. **Work
Group:** 13.14. Vehicle and Facility Mechanical
Work. **Other Jobs in This Work Group:** Aircraft
Mechanics and Service Technicians; Aircraft
Structure, Surfaces, Rigging, and Systems Assem-
blers; Automotive Body and Related Repairers;
Automotive Glass Installers and Repairers;
Automotive Master Mechanics; Automotive Service
Technicians and Mechanics; Automotive Specialty
Technicians; Farm Equipment Mechanics; Fiberglass
Laminators and Fabricators; Mobile Heavy
Equipment Mechanics, Except Engines; Motorboat
Mechanics; Motorcycle Mechanics; Outdoor Power
Equipment and Other Small Engine Mechanics; Rail
Car Repairers; Recreational Vehicle Service
Technicians; Tire Repairers and Changers.

Skills—Repairing: Repairing machines or systems by
using the needed tools. **Equipment Maintenance:**
Performing routine maintenance on equipment and
determining when and what kind of maintenance is
needed. **Troubleshooting:** Determining causes of
operating errors and deciding what to do about them.
Installation: Installing equipment, machines, wiring,
or programs to meet specifications. **Science:** Using
scientific rules and methods to solve problems.
Technology Design: Generating or adapting equipment and technology to serve user needs.

Education and Training Programs: Diesel
Mechanics Technology/Technician Training;
Medium/Heavy Vehicle and Truck Technology/
Technician Training. **Related Knowledge/Courses:**
Mechanical Devices: Machines and tools, including
their designs, uses, repair, and maintenance.
Transportation: Principles and methods for moving
people or goods by air, rail, sea, or road, including the
relative costs and benefits. **Public Safety and
Security:** Relevant equipment, policies, procedures,
and strategies to promote effective local, state, or
national security operations for the protection of people, data, property, and institutions. **Physics:** Physical
principles and laws and their interrelationships and
applications to understanding fluid, material, and
atmospheric dynamics and mechanical, electrical,
atomic, and subatomic structures and processes.

Engineering and Technology: The practical application of engineering science and technology. This includes applying principles, techniques, procedures, and equipment to the design and production of various goods and services. **Law and Government:** Laws, legal codes, court procedures, precedents, government regulations, executive orders, agency rules, and the democratic political process.

Work Environment: Noisy; very bright or dim lighting; contaminants; hazardous equipment; standing; using hands on objects, tools, or controls.

Bus Drivers, School

- Education/Training Required: Short-term on-the-job training
- Annual Earnings: $24,070
- Growth: 13.6%
- Annual Job Openings: 76,000
- Self-Employed: 0.5%
- Part-Time: 38.4%

Level of Solitary Work: 78.0 (out of 100)

Level of Contact with Others: 87.5 (out of 100)

Transport students or special clients, such as the elderly or persons with disabilities. Ensure adherence to safety rules. May assist passengers in boarding or exiting. Follow safety rules as students are boarding and exiting buses and as they cross streets near bus stops. Comply with traffic regulations to operate vehicles in a safe and courteous manner. Check the condition of a vehicle's tires, brakes, windshield wipers, lights, oil, fuel, water, and safety equipment to ensure that everything is in working order. Maintain order among pupils during trips to ensure safety. Pick up and drop off students at regularly scheduled neighborhood locations, following strict time schedules. Report any bus malfunctions or needed repairs. Drive gasoline, diesel, or electrically powered multi-passenger vehicles to transport students between neighborhoods, schools, and school activities. Prepare and submit reports that may include the number of passengers or trips, hours worked, mileage, fuel consumption, and fares received. Maintain knowledge of first-aid procedures. Keep bus interiors clean for passengers. Read maps and follow written and verbal geographic directions. Report delays, accidents, or other traffic and transportation situations, using telephones or mobile two-way radios. Regulate heating, lighting, and ventilation systems for passenger comfort. Escort small children across roads and highways. Make minor repairs to vehicles.

Personality Type: Realistic. Realistic occupations frequently involve work activities that include practical, hands-on problems and solutions. They often deal with plants; animals; and real-world materials such as wood, tools, and machinery. Many of the occupations require working outside and do not involve a lot of paperwork or working closely with others.

GOE—Interest Area: 16. Transportation, Distribution, and Logistics. **Work Group:** 16.06. Other Services Requiring Driving. **Other Jobs in This Work Group:** Ambulance Drivers and Attendants, Except Emergency Medical Technicians; Bus Drivers, Transit and Intercity; Couriers and Messengers; Driver/Sales Workers; Parking Lot Attendants; Postal Service Mail Carriers; Taxi Drivers and Chauffeurs.

Skills—Operation Monitoring: Watching gauges, dials, or other indicators to make sure a machine is working properly. **Equipment Maintenance:** Performing routine maintenance on equipment and determining when and what kind of maintenance is needed. **Operation and Control:** Controlling operations of equipment or systems. **Social Perceptiveness:** Being aware of others' reactions and understanding why they react as they do. **Persuasion:** Persuading others to change their minds or behavior. **Negotiation:** Bringing others together and trying to reconcile differences.

Education and Training Program: Truck and Bus Driver Training/Commercial Vehicle Operation.

Related Knowledge/Courses: **Transportation:** Principles and methods for moving people or goods by air, rail, sea, or road, including the relative costs and benefits. **Psychology:** Human behavior and performance; individual differences in ability, personality, and interests; learning and motivation; psychological research methods; and the assessment and treatment of behavioral and affective disorders. **Public Safety and Security:** Relevant equipment, policies, procedures, and strategies to promote effective local, state, or national security operations for the protection of people, data, property, and institutions. **Law and Government:** Laws, legal codes, court procedures, precedents, government regulations, executive orders, agency rules, and the democratic political process.

Work Environment: Noisy; contaminants; disease or infections; sitting; using hands on objects, tools, or controls; repetitive motions.

Bus Drivers, Transit and Intercity

- Education/Training Required: Moderate-term on-the-job training
- Annual Earnings: $31,010
- Growth: 21.7%
- Annual Job Openings: 34,000
- Self-Employed: 0.5%
- Part-Time: 38.4%

Level of Solitary Work: 75.0 (out of 100)

Level of Contact with Others: 97.0 (out of 100)

Drive bus or motor coach, including regular route operations, charters, and private carriage. May assist passengers with baggage. May collect fares or tickets. Inspect vehicles and check gas, oil, and water levels prior to departure. Drive vehicles over specified routes or to specified destinations according to time schedules to transport passengers, complying with traffic regulations. Park vehicles at loading areas so that passengers can board. Assist passengers with baggage and collect tickets or cash fares. Report delays or accidents. Advise passengers to be seated and orderly while on vehicles. Regulate heating, lighting, and ventilating systems for passenger comfort. Load and unload baggage in baggage compartments. Record cash receipts and ticket fares. Make minor repairs to vehicle and change tires.

Personality Type: Realistic. Realistic occupations frequently involve work activities that include practical, hands-on problems and solutions. They often deal with plants; animals; and real-world materials such as wood, tools, and machinery. Many of the occupations require working outside and do not involve a lot of paperwork or working closely with others.

GOE—Interest Area: 16. Transportation, Distribution, and Logistics. **Work Group:** 16.06. Other Services Requiring Driving. **Other Jobs in This Work Group:** Ambulance Drivers and Attendants, Except Emergency Medical Technicians; Bus Drivers, School; Couriers and Messengers; Driver/Sales Workers; Parking Lot Attendants; Postal Service Mail Carriers; Taxi Drivers and Chauffeurs.

Skills—Equipment Maintenance: Performing routine maintenance on equipment and determining when and what kind of maintenance is needed. **Operation and Control:** Controlling operations of equipment or systems. **Social Perceptiveness:** Being aware of others' reactions and understanding why they react as they do. **Operation Monitoring:** Watching gauges, dials, or other indicators to make sure a machine is working properly. **Troubleshooting:** Determining causes of operating errors and deciding what to do about them. **Repairing:** Repairing machines or systems by using the needed tools.

Education and Training Program: Truck and Bus Driver Training/Commercial Vehicle Operation. **Related Knowledge/Courses:** **Transportation:**

B

Principles and methods for moving people or goods by air, rail, sea, or road, including the relative costs and benefits. **Geography:** Principles and methods for describing the features of land, sea, and air masses, including their physical characteristics; locations; interrelationships; and distribution of plant, animal, and human life. **Public Safety and Security:** Relevant equipment, policies, procedures, and strategies to promote effective local, state, or national security operations for the protection of people, data, property, and institutions. **Customer and Personal Service:** Principles and processes for providing customer and personal services. This includes customer needs assessment, meeting quality standards for services, and evaluation of customer satisfaction. **Psychology:** Human behavior and performance; individual differences in ability, personality, and interests; learning and motivation; psychological research methods; and the assessment and treatment of behavioral and affective disorders. **Law and Government:** Laws, legal codes, court procedures, precedents, government regulations, executive orders, agency rules, and the democratic political process.

Work Environment: Outdoors; noisy; contaminants; sitting; using hands on objects, tools, or controls; repetitive motions.

Butchers and Meat Cutters

- Education/Training Required: Long-term on-the-job training
- Annual Earnings: $26,590
- Growth: 7.9%
- Annual Job Openings: 20,000
- Self-Employed: 1.4%
- Part-Time: 10.5%

Level of Solitary Work: 62.5 (out of 100)

Level of Contact with Others: 83.2 (out of 100)

Cut, trim, or prepare consumer-sized portions of meat for use or sale in retail establishments. Wrap, weigh, label, and price cuts of meat. Prepare and place meat cuts and products in display counter so they will appear attractive and catch the shopper's eye. Prepare special cuts of meat ordered by customers. Cut, trim, bone, tie, and grind meats, such as beef, pork, poultry, and fish, to prepare meat in cooking form. Receive, inspect, and store meat upon delivery to ensure meat quality. Shape, lace, and tie roasts, using boning knife, skewer, and twine. Estimate requirements and order or requisition meat supplies to maintain inventories. Supervise other butchers or meat cutters. Record quantity of meat received and issued to cooks and keep records of meat sales. Negotiate with representatives from supply companies to determine order details. Cure, smoke, tenderize, and preserve meat. Total sales and collect money from customers.

Personality Type: Realistic. Realistic occupations frequently involve work activities that include practical, hands-on problems and solutions. They often deal with plants; animals; and real-world materials such as wood, tools, and machinery. Many of the occupations require working outside and do not involve a lot of paperwork or working closely with others.

GOE—Interest Area: 09. Hospitality, Tourism, and Recreation. **Work Group:** 09.04. Food and Beverage Preparation. **Other Jobs in This Work Group:** Chefs and Head Cooks; Cooks, Fast Food; Cooks, Institution and Cafeteria; Cooks, Private Household; Cooks, Restaurant; Cooks, Short Order; Dishwashers; Food Preparation Workers.

Skills—Equipment Maintenance: Performing routine maintenance on equipment and determining when and what kind of maintenance is needed.

Education and Training Program: Meat Cutting/Meat Cutter Training. **Related Knowledge/ Courses: Food Production:** Techniques and equipment for planting, growing, and harvesting food products (both plant and animal) for consumption, including storage/handling techniques. **Production**

and **Processing:** Raw materials, production processes, quality control, costs, and other techniques for maximizing the effective manufacture and distribution of goods. **Mechanical Devices:** Machines and tools, including their designs, uses, repair, and maintenance. **Sales and Marketing:** Principles and methods for showing, promoting, and selling products or services. This includes marketing strategy and tactics, product demonstration, sales techniques, and sales control systems. **Customer and Personal Service:** Principles and processes for providing customer and personal services. This includes customer needs assessment, meeting quality standards for services, and evaluation of customer satisfaction.

Work Environment: Indoors; very hot or cold; hazardous equipment; standing; using hands on objects, tools, or controls; repetitive motions.

Cabinetmakers and Bench Carpenters

- Education/Training Required: Long-term on-the-job training
- Annual Earnings: $26,020
- Growth: 4.1%
- Annual Job Openings: 12,000
- Self-Employed: 15.7%
- Part-Time: 5.6%

Level of Solitary Work: 62.5 (out of 100)

Level of Contact with Others: 61.0 (out of 100)

Cut, shape, and assemble wooden articles or set up and operate a variety of woodworking machines, such as power saws, jointers, and mortisers, to surface, cut, or shape lumber or to fabricate parts for wood products. Produce and assemble components of articles such as store fixtures, office equipment, cabinets, and high-grade furniture. Verify dimensions and check the quality and fit of pieces to ensure adherence to specifications. Set up and operate machines, including power saws, jointers, mortisers, tenoners, molders, and shapers, to cut, mold, and shape woodstock and wood substitutes. Measure and mark dimensions of parts on paper or lumber stock prior to cutting, following blueprints, to ensure a tight fit and quality product. Reinforce joints with nails or other fasteners to prepare articles for finishing. Attach parts and subassemblies together to form completed units, using glue, dowels, nails, screws, or clamps. Establish the specifications of articles to be constructed or repaired and plan the methods and operations for shaping and assembling parts, based on blueprints, drawings, diagrams, or oral or written instructions. Cut timber to the right size and shape and trim parts of joints to ensure a snug fit, using hand tools such as planes, chisels, or wood files. Trim, sand, and scrape surfaces and joints to prepare articles for finishing. Match materials for color, grain, and texture, giving attention to knots and other features of the wood. Bore holes for insertion of screws or dowels by hand or using boring machines. Program computers to operate machinery. Estimate the amounts, types, and costs of needed materials. Perform final touch-ups with sandpaper and steel wool. Install hardware such as hinges, handles, catches, and drawer pulls, using hand tools. Discuss projects with customers and draw up detailed specifications. Repair or alter wooden furniture, cabinetry, fixtures, paneling, and other pieces. Apply Masonite, formica, and vinyl surfacing materials. Design furniture, using computer-aided drawing programs. Dip, brush, or spray assembled articles with protective or decorative finishes such as stain, varnish, paint, or lacquer.

Personality Type: Realistic. Realistic occupations frequently involve work activities that include practical, hands-on problems and solutions. They often deal with plants; animals; and real-world materials such as wood, tools, and machinery. Many of the occupations require working outside and do not involve a lot of paperwork or working closely with others.

GOE—Interest Area: 13. Manufacturing. **Work Group:** 13.10. Woodworking Technology. **Other Jobs in This Work Group:** Furniture Finishers; Model Makers, Wood; Patternmakers, Wood.

Skills—**Installation:** Installing equipment, machines, wiring, or programs to meet specifications. **Quality Control Analysis:** Conducting tests and inspections of products, services, or processes to evaluate quality or performance. **Instructing:** Teaching others how to do something. **Mathematics:** Using mathematics to solve problems. **Equipment Maintenance:** Performing routine maintenance on equipment and determining when and what kind of maintenance is needed.

Education and Training Program: Cabinetmaking and Millwork/Millwright. **Related Knowledge/Courses: Design:** Design techniques, tools, and principles involved in production of precision technical plans, blueprints, drawings, and models. **Production and Processing:** Raw materials, production processes, quality control, costs, and other techniques for maximizing the effective manufacture and distribution of goods. **Mechanical Devices:** Machines and tools, including their designs, uses, repair, and maintenance. **Building and Construction:** The materials, methods, and tools involved in the construction or repair of houses, buildings, or other structures such as highways and roads. **Engineering and Technology:** The practical application of engineering science and technology. This includes applying principles, techniques, procedures, and equipment to the design and production of various goods and services. **Mathematics:** Arithmetic, algebra, geometry, calculus, and statistics and their applications.

Work Environment: Noisy; contaminants; hazardous equipment; standing; walking and running; using hands on objects, tools, or controls.

Captains, Mates, and Pilots of Water Vessels

See the descriptions of these jobs:

- Mates—Ship, Boat, and Barge
- Pilots, Ship
- Ship and Boat Captains

Cartographers and Photogrammetrists

- Education/Training Required: Bachelor's degree
- Annual Earnings: $48,250
- Growth: 15.2%
- Annual Job Openings: 1,000
- Self-Employed: 2.9%
- Part-Time: 8.1%

Level of Solitary Work: 68.8 (out of 100)

Level of Contact with Others: 64.7 (out of 100)

Collect, analyze, and interpret geographic information provided by geodetic surveys, aerial photographs, and satellite data. Research, study, and prepare maps and other spatial data in digital or graphic form for legal, social, political, educational, and design purposes. May work with Geographic Information Systems (GIS). May design and evaluate algorithms, data structures, and user interfaces for GIS and mapping systems. Identify, scale, and orient geodetic points, elevations, and other planimetric or topographic features, applying standard mathematical formulas. Collect information about specific features of the Earth, using aerial photography and other digital remote sensing techniques. Revise existing maps and charts, making all necessary corrections and adjustments. Compile data required for map preparation, including aerial photographs, survey notes, records, reports, and original maps. Inspect final compositions to ensure completeness and accuracy. Determine map content and layout, as well as production specifications such as scale, size, projection, and colors, and direct production to ensure that specifications are followed. Examine and analyze data from ground surveys, reports, aerial photographs, and satellite images to prepare topographic maps, aerial-photograph mosaics, and related charts. Select aerial photographic and remote sensing techniques and plotting equipment needed to meet required standards of accuracy. Delineate aerial photographic detail such as control points, hydrography, topography, and cultural features, using precision stereoplotting apparatus or drafting instruments. Build and update digital databases. Prepare and alter trace maps, charts, tables, detailed drawings, and three-dimensional optical models of terrain, using stereoscopic plotting and computer graphics equipment. Determine guidelines that specify which source material is acceptable for use. Study legal records to establish boundaries of local, national, and international properties. Travel over photographed areas to observe, identify, record, and verify all relevant features.

Personality Type: Conventional. Conventional occupations frequently involve following set procedures and routines. These occupations can include working with data and details more than with ideas. Usually there is a clear line of authority to follow.

GOE—Interest Area: 15. Scientific Research, Engineering, and Mathematics. **Work Group:** 15.09. Engineering Technology. **Other Jobs in This Work Group:** Aerospace Engineering and Operations Technicians; Civil Engineering Technicians; Electrical and Electronic Engineering Technicians; Electrical and Electronics Drafters; Electrical Drafters; Electrical Engineering Technicians; Electro-Mechanical Technicians; Electronic Drafters; Electronics Engineering Technicians; Environmental Engineering Technicians; Mapping Technicians; Mechanical Drafters; Mechanical Engineering

Technicians; Surveying and Mapping Technicians; Surveying Technicians.

Skills—Science: Using scientific rules and methods to solve problems. **Technology Design:** Generating or adapting equipment and technology to serve user needs. **Mathematics:** Using mathematics to solve problems. **Active Learning:** Understanding the implications of new information for both current and future problem solving and decision making. **Troubleshooting:** Determining causes of operating errors and deciding what to do about them. **Reading Comprehension:** Understanding written sentences and paragraphs in work-related documents.

Education and Training Programs: Cartography; Surveying Technology/Surveying. **Related Knowledge/Courses: Geography:** Principles and methods for describing the features of land, sea, and air masses, including their physical characteristics; locations; interrelationships; and distribution of plant, animal, and human life. **Design:** Design techniques, tools, and principles involved in production of precision technical plans, blueprints, drawings, and models. **Engineering and Technology:** The practical application of engineering science and technology. This includes applying principles, techniques, procedures, and equipment to the design and production of various goods and services. **Computers and Electronics:** Circuit boards, processors, chips, electronic equipment, and computer hardware and software, including applications and programming. **Production and Processing:** Raw materials, production processes, quality control, costs, and other techniques for maximizing the effective manufacture and distribution of goods. **Mathematics:** Arithmetic, algebra, geometry, calculus, and statistics and their applications.

Work Environment: Indoors; sitting; using hands on objects, tools, or controls; repetitive motions.

Cement Masons and Concrete Finishers

- Education/Training Required: Moderate-term on-the-job training
- Annual Earnings: $32,030
- Growth: 15.9%
- Annual Job Openings: 32,000
- Self-Employed: 3.1%
- Part-Time: 8.5%

Level of Solitary Work: 50.0 (out of 100)

Level of Contact with Others: 67.8 (out of 100)

Smooth and finish surfaces of poured concrete, such as floors, walks, sidewalks, roads, or curbs, using a variety of hand and power tools. Align forms for sidewalks, curbs, or gutters; patch voids; and use saws to cut expansion joints. Check the forms that hold the concrete to see that they are properly constructed. Set the forms that hold concrete to the desired pitch and depth and align them. Spread, level, and smooth concrete, using rake, shovel, hand or power trowel, hand or power screed, and float. Mold expansion joints and edges, using edging tools, jointers, and straightedge. Monitor how the wind, heat, or cold affect the curing of the concrete throughout the entire process. Signal truck driver to position truck to facilitate pouring concrete and move chute to direct concrete on forms. Produce rough concrete surface, using broom. Operate power vibrator to compact concrete. Direct the casting of the concrete and supervise laborers who use shovels or special tools to spread it. Mix cement, sand, and water to produce concrete, grout, or slurry, using hoe, trowel, tamper, scraper, or concrete-mixing machine. Cut out damaged areas, drill holes for reinforcing rods, and position reinforcing rods to repair concrete, using power saw and drill. Wet surface to prepare for bonding, fill holes and cracks with grout or slurry, and smooth, using trowel. Wet concrete surface and rub with stone to smooth surface and obtain specified finish. Clean chipped area, using wire brush, and feel and observe surface to determine if it is rough or uneven. Apply hardening and sealing compounds to cure surface of concrete and waterproof or restore surface. Chip, scrape, and grind high spots, ridges, and rough projections to finish concrete, using pneumatic chisels, power grinders, or hand tools. Spread roofing paper on surface of foundation and spread concrete onto roofing paper with trowel to form terrazzo base. Build wooden molds and clamp molds around area to be repaired, using hand tools. Sprinkle colored marble or stone chips, powdered steel, or coloring powder over surface to produce prescribed finish. Cut metal division strips and press them into terrazzo base so that top edges form desired design or pattern. Fabricate concrete beams, columns, and panels. Waterproof or restore concrete surfaces, using appropriate compounds.

Personality Type: Realistic. Realistic occupations frequently involve work activities that include practical, hands-on problems and solutions. They often deal with plants; animals; and real-world materials such as wood, tools, and machinery. Many of the occupations require working outside and do not involve a lot of paperwork or working closely with others.

GOE—Interest Area: 02. Architecture and Construction. **Work Group:** 02.04. Construction Crafts. **Other Jobs in This Work Group:** Boilermakers; Brickmasons and Blockmasons; Carpet Installers; Commercial Divers; Construction Carpenters; Crane and Tower Operators; Drywall and Ceiling Tile Installers; Electricians; Fence Erectors; Floor Layers, Except Carpet, Wood, and Hard Tiles; Floor Sanders and Finishers; Glaziers; Hazardous Materials Removal Workers; Insulation Workers, Floor, Ceiling, and Wall; Insulation Workers, Mechanical; Manufactured Building and Mobile Home Installers; Operating Engineers and Other Construction Equipment Operators; Painters, Construction and Maintenance; Paperhangers; Paving, Surfacing, and Tamping Equipment Operators; Pile-Driver Operators; Pipe Fitters and Steamfitters; Pipelayers; Plasterers and Stucco Masons; Plumbers; Plumbers, Pipefitters, and

Steamfitters; Rail-Track Laying and Maintenance Equipment Operators; Refractory Materials Repairers, Except Brickmasons; Reinforcing Iron and Rebar Workers; Riggers; Roofers; Rough Carpenters; Security and Fire Alarm Systems Installers; Segmental Pavers; Sheet Metal Workers; Stone Cutters and Carvers, Manufacturing; Stonemasons; Structural Iron and Steel Workers; Tapers; Terrazzo Workers and Finishers; Tile and Marble Setters.

Skills—Mathematics: Using mathematics to solve problems. **Installation:** Installing equipment, machines, wiring, or programs to meet specifications. **Repairing:** Repairing machines or systems by using the needed tools. **Equipment Maintenance:** Performing routine maintenance on equipment and determining when and what kind of maintenance is needed. **Coordination:** Adjusting actions in relation to others' actions. **Equipment Selection:** Determining the kind of tools and equipment needed to do a job.

Education and Training Program: Concrete Finishing/Concrete Finisher Training. **Related Knowledge/Courses: Building and Construction:** The materials, methods, and tools involved in the construction or repair of houses, buildings, or other structures such as highways and roads. **Public Safety and Security:** Relevant equipment, policies, procedures, and strategies to promote effective local, state, or national security operations for the protection of people, data, property, and institutions. **Mechanical Devices:** Machines and tools, including their designs, uses, repair, and maintenance. **Design:** Design techniques, tools, and principles involved in production of precision technical plans, blueprints, drawings, and models. **Engineering and Technology:** The practical application of engineering science and technology. This includes applying principles, techniques, procedures, and equipment to the design and production of various goods and services. **Administration and Management:** Business and management principles involved in strategic planning, resource allocation, human resources modeling, leadership technique, production methods, and coordination of people and resources.

Work Environment: Outdoors; noisy; hazardous equipment; standing; using hands on objects, tools, or controls; bending or twisting the body.

Chemical Equipment Operators and Tenders

- Education/Training Required: Moderate-term on-the-job training
- Annual Earnings: $39,030
- Growth: −4.5%
- Annual Job Openings: 6,000
- Self-Employed: 0.8%
- Part-Time: 4.3%

Level of Solitary Work: 57.7 (out of 100)

Level of Contact with Others: 78.0 (out of 100)

Operate or tend equipment to control chemical changes or reactions in the processing of industrial or consumer products. Equipment used includes devulcanizers, steam-jacketed kettles, and reactor vessels. Adjust controls to regulate temperature, pressure, feed, and flow of liquids and gases and times of prescribed reactions according to knowledge of equipment and processes. Observe safety precautions to prevent fires and explosions. Monitor gauges, recording instruments, flowmeters, or products to ensure that specified conditions are maintained. Control and operate equipment in which chemical changes or reactions take place during the processing of industrial or consumer products. Measure, weigh, and mix chemical ingredients according to specifications. Inspect equipment or units to detect leaks and malfunctions, shutting equipment down if necessary. Patrol work areas to detect leaks and equipment malfunctions and to monitor operating conditions. Test product samples for specific gravity, chemical characteristics, pH levels, and concentrations or viscosities or send them to laboratories for testing. Draw samples of products at specified stages so that analyses can be performed. Record operational data such as temperatures, pressures, ingredients used, processing times, or test results. Notify maintenance engineers of equipment malfunctions. Add treating or neutralizing agents to products and pump products through filters or centrifuges to remove impurities or to precipitate products. Open valves or start pumps, agitators, reactors, blowers, or automatic feed of materials. Read plant specifications to determine products, ingredients, and prescribed modifications of plant procedures. Drain equipment and pump water or other solutions through to flush and clean tanks and equipment. Make minor repairs and lubricate and maintain equipment, using hand tools. Flush or clean equipment, using steam hoses or mechanical reamers. Observe colors and consistencies of products and compare them to instrument readings and to laboratory and standard test results. Implement appropriate industrial emergency response procedures. Dump or scoop prescribed solid, granular, or powdered materials into equipment. Estimate materials required for production and manufacturing of products.

Personality Type: Realistic. Realistic occupations frequently involve work activities that include practical, hands-on problems and solutions. They often deal with plants; animals; and real-world materials such as wood, tools, and machinery. Many of the occupations require working outside and do not involve a lot of paperwork or working closely with others.

GOE—Interest Area: 13. Manufacturing. **Work Group:** 13.03. Production Work, Assorted Materials Processing. **Other Jobs in This Work Group:** Bakers; Cementing and Gluing Machine Operators and Tenders; Cleaning, Washing, and Metal Pickling Equipment Operators and Tenders; Coating, Painting, and Spraying Machine Setters, Operators, and Tenders; Cooling and Freezing Equipment Operators and Tenders; Cutting and Slicing Machine Setters, Operators, and Tenders; Extruding and Forming Machine Setters, Operators, and Tenders, Synthetic and Glass Fibers; Extruding, Forming, Pressing, and Compacting Machine Setters, Operators, and Tenders; Food and Tobacco Roasting, Baking, and Drying Machine Operators and Tenders;

Food Batchmakers; Food Cooking Machine Operators and Tenders; Furnace, Kiln, Oven, Drier, and Kettle Operators and Tenders; Heat Treating Equipment Setters, Operators, and Tenders, Metal and Plastic; Helpers—Production Workers; Meat, Poultry, and Fish Cutters and Trimmers; Metal-Refining Furnace Operators and Tenders; Mixing and Blending Machine Setters, Operators, and Tenders; Packaging and Filling Machine Operators and Tenders; Plating and Coating Machine Setters, Operators, and Tenders, Metal and Plastic; Pourers and Casters, Metal; Sawing Machine Setters, Operators, and Tenders, Wood; Separating, Filtering, Clarifying, Precipitating, and Still Machine Setters, Operators, and Tenders; Sewing Machine Operators; Shoe Machine Operators and Tenders; Slaughterers and Meat Packers; Team Assemblers; Textile Bleaching and Dyeing Machine Operators and Tenders; Tire Builders; Woodworking Machine Setters, Operators, and Tenders, Except Sawing.

Skills—Operation Monitoring: Watching gauges, dials, or other indicators to make sure a machine is working properly. **Operation and Control:** Controlling operations of equipment or systems. **Troubleshooting:** Determining causes of operating errors and deciding what to do about them. **Equipment Maintenance:** Performing routine maintenance on equipment and determining when and what kind of maintenance is needed. **Repairing:** Repairing machines or systems by using the needed tools. **Science:** Using scientific rules and methods to solve problems.

Education and Training Program: Chemical Technology/Technician. **Related Knowledge/Courses: Chemistry:** The chemical composition, structure, and properties of substances and of the chemical processes and transformations that they undergo. This includes uses of chemicals and their danger signs, production techniques, and disposal methods. **Mechanical Devices:** Machines and tools, including their designs, uses, repair, and maintenance. **Production and Processing:** Raw materials, production processes, quality control, costs, and other techniques for maximizing the effective manufacture and distribution of goods. **Public Safety and Security:** Relevant equipment, policies, procedures, and strategies to promote effective local, state, or national security operations for the protection of people, data, property, and institutions. **English Language:** The structure and content of the English language, including the meaning and spelling of words, rules of composition, and grammar. **Computers and Electronics:** Circuit boards, processors, chips, electronic equipment, and computer hardware and software, including applications and programming.

Work Environment: More often outdoors than indoors; noisy; very hot or cold; contaminants; hazardous conditions.

Chemists

- ◎ Education/Training Required: Bachelor's degree
- ◎ Annual Earnings: $57,890
- ◎ Growth: 7.3%
- ◎ Annual Job Openings: 5,000
- ◎ Self-Employed: 0.4%
- ◎ Part-Time: 6.6%

Level of Solitary Work: 75.0 (out of 100)

Level of Contact with Others: 77.0 (out of 100)

Conduct qualitative and quantitative chemical analyses or chemical experiments in laboratories for quality or process control or to develop new products or knowledge. Analyze organic and inorganic compounds to determine chemical and physical properties, composition, structure, relationships, and reactions, utilizing chromatography, spectroscopy, and spectrophotometry techniques. Develop, improve, and customize products, equipment, formulas, processes, and analytical methods. Compile and analyze test information to determine process or equipment operating efficiency and to diagnose mal-

functions. Confer with scientists and engineers to conduct analyses of research projects, interpret test results, or develop nonstandard tests. Direct, coordinate, and advise personnel in test procedures for analyzing components and physical properties of materials. Induce changes in composition of substances by introducing heat, light, energy, and chemical catalysts for quantitative and qualitative analysis. Write technical papers and reports and prepare standards and specifications for processes, facilities, products, or tests. Study effects of various methods of processing, preserving, and packaging on composition and properties of foods. Prepare test solutions, compounds, and reagents for laboratory personnel to conduct test.

Personality Type: Investigative. Investigative occupations frequently involve working with ideas and require an extensive amount of thinking. These occupations can involve searching for facts and figuring out problems mentally.

GOE—Interest Area: 15. Scientific Research, Engineering, and Mathematics. **Work Group:** 15.02. Physical Sciences. **Other Jobs in This Work Group:** Astronomers; Atmospheric and Space Scientists; Geographers; Geoscientists, Except Hydrologists and Geographers; Hydrologists; Materials Scientists; Physicists.

Skills—Science: Using scientific rules and methods to solve problems. **Quality Control Analysis:** Conducting tests and inspections of products, services, or processes to evaluate quality or performance. **Technology Design:** Generating or adapting equipment and technology to serve user needs. **Operation Monitoring:** Watching gauges, dials, or other indicators to make sure a machine is working properly. **Management of Financial Resources:** Determining how money will be spent to get the work done and accounting for these expenditures. **Management of Material Resources:** Obtaining and seeing to the appropriate use of equipment, facilities, and materials needed to do certain work.

Education and Training Programs: Analytical Chemistry; Chemical Physics; Chemistry, General;

Chemistry, Other; Inorganic Chemistry; Organic Chemistry; Physical and Theoretical Chemistry; Polymer Chemistry. **Related Knowledge/Courses: Chemistry:** The chemical composition, structure, and properties of substances and of the chemical processes and transformations that they undergo. This includes uses of chemicals and their danger signs, production techniques, and disposal methods. **Mathematics:** Arithmetic, algebra, geometry, calculus, and statistics and their applications. **Engineering and Technology:** The practical application of engineering science and technology. This includes applying principles, techniques, procedures, and equipment to the design and production of various goods and services. **Production and Processing:** Raw materials, production processes, quality control, costs, and other techniques for maximizing the effective manufacture and distribution of goods. **Computers and Electronics:** Circuit boards, processors, chips, electronic equipment, and computer hardware and software, including applications and programming. **Law and Government:** Laws, legal codes, court procedures, precedents, government regulations, executive orders, agency rules, and the democratic political process.

Work Environment: Indoors; contaminants; hazardous conditions; standing.

Civil Drafters

This job can be found in the Part II lists under the title Architectural and Civil Drafters.

- Education/Training Required: Postsecondary vocational training
- Annual Earnings: $40,390
- Growth: 4.6%
- Annual Job Openings: 9,000
- Self-Employed: 6.1%
- Part-Time: 8.4%

The job openings listed here are shared with Architectural Drafters.

Level of Solitary Work: 70.2 (out of 100)

Level of Contact with Others: 73.8 (out of 100)

Prepare drawings and topographical and relief maps used in civil engineering projects, such as highways, bridges, pipelines, flood control projects, and water and sewerage control systems. Produce drawings, using computer-assisted drafting systems (CAD) or drafting machines, or by hand, using compasses, dividers, protractors, triangles, and other drafting devices. Draft plans and detailed drawings for structures, installations, and construction projects such as highways, sewage disposal systems, and dikes, working from sketches or notes. Draw maps, diagrams, and profiles, using cross-sections and surveys, to represent elevations, topographical contours, subsurface formations, and structures. Correlate, interpret, and modify data obtained from topographical surveys, well logs, and geophysical prospecting reports. Finish and duplicate drawings and documentation packages according to required mediums and specifications for reproduction, using blueprinting, photography, or other duplicating methods. Review rough sketches, drawings, specifications, and other engineering data received from civil engineers to ensure that they conform to design concepts. Supervise and train other technologists, technicians, and drafters. Supervise or conduct field surveys, inspections, or technical investigations to obtain data required to revise construction drawings. Determine the order of work and method of presentation, such as orthographic or isometric drawing. Calculate excavation tonnage and prepare graphs and fill-hauling diagrams for use in earth-moving operations. Explain drawings to production or construction teams and provide adjustments as necessary. Locate and identify symbols located on topographical surveys to denote geological and geophysical formations or oilfield installations. Calculate weights, volumes, and stress factors and their implications for technical aspects of designs. Determine quality, cost, strength, and quantity of required materials and enter figures on materials lists.

Plot characteristics of boreholes for oil and gas wells from photographic subsurface survey recordings and other data, representing depth, degree, and direction of inclination.

Personality Type: Realistic. Realistic occupations frequently involve work activities that include practical, hands-on problems and solutions. They often deal with plants; animals; and real-world materials such as wood, tools, and machinery. Many of the occupations require working outside and do not involve a lot of paperwork or working closely with others.

GOE—Interest Area: 02. Architecture and Construction. **Work Group:** 02.03. Architecture/Construction Engineering Technologies. **Other Jobs in This Work Group:** Architectural and Civil Drafters; Architectural Drafters; Surveyors.

Skills—Mathematics: Using mathematics to solve problems. **Operations Analysis:** Analyzing needs and product requirements to create a design. **Technology Design:** Generating or adapting equipment and technology to serve user needs. **Coordination:** Adjusting actions in relation to others' actions. **Active Learning:** Understanding the implications of new information for both current and future problem solving and decision making. **Instructing:** Teaching others how to do something.

Education and Training Programs: Architectural Drafting and Architectural CAD/CADD; Architectural Technology/Technician Training; CAD/CADD Drafting and/or Design Technology/Technician Training; Civil Drafting and Civil Engineering CAD/CADD; Drafting and Design Technology/Technician Training, General. **Related Knowledge/Courses: Design:** Design techniques, tools, and principles involved in production of precision technical plans, blueprints, drawings, and models. **Engineering and Technology:** The practical application of engineering science and technology. This includes applying principles, techniques, procedures, and equipment to the design and production of various goods and services. **Geography:** Principles and methods for describing the features of land, sea, and air

masses, including their physical characteristics; locations; interrelationships; and distribution of plant, animal, and human life. **Computers and Electronics:** Circuit boards, processors, chips, electronic equipment, and computer hardware and software, including applications and programming. **Mathematics:** Arithmetic, algebra, geometry, calculus, and statistics and their applications. **Law and Government:** Laws, legal codes, court procedures, precedents, government regulations, executive orders, agency rules, and the democratic political process.

Work Environment: Indoors; sitting; repetitive motions.

Civil Engineers

- ◎ Education/Training Required: Bachelor's degree
- ◎ Annual Earnings: $66,190
- ◎ Growth: 16.5%
- ◎ Annual Job Openings: 19,000
- ◎ Self-Employed: 4.9%
- ◎ Part-Time: 3.4%

Level of Solitary Work: 34.2 (out of 100)

Level of Contact with Others: 56.5 (out of 100)

Perform engineering duties in planning, designing, and overseeing construction and maintenance of building structures and facilities, such as roads, railroads, airports, bridges, harbors, channels, dams, irrigation projects, pipelines, power plants, water and sewage systems, and waste disposal units. Includes architectural, structural, traffic, ocean, and geo-technical engineers. Analyze survey reports, maps, drawings, blueprints, aerial photography, and other topographical or geologic data to plan projects. Plan and design transportation or hydraulic systems and structures, following construction and government standards and using design software and drawing tools. Compute load and grade requirements, water flow rates, and material stress factors to determine design specifications. Inspect project sites to monitor progress and ensure conformance to design specifications and safety or sanitation standards. Direct construction, operations, and maintenance activities at project site. Direct or participate in surveying to lay out installations and establish reference points, grades, and elevations to guide construction. Estimate quantities and cost of materials, equipment, or labor to determine project feasibility. Prepare or present public reports on topics such as bid proposals, deeds, environmental impact statements, or property and right-of-way descriptions. Test soils and materials to determine the adequacy and strength of foundations, concrete, asphalt, or steel. Provide technical advice regarding design, construction, or program modifications and structural repairs to industrial and managerial personnel. Conduct studies of traffic patterns or environmental conditions to identify engineering problems and assess the potential impact of projects.

Personality Type: Realistic. Realistic occupations frequently involve work activities that include practical, hands-on problems and solutions. They often deal with plants; animals; and real-world materials such as wood, tools, and machinery. Many of the occupations require working outside and do not involve a lot of paperwork or working closely with others.

GOE—Interest Area: 15. Scientific Research, Engineering, and Mathematics. **Work Group:** 15.07. Research and Design Engineering. **Other Jobs in This Work Group:** Aerospace Engineers; Biomedical Engineers; Chemical Engineers; Computer Hardware Engineers; Electrical Engineers; Electronics Engineers, Except Computer; Marine Architects; Marine Engineers; Marine Engineers and Naval Architects; Materials Engineers; Mechanical Engineers; Nuclear Engineers.

Skills—Science: Using scientific rules and methods to solve problems. **Mathematics:** Using mathematics to solve problems. **Operations Analysis:** Analyzing needs and product requirements to create a design.

Coordination: Adjusting actions in relation to others' actions. **Negotiation:** Bringing others together and trying to reconcile differences. **Persuasion:** Persuading others to change their minds or behavior.

Education and Training Programs: Civil Engineering, General; Civil Engineering, Other; Transportation and Highway Engineering; Water Resources Engineering. **Related Knowledge/Courses: Engineering and Technology:** The practical application of engineering science and technology. This includes applying principles, techniques, procedures, and equipment to the design and production of various goods and services. **Design:** Design techniques, tools, and principles involved in production of precision technical plans, blueprints, drawings, and models. **Building and Construction:** The materials, methods, and tools involved in the construction or repair of houses, buildings, or other structures such as highways and roads. **Physics:** Physical principles and laws and their interrelationships and applications to understanding fluid, material, and atmospheric dynamics and mechanical, electrical, atomic, and subatomic structures and processes. **Mathematics:** Arithmetic, algebra, geometry, calculus, and statistics and their applications. **Transportation:** Principles and methods for moving people or goods by air, rail, sea, or road, including the relative costs and benefits.

Work Environment: More often outdoors than indoors; very hot or cold; contaminants; hazardous equipment; sitting.

Clergy

- ◎ Education/Training Required: Master's degree
- ◎ Annual Earnings: $38,540
- ◎ Growth: 12.4%
- ◎ Annual Job Openings: 26,000
- ◎ Self-Employed: 0.3%
- ◎ Part-Time: 10.9%

Level of Solitary Work: 50.0 (out of 100)

Level of Contact with Others: 72.0 (out of 100)

Conduct religious worship and perform other spiritual functions associated with beliefs and practices of religious faith or denomination. Provide spiritual and moral guidance and assistance to members. Pray and promote spirituality. Read from sacred texts such as the Bible, Torah, or Koran. Prepare and deliver sermons and other talks. Organize and lead regular religious services. Share information about religious issues by writing articles, giving speeches, or teaching. Instruct people who seek conversion to a particular faith. Visit people in homes, hospitals, and prisons to provide them with comfort and support. Counsel individuals and groups concerning their spiritual, emotional, and personal needs. Train leaders of church, community, and youth groups. Administer religious rites or ordinances. Study and interpret religious laws, doctrines, or traditions. Conduct special ceremonies such as weddings, funerals, and confirmations. Plan and lead religious education programs for their congregations. Respond to requests for assistance during emergencies or crises. Devise ways in which congregation membership can be expanded. Collaborate with committees and individuals to address financial and administrative issues pertaining to congregations. Prepare people for participation in religious ceremonies. Perform administrative duties such as overseeing building management, ordering supplies, contracting for services and repairs, and supervising the work of staff members and volunteers. Refer people to community support services, psychologists, and doctors as necessary. Participate in fundraising activities to support congregation activities and facilities. Organize and engage in interfaith, community, civic, educational, and recreational activities sponsored by or related to their religion.

Personality Type: Social. Social occupations frequently involve working with, communicating with, and teaching people. These occupations often involve helping or providing service to others.

GOE—Interest Area: 10. Human Service. **Work Group:** 10.02. Religious Work. **Other Jobs in This**

Work Group: Directors, Religious Activities and Education.

Skills—Management of Personnel Resources: Motivating, developing, and directing people as they work; identifying the best people for the job. **Management of Financial Resources:** Determining how money will be spent to get the work done and accounting for these expenditures. **Service Orientation:** Actively looking for ways to help people. **Negotiation:** Bringing others together and trying to reconcile differences. **Persuasion:** Persuading others to change their minds or behavior. **Judgment and Decision Making:** Considering the relative costs and benefits of potential actions to choose the most appropriate one.

Education and Training Programs: Clinical Pastoral Counseling/Patient Counseling; Divinity/Ministry (BD, MDiv.); Pastoral Counseling and Specialized Ministries, Other; Pastoral Studies/Counseling; Pre-Theology/Pre-Ministerial Studies; Rabbinical Studies; Theological and Ministerial Studies, Other; Theology and Religious Vocations, Other; Theology/Theological Studies; Youth Ministry. **Related Knowledge/Courses: Philosophy and Theology:** Different philosophical systems and religions. This includes their basic principles, values, ethics, ways of thinking, customs, and practices and their impact on human culture. **Therapy and Counseling:** Principles, methods, and procedures for diagnosis, treatment, and rehabilitation of physical and mental dysfunctions and for career counseling and guidance. **Sociology and Anthropology:** Group behavior and dynamics, societal trends and influences, human migrations, ethnicity, and cultures and their history and origins. **Psychology:** Human behavior and performance; individual differences in ability, personality, and interests; learning and motivation; psychological research methods; and the assessment and treatment of behavioral and affective disorders. **Customer and Personal Service:** Principles and processes for providing customer and personal services. This includes customer needs assessment, meeting quality standards for services, and evaluation of customer satisfaction. **Public Safety and Security:**

Relevant equipment, policies, procedures, and strategies to promote effective local, state, or national security operations for the protection of people, data, property, and institutions.

Work Environment: Indoors; sitting.

Coating, Painting, and Spraying Machine Setters, Operators, and Tenders

- Education/Training Required: Moderate-term on-the-job training
- Annual Earnings: $26,670
- Growth: –3.4%
- Annual Job Openings: 16,000
- Self-Employed: 6.5%
- Part-Time: 5.7%

Level of Solitary Work: 67.3 (out of 100)

Level of Contact with Others: 56.3 (out of 100)

Set up, operate, or tend machines to coat or paint any of a wide variety of products, including food, glassware, cloth, ceramics, metal, plastic, paper, or wood, with lacquer, silver, copper, rubber, varnish, glaze, enamel, oil, or rustproofing materials. Observe machine gauges and equipment operation to detect defects or deviations from standards and make adjustments as necessary. Determine paint flow, viscosity, and coating quality by performing visual inspections or by using viscometers. Weigh or measure chemicals, coatings, or paints before adding them to machines. Select appropriate coatings, paints, or sprays or prepare them by mixing substances according to formulas, using automated paint mixing equipment. Set up and operate machines to paint or coat products with such materials as silver and copper solution, rubber, paint, glaze, oil, or rustproofing materials. Turn dials, handwheels, valves, or switches to regulate conveyor speeds, machine temperature,

air pressure and circulation, and the flow or spray of coatings or paints. Start and stop operation of machines, using levers or buttons. Record operational data on specified forms. Start pumps to mix solutions and fill tanks. Fill hoppers, reservoirs, troughs, or pans with material used to coat, paint, or spray, using conveyors or pails. Operate auxiliary machines or equipment used in coating or painting processes. Perform test runs to ensure that equipment is set up properly. Clean machines, related equipment, and work areas, using water, solvents, and other cleaning aids. Thread or feed items or products through or around machine rollers and dryers. Attach hoses or nozzles to machines, using wrenches and pliers, and make adjustments to obtain the proper dispersion of spray. Remove materials, parts, or workpieces from painting or coating machines, using hand tools. Transfer completed items or products from machines to drying or storage areas, using handcarts, handtrucks, or cranes. Attach and align machine parts such as rollers, guides, brushes, and blades, using hand tools. Examine, measure, weigh, or test sample products to ensure conformance to specifications. Hold or position spray guns to direct spray onto articles. Place items or products on feedracks, spindles, or reel strands to coat, paint, or spray them, using hands, hoists, or trucklifts. Prepare and apply stencils, computer-generated decals, or other decorative items to finished products.

Personality Type: Realistic. Realistic occupations frequently involve work activities that include practical, hands-on problems and solutions. They often deal with plants; animals; and real-world materials such as wood, tools, and machinery. Many of the occupations require working outside and do not involve a lot of paperwork or working closely with others.

GOE—Interest Area: 13. Manufacturing. **Work Group:** 13.03. Production Work, Assorted Materials Processing. **Other Jobs in This Work Group:** Bakers; Cementing and Gluing Machine Operators and Tenders; Chemical Equipment Operators and Tenders; Cleaning, Washing, and Metal Pickling Equipment Operators and Tenders; Cooling and Freezing Equipment Operators and Tenders; Cutting and Slicing Machine Setters, Operators, and Tenders; Extruding and Forming Machine Setters, Operators, and Tenders, Synthetic and Glass Fibers; Extruding, Forming, Pressing, and Compacting Machine Setters, Operators, and Tenders; Food and Tobacco Roasting, Baking, and Drying Machine Operators and Tenders; Food Batchmakers; Food Cooking Machine Operators and Tenders; Furnace, Kiln, Oven, Drier, and Kettle Operators and Tenders; Heat Treating Equipment Setters, Operators, and Tenders, Metal and Plastic; Helpers—Production Workers; Meat, Poultry, and Fish Cutters and Trimmers; Metal-Refining Furnace Operators and Tenders; Mixing and Blending Machine Setters, Operators, and Tenders; Packaging and Filling Machine Operators and Tenders; Plating and Coating Machine Setters, Operators, and Tenders, Metal and Plastic; Pourers and Casters, Metal; Sawing Machine Setters, Operators, and Tenders, Wood; Separating, Filtering, Clarifying, Precipitating, and Still Machine Setters, Operators, and Tenders; Sewing Machine Operators; Shoe Machine Operators and Tenders; Slaughterers and Meat Packers; Team Assemblers; Textile Bleaching and Dyeing Machine Operators and Tenders; Tire Builders; Woodworking Machine Setters, Operators, and Tenders, Except Sawing.

Skills—Operation Monitoring: Watching gauges, dials, or other indicators to make sure a machine is working properly. **Equipment Maintenance:** Performing routine maintenance on equipment and determining when and what kind of maintenance is needed. **Operation and Control:** Controlling operations of equipment or systems. **Quality Control Analysis:** Conducting tests and inspections of products, services, or processes to evaluate quality or performance. **Installation:** Installing equipment, machines, wiring, or programs to meet specifications. **Repairing:** Repairing machines or systems by using the needed tools.

Education and Training Program: No related CIP programs; this job is learned through informal moderate-term on-the-job training. **Related Knowledge/Courses: Production and Processing:** Raw materials, production processes, quality control,

costs, and other techniques for maximizing the effective manufacture and distribution of goods. **Mechanical Devices:** Machines and tools, including their designs, uses, repair, and maintenance.

Work Environment: Noisy; contaminants; hazardous conditions; standing; using hands on objects, tools, or controls; repetitive motions.

Coin, Vending, and Amusement Machine Servicers and Repairers

- ◎ Education/Training Required: Moderate-term on-the-job training
- ◎ Annual Earnings: $28,200
- ◎ Growth: 2.4%
- ◎ Annual Job Openings: 7,000
- ◎ Self-Employed: 17.5%
- ◎ Part-Time: 13.8%

Level of Solitary Work: 71.7 (out of 100)

Level of Contact with Others: 11.8 (out of 100)

Install, service, adjust, or repair coin, vending, or amusement machines, including video games, jukeboxes, pinball machines, or slot machines. Clean and oil machine parts. Replace malfunctioning parts, such as worn magnetic heads on automatic teller machine (ATM) card readers. Adjust and repair coin, vending, or amusement machines and meters and replace defective mechanical and electrical parts, using hand tools, soldering irons, and diagrams. Collect coins and bills from machines, prepare invoices, and settle accounts with concessionaires. Disassemble and assemble machines according to specifications, using hand and power tools. Fill machines with products, ingredients, money, and other supplies. Inspect machines and meters to determine causes of malfunctions and fix minor problems such as jammed bills or stuck products. Install machines, making the necessary water and electrical connections in compliance with codes. Make service calls to maintain and repair machines. Adjust machine pressure gauges and thermostats. Test machines to determine proper functioning. Refer to manuals and wiring diagrams to gather information needed to repair machines. Contact other repair personnel or make arrangements for the removal of machines in cases where major repairs are required. Count cash and items deposited at automatic teller machines (ATMs) by customers and compare numbers to transactions indicated on transaction tapes. Install automatic teller machine (ATM) hardware, software, and peripheral equipment and check that all components are configured correctly and connected to power sources and communications lines. Keep records of merchandise distributed and money collected. Maintain records of machine maintenance and repair. Order parts needed for machine repairs. Prepare repair cost estimates. Record transaction information on forms or logs and notify designated personnel of discrepancies. Transport machines to installation sites. Shellac or paint dial markings or mechanism exteriors, using brushes or spray guns.

Personality Type: Realistic. Realistic occupations frequently involve work activities that include practical, hands-on problems and solutions. They often deal with plants; animals; and real-world materials such as wood, tools, and machinery. Many of the occupations require working outside and do not involve a lot of paperwork or working closely with others.

GOE—Interest Area: 11. Information Technology. **Work Group:** 11.03. Digital Equipment Repair. **Other Jobs in This Work Group:** Computer, Automated Teller, and Office Machine Repairers.

Skills—Repairing: Repairing machines or systems by using the needed tools. **Installation:** Installing equipment, machines, wiring, or programs to meet specifications. **Equipment Maintenance:** Performing routine maintenance on equipment and determining when and what kind of maintenance is needed.

Education and Training Program: Electrical/Electronics Maintenance and Repair Technology, Other. **Related Knowledge/Courses: Mechanical Devices:** Machines and tools, including their designs, uses, repair, and maintenance.

Work Environment: Indoors; standing; kneeling, crouching, stooping, or crawling; using hands on objects, tools, or controls; bending or twisting the body; repetitive motions.

Commercial and Industrial Designers

- Education/Training Required: Bachelor's degree
- Annual Earnings: $52,200
- Growth: 10.8%
- Annual Job Openings: 7,000
- Self-Employed: 30.1%
- Part-Time: 21.3%

Level of Solitary Work: 65.5 (out of 100)

Level of Contact with Others: 77.8 (out of 100)

Develop and design manufactured products, such as cars, home appliances, and children's toys. Combine artistic talent with research on product use, marketing, and materials to create the most functional and appealing product design. Prepare sketches of ideas, detailed drawings, illustrations, artwork, or blueprints, using drafting instruments, paints and brushes, or computer-aided design equipment. Direct and coordinate the fabrication of models or samples and the drafting of working drawings and specification sheets from sketches. Modify and refine designs, using working models, to conform with customer specifications, production limitations, or changes in design trends. Coordinate the look and function of product lines. Confer with engineering, marketing, production, or sales departments, or with customers, to establish and evaluate design concepts for manufactured products. Present designs and reports to customers or design committees for approval and discuss need for modification. Evaluate feasibility of design ideas based on factors such as appearance, safety, function, serviceability, budget, production costs/methods, and market characteristics. Read publications, attend showings, and study competing products and design styles and motifs to obtain perspective and generate design concepts. Research production specifications, costs, production materials, and manufacturing methods and provide cost estimates and itemized production requirements. Design graphic material for use as ornamentation, illustration, or advertising on manufactured materials and packaging or containers. Develop manufacturing procedures and monitor the manufacture of their designs in a factory to improve operations and product quality. Supervise assistants' work throughout the design process. Fabricate models or samples in paper, wood, glass, fabric, plastic, metal, or other materials, using hand or power tools. Investigate product characteristics such as the product's safety and handling qualities; its market appeal; how efficiently it can be produced; and ways of distributing, using, and maintaining it. Develop industrial standards and regulatory guidelines. Participate in new product planning or market research, including studying the potential need for new products. Advise corporations on issues involving corporate image projects or problems.

Personality Type: Artistic. Artistic occupations frequently involve working with forms, designs, and patterns. They often require self-expression, and the work can be done without following a clear set of rules.

GOE—Interest Area: 03. Arts and Communication. **Work Group:** 03.05. Design. **Other Jobs in This Work Group:** Fashion Designers; Floral Designers; Graphic Designers; Interior Designers; Merchandise Displayers and Window Trimmers; Set and Exhibit Designers.

Skills—Technology Design: Generating or adapting equipment and technology to serve user needs. **Operations Analysis:** Analyzing needs and product requirements to create a design. **Quality Control Analysis:** Conducting tests and inspections of products, services, or processes to evaluate quality or performance. **Troubleshooting:** Determining causes of operating errors and deciding what to do about them. **Installation:** Installing equipment, machines, wiring, or programs to meet specifications. **Systems Evaluation:** Identifying measures or indicators of system performance and the actions needed to improve or correct performance relative to the goals of the system.

Education and Training Programs: Commercial and Advertising Art; Design and Applied Arts, Other; Design and Visual Communications, General; Industrial Design. **Related Knowledge/Courses: Design:** Design techniques, tools, and principles involved in production of precision technical plans, blueprints, drawings, and models. **Engineering and Technology:** The practical application of engineering science and technology. This includes applying principles, techniques, procedures, and equipment to the design and production of various goods and services. **Mathematics:** Arithmetic, algebra, geometry, calculus, and statistics and their applications. **Production and Processing:** Raw materials, production processes, quality control, costs, and other techniques for maximizing the effective manufacture and distribution of goods. **Physics:** Physical principles and laws and their interrelationships and applications to understanding fluid, material, and atmospheric dynamics and mechanical, electrical, atomic, and subatomic structures and processes. **Mechanical Devices:** Machines and tools, including their designs, uses, repair, and maintenance.

Work Environment: Indoors; sitting; using hands on objects, tools, or controls; repetitive motions.

Commercial Divers

◎ Education/Training Required: Moderate-term on-the-job training

◎ Annual Earnings: $37,960

◎ Growth: 9.4%

◎ Annual Job Openings: Fewer than 500

◎ Self-Employed: 6.6%

◎ Part-Time: 13.9%

Level of Solitary Work: 53.0 (out of 100)

Level of Contact with Others: 33.2 (out of 100)

Work below surface of water, using scuba gear to inspect, repair, remove, or install equipment and structures. May use a variety of power and hand tools, such as drills, sledgehammers, torches, and welding equipment. May conduct tests or experiments, rig explosives, or photograph structures or marine life. Perform activities related to underwater search and rescue, salvage, recovery, and cleanup operations. Take appropriate safety precautions, such as monitoring dive lengths and depths and registering with authorities before diving expeditions begin. Set or guide placement of pilings and sandbags to provide support for structures such as docks, bridges, cofferdams, and platforms. Salvage wrecked ships or their cargo, using pneumatic power velocity and hydraulic tools and explosive charges when necessary. Repair ships, bridge foundations, and other structures below the water line, using caulk, bolts, and hand tools. Remove obstructions from strainers and marine railway or launching ways, using pneumatic and power hand tools. Inspect and test docks; ships; buoyage systems; plant intakes and outflows; and underwater pipelines, cables, and sewers, using closed-circuit television, still photography, and testing equipment. Perform offshore oil and gas exploration and extraction duties such as conducting underwater surveys and repairing and maintaining drilling rigs and platforms. Install, inspect, clean, and repair piping and valves. Carry out non-destructive testing such as tests for cracks on the legs of oil rigs at sea. Check and maintain diving equipment such as helmets, masks, air tanks, harnesses, and gauges. Communicate with workers on the surface while underwater, using signal lines or telephones. Cut and weld steel, using underwater welding equipment, jigs, and supports. Descend into water with the aid of diver helpers, using scuba gear or diving suits. Recover objects by placing rigging around sunken objects; hooking rigging to crane lines; and operating winches, derricks, or cranes to raise objects. Install pilings or footings for piers and bridges. Supervise and train other divers, including hobby divers. Obtain information about diving tasks and environmental conditions. Remove rubbish and pollution from the sea. Cultivate and harvest marine species and perform routine work on fish farms. Set up dive sites for recreational instruction. Drill holes in rock and rig explosives for underwater demolitions.

Personality Type: Realistic. Realistic occupations frequently involve work activities that include practical, hands-on problems and solutions. They often deal with plants; animals; and real-world materials such as wood, tools, and machinery. Many of the occupations require working outside and do not involve a lot of paperwork or working closely with others.

GOE—Interest Area: 02. Architecture and Construction. **Work Group:** 02.04. Construction Crafts. **Other Jobs in This Work Group:** Boilermakers; Brickmasons and Blockmasons; Carpet Installers; Cement Masons and Concrete Finishers; Construction Carpenters; Crane and Tower Operators; Drywall and Ceiling Tile Installers; Electricians; Fence Erectors; Floor Layers, Except Carpet, Wood, and Hard Tiles; Floor Sanders and Finishers; Glaziers; Hazardous Materials Removal Workers; Insulation Workers, Floor, Ceiling, and Wall; Insulation Workers, Mechanical; Manufactured Building and Mobile Home Installers; Operating Engineers and Other Construction Equipment Operators; Painters, Construction and Maintenance; Paperhangers; Paving, Surfacing, and Tamping

Equipment Operators; Pile-Driver Operators; Pipe Fitters and Steamfitters; Pipelayers; Plasterers and Stucco Masons; Plumbers; Plumbers, Pipefitters, and Steamfitters; Rail-Track Laying and Maintenance Equipment Operators; Refractory Materials Repairers, Except Brickmasons; Reinforcing Iron and Rebar Workers; Riggers; Roofers; Rough Carpenters; Security and Fire Alarm Systems Installers; Segmental Pavers; Sheet Metal Workers; Stone Cutters and Carvers, Manufacturing; Stonemasons; Structural Iron and Steel Workers; Tapers; Terrazzo Workers and Finishers; Tile and Marble Setters.

Skills—Repairing: Repairing machines or systems by using the needed tools. **Installation:** Installing equipment, machines, wiring, or programs to meet specifications.

Education and Training Program: Diver, Professional and Instructor Training. **Related Knowledge/Courses: Building and Construction:** The materials, methods, and tools involved in the construction or repair of houses, buildings, or other structures such as highways and roads. **Mechanical Devices:** Machines and tools, including their designs, uses, repair, and maintenance. **Physics:** Physical principles and laws and their interrelationships and applications to understanding fluid, material, and atmospheric dynamics and mechanical, electrical, atomic, and subatomic structures and processes. **Engineering and Technology:** The practical application of engineering science and technology. This includes applying principles, techniques, procedures, and equipment to the design and production of various goods and services.

Work Environment: Outdoors; very hot or cold; very bright or dim lighting; minor burns, cuts, bites, or stings; kneeling, crouching, stooping, or crawling; using hands on objects, tools, or controls.

Computer Programmers

- Education/Training Required: Bachelor's degree
- Annual Earnings: $63,420
- Growth: 2.0%
- Annual Job Openings: 28,000
- Self-Employed: 4.5%
- Part-Time: 6.0%

Level of Solitary Work: 59.2 (out of 100)

Level of Contact with Others: 79.8 (out of 100)

Convert project specifications and statements of problems and procedures to detailed logical flow charts for coding into computer language. Develop and write computer programs to store, locate, and retrieve specific documents, data, and information. May program Web sites. Correct errors by making appropriate changes and rechecking the program to ensure that the desired results are produced. Conduct trial runs of programs and software applications to be sure that they will produce the desired information and that the instructions are correct. Compile and write documentation of program development and subsequent revisions, inserting comments in the coded instructions so others can understand the program. Write, update, and maintain computer programs or software packages to handle specific jobs such as tracking inventory, storing or retrieving data, or controlling other equipment. Consult with managerial, engineering, and technical personnel to clarify program intent, identify problems, and suggest changes. Perform or direct revision, repair, or expansion of existing programs to increase operating efficiency or adapt to new requirements. Write, analyze, review, and rewrite programs, using workflow chart and diagram and applying knowledge of computer capabilities, subject matter, and symbolic logic. Write or contribute to instructions or manuals to guide end users. Investigate whether networks, workstations, the central processing unit of the system, or peripheral equipment are responding to a program's instructions. Prepare detailed workflow charts and diagrams that describe input, output, and logical operation and convert them into a series of instructions coded in a computer language. Perform systems analysis and programming tasks to maintain and control the use of computer systems software as a systems programmer. Consult with and assist computer operators or system analysts to define and resolve problems in running computer programs. Assign, coordinate, and review work and activities of programming personnel. Collaborate with computer manufacturers and other users to develop new programming methods. Train subordinates in programming and program coding.

Personality Type: Investigative. Investigative occupations frequently involve working with ideas and require an extensive amount of thinking. These occupations can involve searching for facts and figuring out problems mentally.

GOE—Interest Area: 11. Information Technology. **Work Group:** 11.02. Information Technology Specialties. **Other Jobs in This Work Group:** Computer and Information Scientists, Research; Computer Operators; Computer Security Specialists; Computer Software Engineers, Applications; Computer Software Engineers, Systems Software; Computer Support Specialists; Computer Systems Analysts; Computer Systems Engineers/Architects; Database Administrators; Network Designers; Network Systems and Data Communications Analysts; Software Quality Assurance Engineers and Testers; Web Administrators; Web Developers.

Skills—Programming: Writing computer programs for various purposes. **Operations Analysis:** Analyzing needs and product requirements to create a design. **Technology Design:** Generating or adapting equipment and technology to serve user needs. **Systems Analysis:** Determining how a system should work and how changes in conditions, operations, and the environment will affect outcomes. **Troubleshooting:** Determining causes of operating errors and deciding

what to do about them. **Installation:** Installing equipment, machines, wiring, or programs to meet specifications.

Education and Training Programs: Artificial Intelligence and Robotics; Bioinformatics; Computer Graphics; Computer Programming, Specific Applications; Computer Programming, Vendor/Product Certification; Computer Programming/Programmer, General; E-Commerce/Electronic Commerce; Management Information Systems, General; Medical Informatics; Medical Office Computer Specialist/Assistant Training; Web Page, Digital/Multimedia, and Information Resources Design; Web/Multimedia Management and Webmaster Training. **Related Knowledge/Courses: Computers and Electronics:** Circuit boards, processors, chips, electronic equipment, and computer hardware and software, including applications and programming. **Design:** Design techniques, tools, and principles involved in production of precision technical plans, blueprints, drawings, and models. **Mathematics:** Arithmetic, algebra, geometry, calculus, and statistics and their applications. **Telecommunications:** Transmission, broadcasting, switching, control, and operation of telecommunications systems. **Economics and Accounting:** Economic and accounting principles and practices, the financial markets, banking, and the analysis and reporting of financial data. **Engineering and Technology:** The practical application of engineering science and technology. This includes applying principles, techniques, procedures, and equipment to the design and production of various goods and services.

Work Environment: Indoors; sitting; using hands on objects, tools, or controls; repetitive motions.

Computer Software Engineers, Applications

- ◎ Education/Training Required: Bachelor's degree
- ◎ Annual Earnings: $77,090
- ◎ Growth: 48.4%
- ◎ Annual Job Openings: 54,000
- ◎ Self-Employed: 2.4%
- ◎ Part-Time: 2.5%

Level of Solitary Work: 56.3 (out of 100)

Level of Contact with Others: 67.3 (out of 100)

Develop, create, and modify general computer applications software or specialized utility programs. Analyze user needs and develop software solutions. Design software or customize software for client use with the aim of optimizing operational efficiency. May analyze and design databases within an application area, working individually or coordinating database development as part of a team. Confer with systems analysts, engineers, programmers, and others to design system and to obtain information on project limitations and capabilities, performance requirements, and interfaces. Modify existing software to correct errors, allow it to adapt to new hardware, or improve its performance. Analyze user needs and software requirements to determine feasibility of design within time and cost constraints. Consult with customers about software system design and maintenance. Coordinate software system installation and monitor equipment functioning to ensure specifications are met. Design, develop, and modify software systems, using scientific analysis and mathematical models to predict and measure outcome and consequences of design. Develop and direct software system testing and validation procedures, programming, and documentation. Analyze information to determine, recommend, and plan computer specifications and layouts and peripheral equipment modi-

fications. Supervise the work of programmers, technologists, and technicians and other engineering and scientific personnel. Obtain and evaluate information on factors such as reporting formats required, costs, and security needs to determine hardware configuration. Determine system performance standards. Train users to use new or modified equipment. Store, retrieve, and manipulate data for analysis of system capabilities and requirements. Specify power supply requirements and configuration. Recommend purchase of equipment to control dust, temperature, and humidity in area of system installation.

Personality Type: Investigative. Investigative occupations frequently involve working with ideas and require an extensive amount of thinking. These occupations can involve searching for facts and figuring out problems mentally.

GOE—Interest Area: 11. Information Technology. **Work Group:** 11.02. Information Technology Specialties. **Other Jobs in This Work Group:** Computer and Information Scientists, Research; Computer Operators; Computer Programmers; Computer Security Specialists; Computer Software Engineers, Systems Software; Computer Support Specialists; Computer Systems Analysts; Computer Systems Engineers/Architects; Database Administrators; Network Designers; Network Systems and Data Communications Analysts; Software Quality Assurance Engineers and Testers; Web Administrators; Web Developers.

Skills—Programming: Writing computer programs for various purposes. **Troubleshooting:** Determining causes of operating errors and deciding what to do about them. **Technology Design:** Generating or adapting equipment and technology to serve user needs. **Systems Analysis:** Determining how a system should work and how changes in conditions, operations, and the environment will affect outcomes. **Quality Control Analysis:** Conducting tests and inspections of products, services, or processes to evaluate quality or performance. **Operations Analysis:** Analyzing needs and product requirements to create a design.

Education and Training Programs: Artificial Intelligence and Robotics; Bioinformatics; Computer Engineering Technologies/Technician Training, Other; Computer Engineering, General; Computer Science; Computer Software Engineering; Information Technology; Medical Illustration and Informatics, Other; Medical Informatics. **Related Knowledge/Courses: Computers and Electronics:** Circuit boards, processors, chips, electronic equipment, and computer hardware and software, including applications and programming. **Telecommunications:** Transmission, broadcasting, switching, control, and operation of telecommunications systems. **Engineering and Technology:** The practical application of engineering science and technology. This includes applying principles, techniques, procedures, and equipment to the design and production of various goods and services. **Design:** Design techniques, tools, and principles involved in production of precision technical plans, blueprints, drawings, and models. **Mathematics:** Arithmetic, algebra, geometry, calculus, and statistics and their applications. **Physics:** Physical principles and laws and their interrelationships and applications to understanding fluid, material, and atmospheric dynamics and mechanical, electrical, atomic, and subatomic structures and processes.

Work Environment: Indoors; sitting; using hands on objects, tools, or controls; repetitive motions.

Computer Software Engineers, Systems Software

- Education/Training Required: Bachelor's degree
- Annual Earnings: $82,120
- Growth: 43.0%
- Annual Job Openings: 37,000
- Self-Employed: 2.4%
- Part-Time: 2.5%

Level of Solitary Work: 56.3 (out of 100)

Level of Contact with Others: 79.5 (out of 100)

Research, design, develop, and test operating systems-level software, compilers, and network distribution software for medical, industrial, military, communications, aerospace, business, scientific, and general computing applications. Set operational specifications and formulate and analyze software requirements. Apply principles and techniques of computer science, engineering, and mathematical analysis. Modify existing software to correct errors, to adapt it to new hardware, or to upgrade interfaces and improve performance. Design and develop software systems, using scientific analysis and mathematical models to predict and measure outcome and consequences of design. Consult with engineering staff to evaluate interface between hardware and software, develop specifications and performance requirements, and resolve customer problems. Analyze information to determine, recommend, and plan installation of a new system or modification of an existing system. Develop and direct software system testing and validation procedures. Direct software programming and development of documentation. Consult with customers or other departments on project status, proposals, and technical issues such as software system design and maintenance. Advise customer about, or perform, maintenance of software system. Coordinate installation of software system. Monitor functioning of equipment to ensure system operates in conformance with specifications. Store, retrieve, and manipulate data for analysis of system capabilities and requirements. Confer with data processing and project managers to obtain information on limitations and capabilities for data-processing projects. Prepare reports and correspondence concerning project specifications, activities, and status. Evaluate factors such as reporting formats required, cost constraints, and need for security restrictions to determine hardware configuration. Supervise and assign work to programmers, designers, technologists and technicians, and other engineering and scientific personnel. Train users to use new or modified equipment. Utilize microcontrollers to develop control signals; implement control algorithms; and measure process variables such as temperatures, pressures, and positions. Recommend purchase of equipment to control dust, temperature, and humidity in area of system installation. Specify power supply requirements and configuration.

Personality Type: Investigative. Investigative occupations frequently involve working with ideas and require an extensive amount of thinking. These occupations can involve searching for facts and figuring out problems mentally.

GOE—Interest Area: 11. Information Technology. **Work Group:** 11.02. Information Technology Specialties. **Other Jobs in This Work Group:** Computer and Information Scientists, Research; Computer Operators; Computer Programmers; Computer Security Specialists; Computer Software Engineers, Applications; Computer Support Specialists; Computer Systems Analysts; Computer Systems Engineers/Architects; Database Administrators; Network Designers; Network Systems and Data Communications Analysts; Software Quality Assurance Engineers and Testers; Web Administrators; Web Developers.

Skills—Programming: Writing computer programs for various purposes. **Technology Design:** Generating or adapting equipment and technology to serve user needs. **Systems Analysis:** Determining how a system should work and how changes in conditions, operations, and the environment will affect outcomes. **Troubleshooting:** Determining causes of operating errors and deciding what to do about them. **Operations Analysis:** Analyzing needs and product requirements to create a design. **Complex Problem Solving:** Identifying complex problems and reviewing related information to develop and evaluate options and implement solutions.

Education and Training Programs: Artificial Intelligence and Robotics; Computer Engineering Technologies/Technician Training, Other; Computer Engineering, General; Computer Science; Information Science/Studies; Information Technology; System, Networking, and LAN/WAN Management/Manager Training. **Related Knowledge/Courses: Computers and Electronics:** Circuit boards, processors, chips, electronic equipment, and computer hardware and software, including applications and programming. **Design:** Design techniques, tools, and principles involved in production of precision technical plans, blueprints, drawings, and models. **Engineering and Technology:** The practical application of engineering science and technology. This includes applying principles, techniques, procedures, and equipment to the design and production of various goods and services. **Telecommunications:** Transmission, broadcasting, switching, control, and operation of telecommunications systems. **Mathematics:** Arithmetic, algebra, geometry, calculus, and statistics and their applications. **Education and Training:** Principles and methods for curriculum and training design, teaching and instruction for individuals and groups, and the measurement of training effects.

Work Environment: Indoors; sitting; using hands on objects, tools, or controls; repetitive motions.

Computer Systems Analysts

- ◎ Education/Training Required: Bachelor's degree
- ◎ Annual Earnings: $68,300
- ◎ Growth: 31.4%
- ◎ Annual Job Openings: 56,000
- ◎ Self-Employed: 5.0%
- ◎ Part-Time: 6.2%

Level of Solitary Work: 62.5 (out of 100)

Level of Contact with Others: 74.0 (out of 100)

Analyze science, engineering, business, and all other data-processing problems for application to electronic data-processing systems. Analyze user requirements, procedures, and problems to automate or improve existing systems and review computer system capabilities, workflow, and scheduling limitations. May analyze or recommend commercially available software. May supervise computer programmers. Provide staff and users with assistance solving computer-related problems, such as malfunctions and program problems. Test, maintain, and monitor computer programs and systems, including coordinating the installation of computer programs and systems. Use object-oriented programming languages as well as client and server applications development processes and multimedia and Internet technology. Confer with clients regarding the nature of the information processing or computation needs a computer program is to address. Coordinate and link the computer systems within an organization to increase compatibility and so information can be shared. Consult with management to ensure agreement on system principles. Expand or modify system to serve new purposes or improve workflow. Interview or survey workers, observe job performance, or perform the job to determine what informa-

tion is processed and how it is processed. Determine computer software or hardware needed to set up or alter system. Train staff and users to work with computer systems and programs. Analyze information processing or computation needs and plan and design computer systems, using techniques such as structured analysis, data modeling, and information engineering. Assess the usefulness of pre-developed application packages and adapt them to a user environment. Define the goals of the system and devise flow charts and diagrams describing logical operational steps of programs. Develop, document, and revise system design procedures, test procedures, and quality standards. Review and analyze computer printouts and performance indicators to locate code problems; correct errors by correcting codes. Recommend new equipment or software packages. Read manuals, periodicals, and technical reports to learn how to develop programs that meet staff and user requirements. Supervise computer programmers or other systems analysts or serve as project leaders for particular systems projects. Utilize the computer in the analysis and solution of business problems such as development of integrated production and inventory control and cost analysis systems.

Personality Type: Investigative. Investigative occupations frequently involve working with ideas and require an extensive amount of thinking. These occupations can involve searching for facts and figuring out problems mentally.

GOE—Interest Area: 11. Information Technology. **Work Group:** 11.02. Information Technology Specialties. **Other Jobs in This Work Group:** Computer and Information Scientists, Research; Computer Operators; Computer Programmers; Computer Security Specialists; Computer Software Engineers, Applications; Computer Software Engineers, Systems Software; Computer Support Specialists; Computer Systems Engineers/Architects; Database Administrators; Network Designers; Network Systems and Data Communications Analysts; Software Quality Assurance Engineers and Testers; Web Administrators; Web Developers.

Skills—**Installation:** Installing equipment, machines, wiring, or programs to meet specifications. **Quality Control Analysis:** Conducting tests and inspections of products, services, or processes to evaluate quality or performance. **Systems Analysis:** Determining how a system should work and how changes in conditions, operations, and the environment will affect outcomes. **Programming:** Writing computer programs for various purposes. **Technology Design:** Generating or adapting equipment and technology to serve user needs. **Troubleshooting:** Determining causes of operating errors and deciding what to do about them.

Education and Training Programs: Computer and Information Sciences, General; Computer Systems Analysis/Analyst Training; Information Technology; Web/Multimedia Management and Webmaster Training. **Related Knowledge/Courses: Computers and Electronics:** Circuit boards, processors, chips, electronic equipment, and computer hardware and software, including applications and programming. **Telecommunications:** Transmission, broadcasting, switching, control, and operation of telecommunications systems. **Design:** Design techniques, tools, and principles involved in production of precision technical plans, blueprints, drawings, and models. **Customer and Personal Service:** Principles and processes for providing customer and personal services. This includes customer needs assessment, meeting quality standards for services, and evaluation of customer satisfaction. **Law and Government:** Laws, legal codes, court procedures, precedents, government regulations, executive orders, agency rules, and the democratic political process. **Education and Training:** Principles and methods for curriculum and training design, teaching and instruction for individuals and groups, and the measurement of training effects.

Work Environment: Indoors; sitting.

Computer, Automated Teller, and Office Machine Repairers

- Education/Training Required: Postsecondary vocational training
- Annual Earnings: $36,060
- Growth: 3.8%
- Annual Job Openings: 31,000
- Self-Employed: 13.7%
- Part-Time: 9.9%

Level of Solitary Work: 64.0 (out of 100)

Level of Contact with Others: 86.7 (out of 100)

Repair, maintain, or install computers; word-processing systems; automated teller machines;, and electronic office machines, such as duplicating and fax machines. Converse with customers to determine details of equipment problems. Reassemble machines after making repairs or replacing parts. Travel to customers' stores or offices to service machines or to provide emergency repair service. Reinstall software programs or adjust settings on existing software to fix machine malfunctions. Advise customers concerning equipment operation, maintenance, and programming. Assemble machines according to specifications, using hand tools, power tools, and measuring devices. Test new systems to ensure that they are in working order. Operate machines to test functioning of parts and mechanisms. Maintain records of equipment maintenance work and repairs. Install and configure new equipment, including operating software and peripheral equipment. Maintain parts inventories and order any additional parts needed for repairs. Update existing equipment, performing tasks such as installing updated circuit boards or additional memory. Test components and circuits of faulty equipment to locate defects, using oscilloscopes, signal generators, ammeters, voltmeters, or special diagnostic software programs. Align, adjust, and calibrate equipment according to specifications. Repair, adjust, or replace electrical and mechanical components and parts, using hand tools, power tools, and soldering or welding equipment. Complete repair bills, shop records, time cards, and expense reports. Disassemble machine to examine parts such as wires, gears, and bearings for wear and defects, using hand tools, power tools, and measuring devices. Clean, oil, and adjust mechanical parts to maintain machines' operating efficiency and to prevent breakdowns. Enter information into computers to copy programs from one electronic component to another or to draw, modify, or store schematics. Read specifications such as blueprints, charts, and schematics to determine machine settings and adjustments. Lay cable and hook up electrical connections between machines, power sources, and phone lines. Analyze equipment performance records to assess equipment functioning.

Personality Type: Realistic. Realistic occupations frequently involve work activities that include practical, hands-on problems and solutions. They often deal with plants; animals; and real-world materials such as wood, tools, and machinery. Many of the occupations require working outside and do not involve a lot of paperwork or working closely with others.

GOE—Interest Area: 11. Information Technology. **Work Group:** 11.03. Digital Equipment Repair. **Other Jobs in This Work Group:** Coin, Vending, and Amusement Machine Servicers and Repairers.

Skills—Installation: Installing equipment, machines, wiring, or programs to meet specifications. **Repairing:** Repairing machines or systems by using the needed tools. **Troubleshooting:** Determining causes of operating errors and deciding what to do about them. **Equipment Maintenance:** Performing routine maintenance on equipment and determining when and what kind of maintenance is needed. **Management of Material Resources:** Obtaining and seeing to the appropriate use of equipment, facilities, and materials needed to do certain work. **Programming:** Writing computer programs for various purposes.

Education and Training Programs: Business Machine Repair; Computer Installation and Repair Technology/Technician Training. **Related Knowledge/Courses: Computers and Electronics:** Circuit boards, processors, chips, electronic equipment, and computer hardware and software, including applications and programming. **Telecommunications:** Transmission, broadcasting, switching, control, and operation of telecommunications systems. **Customer and Personal Service:** Principles and processes for providing customer and personal services. This includes customer needs assessment, meeting quality standards for services, and evaluation of customer satisfaction. **Mechanical Devices:** Machines and tools, including their designs, uses, repair, and maintenance. **Engineering and Technology:** The practical application of engineering science and technology. This includes applying principles, techniques, procedures, and equipment to the design and production of various goods and services. **Sales and Marketing:** Principles and methods for showing, promoting, and selling products or services. This includes marketing strategy and tactics, product demonstration, sales techniques, and sales control systems.

Work Environment: Indoors; sitting; using hands on objects, tools, or controls; repetitive motions.

Computer-Controlled Machine Tool Operators, Metal and Plastic

- Education/Training Required: Moderate-term on-the-job training
- Annual Earnings: $31,010
- Growth: –1.2%
- Annual Job Openings: 13,000
- Self-Employed: 0.0%
- Part-Time: 0.3%

Level of Solitary Work: 62.5 (out of 100)

Level of Contact with Others: 66.0 (out of 100)

Operate computer-controlled machines or robots to perform one or more machine functions on metal or plastic workpieces. Measure dimensions of finished workpieces to ensure conformance to specifications, using precision measuring instruments, templates, and fixtures. Remove and replace dull cutting tools. Mount, install, align, and secure tools, attachments, fixtures, and workpieces on machines, using hand tools and precision measuring instruments. Listen to machines during operation to detect sounds such as those made by dull cutting tools or excessive vibration and adjust machines to compensate for problems. Adjust machine feed and speed, change cutting tools, or adjust machine controls when automatic programming is faulty or if machines malfunction. Stop machines to remove finished workpieces or to change tooling, setup, or workpiece placement according to required machining sequences. Lift workpieces to machines manually or with hoists or cranes. Modify cutting programs to account for problems encountered during operation and save modified programs. Calculate machine speed and feed ratios and the size and position of cuts. Insert control instructions into machine control units to start operation. Check to ensure that workpieces are properly lubricated and cooled during machine operation. Input initial part dimensions into machine control panels. Set up and operate computer-controlled machines or robots to perform one or more machine functions on metal or plastic workpieces. Confer with supervisors or programmers to resolve machine malfunctions and production errors and to obtain approval to continue production. Review program specifications or blueprints to determine and set machine operations and sequencing, finished workpiece dimensions, or numerical control sequences. Monitor machine operation and control panel displays and compare readings to specifications to detect malfunctions. Control coolant systems. Maintain machines and remove and replace broken or worn machine tools, using hand tools. Stack or load finished items or place items on conveyor systems. Clean machines, tooling, and parts, using solvents or solutions and rags. Enter commands or load control media such as tapes, cards, or disks into machine controllers to retrieve programmed instructions.

Personality Type: Realistic. Realistic occupations frequently involve work activities that include practical, hands-on problems and solutions. They often deal with plants; animals; and real-world materials such as wood, tools, and machinery. Many of the occupations require working outside and do not involve a lot of paperwork or working closely with others.

GOE—Interest Area: 13. Manufacturing. **Work Group:** 13.05. Production Machining Technology. **Other Jobs in This Work Group:** Foundry Mold and Coremakers; Lay-Out Workers, Metal and Plastic; Machinists; Model Makers, Metal and Plastic; Numerical Tool and Process Control Programmers; Patternmakers, Metal and Plastic; Tool and Die Makers; Tool Grinders, Filers, and Sharpeners.

Skills—Operation Monitoring: Watching gauges, dials, or other indicators to make sure a machine is working properly. **Operation and Control:** Controlling operations of equipment or systems. **Equipment Maintenance:** Performing routine maintenance on equipment and determining when and what kind of maintenance is needed. **Quality Control Analysis:** Conducting tests and inspections of products, services, or processes to evaluate quality or performance. **Programming:** Writing computer programs for various purposes. **Troubleshooting:** Determining causes of operating errors and deciding what to do about them.

Education and Training Program: Machine Shop Technology/Assistant. **Related Knowledge/Courses: Mechanical Devices:** Machines and tools, including their designs, uses, repair, and maintenance. **Production and Processing:** Raw materials, production processes, quality control, costs, and other techniques for maximizing the effective manufacture and distribution of goods. **Engineering and Technology:** The practical application of engineering science and technology. This includes applying principles, techniques, procedures, and equipment to the design and production of various goods and services. **Design:** Design techniques, tools, and principles involved in production of precision technical plans, blueprints, drawings, and models. **Mathematics:** Arithmetic, algebra, geometry, calculus, and statistics and their applications. **Computers and Electronics:** Circuit boards, processors, chips, electronic equipment, and computer hardware and software, including applications and programming.

Work Environment: Noisy; contaminants; hazardous equipment; standing; using hands on objects, tools, or controls; repetitive motions.

Conservation Scientists

See the descriptions of these jobs:

- Park Naturalists
- Range Managers
- Soil and Water Conservationists

Control and Valve Installers and Repairers, Except Mechanical Door

- Education/Training Required: Moderate-term on-the-job training
- Annual Earnings: $44,120
- Growth: 4.9%
- Annual Job Openings: 4,000
- Self-Employed: 0.0%
- Part-Time: No data available

Level of Solitary Work: 76.0 (out of 100)

Level of Contact with Others: 79.3 (out of 100)

Install, repair, and maintain mechanical regulating and controlling devices, such as electric meters, gas regulators, thermostats, safety and flow valves, and other mechanical governors. Turn meters on or off to establish or close service. Turn valves to allow measured amounts of air or gas to pass through meters at specified flow rates. Report hazardous field situations and damaged or missing meters. Record meter readings and installation data on meter cards, work orders, or field service orders or enter data into handheld computers. Connect regulators to test stands and turn screw adjustments until gauges indicate that inlet and outlet pressures meet specifications. Disassemble and repair mechanical control devices or valves, such as regulators, thermostats, or hydrants, using power tools, hand tools, and cutting torches. Record maintenance information, including test results, material usage, and repairs made. Disconnect and/or remove defective or unauthorized meters, using hand tools. Lubricate wearing surfaces of mechanical parts, using oils or other lubricants. Test valves and regulators for leaks and accurate temperature and pressure settings, using precision testing equipment. Install regulators and related equipment such as gas meters, odorization units, and gas pressure telemetering equipment. Shut off service and notify repair crews when major repairs are required, such as the replacement of underground pipes or wiring. Examine valves or mechanical control device parts for defects, dents, or loose attachments and mark malfunctioning areas of defective units. Attach air hoses to meter inlets; then plug outlets and observe gauges for pressure losses to test internal seams for leaks. Dismantle meters and replace or adjust defective parts such as cases, shafts, gears, disks, and recording mechanisms, using soldering irons and hand tools. Advise customers on proper installation of valves or regulators and related equipment. Connect hoses from provers to meter inlets and outlets and raise prover bells until prover gauges register zero. Make adjustments to meter components, such as setscrews or timing mechanisms, so that they conform to specifications. Replace defective parts, such as bellows, range springs, and toggle switches, and reassemble units according to blueprints, using cam presses and hand tools.

Personality Type: Realistic. Realistic occupations frequently involve work activities that include practical, hands-on problems and solutions. They often deal with plants; animals; and real-world materials such as wood, tools, and machinery. Many of the occupations require working outside and do not involve a lot of paperwork or working closely with others.

GOE—Interest Area: 13. Manufacturing. **Work Group:** 13.13. Machinery Repair. **Other Jobs in This Work Group:** Bicycle Repairers; Home Appliance Repairers; Industrial Machinery Mechanics; Locksmiths and Safe Repairers; Maintenance Workers, Machinery; Mechanical Door Repairers; Millwrights; Signal and Track Switch Repairers.

Skills—Installation: Installing equipment, machines, wiring, or programs to meet specifications. **Repairing:** Repairing machines or systems by using the needed tools. **Equipment Maintenance:** Performing routine maintenance on equipment and determining when and what kind of maintenance is needed. **Operation Monitoring:** Watching gauges, dials, or other indicators to make sure a machine is working properly. **Troubleshooting:** Determining causes of operating errors and deciding what to do about them. **Quality Control Analysis:** Conducting tests and inspections of products, services, or processes to evaluate quality or performance.

Education and Training Program: Instrumentation Technology/Technician Training. **Related Knowledge/Courses: Mechanical Devices:** Machines and tools, including their designs, uses, repair, and maintenance. **Transportation:** Principles and methods for moving people or goods by air, rail, sea, or road, including the relative costs and benefits. **Public Safety and Security:** Relevant equipment, policies, procedures, and strategies to promote effective local, state, or national security operations for the protection of people, data, property, and institutions. **Physics:** Physical principles and laws and their interrelationships and applications to understanding fluid, material, and atmospheric dynamics and mechanical, electrical, atomic, and subatomic structures and processes. **Design:** Design techniques, tools, and

principles involved in production of precision technical plans, blueprints, drawings, and models. **Chemistry:** The chemical composition, structure, and properties of substances and of the chemical processes and transformations that they undergo. This includes uses of chemicals and their danger signs, production techniques, and disposal methods.

Work Environment: Outdoors; very hot or cold; very bright or dim lighting; contaminants; cramped work space, awkward positions; hazardous conditions.

Copy Writers

This job can be found in the Part II lists under the title Writers and Authors.

- ◉ Education/Training Required: Bachelor's degree
- ◉ Annual Earnings: $46,420
- ◉ Growth: 17.7%
- ◉ Annual Job Openings: 14,000
- ◉ Self-Employed: 67.7%
- ◉ Part-Time: 30.7%

The job openings listed here are shared with Poets, Lyricists, and Creative Writers.

Level of Solitary Work: 72.6 (out of 100)

Level of Contact with Others: 67.4 (out of 100)

Write advertising copy for use by publication or broadcast media to promote sale of goods and services. Write advertising copy for use by publication, broadcast, or Internet media to promote the sale of goods and services. Present drafts and ideas to clients. Discuss with the client the product, advertising themes and methods, and any changes that should be made in advertising copy. Consult with sales, media, and marketing representatives to obtain information on product or service and discuss style and length of advertising copy. Vary language and tone of messages based on product and medium. Edit or rewrite existing copy as necessary and submit copy for approval by supervisor. Write to customers in their terms and on their level so that the advertiser's sales message is more readily received. Write articles; bulletins; sales letters; speeches; and other related informative, marketing, and promotional material. Invent names for products and write the slogans that appear on packaging, brochures, and other promotional material. Review advertising trends, consumer surveys, and other data regarding marketing of goods and services to determine the best way to promote products. Develop advertising campaigns for a wide range of clients, working with an advertising agency's creative director and art director to determine the best way to present advertising information. Conduct research and interviews to determine which of a product's selling features should be promoted.

Personality Type: Artistic. Artistic occupations frequently involve working with forms, designs, and patterns. They often require self-expression, and the work can be done without following a clear set of rules.

GOE—Interest Area: 03. Arts and Communication. **Work Group:** 03.02. Writing and Editing. **Other Jobs in This Work Group:** Editors; Poets, Lyricists, and Creative Writers; Technical Writers; Writers and Authors.

Skills—Persuasion: Persuading others to change their minds or behavior. **Technology Design:** Generating or adapting equipment and technology to serve user needs. **Time Management:** Managing one's own time and the time of others. **Equipment Selection:** Determining the kind of tools and equipment needed to do a job. **Quality Control Analysis:** Conducting tests and inspections of products, services, or processes to evaluate quality or performance. **Negotiation:** Bringing others together and trying to reconcile differences.

Education and Training Programs: Broadcast Journalism; Communication Studies/Speech Communication and Rhetoric; Communication, Journalism, and Related Programs, Other; English

Composition; Journalism; Mass Communication/Media Studies. **Related Knowledge/Courses: Sales and Marketing:** Principles and methods for showing, promoting, and selling products or services. This includes marketing strategy and tactics, product demonstration, sales techniques, and sales control systems. **Communications and Media:** Media production, communication, and dissemination techniques and methods. This includes alternative ways to inform and entertain via written, oral, and visual media. **Sociology and Anthropology:** Group behavior and dynamics, societal trends and influences, human migrations, ethnicity, and cultures and their history and origins. **English Language:** The structure and content of the English language, including the meaning and spelling of words, rules of composition, and grammar. **Computers and Electronics:** Circuit boards, processors, chips, electronic equipment, and computer hardware and software, including applications and programming. **Psychology:** Human behavior and performance; individual differences in ability, personality, and interests; learning and motivation; psychological research methods; and the assessment and treatment of behavioral and affective disorders.

Work Environment: Indoors; sitting; using hands on objects, tools, or controls; repetitive motions.

Cost Estimators

- Education/Training Required: Work experience in a related occupation
- Annual Earnings: $52,020
- Growth: 18.2%
- Annual Job Openings: 15,000
- Self-Employed: 2.2%
- Part-Time: 5.9%

Level of Solitary Work: 65.5 (out of 100)

Level of Contact with Others: 84.5 (out of 100)

Prepare cost estimates for product manufacturing, construction projects, or services to aid management in bidding on or determining price of product or service. May specialize according to particular service performed or type of product manufactured. Analyze blueprints and other documentation to prepare time, cost, materials, and labor estimates. Assess cost-effectiveness of products, projects, or services, tracking actual costs relative to bids as the project develops. Consult with clients, vendors, personnel in other departments, or construction foremen to discuss and formulate estimates and resolve issues. Confer with engineers, architects, owners, contractors, and subcontractors on changes and adjustments to cost estimates. Prepare estimates used by management for purposes such as planning, organizing, and scheduling work. Prepare estimates for use in selecting vendors or subcontractors. Review material and labor requirements to decide whether it is more cost-effective to produce or purchase components. Prepare cost and expenditure statements and other necessary documentation at regular intervals for the duration of the project. Prepare and maintain a directory of suppliers, contractors, and subcontractors. Set up cost-monitoring and -reporting systems and procedures. Establish and maintain tendering process and conduct negotiations. Conduct special studies to develop and establish standard hour and related cost data or to effect cost reduction. Visit site and record information about access, drainage and topography, and availability of services such as water and electricity.

Personality Type: Conventional. Conventional occupations frequently involve following set procedures and routines. These occupations can include working with data and details more than with ideas. Usually there is a clear line of authority to follow.

GOE—Interest Area: 06. Finance and Insurance. **Work Group:** 06.02. Finance/Insurance Investigation and Analysis. **Other Jobs in This Work Group:** Appraisers and Assessors of Real Estate; Appraisers, Real Estate; Assessors; Claims Adjusters, Examiners, and Investigators; Claims Examiners, Property and Casualty Insurance; Credit Analysts; Financial Analysts; Insurance Adjusters, Examiners, and Investigators; Insurance Appraisers, Auto

Damage; Insurance Underwriters; Loan Counselors; Loan Officers; Market Research Analysts; Survey Researchers.

Skills—Management of Financial Resources: Determining how money will be spent to get the work done and accounting for these expenditures. **Mathematics:** Using mathematics to solve problems. **Management of Personnel Resources:** Motivating, developing, and directing people as they work; identifying the best people for the job. **Negotiation:** Bringing others together and trying to reconcile differences. **Operations Analysis:** Analyzing needs and product requirements to create a design. **Equipment Selection:** Determining the kind of tools and equipment needed to do a job.

Education and Training Programs: Business Administration and Management, General; Business/Commerce, General; Construction Engineering; Construction Engineering Technology/Technician Training; Manufacturing Engineering; Materials Engineering; Mechanical Engineering. **Related Knowledge/Courses: Economics and Accounting:** Economic and accounting principles and practices, the financial markets, banking, and the analysis and reporting of financial data. **Production and Processing:** Raw materials, production processes, quality control, costs, and other techniques for maximizing the effective manufacture and distribution of goods. **Administration and Management:** Business and management principles involved in strategic planning, resource allocation, human resources modeling, leadership technique, production methods, and coordination of people and resources. **Sales and Marketing:** Principles and methods for showing, promoting, and selling products or services. This includes marketing strategy and tactics, product demonstration, sales techniques, and sales control systems. **Clerical Practices:** Administrative and clerical procedures and systems such as word processing, managing files and records, stenography and transcription, designing forms, and other office procedures and terminology. **Personnel and Human Resources:** Principles and procedures for personnel recruitment, selection, training, compensation and benefits, labor relations and negotiation, and personnel information systems.

Work Environment: Indoors; contaminants; sitting.

Credit Analysts

- ◎ Education/Training Required: Bachelor's degree
- ◎ Annual Earnings: $50,370
- ◎ Growth: 3.6%
- ◎ Annual Job Openings: 3,000
- ◎ Self-Employed: 0.0%
- ◎ Part-Time: 4.2%

Level of Solitary Work: 59.2 (out of 100)

Level of Contact with Others: 67.3 (out of 100)

Analyze current credit data and financial statements of individuals or firms to determine the degree of risk involved in extending credit or lending money. Prepare reports with this credit information for use in decision-making. Evaluate customer records and recommend payment plans based on earnings, savings data, payment history, and purchase activity. Confer with credit association and other business representatives to exchange credit information. Complete loan applications, including credit analyses and summaries of loan requests, and submit to loan committees for approval. Generate financial ratios, using computer programs, to evaluate customers' financial status. Review individual or commercial customer files to identify and select delinquent accounts for collection. Compare liquidity, profitability, and credit histories of establishments being evaluated with those of similar establishments in the same industries and geographic locations. Consult with customers to resolve complaints and verify financial and credit transactions. Analyze financial data such as income growth, quality of management, and market share to determine expected profitability of loans.

Personality Type: Conventional. Conventional occupations frequently involve following set procedures and routines. These occupations can include working with data and details more than with ideas. Usually there is a clear line of authority to follow.

GOE—Interest Area: 06. Finance and Insurance. **Work Group:** 06.02. Finance/Insurance Investigation and Analysis. **Other Jobs in This Work Group:** Appraisers and Assessors of Real Estate; Appraisers, Real Estate; Assessors; Claims Adjusters, Examiners, and Investigators; Claims Examiners, Property and Casualty Insurance; Cost Estimators; Financial Analysts; Insurance Adjusters, Examiners, and Investigators; Insurance Appraisers, Auto Damage; Insurance Underwriters; Loan Counselors; Loan Officers; Market Research Analysts; Survey Researchers.

Skills—Speaking: Talking to others to convey information effectively. **Writing:** Communicating effectively in writing as appropriate for the needs of the audience. **Operations Analysis:** Analyzing needs and product requirements to create a design. **Negotiation:** Bringing others together and trying to reconcile differences. **Active Listening:** Giving full attention to what other people are saying, taking time to understand the points being made, asking questions as appropriate, and not interrupting at inappropriate times. **Systems Evaluation:** Identifying measures or indicators of system performance and the actions needed to improve or correct performance relative to the goals of the system.

Education and Training Programs: Accounting; Credit Management; Finance, General. **Related Knowledge/Courses: Economics and Accounting:** Economic and accounting principles and practices, the financial markets, banking, and the analysis and reporting of financial data. **Clerical Practices:** Administrative and clerical procedures and systems such as word processing, managing files and records, stenography and transcription, designing forms, and other office procedures and terminology. **Mathematics:** Arithmetic, algebra, geometry, calculus, and statistics and their applications. **Law and**

Government: Laws, legal codes, court procedures, precedents, government regulations, executive orders, agency rules, and the democratic political process. **Administration and Management:** Business and management principles involved in strategic planning, resource allocation, human resources modeling, leadership technique, production methods, and coordination of people and resources. **Customer and Personal Service:** Principles and processes for providing customer and personal services. This includes customer needs assessment, meeting quality standards for services, and evaluation of customer satisfaction.

Work Environment: Indoors; sitting; repetitive motions.

Crossing Guards

- Education/Training Required: Short-term on-the-job training
- Annual Earnings: $20,050
- Growth: 19.7%
- Annual Job Openings: 26,000
- Self-Employed: 0.0%
- Part-Time: 53.9%

Level of Solitary Work: 71.7 (out of 100)

Level of Contact with Others: 89.5 (out of 100)

Guide or control vehicular or pedestrian traffic at such places as streets, schools, railroad crossings, or construction sites. Monitor traffic flow to locate safe gaps through which pedestrians can cross streets. Direct or escort pedestrians across streets, stopping traffic as necessary. Guide or control vehicular or pedestrian traffic at such places as street and railroad crossings and construction sites. Communicate traffic and crossing rules and other information to students and adults. Report unsafe behavior of children to school officials. Record license numbers of vehicles disregarding traffic signals and report infractions to appropriate authorities. Direct traffic movement or warn of hazards, using signs, flags, lanterns, and hand signals. Learn the location and purpose of street traffic signs within assigned patrol areas. Stop speeding vehicles to warn drivers of traffic laws. Distribute traffic control signs and markers at designated points. Discuss traffic routing plans and control point locations with superiors. Inform drivers of detour routes through construction sites.

Personality Type: Social. Social occupations frequently involve working with, communicating with, and teaching people. These occupations often involve helping or providing service to others.

GOE—Interest Area: 12. Law and Public Safety. **Work Group:** 12.05. Safety and Security. **Other Jobs in This Work Group:** Animal Control Workers; Gaming Surveillance Officers and Gaming Investigators; Lifeguards, Ski Patrol, and Other Recreational Protective Service Workers; Private Detectives and Investigators; Security Guards; Transportation Security Screeners.

Skills—None met the criteria.

Education and Training Program: Security and Protective Services, Other. **Related Knowledge/Courses: Public Safety and Security:** Relevant equipment, policies, procedures, and strategies to promote effective local, state, or national security operations for the protection of people, data, property, and institutions.

Work Environment: Outdoors; contaminants; hazardous equipment; standing; walking and running; using hands on objects, tools, or controls.

Data Entry Keyers

◎ Education/Training Required: Moderate-term on-the-job training

◎ Annual Earnings: $23,810

◎ Growth: –0.7%

◎ Annual Job Openings: 85,000

◎ Self-Employed: 1.0%

◎ Part-Time: 20.9%

Level of Solitary Work: 81.2 (out of 100)

Level of Contact with Others: 83.5 (out of 100)

Operate data entry device, such as keyboard or photo-composing perforator. Duties may include verifying data and preparing materials for printing. Read source documents such as canceled checks, sales reports, or bills and enter data in specific data fields or onto tapes or disks for subsequent entry, using keyboards or scanners. Compile, sort, and verify the accuracy of data before it is entered. Compare data with source documents or re-enter data in verification format to detect errors. Store completed documents in appropriate locations. Locate and correct data entry errors or report them to supervisors. Maintain logs of activities and completed work. Select materials needed to complete work assignments. Load machines with required input or output media such as paper, cards, disks, tape, or Braille media. Resolve garbled or indecipherable messages, using cryptographic procedures and equipment.

Personality Type: Conventional. Conventional occupations frequently involve following set procedures and routines. These occupations can include working with data and details more than with ideas. Usually there is a clear line of authority to follow.

GOE—Interest Area: 04. Business and Administration. **Work Group:** 04.08. Clerical Machine Operation. **Other Jobs in This Work Group:** Billing, Posting, and Calculating Machine Operators; Mail Clerks and Mail Machine Operators, Except Postal Service; Office Machine Operators, Except Computer; Switchboard Operators, Including Answering Service; Word Processors and Typists.

Skills—Service Orientation: Actively looking for ways to help people. **Social Perceptiveness:** Being aware of others' reactions and understanding why they react as they do.

Education and Training Programs: Business/Office Automation/Technology/Data Entry; Data Entry/Microcomputer Applications, General; Graphic and Printing Equipment Operator, General Production. **Related Knowledge/Courses: Clerical Practices:** Administrative and clerical procedures and systems such as word processing, managing files and records, stenography and transcription, designing forms, and other office procedures and terminology. **Economics and Accounting:** Economic and accounting principles and practices, the financial markets, banking, and the analysis and reporting of financial data. **Computers and Electronics:** Circuit boards, processors, chips, electronic equipment, and computer hardware and software, including applications and programming. **Customer and Personal Service:** Principles and processes for providing customer and personal services. This includes customer needs assessment, meeting quality standards for services, and evaluation of customer satisfaction. **Personnel and Human Resources:** Principles and procedures for personnel recruitment, selection, training, compensation and benefits, labor relations and negotiation, and personnel information systems. **Administration and Management:** Business and management principles involved in strategic planning, resource allocation, human resources modeling, leadership technique, production methods, and coordination of people and resources.

Work Environment: Indoors; noisy; sitting; using hands on objects, tools, or controls; repetitive motions.

Database Administrators

- Education/Training Required: Bachelor's degree
- Annual Earnings: $63,250
- Growth: 38.2%
- Annual Job Openings: 9,000
- Self-Employed: 0.5%
- Part-Time: 5.0%

Level of Solitary Work: 53.0 (out of 100)

Level of Contact with Others: 74.0 (out of 100)

Coordinate changes to computer databases; test and implement the database, applying knowledge of database management systems. May plan, coordinate, and implement security measures to safeguard computer databases. Develop standards and guidelines to guide the use and acquisition of software and to protect vulnerable information. Modify existing databases and database management systems or direct programmers and analysts to make changes. Test programs or databases, correct errors, and make necessary modifications. Plan, coordinate, and implement security measures to safeguard information in computer files against accidental or unauthorized damage, modification, or disclosure. Approve, schedule, plan, and supervise the installation and testing of new products and improvements to computer systems, such as the installation of new databases. Train users and answer questions. Establish and calculate optimum values for database parameters, using manuals and calculator. Specify users and user access levels for each segment of database. Develop data model describing data elements and how they are used, following procedures and using pen, template, or computer software. Develop methods for integrating different products so they work properly together, such as customizing commercial databases to fit specific needs. Review project requests describing data-base user needs to estimate time and cost required to accomplish project. Review procedures in database management system manuals for making changes to database. Work as part of a project team to coordinate database development and determine project scope and limitations. Select and enter codes to monitor database performance and to create production database. Identify and evaluate industry trends in database systems to serve as a source of information and advice for upper management. Write and code logical and physical database descriptions and specify identifiers of database to management system or direct others in coding descriptions. Review workflow charts developed by programmer analyst to understand tasks computer will perform, such as updating records. Revise company definition of data as defined in data dictionary.

Personality Type: Investigative. Investigative occupations frequently involve working with ideas and require an extensive amount of thinking. These occupations can involve searching for facts and figuring out problems mentally.

GOE—Interest Area: 11. Information Technology. **Work Group:** 11.02. Information Technology Specialties. **Other Jobs in This Work Group:** Computer and Information Scientists, Research; Computer Operators; Computer Programmers; Computer Security Specialists; Computer Software Engineers, Applications; Computer Software Engineers, Systems Software; Computer Support Specialists; Computer Systems Analysts; Computer Systems Engineers/Architects; Network Designers; Network Systems and Data Communications Analysts; Software Quality Assurance Engineers and Testers; Web Administrators; Web Developers.

Skills—Troubleshooting: Determining causes of operating errors and deciding what to do about them. **Systems Evaluation:** Identifying measures or indicators of system performance and the actions needed to improve or correct performance relative to the goals of the system. **Operations Analysis:** Analyzing needs and product requirements to create a design. **Persuasion:** Persuading others to change their minds or behavior. **Systems Analysis:** Determining how a system should work and how changes in conditions, operations, and the environment will affect outcomes. **Programming:** Writing computer programs for various purposes.

Education and Training Programs: Computer and Information Sciences, General; Computer and Information Systems Security; Computer Systems Analysis/Analyst Training; Data Modeling/Warehousing and Database Administration; Management Information Systems, General. **Related Knowledge/Courses: Computers and Electronics:** Circuit boards, processors, chips, electronic equipment, and computer hardware and software, including applications and programming. **Economics and Accounting:** Economic and accounting principles and practices, the financial markets, banking, and the analysis and reporting of financial data. **Clerical Practices:** Administrative and clerical procedures and systems such as word processing, managing files and records, stenography and transcription, designing forms, and other office procedures and terminology. **Administration and Management:** Business and management principles involved in strategic planning, resource allocation, human resources modeling, leadership technique, production methods, and coordination of people and resources. **Mathematics:** Arithmetic, algebra, geometry, calculus, and statistics and their applications. **Customer and Personal Service:** Principles and processes for providing customer and personal services. This includes customer needs assessment, meeting quality standards for services, and evaluation of customer satisfaction.

Work Environment: Indoors; noisy; sitting; using hands on objects, tools, or controls; repetitive motions.

Dental Laboratory Technicians

- Education/Training Required: Long-term on-the-job training
- Annual Earnings: $32,240
- Growth: 7.6%
- Annual Job Openings: 3,000
- Self-Employed: 10.2%
- Part-Time: 11.2%

Level of Solitary Work: 75.0 (out of 100)

Level of Contact with Others: 74.8 (out of 100)

Construct and repair full or partial dentures or dental appliances. Read prescriptions or specifications and examine models and impressions to determine the design of dental products to be constructed. Fabricate, alter, and repair dental devices such as dentures, crowns, bridges, inlays, and appliances for straightening teeth. Place tooth models on apparatus that mimics bite and movement of patient's jaw to evaluate functionality of model. Test appliances for conformance to specifications and accuracy of occlusion, using articulators and micrometers. Melt metals or mix plaster, porcelain, or acrylic pastes and pour materials into molds or over frameworks to form dental prostheses or apparatus. Prepare metal surfaces for bonding with porcelain to create artificial teeth, using small hand tools. Remove excess metal or porcelain and polish surfaces of prostheses or frameworks, using polishing machines. Create a model of patient's mouth by pouring plaster into a dental impression and allowing plaster to set. Load newly constructed teeth into porcelain furnaces to bake the porcelain onto the metal framework. Build and shape wax teeth, using small hand instruments and information from observations or dentists' specifications. Apply porcelain paste or wax over prosthesis frameworks or setups, using brushes and spatulas. Fill chipped or low spots in surfaces of devices, using acrylic resins. Prepare wax bite-blocks and impression trays for use. Mold wax over denture set-ups to form the full contours of artificial gums. Train and supervise other dental technicians or dental laboratory bench workers. Rebuild or replace linings, wire sections, and missing teeth to repair dentures. Shape and solder wire and metal frames or bands for dental products, using soldering irons and hand tools.

Personality Type: Realistic. Realistic occupations frequently involve work activities that include practical, hands-on problems and solutions. They often deal with plants; animals; and real-world materials such as wood, tools, and machinery. Many of the occupations require working outside and do not involve a lot of paperwork or working closely with others.

GOE—Interest Area: 13. Manufacturing. **Work Group:** 13.06. Production Precision Work. **Other Jobs in This Work Group:** Bookbinders; Electrical and Electronic Equipment Assemblers; Electromechanical Equipment Assemblers; Engine and Other Machine Assemblers; Gem and Diamond Workers; Jewelers; Jewelers and Precious Stone and Metal Workers; Medical Appliance Technicians; Molding, Coremaking, and Casting Machine Setters, Operators, and Tenders, Metal and Plastic; Ophthalmic Laboratory Technicians; Precious Metal Workers; Semiconductor Processors; Timing Device Assemblers, Adjusters, and Calibrators.

Skills—Equipment Maintenance: Performing routine maintenance on equipment and determining when and what kind of maintenance is needed. **Equipment Selection:** Determining the kind of tools and equipment needed to do a job. **Management of Material Resources:** Obtaining and seeing to the appropriate use of equipment, facilities, and materials needed to do certain work. **Repairing:** Repairing machines or systems by using the needed tools. **Quality Control Analysis:** Conducting tests and inspections of products, services, or processes to evaluate quality or performance. **Operation Monitoring:** Watching gauges, dials, or other indicators to make sure a machine is working properly.

Education and Training Program: Dental Laboratory Technology/Technician Training. **Related Knowledge/Courses: Medicine and Dentistry:** The information and techniques needed to diagnose and treat human injuries, diseases, and deformities. This includes symptoms, treatment alternatives, drug properties and interactions, and preventive healthcare measures. **Design:** Design techniques, tools, and principles involved in production of precision technical plans, blueprints, drawings, and models. **Production and Processing:** Raw materials, production processes, quality control, costs, and other techniques for maximizing the effective manufacture and distribution of goods. **Engineering and Technology:** The practical application of engineering science and technology. This includes applying principles, techniques, procedures, and equipment to the design and production of various goods and services. **Mechanical Devices:** Machines and tools, including their designs, uses, repair, and maintenance. **Chemistry:** The chemical composition, structure, and properties of substances and of the chemical processes and transformations that they undergo. This includes uses of chemicals and their danger signs, production techniques, and disposal methods.

Work Environment: Indoors; noisy; contaminants; sitting; using hands on objects, tools, or controls; repetitive motions.

Desktop Publishers

- Education/Training Required: Postsecondary vocational training
- Annual Earnings: $32,800
- Growth: 23.2%
- Annual Job Openings: 8,000
- Self-Employed: 1.1%
- Part-Time: 4.7%

Level of Solitary Work: 71.7 (out of 100)

Level of Contact with Others: 76.5 (out of 100)

Format typescript and graphic elements, using computer software to produce publication-ready material. Check preliminary and final proofs for errors and make necessary corrections. Operate desktop publishing software and equipment to design, lay out, and produce camera-ready copy. View monitors for visual representation of work in progress and for instructions and feedback throughout process, making modifications as necessary. Enter text into computer keyboard and select the size and style of type, column width, and appropriate spacing for printed materials. Store copies of publications on paper, magnetic tape, film, or diskette. Position text and art elements from a variety of databases in a visually appealing way to design print or Web pages, using knowledge of type styles and size and layout patterns. Enter digitized data into electronic prepress system computer memory, using scanner, camera, keyboard, or mouse. Edit graphics and photos, using pixel or bitmap editing, airbrushing, masking, or image retouching. Import text and art elements such as electronic clip art or electronic files from photographs that have been scanned or produced with a digital camera, using computer software. Prepare sample layouts for approval, using computer software. Study layout or other design instructions to determine work to be done and sequence of operations. Load floppy disks or tapes containing information into system. Convert various types of files for printing or for the Internet, using computer software. Enter data, such as coordinates of images and color specifications, into system to retouch and make color corrections. Select number of colors and determine color separations. Transmit, deliver, or mail publication master to printer for production into film and plates. Collaborate with graphic artists, editors, and writers to produce master copies according to design specifications. Create special effects such as vignettes, mosaics, and image combining and add elements such as sound and animation to electronic publications.

Personality Type: Realistic. Realistic occupations frequently involve work activities that include practical, hands-on problems and solutions. They often deal with plants; animals; and real-world materials such as wood, tools, and machinery. Many of the occupations require working outside and do not involve a lot of paperwork or working closely with others.

GOE—Interest Area: 13. Manufacturing. **Work Group:** 13.08. Graphic Arts Production. **Other Jobs in This Work Group:** Bindery Workers; Etchers and Engravers; Job Printers; Photographic Process Workers; Photographic Processing Machine Operators; Prepress Technicians and Workers; Printing Machine Operators.

Skills—Operation and Control: Controlling operations of equipment or systems. **Operations Analysis:** Analyzing needs and product requirements to create a design. **Time Management:** Managing one's own time and the time of others. **Service Orientation:** Actively looking for ways to help people. **Active Listening:** Giving full attention to what other people are saying, taking time to understand the points being made, asking questions as appropriate, and not interrupting at inappropriate times. **Writing:** Communicating effectively in writing as appropriate for the needs of the audience.

Education and Training Program: Prepress/Desktop Publishing and Digital Imaging Design. **Related Knowledge/Courses: Computers and Electronics:** Circuit boards, processors, chips, electronic equipment, and computer hardware and software, including applications and programming. **Production and Processing:** Raw materials, production processes, quality control, costs, and other techniques for maximizing the effective manufacture and distribution of goods. **English Language:** The structure and content of the English language, including the meaning and spelling of words, rules of composition, and grammar.

Work Environment: Indoors; sitting; repetitive motions.

Driver/Sales Workers

- Education/Training Required: Short-term on-the-job training
- Annual Earnings: $20,120
- Growth: 13.8%
- Annual Job Openings: 72,000
- Self-Employed: 8.8%
- Part-Time: 9.1%

Level of Solitary Work: 71.7 (out of 100)

Level of Contact with Others: 83.0 (out of 100)

Drive truck or other vehicle over established routes or within an established territory and sell goods such as food products, including restaurant take-out items, or pick up and deliver items such as laundry. May also take orders and collect payments. Includes newspaper delivery drivers. Collect money from customers, make change, and record transactions on customer receipts. Listen to and resolve customers' complaints regarding products or services. Inform regular customers of new products or services and price changes. Write customer orders and sales contracts according to company guidelines. Drive trucks to deliver such items as food, medical supplies, or newspapers. Collect coins from vending machines, refill machines, and remove aged merchandise. Call on prospective customers to explain company services and to solicit new business. Record sales or delivery information on daily sales or delivery record. Review lists of dealers, customers, or station drops and load trucks. Arrange merchandise and sales promotion displays or issue sales promotion materials to customers. Maintain trucks and food-dispensing equipment and clean inside of machines that dispense food or beverages. Sell food specialties, such as sandwiches and beverages, to office workers and patrons of sports events.

Personality Type: Enterprising. Enterprising occupations frequently involve starting up and carrying out projects. These occupations can involve leading peo-

ple and making many decisions. They sometimes require risk taking and often deal with business.

GOE—Interest Area: 16. Transportation, Distribution, and Logistics. **Work Group:** 16.06. Other Services Requiring Driving. **Other Jobs in This Work Group:** Ambulance Drivers and Attendants, Except Emergency Medical Technicians; Bus Drivers, School; Bus Drivers, Transit and Intercity; Couriers and Messengers; Parking Lot Attendants; Postal Service Mail Carriers; Taxi Drivers and Chauffeurs.

Skills—None met the criteria.

Education and Training Program: Retailing and Retail Operations. **Related Knowledge/Courses: Transportation:** Principles and methods for moving people or goods by air, rail, sea, or road, including the relative costs and benefits. **Sales and Marketing:** Principles and methods for showing, promoting, and selling products or services. This includes marketing strategy and tactics, product demonstration, sales techniques, and sales control systems. **Public Safety and Security:** Relevant equipment, policies, procedures, and strategies to promote effective local, state, or national security operations for the protection of people, data, property, and institutions.

Work Environment: More often outdoors than indoors; very hot or cold; sitting; using hands on objects, tools, or controls; repetitive motions.

Drywall and Ceiling Tile Installers

- Education/Training Required: Moderate-term on-the-job training
- Annual Earnings: $34,740
- Growth: 9.0%
- Annual Job Openings: 17,000
- Self-Employed: 23.4%
- Part-Time: 8.0%

Level of Solitary Work: 57.7 (out of 100)

Level of Contact with Others: 9.5 (out of 100)

Apply plasterboard or other wallboard to ceilings or interior walls of buildings. Apply or mount acoustical tiles or blocks, strips, or sheets of shock-absorbing materials to ceilings and walls of buildings to reduce or reflect sound. Materials may be of decorative quality. Includes lathers who fasten wooden, metal, or rockboard lath to walls, ceilings, or partitions of buildings to provide support base for plaster, fireproofing, or acoustical material. Fasten metal or rockboard lath to the structural framework of walls, ceilings, and partitions of buildings, using nails, screws, staples, or wire-ties. Apply cement to backs of tiles and press tiles into place, aligning them with layout marks or joints of previously laid tile. Apply or mount acoustical tile or blocks, strips, or sheets of shock-absorbing materials to ceilings and walls of buildings to reduce reflection of sound or to decorate rooms. Assemble and install metal framing and decorative trim for windows, doorways, and vents. Cut and screw together metal channels to make floor and ceiling frames according to plans for the location of rooms and hallways. Cut metal or wood framing and trim to size, using cutting tools. Measure and cut openings in panels or tiles for electrical outlets, windows, vents, and plumbing and other fixtures, using keyhole saws or other cutting tools. Fit and fasten wallboard or drywall into position on wood or metal frameworks, using glue, nails, or screws. Hang dry lines (stretched string) to wall moldings in order to guide positioning of main runners. Hang drywall panels on metal frameworks of walls and ceilings in offices, schools, and other large buildings, using lifts or hoists to adjust panel heights when necessary. Inspect furrings, mechanical mountings, and masonry surface for plumbness and level, using spirit or water levels. Install horizontal and vertical metal or wooden studs to frames so that wallboard can be attached to interior walls. Measure and mark surfaces to lay out work according to blueprints and drawings, using tape measures, straightedges or squares, and marking devices. Nail channels or wood furring strips to surfaces to provide mounting for tile.

Read blueprints and other specifications to determine methods of installation, work procedures, and material and tool requirements. Scribe and cut edges of tile to fit walls where wall molding is not specified. Seal joints between ceiling tiles and walls. Cut fixture and border tiles to size, using keyhole saws, and insert them into surrounding frameworks. Suspend angle iron grids and channel irons from ceilings, using wire.

Personality Type: Realistic. Realistic occupations frequently involve work activities that include practical, hands-on problems and solutions. They often deal with plants; animals; and real-world materials such as wood, tools, and machinery. Many of the occupations require working outside and do not involve a lot of paperwork or working closely with others.

GOE—Interest Area: 02. Architecture and Construction. **Work Group:** 02.04. Construction Crafts. **Other Jobs in This Work Group:** Boilermakers; Brickmasons and Blockmasons; Carpet Installers; Cement Masons and Concrete Finishers; Commercial Divers; Construction Carpenters; Crane and Tower Operators; Electricians; Fence Erectors; Floor Layers, Except Carpet, Wood, and Hard Tiles; Floor Sanders and Finishers; Glaziers; Hazardous Materials Removal Workers; Insulation Workers, Floor, Ceiling, and Wall; Insulation Workers, Mechanical; Manufactured Building and Mobile Home Installers; Operating Engineers and Other Construction Equipment Operators; Painters, Construction and Maintenance; Paperhangers; Paving, Surfacing, and Tamping Equipment Operators; Pile-Driver Operators; Pipe Fitters and Steamfitters; Pipelayers; Plasterers and Stucco Masons; Plumbers; Plumbers, Pipefitters, and Steamfitters; Rail-Track Laying and Maintenance Equipment Operators; Refractory Materials Repairers, Except Brickmasons; Reinforcing Iron and Rebar Workers; Riggers; Roofers; Rough Carpenters; Security and Fire Alarm Systems Installers; Segmental Pavers; Sheet Metal Workers; Stone Cutters and Carvers, Manufacturing; Stonemasons; Structural Iron and Steel Workers; Tapers; Terrazzo Workers and Finishers; Tile and Marble Setters.

Skills—**Installation:** Installing equipment, machines, wiring, or programs to meet specifications.

Education and Training Program: Drywall Installation/Drywaller Training. **Related Knowledge/Courses: Building and Construction:** The materials, methods, and tools involved in the construction or repair of houses, buildings, or other structures such as highways and roads. **Design:** Design techniques, tools, and principles involved in production of precision technical plans, blueprints, drawings, and models.

Work Environment: Indoors; contaminants; hazardous equipment; minor burns, cuts, bites, or stings; standing; using hands on objects, tools, or controls.

Earth Drillers, Except Oil and Gas

- ◎ Education/Training Required: Moderate-term on-the-job training
- ◎ Annual Earnings: $33,770
- ◎ Growth: 7.9%
- ◎ Annual Job Openings: 4,000
- ◎ Self-Employed: 10.5%
- ◎ Part-Time: 0.5%

Level of Solitary Work: 51.5 (out of 100)

Level of Contact with Others: 15.5 (out of 100)

Operate a variety of drills—such as rotary, churn, and pneumatic—to tap sub-surface water and salt deposits, to remove core samples during mineral exploration or soil testing, and to facilitate the use of explosives in mining or construction. May use explosives. Includes horizontal and earth boring machine operators. Drive or guide truck-mounted equipment into position, level and stabilize rigs, and extend telescoping derricks. Operate hoists to lift power line poles into position. Fabricate well casings. Disinfect, reconstruct, and redevelop contaminated wells and water pumping systems and clean and disinfect new wells in preparation for use. Design well pumping systems. Assemble and position machines, augers, casing pipes, and other equipment, using hand and power tools. Signal crane operators to move equipment. Record drilling progress and geological data. Retrieve lost equipment from bore holes, using retrieval tools and equipment. Review client requirements and proposed locations for drilling operations to determine feasibility and cost estimates. Perform routine maintenance and upgrade work on machines and equipment, such as replacing parts, building up drill bits, and lubricating machinery. Perform pumping tests to assess well performance. Drive trucks, tractors, or truck-mounted drills to and from worksites. Verify depths and alignments of boring positions. Withdraw drill rods from holes and extract core samples. Operate water-well drilling rigs and other equipment to drill, bore, and dig for water wells or for environmental assessment purposes. Drill or bore holes in rock for blasting, grouting, anchoring, or building foundations. Inspect core samples to determine nature of strata or take samples to laboratories for analysis. Monitor drilling operations, checking gauges and listening to equipment to assess drilling conditions and to determine the need to adjust drilling or alter equipment. Observe electronic graph recorders and flow meters that monitor the water used to flush debris from holes. Document geological formations encountered during work. Operate machines to flush earth cuttings or to blow dust from holes. Start, stop, and control drilling speed of machines and insertion of casings into holes. Select the appropriate drill for the job, using knowledge of rock or soil conditions. Operate controls to stabilize machines and to position and align drills. Place and install screens, casings, pumps, and other well fixtures to develop wells. Pour water into wells or pump water or slush into wells to cool drill bits and to remove drillings.

Personality Type: Realistic. Realistic occupations frequently involve work activities that include practical, hands-on problems and solutions. They often deal with plants; animals; and real-world materials such as wood, tools, and machinery. Many of the occupations require working outside and do not involve a lot of paperwork or working closely with others.

GOE—Interest Area: 01. Agriculture and Natural Resources. **Work Group:** 01.08. Mining and Drilling. **Other Jobs in This Work Group:** Continuous Mining Machine Operators; Derrick Operators, Oil and Gas; Excavating and Loading Machine and Dragline Operators; Explosives Workers, Ordnance Handling Experts, and Blasters; Helpers—Extraction Workers; Loading Machine Operators, Underground Mining; Mine Cutting and Channeling Machine Operators; Rock Splitters, Quarry; Roof Bolters, Mining; Rotary Drill Operators, Oil and Gas; Roustabouts, Oil and Gas; Service Unit Operators, Oil, Gas, and Mining; Shuttle Car Operators; Wellhead Pumpers.

Skills—Operation Monitoring: Watching gauges, dials, or other indicators to make sure a machine is working properly. **Operation and Control:** Controlling operations of equipment or systems. **Equipment Maintenance:** Performing routine maintenance on equipment and determining when and what kind of maintenance is needed.

Education and Training Programs: Construction/ Heavy Equipment/Earthmoving Equipment Operation; Well Drilling/Driller Training. **Related Knowledge/Courses: Mechanical Devices:** Machines and tools, including their designs, uses, repair, and maintenance. **Transportation:** Principles and methods for moving people or goods by air, rail, sea, or road, including the relative costs and benefits. **Physics:** Physical principles and laws and their interrelationships and applications to understanding fluid, material, and atmospheric dynamics and mechanical, electrical, atomic, and subatomic structures and processes. **Engineering and Technology:** The practical application of engineering science and technology. This includes applying principles, techniques, procedures, and equipment to the design and production of various goods and services.

Work Environment: Outdoors; noisy; contaminants; hazardous equipment; standing; using hands on objects, tools, or controls.

Economists

- ◎ Education/Training Required: Master's degree
- ◎ Annual Earnings: $73,690
- ◎ Growth: 5.6%
- ◎ Annual Job Openings: 1,000
- ◎ Self-Employed: 0.0%
- ◎ Part-Time: 2.4%

Level of Solitary Work: 71.7 (out of 100)

Level of Contact with Others: 68.8 (out of 100)

Conduct research, prepare reports, or formulate plans to aid in solution of economic problems arising from production and distribution of goods and services. May collect and process economic and statistical data, using econometric and sampling techniques. Study economic and statistical data in area of specialization, such as finance, labor, or agriculture. Provide advice and consultation on economic relationships to businesses, public and private agencies, and other employers. Compile, analyze, and report data to explain economic phenomena and forecast market trends, applying mathematical models and statistical techniques. Formulate recommendations, policies, or plans to solve economic problems or to interpret markets. Develop economic guidelines and standards and prepare points of view used in forecasting trends and formulating economic policy. Testify at regulatory or legislative hearings concerning the estimated effects of changes in legislation or public policy and present recommendations based on cost-benefit analyses. Supervise research projects and students' study projects. Forecast production and consumption of renewable resources and supply, consumption, and depletion of non-renewable resources. Teach theories, principles, and methods of economics.

Personality Type: Investigative. Investigative occupations frequently involve working with ideas and require an extensive amount of thinking. These occupations can involve searching for facts and figuring out problems mentally.

GOE—Interest Area: 15. Scientific Research, Engineering, and Mathematics. **Work Group:** 15.04. Social Sciences. **Other Jobs in This Work Group:** Anthropologists; Anthropologists and Archeologists; Archeologists; Historians; Industrial-Organizational Psychologists; Political Scientists; School Psychologists; Sociologists.

Skills—Mathematics: Using mathematics to solve problems. **Programming:** Writing computer programs for various purposes. **Persuasion:** Persuading others to change their minds or behavior. **Judgment and Decision Making:** Considering the relative costs and benefits of potential actions to choose the most appropriate one. **Complex Problem Solving:** Identifying complex problems and reviewing related information to develop and evaluate options and implement solutions. **Writing:** Communicating effectively in writing as appropriate for the needs of the audience.

Education and Training Programs: Agricultural Economics; Applied Economics; Business/Managerial Economics; Development Economics and International Development; Econometrics and Quantitative Economics; Economics, General; Economics, Other; International Economics. **Related Knowledge/Courses: Economics and Accounting:** Economic and accounting principles and practices, the financial markets, banking, and the analysis and reporting of financial data. **Mathematics:** Arithmetic, algebra, geometry, calculus, and statistics and their applications. **Sales and Marketing:** Principles and methods for showing, promoting, and selling products or services. This includes marketing strategy and tactics, product demonstration, sales techniques, and sales control systems. **Geography:** Principles and methods for describing the features of land, sea, and air masses, including their physical characteristics; locations; interrelationships; and distribution of plant, animal, and human life. **Computers and Electronics:** Circuit boards, processors, chips, electronic equipment, and computer hardware and software, including applications and programming.

English Language: The structure and content of the English language, including the meaning and spelling of words, rules of composition, and grammar.

Work Environment: Indoors; sitting.

Editors

- Education/Training Required: Bachelor's degree
- Annual Earnings: $45,510
- Growth: 14.8%
- Annual Job Openings: 16,000
- Self-Employed: 14.8%
- Part-Time: 17.0%

Level of Solitary Work: 62.5 (out of 100)

Level of Contact with Others: 77.8 (out of 100)

Perform variety of editorial duties, such as laying out, indexing, and revising content of written materials, in preparation for final publication. Prepare, rewrite, and edit copy to improve readability or supervise others who do this work. Read copy or proof to detect and correct errors in spelling, punctuation, and syntax. Allocate print space for story text, photos, and illustrations according to space parameters and copy significance, using knowledge of layout principles. Plan the contents of publications according to the publication's style, editorial policy, and publishing requirements. Verify facts, dates, and statistics, using standard reference sources. Review and approve proofs submitted by composing room prior to publication production. Develop story or content ideas, considering reader or audience appeal. Oversee publication production, including artwork, layout, computer typesetting, and printing, ensuring adherence to deadlines and budget requirements. Confer with management and editorial staff members regarding placement and emphasis of developing news stories. Assign topics, events, and stories to individual writers or reporters for coverage. Read,

E

evaluate, and edit manuscripts or other materials submitted for publication and confer with authors regarding changes in content, style or organization, or publication. Monitor news-gathering operations to ensure utilization of all news sources, such as press releases, telephone contacts, radio, television, wire services, and other reporters. Meet frequently with artists, typesetters, layout personnel, marketing directors, and production managers to discuss projects and resolve problems. Supervise and coordinate work of reporters and other editors. Make manuscript acceptance or revision recommendations to the publisher. Select local, state, national, and international news items received from wire services based on assessment of items' significance and interest value. Interview and hire writers and reporters or negotiate contracts, royalties, and payments for authors or freelancers. Direct the policies and departments of newspapers, magazines, and other publishing establishments. Arrange for copyright permissions. Read material to determine index items and arrange them alphabetically or topically, indicating page or chapter location.

Personality Type: Artistic. Artistic occupations frequently involve working with forms, designs, and patterns. They often require self-expression, and the work can be done without following a clear set of rules.

GOE—Interest Area: 03. Arts and Communication. **Work Group:** 03.02. Writing and Editing. **Other Jobs in This Work Group:** Copy Writers; Poets, Lyricists, and Creative Writers; Technical Writers; Writers and Authors.

Skills—Writing: Communicating effectively in writing as appropriate for the needs of the audience. **Reading Comprehension:** Understanding written sentences and paragraphs in work-related documents. **Active Listening:** Giving full attention to what other people are saying, taking time to understand the points being made, asking questions as appropriate, and not interrupting at inappropriate times. **Persuasion:** Persuading others to change their minds or behavior. **Time Management:** Managing one's own time and the time of others. **Critical Thinking:** Using logic and reasoning to identify the strengths and weaknesses of alternative solutions, conclusions, or approaches to problems.

Education and Training Programs: Broadcast Journalism; Business/Corporate Communications; Communication, Journalism, and Related Programs, Other; Creative Writing; Family and Consumer Sciences/Human Sciences Communication; Journalism; Mass Communication/Media Studies; Publishing; Technical and Business Writing. **Related Knowledge/Courses: Communications and Media:** Media production, communication, and dissemination techniques and methods. This includes alternative ways to inform and entertain via written, oral, and visual media. **History and Archeology:** Historical events and their causes, indicators, and effects on civilizations and cultures. **Geography:** Principles and methods for describing the features of land, sea, and air masses, including their physical characteristics; locations; interrelationships; and distribution of plant, animal, and human life. **English Language:** The structure and content of the English language, including the meaning and spelling of words, rules of composition, and grammar. **Sales and Marketing:** Principles and methods for showing, promoting, and selling products or services. This includes marketing strategy and tactics, product demonstration, sales techniques, and sales control systems. **Clerical Practices:** Administrative and clerical procedures and systems such as word processing, managing files and records, stenography and transcription, designing forms, and other office procedures and terminology.

Work Environment: Indoors; sitting; using hands on objects, tools, or controls; repetitive motions.

Electric Motor, Power Tool, and Related Repairers

- ◎ Education/Training Required: Postsecondary vocational training
- ◎ Annual Earnings: $33,460
- ◎ Growth: 4.1%
- ◎ Annual Job Openings: 3,000
- ◎ Self-Employed: 21.2%
- ◎ Part-Time: 7.1%

Level of Solitary Work: 66.3 (out of 100)

Level of Contact with Others: 75.3 (out of 100)

Repair, maintain, or install electric motors, wiring, or switches. Measure velocity, horsepower, revolutions per minute (rpm), amperage, circuitry, and voltage of units or parts to diagnose problems, using ammeters, voltmeters, wattmeters, and other testing devices. Record repairs required, parts used, and labor time. Reassemble repaired electric motors to specified requirements and ratings, using hand tools and electrical meters. Maintain stocks of parts. Repair and rebuild defective mechanical parts in electric motors, generators, and related equipment, using hand tools and power tools. Rewire electrical systems and repair or replace electrical accessories. Inspect electrical connections, wiring, relays, charging resistance boxes, and storage batteries, following wiring diagrams. Read service guides to find information needed to perform repairs. Inspect and test equipment to locate damage or worn parts and diagnose malfunctions or read work orders or schematic drawings to determine required repairs. Solder, wrap, and coat wires to ensure proper insulation. Assemble electrical parts such as alternators, generators, starting devices, and switches, following schematic drawings and using hand, machine, and power tools. Lubricate moving parts. Remove and replace defective parts such as coil leads, carbon brushes, and wires, using soldering equipment. Disassemble defective equipment so that repairs can be made, using hand tools.

Lift units or parts such as motors or generators, using cranes or chain hoists, or signal crane operators to lift heavy parts or subassemblies. Weld, braze, or solder electrical connections. Reface, ream, and polish commutators and machine parts to specified tolerances, using machine tools. Adjust working parts, such as fan belts, contacts, and springs, using hand tools and gauges. Clean cells, cell assemblies, glassware, leads, electrical connections, and battery poles, using scrapers, steam, water, emery cloths, power grinders, or acid. Scrape and clean units or parts, using cleaning solvents and equipment such as buffing wheels. Rewind coils on cores in slots or make replacement coils, using coil-winding machines.

Personality Type: Realistic. Realistic occupations frequently involve work activities that include practical, hands-on problems and solutions. They often deal with plants; animals; and real-world materials such as wood, tools, and machinery. Many of the occupations require working outside and do not involve a lot of paperwork or working closely with others.

GOE—Interest Area: 13. Manufacturing. **Work Group:** 13.12. Electrical and Electronic Repair. **Other Jobs in This Work Group:** Avionics Technicians; Electrical and Electronics Installers and Repairers, Transportation Equipment; Electrical and Electronics Repairers, Commercial and Industrial Equipment; Electronic Equipment Installers and Repairers, Motor Vehicles; Electronic Home Entertainment Equipment Installers and Repairers; Radio Mechanics.

Skills—Installation: Installing equipment, machines, wiring, or programs to meet specifications. **Repairing:** Repairing machines or systems by using the needed tools. **Troubleshooting:** Determining causes of operating errors and deciding what to do about them. **Equipment Maintenance:** Performing routine maintenance on equipment and determining when and what kind of maintenance is needed. **Technology Design:** Generating or adapting equipment and technology to serve user needs. **Operation Monitoring:** Watching gauges, dials, or other indicators to make sure a machine is working properly.

E

Education and Training Program: Electrical/Electronics Equipment Installation and Repair, General. **Related Knowledge/Courses: Mechanical Devices:** Machines and tools, including their designs, uses, repair, and maintenance. **Engineering and Technology:** The practical application of engineering science and technology. This includes applying principles, techniques, procedures, and equipment to the design and production of various goods and services. **Design:** Design techniques, tools, and principles involved in production of precision technical plans, blueprints, drawings, and models. **Production and Processing:** Raw materials, production processes, quality control, costs, and other techniques for maximizing the effective manufacture and distribution of goods.

Work Environment: Noisy; contaminants; hazardous conditions; hazardous equipment; standing; using hands on objects, tools, or controls.

Electrical and Electronic Engineering Technicians

See the descriptions of these jobs:

- Electrical Engineering Technicians
- Electronics Engineering Technicians

Electrical and Electronics Drafters

See the descriptions of these jobs:

- Electrical Drafters
- Electronic Drafters

Electrical and Electronics Repairers, Powerhouse, Substation, and Relay

- Education/Training Required: Postsecondary vocational training
- Annual Earnings: $54,970
- Growth: –0.4%
- Annual Job Openings: 2,000
- Self-Employed: 0.0%
- Part-Time: 5.5%

Level of Solitary Work: 59.2 (out of 100)

Level of Contact with Others: 77.8 (out of 100)

Inspect, test, repair, or maintain electrical equipment in generating stations, substations, and in-service relays. Construct, test, maintain, and repair substation relay and control systems. Inspect and test equipment and circuits to identify malfunctions or defects, using wiring diagrams and testing devices such as ohmmeters, voltmeters, or ammeters. Consult manuals, schematics, wiring diagrams, and engineering personnel to troubleshoot and solve equipment problems and to determine optimum equipment functioning. Notify facility personnel of equipment shutdowns. Open and close switches to isolate defective relays; then perform adjustments or repairs. Prepare and maintain records detailing tests, repairs, and maintenance. Analyze test data to diagnose malfunctions, to determine performance characteristics of systems, and to evaluate effects of system modifications. Test insulators and bushings of equipment by inducing voltage across insulation, testing current, and calculating insulation loss. Repair, replace, and clean equipment and components such as circuit breakers, brushes, and commutators. Disconnect voltage regulators, bolts, and screws and connect replacement regulators to high-voltage lines. Schedule and supervise the construction and testing of special devices and the implementation of unique monitoring or control systems. Run signal quality and connectivity tests for individual cables and record results. Schedule and supervise splicing or termination of cables in color-code order. Test oil in circuit breakers and transformers for dielectric strength, refilling oil periodically. Maintain inventories of spare parts for all equipment, requisitioning parts as necessary. Set forms and pour concrete footings for installation of heavy equipment.

Personality Type: Realistic. Realistic occupations frequently involve work activities that include practical, hands-on problems and solutions. They often deal with plants; animals; and real-world materials such as wood, tools, and machinery. Many of the occupations require working outside and do not involve a lot of paperwork or working closely with others.

GOE—Interest Area: 02. Architecture and Construction. **Work Group:** 02.05. Systems and Equipment Installation, Maintenance, and Repair. **Other Jobs in This Work Group:** Electrical Power-Line Installers and Repairers; Elevator Installers and Repairers; Heating and Air Conditioning Mechanics and Installers; Maintenance and Repair Workers, General; Refrigeration Mechanics and Installers; Telecommunications Equipment Installers and Repairers, Except Line Installers; Telecommunications Line Installers and Repairers.

Skills—Installation: Installing equipment, machines, wiring, or programs to meet specifications. **Repairing:** Repairing machines or systems by using the needed tools. **Equipment Maintenance:** Performing routine maintenance on equipment and determining when and what kind of maintenance is needed. **Troubleshooting:** Determining causes of operating errors and deciding what to do about them. **Operation Monitoring:** Watching gauges, dials, or other indicators to make sure a machine is working properly. **Operation and Control:** Controlling operations of equipment or systems.

Education and Training Program: Mechanic and Repair Technologies/Technician Training, Other. **Related Knowledge/Courses:** Mechanical Devices:

Machines and tools, including their designs, uses, repair, and maintenance. **Design:** Design techniques, tools, and principles involved in production of precision technical plans, blueprints, drawings, and models. **Telecommunications:** Transmission, broadcasting, switching, control, and operation of telecommunications systems. **Building and Construction:** The materials, methods, and tools involved in the construction or repair of houses, buildings, or other structures such as highways and roads. **Physics:** Physical principles and laws and their interrelationships and applications to understanding fluid, material, and atmospheric dynamics and mechanical, electrical, atomic, and subatomic structures and processes. **Public Safety and Security:** Relevant equipment, policies, procedures, and strategies to promote effective local, state, or national security operations for the protection of people, data, property, and institutions.

Work Environment: Outdoors; noisy; very bright or dim lighting; hazardous conditions; standing; using hands on objects, tools, or controls.

Electrical Drafters

This job can be found in the Part II lists under the title Electrical and Electronics Drafters.

- Education/Training Required: Postsecondary vocational training
- Annual Earnings: $45,550
- Growth: 1.2%
- Annual Job Openings: 3,000
- Self-Employed: 6.4%
- Part-Time: 8.4%

The job openings listed here are shared with Electronic Drafters.

Level of Solitary Work: 54.6 (out of 100)

Level of Contact with Others: 74.8 (out of 100)

Develop specifications and instructions for installation of voltage transformers, overhead or underground cables, and related electrical equipment used to conduct electrical energy from transmission lines or high-voltage distribution lines to consumers. Use computer-aided drafting equipment and/or conventional drafting stations; technical handbooks; tables; calculators; and traditional drafting tools such as boards, pencils, protractors, and T-squares. Draft working drawings, wiring diagrams, wiring connection specifications, or cross-sections of underground cables as required for instructions to installation crew. Confer with engineering staff and other personnel to resolve problems. Draw master sketches to scale, showing relation of proposed installations to existing facilities and exact specifications and dimensions. Measure factors that affect installation and arrangement of equipment, such as distances to be spanned by wire and cable. Assemble documentation packages and produce drawing sets, which are then checked by an engineer or an architect. Review completed construction drawings and cost estimates for accuracy and conformity to standards and regulations. Prepare and interpret specifications, calculating weights, volumes, and stress factors. Explain drawings to production or construction teams and provide adjustments as necessary. Supervise and train other technologists, technicians, and drafters. Study work order requests to determine type of service, such as lighting or power, demanded by installation. Visit proposed installation sites and draw rough sketches of location. Determine the order of work and the method of presentation, such as orthographic or isometric drawing. Reproduce working drawings on copy machines or trace drawings in ink. Write technical reports and draw charts that display statistics and data.

Personality Type: Conventional. Conventional occupations frequently involve following set procedures and routines. These occupations can include working with data and details more than with ideas. Usually there is a clear line of authority to follow.

GOE—Interest Area: 15. Scientific Research, Engineering, and Mathematics. **Work Group:** 15.09. Engineering Technology. **Other Jobs in This Work**

Group: Aerospace Engineering and Operations Technicians; Cartographers and Photogrammetrists; Civil Engineering Technicians; Electrical and Electronic Engineering Technicians; Electrical and Electronics Drafters; Electrical Engineering Technicians; Electro-Mechanical Technicians; Electronic Drafters; Electronics Engineering Technicians; Environmental Engineering Technicians; Mapping Technicians; Mechanical Drafters; Mechanical Engineering Technicians; Surveying and Mapping Technicians; Surveying Technicians.

Skills—Mathematics: Using mathematics to solve problems. **Active Learning:** Understanding the implications of new information for both current and future problem solving and decision making. **Installation:** Installing equipment, machines, wiring, or programs to meet specifications. **Critical Thinking:** Using logic and reasoning to identify the strengths and weaknesses of alternative solutions, conclusions, or approaches to problems. **Management of Personnel Resources:** Motivating, developing, and directing people as they work; identifying the best people for the job. **Quality Control Analysis:** Conducting tests and inspections of products, services, or processes to evaluate quality or performance.

Education and Training Program: Electrical/Electronics Drafting and Electrical/Electronics CAD/CADD. **Related Knowledge/Courses: Design:** Design techniques, tools, and principles involved in production of precision technical plans, blueprints, drawings, and models. **Engineering and Technology:** The practical application of engineering science and technology. This includes applying principles, techniques, procedures, and equipment to the design and production of various goods and services. **Building and Construction:** The materials, methods, and tools involved in the construction or repair of houses, buildings, or other structures such as highways and roads. **Computers and Electronics:** Circuit boards, processors, chips, electronic equipment, and computer hardware and software, including applications and programming. **Telecommunications:** Transmission, broadcasting, switching, control, and operation of telecommunications systems. **Clerical Practices:** Administrative and clerical procedures and systems such as word processing, managing files and records, stenography and transcription, designing forms, and other office procedures and terminology.

Work Environment: Indoors; sitting.

Electrical Engineering Technicians

This job can be found in the Part II lists under the title Electrical and Electronic Engineering Technicians.

- Education/Training Required: Associate degree
- Annual Earnings: $48,040
- Growth: 9.8%
- Annual Job Openings: 18,000
- Self-Employed: 0.4%
- Part-Time: 6.7%

The job openings listed here are shared with Electronics Engineering Technicians.

Level of Solitary Work: 49.9 (out of 100)

Level of Contact with Others: 72.2 (out of 100)

Apply electrical theory and related knowledge to test and modify developmental or operational electrical machinery and electrical control equipment and circuitry in industrial or commercial plants and laboratories. Usually work under direction of engineering staff. Assemble electrical and electronic systems and prototypes according to engineering data and knowledge of electrical principles, using hand tools and measuring instruments. Provide technical assistance and resolution when electrical or engineering problems are encountered before, during, and after construction. Install and maintain electrical control systems and solid state equipment. Modify electrical prototypes, parts, assemblies, and systems to correct functional deviations. Set up and operate test equipment to evaluate performance of developmental parts, assemblies, or systems under simulated operating conditions and record results. Collaborate with electrical engineers and other personnel to identify, define, and solve developmental problems. Build, calibrate, maintain, troubleshoot, and repair electrical instruments or testing equipment. Analyze and interpret test information to resolve design-related problems. Write commissioning procedures for electrical installations. Prepare project cost and work-time estimates. Evaluate engineering proposals, shop drawings, and design comments for sound electrical engineering practice and conformance with established safety and design criteria and recommend approval or disapproval. Draw or modify diagrams and write engineering specifications to clarify design details and functional criteria of experimental electronics units. Conduct inspections for quality control and assurance programs, reporting findings and recommendations. Prepare contracts and initiate, review, and coordinate modifications to contract specifications and plans throughout the construction process. Plan, schedule, and monitor work of support personnel to assist supervisor. Review existing electrical engineering criteria to identify necessary revisions, deletions, or amendments to outdated material. Perform supervisory duties such as recommending work assignments, approving leaves, and completing performance evaluations. Plan method and sequence of operations for developing and testing experimental electronic and electrical equipment. Visit construction sites to observe conditions impacting design and to identify solutions to technical design problems involving electrical systems equipment that arise during construction.

Personality Type: Realistic. Realistic occupations frequently involve work activities that include practical, hands-on problems and solutions. They often deal with plants; animals; and real-world materials such as wood, tools, and machinery. Many of the occupations require working outside and do not involve a lot of paperwork or working closely with others.

E

GOE—Interest Area: 15. Scientific Research, Engineering, and Mathematics. **Work Group:** 15.09. Engineering Technology. **Other Jobs in This Work Group:** Aerospace Engineering and Operations Technicians; Cartographers and Photogrammetrists; Civil Engineering Technicians; Electrical and Electronic Engineering Technicians; Electrical and Electronics Drafters; Electrical Drafters; Electro-Mechanical Technicians; Electronic Drafters; Electronics Engineering Technicians; Environmental Engineering Technicians; Mapping Technicians; Mechanical Drafters; Mechanical Engineering Technicians; Surveying and Mapping Technicians; Surveying Technicians.

Skills—Repairing: Repairing machines or systems by using the needed tools. **Installation:** Installing equipment, machines, wiring, or programs to meet specifications. **Troubleshooting:** Determining causes of operating errors and deciding what to do about them. **Science:** Using scientific rules and methods to solve problems. **Mathematics:** Using mathematics to solve problems. **Equipment Maintenance:** Performing routine maintenance on equipment and determining when and what kind of maintenance is needed.

Education and Training Programs: Computer Engineering Technology/Technician Training; Computer Technology/Computer Systems Technology; Electrical and Electronic Engineering Technologies/Technician Training, Other; Electrical, Electronic, and Communications Engineering Technology/Technician Training; Telecommunications Technology/Technician Training. **Related Knowledge/Courses: Engineering and Technology:** The practical application of engineering science and technology. This includes applying principles, techniques, procedures, and equipment to the design and production of various goods and services. **Design:** Design techniques, tools, and principles involved in production of precision technical plans, blueprints, drawings, and models. **Computers and Electronics:** Circuit boards, processors, chips, electronic equipment, and computer hardware and software, including applications and programming. **Physics:** Physical

principles and laws and their interrelationships and applications to understanding fluid, material, and atmospheric dynamics and mechanical, electrical, atomic, and subatomic structures and processes. **Mechanical Devices:** Machines and tools, including their designs, uses, repair, and maintenance. **Telecommunications:** Transmission, broadcasting, switching, control, and operation of telecommunications systems.

Work Environment: Indoors; noisy; sitting; using hands on objects, tools, or controls.

Electrical Engineers

- ◎ Education/Training Required: Bachelor's degree
- ◎ Annual Earnings: $73,510
- ◎ Growth: 11.8%
- ◎ Annual Job Openings: 12,000
- ◎ Self-Employed: 3.3%
- ◎ Part-Time: 2.1%

Level of Solitary Work: 46.7 (out of 100)

Level of Contact with Others: 58.7 (out of 100)

Design, develop, test, or supervise the manufacturing and installation of electrical equipment, components, or systems for commercial, industrial, military, or scientific use. Confer with engineers, customers, and others to discuss existing or potential engineering projects and products. Design, implement, maintain, and improve electrical instruments, equipment, facilities, components, products, and systems for commercial, industrial, and domestic purposes. Operate computer-assisted engineering and design software and equipment to perform engineering tasks. Direct and coordinate manufacturing, construction, installation, maintenance, support, documentation, and testing activities to ensure compliance with specifications, codes, and customer requirements. Perform detailed calculations to compute and establish manufacturing, construction, and installation standards and specifications. Inspect completed installations and observe operations to ensure conformance to design and equipment specifications and compliance with operational and safety standards. Plan and implement research methodology and procedures to apply principles of electrical theory to engineering projects. Prepare specifications for purchase of materials and equipment. Supervise and train project team members as necessary. Investigate and test vendors' and competitors' products. Oversee project production efforts to assure projects are completed satisfactorily, on time, and within budget. Prepare and study technical drawings, specifications of electrical systems, and topographical maps to ensure that installation and operations conform to standards and customer requirements. Investigate customer or public complaints, determine nature and extent of problem, and recommend remedial measures. Plan layout of electric-power-generating plants and distribution lines and stations. Assist in developing capital project programs for new equipment and major repairs. Develop budgets, estimating labor, material, and construction costs. Compile data and write reports regarding existing and potential engineering studies and projects. Collect data relating to commercial and residential development, population, and power system interconnection to determine operating efficiency of electrical systems. Conduct field surveys and study maps, graphs, diagrams, and other data to identify and correct power system problems.

Personality Type: Investigative. Investigative occupations frequently involve working with ideas and require an extensive amount of thinking. These occupations can involve searching for facts and figuring out problems mentally.

GOE—Interest Area: 15. Scientific Research, Engineering, and Mathematics. **Work Group:** 15.07. Research and Design Engineering. **Other Jobs in This Work Group:** Aerospace Engineers; Biomedical Engineers; Chemical Engineers; Civil Engineers; Computer Hardware Engineers; Electronics Engineers, Except Computer; Marine Architects; Marine Engineers; Marine Engineers and Naval Architects; Materials Engineers; Mechanical Engineers; Nuclear Engineers.

Skills—Technology Design: Generating or adapting equipment and technology to serve user needs. **Systems Analysis:** Determining how a system should work and how changes in conditions, operations, and the environment will affect outcomes. **Troubleshooting:** Determining causes of operating errors and deciding what to do about them. **Science:** Using scientific rules and methods to solve problems. **Systems Evaluation:** Identifying measures or indicators of system performance and the actions needed to improve or correct performance relative to the goals of the system. **Equipment Selection:** Determining the kind of tools and equipment needed to do a job.

Education and Training Program: Electrical, Electronics, and Communications Engineering. **Related Knowledge/Courses: Engineering and Technology:** The practical application of engineering science and technology. This includes applying principles, techniques, procedures, and equipment to the design and production of various goods and services. **Design:** Design techniques, tools, and principles involved in production of precision technical plans, blueprints, drawings, and models. **Physics:** Physical principles and laws and their interrelationships and applications to understanding fluid, material, and atmospheric dynamics and mechanical, electrical, atomic, and subatomic structures and processes. **Telecommunications:** Transmission, broadcasting, switching, control, and operation of telecommunications systems. **Computers and Electronics:** Circuit boards, processors, chips, electronic equipment, and computer hardware and software, including applications and programming. **Mathematics:** Arithmetic, algebra, geometry, calculus, and statistics and their applications.

Work Environment: Indoors; sitting.

E

Electrical Power-Line Installers and Repairers

- Education/Training Required: Long-term on-the-job training
- Annual Earnings: $50,150
- Growth: 2.5%
- Annual Job Openings: 11,000
- Self-Employed: 2.3%
- Part-Time: 0.9%

Level of Solitary Work: 62.5 (out of 100)

Level of Contact with Others: 84.2 (out of 100)

Install or repair cables or wires used in electrical power or distribution systems. May erect poles and light- or heavy-duty transmission towers. Adhere to safety practices and procedures, such as checking equipment regularly and erecting barriers around work areas. Open switches or attach grounding devices to remove electrical hazards from disturbed or fallen lines or to facilitate repairs. Climb poles or use truck-mounted buckets to access equipment. Place insulating or fireproofing materials over conductors and joints. Install, maintain, and repair electrical distribution and transmission systems, including conduits; cables; wires; and related equipment such as transformers, circuit breakers, and switches. Identify defective sectionalizing devices, circuit breakers, fuses, voltage regulators, transformers, switches, relays, or wiring, using wiring diagrams and electrical-testing instruments. Drive vehicles equipped with tools and materials to job sites. Coordinate work assignment preparation and completion with other workers. String wire conductors and cables between poles, towers, trenches, pylons, and buildings, setting lines in place and using winches to adjust tension. Inspect and test power lines and auxiliary equipment to locate and identify problems, using reading and testing instruments. Test conductors according to electrical diagrams and specifications to identify corresponding conductors and to prevent incorrect connections. Replace damaged poles with new poles and straighten the poles. Install watt-hour meters and connect service drops between power lines and consumers' facilities. Attach crossarms, insulators, and auxiliary equipment to poles prior to installing them. Travel in trucks, helicopters, and airplanes to inspect lines for freedom from obstruction and adequacy of insulation. Dig holes, using augers, and set poles, using cranes and power equipment. Trim trees that could be hazardous to the functioning of cables or wires. Splice or solder cables together or to overhead transmission lines, customer service lines, or street light lines, using hand tools, epoxies, or specialized equipment. Cut and peel lead sheathing and insulation from defective or newly installed cables and conduits prior to splicing.

Personality Type: Realistic. Realistic occupations frequently involve work activities that include practical, hands-on problems and solutions. They often deal with plants; animals; and real-world materials such as wood, tools, and machinery. Many of the occupations require working outside and do not involve a lot of paperwork or working closely with others.

GOE—Interest Area: 02. Architecture and Construction. **Work Group:** 02.05. Systems and Equipment Installation, Maintenance, and Repair. **Other Jobs in This Work Group:** Electrical and Electronics Repairers, Powerhouse, Substation, and Relay; Elevator Installers and Repairers; Heating and Air Conditioning Mechanics and Installers; Maintenance and Repair Workers, General; Refrigeration Mechanics and Installers; Telecommunications Equipment Installers and Repairers, Except Line Installers; Telecommunications Line Installers and Repairers.

Skills—Repairing: Repairing machines or systems by using the needed tools. **Installation:** Installing equipment, machines, wiring, or programs to meet specifications. **Equipment Maintenance:** Performing routine maintenance on equipment and determining when and what kind of maintenance is needed. **Operation Monitoring:** Watching gauges, dials, or other indicators to make sure a machine is working properly. **Troubleshooting:** Determining causes of operating errors and deciding what to do about them. **Operation and Control:** Controlling operations of equipment or systems.

Education and Training Programs: Electrical and Power Transmission Installation/Installer Training, General; Electrical and Power Transmission Installer Training, Other; Lineworker Training. **Related Knowledge/Courses: Building and Construction:** The materials, methods, and tools involved in the construction or repair of houses, buildings, or other structures such as highways and roads. **Mechanical Devices:** Machines and tools, including their designs, uses, repair, and maintenance. **Customer and Personal Service:** Principles and processes for providing customer and personal services. This includes customer needs assessment, meeting quality standards for services, and evaluation of customer satisfaction. **Engineering and Technology:** The practical application of engineering science and technology. This includes applying principles, techniques, procedures, and equipment to the design and production of various goods and services. **Transportation:** Principles and methods for moving people or goods by air, rail, sea, or road, including the relative costs and benefits. **Design:** Design techniques, tools, and principles involved in production of precision technical plans, blueprints, drawings, and models.

Work Environment: Outdoors; very hot or cold; high places; hazardous conditions; hazardous equipment; using hands on objects, tools, or controls.

Electro-Mechanical Technicians

- Education/Training Required: Associate degree
- Annual Earnings: $43,880
- Growth: 9.7%
- Annual Job Openings: 2,000
- Self-Employed: 0.5%
- Part-Time: 6.7%

Level of Solitary Work: 75.0 (out of 100)

Level of Contact with Others: 58.7 (out of 100)

Operate, test, and maintain unmanned, automated, servo-mechanical, or electromechanical equipment. May operate unmanned submarines, aircraft, or other equipment at worksites, such as oil rigs, deep ocean exploration, or hazardous waste removal. May assist engineers in testing and designing robotics equipment. Test performance of electromechanical assemblies, using test instruments such as oscilloscopes, electronic voltmeters, and bridges. Read blueprints, schematics, diagrams, and technical orders to determine methods and sequences of assembly. Install electrical and electronic parts and hardware in housings or assemblies, using soldering equipment and hand tools. Align, fit, and assemble component parts, using hand tools, power tools, fixtures, templates, and microscopes. Inspect parts for surface defects. Analyze and record test results and prepare written testing documentation. Verify dimensions and clearances of parts to ensure conformance to specifications, using precision measuring instruments. Operate metalworking machines to fabricate housings, jigs, fittings, and fixtures. Repair, rework, and calibrate hydraulic and pneumatic assemblies and systems to meet operational specifications and tolerances. Train others to install, use, and maintain robots. Develop, test, and program new robots.

E

Personality Type: Realistic. Realistic occupations frequently involve work activities that include practical, hands-on problems and solutions. They often deal with plants; animals; and real-world materials such as wood, tools, and machinery. Many of the occupations require working outside and do not involve a lot of paperwork or working closely with others.

GOE—Interest Area: 15. Scientific Research, Engineering, and Mathematics. **Work Group:** 15.09. Engineering Technology. **Other Jobs in This Work Group:** Aerospace Engineering and Operations Technicians; Cartographers and Photogrammetrists; Civil Engineering Technicians; Electrical and Electronic Engineering Technicians; Electrical and Electronics Drafters; Electrical Drafters; Electrical Engineering Technicians; Electronic Drafters; Electronics Engineering Technicians; Environmental Engineering Technicians; Mapping Technicians; Mechanical Drafters; Mechanical Engineering Technicians; Surveying and Mapping Technicians; Surveying Technicians.

Skills—Equipment Maintenance: Performing routine maintenance on equipment and determining when and what kind of maintenance is needed. **Operation Monitoring:** Watching gauges, dials, or other indicators to make sure a machine is working properly. **Installation:** Installing equipment, machines, wiring, or programs to meet specifications. **Quality Control Analysis:** Conducting tests and inspections of products, services, or processes to evaluate quality or performance. **Operation and Control:** Controlling operations of equipment or systems. **Troubleshooting:** Determining causes of operating errors and deciding what to do about them.

Education and Training Program: Engineering Technologies/Technician Training, Other. **Related Knowledge/Courses: Mechanical Devices:** Machines and tools, including their designs, uses, repair, and maintenance. **Engineering and Technology:** The practical application of engineering science and technology. This includes applying principles, techniques, procedures, and equipment to the design and production of various goods and services. **Computers and Electronics:** Circuit boards, processors, chips, electronic equipment, and computer hardware and software, including applications and programming. **Mathematics:** Arithmetic, algebra, geometry, calculus, and statistics and their applications. **Design:** Design techniques, tools, and principles involved in production of precision technical plans, blueprints, drawings, and models. **Physics:** Physical principles and laws and their interrelationships and applications to understanding fluid, material, and atmospheric dynamics and mechanical, electrical, atomic, and subatomic structures and processes.

Work Environment: Indoors; noisy; contaminants; hazardous equipment; standing; using hands on objects, tools, or controls.

Electronic Drafters

This job can be found in the Part II lists under the title Electrical and Electronics Drafters.

- Education/Training Required: Postsecondary vocational training
- Annual Earnings: $45,550
- Growth: 1.2%
- Annual Job Openings: 3,000
- Self-Employed: 6.4%
- Part-Time: 8.4%

The job openings listed here are shared with Electrical Drafters.

Level of Solitary Work: 54.6 (out of 100)

Level of Contact with Others: 74.8 (out of 100)

Draw wiring diagrams, circuit board assembly diagrams, schematics, and layout drawings used for manufacture, installation, and repair of electronic equipment. Draft detail and assembly drawings of design components, circuitry, and printed circuit boards, using computer-assisted equipment or standard drafting techniques and devices. Consult with engineers to discuss and interpret design concepts and determine requirements of detailed working drawings. Locate files relating to specified design project in database library, load program into computer, and record completed job data. Examine electronic schematics and supporting documents to develop, compute, and verify specifications for drafting data, such as configuration of parts, dimensions, and tolerances. Supervise and coordinate work activities of workers engaged in drafting, designing layouts, assembling, and testing printed circuit boards. Compare logic element configuration on display screen with engineering schematics and calculate figures to convert, redesign, and modify element. Review work orders and procedural manuals and confer with vendors and design staff to resolve problems and modify design. Review blueprints to determine customer requirements and consult with assembler regarding schematics, wiring procedures, and conductor paths. Train students to use drafting machines and to prepare schematic diagrams, block diagrams, control drawings, logic diagrams, integrated circuit drawings, and interconnection diagrams. Generate computer tapes of final layout design to produce layered photo masks and photo plotting design onto film. Select drill size to drill test head, according to test design and specifications, and submit guide layout to designated department. Key and program specified commands and engineering specifications into computer system to change functions and test final layout. Copy drawings of printed circuit board fabrication, using print machine or blueprinting procedure. Plot electrical test points on layout sheets and draw schematics for wiring test fixture heads to frames.

Personality Type: Realistic. Realistic occupations frequently involve work activities that include practical, hands-on problems and solutions. They often deal with plants; animals; and real-world materials such as wood, tools, and machinery. Many of the occupations require working outside and do not involve a lot of paperwork or working closely with others.

GOE—Interest Area: 15. Scientific Research, Engineering, and Mathematics. **Work Group:** 15.09.

Engineering Technology. **Other Jobs in This Work Group:** Aerospace Engineering and Operations Technicians; Cartographers and Photogrammetrists; Civil Engineering Technicians; Electrical and Electronic Engineering Technicians; Electrical and Electronics Drafters; Electrical Drafters; Electrical Engineering Technicians; Electro-Mechanical Technicians; Electronics Engineering Technicians; Environmental Engineering Technicians; Mapping Technicians; Mechanical Drafters; Mechanical Engineering Technicians; Surveying and Mapping Technicians; Surveying Technicians.

Skills—Technology Design: Generating or adapting equipment and technology to serve user needs. **Operations Analysis:** Analyzing needs and product requirements to create a design. **Installation:** Installing equipment, machines, wiring, or programs to meet specifications. **Mathematics:** Using mathematics to solve problems. **Equipment Selection:** Determining the kind of tools and equipment needed to do a job. **Negotiation:** Bringing others together and trying to reconcile differences.

Education and Training Program: Electrical/Electronics Drafting and Electrical/Electronics CAD/CADD. **Related Knowledge/Courses: Design:** Design techniques, tools, and principles involved in production of precision technical plans, blueprints, drawings, and models. **Engineering and Technology:** The practical application of engineering science and technology. This includes applying principles, techniques, procedures, and equipment to the design and production of various goods and services. **Mechanical Devices:** Machines and tools, including their designs, uses, repair, and maintenance. **Physics:** Physical principles and laws and their interrelationships and applications to understanding fluid, material, and atmospheric dynamics and mechanical, electrical, atomic, and subatomic structures and processes. **Telecommunications:** Transmission, broadcasting, switching, control, and operation of telecommunications systems. **Mathematics:** Arithmetic, algebra, geometry, calculus, and statistics and their applications.

Work Environment: Indoors; noisy; sitting; using hands on objects, tools, or controls; repetitive motions.

Electronic Home Entertainment Equipment Installers and Repairers

◎ Education/Training Required: Postsecondary vocational training

◎ Annual Earnings: $28,940

◎ Growth: 4.7%

◎ Annual Job Openings: 6,000

◎ Self-Employed: 30.7%

◎ Part-Time: 8.4%

Level of Solitary Work: 65.5 (out of 100)

Level of Contact with Others: 33.2 (out of 100)

Repair, adjust, or install audio or television receivers, stereo systems, camcorders, video systems, or other electronic home entertainment equipment. Read and interpret electronic circuit diagrams, function block diagrams, specifications, engineering drawings, and service manuals. Install, service, and repair electronic equipment or instruments such as televisions, radios, and videocassette recorders. Position or mount speakers and wire speakers to consoles. Calibrate and test equipment and locate circuit and component faults, using hand and power tools and measuring and testing instruments such as resistance meters and oscilloscopes. Compute cost estimates for labor and materials. Disassemble entertainment equipment and repair or replace loose, worn, or defective components and wiring, using hand tools and soldering irons. Make service calls to repair units in customers' homes or return units to shops for major repairs. Tune or adjust equipment and instruments to obtain optimum visual or auditory reception according to specifications, manuals, and drawings. Instruct customers on the safe and proper use of equipment. Keep records of work orders and test and maintenance reports. Confer with customers to determine the nature of problems or to explain repairs.

Personality Type: Realistic. Realistic occupations frequently involve work activities that include practical, hands-on problems and solutions. They often deal with plants; animals; and real-world materials such as wood, tools, and machinery. Many of the occupations require working outside and do not involve a lot of paperwork or working closely with others.

GOE—Interest Area: 13. Manufacturing. **Work Group:** 13.12. Electrical and Electronic Repair. **Other Jobs in This Work Group:** Avionics Technicians; Electric Motor, Power Tool, and Related Repairers; Electrical and Electronics Installers and Repairers, Transportation Equipment; Electrical and Electronics Repairers, Commercial and Industrial Equipment; Electronic Equipment Installers and Repairers, Motor Vehicles; Radio Mechanics.

Skills—Installation: Installing equipment, machines, wiring, or programs to meet specifications. **Science:** Using scientific rules and methods to solve problems. **Repairing:** Repairing machines or systems by using the needed tools. **Equipment Maintenance:** Performing routine maintenance on equipment and determining when and what kind of maintenance is needed. **Troubleshooting:** Determining causes of operating errors and deciding what to do about them. **Technology Design:** Generating or adapting equipment and technology to serve user needs.

Education and Training Program: Communications Systems Installation and Repair Technology. **Related Knowledge/Courses: Computers and Electronics:** Circuit boards, processors, chips, electronic equipment, and computer hardware and software, including applications and programming. **Telecommunications:** Transmission, broadcasting, switching, control, and operation of telecommunications systems. **Design:** Design techniques, tools, and principles involved in production of precision technical plans, blueprints, drawings, and models. **Mechanical Devices:** Machines and tools, including their designs, uses, repair, and maintenance. **Engineering and Technology:** The practical application of engineering science and technology. This includes applying principles, techniques, procedures, and equipment to the design and production of various goods and services.

Work Environment: Indoors; sitting; using hands on objects, tools, or controls; bending or twisting the body.

Electronics Engineering Technicians

This job can be found in the Part II lists under the title Electrical and Electronic Engineering Technicians.

- Education/Training Required: Associate degree
- Annual Earnings: $48,040
- Growth: 9.8%
- Annual Job Openings: 18,000
- Self-Employed: 0.4%
- Part-Time: 6.7%

The job openings listed here are shared with Electrical Engineering Technicians.

Level of Solitary Work: 49.9 (out of 100)

Level of Contact with Others: 72.2 (out of 100)

Lay out, build, test, troubleshoot, repair, and modify developmental and production electronic components, parts, equipment, and systems, such as computer equipment, missile control instrumentation, electron tubes, test equipment, and machine tool numerical controls, applying principles and theories of electronics, electrical circuitry, engineering mathematics, electronic and electrical testing, and physics. Usually work under direction of engineering staff. Test electronics units, using standard test equipment, and analyze results to evaluate performance and determine need for adjustment.

Perform preventative maintenance and calibration of equipment and systems. Read blueprints, wiring diagrams, schematic drawings, and engineering instructions for assembling electronics units, applying knowledge of electronic theory and components. Identify and resolve equipment malfunctions, working with manufacturers and field representatives as necessary to procure replacement parts. Maintain system logs and manuals to document testing and operation of equipment. Assemble, test, and maintain circuitry or electronic components according to engineering instructions, technical manuals, and knowledge of electronics, using hand and power tools. Adjust and replace defective or improperly functioning circuitry and electronics components, using hand tools and soldering iron. Procure parts and maintain inventory and related documentation. Maintain working knowledge of state-of-the-art tools or software by reading or attending conferences, workshops, or other training. Provide user applications and engineering support and recommendations for new and existing equipment with regard to installation, upgrades, and enhancement. Write reports and record data on testing techniques, laboratory equipment, and specifications to assist engineers. Provide customer support and education, working with users to identify needs, determine sources of problems, and provide information on product use. Design basic circuitry and draft sketches for clarification of details and design documentation under engineers' direction, using drafting instruments and computer-aided design (CAD) equipment. Build prototypes from rough sketches or plans. Develop and upgrade preventative maintenance procedures for components, equipment, parts, and systems. Fabricate parts, such as coils, terminal boards, and chassis, using bench lathes, drills, or other machine tools. Research equipment and component needs, sources, competitive prices, delivery times, and ongoing operational costs. Write computer or microprocessor software programs.

Personality Type: Realistic. Realistic occupations frequently involve work activities that include practical, hands-on problems and solutions. They often deal with plants; animals; and real-world materials such as

E

wood, tools, and machinery. Many of the occupations require working outside and do not involve a lot of paperwork or working closely with others.

GOE—Interest Area: 15. Scientific Research, Engineer-ing, and Mathematics. Work Group: 15.09. Engineering Technology. Other Jobs in This Work Group: Aerospace Engineering and Operations Technicians; Cartographers and Photogrammetrists; Civil Engineering Technicians; Electrical and Electronic Engineering Technicians; Electrical and Electronics Drafters; Electrical Drafters; Electrical Engineering Technicians; Electro-Mechanical Technicians; Electronic Drafters; Environmental Engineering Technicians; Mapping Technicians; Mechanical Drafters; Mechanical Engineering Technicians; Surveying and Mapping Technicians; Surveying Technicians.

Skills—Repairing: Repairing machines or systems by using the needed tools. Installation: Installing equipment, machines, wiring, or programs to meet specifications. Equipment Maintenance: Performing routine maintenance on equipment and determining when and what kind of maintenance is needed. Troubleshooting: Determining causes of operating errors and deciding what to do about them. Operation Monitoring: Watching gauges, dials, or other indicators to make sure a machine is working properly. Technology Design: Generating or adapting equipment and technology to serve user needs.

Education and Training Programs: Computer Engineering Technology/Technician Training; Electrical and Electronic Engineering Technologies/ Technician Training, Other; Electrical, Electronic, and Communications Engineering Technology/ Technician Training; Telecommunications Technology/Technician Training. Related Knowledge/ Courses: Engineering and Technology: The practical application of engineering science and technology. This includes applying principles, techniques, procedures, and equipment to the design and production of various goods and services. Mechanical Devices: Machines and tools, including their designs, uses, repair, and maintenance. Computers and Electronics: Circuit boards, processors, chips, elec-

tronic equipment, and computer hardware and software, including applications and programming. Design: Design techniques, tools, and principles involved in production of precision technical plans, blueprints, drawings, and models. Telecommunications: Transmission, broadcasting, switching, control, and operation of telecommunications systems. Mathematics: Arithmetic, algebra, geometry, calculus, and statistics and their applications.

Work Environment: Indoors; contaminants; hazardous conditions; hazardous equipment; sitting; using hands on objects, tools, or controls.

Electronics Engineers, Except Computer

- Education/Training Required: Bachelor's degree
- Annual Earnings: $78,030
- Growth: 9.7%
- Annual Job Openings: 11,000
- Self-Employed: 3.2%
- Part-Time: 2.1%

Level of Solitary Work: 53.0 (out of 100)

Level of Contact with Others: 74.8 (out of 100)

Research, design, develop, and test electronic components and systems for commercial, industrial, military, or scientific use, utilizing knowledge of electronic theory and materials properties. Design electronic circuits and components for use in fields such as telecommunications, aerospace guidance and propulsion control, acoustics, or instruments and controls. Design electronic components, software, products, or systems for commercial, industrial, medical, military, or scientific applications. Provide technical support and instruction to staff or customers regarding equipment standards, assisting with specific, difficult in-service engineering. Operate computer-assisted engineering and design software and equipment to perform engineering tasks. Analyze system requirements, capacity, cost, and customer needs to determine feasibility of project and develop system plan. Confer with engineers, customers, vendors, or others to discuss existing and potential engineering projects or products. Review and evaluate work of others inside and outside the organization to ensure effectiveness, technical adequacy, and compatibility in the resolution of complex engineering problems. Determine material and equipment needs and order supplies. Inspect electronic equipment, instruments, products, and systems to ensure conformance to specifications, safety standards, and applicable codes and regulations. Evaluate operational systems, prototypes, and proposals and recommend repair or design modifications based on factors such as environment, service, cost, and system capabilities. Prepare documentation containing information such as confidential descriptions and specifications of proprietary hardware and software, product development and introduction schedules, product costs, and information about product performance weaknesses. Direct and coordinate activities concerned with manufacture, construction, installation, maintenance, operation, and modification of electronic equipment, products, and systems. Develop and perform operational, maintenance, and testing procedures for electronic products, components, equipment, and systems. Plan and develop applications and modifications for electronic properties used in components, products, and systems to improve technical performance. Plan and implement research, methodology, and procedures to apply principles of electronic theory to engineering projects. Prepare engineering sketches and specifications for construction, relocation, and installation of equipment, facilities, products, and systems.

Personality Type: Investigative. Investigative occupations frequently involve working with ideas and require an extensive amount of thinking. These occupations can involve searching for facts and figuring out problems mentally.

GOE—Interest Area: 15. Scientific Research, Engineering, and Mathematics. **Work Group:** 15.07. Research and Design Engineering. **Other Jobs in This Work Group:** Aerospace Engineers; Biomedical Engineers; Chemical Engineers; Civil Engineers; Computer Hardware Engineers; Electrical Engineers; Marine Architects; Marine Engineers; Marine Engineers and Naval Architects; Materials Engineers; Mechanical Engineers; Nuclear Engineers.

Skills—Troubleshooting: Determining causes of operating errors and deciding what to do about them. **Installation:** Installing equipment, machines, wiring, or programs to meet specifications. **Technology Design:** Generating or adapting equipment and technology to serve user needs. **Operations Analysis:** Analyzing needs and product requirements to create a design. **Science:** Using scientific rules and methods to solve problems. **Systems Evaluation:** Identifying measures or indicators of system performance and the actions needed to improve or correct performance relative to the goals of the system.

Education and Training Program: Electrical, Electronics, and Communications Engineering. **Related Knowledge/Courses: Engineering and Technology:** The practical application of engineering science and technology. This includes applying principles, techniques, procedures, and equipment to the design and production of various goods and services. **Design:** Design techniques, tools, and principles involved in production of precision technical plans, blueprints, drawings, and models. **Computers and Electronics:** Circuit boards, processors, chips, electronic equipment, and computer hardware and software, including applications and programming. **Physics:** Physical principles and laws and their interrelationships and applications to understanding fluid, material, and atmospheric dynamics and mechanical, electrical, atomic, and subatomic structures and processes. **Telecommunications:** Transmission, broadcasting, switching, control, and operation of telecommunications systems. **Production and Processing:** Raw materials, production processes, quality control, costs, and other techniques for maximizing the effective manufacture and distribution of goods.

Work Environment: Indoors; noisy; sitting.

Elevator Installers and Repairers

- Education/Training Required: Long-term on-the-job training
- Annual Earnings: $59,190
- Growth: 14.8%
- Annual Job Openings: 3,000
- Self-Employed: 0.4%
- Part-Time: No data available

Level of Solitary Work: 71.7 (out of 100)

Level of Contact with Others: 76.8 (out of 100)

Assemble, install, repair, or maintain electric or hydraulic freight or passenger elevators, escalators, or dumbwaiters. Assemble, install, repair, and maintain elevators, escalators, moving sidewalks, and dumbwaiters, using hand and power tools and testing devices such as test lamps, ammeters, and voltmeters. Test newly installed equipment to ensure that it meets specifications, such as stopping at floors for set amounts of time. Locate malfunctions in brakes, motors, switches, and signal and control systems, using test equipment. Check that safety regulations and building codes are met and complete service reports verifying conformance to standards. Connect electrical wiring to control panels and electric motors. Read and interpret blueprints to determine the layout of system components, frameworks, and foundations and to select installation equipment. Adjust safety controls; counterweights; door mechanisms; and components such as valves, ratchets, seals, and brake linings. Inspect wiring connections, control panel hookups, door installations, and align-

ments and clearances of cars and hoistways to ensure that equipment will operate properly. Disassemble defective units and repair or replace parts such as locks, gears, cables, and electric wiring. Maintain logbooks that detail all repairs and checks performed. Participate in additional training to keep skills up to date. Attach guide shoes and rollers to minimize the lateral motion of cars as they travel through shafts. Connect car frames to counterweights, using steel cables. Bolt or weld steel rails to the walls of shafts to guide elevators, working from scaffolding or platforms. Assemble elevator cars, installing each car's platform, walls, and doors. Install outer doors and door frames at elevator entrances on each floor of a structure. Install electrical wires and controls by attaching conduit along shaft walls from floor to floor and then pulling plastic-covered wires through the conduit. Cut prefabricated sections of framework, rails, and other components to specified dimensions. Operate elevators to determine power demands and test power consumption to detect overload factors. Assemble electrically powered stairs, steel frameworks, and tracks and install associated motors and electrical wiring.

Personality Type: Realistic. Realistic occupations frequently involve work activities that include practical, hands-on problems and solutions. They often deal with plants; animals; and real-world materials such as wood, tools, and machinery. Many of the occupations require working outside and do not involve a lot of paperwork or working closely with others.

GOE—Interest Area: 02. Architecture and Construction. **Work Group:** 02.05. Systems and Equipment Installation, Maintenance, and Repair. **Other Jobs in This Work Group:** Electrical and Electronics Repairers, Powerhouse, Substation, and Relay; Electrical Power-Line Installers and Repairers; Heating and Air Conditioning Mechanics and Installers; Maintenance and Repair Workers, General; Refrigeration Mechanics and Installers; Telecommunications Equipment Installers and Repairers, Except Line Installers; Telecommunications Line Installers and Repairers.

Skills—**Installation:** Installing equipment, machines, wiring, or programs to meet specifications. **Repairing:** Repairing machines or systems by using the needed tools. **Troubleshooting:** Determining causes of operating errors and deciding what to do about them. **Equipment Maintenance:** Performing routine maintenance on equipment and determining when and what kind of maintenance is needed. **Quality Control Analysis:** Conducting tests and inspections of products, services, or processes to evaluate quality or performance. **Technology Design:** Generating or adapting equipment and technology to serve user needs.

Education and Training Program: Industrial Mechanics and Maintenance Technology. **Related Knowledge/Courses: Building and Construction:** The materials, methods, and tools involved in the construction or repair of houses, buildings, or other structures such as highways and roads. **Mechanical Devices:** Machines and tools, including their designs, uses, repair, and maintenance. **Design:** Design techniques, tools, and principles involved in production of precision technical plans, blueprints, drawings, and models. **Physics:** Physical principles and laws and their interrelationships and applications to understanding fluid, material, and atmospheric dynamics and mechanical, electrical, atomic, and subatomic structures and processes. **Engineering and Technology:** The practical application of engineering science and technology. This includes applying principles, techniques, procedures, and equipment to the design and production of various goods and services. **Customer and Personal Service:** Principles and processes for providing customer and personal services. This includes customer needs assessment, meeting quality standards for services, and evaluation of customer satisfaction.

Work Environment: Contaminants; high places; hazardous conditions; hazardous equipment; standing; using hands on objects, tools, or controls.

Embalmers

- Education/Training Required: Postsecondary vocational training
- Annual Earnings: $36,960
- Growth: 15.7%
- Annual Job Openings: 2,000
- Self-Employed: 0.0%
- Part-Time: 44.0%

Level of Solitary Work: 75.0 (out of 100)

Level of Contact with Others: 90.0 (out of 100)

Prepare bodies for interment in conformity with legal requirements. Conform to laws of health and sanitation and ensure that legal requirements concerning embalming are met. Apply cosmetics to impart lifelike appearance to the deceased. Incise stomach and abdominal walls and probe internal organs, using trocar, to withdraw blood and waste matter from organs. Close incisions, using needles and sutures. Reshape or reconstruct disfigured or maimed bodies when necessary, using derma-surgery techniques and materials such as clay, cotton, plaster of paris, and wax. Make incisions in arms or thighs and drain blood from circulatory system and replace it with embalming fluid, using pump. Dress bodies and place them in caskets. Join lips, using needles and thread or wire. Conduct interviews to arrange for the preparation of obituary notices, to assist with the selection of caskets or urns, and to determine the location and time of burials or cremations. Perform the duties of funeral directors, including coordinating funeral activities. Attach trocar to pump-tube, start pump, and repeat probing to force embalming fluid into organs. Perform special procedures necessary for remains that are to be transported to other states or overseas or where death was caused by infectious disease. Maintain records such as itemized lists of clothing or valuables delivered with body and names of persons embalmed. Insert convex celluloid or cotton between eyeballs and eyelids to prevent slipping and sinking of eyelids. Wash and dry bodies, using germicidal soap and towels or hot air dryers. Arrange for transporting the deceased to another state for interment. Supervise funeral attendants and other funeral home staff. Pack body orifices with cotton saturated with embalming fluid to prevent escape of gases or waste matter. Assist with placing caskets in hearses and organize cemetery processions. Serve as pallbearers, attend visiting rooms, and provide other assistance to the bereaved. Direct casket and floral display placement and arrange guest seating. Arrange funeral home equipment and perform general maintenance. Assist coroners at death scenes or at autopsies, file police reports, and testify at inquests or in court if employed by a coroner.

Personality Type: Realistic. Realistic occupations frequently involve work activities that include practical, hands-on problems and solutions. They often deal with plants; animals; and real-world materials such as wood, tools, and machinery. Many of the occupations require working outside and do not involve a lot of paperwork or working closely with others.

GOE—Interest Area: 08. Health Science. **Work Group:** 08.09. Health Protection and Promotion. **Other Jobs in This Work Group:** Athletic Trainers; Dietetic Technicians; Dietitians and Nutritionists.

Skills—Service Orientation: Actively looking for ways to help people. **Science:** Using scientific rules and methods to solve problems. **Management of Financial Resources:** Determining how money will be spent to get the work done and accounting for these expenditures. **Management of Material Resources:** Obtaining and seeing to the appropriate use of equipment, facilities, and materials needed to do certain work. **Social Perceptiveness:** Being aware of others' reactions and understanding why they react as they do. **Equipment Maintenance:** Performing routine maintenance on equipment and determining when and what kind of maintenance is needed.

Education and Training Programs: Funeral Service and Mortuary Science, General; Mortuary Science and Embalming/Embalmer Training. **Related Knowledge/Courses: Chemistry:** The chemical composition, structure, and properties of substances and

of the chemical processes and transformations that they undergo. This includes uses of chemicals and their danger signs, production techniques, and disposal methods. **Biology:** Plant and animal organisms and their tissues, cells, functions, interdependencies, and interactions with each other and the environment. **Customer and Personal Service:** Principles and processes for providing customer and personal services. This includes customer needs assessment, meeting quality standards for services, and evaluation of customer satisfaction. **Philosophy and Theology:** Different philosophical systems and religions. This includes their basic principles, values, ethics, ways of thinking, customs, and practices and their impact on human culture. **Therapy and Counseling:** Principles, methods, and procedures for diagnosis, treatment, and rehabilitation of physical and mental dysfunctions and for career counseling and guidance. **Medicine and Dentistry:** The information and techniques needed to diagnose and treat human injuries, diseases, and deformities. This includes symptoms, treatment alternatives, drug properties and interactions, and preventive health-care measures.

Work Environment: Indoors; contaminants; disease or infections; hazardous conditions; standing; using hands on objects, tools, or controls.

Environmental Science and Protection Technicians, Including Health

- ◉ Education/Training Required: Associate degree
- ◉ Annual Earnings: $36,260
- ◉ Growth: 16.3%
- ◉ Annual Job Openings: 6,000
- ◉ Self-Employed: 1.4%
- ◉ Part-Time: 22.7%

Level of Solitary Work: 65.5 (out of 100)

Level of Contact with Others: 80.8 (out of 100)

Perform laboratory and field tests to monitor the environment and investigate sources of pollution, including those that affect health. Under direction of an environmental scientist or specialist, may collect samples of gases, soil, water, and other materials for testing and take corrective actions as assigned. Record test data and prepare reports, summaries, and charts that interpret test results. Collect samples of gases, soils, water, industrial wastewater, and asbestos products to conduct tests on pollutant levels and identify sources of pollution. Respond to and investigate hazardous conditions or spills or outbreaks of disease or food poisoning, collecting samples for analysis. Provide information and technical and program assistance to government representatives, employers, and the general public on the issues of public health, environmental protection, or workplace safety. Calibrate microscopes and test instruments. Make recommendations to control or eliminate unsafe conditions at workplaces or public facilities. Inspect sanitary conditions at public facilities. Prepare samples or photomicrographs for testing and analysis. Calculate amount of pollutant in samples or compute air pollution or gas flow in industrial processes, using chemical and mathematical formulas. Initiate procedures to close down or fine establishments violating environmental or health regulations. Determine amounts and kinds of chemicals to use in destroying harmful organisms and removing impurities from purification systems. Discuss test results and analyses with customers. Maintain files such as hazardous waste databases, chemical usage data, personnel exposure information, and diagrams showing equipment locations. Perform statistical analysis of environmental data. Set up equipment or stations to monitor and collect pollutants from sites such as smokestacks, manufacturing plants, or mechanical equipment. Distribute permits, closure plans, and cleanup plans. Inspect workplaces to ensure the absence of health and safety hazards such as high noise levels, radiation, or potential lighting hazards. Weigh, analyze, and measure collected sample particles, such as lead, coal dust, or rock, to determine concentration of pollutants. Examine and analyze material for presence and concentration of contaminants such as asbestos, using variety of microscopes. Develop testing procedures or direct activities of workers in laboratory.

Personality Type: Investigative. Investigative occupations frequently involve working with ideas and require an extensive amount of thinking. These occupations can involve searching for facts and figuring out problems mentally.

GOE—Interest Area: 01. Agriculture and Natural Resources. **Work Group:** 01.03. Resource Technologies for Plants, Animals, and the Environment. **Other Jobs in This Work Group:** Agricultural and Food Science Technicians; Agricultural Technicians; Food Science Technicians; Food Scientists and Technologists; Geological and Petroleum Technicians; Geological Sample Test Technicians; Geophysical Data Technicians.

Skills—Science: Using scientific rules and methods to solve problems. **Persuasion:** Persuading others to change their minds or behavior. **Active Learning:** Understanding the implications of new information for both current and future problem solving and decision making. **Mathematics:** Using mathematics to solve problems. **Reading Comprehension:** Understanding written sentences and paragraphs in work-related documents. **Quality Control Analysis:** Conducting tests and inspections of products, services, or processes to evaluate quality or performance.

Education and Training Programs: Environmental Science; Environmental Studies; Physical Science Technologies/Technician Training, Other; Science Technologies/Technician Training, Other. **Related Knowledge/Courses: Biology:** Plant and animal organisms and their tissues, cells, functions, interdependencies, and interactions with each other and the environment. **Engineering and Technology:** The practical application of engineering science and technology. This includes applying principles, techniques, procedures, and equipment to the design and production of various goods and services. **Chemistry:**

The chemical composition, structure, and properties of substances and of the chemical processes and transformations that they undergo. This includes uses of chemicals and their danger signs, production techniques, and disposal methods. **Physics:** Physical principles and laws and their interrelationships and applications to understanding fluid, material, and atmospheric dynamics and mechanical, electrical, atomic, and subatomic structures and processes. **Building and Construction:** The materials, methods, and tools involved in the construction or repair of houses, buildings, or other structures such as highways and roads. **Design:** Design techniques, tools, and principles involved in production of precision technical plans, blueprints, drawings, and models.

Work Environment: More often indoors than outdoors; noisy; very hot or cold; contaminants; sitting.

Environmental Scientists and Specialists, Including Health

- ◎ Education/Training Required: Master's degree
- ◎ Annual Earnings: $52,630
- ◎ Growth: 17.1%
- ◎ Annual Job Openings: 8,000
- ◎ Self-Employed: 4.2%
- ◎ Part-Time: 5.7%

Level of Solitary Work: 71.7 (out of 100)

Level of Contact with Others: 89.8 (out of 100)

Conduct research or perform investigation for the purpose of identifying, abating, or eliminating sources of pollutants or hazards that affect either the environment or the health of the population. Utilizing knowledge of various scientific disciplines, may collect, synthesize, study, report, and take action based on data derived from measurements or observations of air, food, soil, water, and other sources. **Conduct environmental audits and inspections and investigations of violations. Evaluate violations or problems discovered during inspections to determine appropriate regulatory actions or to provide advice on the development and prosecution of regulatory cases. Communicate scientific and technical information through oral briefings, written documents, workshops, conferences, and public hearings. Review and implement environmental technical standards, guidelines, policies, and formal regulations that meet all appropriate requirements. Provide technical guidance, support, and oversight to environmental programs, industry, and the public. Provide advice on proper standards and regulations or the development of policies, strategies, and codes of practice for environmental management. Analyze data to determine validity, quality, and scientific significance and to interpret correlations between human activities and environmental effects. Collect, synthesize, and analyze data derived from pollution emission measurements, atmospheric monitoring, meteorological and mineralogical information, and soil or water samples. Determine data collection methods to be employed in research projects and surveys. Prepare charts or graphs from data samples, providing summary information on the environmental relevance of the data. Develop the technical portions of legal documents, administrative orders, or consent decrees. Investigate and report on accidents affecting the environment. Monitor environmental impacts of development activities. Supervise environmental technologists and technicians. Develop programs designed to obtain the most productive, non-damaging use of land. Research sources of pollution to determine their effects on the environment and to develop theories or methods of pollution abatement or control. Monitor effects of pollution and land degradation and recommend means of prevention or control. Design and direct studies to obtain technical environmental information about planned projects. Conduct applied research on topics such as waste control and treatment and pollution control methods.**

Personality Type: Investigative. Investigative occupations frequently involve working with ideas and require an extensive amount of thinking. These occupations can involve searching for facts and figuring out problems mentally.

GOE—Interest Area: 15. Scientific Research, Engineering, and Mathematics. **Work Group:** 15.03. Life Sciences. **Other Jobs in This Work Group:** Biochemists and Biophysicists; Biologists; Epidemiologists; Medical Scientists, Except Epidemiologists; Microbiologists.

Skills—Science: Using scientific rules and methods to solve problems. **Service Orientation:** Actively looking for ways to help people. **Negotiation:** Bringing others together and trying to reconcile differences. **Coordination:** Adjusting actions in relation to others' actions. **Reading Comprehension:** Understanding written sentences and paragraphs in work-related documents. **Complex Problem Solving:** Identifying complex problems and reviewing related information to develop and evaluate options and implement solutions.

Education and Training Programs: Environmental Science; Environmental Studies. **Related Knowledge/Courses: Biology:** Plant and animal organisms and their tissues, cells, functions, interdependencies, and interactions with each other and the environment. **Geography:** Principles and methods for describing the features of land, sea, and air masses, including their physical characteristics; locations; interrelationships; and distribution of plant, animal, and human life. **Chemistry:** The chemical composition, structure, and properties of substances and of the chemical processes and transformations that they undergo. This includes uses of chemicals and their danger signs, production techniques, and disposal methods. **Law and Government:** Laws, legal codes, court procedures, precedents, government regulations, executive orders, agency rules, and the democratic political process. **Engineering and Technology:** The practical application of engineering science and technology. This includes applying principles, techniques, procedures, and equipment to the design and production of various goods and services.

Physics: Physical principles and laws and their interrelationships and applications to understanding fluid, material, and atmospheric dynamics and mechanical, electrical, atomic, and subatomic structures and processes.

Work Environment: More often indoors than outdoors; noisy; sitting.

Epidemiologists

- Education/Training Required: Master's degree
- Annual Earnings: $52,170
- Growth: 26.2%
- Annual Job Openings: 1,000
- Self-Employed: 0.4%
- Part-Time: 5.5%

Level of Solitary Work: 62.5 (out of 100)

Level of Contact with Others: 81.5 (out of 100)

Investigate and describe the determinants and distribution of disease, disability, and other health outcomes and develop the means for prevention and control. Oversee public health programs, including statistical analysis, health-care planning, surveillance systems, and public health improvement. Investigate diseases or parasites to determine cause and risk factors, progress, life cycle, or mode of transmission. Plan and direct studies to investigate human or animal disease, preventive methods, and treatments for disease. Plan, administer, and evaluate health safety standards and programs to improve public health, conferring with health department, industry personnel, physicians, and others. Provide expertise in the design, management, and evaluation of study protocols and health status questionnaires, sample selection, and analysis. Conduct research to develop methodologies, instrumentation, and procedures for medical application, analyzing data and presenting findings. Consult with and advise physicians, educators, researchers, government health officials, and others regarding medical applications of sciences such as physics, biology, and chemistry. Supervise professional, technical, and clerical personnel. Identify and analyze public health issues related to foodborne parasitic diseases and their impact on public policies or scientific studies or surveys. Teach principles of medicine and medical and laboratory procedures to physicians, residents, students, and technicians. Standardize drug dosages, methods of immunization, and procedures for manufacture of drugs and medicinal compounds. Prepare and analyze samples to study effects of drugs, gases, pesticides, or microorganisms on cell structure and tissue.

Personality Type: Investigative. Investigative occupations frequently involve working with ideas and require an extensive amount of thinking. These occupations can involve searching for facts and figuring out problems mentally.

GOE—Interest Area: 15. Scientific Research, Engineering, and Mathematics. **Work Group:** 15.03. Life Sciences. **Other Jobs in This Work Group:** Biochemists and Biophysicists; Biologists; Environmental Scientists and Specialists, Including Health; Medical Scientists, Except Epidemiologists; Microbiologists.

Skills—Science: Using scientific rules and methods to solve problems. **Programming:** Writing computer programs for various purposes. **Reading Comprehension:** Understanding written sentences and paragraphs in work-related documents. **Mathematics:** Using mathematics to solve problems. **Writing:** Communicating effectively in writing as appropriate for the needs of the audience. **Complex Problem Solving:** Identifying complex problems and reviewing related information to develop and evaluate options and implement solutions.

Education and Training Programs: Biophysics; Cell/Cellular Biology and Histology; Epidemiology; Medical Scientist (MS, PhD). **Related Knowledge/ Courses: Biology:** Plant and animal organisms and their tissues, cells, functions, interdependencies, and interactions with each other and the environment.

Sociology and Anthropology: Group behavior and dynamics, societal trends and influences, human migrations, ethnicity, and cultures and their history and origins. **Medicine and Dentistry:** The information and techniques needed to diagnose and treat human injuries, diseases, and deformities. This includes symptoms, treatment alternatives, drug properties and interactions, and preventive healthcare measures. **English Language:** The structure and content of the English language, including the meaning and spelling of words, rules of composition, and grammar. **Mathematics:** Arithmetic, algebra, geometry, calculus, and statistics and their applications. **Computers and Electronics:** Circuit boards, processors, chips, electronic equipment, and computer hardware and software, including applications and programming.

Work Environment: Indoors; noisy; sitting; repetitive motions.

Excavating and Loading Machine and Dragline Operators

- ◎ Education/Training Required: Moderate-term on-the-job training
- ◎ Annual Earnings: $32,380
- ◎ Growth: 8.0%
- ◎ Annual Job Openings: 11,000
- ◎ Self-Employed: 19.1%
- ◎ Part-Time: 3.6%

Level of Solitary Work: 48.5 (out of 100)

Level of Contact with Others: 70.7 (out of 100)

Operate or tend machinery equipped with scoops, shovels, or buckets to excavate and load loose materials. Move levers, depress foot pedals, and turn dials to operate power machinery such as power shovels, stripping shovels, scraper loaders, or backhoes. Set up and inspect equipment prior to operation. Observe hand signals, grade stakes, and other markings when operating machines so that work can be performed to specifications. Become familiar with digging plans, machine capabilities and limitations, and efficient and safe digging procedures in a given application. Operate machinery to perform activities such as backfilling excavations, vibrating or breaking rock or concrete, and making winter roads. Create and maintain inclines and ramps and handle slides, mud, and pit cleanings and maintenance. Lubricate, adjust, and repair machinery and replace parts such as gears, bearings, and bucket teeth. Move materials over short distances, such as around a construction site, factory, or warehouse. Measure and verify levels of rock or gravel, bases, and other excavated material. Receive written or oral instructions regarding material movement or excavation. Adjust dig face angles for varying overburden depths and set lengths. Drive machines to worksites. Perform manual labor to prepare or finish sites, such as shoveling materials by hand. Direct ground workers engaged in activities such as moving stakes or markers or changing positions of towers. Direct workers engaged in placing blocks and outriggers to prevent capsizing of machines when lifting heavy loads.

Personality Type: Realistic. Realistic occupations frequently involve work activities that include practical, hands-on problems and solutions. They often deal with plants; animals; and real-world materials such as wood, tools, and machinery. Many of the occupations require working outside and do not involve a lot of paperwork or working closely with others.

GOE—Interest Area: 01. Agriculture and Natural Resources. **Work Group:** 01.08. Mining and Drilling. **Other Jobs in This Work Group:** Continuous Mining Machine Operators; Derrick Operators, Oil and Gas; Earth Drillers, Except Oil and Gas; Explosives Workers, Ordnance Handling Experts, and Blasters; Helpers—Extraction Workers; Loading Machine Operators, Underground Mining; Mine Cutting and Channeling Machine Operators; Rock Splitters, Quarry; Roof Bolters, Mining; Rotary Drill Operators, Oil and Gas; Roustabouts, Oil and Gas; Service Unit Operators, Oil, Gas, and Mining; Shuttle Car Operators; Wellhead Pumpers.

Skills—Repairing: Repairing machines or systems by using the needed tools. **Operation Monitoring:** Watching gauges, dials, or other indicators to make sure a machine is working properly. **Equipment Maintenance:** Performing routine maintenance on equipment and determining when and what kind of maintenance is needed. **Operation and Control:** Controlling operations of equipment or systems. **Installation:** Installing equipment, machines, wiring, or programs to meet specifications. **Systems Analysis:** Determining how a system should work and how changes in conditions, operations, and the environment will affect outcomes.

Education and Training Program: Construction/ Heavy Equipment/Earthmoving Equipment Operation. **Related Knowledge/Courses: Building and Construction:** The materials, methods, and tools involved in the construction or repair of houses, buildings, or other structures such as highways and roads. **Mechanical Devices:** Machines and tools, including their designs, uses, repair, and maintenance. **Transportation:** Principles and methods for moving people or goods by air, rail, sea, or road, including the relative costs and benefits. **Production and Processing:** Raw materials, production processes, quality control, costs, and other techniques for maximizing the effective manufacture and distribution of goods. **Public Safety and Security:** Relevant equipment, policies, procedures, and strategies to promote effective local, state, or national security operations for the protection of people, data, property, and institutions. **Engineering and Technology:** The practical application of engineering science and technology. This includes applying principles, techniques, procedures, and equipment to the design and production of various goods and services.

Work Environment: Outdoors; noisy; contaminants; whole-body vibration; sitting; using hands on objects, tools, or controls.

Farmers and Ranchers

- ◉ Education/Training Required: Long-term on-the-job training
- ◉ Annual Earnings: $34,140
- ◉ Growth: –14.5%
- ◉ Annual Job Openings: 96,000
- ◉ Self-Employed: 100.0%
- ◉ Part-Time: 23.6%

Level of Solitary Work: 40.5 (out of 100)

Level of Contact with Others: 35.0 (out of 100)

On an ownership or rental basis, operate farms, ranches, greenhouses, nurseries, timber tracts, or other agricultural production establishments that produce crops, horticultural specialties, livestock, poultry, finfish, shellfish, or animal specialties. May plant, cultivate, harvest, perform post-harvest activities on, and market crops and livestock; may hire, train, and supervise farm workers or supervise a farm labor contractor; may prepare cost, production, and other records. May maintain and operate machinery and perform physical work. Monitor crops as they grow in order to ensure that they are growing properly and are free from diseases and contaminants. Select animals for market and provide transportation of livestock to market. Select and purchase supplies and equipment such as seed, fertilizers, and farm machinery. Remove lower-quality or older animals from herds and purchase other livestock to replace culled animals. Purchase and store livestock feed. Plan crop activities based on factors such as crop maturity and weather conditions. Negotiate and arrange with buyers for the sale, storage, and shipment of crops. Determine types and quantities of crops or livestock to be raised according to factors such as market conditions, federal program availability, and soil conditions. Milk cows, using milking machinery. Maintain pastures or grazing lands to ensure that animals have enough feed, employing pasture-conservation measures such as arranging

rotational grazing. Install and shift irrigation systems to irrigate fields evenly or according to crop need. Harvest crops and collect specialty products such as royal jelly, wax, pollen, and honey from bee colonies. Evaluate product marketing alternatives and then promote and market farm products, acting as the sales agent for livestock and crops. Assist in animal births and care for newborn livestock. Breed and raise stock such as cattle, poultry, and honeybees, using recognized breeding practices to ensure continued improvement in stock. Clean and disinfect buildings and yards and remove manure. Clean and sanitize milking equipment, storage tanks, collection cups, and cows' udders or ensure that procedures are followed to maintain sanitary conditions for handling of milk. Clean, grade, and package crops for marketing. Control the spread of disease and parasites in herds by using vaccination and medication and by separating sick animals. Destroy diseased or superfluous crops. Perform crop production duties such as planning, tilling, planting, fertilizing, cultivating, spraying, and harvesting. Set up and operate farm machinery to cultivate, harvest, and haul crops.

Personality Type: Realistic. Realistic occupations frequently involve work activities that include practical, hands-on problems and solutions. They often deal with plants; animals; and real-world materials such as wood, tools, and machinery. Many of the occupations require working outside and do not involve a lot of paperwork or working closely with others.

GOE—Interest Area: 01. Agriculture and Natural Resources. **Work Group:** 01.01. Managerial Work in Agriculture and Natural Resources. **Other Jobs in This Work Group:** Aquacultural Managers; Crop and Livestock Managers; Farm Labor Contractors; Farm, Ranch, and Other Agricultural Managers; First-Line Supervisors/Managers of Agricultural Crop and Horticultural Workers; First-Line Supervisors/Managers of Animal Husbandry and Animal Care Workers; First-Line Supervisors/Managers of Aquacultural Workers; First-Line Supervisors/Managers of Construction Trades and Extraction Workers; First-Line Supervisors/Managers of Farming, Fishing, and Forestry Workers; First-Line

Supervisors/Managers of Landscaping, Lawn Service, and Groundskeeping Workers; First-Line Supervisors/Managers of Logging Workers; Nursery and Greenhouse Managers; Park Naturalists; Purchasing Agents and Buyers, Farm Products.

Skills—Management of Financial Resources: Determining how money will be spent to get the work done and accounting for these expenditures. **Operation and Control:** Controlling operations of equipment or systems. **Installation:** Installing equipment, machines, wiring, or programs to meet specifications. **Management of Material Resources:** Obtaining and seeing to the appropriate use of equipment, facilities, and materials needed to do certain work. **Equipment Selection:** Determining the kind of tools and equipment needed to do a job. **Management of Personnel Resources:** Motivating, developing, and directing people as they work; identifying the best people for the job.

Education and Training Programs: Agribusiness/Agricultural Business Operations; Agricultural Animal Breeding; Agricultural Business and Management, General; Agronomy and Crop Science; Animal Nutrition; Animal Sciences, General; Aquaculture; Crop Production; Dairy Science; Farm/Farm and Ranch Management; Greenhouse Operations and Management; Horticultural Science; Livestock Management; Ornamental Horticulture; Plant Nursery Operations and Management; Poultry Science; Range Science and Management; others. **Related Knowledge/Courses: Food Production:** Techniques and equipment for planting, growing, and harvesting food products (both plant and animal) for consumption, including storage/handling techniques. **Economics and Accounting:** Economic and accounting principles and practices, the financial markets, banking, and the analysis and reporting of financial data. **Personnel and Human Resources:** Principles and procedures for personnel recruitment, selection, training, compensation and benefits, labor relations and negotiation, and personnel information systems. **Production and Processing:** Raw materials, production processes, quality control, costs, and other techniques for maximizing the effective manu-

facture and distribution of goods. **Biology:** Plant and animal organisms and their tissues, cells, functions, interdependencies, and interactions with each other and the environment. **Sales and Marketing:** Principles and methods for showing, promoting, and selling products or services. This includes marketing strategy and tactics, product demonstration, sales techniques, and sales control systems.

Work Environment: Outdoors; contaminants; hazardous equipment; minor burns, cuts, bites, or stings; standing; using hands on objects, tools, or controls.

Fashion Designers

- ◎ Education/Training Required: Associate degree
- ◎ Annual Earnings: $60,860
- ◎ Growth: 8.4%
- ◎ Annual Job Openings: 2,000
- ◎ Self-Employed: 26.5%
- ◎ Part-Time: 21.3%

Level of Solitary Work: 65.5 (out of 100)

Level of Contact with Others: 60.0 (out of 100)

Design clothing and accessories. Create original garments or design garments that follow well-established fashion trends. May develop the line of color and kinds of materials. Identify target markets for designs, looking at factors such as age, gender, and socioeconomic status. Provide sample garments to agents and sales representatives and arrange for showings of sample garments at sales meetings or fashion shows. Purchase new or used clothing and accessory items as needed to complete designs. Read scripts and consult directors and other production staff in order to develop design concepts and plan productions. Research the styles and periods of clothing needed for film or theatrical productions. Sew together sections of material to form mockups or samples of garments or articles, using sewing equipment. Test fabrics or oversee testing so that garment care labels can be created. Direct and coordinate workers involved in drawing and cutting patterns and constructing samples or finished garments. Sketch rough and detailed drawings of apparel or accessories and write specifications such as color schemes, construction, material types, and accessory requirements. Visit textile showrooms to keep up to date on the latest fabrics. Determine prices for styles. Confer with sales and management executives or with clients to discuss design ideas. Design custom clothing and accessories for individuals; retailers; or theatrical, television, or film productions. Adapt other designers' ideas for the mass market. Collaborate with other designers to coordinate special products and designs. Draw patterns for articles designed; then cut patterns and cut material according to patterns, using measuring instruments and scissors. Develop a group of products or accessories and market them through venues such as boutiques or mail-order catalogs. Examine sample garments on and off models; then modify designs to achieve desired effects. Select materials and production techniques to be used for products. Attend fashion shows and review garment magazines and manuals to gather information about fashion trends and consumer preferences.

Personality Type: Artistic. Artistic occupations frequently involve working with forms, designs, and patterns. They often require self-expression, and the work can be done without following a clear set of rules.

GOE—Interest Area: 03. Arts and Communication. **Work Group:** 03.05. Design. **Other Jobs in This Work Group:** Commercial and Industrial Designers; Floral Designers; Graphic Designers; Interior Designers; Merchandise Displayers and Window Trimmers; Set and Exhibit Designers.

Skills—Systems Analysis: Determining how a system should work and how changes in conditions, operations, and the environment will affect outcomes. **Operations Analysis:** Analyzing needs and product requirements to create a design. **Management of Financial Resources:** Determining how money will be spent to get the work done and

accounting for these expenditures. **Systems Evaluation:** Identifying measures or indicators of system performance and the actions needed to improve or correct performance relative to the goals of the system. **Management of Material Resources:** Obtaining and seeing to the appropriate use of equipment, facilities, and materials needed to do certain work. **Persuasion:** Persuading others to change their minds or behavior.

Education and Training Programs: Apparel and Textile Manufacture; Fashion and Fabric Consultant; Fashion/Apparel Design; Textile Science. **Related Knowledge/Courses: Fine Arts:** The theory and techniques required to compose, produce, and perform works of music, dance, visual arts, drama, and sculpture. **Design:** Design techniques, tools, and principles involved in production of precision technical plans, blueprints, drawings, and models. **Sales and Marketing:** Principles and methods for showing, promoting, and selling products or services. This includes marketing strategy and tactics, product demonstration, sales techniques, and sales control systems. **Education and Training:** Principles and methods for curriculum and training design, teaching and instruction for individuals and groups, and the measurement of training effects.

Work Environment: Indoors; sitting; using hands on objects, tools, or controls.

Fence Erectors

- Education/Training Required: Moderate-term on-the-job training
- Annual Earnings: $24,930
- Growth: 9.9%
- Annual Job Openings: 5,000
- Self-Employed: 34.6%
- Part-Time: 9.9%

Level of Solitary Work: 46.7 (out of 100)

Level of Contact with Others: 10.5 (out of 100)

Erect and repair metal and wooden fences and fence gates around highways, industrial establishments, residences, or farms, using hand and power tools. Insert metal tubing through rail supports. Discuss fencing needs with customers and estimate and quote prices. Weld metal parts together, using portable gas welding equipment. Stretch wire, wire mesh, or chain link fencing between posts and attach fencing to frames. Set metal or wooden posts in upright positions in postholes. Nail top and bottom rails to fence posts or insert them in slots on posts. Nail pointed slats to rails to construct picket fences. Mix and pour concrete around bases of posts or tamp soil into postholes to embed posts. Blast rock formations and rocky areas with dynamite to facilitate posthole digging. Make rails for fences by sawing lumber or by cutting metal tubing to required lengths. Establish the location for a fence and gather information needed to ensure that there are no electric cables or water lines in the area. Erect alternate panel, basket weave, and louvered fences. Construct and repair barriers, retaining walls, trellises, and other types of fences, walls, and gates. Align posts, using lines or by sighting, and verify vertical alignment of posts, using plumb bobs or spirit levels. Assemble gates and fasten gates into position, using hand tools. Attach fence rail supports to posts, using hammers and pliers. Complete top fence rails of metal fences by connecting tube sections, using metal sleeves. Attach rails or tension wire along bottoms of posts to form fencing frames. Measure and lay out fence lines and mark posthole positions, following instructions, drawings, or specifications. Dig postholes, using spades, posthole diggers, or power-driven augers.

Personality Type: Realistic. Realistic occupations frequently involve work activities that include practical, hands-on problems and solutions. They often deal with plants; animals; and real-world materials such as wood, tools, and machinery. Many of the occupations require working outside and do not involve a lot of paperwork or working closely with others.

GOE—Interest Area: 02. Architecture and Construction. **Work Group:** 02.04. Construction Crafts. **Other Jobs in This Work Group:** Boilermakers; Brickmasons and Blockmasons; Carpet Installers; Cement Masons and Concrete Finishers; Commercial Divers; Construction Carpenters; Crane and Tower Operators; Drywall and Ceiling Tile Installers; Electricians; Floor Layers, Except Carpet, Wood, and Hard Tiles; Floor Sanders and Finishers; Glaziers; Hazardous Materials Removal Workers; Insulation Workers, Floor, Ceiling, and Wall; Insulation Workers, Mechanical; Manufactured Building and Mobile Home Installers; Operating Engineers and Other Construction Equipment Operators; Painters, Construction and Maintenance; Paperhangers; Paving, Surfacing, and Tamping Equipment Operators; Pile-Driver Operators; Pipe Fitters and Steamfitters; Pipelayers; Plasterers and Stucco Masons; Plumbers; Plumbers, Pipefitters, and Steamfitters; Rail-Track Laying and Maintenance Equipment Operators; Refractory Materials Repairers, Except Brickmasons; Reinforcing Iron and Rebar Workers; Riggers; Roofers; Rough Carpenters; Security and Fire Alarm Systems Installers; Segmental Pavers; Sheet Metal Workers; Stone Cutters and Carvers, Manufacturing; Stonemasons; Structural Iron and Steel Workers; Tapers; Terrazzo Workers and Finishers; Tile and Marble Setters.

Skills—Repairing: Repairing machines or systems by using the needed tools.

Education and Training Program: Construction Trades, Other. **Related Knowledge/Courses: Building and Construction:** The materials, methods, and tools involved in the construction or repair of houses, buildings, or other structures such as highways and roads.

Work Environment: Outdoors; noisy; minor burns, cuts, bites, or stings; standing; kneeling, crouching, stooping, or crawling; using hands on objects, tools, or controls.

Financial Analysts

- ◎ Education/Training Required: Bachelor's degree
- ◎ Annual Earnings: $63,860
- ◎ Growth: 17.3%
- ◎ Annual Job Openings: 28,000
- ◎ Self-Employed: 6.7%
- ◎ Part-Time: 9.8%

Level of Solitary Work: 65.5 (out of 100)

Level of Contact with Others: 79.0 (out of 100)

Conduct quantitative analyses of information affecting investment programs of public or private institutions. Assemble spreadsheets and draw charts and graphs used to illustrate technical reports, using computer. Analyze financial information to produce forecasts of business, industry, and economic conditions for use in making investment decisions. Maintain knowledge and stay abreast of developments in the fields of industrial technology, business, finance, and economic theory. Interpret data affecting investment programs, such as price, yield, stability, future trends in investment risks, and economic influences. Monitor fundamental economic, industrial, and corporate developments through the analysis of information obtained from financial publications and services, investment banking firms, government agencies, trade publications, company sources, and personal interviews. Recommend investments and investment timing to companies, investment firm staff, or the investing public. Determine the prices at which securities should be syndicated and offered to the public. Prepare plans of action for investment based on financial analyses. Evaluate and compare the relative quality of various securities in a given industry. Present oral and written reports on general economic trends, individual corporations, and entire industries. Contact brokers and purchase investments for companies according to company policy. Collaborate with investment bankers to attract new corporate clients to securities firms.

Personality Type: Investigative. Investigative occupations frequently involve working with ideas and require an extensive amount of thinking. These occupations can involve searching for facts and figuring out problems mentally.

GOE—Interest Area: 06. Finance and Insurance. **Work Group:** 06.02. Finance/Insurance Investigation and Analysis. **Other Jobs in This Work Group:** Appraisers and Assessors of Real Estate; Appraisers, Real Estate; Assessors; Claims Adjusters, Examiners, and Investigators; Claims Examiners, Property and Casualty Insurance; Cost Estimators; Credit Analysts; Insurance Adjusters, Examiners, and Investigators; Insurance Appraisers, Auto Damage; Insurance Underwriters; Loan Counselors; Loan Officers; Market Research Analysts; Survey Researchers.

Skills—Management of Financial Resources: Determining how money will be spent to get the work done and accounting for these expenditures. **Judgment and Decision Making:** Considering the relative costs and benefits of potential actions to choose the most appropriate one. **Systems Evaluation:** Identifying measures or indicators of system performance and the actions needed to improve or correct performance relative to the goals of the system. **Programming:** Writing computer programs for various purposes. **Complex Problem Solving:** Identifying complex problems and reviewing related information to develop and evaluate options and implement solutions. **Mathematics:** Using mathematics to solve problems.

Education and Training Programs: Accounting and Business/Management; Accounting and Finance; Finance, General. **Related Knowledge/Courses: Economics and Accounting:** Economic and accounting principles and practices, the financial markets, banking, and the analysis and reporting of financial data. **Mathematics:** Arithmetic, algebra, geometry, calculus, and statistics and their applications. **Law and Government:** Laws, legal codes, court procedures, precedents, government regulations, executive orders, agency rules, and the democratic political process. **Administration and Management:** Business and management principles involved in strategic planning, resource allocation, human resources modeling, leadership technique, production methods, and coordination of people and resources. **Clerical Practices:** Administrative and clerical procedures and systems such as word processing, managing files and records, stenography and transcription, designing forms, and other office procedures and terminology. **English Language:** The structure and content of the English language, including the meaning and spelling of words, rules of composition, and grammar.

Work Environment: Indoors; sitting.

Financial Examiners

- ◎ Education/Training Required: Bachelor's degree
- ◎ Annual Earnings: $63,090
- ◎ Growth: 9.5%
- ◎ Annual Job Openings: 3,000
- ◎ Self-Employed: 0.0%
- ◎ Part-Time: No data available

Level of Solitary Work: 62.5 (out of 100)

Level of Contact with Others: 83.7 (out of 100)

Enforce or ensure compliance with laws and regulations governing financial and securities institutions and financial and real estate transactions. May examine, verify correctness of, or establish authenticity of records. Investigate activities of institutions in order to enforce laws and regulations and to ensure legality of transactions and operations or financial solvency. Review and analyze new, proposed, or revised laws, regulations, policies, and procedures in order to interpret their meaning and determine their impact. Plan, supervise, and review work of assigned subordinates. Recommend actions to ensure compliance with laws and regulations or to protect solvency of institutions. Examine the minutes of meetings of directors, stockholders, and committees in order to

investigate the specific authority extended at various levels of management. Prepare reports, exhibits, and other supporting schedules that detail an institution's safety and soundness, compliance with laws and regulations, and recommended solutions to questionable financial conditions. Review balance sheets, operating income and expense accounts, and loan documentation in order to confirm institution assets and liabilities. Review audit reports of internal and external auditors in order to monitor adequacy of scope of reports or to discover specific weaknesses in internal routines. Train other examiners in the financial examination process. Establish guidelines for procedures and policies that comply with new and revised regulations and direct their implementation. Direct and participate in formal and informal meetings with bank directors, trustees, senior management, counsels, outside accountants, and consultants in order to gather information and discuss findings. Verify and inspect cash reserves, assigned collateral, and bank-owned securities in order to check internal control procedures. Review applications for mergers, acquisitions, establishment of new institutions, acceptance in Federal Reserve System, or registration of securities sales in order to determine their public interest value and conformance to regulations and recommend acceptance or rejection. Resolve problems concerning the overall financial integrity of banking institutions, including loan investment portfolios, capital, earnings, and specific or large troubled accounts.

Personality Type: Enterprising. Enterprising occupations frequently involve starting up and carrying out projects. These occupations can involve leading people and making many decisions. They sometimes require risk taking and often deal with business.

GOE—Interest Area: 07. Government and Public Administration. **Work Group:** 07.03. Regulations Enforcement. **Other Jobs in This Work Group:** Agricultural Inspectors; Aviation Inspectors; Compliance Officers, Except Agriculture, Construction, Health and Safety, and Transportation; Construction and Building Inspectors; Environmental Compliance Inspectors; Equal Opportunity Representatives and Officers; Fire Inspectors; Fish and Game Wardens;

Forest Fire Inspectors and Prevention Specialists; Freight and Cargo Inspectors; Government Property Inspectors and Investigators; Immigration and Customs Inspectors; Licensing Examiners and Inspectors; Nuclear Monitoring Technicians; Occupational Health and Safety Specialists; Occupational Health and Safety Technicians; Tax Examiners, Collectors, and Revenue Agents; Transportation Vehicle, Equipment, and Systems Inspectors, Except Aviation.

Skills—Monitoring: Monitoring or assessing your own performance or that of other individuals or organizations to make improvements or take corrective action. **Management of Financial Resources:** Determining how money will be spent to get the work done and accounting for these expenditures. **Quality Control Analysis:** Conducting tests and inspections of products, services, or processes to evaluate quality or performance. **Systems Analysis:** Determining how a system should work and how changes in conditions, operations, and the environment will affect outcomes. **Systems Evaluation:** Identifying measures or indicators of system performance and the actions needed to improve or correct performance relative to the goals of the system. **Operations Analysis:** Analyzing needs and product requirements to create a design.

Education and Training Programs: Accounting; Taxation. **Related Knowledge/Courses: Economics and Accounting:** Economic and accounting principles and practices, the financial markets, banking, and the analysis and reporting of financial data. **Law and Government:** Laws, legal codes, court procedures, precedents, government regulations, executive orders, agency rules, and the democratic political process. **Clerical Practices:** Administrative and clerical procedures and systems such as word processing, managing files and records, stenography and transcription, designing forms, and other office procedures and terminology. **Mathematics:** Arithmetic, algebra, geometry, calculus, and statistics and their applications. **English Language:** The structure and content of the English language, including the mean-

ing and spelling of words, rules of composition, and grammar. **Administration and Management:** Business and management principles involved in strategic planning, resource allocation, human resources modeling, leadership technique, production methods, and coordination of people and resources.

Work Environment: Indoors; sitting.

Fine Artists, Including Painters, Sculptors, and Illustrators

- Education/Training Required: Long-term on-the-job training
- Annual Earnings: $41,280
- Growth: 10.2%
- Annual Job Openings: 4,000
- Self-Employed: 61.9%
- Part-Time: 30.9%

Level of Solitary Work: 83.5 (out of 100)

Level of Contact with Others: 53.3 (out of 100)

Create original artwork, using any of a wide variety of mediums and techniques such as painting and sculpture. Use materials such as pens and ink, watercolors, charcoal, oil, or computer software to create artwork. Integrate and develop visual elements, such as line, space, mass, color, and perspective, to produce desired effects such as the illustration of ideas, emotions, or moods. Confer with clients, editors, writers, art directors, and other interested parties regarding the nature and content of artwork to be produced. Submit preliminary or finished artwork or project plans to clients for approval, incorporating changes as necessary. Maintain portfolios of artistic work to demonstrate styles, interests, and abilities. Create finished artwork as decoration or to elucidate or substitute for spoken or written messages. Cut, bend, laminate, arrange, and fasten individual or mixed raw and manufactured materials and products to form works of art. Monitor events, trends, and other circumstances; research specific subject areas; attend art exhibitions; and read art publications to develop ideas and keep current on art world activities. Study different techniques to learn how to apply them to artistic endeavors. Render drawings, illustrations, and sketches of buildings, manufactured products, or models, working from sketches, blueprints, memory, models, or reference materials. Create sculptures, statues, and other three-dimensional artwork by using abrasives and tools to shape, carve, and fabricate materials such as clay, stone, wood, or metal. Create sketches, profiles, or likenesses of posed subjects or photographs, using any combination of freehand drawing, mechanical assembly kits, and computer imaging. Study styles, techniques, colors, textures, and materials used in works undergoing restoration to ensure consistency during the restoration process. Develop project budgets for approval, estimating timelines and material costs. Shade and fill in sketch outlines and backgrounds, using a variety of media such as watercolors, markers, and transparent washes, labeling designated colors when necessary. Collaborate with engineers, mechanics, and other technical experts as necessary to build and install creations.

Personality Type: Artistic. Artistic occupations frequently involve working with forms, designs, and patterns. They often require self-expression, and the work can be done without following a clear set of rules.

GOE—Interest Area: 03. Arts and Communication. **Work Group:** 03.04. Studio Art. **Other Jobs in This Work Group:** Craft Artists; Potters, Manufacturing.

Skills—Management of Financial Resources: Determining how money will be spent to get the work done and accounting for these expenditures.

Equipment Selection: Determining the kind of tools and equipment needed to do a job. **Operations Analysis:** Analyzing needs and product requirements to create a design. **Repairing:** Repairing machines or systems by using the needed tools. **Equipment Maintenance:** Performing routine maintenance on equipment and determining when and what kind of maintenance is needed. **Complex Problem Solving:** Identifying complex problems and reviewing related information to develop and evaluate options and implement solutions.

Education and Training Programs: Art/Art Studies, General; Drawing; Fine/Studio Arts, General; Fine Arts and Art Studies, Other; Painting; Visual and Performing Arts, General. **Related Knowledge/ Courses: Fine Arts:** The theory and techniques required to compose, produce, and perform works of music, dance, visual arts, drama, and sculpture. **Design:** Design techniques, tools, and principles involved in production of precision technical plans, blueprints, drawings, and models. **Sales and Marketing:** Principles and methods for showing, promoting, and selling products or services. This includes marketing strategy and tactics, product demonstration, sales techniques, and sales control systems. **Production and Processing:** Raw materials, production processes, quality control, costs, and other techniques for maximizing the effective manufacture and distribution of goods. **Economics and Accounting:** Economic and accounting principles and practices, the financial markets, banking, and the analysis and reporting of financial data. **Communications and Media:** Media production, communication, and dissemination techniques and methods. This includes alternative ways to inform and entertain via written, oral, and visual media.

Work Environment: Indoors; contaminants; standing; using hands on objects, tools, or controls; repetitive motions.

Fire-Prevention and Protection Engineers

This job can be found in the Part II lists under the title Health and Safety Engineers, Except Mining Safety Engineers and Inspectors.

- ◎ Education/Training Required: Bachelor's degree
- ◎ Annual Earnings: $65,210
- ◎ Growth: 13.4%
- ◎ Annual Job Openings: 2,000
- ◎ Self-Employed: 0.5%
- ◎ Part-Time: 2.6%

The job openings listed here are shared with Industrial Safety and Health Engineers and with Product Safety Engineers.

Level of Solitary Work: 47.8 (out of 100)

Level of Contact with Others: 66.7 (out of 100)

Research causes of fires, determine fire protection methods, and design or recommend materials or equipment such as structural components or fire-detection equipment to assist organizations in safeguarding life and property against fire, explosion, and related hazards. Design fire detection equipment, alarm systems, and fire extinguishing devices and systems. Inspect buildings or building designs to determine fire protection system requirements and potential problems in areas such as water supplies, exit locations, and construction materials. Advise architects, builders, and other construction personnel on fire prevention equipment and techniques and on fire code and standard interpretation and compliance. Prepare and write reports detailing specific fire prevention and protection issues, such as work performed and proposed review schedules. Determine causes of fires and ways in which they could have been prevented. Direct the purchase, modification, installation, maintenance, and operation of fire pro-

tection systems. Consult with authorities to discuss safety regulations and to recommend changes as necessary. Develop plans for the prevention of destruction by fire, wind, and water. Study the relationships between ignition sources and materials to determine how fires start. Attend workshops, seminars, or conferences to present or obtain information regarding fire prevention and protection. Develop training materials and conduct training sessions on fire protection. Evaluate fire department performance and the laws and regulations affecting fire prevention or fire safety. Conduct research on fire retardants and the fire safety of materials and devices.

Personality Type: Investigative. Investigative occupations frequently involve working with ideas and require an extensive amount of thinking. These occupations can involve searching for facts and figuring out problems mentally.

GOE—Interest Area: 15. Scientific Research, Engineering, and Mathematics. **Work Group:** 15.08. Industrial and Safety Engineering. **Other Jobs in This Work Group:** Health and Safety Engineers, Except Mining Safety Engineers and Inspectors; Industrial Engineers; Industrial Safety and Health Engineers; Product Safety Engineers.

Skills—Science: Using scientific rules and methods to solve problems. **Management of Financial Resources:** Determining how money will be spent to get the work done and accounting for these expenditures. **Operations Analysis:** Analyzing needs and product requirements to create a design. **Mathematics:** Using mathematics to solve problems. **Systems Analysis:** Determining how a system should work and how changes in conditions, operations, and the environment will affect outcomes. **Negotiation:** Bringing others together and trying to reconcile differences.

Education and Training Program: Environmental/Environmental Health Engineering. **Related Knowledge/Courses: Design:** Design techniques, tools, and principles involved in production of precision technical plans, blueprints, drawings, and models. **Engineering and Technology:** The practical application of engineering science and technology. This includes applying principles, techniques, procedures, and equipment to the design and production of various goods and services. **Building and Construction:** The materials, methods, and tools involved in the construction or repair of houses, buildings, or other structures such as highways and roads. **Physics:** Physical principles and laws and their interrelationships and applications to understanding fluid, material, and atmospheric dynamics and mechanical, electrical, atomic, and subatomic structures and processes. **Chemistry:** The chemical composition, structure, and properties of substances and of the chemical processes and transformations that they undergo. This includes uses of chemicals and their danger signs, production techniques, and disposal methods. **Public Safety and Security:** Relevant equipment, policies, procedures, and strategies to promote effective local, state, or national security operations for the protection of people, data, property, and institutions.

Work Environment: Indoors; sitting.

Food Scientists and Technologists

- ◉ Education/Training Required: Bachelor's degree
- ◉ Annual Earnings: $51,440
- ◉ Growth: 10.9%
- ◉ Annual Job Openings: 1,000
- ◉ Self-Employed: 28.8%
- ◉ Part-Time: No data available

Level of Solitary Work: 68.8 (out of 100)

Level of Contact with Others: 83.0 (out of 100)

Use chemistry, microbiology, engineering, and other sciences to study the principles underlying the processing and deterioration of foods; analyze food content to determine levels of vitamins, fat, sugar, and protein; discover new food sources; research ways to make processed foods safe, palatable, and healthful; and apply food science knowledge to determine the best ways to process, package, preserve, store, and distribute food. Test new products for flavor, texture, color, nutritional content, and adherence to government and industry standards. Check raw ingredients for maturity or stability for processing and finished products for safety, quality, and nutritional value. Confer with process engineers, plant operators, flavor experts, and packaging and marketing specialists in order to resolve problems in product development. Evaluate food processing and storage operations and assist in the development of quality assurance programs for such operations. Study methods to improve aspects of foods such as chemical composition, flavor, color, texture, nutritional value, and convenience. Study the structure and composition of food or the changes foods undergo in storage and processing. Develop new or improved ways of preserving, processing, packaging, storing, and delivering foods, using knowledge of chemistry, microbiology, and other sciences. Develop food standards and production specifications, safety and sanitary regulations, and waste management and water supply specifications. Demonstrate products to clients. Inspect food processing areas in order to ensure compliance with government regulations and standards for sanitation, safety, quality, and waste management standards. Search for substitutes for harmful or undesirable additives, such as nitrites.

Personality Type: Investigative. Investigative occupations frequently involve working with ideas and require an extensive amount of thinking. These occupations can involve searching for facts and figuring out problems mentally.

GOE—Interest Area: 01. Agriculture and Natural Resources. **Work Group:** 01.03. Resource Technologies for Plants, Animals, and the Environment. **Other Jobs in This Work Group:** Agricultural and Food Science Technicians; Agricultural Technicians; Environmental Science and Protection Technicians, Including Health; Food Science Technicians;

Geological and Petroleum Technicians; Geological Sample Test Technicians; Geophysical Data Technicians.

Skills—Quality Control Analysis: Conducting tests and inspections of products, services, or processes to evaluate quality or performance. **Science:** Using scientific rules and methods to solve problems. **Troubleshooting:** Determining causes of operating errors and deciding what to do about them. **Operation Monitoring:** Watching gauges, dials, or other indicators to make sure a machine is working properly. **Monitoring:** Monitoring or assessing your own performance or that of other individuals or organizations to make improvements or take corrective action. **Reading Comprehension:** Understanding written sentences and paragraphs in work-related documents.

Education and Training Programs: Agriculture, General; Food Science; Food Technology and Processing; International Agriculture. **Related Knowledge/ Courses: Food Production:** Techniques and equipment for planting, growing, and harvesting food products (both plant and animal) for consumption, including storage/handling techniques. **Chemistry:** The chemical composition, structure, and properties of substances and of the chemical processes and transformations that they undergo. This includes uses of chemicals and their danger signs, production techniques, and disposal methods. **Production and Processing:** Raw materials, production processes, quality control, costs, and other techniques for maximizing the effective manufacture and distribution of goods. **Biology:** Plant and animal organisms and their tissues, cells, functions, interdependencies, and interactions with each other and the environment. **Physics:** Physical principles and laws and their interrelationships and applications to understanding fluid, material, and atmospheric dynamics and mechanical, electrical, atomic, and subatomic structures and processes. **Mathematics:** Arithmetic, algebra, geometry, calculus, and statistics and their applications.

Work Environment: Indoors; noisy; hazardous conditions; sitting.

Foresters

- Education/Training Required: Bachelor's degree
- Annual Earnings: $48,670
- Growth: 6.7%
- Annual Job Openings: 1,000
- Self-Employed: 9.1%
- Part-Time: 6.7%

Level of Solitary Work: 59.2 (out of 100)

Level of Contact with Others: 75.0 (out of 100)

Manage forested lands for economic, recreational, and conservation purposes. May inventory the type, amount, and location of standing timber; appraise the timber's worth; negotiate the purchase; and draw up contracts for procurement. May determine how to conserve wildlife habitats, creek beds, water quality, and soil stability and how best to comply with environmental regulations. May devise plans for planting and growing new trees, monitor trees for healthy growth, and determine the best time for harvesting. Develop forest management plans for public and privately owned forested lands. Monitor contract compliance and results of forestry activities to assure adherence to government regulations. Establish short- and long-term plans for management of forest lands and forest resources. Supervise activities of other forestry workers. Choose and prepare sites for new trees, using controlled burning, bulldozers, or herbicides to clear weeds, brush, and logging debris. Plan and supervise forestry projects, such as determining the type, number, and placement of trees to be planted; managing tree nurseries; thinning forest; and monitoring growth of new seedlings. Negotiate terms and conditions of agreements and contracts for forest harvesting, forest management, and leasing of forest lands. Direct and participate in forest-fire suppression. Determine methods of cutting and removing timber with minimum waste and environmental damage. Analyze effect of forest conditions on tree growth rates and tree species prevalence and the yield, duration, seed production, growth viability, and germination of different species. Monitor forest-cleared lands to ensure that they are reclaimed to their most suitable end use. Plan and implement projects for conservation of wildlife habitats and soil and water quality. Plan and direct forest surveys and related studies and prepare reports and recommendations. Perform inspections of forests or forest nurseries. Map forest area soils and vegetation to estimate the amount of standing timber and future value and growth. Conduct public educational programs on forest care and conservation. Procure timber from private landowners. Subcontract with loggers or pulpwood cutters for tree removal and to aid in road layout. Plan cutting programs and manage timber sales from harvested areas, helping companies to achieve production goals. Monitor wildlife populations and assess the impacts of forest operations on population and habitats. Plan and direct construction and maintenance of recreation facilities, fire towers, trails, roads, and bridges, ensuring that they comply with guidelines and regulations set for forested public lands. Contact local forest owners and gain permission to take inventory of the type, amount, and location of all standing timber on the property.

Personality Type: Realistic. Realistic occupations frequently involve work activities that include practical, hands-on problems and solutions. They often deal with plants; animals; and real-world materials such as wood, tools, and machinery. Many of the occupations require working outside and do not involve a lot of paperwork or working closely with others.

GOE—Interest Area: 01. Agriculture and Natural Resources. **Work Group:** 01.02. Resource Science/Engineering for Plants, Animals, and the Environment. **Other Jobs in This Work Group:** Agricultural Engineers; Animal Scientists; Conservation Scientists; Environmental Engineers; Mining and Geological Engineers, Including Mining Safety Engineers; Petroleum Engineers; Range Managers; Soil and Plant Scientists; Soil and Water Conservationists; Zoologists and Wildlife Biologists.

Skills—Management of Financial Resources: Determining how money will be spent to get the work done and accounting for these expenditures. **Science:** Using scientific rules and methods to solve problems. **Programming:** Writing computer programs for various purposes. **Quality Control Analysis:** Conducting tests and inspections of products, services, or processes to evaluate quality or performance. **Mathematics:** Using mathematics to solve problems. **Operations Analysis:** Analyzing needs and product requirements to create a design.

Education and Training Programs: Forest Management/Forest Resources Management; Forest Resources Production and Management; Forest Sciences and Biology; Forestry, General; Forestry, Other; Natural Resources and Conservation, Other; Natural Resources Management and Policy; Natural Resources Management and Policy, Other; Natural Resources/Conservation, General; Urban Forestry; Wood Science and Wood Products/Pulp and Paper Technology. **Related Knowledge/Courses: Biology:** Plant and animal organisms and their tissues, cells, functions, interdependencies, and interactions with each other and the environment. **Geography:** Principles and methods for describing the features of land, sea, and air masses, including their physical characteristics; locations; interrelationships; and distribution of plant, animal, and human life. **Mathematics:** Arithmetic, algebra, geometry, calculus, and statistics and their applications. **Law and Government:** Laws, legal codes, court procedures, precedents, government regulations, executive orders, agency rules, and the democratic political process. **Computers and Electronics:** Circuit boards, processors, chips, electronic equipment, and computer hardware and software, including applications and programming. **English Language:** The structure and content of the English language, including the meaning and spelling of words, rules of composition, and grammar.

Work Environment: More often indoors than outdoors; noisy; sitting.

Freight and Cargo Inspectors

This job can be found in the Part II lists under the title Transportation Inspectors.

- ◎ Education/Training Required: Work experience in a related occupation
- ◎ Annual Earnings: $49,490
- ◎ Growth: 11.4%
- ◎ Annual Job Openings: 2,000
- ◎ Self-Employed: 1.9%
- ◎ Part-Time: 2.3%

The job openings listed here are shared with Aviation Inspectors and with Transportation Vehicle, Equipment, and Systems Inspectors, Except Aviation.

Level of Solitary Work: 58.9 (out of 100)

Level of Contact with Others: 57.6 (out of 100)

Inspect the handling, storage, and stowing of freight and cargoes. Review commercial vehicle logs, shipping papers, and driver and equipment records to detect any problems and to ensure compliance with regulations. Prepare and submit reports after completion of freight shipments. Recommend remedial procedures to correct any violations found during inspections. Record details about freight conditions, handling of freight, and any problems encountered. Calculate gross and net tonnage, hold capacities, volumes of stored fuel and water, cargo weights, and ship stability factors, using mathematical formulas. Evaluate new methods of packaging, testing, shipping, and transporting hazardous materials to ensure adequate public safety protection. Measure ships' holds and depths of fuel and water in tanks, using sounding lines and tape measures. Write certificates of admeasurement that list details such as designs, lengths, depths, and breadths of vessels and methods of propulsion. Read draft markings to determine depths of vessels in water. Post warning signs on vehi-cles containing explosives or flammable or radioactive materials. Negotiate with authorities, such as local government officials, to eliminate hazards along transportation routes. Observe loading of freight to ensure that crews comply with procedures. Notify workers of any special treatment required for shipments. Measure heights and widths of loads to ensure they will pass over bridges or through tunnels on scheduled routes. Issue certificates of compliance for vessels without violations. Inspect shipments to ensure that freight is securely braced and blocked. Inspect loaded cargo, cargo lashed to decks or in storage facilities, and cargo-handling devices to determine compliance with health and safety regulations and need for maintenance. Direct crews to reload freight or to insert additional bracing or packing as necessary. Determine types of licenses and safety equipment required and compute applicable fees such as tolls and wharfage fees. Determine cargo transportation capabilities by reading documents that set forth cargo loading and securing procedures, capacities, and stability factors.

Personality Type: Conventional. Conventional occupations frequently involve following set procedures and routines. These occupations can include working with data and details more than with ideas. Usually there is a clear line of authority to follow.

GOE—Interest Area: 07. Government and Public Administration. **Work Group:** 07.03. Regulations Enforcement. **Other Jobs in This Work Group:** Agricultural Inspectors; Aviation Inspectors; Compliance Officers, Except Agriculture, Construction, Health and Safety, and Transportation; Construction and Building Inspectors; Environmental Compliance Inspectors; Equal Opportunity Representatives and Officers; Financial Examiners; Fire Inspectors; Fish and Game Wardens; Forest Fire Inspectors and Prevention Specialists; Government Property Inspectors and Investigators; Immigration and Customs Inspectors; Licensing Examiners and Inspectors; Nuclear Monitoring Technicians; Occupational Health and Safety Specialists; Occupational Health and Safety Technicians; Tax Examiners, Collectors, and Revenue Agents;

Transportation Vehicle, Equipment, and Systems Inspectors, Except Aviation.

Skills—Mathematics: Using mathematics to solve problems.

Education and Training Programs: No related CIP programs; this job is learned through work experience in a related occupation. **Related Knowledge/Courses: Transportation:** Principles and methods for moving people or goods by air, rail, sea, or road, including the relative costs and benefits. **Public Safety and Security:** Relevant equipment, policies, procedures, and strategies to promote effective local, state, or national security operations for the protection of people, data, property, and institutions. **Mathematics:** Arithmetic, algebra, geometry, calculus, and statistics and their applications.

Work Environment: Outdoors; standing; walking and running; using hands on objects, tools, or controls.

Gas Plant Operators

- Education/Training Required: Long-term on-the-job training
- Annual Earnings: $51,920
- Growth: 7.7%
- Annual Job Openings: 2,000
- Self-Employed: 0.1%
- Part-Time: 0.8%

Level of Solitary Work: 54.8 (out of 100)

Level of Contact with Others: 12.5 (out of 100)

Distribute or process gas for utility companies and others by controlling compressors to maintain specified pressures on main pipelines. Determine causes of abnormal pressure variances and make corrective recommendations such as installation of pipes to relieve overloading. Distribute or process gas for utility companies or industrial plants, using panel boards, control boards, and semi-automatic equipment. Start and shut down plant equipment. Test gas, chemicals, and air during processing to assess factors such as purity and moisture content and to detect quality problems or gas or chemical leaks. Adjust temperature, pressure, vacuum, level, flow rate, and transfer of gas to maintain processes at required levels or to correct problems. Change charts in recording meters. Calculate gas ratios to detect deviations from specifications, using testing apparatus. Clean, maintain, and repair equipment, using hand tools, or request that repair and maintenance work be performed. Collaborate with other operators to solve unit problems. Monitor equipment functioning; observe temperature, level, and flow gauges; and perform regular unit checks to ensure that all equipment is operating as it should. Control fractioning columns, compressors, purifying towers, heat exchangers, and related equipment to extract nitrogen and oxygen from air. Control equipment to regulate flow and pressure of gas to feedlines of boilers, furnaces, and related steam-generating or heating equipment. Operate construction equipment to install and maintain gas distribution systems. Signal or direct workers who tend auxiliary equipment. Record, review, and compile operations records; test results; and gauge readings such as temperatures, pressures, concentrations, and flows. Read logsheets to determine product demand and disposition or to detect malfunctions. Monitor transportation and storage of flammable and other potentially dangerous products to ensure that safety guidelines are followed. Contact maintenance crews when necessary. Control operation of compressors, scrubbers, evaporators, and refrigeration equipment to liquefy, compress, or regasify natural gas.

Personality Type: Realistic. Realistic occupations frequently involve work activities that include practical, hands-on problems and solutions. They often deal with plants; animals; and real-world materials such as wood, tools, and machinery. Many of the occupations require working outside and do not involve a lot of paperwork or working closely with others.

GOE—Interest Area: 13. Manufacturing. Work Group: 13.16. Utility Operation and Energy Distribution. Other Jobs in This Work Group: Chemical Plant and System Operators; Gas Compressor and Gas Pumping Station Operators; Nuclear Power Reactor Operators; Petroleum Pump System Operators, Refinery Operators, and Gaugers; Power Distributors and Dispatchers; Power Plant Operators; Ship Engineers; Stationary Engineers and Boiler Operators; Water and Liquid Waste Treatment Plant and System Operators.

Skills—Operation Monitoring: Watching gauges, dials, or other indicators to make sure a machine is working properly. Operation and Control: Controlling operations of equipment or systems. Repairing: Repairing machines or systems by using the needed tools. Equipment Maintenance: Performing routine maintenance on equipment and determining when and what kind of maintenance is needed. Troubleshooting: Determining causes of operating errors and deciding what to do about them.

Education and Training Program: Mechanic and Repair Technologies/Technician Training, Other. Related Knowledge/Courses: Mechanical Devices: Machines and tools, including their designs, uses, repair, and maintenance. Physics: Physical principles and laws and their interrelationships and applications to understanding fluid, material, and atmospheric dynamics and mechanical, electrical, atomic, and subatomic structures and processes. Engineering and Technology: The practical application of engineering science and technology. This includes applying principles, techniques, procedures, and equipment to the design and production of various goods and services. Production and Processing: Raw materials, production processes, quality control, costs, and other techniques for maximizing the effective manufacture and distribution of goods. Chemistry: The chemical composition, structure, and properties of substances and of the chemical processes and transformations that they undergo. This includes uses of chemicals and their danger signs, production techniques, and disposal methods.

Work Environment: Indoors; contaminants; hazardous conditions; standing; using hands on objects, tools, or controls.

Geographers

- Education/Training Required: Master's degree
- Annual Earnings: $63,550
- Growth: 6.8%
- Annual Job Openings: Fewer than 500
- Self-Employed: 4.2%
- Part-Time: 14.8%

Level of Solitary Work: 65.5 (out of 100)

Level of Contact with Others: 70.7 (out of 100)

Study nature and use of areas of earth's surface, relating and interpreting interactions of physical and cultural phenomena. Conduct research on physical aspects of a region, including land forms, climates, soils, plants, and animals, and conduct research on the spatial implications of human activities within a given area, including social characteristics, economic activities, and political organization, as well as researching interdependence between regions at scales ranging from local to global. Create and modify maps, graphs, or diagrams, using geographical information software and related equipment and principles of cartography such as coordinate systems, longitude, latitude, elevation, topography, and map scales. Write and present reports of research findings. Develop, operate, and maintain geographical information (GIS) computer systems, including hardware, software, plotters, digitizers, printers, and video cameras. Locate and obtain existing geographic information databases. Analyze geographic distributions of physical and cultural phenomena on local, regional, continental, or global scales. Teach geography. Gather and compile geographic data from sources including censuses, field observations, satellite imagery, aerial photographs, and existing maps. Conduct fieldwork at outdoor sites. Study the economic, political, and cultural characteristics of a specific region's population. Provide consulting services in fields including resource development and management, business location and market area analysis, environmental hazards, regional cultural history, and urban social planning. Collect data on physical characteristics of specified areas, such as geological formations, climates, and vegetation, using surveying or meteorological equipment. Provide geographical information systems support to the private and public sectors.

Personality Type: Investigative. Investigative occupations frequently involve working with ideas and require an extensive amount of thinking. These occupations can involve searching for facts and figuring out problems mentally.

GOE—Interest Area: 15. Scientific Research, Engineering, and Mathematics. **Work Group:** 15.02. Physical Sciences. **Other Jobs in This Work Group:** Astronomers; Atmospheric and Space Scientists; Chemists; Geoscientists, Except Hydrologists and Geographers; Hydrologists; Materials Scientists; Physicists.

Skills—Programming: Writing computer programs for various purposes. **Science:** Using scientific rules and methods to solve problems. **Complex Problem Solving:** Identifying complex problems and reviewing related information to develop and evaluate options and implement solutions. **Writing:** Communicating effectively in writing as appropriate for the needs of the audience. **Management of Financial Resources:** Determining how money will be spent to get the work done and accounting for these expenditures. **Reading Comprehension:** Understanding written sentences and paragraphs in work-related documents.

Education and Training Program: Geography. **Related Knowledge/Courses: Geography:** Principles and methods for describing the features of land, sea, and air masses, including their physical characteristics; locations; interrelationships; and distribution of

plant, animal, and human life. **Sociology and Anthropology:** Group behavior and dynamics, societal trends and influences, human migrations, ethnicity, and cultures and their history and origins. **History and Archeology:** Historical events and their causes, indicators, and effects on civilizations and cultures. **Biology:** Plant and animal organisms and their tissues, cells, functions, interdependencies, and interactions with each other and the environment. **Education and Training:** Principles and methods for curriculum and training design, teaching and instruction for individuals and groups, and the measurement of training effects. **Philosophy and Theology:** Different philosophical systems and religions. This includes their basic principles, values, ethics, ways of thinking, customs, and practices and their impact on human culture.

Work Environment: Indoors; sitting.

Geoscientists, Except Hydrologists and Geographers

- Education/Training Required: Master's degree
- Annual Earnings: $71,640
- Growth: 8.3%
- Annual Job Openings: 2,000
- Self-Employed: 5.1%
- Part-Time: 5.7%

Level of Solitary Work: 68.8 (out of 100)

Level of Contact with Others: 83.0 (out of 100)

Study the composition, structure, and other physical aspects of the earth. May use geological, physics, and mathematics knowledge in exploration for oil, gas, minerals, or underground water or in waste disposal, land reclamation, or other environmental problems. May study the earth's internal

composition, atmospheres, and oceans and its magnetic, electrical, and gravitational forces. Includes mineralogists, crystallographers, paleontologists, stratigraphers, geodesists, and seismologists. Analyze and interpret geological, geochemical, and geophysical information from sources such as survey data, well logs, bore holes, and aerial photos. Plan and conduct geological, geochemical, and geophysical field studies and surveys, sample collection, or drilling and testing programs used to collect data for research or application. Investigate the composition, structure, and history of the Earth's crust through the collection, examination, measurement, and classification of soils, minerals, rocks, or fossil remains. Prepare geological maps, cross-sectional diagrams, charts, and reports concerning mineral extraction, land use, and resource management, using results of fieldwork and laboratory research. Locate and estimate probable natural gas, oil, and mineral ore deposits and underground water resources, using aerial photographs, charts, or research and survey results. Assess ground and surface water movement to provide advice regarding issues such as waste management, route and site selection, and the restoration of contaminated sites. Identify risks for natural disasters such as mud slides, earthquakes, and volcanic eruptions, providing advice on mitigation of potential damage. Conduct geological and geophysical studies to provide information for use in regional development, site selection, and development of public works projects. Inspect construction projects to analyze engineering problems, applying geological knowledge and using test equipment and drilling machinery. Advise construction firms and government agencies on dam and road construction, foundation design, or land use and resource management. Communicate geological findings by writing research papers, participating in conferences, or teaching geological science at universities. Measure characteristics of the Earth, such as gravity and magnetic fields, using equipment such as seismographs, gravimeters, torsion balances, and magnetometers. Test industrial diamonds and abrasives, soil, or rocks to determine their geological characteristics, using optical, X-ray, heat, acid, and precision instruments. Identify

deposits of construction materials and assess the materials' characteristics and suitability for use as concrete aggregates, as road fill, or in other applications.

Personality Type: Investigative. Investigative occupations frequently involve working with ideas and require an extensive amount of thinking. These occupations can involve searching for facts and figuring out problems mentally.

GOE—Interest Area: 15. Scientific Research, Engineering, and Mathematics. **Work Group:** 15.02. Physical Sciences. **Other Jobs in This Work Group:** Astronomers; Atmospheric and Space Scientists; Chemists; Geographers; Hydrologists; Materials Scientists; Physicists.

Skills—Science: Using scientific rules and methods to solve problems. **Management of Financial Resources:** Determining how money will be spent to get the work done and accounting for these expenditures. **Active Learning:** Understanding the implications of new information for both current and future problem solving and decision making. **Time Management:** Managing one's own time and the time of others. **Coordination:** Adjusting actions in relation to others' actions. **Equipment Selection:** Determining the kind of tools and equipment needed to do a job.

Education and Training Programs: Geochemistry; Geochemistry and Petrology; Geological and Earth Sciences/Geosciences, Other; Geology/Earth Science, General; Geophysics and Seismology; Oceanography, Chemical and Physical; Paleontology. **Related Knowledge/Courses: Geography:** Principles and methods for describing the features of land, sea, and air masses, including their physical characteristics; locations; interrelationships; and distribution of plant, animal, and human life. **Physics:** Physical principles and laws and their interrelationships and applications to understanding fluid, material, and atmospheric dynamics and mechanical, electrical, atomic, and subatomic structures and processes. **Chemistry:** The chemical composition, structure, and properties of substances and of the chemical processes and transformations that they undergo. This includes uses of chemicals and their danger signs, production techniques, and disposal methods. **Biology:** Plant and animal organisms and their tissues, cells, functions, interdependencies, and interactions with each other and the environment. **Engineering and Technology:** The practical application of engineering science and technology. This includes applying principles, techniques, procedures, and equipment to the design and production of various goods and services. **Mathematics:** Arithmetic, algebra, geometry, calculus, and statistics and their applications.

Work Environment: More often indoors than outdoors; sitting.

Graphic Designers

- Education/Training Required: Bachelor's degree
- Annual Earnings: $38,390
- Growth: 15.2%
- Annual Job Openings: 35,000
- Self-Employed: 25.6%
- Part-Time: 21.3%

Level of Solitary Work: 71.7 (out of 100)

Level of Contact with Others: 89.8 (out of 100)

Design or create graphics to meet specific commercial or promotional needs, such as packaging, displays, or logos. May use a variety of media to achieve artistic or decorative effects. Create designs, concepts, and sample layouts based on knowledge of layout principles and esthetic design concepts. Determine size and arrangement of illustrative material and copy and select style and size of type. Use computer software to generate new images. Mark up, paste, and assemble final layouts to prepare layouts for printer. Draw and print charts, graphs, illustrations, and other artwork, using computer. Review final layouts and suggest improvements as needed. Confer with clients to discuss and determine layout design. Develop graphics and layouts for product illustrations, company logos, and Internet Web sites. Key information into computer equipment to create layouts for client or supervisor. Prepare illustrations or rough sketches of material, discussing them with clients or supervisors and making necessary changes. Study illustrations and photographs to plan presentation of materials, products, or services. Prepare notes and instructions for workers who assemble and prepare final layouts for printing. Develop negatives and prints to produce layout photographs, using negative and print developing equipment and tools. Photograph layouts, using camera, to make layout prints for supervisors or clients. Produce still and animated graphics for on-air and taped portions of television news broadcasts, using electronic video equipment.

Personality Type: Artistic. Artistic occupations frequently involve working with forms, designs, and patterns. They often require self-expression, and the work can be done without following a clear set of rules.

GOE—Interest Area: 03. Arts and Communication. **Work Group:** 03.05. Design. **Other Jobs in This Work Group:** Commercial and Industrial Designers; Fashion Designers; Floral Designers; Interior Designers; Merchandise Displayers and Window Trimmers; Set and Exhibit Designers.

Skills—Persuasion: Persuading others to change their minds or behavior. **Operations Analysis:** Analyzing needs and product requirements to create a design. **Troubleshooting:** Determining causes of operating errors and deciding what to do about them. **Time Management:** Managing one's own time and the time of others. **Complex Problem Solving:** Identifying complex problems and reviewing related information to develop and evaluate options and implement solutions. **Quality Control Analysis:** Conducting tests and inspections of products, services, or processes to evaluate quality or performance.

Education and Training Programs: Agricultural Communication/Journalism; Commercial and Advertising Art; Computer Graphics; Design and Visual Communications, General; Graphic Design; Industrial Design; Web Page, Digital/Multimedia, and Information Resources Design. **Related Knowledge/Courses: Fine Arts:** The theory and techniques required to compose, produce, and perform works of music, dance, visual arts, drama, and sculpture. **Design:** Design techniques, tools, and principles involved in production of precision technical plans, blueprints, drawings, and models. **Communications and Media:** Media production, communication, and dissemination techniques and methods. This includes alternative ways to inform and entertain via written, oral, and visual media. **Sales and Marketing:** Principles and methods for showing, promoting, and selling products or services. This includes marketing strategy and tactics, product demonstration, sales techniques, and sales control systems. **Computers and Electronics:** Circuit boards, processors, chips, electronic equipment, and computer hardware and software, including applications and programming. **Clerical Practices:** Administrative and clerical procedures and systems such as word processing, managing files and records, stenography and transcription, designing forms, and other office procedures and terminology.

Work Environment: Indoors; sitting; using hands on objects, tools, or controls; repetitive motions.

Hazardous Materials Removal Workers

- Education/Training Required: Moderate-term on-the-job training
- Annual Earnings: $33,690
- Growth: 31.2%
- Annual Job Openings: 11,000
- Self-Employed: 0.0%
- Part-Time: 5.0%

Level of Solitary Work: 62.5 (out of 100)

Level of Contact with Others: 80.8 (out of 100)

Identify, remove, pack, transport, or dispose of hazardous materials, including asbestos, lead-based paint, waste oil, fuel, transmission fluid, radioactive materials, contaminated soil, and so on. Specialized training and certification in hazardous materials handling or a confined entry permit are generally required. May operate earth-moving equipment or trucks. Follow prescribed safety procedures and comply with federal laws regulating waste disposal methods. Record numbers of containers stored at disposal sites and specify amounts and types of equipment and waste disposed. Drive trucks or other heavy equipment to convey contaminated waste to designated sea or ground locations. Operate machines and equipment to remove, package, store, or transport loads of waste materials. Load and unload materials into containers and onto trucks, using hoists or forklifts. Clean contaminated equipment or areas for re-use, using detergents and solvents, sandblasters, filter pumps, and steam cleaners. Construct scaffolding or build containment areas prior to beginning abatement or decontamination work. Remove asbestos or lead from surfaces, using hand and power tools such as scrapers, vacuums, and high-pressure sprayers. Unload baskets of irradiated elements onto packaging machines that automatically insert fuel elements into canisters and secure lids. Apply chemical compounds to lead-based paint, allow compounds to dry; then scrape the hazardous material into containers for removal or storage. Identify asbestos, lead, or other hazardous materials that need to be removed, using monitoring devices. Pull tram cars along underwater tracks and position cars to receive irradiated fuel elements; then pull loaded cars to mechanisms that automatically unload elements onto underwater tables. Package, store, and move irradiated fuel elements in the underwater storage basin of a nuclear reactor plant, using machines and equipment. Organize and track the locations of hazardous items in landfills. Operate cranes to move and load baskets, casks, and canisters. Manipulate handgrips of mechanical arms to place irradiated fuel elements into baskets. Mix and pour concrete into forms to encase waste material for disposal.

Personality Type: Realistic. Realistic occupations frequently involve work activities that include practical, hands-on problems and solutions. They often deal with plants; animals; and real-world materials such as wood, tools, and machinery. Many of the occupations require working outside and do not involve a lot of paperwork or working closely with others.

GOE—Interest Area: 02. Architecture and Construction. **Work Group:** 02.04. Construction Crafts. **Other Jobs in This Work Group:** Boilermakers; Brickmasons and Blockmasons; Carpet Installers; Cement Masons and Concrete Finishers; Commercial Divers; Construction Carpenters; Crane and Tower Operators; Drywall and Ceiling Tile Installers; Electricians; Fence Erectors; Floor Layers, Except Carpet, Wood, and Hard Tiles; Floor Sanders and Finishers; Glaziers; Insulation Workers, Floor, Ceiling, and Wall; Insulation Workers, Mechanical; Manufactured Building and Mobile Home Installers; Operating Engineers and Other Construction Equipment Operators; Painters, Construction and Maintenance; Paperhangers; Paving, Surfacing, and Tamping Equipment Operators; Pile-Driver Operators; Pipe Fitters and Steamfitters; Pipelayers; Plasterers and Stucco Masons; Plumbers; Plumbers, Pipefitters, and Steamfitters; Rail-Track Laying and Maintenance Equipment Operators; Refractory Materials Repairers, Except Brickmasons; Reinforcing Iron and Rebar Workers; Riggers; Roofers; Rough Carpenters; Security and Fire Alarm Systems Installers; Segmental Pavers; Sheet Metal Workers; Stone Cutters and Carvers, Manufacturing; Stonemasons; Structural Iron and Steel Workers; Tapers; Terrazzo Workers and Finishers; Tile and Marble Setters.

Skills—Operation Monitoring: Watching gauges, dials, or other indicators to make sure a machine is working properly. **Equipment Maintenance:** Performing routine maintenance on equipment and determining when and what kind of maintenance is needed. **Repairing:** Repairing machines or systems by using the needed tools. **Operation and Control:** Controlling operations of equipment or systems. **Troubleshooting:** Determining causes of operating errors and deciding what to do about them. **Science:** Using scientific rules and methods to solve problems.

Education and Training Programs: Construction Trades, Other; Hazardous Materials Management and Waste Technology/Technician Training; Mechanic and Repair Technologies/Technician Training, Other. **Related Knowledge/Courses: Chemistry:** The chemical composition, structure, and properties of substances and of the chemical processes and transformations that they undergo. This includes uses of chemicals and their danger signs, production techniques, and disposal methods. **Building and Construction:** The materials, methods, and tools involved in the construction or repair of houses, buildings, or other structures such as highways and roads. **Mechanical Devices:** Machines and tools, including their designs, uses, repair, and maintenance. **Transportation:** Principles and methods for moving people or goods by air, rail, sea, or road, including the relative costs and benefits. **Physics:** Physical principles and laws and their interrelationships and applications to understanding fluid, material, and atmospheric dynamics and mechanical, electrical, atomic, and subatomic structures and processes. **Education and Training:** Principles and methods for curriculum and training design, teaching and instruction for individuals and groups, and the measurement of training effects.

Work Environment: Outdoors; very hot or cold; contaminants; hazardous conditions; using hands on objects, tools, or controls; repetitive motions.

Health and Safety Engineers, Except Mining Safety Engineers and Inspectors

See the descriptions of these jobs:

- Fire-Prevention and Protection Engineers
- Industrial Safety and Health Engineers
- Product Safety Engineers

Heating and Air Conditioning Mechanics and Installers

This job can be found in the Part II lists under the title Heating, Air Conditioning, and Refrigeration Mechanics and Installers.

- Education/Training Required: Long-term on-the-job training
- Annual Earnings: $37,040
- Growth: 19.0%
- Annual Job Openings: 33,000
- Self-Employed: 13.1%
- Part-Time: 3.6%

The job openings listed here are shared with Refrigeration Mechanics and Installers.

Level of Solitary Work: 68.8 (out of 100)

Level of Contact with Others: 83.0 (out of 100)

Install, service, and repair heating and air conditioning systems in residences and commercial establishments. Obtain and maintain required certifications. Comply with all applicable standards, policies, and procedures, including safety procedures and the maintenance of a clean work area. Repair or replace defective equipment, components, or wiring. Test electrical circuits and components for continuity, using electrical test equipment. Reassemble and test equipment following repairs. Inspect and test system to verify system compliance with plans and specifications and to detect and locate malfunctions. Discuss heating-cooling system malfunctions with users to isolate problems or to verify that malfunctions have been corrected. Test pipe or tubing joints and connections for leaks, using pressure gauge or soap-and-water solution. Record and report all faults, deficiencies, and other unusual occurrences, as well as the time and materials expended on work orders. Adjust system controls to setting recommended by manufacturer to balance system, using hand tools. Recommend, develop, and perform preventive and general maintenance procedures such as cleaning, power-washing, and vacuuming equipment; oiling parts; and changing filters. Lay out and connect electrical wiring between controls and equipment according to wiring diagram, using electrician's hand tools. Install auxiliary components to heating-cooling equipment, such as expansion and discharge valves, air ducts, pipes, blowers, dampers, flues, and stokers, following blueprints. Assist with other work in coordination with repair and maintenance teams. Install, connect, and adjust thermostats, humidistats, and timers, using hand tools. Generate work orders that address deficiencies in need of correction. Join pipes or tubing to equipment and to fuel, water, or refrigerant source to form complete circuit. Assemble, position, and mount heating or cooling equipment, following blueprints. Study blueprints, design specifications, and manufacturers' recommendations to ascertain the configuration of heating or cooling equipment components and to ensure the proper installation of components. Cut and drill holes in floors, walls, and roof to install equipment, using power saws and drills.

Personality Type: Realistic. Realistic occupations frequently involve work activities that include practical, hands-on problems and solutions. They often deal with plants; animals; and real-world materials such as wood, tools, and machinery. Many of the occupations require working outside and do not involve a lot of paperwork or working closely with others.

GOE—Interest Area: 02. Architecture and Construction. **Work Group:** 02.05. Systems and Equipment Installation, Maintenance, and Repair. **Other Jobs in This Work Group:** Electrical and Electronics Repairers, Powerhouse, Substation, and Relay; Electrical Power-Line Installers and Repairers; Elevator Installers and Repairers; Maintenance and Repair Workers, General; Refrigeration Mechanics and Installers; Telecommunications Equipment Installers and Repairers, Except Line Installers; Telecommunications Line Installers and Repairers.

Skills—Repairing: Repairing machines or systems by using the needed tools. **Installation:** Installing equipment, machines, wiring, or programs to meet specifications. **Equipment Maintenance:** Performing routine maintenance on equipment and determining when and what kind of maintenance is needed. **Troubleshooting:** Determining causes of operating errors and deciding what to do about them. **Systems Evaluation:** Identifying measures or indicators of system performance and the actions needed to improve or correct performance relative to the goals of the system. **Systems Analysis:** Determining how a system should work and how changes in conditions, operations, and the environment will affect outcomes.

Education and Training Programs: Heating, Air Conditioning, and Refrigeration Technology/Technician Training (ACH/ACR/ACHR/HRAC/HVAC); Heating, Air Conditioning, Ventilation, and Refrigeration Maintenance Technology/Technician Training; Solar Energy Technology/Technician Training. **Related Knowledge/Courses: Mechanical Devices:** Machines and tools, including their designs, uses, repair, and maintenance. **Building and**

Construction: The materials, methods, and tools involved in the construction or repair of houses, buildings, or other structures such as highways and roads. **Design:** Design techniques, tools, and principles involved in production of precision technical plans, blueprints, drawings, and models. **Physics:** Physical principles and laws and their interrelationships and applications to understanding fluid, material, and atmospheric dynamics and mechanical, electrical, atomic, and subatomic structures and processes. **Engineering and Technology:** The practical application of engineering science and technology. This includes applying principles, techniques, procedures, and equipment to the design and production of various goods and services. **Sales and Marketing:** Principles and methods for showing, promoting, and selling products or services. This includes marketing strategy and tactics, product demonstration, sales techniques, and sales control systems.

Work Environment: Outdoors; very hot or cold; contaminants; hazardous conditions; minor burns, cuts, bites, or stings; using hands on objects, tools, or controls.

Heating, Air Conditioning, and Refrigeration Mechanics and Installers

See the descriptions of these jobs:

- Heating and Air Conditioning Mechanics and Installers
- Refrigeration Mechanics and Installers

Helpers—Brickmasons, Blockmasons, Stonemasons, and Tile and Marble Setters

- Education/Training Required: Short-term on-the-job training
- Annual Earnings: $24,600
- Growth: 14.9%
- Annual Job Openings: 14,000
- Self-Employed: 0.8%
- Part-Time: 13.1%

Level of Solitary Work: 28.0 (out of 100)

Level of Contact with Others: 25.0 (out of 100)

Help brickmasons, blockmasons, stonemasons, or tile and marble setters by performing duties of lesser skill. Duties include using, supplying, or holding materials or tools and cleaning work area and equipment. Transport materials, tools, and machines to installation sites manually or by using conveyance equipment. Mix mortar, plaster, and grout manually or by using machines according to standard formulas. Erect scaffolding or other installation structures. Cut materials to specified sizes for installation, using power saws or tile cutters. Clean installation surfaces, equipment, tools, worksites, and storage areas, using water, chemical solutions, oxygen lances, or polishing machines. Move or position materials such as marble slabs, using cranes, hoists, or dollies. Modify material moving, mixing, grouting, grinding, polishing, or cleaning procedures according to installation or material requirements. Correct surface imperfections or fill chipped, cracked, or broken bricks or tiles, using fillers, adhesives, and grouting materials. Arrange and store materials, machines, tools, and equipment. Apply grout between joints of bricks or tiles, using grouting trowels. Apply caulk, sealants, or other agents to installed surfaces. Select or locate and supply materials to masons for installation, following drawings or numbered sequences. Remove excess grout and residue from tile or brick joints, using sponges or trowels. Remove damaged tile, brick, or mortar and clean and prepare surfaces, using pliers, hammers, chisels, drills, wire brushes, and metal wire anchors. Provide assistance in the preparation, installation, repair, or rebuilding of tile, brick, or stone surfaces. Mix mortar, plaster, and grout manually or by using machines according to standard formulas.

Personality Type: Realistic. Realistic occupations frequently involve work activities that include practical, hands-on problems and solutions. They often deal with plants; animals; and real-world materials such as wood, tools, and machinery. Many of the occupations require working outside and do not involve a lot of paperwork or working closely with others.

GOE—Interest Area: 02. Architecture and Construction. **Work Group:** 02.06. Construction Support/Labor. **Other Jobs in This Work Group:** Construction Laborers; Helpers—Carpenters; Helpers—Electricians; Helpers—Installation, Maintenance, and Repair Workers; Helpers—Painters, Paperhangers, Plasterers, and Stucco Masons; Helpers—Pipelayers, Plumbers, Pipefitters, and Steamfitters; Helpers—Roofers; Highway Maintenance Workers; Septic Tank Servicers and Sewer Pipe Cleaners.

Skills—Installation: Installing equipment, machines, wiring, or programs to meet specifications.

Education and Training Program: Mason Training/Masonry. **Related Knowledge/Courses: Building and Construction:** The materials, methods, and tools involved in the construction or repair of houses, buildings, or other structures such as highways and roads. **Mechanical Devices:** Machines and tools, including their designs, uses, repair, and maintenance.

Work Environment: Outdoors; standing; walking and running; kneeling, crouching, stooping, or crawling; using hands on objects, tools, or controls; repetitive motions.

Helpers—Painters, Paperhangers, Plasterers, and Stucco Masons

- Education/Training Required: Short-term on-the-job training
- Annual Earnings: $20,560
- Growth: 11.5%
- Annual Job Openings: 6,000
- Self-Employed: 0.9%
- Part-Time: 13.1%

Level of Solitary Work: 25.0 (out of 100)

Level of Contact with Others: 28.3 (out of 100)

Help painters, paperhangers, plasterers, or stucco masons by performing duties of lesser skill. Duties include using, supplying, or holding materials or tools and cleaning work area and equipment. Fill cracks or breaks in surfaces of plaster articles or areas with putty or epoxy compounds. Clean work areas and equipment. Apply protective coverings such as masking tape to articles or areas that could be damaged or stained by work processes. Supply or hold tools and materials. Place articles to be stripped into stripping tanks. Pour specified amounts of chemical solutions into stripping tanks. Smooth surfaces of articles to be painted, using sanding and buffing tools and equipment. Mix plaster and carry plaster to plasterers. Perform support duties to assist painters, paperhangers, plasterers, or masons. Remove articles such as cabinets, metal furniture, and paint containers from stripping tanks after prescribed periods of time. Erect scaffolding.

Personality Type: Realistic. Realistic occupations frequently involve work activities that include practical, hands-on problems and solutions. They often deal with plants; animals; and real-world materials such as wood, tools, and machinery. Many of the occupations require working outside and do not involve a lot of paperwork or working closely with others.

GOE—Interest Area: 02. Architecture and Construction. **Work Group:** 02.06. Construction Support/Labor. **Other Jobs in This Work Group:** Construction Laborers; Helpers—Brickmasons, Blockmasons, Stonemasons, and Tile and Marble Setters; Helpers—Carpenters; Helpers—Electricians; Helpers—Installation, Maintenance, and Repair Workers; Helpers—Pipelayers, Plumbers, Pipefitters, and Steamfitters; Helpers—Roofers; Highway Maintenance Workers; Septic Tank Servicers and Sewer Pipe Cleaners.

Skills—None met the criteria.

Education and Training Program: Painting/Painter and Wall Coverer Training. **Related Knowledge/Courses: Building and Construction:** The materials, methods, and tools involved in the construction or repair of houses, buildings, or other structures such as highways and roads.

Work Environment: Indoors; contaminants; standing; climbing ladders, scaffolds, or poles; using hands on objects, tools, or controls; repetitive motions.

Helpers—Production Workers

- Education/Training Required: Short-term on-the-job training
- Annual Earnings: $20,390
- Growth: 7.9%
- Annual Job Openings: 107,000
- Self-Employed: 0.1%
- Part-Time: 23.3%

Level of Solitary Work: 40.8 (out of 100)

Level of Contact with Others: 60.3 (out of 100)

Help production workers by performing duties of lesser skill. Duties include supplying or holding materials or tools and cleaning work area and equipment. Operate machinery used in the production process or assist machine operators. Examine products to verify conformance to quality standards. Observe equipment operations so that malfunctions can be detected and notify operators of any malfunctions. Lift raw materials, finished products, and packed items manually or using hoists. Count finished products to determine if product orders are complete. Mark or tag identification on parts. Load and unload items from machines, conveyors, and conveyances. Help production workers by performing duties of lesser skill, such as supplying or holding materials or tools and cleaning work areas and equipment. Clean and lubricate equipment. Record information such as the number of products tested, meter readings, and dates and times of product production. Start machines or equipment to begin production processes. Separate products according to weight, grade, size, and composition of materials used to produce them. Turn valves to regulate flow of liquids or air, to reverse machines, to start pumps, or to regulate equipment. Place products in equipment or on work surfaces for further processing, inspecting, or wrapping. Pack and store materials and products. Remove products, machine attachments, and waste material from machines. Tie products in bundles for further processing or shipment, following prescribed procedures. Transfer finished products, raw materials, tools, or equipment between storage and work areas of plants and warehouses by hand or using hand trucks or powered lift trucks. Signal co-workers to direct them to move products during the production process. Prepare raw materials for processing. Measure amounts of products, lengths of extruded articles, or weights of filled containers to ensure conformance to specifications. Thread ends of items such as thread, cloth, and lace through needles and rollers and around take-up tubes. Read gauges and charts and record data obtained. Mix ingredients according to specified procedures and formulas. Position spouts or chutes of storage bins so that containers can be filled. Fold products and product parts during processing.

Personality Type: Realistic. Realistic occupations frequently involve work activities that include practical, hands-on problems and solutions. They often deal with plants; animals; and real-world materials such as wood, tools, and machinery. Many of the occupations require working outside and do not involve a lot of paperwork or working closely with others.

GOE—Interest Area: 13. Manufacturing. **Work Group:** 13.03. Production Work, Assorted Materials Processing. **Other Jobs in This Work Group:** Bakers; Cementing and Gluing Machine Operators and Tenders; Chemical Equipment Operators and Tenders; Cleaning, Washing, and Metal Pickling Equipment Operators and Tenders; Coating, Painting, and Spraying Machine Setters, Operators, and Tenders; Cooling and Freezing Equipment Operators and Tenders; Cutting and Slicing Machine Setters, Operators, and Tenders; Extruding and Forming Machine Setters, Operators, and Tenders, Synthetic and Glass Fibers; Extruding, Forming, Pressing, and Compacting Machine Setters, Operators, and Tenders; Food and Tobacco Roasting, Baking, and Drying Machine Operators and Tenders; Food Batchmakers; Food Cooking Machine Operators and Tenders; Furnace, Kiln, Oven, Drier, and Kettle Operators and Tenders; Heat Treating Equipment Setters, Operators, and Tenders, Metal and Plastic; Meat, Poultry, and Fish Cutters and Trimmers; Metal-Refining Furnace Operators and Tenders; Mixing and Blending Machine Setters, Operators, and Tenders; Packaging and Filling Machine Operators and Tenders; Plating and Coating Machine Setters, Operators, and Tenders, Metal and Plastic; Pourers and Casters, Metal; Sawing Machine Setters, Operators, and Tenders, Wood; Separating, Filtering, Clarifying, Precipitating, and Still Machine Setters, Operators, and Tenders; Sewing Machine Operators; Shoe Machine Operators and Tenders; Slaughterers and Meat Packers; Team Assemblers; Textile Bleaching and Dyeing Machine Operators and Tenders; Tire Builders; Woodworking Machine Setters, Operators, and Tenders, Except Sawing.

Skills—Equipment Selection: Determining the kind of tools and equipment needed to do a job. **Equipment Maintenance:** Performing routine maintenance on equipment and determining when and what kind of maintenance is needed. **Installation:** Installing equipment, machines, wiring, or programs to meet specifications. **Troubleshooting:** Determining causes of operating errors and deciding what to do about them. **Management of Material Resources:** Obtaining and seeing to the appropriate use of equipment, facilities, and materials needed to do certain work. **Quality Control Analysis:** Conducting tests and inspections of products, services, or processes to evaluate quality or performance.

Education and Training Programs: No related CIP programs; this job is learned through informal short-term on-the-job training. **Related Knowledge/ Courses: Food Production:** Techniques and equipment for planting, growing, and harvesting food products (both plant and animal) for consumption, including storage/handling techniques. **Production and Processing:** Raw materials, production processes, quality control, costs, and other techniques for maximizing the effective manufacture and distribution of goods.

Work Environment: Noisy; contaminants; minor burns, cuts, bites, or stings; standing; using hands on objects, tools, or controls; bending or twisting the body.

Historians

- ◉ Education/Training Required: Master's degree
- ◉ Annual Earnings: $44,400
- ◉ Growth: 4.3%
- ◉ Annual Job Openings: Fewer than 500
- ◉ Self-Employed: 3.6%
- ◉ Part-Time: 14.8%

Level of Solitary Work: 68.8 (out of 100)

Level of Contact with Others: 92.0 (out of 100)

Research, analyze, record, and interpret the past as recorded in sources such as government and institu- tional records; newspapers and other periodicals; photographs; interviews; films; and unpublished manuscripts, such as personal diaries and letters. Gather historical data from sources such as archives, court records, diaries, news files, and photographs, as well as collect data sources such as books, pamphlets, and periodicals. Organize data and analyze and interpret its authenticity and relative significance. Trace historical development in a particular field, such as social, cultural, political, or diplomatic history. Conduct historical research as a basis for the identification, conservation, and reconstruction of historic places and materials. Teach and conduct research in colleges, universities, museums, and other research agencies and schools. Conduct historical research and publish or present findings and theories. Speak to various groups, organizations, and clubs to promote the aims and activities of historical societies. Prepare publications and exhibits or review those prepared by others in order to ensure their historical accuracy. Research the history of a particular country or region or of a specific time period. Determine which topics to research or pursue research topics specified by clients or employers. Present historical accounts in terms of individuals or social, ethnic, political, economic, or geographic groupings. Organize information for publication and for other means of dissemination, such as use in CD-ROMs or Internet sites. Research and prepare manuscripts in support of public programming and the development of exhibits at historic sites, museums, libraries, and archives. Advise or consult with individuals and institutions regarding issues such as the historical authenticity of materials or the customs of a specific historical period. Translate or request translation of reference materials. Collect detailed information on individuals for use in biographies. Interview people in order to gather information about historical events and to record oral histories. Recommend actions related to historical art, such as which items to add to a collection or which items to display in an exhibit. Coordinate activities of workers engaged in cataloging and filing materials. Edit historical society publications.

Personality Type: Investigative. Investigative occupations frequently involve working with ideas and require an extensive amount of thinking. These occupations can involve searching for facts and figuring out problems mentally.

GOE—Interest Area: 15. Scientific Research, Engineering, and Mathematics. **Work Group:** 15.04. Social Sciences. **Other Jobs in This Work Group:** Anthropologists; Anthropologists and Archeologists; Archeologists; Economists; Industrial-Organizational Psychologists; Political Scientists; School Psychologists; Sociologists.

Skills—Reading Comprehension: Understanding written sentences and paragraphs in work-related documents. **Management of Financial Resources:** Determining how money will be spent to get the work done and accounting for these expenditures. **Writing:** Communicating effectively in writing as appropriate for the needs of the audience. **Management of Personnel Resources:** Motivating, developing, and directing people as they work; identifying the best people for the job. **Speaking:** Talking to others to convey information effectively. **Social Perceptiveness:** Being aware of others' reactions and understanding why they react as they do.

Education and Training Programs: American History; Ancient Civilization; Architectural History and Criticism, General; Asian History; Canadian History; Classical, Ancient Mediterranean, and Near Eastern Studies and Archaeology; Cultural Resource Management and Policy Analysis; European History; Historic Preservation and Conservation; Historic Preservation and Conservation, Other; History and Philosophy of Science and Technology; History, General; History, Other; Holocaust and Related Studies; Medieval and Renaissance Studies. **Related Knowledge/Courses: History and Archeology:** Historical events and their causes, indicators, and effects on civilizations and cultures. **Computers and Electronics:** Circuit boards, processors, chips, electronic equipment, and computer hardware and software, including applications and programming. **English Language:** The structure and content of the English language, including the meaning and spelling of words, rules of composition, and grammar. **Geography:** Principles and methods for describing

the features of land, sea, and air masses, including their physical characteristics; locations; interrelationships; and distribution of plant, animal, and human life. **Communications and Media:** Media production, communication, and dissemination techniques and methods. This includes alternative ways to inform and entertain via written, oral, and visual media. **Clerical Practices:** Administrative and clerical procedures and systems such as word processing, managing files and records, stenography and transcription, designing forms, and other office procedures and terminology.

Work Environment: Indoors; noisy; very bright or dim lighting; contaminants; cramped work space, awkward positions; using hands on objects, tools, or controls.

Home Appliance Repairers

- Education/Training Required: Long-term on-the-job training
- Annual Earnings: $32,980
- Growth: 2.6%
- Annual Job Openings: 3,000
- Self-Employed: 18.0%
- Part-Time: 13.4%

Level of Solitary Work: 62.5 (out of 100)

Level of Contact with Others: 25.5 (out of 100)

Repair, adjust, or install all types of electric or gas household appliances, such as refrigerators, washers, dryers, and ovens. Clean, lubricate, and touch up minor defects on newly installed or repaired appliances. Observe and test operation of appliances following installation and make any initial installation adjustments that are necessary. Level refrigerators, adjust doors, and connect water lines to water pipes for ice makers and water dispensers, using hand tools. Level washing machines and connect hoses to water pipes, using hand tools. Maintain stocks of parts used in on-site installation, maintenance, and repair of appliances. Instruct customers regarding operation and care of appliances and provide information such as emergency service numbers. Provide repair cost estimates and recommend whether appliance repair or replacement is a better choice. Conserve, recover, and recycle refrigerants used in cooling systems. Contact supervisors or offices to receive repair assignments. Install gas pipes and water lines to connect appliances to existing gas lines or plumbing. Record maintenance and repair work performed on appliances. Respond to emergency calls for problems such as gas leaks. Assemble new or reconditioned appliances. Disassemble and reinstall existing kitchen cabinets or assemble and install prefabricated kitchen cabinets and trim in conjunction with appliance installation. Hang steel supports from beams or joists to hold hoses, vents, and gas pipes in place. Install appliances such as refrigerators, washing machines, and stoves. Set appliance thermostats and check to ensure that they are functioning properly. Disassemble and reinstall existing kitchen cabinets or assemble and install prefabricated kitchen cabinets and trim in conjunction with appliance installation. Refer to schematic drawings, product manuals, and troubleshooting guides to diagnose and repair problems. Clean and reinstall parts. Disassemble appliances so that problems can be diagnosed and repairs can be made. Light and adjust pilot lights on gas stoves and examine valves and burners for gas leakage and specified flame. Test and examine gas pipelines and equipment to locate leaks and faulty connections and to determine the pressure and flow of gas. Take measurements to determine if appliances will fit in installation locations; perform minor carpentry work when necessary to ensure proper installation. Measure, cut, and thread pipe and connect it to feeder lines and equipment or appliances, using rules and hand tools. Reassemble units after repairs are made, making adjustments and cleaning and lubricating parts as needed.

Personality Type: Realistic. Realistic occupations frequently involve work activities that include practical, hands-on problems and solutions. They often deal with plants; animals; and real-world materials such as wood, tools, and machinery. Many of the occupations require working outside and do not involve a lot of paperwork or working closely with others.

GOE—Interest Area: 13. Manufacturing. **Work Group:** 13.13. Machinery Repair. **Other Jobs in This Work Group:** Bicycle Repairers; Control and Valve Installers and Repairers, Except Mechanical Door; Industrial Machinery Mechanics; Locksmiths and Safe Repairers; Maintenance Workers, Machinery; Mechanical Door Repairers; Millwrights; Signal and Track Switch Repairers.

Skills—Installation: Installing equipment, machines, wiring, or programs to meet specifications. **Repairing:** Repairing machines or systems by using the needed tools. **Troubleshooting:** Determining causes of operating errors and deciding what to do about them. **Operation Monitoring:** Watching gauges, dials, or other indicators to make sure a machine is working properly. **Equipment Maintenance:** Performing routine maintenance on equipment and determining when and what kind of maintenance is needed.

Education and Training Programs: Appliance Installation and Repair Technology/Technician; Electrical/Electronics Equipment Installation and Repair, General; Home Furnishings and Equipment Installers. **Related Knowledge/Courses: Mechanical Devices:** Machines and tools, including their designs, uses, repair, and maintenance. **Building and Construction:** The materials, methods, and tools involved in the construction or repair of houses, buildings, or other structures such as highways and roads. **Engineering and Technology:** The practical application of engineering science and technology. This includes applying principles, techniques, procedures, and equipment to the design and production of various goods and services.

Work Environment: Indoors; standing; kneeling, crouching, stooping, or crawling; using hands on objects, tools, or controls.

Hydrologists

- ◎ Education/Training Required: Master's degree
- ◎ Annual Earnings: $63,820
- ◎ Growth: 31.6%
- ◎ Annual Job Openings: 1,000
- ◎ Self-Employed: 4.3%
- ◎ Part-Time: 5.7%

Level of Solitary Work: 75.0 (out of 100)

Level of Contact with Others: 68.8 (out of 100)

Research the distribution, circulation, and physical properties of underground and surface waters; study the form and intensity of precipitation, its rate of infiltration into the soil, its movement through the earth, and its return to the ocean and atmosphere. Study and document quantities, distribution, disposition, and development of underground and surface waters. Draft final reports describing research results, including illustrations, appendices, maps, and other attachments. Coordinate and supervise the work of professional and technical staff, including research assistants, technologists, and technicians. Prepare hydrogeologic evaluations of known or suspected hazardous waste sites and land treatment and feedlot facilities. Design and conduct scientific hydrogeological investigations to ensure that accurate and appropriate information is available for use in water resource management decisions. Study public water supply issues, including flood and drought risks, water quality, wastewater, and impacts on wetland habitats. Collect and analyze water samples as part of field investigations and/or to validate data from automatic monitors. Apply research findings to help minimize the environmental impacts of pollution, water-borne diseases, erosion, and sedimentation. Measure and graph phenomena such as lake levels, stream flows, and changes in water volumes. Investigate complaints or conflicts related to the alteration of public waters, gathering information, recommending alternatives, informing participants of progress, and preparing draft orders. Develop or modify methods of conducting hydrologic studies. Answer questions and provide technical assistance and information to contractors and/or the public regarding issues such as well drilling, code requirements, hydrology, and geology. Install, maintain, and calibrate instruments such as those that monitor water levels, rainfall, and sediments. Evaluate data and provide recommendations regarding the feasibility of municipal projects such as hydroelectric power plants, irrigation systems, flood warning systems, and waste treatment facilities. Conduct short-term and long-term climate assessments and study storm occurrences. Study and analyze the physical aspects of the Earth in terms of the hydrological components, including atmosphere, hydrosphere, and interior structure. Conduct research and communicate information to promote the conservation and preservation of water resources.

Personality Type: Investigative. Investigative occupations frequently involve working with ideas and require an extensive amount of thinking. These occupations can involve searching for facts and figuring out problems mentally.

GOE—Interest Area: 15. Scientific Research, Engineering, and Mathematics. **Work Group:** 15.02. Physical Sciences. **Other Jobs in This Work Group:** Astronomers; Atmospheric and Space Scientists; Chemists; Geographers; Geoscientists, Except Hydrologists and Geographers; Materials Scientists; Physicists.

Skills—Science: Using scientific rules and methods to solve problems. **Programming:** Writing computer programs for various purposes. **Management of Financial Resources:** Determining how money will be spent to get the work done and accounting for these expenditures. **Mathematics:** Using mathematics to solve problems. **Management of Personnel Resources:** Motivating, developing, and directing people as they work; identifying the best people for the job. **Complex Problem Solving:** Identifying complex problems and reviewing related information to develop and evaluate options and implement solutions.

Education and Training Programs: Geology/Earth Science, General; Hydrology and Water Resources Science; Oceanography, Chemical and Physical. **Related Knowledge/Courses: Geography:** Principles and methods for describing the features of land, sea, and air masses, including their physical characteristics; locations; interrelationships; and distribution of plant, animal, and human life. **Physics:** Physical principles and laws and their interrelationships and applications to understanding fluid, material, and atmospheric dynamics and mechanical, electrical, atomic, and subatomic structures and processes. **Engineering and Technology:** The practical application of engineering science and technology. This includes applying principles, techniques, procedures, and equipment to the design and production of various goods and services. **Chemistry:** The chemical composition, structure, and properties of substances and of the chemical processes and transformations that they undergo. This includes uses of chemicals and their danger signs, production techniques, and disposal methods. **Biology:** Plant and animal organisms and their tissues, cells, functions, interdependencies, and interactions with each other and the environment. **Mathematics:** Arithmetic, algebra, geometry, calculus, and statistics and their applications.

Work Environment: More often indoors than outdoors; sitting.

Industrial Machinery Mechanics

- ◎ Education/Training Required: Long-term on-the-job training
- ◎ Annual Earnings: $39,740
- ◎ Growth: –0.2%
- ◎ Annual Job Openings: 13,000
- ◎ Self-Employed: 2.3%
- ◎ Part-Time: 1.5%

Level of Solitary Work: 65.5 (out of 100)

Level of Contact with Others: 71.7 (out of 100)

Repair, install, adjust, or maintain industrial production and processing machinery or refinery and pipeline distribution systems. Disassemble machinery and equipment to remove parts and make repairs. Repair and replace broken or malfunctioning components of machinery and equipment. Examine parts for defects such as breakage and excessive wear. Repair and maintain the operating condition of industrial production and processing machinery and equipment. Reassemble equipment after completion of inspections, testing, or repairs. Observe and test the operation of machinery and equipment to diagnose malfunctions, using voltmeters and other testing devices. Operate newly repaired machinery and equipment to verify the adequacy of repairs. Clean, lubricate, and adjust parts, equipment, and machinery. Analyze test results, machine error messages, and information obtained from operators to diagnose equipment problems. Record repairs and maintenance performed. Study blueprints and manufacturers' manuals to determine correct installation and operation of machinery. Record parts and materials used and order or requisition new parts and materials as necessary. Cut and weld metal to repair broken metal parts, fabricate new parts, and assemble new equipment. Demonstrate equipment functions and features to machine operators. Enter codes and instructions to program computer-controlled machinery.

Personality Type: Realistic. Realistic occupations frequently involve work activities that include practical, hands-on problems and solutions. They often deal with plants; animals; and real-world materials such as wood, tools, and machinery. Many of the occupations require working outside and do not involve a lot of paperwork or working closely with others.

GOE—Interest Area: 13. Manufacturing. **Work Group:** 13.13. Machinery Repair. **Other Jobs in This Work Group:** Bicycle Repairers; Control and Valve Installers and Repairers, Except Mechanical Door; Home Appliance Repairers; Locksmiths and

Safe Repairers; Maintenance Workers, Machinery; Mechanical Door Repairers; Millwrights; Signal and Track Switch Repairers.

Skills—Repairing: Repairing machines or systems by using the needed tools. **Installation:** Installing equipment, machines, wiring, or programs to meet specifications. **Equipment Maintenance:** Performing routine maintenance on equipment and determining when and what kind of maintenance is needed. **Operation Monitoring:** Watching gauges, dials, or other indicators to make sure a machine is working properly. **Troubleshooting:** Determining causes of operating errors and deciding what to do about them. **Technology Design:** Generating or adapting equipment and technology to serve user needs.

Education and Training Programs: Heavy/Industrial Equipment Maintenance Technologies, Other; Industrial Mechanics and Maintenance Technology. **Related Knowledge/Courses: Mechanical Devices:** Machines and tools, including their designs, uses, repair, and maintenance. **Engineering and Technology:** The practical application of engineering science and technology. This includes applying principles, techniques, procedures, and equipment to the design and production of various goods and services. **Building and Construction:** The materials, methods, and tools involved in the construction or repair of houses, buildings, or other structures such as highways and roads. **Design:** Design techniques, tools, and principles involved in production of precision technical plans, blueprints, drawings, and models. **Chemistry:** The chemical composition, structure, and properties of substances and of the chemical processes and transformations that they undergo. This includes uses of chemicals and their danger signs, production techniques, and disposal methods. **Physics:** Physical principles and laws and their inter-relationships and applications to understanding fluid, material, and atmospheric dynamics and mechanical, electrical, atomic, and subatomic structures and processes.

Work Environment: Noisy; contaminants; hazardous conditions; hazardous equipment; standing; using hands on objects, tools, or controls.

Industrial Safety and Health Engineers

This job can be found in the Part II lists under the title Health and Safety Engineers, Except Mining Safety Engineers and Inspectors.

- Education/Training Required: Bachelor's degree
- Annual Earnings: $65,210
- Growth: 13.4%
- Annual Job Openings: 2,000
- Self-Employed: 0.5%
- Part-Time: 2.6%

The job openings listed here are shared with Fire-Prevention and Protection Engineers and with Product Safety Engineers.

Level of Solitary Work: 47.8 (out of 100)

Level of Contact with Others: 66.7 (out of 100)

Plan, implement, and coordinate safety programs requiring application of engineering principles and technology to prevent or correct unsafe environmental working conditions. Investigate industrial accidents, injuries, or occupational diseases to determine causes and preventive measures. Report or review findings from accident investigations, facilities inspections, or environmental testing. Maintain and apply knowledge of current policies, regulations, and industrial processes. Inspect facilities, machinery, and safety equipment to identify and correct potential hazards and to ensure safety regulation compliance. Conduct or coordinate worker training in areas such as safety laws and regulations, hazardous condition monitoring, and use of safety equipment. Review employee safety programs to determine their adequacy. Interview employers and employees to obtain information about work environments and workplace incidents. Review plans and specifications for construction of new machinery or equipment to determine whether all safety requirements have been met. Compile, analyze, and interpret statistical data related to occupational illnesses and accidents. Interpret safety regulations for others interested in industrial safety, such as safety engineers, labor representatives, and safety inspectors. Recommend process and product safety features that will reduce employees' exposure to chemical, physical, and biological work hazards. Conduct or direct testing of air quality, noise, temperature, or radiation levels to verify compliance with health and safety regulations. Provide technical advice and guidance to organizations on how to handle health-related problems and make needed changes. Confer with medical professionals to assess health risks and to develop ways to manage health issues and concerns. Install safety devices on machinery or direct device installation. Maintain liaisons with outside organizations such as fire departments, mutual aid societies, and rescue teams so that emergency responses can be facilitated. Evaluate adequacy of actions taken to correct health inspection violations. Write and revise safety regulations and codes. Check floors of plants to ensure that they are strong enough to support heavy machinery. Plan and conduct industrial hygiene research.

Personality Type: Investigative. Investigative occupations frequently involve working with ideas and require an extensive amount of thinking. These occupations can involve searching for facts and figuring out problems mentally.

GOE—Interest Area: 15. Scientific Research, Engineering, and Mathematics. **Work Group:** 15.08. Industrial and Safety Engineering. **Other Jobs in This Work Group:** Fire-Prevention and Protection Engineers; Health and Safety Engineers, Except Mining Safety Engineers and Inspectors; Industrial Engineers; Product Safety Engineers.

Skills—Management of Financial Resources: Determining how money will be spent to get the work done and accounting for these expenditures. **Science:** Using scientific rules and methods to solve problems. **Systems Analysis:** Determining how a system should work and how changes in conditions, operations, and the environment will affect outcomes. **Persuasion:** Persuading others to change their minds or behavior. **Systems Evaluation:** Identifying measures or indicators of system performance and the actions needed to improve or correct performance relative to the goals of the system. **Management of Personnel Resources:** Motivating, developing, and directing people as they work; identifying the best people for the job.

Education and Training Program: Environmental/ Environmental Health Engineering. **Related Knowledge/Courses: Building and Construction:** The materials, methods, and tools involved in the construction or repair of houses, buildings, or other structures such as highways and roads. **Education and Training:** Principles and methods for curriculum and training design, teaching and instruction for individuals and groups, and the measurement of training effects. **Chemistry:** The chemical composition, structure, and properties of substances and of the chemical processes and transformations that they undergo. This includes uses of chemicals and their danger signs, production techniques, and disposal methods. **Physics:** Physical principles and laws and their interrelationships and applications to understanding fluid, material, and atmospheric dynamics and mechanical, electrical, atomic, and subatomic structures and processes. **Engineering and Technology:** The practical application of engineering science and technology. This includes applying principles, techniques, procedures, and equipment to the design and production of various goods and services. **Biology:** Plant and animal organisms and their tissues, cells, functions, interdependencies, and interactions with each other and the environment.

Work Environment: More often indoors than outdoors; noisy; sitting.

Inspectors, Testers, Sorters, Samplers, and Weighers

- ◎ Education/Training Required: Moderate-term on-the-job training
- ◎ Annual Earnings: $29,200
- ◎ Growth: –2.6%
- ◎ Annual Job Openings: 85,000
- ◎ Self-Employed: 1.9%
- ◎ Part-Time: 6.7%

Level of Solitary Work: 63.7 (out of 100)

Level of Contact with Others: 70.5 (out of 100)

Inspect, test, sort, sample, or weigh nonagricultural raw materials or processed, machined, fabricated, or assembled parts or products for defects, wear, and deviations from specifications. May use precision measuring instruments and complex test equipment. Discard or reject products, materials, and equipment not meeting specifications. Analyze and interpret blueprints, data, manuals, and other materials to determine specifications, inspection and testing procedures, adjustment and certification methods, formulas, and measuring instruments required. Inspect, test, or measure materials, products, installations, and work for conformance to specifications. Notify supervisors and other personnel of production problems and assist in identifying and correcting these problems. Discuss inspection results with those responsible for products and recommend necessary corrective actions. Record inspection or test data, such as weights, temperatures, grades, or moisture content and quantities inspected or graded. Mark items with details such as grade and acceptance or rejection status. Observe and monitor production operations and equipment to ensure conformance to specifications and make or order necessary process or assembly adjustments. Measure dimensions of products to verify conformance to specifications, using measuring instruments such as rulers, calipers, gauges, or micrometers. Analyze test data and make computations as necessary to determine test results. Collect or select samples for testing or for use as models. Check arriving materials to ensure that they match purchase orders and submit discrepancy reports when problems are found. Compare colors, shapes, textures, or grades of products or materials with color charts, templates, or samples to verify conformance to standards. Write test and inspection reports describing results, recommendations, and needed repairs. Read dials and meters to verify that equipment is functioning at specified levels. Remove defects, such as chips and burrs, and lap corroded or pitted surfaces. Clean, maintain, repair, and calibrate measuring instruments and test equipment such as dial indicators, fixed gauges, and height gauges. Adjust, clean, or repair products or processing equipment to correct defects found during inspections. Stack and arrange tested products for further processing, shipping, or packaging and transport products to other workstations as necessary.

Personality Type: Realistic. Realistic occupations frequently involve work activities that include practical, hands-on problems and solutions. They often deal with plants; animals; and real-world materials such as wood, tools, and machinery. Many of the occupations require working outside and do not involve a lot of paperwork or working closely with others.

GOE—Interest Area: 13. Manufacturing. **Work Group:** 13.07. Production Quality Control. **Other Jobs in This Work Group:** Graders and Sorters, Agricultural Products.

Skills—Quality Control Analysis: Conducting tests and inspections of products, services, or processes to evaluate quality or performance. **Operation Monitoring:** Watching gauges, dials, or other indicators to make sure a machine is working properly. **Operation and Control:** Controlling operations of equipment or systems. **Repairing:** Repairing machines or systems by using the needed tools. **Instructing:** Teaching others how to do something. **Systems Evaluation:** Identifying measures or indicators of system performance and the actions needed to improve or correct performance relative to the goals of the system.

Education and Training Program: Quality Control Technology/Technician. **Related Knowledge/ Courses: Production and Processing:** Raw materials, production processes, quality control, costs, and other techniques for maximizing the effective manufacture and distribution of goods.

Work Environment: Noisy; standing; using hands on objects, tools, or controls; repetitive motions.

Insulation Workers, Floor, Ceiling, and Wall

- ◎ Education/Training Required: Moderate-term on-the-job training
- ◎ Annual Earnings: $31,360
- ◎ Growth: 3.0%
- ◎ Annual Job Openings: 4,000
- ◎ Self-Employed: 11.0%
- ◎ Part-Time: 3.7%

Level of Solitary Work: 59.2 (out of 100)

Level of Contact with Others: 16.5 (out of 100)

Line and cover structures with insulating materials. May work with batt, roll, or blown insulation materials. Distribute insulating materials evenly into small spaces within floors, ceilings, or walls, using blowers and hose attachments or cement mortars. Cover and line structures with blown or rolled forms of materials to insulate against cold, heat, or moisture, using saws, knives, rasps, trowels, blowers, and other tools and implements. Move controls, buttons, or levers to start blowers and regulate flow of materials through nozzles. Remove old insulation such as asbestos, following safety procedures. Read blueprints and select appropriate insulation, based on space characteristics and the heat-retaining or -excluding characteristics of the material. Prepare surfaces for insulation application by brushing or spreading on adhesives, cement,

or asphalt or by attaching metal pins to surfaces. Measure and cut insulation for covering surfaces, using tape measures, hand saws, power saws, knives, or scissors. Fit, wrap, staple, or glue insulating materials to structures or surfaces, using hand tools or wires. Fill blower hoppers with insulating materials. Cover, seal, or finish insulated surfaces or access holes with plastic covers, canvas strips, sealants, tape, cement, or asphalt mastic.

Personality Type: Realistic. Realistic occupations frequently involve work activities that include practical, hands-on problems and solutions. They often deal with plants; animals; and real-world materials such as wood, tools, and machinery. Many of the occupations require working outside and do not involve a lot of paperwork or working closely with others.

GOE—Interest Area: 02. Architecture and Construction. **Work Group:** 02.04. Construction Crafts. **Other Jobs in This Work Group:** Boilermakers; Brickmasons and Blockmasons; Carpet Installers; Cement Masons and Concrete Finishers; Commercial Divers; Construction Carpenters; Crane and Tower Operators; Drywall and Ceiling Tile Installers; Electricians; Fence Erectors; Floor Layers, Except Carpet, Wood, and Hard Tiles; Floor Sanders and Finishers; Glaziers; Hazardous Materials Removal Workers; Insulation Workers, Mechanical; Manufactured Building and Mobile Home Installers; Operating Engineers and Other Construction Equipment Operators; Painters, Construction and Maintenance; Paperhangers; Paving, Surfacing, and Tamping Equipment Operators; Pile-Driver Operators; Pipe Fitters and Steamfitters; Pipelayers; Plasterers and Stucco Masons; Plumbers; Plumbers, Pipefitters, and Steamfitters; Rail-Track Laying and Maintenance Equipment Operators; Refractory Materials Repairers, Except Brickmasons; Reinforcing Iron and Rebar Workers; Riggers; Roofers; Rough Carpenters; Security and Fire Alarm Systems Installers; Segmental Pavers; Sheet Metal Workers; Stone Cutters and Carvers, Manufacturing; Stonemasons; Structural Iron and Steel Workers; Tapers; Terrazzo Workers and Finishers; Tile and Marble Setters.

Skills—None met the criteria.

Education and Training Program: Construction Trades, Other. **Related Knowledge/Courses: Building and Construction:** The materials, methods, and tools involved in the construction or repair of houses, buildings, or other structures such as highways and roads. **Mechanical Devices:** Machines and tools, including their designs, uses, repair, and maintenance.

Work Environment: Indoors; contaminants; standing; using hands on objects, tools, or controls.

Insulation Workers, Mechanical

- ◎ Education/Training Required: Moderateterm on-the-job training
- ◎ Annual Earnings: $35,510
- ◎ Growth: 1.0%
- ◎ Annual Job Openings: 2,000
- ◎ Self-Employed: 6.8%
- ◎ Part-Time: 3.7%

Level of Solitary Work: 59.2 (out of 100)

Level of Contact with Others: 16.5 (out of 100)

Apply insulating materials to pipes or ductwork or other mechanical systems to help control and maintain temperature. Read blueprints and specifications to determine job requirements. Remove or seal off old asbestos insulation, following safety procedures. Fill blower hoppers with insulating materials. Distribute insulating materials evenly into small spaces within floors, ceilings, or walls, using blowers and hose attachments or cement mortar. Select appropriate insulation such as fiberglass, Styrofoam, or cork, based on the heat-retaining or -excluding characteristics of the material. Move controls, buttons, or levers to start blowers and to regulate flow of materials through nozzles. Apply, remove, and repair

insulation on industrial equipment; pipes; ductwork; or other mechanical systems such as heat exchangers, tanks, and vessels to help control noise and maintain temperatures. Measure and cut insulation for covering surfaces, using tape measures, handsaws, knives, and scissors. Install sheet metal around insulated pipes with screws to protect the insulation from weather conditions or physical damage. Fit insulation around obstructions and shape insulating materials and protective coverings as required. Determine the amounts and types of insulation needed and methods of installation based on factors such as location, surface shape, and equipment use. Prepare surfaces for insulation application by brushing or spreading on adhesives, cement, or asphalt or by attaching metal pins to surfaces. Cover, seal, or finish insulated surfaces or access holes with plastic covers, canvas strips, sealants, tape, cement, or asphalt mastic.

Personality Type: Realistic. Realistic occupations frequently involve work activities that include practical, hands-on problems and solutions. They often deal with plants; animals; and real-world materials such as wood, tools, and machinery. Many of the occupations require working outside and do not involve a lot of paperwork or working closely with others.

GOE—Interest Area: 02. Architecture and Construction. **Work Group:** 02.04. Construction Crafts. **Other Jobs in This Work Group:** Boilermakers; Brickmasons and Blockmasons; Carpet Installers; Cement Masons and Concrete Finishers; Commercial Divers; Construction Carpenters; Crane and Tower Operators; Drywall and Ceiling Tile Installers; Electricians; Fence Erectors; Floor Layers, Except Carpet, Wood, and Hard Tiles; Floor Sanders and Finishers; Glaziers; Hazardous Materials Removal Workers; Insulation Workers, Floor, Ceiling, and Wall; Manufactured Building and Mobile Home Installers; Operating Engineers and Other Construction Equipment Operators; Painters, Construction and Maintenance; Paperhangers; Paving, Surfacing, and Tamping Equipment Operators; Pile-Driver Operators; Pipe Fitters and Steamfitters; Pipelayers; Plasterers and Stucco Masons; Plumbers; Plumbers, Pipefitters, and

Steamfitters; Rail-Track Laying and Maintenance Equipment Operators; Refractory Materials Repairers, Except Brickmasons; Reinforcing Iron and Rebar Workers; Riggers; Roofers; Rough Carpenters; Security and Fire Alarm Systems Installers; Segmental Pavers; Sheet Metal Workers; Stone Cutters and Carvers, Manufacturing; Stonemasons; Structural Iron and Steel Workers; Tapers; Terrazzo Workers and Finishers; Tile and Marble Setters.

Skills—None met the criteria.

Education and Training Program: Construction Trades, Other. **Related Knowledge/Courses: Building and Construction:** The materials, methods, and tools involved in the construction or repair of houses, buildings, or other structures such as highways and roads. **Mechanical Devices:** Machines and tools, including their designs, uses, repair, and maintenance.

Work Environment: Indoors; contaminants; standing; using hands on objects, tools, or controls.

Interior Designers

- ◎ Education/Training Required: Associate degree
- ◎ Annual Earnings: $41,350
- ◎ Growth: 15.5%
- ◎ Annual Job Openings: 10,000
- ◎ Self-Employed: 25.3%
- ◎ Part-Time: 21.3%

Level of Solitary Work: 68.8 (out of 100)

Level of Contact with Others: 86.7 (out of 100)

Plan, design, and furnish interiors of residential, commercial, or industrial buildings. Formulate design that is practical, aesthetic, and conducive to intended purposes, such as raising productivity, selling merchandise, or improving lifestyle. May spe-cialize in a particular field, style, or phase of interior design.** Estimate material requirements and costs and present design to client for approval. Confer with client to determine factors affecting planning interior environments, such as budget, architectural preferences, and purpose and function. Advise client on interior design factors such as space planning, layout, and utilization of furnishings or equipment and color coordination. Select or design and purchase furnishings, artwork, and accessories. Formulate environmental plan to be practical, esthetic, and conducive to intended purposes such as raising productivity or selling merchandise. Subcontract fabrication, installation, and arrangement of carpeting, fixtures, accessories, draperies, paint and wall coverings, artwork, furniture, and related items. Render design ideas in form of paste-ups or drawings. Plan and design interior environments for boats, planes, buses, trains, and other enclosed spaces.

Personality Type: Artistic. Artistic occupations frequently involve working with forms, designs, and patterns. They often require self-expression, and the work can be done without following a clear set of rules.

GOE—Interest Area: 03. Arts and Communication. **Work Group:** 03.05. Design. **Other Jobs in This Work Group:** Commercial and Industrial Designers; Fashion Designers; Floral Designers; Graphic Designers; Merchandise Displayers and Window Trimmers; Set and Exhibit Designers.

Skills—Installation: Installing equipment, machines, wiring, or programs to meet specifications. **Persuasion:** Persuading others to change their minds or behavior. **Management of Financial Resources:** Determining how money will be spent to get the work done and accounting for these expenditures. **Negotiation:** Bringing others together and trying to reconcile differences. **Active Learning:** Understanding the implications of new information for both current and future problem solving and decision making. **Mathematics:** Using mathematics to solve problems.

Education and Training Programs: Facilities Planning and Management; Interior Architecture; Interior Design; Textile Science. **Related Knowledge/Courses: Design:** Design techniques, tools, and principles involved in production of precision technical plans, blueprints, drawings, and models. **Sales and Marketing:** Principles and methods for showing, promoting, and selling products or services. This includes marketing strategy and tactics, product demonstration, sales techniques, and sales control systems. **Building and Construction:** The materials, methods, and tools involved in the construction or repair of houses, buildings, or other structures such as highways and roads. **Administration and Management:** Business and management principles involved in strategic planning, resource allocation, human resources modeling, leadership technique, production methods, and coordination of people and resources. **Clerical Practices:** Administrative and clerical procedures and systems such as word processing, managing files and records, stenography and transcription, designing forms, and other office procedures and terminology. **Fine Arts:** The theory and techniques required to compose, produce, and perform works of music, dance, visual arts, drama, and sculpture.

Work Environment: Indoors; sitting.

Job Printers

- ◎ Education/Training Required: Long-term on-the-job training
- ◎ Annual Earnings: $31,920
- ◎ Growth: 1.8%
- ◎ Annual Job Openings: 8,000
- ◎ Self-Employed: 8.0%
- ◎ Part-Time: 6.7%

Level of Solitary Work: 68.8 (out of 100)

Level of Contact with Others: 79.0 (out of 100)

Set type according to copy, operate press to print job order, read proof for errors and clarity of impression, and correct imperfections. Job printers are often found in small establishments where work combines several job skills. Examine proofs or printed sheets to detect errors and to evaluate the adequacy of impression clarity. Fill ink fountains and move levers to adjust the flow of ink. Set feed guides according to sizes and thicknesses of paper. Operate cylinder or automatic platen presses to print job orders. Clean ink rollers after runs are completed. Position forms (type in locked chases) on beds of presses; then tighten clamps, using wrenches. Lay forms on proof presses; then ink type, fasten paper to press rollers, and pull rollers over forms to make proof copies. Design and set up product compositions and page layouts. Reset type to correct typographical errors.

Personality Type: Realistic. Realistic occupations frequently involve work activities that include practical, hands-on problems and solutions. They often deal with plants; animals; and real-world materials such as wood, tools, and machinery. Many of the occupations require working outside and do not involve a lot of paperwork or working closely with others.

GOE—Interest Area: 13. Manufacturing. **Work Group:** 13.08. Graphic Arts Production. **Other Jobs in This Work Group:** Bindery Workers; Desktop Publishers; Etchers and Engravers; Photographic Process Workers; Photographic Processing Machine Operators; Prepress Technicians and Workers; Printing Machine Operators.

Skills—Operation Monitoring: Watching gauges, dials, or other indicators to make sure a machine is working properly. **Equipment Maintenance:** Performing routine maintenance on equipment and determining when and what kind of maintenance is needed. **Operation and Control:** Controlling operations of equipment or systems. **Repairing:** Repairing machines or systems by using the needed tools. **Quality Control Analysis:** Conducting tests and inspections of products, services, or processes to evaluate quality or performance. **Troubleshooting:**

Determining causes of operating errors and deciding what to do about them.

Education and Training Programs: Graphic and Printing Equipment Operator, General Production; Printing Management. **Related Knowledge/Courses: Production and Processing:** Raw materials, production processes, quality control, costs, and other techniques for maximizing the effective manufacture and distribution of goods. **Mechanical Devices:** Machines and tools, including their designs, uses, repair, and maintenance. **Chemistry:** The chemical composition, structure, and properties of substances and of the chemical processes and transformations that they undergo. This includes uses of chemicals and their danger signs, production techniques, and disposal methods. **Design:** Design techniques, tools, and principles involved in production of precision technical plans, blueprints, drawings, and models. **Education and Training:** Principles and methods for curriculum and training design, teaching and instruction for individuals and groups, and the measurement of training effects. **Engineering and Technology:** The practical application of engineering science and technology. This includes applying principles, techniques, procedures, and equipment to the design and production of various goods and services.

Work Environment: Indoors; contaminants; hazardous conditions; standing; using hands on objects, tools, or controls; repetitive motions.

Landscaping and Groundskeeping Workers

- ◎ Education/Training Required: Short-term on-the-job training
- ◎ Annual Earnings: $20,670
- ◎ Growth: 19.5%
- ◎ Annual Job Openings: 243,000
- ◎ Self-Employed: 20.5%
- ◎ Part-Time: 24.4%

Level of Solitary Work: 62.5 (out of 100)

Level of Contact with Others: 52.2 (out of 100)

Landscape or maintain grounds of property, using hand or power tools or equipment. Workers typically perform a variety of tasks, which may include any combination of the following: sod laying, mowing, trimming, planting, watering, fertilizing, digging, raking, sprinkler installation, and installation of mortarless segmental concrete masonry wall units. Operate powered equipment such as mowers, tractors, twin-axle vehicles, snowblowers, chain saws, electric clippers, sod cutters, and pruning saws. Mow and edge lawns, using power mowers and edgers. Shovel snow from walks, driveways, and parking lots and spread salt in those areas. Care for established lawns by mulching; aerating; weeding; grubbing and removing thatch; and trimming and edging around flower beds, walks, and walls. Use hand tools such as shovels, rakes, pruning saws, saws, hedge and brush trimmers, and axes. Prune and trim trees, shrubs, and hedges, using shears, pruners, or chain saws. Maintain and repair tools; equipment; and structures such as buildings, greenhouses, fences, and benches, using hand and power tools. Gather and remove litter. Mix and spray or spread fertilizers, herbicides, or insecticides onto grass, shrubs, and trees, using hand or automatic sprayers or spreaders. Provide proper upkeep of sidewalks, driveways, parking lots, fountains, planters, burial sites, and other grounds features. Water lawns, trees, and plants, using portable sprinkler systems, hoses, or watering cans. Trim and pick flowers and clean flowerbeds. Rake, mulch, and compost leaves. Plant seeds, bulbs, foliage, flowering plants, grass, ground covers, trees, and shrubs and apply mulch for protection, using gardening tools. Follow planned landscaping designs to determine where to lay sod, sow grass, or plant flowers and foliage. Decorate gardens with stones and plants. Maintain irrigation systems, including winterizing the systems and starting them up in spring. Care for natural turf fields, making sure the underlying soil has the required composition to allow proper drainage and to support the grasses used on the fields. Use irrigation methods to adjust the amount of water consumption and to prevent waste. Haul or spread topsoil and spread straw over seeded soil to hold soil in place. Advise customers on plant selection and care. Care for artificial turf fields, periodically removing the turf and replacing cushioning pads and vacuuming and disinfecting the turf after use to prevent the growth of harmful bacteria.

Personality Type: Realistic. Realistic occupations frequently involve work activities that include practical, hands-on problems and solutions. They often deal with plants; animals; and real-world materials such as wood, tools, and machinery. Many of the occupations require working outside and do not involve a lot of paperwork or working closely with others.

GOE—Interest Area: 01. Agriculture and Natural Resources. **Work Group:** 01.05. Nursery, Groundskeeping, and Pest Control. **Other Jobs in This Work Group:** Nursery Workers; Pest Control Workers; Pesticide Handlers, Sprayers, and Applicators, Vegetation; Tree Trimmers and Pruners.

Skills—Equipment Maintenance: Performing routine maintenance on equipment and determining when and what kind of maintenance is needed. **Repairing:** Repairing machines or systems by using the needed tools. **Operation Monitoring:** Watching gauges, dials, or other indicators to make sure a machine is working properly. **Installation:** Installing equipment, machines, wiring, or programs to meet specifications. **Troubleshooting:** Determining causes of operating errors and deciding what to do about them.

Education and Training Programs: Landscaping and Groundskeeping; Turf and Turfgrass Management. **Related Knowledge/Courses: Mechanical Devices:** Machines and tools, including their designs, uses, repair, and maintenance.

Work Environment: Outdoors; noisy; very hot or cold; contaminants; standing; using hands on objects, tools, or controls.

Lathe and Turning Machine Tool Setters, Operators, and Tenders, Metal and Plastic

- Education/Training Required: Moderate-term on-the-job training
- Annual Earnings: $31,750
- Growth: –9.0%
- Annual Job Openings: 7,000
- Self-Employed: 0.0%
- Part-Time: No data available

Level of Solitary Work: 71.7 (out of 100)

Level of Contact with Others: 64.5 (out of 100)

Set up, operate, or tend lathe and turning machines to turn, bore, thread, form, or face metal or plastic materials, such as wire, rod, or bar stock. Inspect sample workpieces to verify conformance with specifications, using instruments such as gauges, micrometers, and dial indicators. Study blueprints, layouts or charts, and job orders for information on specifications and tooling instructions and to determine material requirements and operational sequences. Adjust machine controls and change tool settings to keep dimensions within specified tolerances. Start lath or turning machines and observe operations to ensure that specifications are met. Move controls to set cutting speeds and depths and feed rates and to position tools in relation to workpieces. Select cutting tools and tooling instructions according to written specifications or knowledge of metal properties and shop mathematics. Crank machines through cycles, stopping to adjust tool positions and machine controls to ensure specified timing, clearances, and tolerances. Lift metal stock or workpieces manually or by using hoists and position and secure them in machines, using fasteners and hand tools. Replace worn tools and sharpen dull cutting tools and dies, using bench grinders or cutter-grinding machines. Position, secure, and align cutting tools in toolholders on machines, using hand tools, and verify their positions with measuring instruments. Compute unspecified dimensions and machine settings, using knowledge of metal properties and shop mathematics. Install holding fixtures, cams, gears, and stops to control stock and tool movement, using hand tools, power tools, and measuring instruments. Move toolholders manually or by turning handwheels or engage automatic feeding mechanisms to feed tools to and along workpieces. Turn valve handles to direct the flow of coolant onto work areas or to coat disks with spinning compounds. Mount attachments, such as relieving or tracing attachments, to perform operations such as duplicating contours of templates or trimming workpieces.

Personality Type: Realistic. Realistic occupations frequently involve work activities that include practical, hands-on problems and solutions. They often deal with plants; animals; and real-world materials such as wood, tools, and machinery. Many of the occupations require working outside and do not involve a lot of paperwork or working closely with others.

GOE—Interest Area: 13. Manufacturing. **Work Group:** 13.02. Machine Setup and Operation. **Other Jobs in This Work Group:** Crushing, Grinding, and Polishing Machine Setters, Operators, and Tenders; Cutting, Punching, and Press Machine Setters, Operators, and Tenders, Metal and Plastic; Drilling and Boring Machine Tool Setters, Operators, and Tenders, Metal and Plastic; Extruding and Drawing Machine Setters, Operators, and Tenders, Metal and Plastic; Forging Machine Setters, Operators, and Tenders, Metal and Plastic; Grinding, Lapping, Polishing, and Buffing Machine Tool Setters, Operators, and Tenders, Metal and Plastic; Milling and Planing Machine Setters, Operators, and Tenders, Metal and Plastic; Multiple Machine Tool Setters, Operators, and Tenders, Metal and Plastic; Paper Goods Machine Setters, Operators, and Tenders; Rolling Machine Setters, Operators, and Tenders, Metal and Plastic; Textile Cutting Machine Setters, Operators, and Tenders; Textile Knitting and Weaving Machine Setters, Operators, and Tenders; Textile Winding, Twisting, and Drawing Out Machine Setters, Operators, and Tenders.

Skills—Operation Monitoring: Watching gauges, dials, or other indicators to make sure a machine is working properly. **Equipment Maintenance:** Performing routine maintenance on equipment and determining when and what kind of maintenance is needed. **Repairing:** Repairing machines or systems by using the needed tools. **Quality Control Analysis:** Conducting tests and inspections of products, services, or processes to evaluate quality or performance. **Operation and Control:** Controlling operations of equipment or systems. **Programming:** Writing computer programs for various purposes.

Education and Training Program: Machine Tool Technology/Machinist Training. **Related Knowledge/Courses: Mechanical Devices:** Machines and tools, including their designs, uses, repair, and maintenance. **Design:** Design techniques, tools, and principles involved in production of precision technical plans, blueprints, drawings, and models. **Engineering and Technology:** The practical application of engineering science and technology. This includes applying principles, techniques, procedures, and equipment to the design and production of various goods and services. **Mathematics:** Arithmetic, algebra, geometry, calculus, and statistics and their applications. **Production and Processing:** Raw materials, production processes, quality control, costs, and other techniques for maximizing the effective manufacture and distribution of goods. **Computers and Electronics:** Circuit boards, processors, chips, electronic equipment, and computer hardware and software, including applications and programming.

Work Environment: Noisy; contaminants; hazardous equipment; minor burns, cuts, bites, or stings; standing; using hands on objects, tools, or controls.

Lawyers

- Education/Training Required: First professional degree
- Annual Earnings: $98,930
- Growth: 15.0%
- Annual Job Openings: 40,000
- Self-Employed: 24.1%
- Part-Time: 6.8%

Level of Solitary Work: 59.2 (out of 100)

Level of Contact with Others: 85.5 (out of 100)

Represent clients in criminal and civil litigation and other legal proceedings, draw up legal documents, and manage or advise clients on legal transactions. May specialize in a single area or may practice broadly in many areas of law. Advise clients concerning business transactions, claim liability, advisability of prosecuting or defending lawsuits, or legal rights and obligations. Interpret laws, rulings, and regulations for individuals and businesses. Analyze the probable outcomes of cases, using knowledge of legal precedents. Present and summarize cases to judges and juries. Gather evidence to formulate defense or to initiate legal actions by such means as interviewing clients and witnesses to ascertain the facts of a case. Evaluate findings and develop strategies and arguments in preparation for presentation of cases. Represent clients in court or before government agencies. Examine legal data to determine advisability of defending or prosecuting lawsuit. Select jurors, argue motions, meet with judges, and question witnesses during the course of a trial. Present evidence to defend clients or prosecute defendants in criminal or civil litigation. Study Constitution, statutes, decisions, regulations, and ordinances of quasi-judicial bodies to determine ramifications for cases. Prepare and draft legal documents, such as wills, deeds, patent applications, mortgages, leases, and contracts. Prepare legal briefs

and opinions and file appeals in state and federal courts of appeal. Negotiate settlements of civil disputes. Confer with colleagues with specialties in appropriate areas of legal issue to establish and verify bases for legal proceedings. Search for and examine public and other legal records to write opinions or establish ownership. Supervise legal assistants. Perform administrative and management functions related to the practice of law. Act as agent, trustee, guardian, or executor for businesses or individuals. Probate wills and represent and advise executors and administrators of estates. Help develop federal and state programs, draft and interpret laws and legislation, and establish enforcement procedures. Work in environmental law, representing public interest groups, waste disposal companies, or construction firms in their dealings with state and federal agencies.

Personality Type: Enterprising. Enterprising occupations frequently involve starting up and carrying out projects. These occupations can involve leading people and making many decisions. They sometimes require risk taking and often deal with business.

GOE—Interest Area: 12. Law and Public Safety. **Work Group:** 12.02. Legal Practice and Justice Administration. **Other Jobs in This Work Group:** Administrative Law Judges, Adjudicators, and Hearing Officers; Arbitrators, Mediators, and Conciliators; Judges, Magistrate Judges, and Magistrates.

Skills—Persuasion: Persuading others to change their minds or behavior. **Negotiation:** Bringing others together and trying to reconcile differences. **Writing:** Communicating effectively in writing as appropriate for the needs of the audience. **Judgment and Decision Making:** Considering the relative costs and benefits of potential actions to choose the most appropriate one. **Critical Thinking:** Using logic and reasoning to identify the strengths and weaknesses of alternative solutions, conclusions, or approaches to problems. **Speaking:** Talking to others to convey information effectively.

Education and Training Programs: American/U.S. Law/Legal Studies/Jurisprudence (LL.M., M.C.J., J.S.D./S.J.D.); Banking, Corporate, Finance, and Securities Law (LL.M., J.S.D./S.J.D.); Comparative Law (LL.M., M.C.L., J.S.D./S.J.D.); Energy, Environment, and Natural Resources Law (LL.M., M.S., J.S.D./S.J.D.); Health Law (LL.M., M.J., J.S.D./S.J.D.); International Law and Legal Studies (LL.M., J.S.D./S.J.D.); Law (LL.B., J.D.); Programs for Foreign Lawyers (LL.M., M.C.L.); Tax Law/Taxation (LL.M., J.S.D./S.J.D.); others. **Related Knowledge/Courses: Law and Government:** Laws, legal codes, court procedures, precedents, government regulations, executive orders, agency rules, and the democratic political process. **English Language:** The structure and content of the English language, including the meaning and spelling of words, rules of composition, and grammar. **Personnel and Human Resources:** Principles and procedures for personnel recruitment, selection, training, compensation and benefits, labor relations and negotiation, and personnel information systems. **Economics and Accounting:** Economic and accounting principles and practices, the financial markets, banking, and the analysis and reporting of financial data. **Psychology:** Human behavior and performance; individual differences in ability, personality, and interests; learning and motivation; psychological research methods; and the assessment and treatment of behavioral and affective disorders. **Administration and Management:** Business and management principles involved in strategic planning, resource allocation, human resources modeling, leadership technique, production methods, and coordination of people and resources.

Work Environment: Indoors; sitting.

Locksmiths and Safe Repairers

- Education/Training Required: Moderate-term on-the-job training
- Annual Earnings: $30,880
- Growth: 16.1%
- Annual Job Openings: 5,000
- Self-Employed: 37.6%
- Part-Time: 18.2%

Level of Solitary Work: 81.2 (out of 100)

Level of Contact with Others: 83.7 (out of 100)

Repair and open locks, make keys, change locks and safe combinations, and install and repair safes. Cut new or duplicate keys, using keycutting machines. Keep records of company locks and keys. Insert new or repaired tumblers into locks to change combinations. Move picklocks in cylinders to open door locks without keys. Disassemble mechanical or electrical locking devices and repair or replace worn tumblers, springs, and other parts, using hand tools. Repair and adjust safes, vault doors, and vault components, using hand tools, lathes, drill presses, and welding and acetylene cutting apparatus. Install safes, vault doors, and deposit boxes according to blueprints, using equipment such as powered drills, taps, dies, truck cranes, and dollies. Open safe locks by drilling. Remove interior and exterior finishes on safes and vaults and spray on new finishes.

Personality Type: Realistic. Realistic occupations frequently involve work activities that include practical, hands-on problems and solutions. They often deal with plants; animals; and real-world materials such as wood, tools, and machinery. Many of the occupations require working outside and do not involve a lot of paperwork or working closely with others.

GOE—Interest Area: 13. Manufacturing. **Work Group:** 13.13. Machinery Repair. **Other Jobs in This Work Group:** Bicycle Repairers; Control and Valve Installers and Repairers, Except Mechanical Door; Home Appliance Repairers; Industrial Machinery Mechanics; Maintenance Workers, Machinery; Mechanical Door Repairers; Millwrights; Signal and Track Switch Repairers.

Skills—Installation: Installing equipment, machines, wiring, or programs to meet specifications. **Repairing:** Repairing machines or systems by using the needed tools. **Equipment Maintenance:** Performing routine maintenance on equipment and determining when and what kind of maintenance is needed. **Troubleshooting:** Determining causes of operating errors and deciding what to do about them. **Equipment Selection:** Determining the kind of tools and equipment needed to do a job. **Service Orientation:** Actively looking for ways to help people.

Education and Training Program: Locksmithing and Safe Repair. **Related Knowledge/Courses: Customer and Personal Service:** Principles and processes for providing customer and personal services. This includes customer needs assessment, meeting quality standards for services, and evaluation of customer satisfaction. **Sales and Marketing:** Principles and methods for showing, promoting, and selling products or services. This includes marketing strategy and tactics, product demonstration, sales techniques, and sales control systems. **Clerical Practices:** Administrative and clerical procedures and systems such as word processing, managing files and records, stenography and transcription, designing forms, and other office procedures and terminology. **Administration and Management:** Business and management principles involved in strategic planning, resource allocation, human resources modeling, leadership technique, production methods, and coordination of people and resources. **Mechanical Devices:** Machines and tools, including their designs, uses, repair, and maintenance. **Public Safety and Security:** Relevant equipment, policies, procedures, and strategies to promote effective local, state, or national security operations for the protection of people, data, property, and institutions.

Work Environment: More often outdoors than indoors; noisy; very bright or dim lighting; standing; using hands on objects, tools, or controls.

Logging Equipment Operators

- Education/Training Required: Moderate-term on-the-job training
- Annual Earnings: $28,920
- Growth: 3.4%
- Annual Job Openings: 9,000
- Self-Employed: 31.7%
- Part-Time: 6.3%

Level of Solitary Work: 50.0 (out of 100)

Level of Contact with Others: 63.0 (out of 100)

Drive logging tractor or wheeled vehicle equipped with one or more accessories, such as bulldozer blade, frontal shear, grapple, logging arch, cable winches, hoisting rack, or crane boom, to fell tree; to skid, load, unload, or stack logs; or to pull stumps or clear brush. Inspect equipment for safety prior to use and perform necessary basic maintenance tasks. Drive straight or articulated tractors equipped with accessories such as bulldozer blades, grapples, logging arches, cable winches, and crane booms to skid, load, unload, or stack logs; pull stumps; or clear brush. Drive crawler or wheeled tractors to drag or transport logs from felling sites to log landing areas for processing and loading. Drive tractors for the purpose of building or repairing logging and skid roads. Grade logs according to characteristics such as knot size and straightness and according to established industry or company standards. Control hydraulic tractors equipped with tree clamps and booms to lift, swing, and bunch sheared trees. Drive and maneuver tractors and tree harvesters to shear the tops off of trees, cut and limb the trees, and then cut the logs into desired lengths. Fill out required job or shift report forms. Calculate total board feet, cordage, or other wood measurement units, using conversion tables.

Personality Type: Realistic. Realistic occupations frequently involve work activities that include practical, hands-on problems and solutions. They often deal with plants; animals; and real-world materials such as wood, tools, and machinery. Many of the occupations require working outside and do not involve a lot of paperwork or working closely with others.

GOE—Interest Area: 01. Agriculture and Natural Resources. **Work Group:** 01.06. Forestry and Logging. **Other Jobs in This Work Group:** Fallers; Forest and Conservation Technicians; Forest and Conservation Workers; Log Graders and Scalers.

Skills—Repairing: Repairing machines or systems by using the needed tools. **Equipment Maintenance:** Performing routine maintenance on equipment and determining when and what kind of maintenance is needed. **Operation Monitoring:** Watching gauges, dials, or other indicators to make sure a machine is working properly. **Troubleshooting:** Determining causes of operating errors and deciding what to do about them. **Operation and Control:** Controlling operations of equipment or systems. **Installation:** Installing equipment, machines, wiring, or programs to meet specifications.

Education and Training Program: Forest Resources Production and Management. **Related Knowledge/ Courses: Mechanical Devices:** Machines and tools, including their designs, uses, repair, and maintenance. **Transportation:** Principles and methods for moving people or goods by air, rail, sea, or road, including the relative costs and benefits. **Production and Processing:** Raw materials, production processes, quality control, costs, and other techniques for maximizing the effective manufacture and distribution of goods. **Public Safety and Security:** Relevant equip-

ment, policies, procedures, and strategies to promote effective local, state, or national security operations for the protection of people, data, property, and institutions. **Administration and Management:** Business and management principles involved in strategic planning, resource allocation, human resources modeling, leadership technique, production methods, and coordination of people and resources.

Work Environment: Outdoors; noisy; contaminants; hazardous equipment; sitting; using hands on objects, tools, or controls.

Machinists

- Education/Training Required: Long-term on-the-job training
- Annual Earnings: $34,350
- Growth: 4.3%
- Annual Job Openings: 33,000
- Self-Employed: 1.0%
- Part-Time: 1.8%

Level of Solitary Work: 53.0 (out of 100)

Level of Contact with Others: 77.3 (out of 100)

Set up and operate a variety of machine tools to produce precision parts and instruments. Includes precision instrument makers who fabricate, modify, or repair mechanical instruments. May also fabricate and modify parts to make or repair machine tools or maintain industrial machines, applying knowledge of mechanics, shop mathematics, metal properties, layout, and machining procedures. Calculate dimensions and tolerances, using knowledge of mathematics and instruments such as micrometers and vernier calipers. Machine parts to specifications, using machine tools such as lathes, milling machines, shapers, or grinders. Measure, examine, and test completed units to detect defects and ensure conformance to specifications, using precision instruments such as micrometers. Set up, adjust, and operate all of the basic machine tools and many specialized or advanced variation tools to perform precision machining operations. Align and secure holding fixtures, cutting tools, attachments, accessories, and materials onto machines. Monitor the feed and speed of machines during the machining process. Study sample parts, blueprints, drawings, and engineering information to determine methods and sequences of operations needed to fabricate products and determine product dimensions and tolerances. Select the appropriate tools, machines, and materials to be used in preparation of machinery work. Lay out, measure, and mark metal stock to display placement of cuts. Observe and listen to operating machines or equipment to diagnose machine malfunctions and to determine need for adjustments or repairs. Check workpieces to ensure that they are properly lubricated and cooled. Maintain industrial machines, applying knowledge of mechanics, shop mathematics, metal properties, layout, and machining procedures. Position and fasten workpieces. Operate equipment to verify operational efficiency. Install repaired parts into equipment or install new equipment. Clean and lubricate machines, tools, and equipment to remove grease, rust, stains, and foreign matter. Advise clients about the materials being used for finished products. Program computers and electronic instruments such as numerically controlled machine tools. Set controls to regulate machining or enter commands to retrieve, input, or edit computerized machine control media. Confer with engineering, supervisory, and manufacturing personnel to exchange technical information. Dismantle machines or equipment, using hand tools and power tools, to examine parts for defects and replace defective parts where needed.

Personality Type: Realistic. Realistic occupations frequently involve work activities that include practical, hands-on problems and solutions. They often deal with plants; animals; and real-world materials such as wood, tools, and machinery. Many of the occupations require working outside and do not involve a lot of paperwork or working closely with others.

GOE—Interest Area: 13. Manufacturing. **Work Group:** 13.05. Production Machining Technology. **Other Jobs in This Work Group:** Computer-Controlled Machine Tool Operators, Metal and Plastic; Foundry Mold and Coremakers; Lay-Out Workers, Metal and Plastic; Model Makers, Metal and Plastic; Numerical Tool and Process Control Programmers; Patternmakers, Metal and Plastic; Tool and Die Makers; Tool Grinders, Filers, and Sharpeners.

Skills—Operation Monitoring: Watching gauges, dials, or other indicators to make sure a machine is working properly. **Operation and Control:** Controlling operations of equipment or systems. **Equipment Maintenance:** Performing routine maintenance on equipment and determining when and what kind of maintenance is needed. **Quality Control Analysis:** Conducting tests and inspections of products, services, or processes to evaluate quality or performance. **Installation:** Installing equipment, machines, wiring, or programs to meet specifications. **Equipment Selection:** Determining the kind of tools and equipment needed to do a job.

Education and Training Programs: Machine Shop Technology/Assistant Training; Machine Tool Technology/Machinist Training. **Related Knowledge/Courses: Mechanical Devices:** Machines and tools, including their designs, uses, repair, and maintenance. **Engineering and Technology:** The practical application of engineering science and technology. This includes applying principles, techniques, procedures, and equipment to the design and production of various goods and services. **Mathematics:** Arithmetic, algebra, geometry, calculus, and statistics and their applications. **Design:** Design techniques, tools, and principles involved in production of precision technical plans, blueprints, drawings, and models. **Production and Processing:** Raw materials, production processes, quality control, costs, and other techniques for maximizing the effective manufacture and distribution of goods. **Computers and Electronics:** Circuit boards, processors, chips, electronic equipment, and computer hardware and software, including applications and programming.

Work Environment: Indoors; noisy; hazardous equipment; standing; using hands on objects, tools, or controls; repetitive motions.

Maintenance and Repair Workers, General

- Education/Training Required: Moderate-term on-the-job training
- Annual Earnings: $31,210
- Growth: 15.2%
- Annual Job Openings: 154,000
- Self-Employed: 0.6%
- Part-Time: 6.0%

Level of Solitary Work: 62.5 (out of 100)

Level of Contact with Others: 79.8 (out of 100)

Perform work involving the skills of two or more maintenance or craft occupations to keep machines, mechanical equipment, or the structure of an establishment in repair. Duties may involve pipe fitting; boiler making; insulating; welding; machining; carpentry; repairing electrical or mechanical equipment; installing, aligning, and balancing new equipment; and repairing buildings, floors, or stairs. Repair or replace defective equipment parts, using hand tools and power tools, and reassemble equipment. Perform routine preventive maintenance to ensure that machines continue to run smoothly, building systems operate efficiently, and the physical condition of buildings does not deteriorate. Inspect drives, motors, and belts; check fluid levels; replace filters; and perform other maintenance actions, following checklists. Use tools ranging from common hand and power tools, such as hammers, hoists, saws, drills, and wrenches, to precision measuring instruments and electrical and electronic testing devices.

Assemble, install, or repair wiring, electrical and electronic components, pipe systems and plumbing, machinery, and equipment. Diagnose mechanical problems and determine how to correct them, checking blueprints, repair manuals, and parts catalogs as necessary. Inspect, operate, and test machinery and equipment to diagnose machine malfunctions. Record maintenance and repair work performed and the costs of the work. Clean and lubricate shafts, bearings, gears, and other parts of machinery. Dismantle devices to gain access to and remove defective parts, using hoists, cranes, hand tools, and power tools. Plan and lay out repair work, using diagrams, drawings, blueprints, maintenance manuals, and schematic diagrams. Adjust functional parts of devices and control instruments, using hand tools, levels, plumb bobs, and straightedges. Order parts, supplies, and equipment from catalogs and suppliers or obtain them from storerooms. Paint and repair roofs, windows, doors, floors, woodwork, plaster, drywall, and other parts of building structures. Operate cutting torches or welding equipment to cut or join metal parts. Align and balance new equipment after installation. Inspect used parts to determine changes in dimensional requirements, using rules, calipers, micrometers, and other measuring instruments. Set up and operate machine tools to repair or fabricate machine parts, jigs and fixtures, and tools. Maintain and repair specialized equipment and machinery found in cafeterias, laundries, hospitals, stores, offices, and factories.

Personality Type: Realistic. Realistic occupations frequently involve work activities that include practical, hands-on problems and solutions. They often deal with plants; animals; and real-world materials such as wood, tools, and machinery. Many of the occupations require working outside and do not involve a lot of paperwork or working closely with others.

GOE—Interest Area: 02. Architecture and Construc-tion. **Work Group:** 02.05. Systems and Equipment Installation, Maintenance, and Repair. **Other Jobs in This Work Group:** Electrical and Electronics Repairers, Powerhouse, Substation, and

Relay; Electrical Power-Line Installers and Repairers; Elevator Installers and Repairers; Heating and Air Conditioning Mechanics and Installers; Refrigeration Mechanics and Installers; Telecommunications Equipment Installers and Repairers, Except Line Installers; Telecommunications Line Installers and Repairers.

Skills—Equipment Maintenance: Performing routine maintenance on equipment and determining when and what kind of maintenance is needed. **Installation:** Installing equipment, machines, wiring, or programs to meet specifications. **Repairing:** Repairing machines or systems by using the needed tools. **Troubleshooting:** Determining causes of operating errors and deciding what to do about them. **Operation Monitoring:** Watching gauges, dials, or other indicators to make sure a machine is working properly. **Operation and Control:** Controlling operations of equipment or systems.

Education and Training Program: Building/ Construction Site Management/Manager Training. **Related Knowledge/Courses: Building and Construction:** The materials, methods, and tools involved in the construction or repair of houses, buildings, or other structures such as highways and roads. **Mechanical Devices:** Machines and tools, including their designs, uses, repair, and maintenance. **Design:** Design techniques, tools, and principles involved in production of precision technical plans, blueprints, drawings, and models. **Physics:** Physical principles and laws and their interrelationships and applications to understanding fluid, material, and atmospheric dynamics and mechanical, electrical, atomic, and subatomic structures and processes. **Engineering and Technology:** The practical application of engineering science and technology. This includes applying principles, techniques, procedures, and equipment to the design and production of various goods and services. **Public Safety and Security:** Relevant equipment, policies, procedures, and strategies to promote effective local, state, or national security operations for the protection of people, data, property, and institutions.

Work Environment: Indoors; noisy; minor burns, cuts, bites, or stings; standing; walking and running; using hands on objects, tools, or controls.

Maintenance Workers, Machinery

- Education/Training Required: Short-term on-the-job training
- Annual Earnings: $33,650
- Growth: 2.8%
- Annual Job Openings: 6,000
- Self-Employed: 0.0%
- Part-Time: 4.5%

Level of Solitary Work: 56.3 (out of 100)

Level of Contact with Others: 81.7 (out of 100)

Lubricate machinery, change parts, or perform other routine machinery maintenance. Reassemble machines after the completion of repair or maintenance work. Start machines and observe mechanical operation to determine efficiency and to detect problems. Inspect or test damaged machine parts and mark defective areas or advise supervisors of repair needs. Lubricate or apply adhesives or other materials to machines, machine parts, or other equipment according to specified procedures. Install, replace, or change machine parts and attachments according to production specifications. Dismantle machines and remove parts for repair, using hand tools, chain falls, jacks, cranes, or hoists. Record production, repair, and machine maintenance information. Read work orders and specifications to determine machines and equipment requiring repair or maintenance. Set up and operate machines and adjust controls to regulate operations. Collaborate with other workers to repair or move machines, machine parts, or equipment. Inventory and requisition machine parts, equipment, and other supplies so that stock can be maintained and replenished. Transport machine parts, tools, equipment, and other material between work areas and storage, using cranes, hoists, or dollies. Collect and discard worn machine parts and other refuse to maintain machinery and work areas. Clean machines and machine parts, using cleaning solvents, cloths, air guns, hoses, vacuums, or other equipment. Replace or repair metal, wood, leather, glass, or other lining in machines or in equipment compartments or containers. Remove hardened material from machines or machine parts, using abrasives, power and hand tools, jackhammers, sledgehammers, or other equipment. Measure, mix, prepare, and test chemical solutions used to clean or repair machinery and equipment. Replace, empty, or replenish machine and equipment containers such as gas tanks or boxes.

Personality Type: Realistic. Realistic occupations frequently involve work activities that include practical, hands-on problems and solutions. They often deal with plants; animals; and real-world materials such as wood, tools, and machinery. Many of the occupations require working outside and do not involve a lot of paperwork or working closely with others.

GOE—Interest Area: 13. Manufacturing. **Work Group:** 13.13. Machinery Repair. **Other Jobs in This Work Group:** Bicycle Repairers; Control and Valve Installers and Repairers, Except Mechanical Door; Home Appliance Repairers; Industrial Machinery Mechanics; Locksmiths and Safe Repairers; Mechanical Door Repairers; Millwrights; Signal and Track Switch Repairers.

Skills—Installation: Installing equipment, machines, wiring, or programs to meet specifications. **Repairing:** Repairing machines or systems by using the needed tools. **Equipment Maintenance:** Performing routine maintenance on equipment and determining when and what kind of maintenance is needed. **Troubleshooting:** Determining causes of operating errors and deciding what to do about them. **Operation Monitoring:** Watching gauges, dials, or other indicators to make sure a machine is working properly. **Operation and Control:** Controlling operations of equipment or systems.

Education and Training Programs: Heavy/Industrial Equipment Maintenance Technologies, Other; Industrial Mechanics and Maintenance Technology. **Related Knowledge/Courses: Mechanical Devices:** Machines and tools, including their designs, uses, repair, and maintenance. **Building and Construction:** The materials, methods, and tools involved in the construction or repair of houses, buildings, or other structures such as highways and roads. **Engineering and Technology:** The practical application of engineering science and technology. This includes applying principles, techniques, procedures, and equipment to the design and production of various goods and services. **Physics:** Physical principles and laws and their interrelationships and applications to understanding fluid, material, and atmospheric dynamics and mechanical, electrical, atomic, and subatomic structures and processes. **Chemistry:** The chemical composition, structure, and properties of substances and of the chemical processes and transformations that they undergo. This includes uses of chemicals and their danger signs, production techniques, and disposal methods. **Design:** Design techniques, tools, and principles involved in production of precision technical plans, blueprints, drawings, and models.

Work Environment: Noisy; very hot or cold; contaminants; hazardous equipment; standing; using hands on objects, tools, or controls.

Mapping Technicians

This job can be found in the Part II lists under the title Surveying and Mapping Technicians.

- Education/Training Required: Moderate-term on-the-job training
- Annual Earnings: $31,290
- Growth: 9.6%
- Annual Job Openings: 9,000
- Self-Employed: 4.3%
- Part-Time: 4.3%

The job openings listed here are shared with Surveying Technicians.

Level of Solitary Work: 51.5 (out of 100)

Level of Contact with Others: 71.6 (out of 100)

Calculate mapmaking information from field notes and draw and verify accuracy of topographical maps. Check all layers of maps to ensure accuracy, identifying and marking errors and making corrections. Determine scales, line sizes, and colors to be used for hard copies of computerized maps, using plotters. Monitor mapping work and the updating of maps to ensure accuracy, the inclusion of new and/or changed information, and compliance with rules and regulations. Identify and compile database information to create maps in response to requests. Produce and update overlay maps to show information boundaries, water locations, and topographic features on various base maps and at different scales. Trace contours and topographic details to generate maps that denote specific land and property locations and geographic attributes. Lay out and match aerial photographs in sequences in which they were taken and identify any areas missing from photographs. Compare topographical features and contour lines with images from aerial photographs, old maps, and other reference materials to verify the accuracy of their identification. Compute and measure scaled distances between reference points to establish relative positions of adjoining prints and enable the creation of photographic mosaics. Research resources such as survey maps and legal descriptions to verify property lines and to obtain information needed for mapping. Form three-dimensional images of aerial photographs taken from different locations, using mathematical techniques and plotting instruments. Enter GPS data, legal deeds, field notes, and land survey reports into GIS workstations so that information can be transformed into graphic land descriptions such as maps and drawings. Analyze aerial photographs to detect and interpret significant military, industrial, resource, or topographical data. Redraw and correct maps, such as revising parcel maps to reflect tax code area changes, using information from official records and surveys. Train staff members in duties such as tax mapping, the use of computerized mapping equipment, and the interpretation of source documents.

Personality Type: Conventional. Conventional occupations frequently involve following set procedures and routines. These occupations can include working with data and details more than with ideas. Usually there is a clear line of authority to follow.

GOE—Interest Area: 15. Scientific Research, Engineering, and Mathematics. **Work Group:** 15.09. Engineering Technology. **Other Jobs in This Work Group:** Aerospace Engineering and Operations Technicians; Cartographers and Photogrammetrists; Civil Engineering Technicians; Electrical and Electronic Engineering Technicians; Electrical and Electronics Drafters; Electrical Drafters; Electrical Engineering Technicians; Electro-Mechanical Technicians; Electronic Drafters; Electronics Engineering Technicians; Environmental Engineering Technicians; Mechanical Drafters; Mechanical Engineering Technicians; Surveying and Mapping Technicians; Surveying Technicians.

Skills—Programming: Writing computer programs for various purposes. **Technology Design:** Generating or adapting equipment and technology to serve user needs. **Quality Control Analysis:** Conducting tests and inspections of products, services, or processes to evaluate quality or performance. **Operations Analysis:** Analyzing needs and product requirements to create a design. **Troubleshooting:** Determining causes of operating errors and deciding what to do about them. **Mathematics:** Using mathematics to solve problems.

Education and Training Programs: Cartography; Surveying Technology/Surveying. **Related Knowledge/Courses: Geography:** Principles and methods for describing the features of land, sea, and air masses, including their physical characteristics; locations; interrelationships; and distribution of plant, animal, and human life. **Design:** Design techniques, tools, and principles involved in production of precision technical plans, blueprints, drawings, and models. **Computers and Electronics:** Circuit boards, processors, chips, electronic equipment, and computer hardware and software, including applications and programming. **Engineering and Technology:** The practical application of engineering science and technology. This includes applying principles, techniques, procedures, and equipment to the design and production of various goods and services. **Mathematics:** Arithmetic, algebra, geometry, calculus, and statistics and their applications. **Clerical Practices:** Administrative and clerical procedures and systems such as word processing, managing files and records, stenography and transcription, designing forms, and other office procedures and terminology.

Work Environment: Indoors; sitting; using hands on objects, tools, or controls; repetitive motions.

Marine Architects

This job can be found in the Part II lists under the title Marine Engineers and Naval Architects.

- ◎ Education/Training Required: Bachelor's degree
- ◎ Annual Earnings: $72,920
- ◎ Growth: 8.5%
- ◎ Annual Job Openings: Fewer than 500
- ◎ Self-Employed: 0.0%
- ◎ Part-Time: 1.9%

The job openings listed here are shared with Marine Engineers.

Level of Solitary Work: 53.0 (out of 100)

Level of Contact with Others: 76.2 (out of 100)

Design and oversee construction and repair of marine craft and floating structures such as ships, barges, tugs, dredges, submarines, torpedoes, floats, and buoys. May confer with marine engineers. Design complete hull and superstructure according to specifications and test data and in conformity with standards of safety, efficiency, and economy. Design layout of craft interior, including cargo space, passenger compartments, ladder wells, and elevators. Study design proposals and specifications to establish basic characteristics of craft, such as size, weight, speed, propulsion, displacement, and draft. Confer with marine engineering personnel to establish arrangement of boiler room equipment and propulsion machinery, heating and ventilating systems, refrigeration equipment, piping, and other functional equipment. Evaluate performance of craft during dock and sea trials to determine design changes and conformance with national and international standards. Oversee construction and testing of prototype in model basin and develop sectional and waterline curves of hull to establish center of gravity, ideal hull form, and buoyancy and stability data.

Personality Type: Realistic. Realistic occupations frequently involve work activities that include practical, hands-on problems and solutions. They often deal with plants; animals; and real-world materials such as wood, tools, and machinery. Many of the occupations require working outside and do not involve a lot of paperwork or working closely with others.

GOE—Interest Area: 15. Scientific Research, Engineering, and Mathematics. **Work Group:** 15.07. Research and Design Engineering. **Other Jobs in This Work Group:** Aerospace Engineers; Biomedical Engineers; Chemical Engineers; Civil Engineers; Computer Hardware Engineers; Electrical Engineers; Electronics Engineers, Except Computer; Marine Engineers; Marine Engineers and Naval Architects; Materials Engineers; Mechanical Engineers; Nuclear Engineers.

Skills—Science: Using scientific rules and methods to solve problems. **Mathematics:** Using mathematics to solve problems. **Operations Analysis:** Analyzing needs and product requirements to create a design. **Technology Design:** Generating or adapting equipment and technology to serve user needs. **Complex Problem Solving:** Identifying complex problems and reviewing related information to develop and evaluate options and implement solutions. **Systems Analysis:** Determining how a system should work and how changes in conditions, operations, and the environment will affect outcomes.

Education and Training Program: Naval Architecture and Marine Engineering. **Related Knowledge/Courses: Engineering and Technology:** The practical application of engineering science and technology. This includes applying principles, techniques, procedures, and equipment to the design and production of various goods and services. **Design:** Design techniques, tools, and principles involved in production of precision technical plans, blueprints, drawings, and models. **Physics:** Physical principles and laws and their interrelationships and applications to understanding fluid, material, and atmospheric dynamics and mechanical, electrical, atomic, and subatomic structures and processes. **Building and Construction:** The materials, methods, and tools involved in the construction or repair of houses, buildings, or other structures such as highways and roads. **Mechanical Devices:** Machines and tools, including their designs, uses, repair, and maintenance. **Production and Processing:** Raw materials, production processes, quality control, costs, and other techniques for maximizing the effective manufacture and distribution of goods.

Work Environment: Indoors; sitting.

Marine Engineers

This job can be found in the Part II lists under the title Marine Engineers and Naval Architects.

- ◎ Education/Training Required: Bachelor's degree
- ◎ Annual Earnings: $72,920
- ◎ Growth: 8.5%
- ◎ Annual Job Openings: Fewer than 500
- ◎ Self-Employed: 0.0%
- ◎ Part-Time: 1.9%

The job openings listed here are shared with Marine Architects.

Level of Solitary Work: 53.0 (out of 100)

Level of Contact with Others: 76.2 (out of 100)

Design, develop, and take responsibility for the installation of ship machinery and related equipment, including propulsion machines and power supply systems. Prepare, or direct the preparation of, product or system layouts and detailed drawings and schematics. Inspect marine equipment and machinery in order to draw up work requests and job specifications. Conduct analytical, environmental, operational, or performance studies in order to develop designs for products such as marine engines, equipment, and structures. Design and oversee testing, installation, and repair of marine apparatus and equipment. Prepare plans, estimates, design and construction schedules, and contract specifications, including any special provisions. Investigate and observe tests on machinery and equipment for compliance with standards. Coordinate activities with regulatory bodies in order to ensure repairs and alterations are at minimum cost consistent with safety. Prepare technical reports for use by engineering, management, or sales personnel. Conduct environmental, operational, or performance tests on marine machinery and equipment. Maintain contact with, and formulate reports for, contractors and clients to ensure completion of work at minimum cost. Evaluate operation of marine equipment during acceptance testing and shakedown cruises. Analyze data in order to determine feasibility of product proposals. Determine conditions under which tests are to be conducted, as well as sequences and phases of test operations. Procure materials needed to repair marine equipment and machinery. Confer with research personnel to clarify or resolve problems and to develop or modify designs. Review work requests and compare them with previous work completed on ships to ensure that costs are economically sound. Act as liaisons between ships' captains and shore personnel to ensure that schedules and budgets are maintained and that ships are operated safely and efficiently. Perform monitoring activities to ensure that ships comply with international regulations and standards for lifesaving equipment and pollution preventatives. Check, test, and maintain automatic controls and alarm systems. Supervise other engineers and crewmembers and train them for routine and emergency duties.

Personality Type: Realistic. Realistic occupations frequently involve work activities that include practical, hands-on problems and solutions. They often deal with plants; animals; and real-world materials such as wood, tools, and machinery. Many of the occupations require working outside and do not involve a lot of paperwork or working closely with others.

GOE—Interest Area: 15. Scientific Research, Engineering, and Mathematics. **Work Group:** 15.07. Research and Design Engineering. **Other Jobs in This Work Group:** Aerospace Engineers; Biomedical Engineers; Chemical Engineers; Civil Engineers; Computer Hardware Engineers; Electrical Engineers; Electronics Engineers, Except Computer; Marine Architects; Marine Engineers and Naval Architects; Materials Engineers; Mechanical Engineers; Nuclear Engineers.

Skills—Science: Using scientific rules and methods to solve problems. **Technology Design:** Generating or adapting equipment and technology to serve user needs. **Installation:** Installing equipment, machines, wiring, or programs to meet specifications. **Mathematics:** Using mathematics to solve problems. **Operations Analysis:** Analyzing needs and product requirements to create a design. **Systems Analysis:** Determining how a system should work and how changes in conditions, operations, and the environment will affect outcomes.

Education and Training Program: Naval Architecture and Marine Engineering. **Related Knowledge/ Courses: Design:** Design techniques, tools, and principles involved in production of precision technical plans, blueprints, drawings, and models. **Engineering and Technology:** The practical application of engineering science and technology.

This includes applying principles, techniques, procedures, and equipment to the design and production of various goods and services. **Mechanical Devices:** Machines and tools, including their designs, uses, repair, and maintenance. **Physics:** Physical principles and laws and their interrelationships and applications to understanding fluid, material, and atmospheric dynamics and mechanical, electrical, atomic, and subatomic structures and processes. **Building and Construction:** The materials, methods, and tools involved in the construction or repair of houses, buildings, or other structures such as highways and roads. **Computers and Electronics:** Circuit boards, processors, chips, electronic equipment, and computer hardware and software, including applications and programming.

Work Environment: Outdoors; noisy; sitting.

Marine Engineers and Naval Architects

See the descriptions of these jobs:

- ◎ **Marine Architects**
- ◎ **Marine Engineers**

Market Research Analysts

- ◎ Education/Training Required: Bachelor's degree
- ◎ Annual Earnings: $57,300
- ◎ Growth: 19.6%
- ◎ Annual Job Openings: 20,000
- ◎ Self-Employed: 7.2%
- ◎ Part-Time: 13.8%

Level of Solitary Work: 56.3 (out of 100)

Level of Contact with Others: 72.0 (out of 100)

Research market conditions in local, regional, or national areas to determine potential sales of a product or service. May gather information on competitors, prices, sales, and methods of marketing and distribution. May use survey results to create a marketing campaign based on regional preferences and buying habits. Collect and analyze data on customer demographics, preferences, needs, and buying habits to identify potential markets and factors affecting product demand. Prepare reports of findings, illustrating data graphically and translating complex findings into written text. Measure and assess customer and employee satisfaction. Forecast and track marketing and sales trends, analyzing collected data. Seek and provide information to help companies determine their position in the marketplace. Measure the effectiveness of marketing, advertising, and communications programs and strategies. Conduct research on consumer opinions and marketing strategies, collaborating with marketing professionals, statisticians, pollsters, and other professionals. Attend staff conferences to provide management with information and proposals concerning the promotion, distribution, design, and pricing of company products or services. Gather data on competitors and analyze their prices, sales, and method of marketing and distribution. Monitor industry statistics and follow trends in trade literature. Devise and evaluate methods and procedures for collecting data, such as surveys, opinion polls, or questionnaires, or arrange to obtain existing data. Develop and implement procedures for identifying advertising needs. Direct trained survey interviewers.

Personality Type: Investigative. Investigative occupations frequently involve working with ideas and require an extensive amount of thinking. These occupations can involve searching for facts and figuring out problems mentally.

GOE—Interest Area: 06. Finance and Insurance. **Work Group:** 06.02. Finance/Insurance Investigation and Analysis. **Other Jobs in This Work Group:** Appraisers and Assessors of Real Estate; Appraisers, Real Estate; Assessors; Claims Adjusters, Examiners, and Investigators; Claims Examiners, Property and Casualty Insurance; Cost Estimators; Credit Analysts; Financial Analysts; Insurance Adjusters, Examiners, and Investigators; Insurance Appraisers, Auto Damage; Insurance Underwriters; Loan Counselors; Loan Officers; Survey Researchers.

Skills—Negotiation: Bringing others together and trying to reconcile differences. **Persuasion:** Persuading others to change their minds or behavior. **Writing:** Communicating effectively in writing as appropriate for the needs of the audience. **Judgment and Decision Making:** Considering the relative costs and benefits of potential actions to choose the most appropriate one. **Reading Comprehension:** Understanding written sentences and paragraphs in work-related documents. **Coordination:** Adjusting actions in relation to others' actions.

Education and Training Programs: Applied Economics; Business/Managerial Economics; Econometrics and Quantitative Economics; Economics, General; International Economics; Marketing Research. **Related Knowledge/Courses: Sales and Marketing:** Principles and methods for showing, promoting, and selling products or services. This includes marketing strategy and tactics, product demonstration, sales techniques, and sales control systems. **Administration and Management:** Business and management principles involved in strategic planning, resource allocation, human resources modeling, leadership technique, production methods, and coordination of people and resources. **Communications and Media:** Media production, communication, and dissemination techniques and methods. This includes alternative ways to inform and entertain via written, oral, and visual media. **Economics and Accounting:** Economic and accounting principles and practices, the financial markets, banking, and the analysis and reporting of financial data. **Clerical Practices:** Administrative and clerical procedures and systems such as word processing, managing files and records, stenography and transcription, designing forms, and other office procedures and terminology. **Computers and Electronics:** Circuit boards, processors, chips, electronic equipment, and computer hardware and software, including applications and programming.

Work Environment: Indoors; sitting.

Materials Engineers

- ◉ Education/Training Required: Bachelor's degree
- ◉ Annual Earnings: $69,660
- ◉ Growth: 12.2%
- ◉ Annual Job Openings: 2,000
- ◉ Self-Employed: 0.0%
- ◉ Part-Time: 2.4%

Level of Solitary Work: 56.3 (out of 100)

Level of Contact with Others: 72.3 (out of 100)

Evaluate materials and develop machinery and processes to manufacture materials for use in products that must meet specialized design and performance specifications. Develop new uses for known materials. Includes those working with composite materials or specializing in one type of material, such as graphite, metal and metal alloys, ceramics and glass, plastics and polymers, and naturally occurring materials. Analyze product failure data and laboratory test results in order to determine causes of problems and develop solutions. Monitor material performance and evaluate material deterioration. Supervise the work of technologists, technicians, and other engineers and scientists. Design and direct the testing and/or control of processing procedures. Evaluate technical specifications and economic factors relating to process or product design objectives. Conduct or supervise tests on raw materials or finished products in order to ensure their quality. Perform managerial functions such as preparing proposals and budgets, analyzing labor costs, and writing reports. Solve problems in a number of engineering fields, such as mechanical, chemical, electrical, civil, nuclear, and aerospace. Plan and evaluate new projects, consulting with other engineers and corporate executives as necessary. Review new product plans and make recommendations for material selection based on design objectives, such as strength, weight, heat resistance, electrical conductivity, and cost. Design processing plants and equipment. Modify properties of metal alloys, using thermal and mechanical treatments. Guide technical staff engaged in developing materials for specific uses in projected products or devices. Plan and implement laboratory operations for the purpose of developing material and fabrication procedures that meet cost, product specification, and performance standards. Determine appropriate methods for fabricating and joining materials. Conduct training sessions on new material products, applications, or manufacturing methods for customers and their employees. Supervise production and testing processes in industrial settings such as metal refining facilities, smelting or foundry operations, or non-metallic materials production operations. Write for technical magazines, journals, and trade association publications. Replicate the characteristics of materials and their components with computers. Teach in colleges and universities.

Personality Type: Investigative. Investigative occupations frequently involve working with ideas and require an extensive amount of thinking. These occupations can involve searching for facts and figuring out problems mentally.

GOE—Interest Area: 15. Scientific Research, Engineering, and Mathematics. **Work Group:** 15.07. Research and Design Engineering. **Other Jobs in This Work Group:** Aerospace Engineers; Biomedical Engineers; Chemical Engineers; Civil Engineers; Computer Hardware Engineers; Electrical Engineers; Electronics Engineers, Except Computer; Marine Architects; Marine Engineers; Marine Engineers and Naval Architects; Mechanical Engineers; Nuclear Engineers.

Skills—Science: Using scientific rules and methods to solve problems. **Mathematics:** Using mathematics to solve problems. **Quality Control Analysis:** Conducting tests and inspections of products, services, or processes to evaluate quality or performance. **Reading Comprehension:** Understanding written sentences and paragraphs in work-related documents. **Troubleshooting:** Determining causes of operating errors and deciding what to do about them. **Technology Design:** Generating or adapting equipment and technology to serve user needs.

Education and Training Programs: Ceramic Sciences and Engineering; Materials Engineering; Metallurgical Engineering. **Related Knowledge/ Courses: Engineering and Technology:** The practical application of engineering science and technology. This includes applying principles, techniques, procedures, and equipment to the design and production of various goods and services. **Chemistry:** The chemical composition, structure, and properties of substances and of the chemical processes and transformations that they undergo. This includes uses of chemicals and their danger signs, production techniques, and disposal methods. **Physics:** Physical principles and laws and their interrelationships and applications to understanding fluid, material, and atmospheric dynamics and mechanical, electrical, atomic, and subatomic structures and processes. **Design:** Design techniques, tools, and principles involved in production of precision technical plans, blueprints, drawings, and models. **Mathematics:** Arithmetic, algebra, geometry, calculus, and statistics and their applications. **Mechanical Devices:** Machines and tools, including their designs, uses, repair, and maintenance.

Work Environment: Indoors; noisy; contaminants; sitting.

Materials Scientists

- ◎ Education/Training Required: Bachelor's degree
- ◎ Annual Earnings: $71,450
- ◎ Growth: 8.0%
- ◎ Annual Job Openings: Fewer than 500
- ◎ Self-Employed: 0.4%
- ◎ Part-Time: 6.6%

Level of Solitary Work: 62.5 (out of 100)

Level of Contact with Others: 88.5 (out of 100)

Research and study the structures and chemical properties of various natural and manmade materials, including metals, alloys, rubber, ceramics, semiconductors, polymers, and glass. Determine ways to strengthen or combine materials or develop new materials with new or specific properties for use in a variety of products and applications. Plan laboratory experiments to confirm feasibility of processes and techniques used in the production of materials having special characteristics. Confer with customers in order to determine how materials can be tailored to suit their needs. Conduct research into the structures and properties of materials such as metals, alloys, polymers, and ceramics to obtain information that could be used to develop new products or enhance existing ones. Prepare reports of materials study findings for the use of other scientists and requestors. Devise testing methods to evaluate the effects of various conditions on particular materials. Determine ways to strengthen or combine materials or develop new materials with new or specific properties for use in a variety of products and applications. Recommend materials for reliable performance in various environments. Test individual parts and products to ensure that manufacturer and governmental quality and safety standards are met. Visit suppliers of materials or users of products to gather specific information. Research methods of processing, forming, and firing materials to develop such products as ceramic fillings for teeth, unbreakable dinner plates, and telescope lenses. Study the nature, structure, and physical properties of metals and their alloys and their responses to applied forces. Monitor production processes to ensure that equipment is used efficiently and that projects are completed within appropriate time frames and budgets. Test material samples for tolerance under tension, compression, and shear to determine the cause of metal failures. Test metals to determine whether they meet specifications of mechanical strength; strength-weight ratio; ductility; magnetic and electrical properties; and resistance to abrasion, corrosion, heat, and cold. Teach in colleges and universities.

Personality Type: Investigative. Investigative occupations frequently involve working with ideas and require an extensive amount of thinking. These occupations can involve searching for facts and figuring out problems mentally.

GOE—Interest Area: 15. Scientific Research, Engineering, and Mathematics. **Work Group:** 15.02. Physical Sciences. **Other Jobs in This Work Group:** Astronomers; Atmospheric and Space Scientists; Chemists; Geographers; Geoscientists, Except Hydrologists and Geographers; Hydrologists; Physicists.

Skills—Science: Using scientific rules and methods to solve problems. **Programming:** Writing computer programs for various purposes. **Technology Design:** Generating or adapting equipment and technology to serve user needs. **Quality Control Analysis:** Conducting tests and inspections of products, services, or processes to evaluate quality or performance. **Mathematics:** Using mathematics to solve problems. **Installation:** Installing equipment, machines, wiring, or programs to meet specifications.

Education and Training Program: Materials Science. **Related Knowledge/Courses: Chemistry:** The chemical composition, structure, and properties of substances and of the chemical processes and transformations that they undergo. This includes uses of chemicals and their danger signs, production techniques, and disposal methods. **Engineering and Technology:** The practical application of engineering science and technology. This includes applying principles, techniques, procedures, and equipment to the design and production of various goods and services. **Mathematics:** Arithmetic, algebra, geometry, calculus, and statistics and their applications. **Physics:** Physical principles and laws and their interrelationships and applications to understanding fluid, material, and atmospheric dynamics and mechanical, electrical, atomic, and subatomic structures and processes. **Production and Processing:** Raw materials, production processes, quality control, costs, and other techniques for maximizing the effective manufacture and distribution of goods. **Administration and Management:** Business and management principles involved in strategic planning, resource allocation, human resources modeling, leadership technique, production methods, and coordination of people and resources.

Work Environment: Indoors; noisy; hazardous conditions; sitting.

Mates—Ship, Boat, and Barge

This job can be found in the Part II lists under the title Captains, Mates, and Pilots of Water Vessels.

- Education/Training Required: Work experience in a related occupation
- Annual Earnings: $50,940
- Growth: 4.8%
- Annual Job Openings: 2,000
- Self-Employed: 5.4%
- Part-Time: 8.7%

The job openings listed here are shared with Pilots, Ship and with Ship and Boat Captains.

Level of Solitary Work: 34.2 (out of 100)

Level of Contact with Others: 57.2 (out of 100)

Supervise and coordinate activities of crew aboard ships, boats, barges, or dredges. Participate in activities related to maintenance of vessel security. Assume command of vessels in the event that ships' masters become incapacitated. Arrange for ships to be stocked, fueled, and repaired. Supervise crews in cleaning and maintaining decks, superstructures, and bridges. Determine geographical positions of ships, using lorans, azimuths of celestial bodies, or computers, and use this information to determine the course and speed of a ship. Inspect equipment such as cargo-handling gear; lifesaving equipment; visual-signaling equipment; and fishing, towing, or dredging gear to detect problems. Observe loading and unloading of cargo and equipment to ensure that handling and storage are performed according to specifications. Observe water from ships' mastheads to advise on navigational direction. Steer vessels, utilizing navigational devices such as compasses and sextons and navigational aids such as lighthouses and buoys. Supervise crew members in the repair or replacement of defective gear and equipment. Stand watches on vessels during specified periods while vessels are under way.

Personality Type: Realistic. Realistic occupations frequently involve work activities that include practical, hands-on problems and solutions. They often deal with plants; animals; and real-world materials such as wood, tools, and machinery. Many of the occupations require working outside and do not involve a lot of paperwork or working closely with others.

GOE—Interest Area: 16. Transportation, Distribution, and Logistics. **Work Group:** 16.05. Water Vehicle Operation. **Other Jobs in This Work Group:** Captains, Mates, and Pilots of Water Vessels; Dredge Operators; Motorboat Operators; Pilots, Ship; Sailors and Marine Oilers; Ship and Boat Captains.

Skills—Operation and Control: Controlling operations of equipment or systems. **Repairing:** Repairing machines or systems by using the needed tools. **Management of Personnel Resources:** Motivating, developing, and directing people as they work; identifying the best people for the job. **Operation Monitoring:** Watching gauges, dials, or other indicators to make sure a machine is working properly. **Systems Analysis:** Determining how a system should work and how changes in conditions, operations, and the environment will affect outcomes. **Systems Evaluation:** Identifying measures or indicators of system performance and the actions needed to improve or correct performance relative to the goals of the system.

Education and Training Programs: Commercial Fishing; Marine Science/Merchant Marine Officer Training; Marine Transportation, Other. **Related Knowledge/Courses: Transportation:** Principles and methods for moving people or goods by air, rail, sea, or road, including the relative costs and benefits. **Geography:** Principles and methods for describing the features of land, sea, and air masses, including their physical characteristics; locations; interrelationships; and distribution of plant, animal, and human life. **Mechanical Devices:** Machines and tools, including their designs, uses, repair, and maintenance. **Physics:** Physical principles and laws and their interrelationships and applications to understanding fluid, material, and atmospheric dynamics and mechanical, electrical, atomic, and subatomic structures and processes. **Public Safety and Security:** Relevant equipment, policies, procedures, and strategies to promote effective local, state, or national security operations for the protection of people, data, property, and institutions. **Administration and Management:** Business and management principles involved in strategic planning, resource allocation, human resources modeling, leadership technique, production methods, and coordination of people and resources.

Work Environment: More often outdoors than indoors; very hot or cold; standing; using hands on objects, tools, or controls.

Mechanical Door Repairers

- Education/Training Required: Moderate-term on-the-job training
- Annual Earnings: $30,310
- Growth: 15.8%
- Annual Job Openings: 1,000
- Self-Employed: 0.0%
- Part-Time: No data available

Level of Solitary Work: 75.0 (out of 100)

Level of Contact with Others: 76.5 (out of 100)

Install, service, or repair opening and closing mechanisms of automatic doors and hydraulic door closers. Includes garage door mechanics. Adjust doors to open or close with the correct amount of effort and make simple adjustments to electric openers. Wind large springs with upward motion of arm. Inspect job sites, assessing headroom, side room, and other conditions to determine appropriateness of door for a given location. Collect payment upon job completion. Complete required paperwork, such as work orders, according to services performed or required. Fasten angle iron back-hangers to ceilings and tracks, using fasteners or welding equipment. Repair or replace worn or broken door parts, using hand tools. Carry springs to tops of doors, using ladders or scaffolding, and attach springs to tracks in order to install spring systems. Set doors into place or stack hardware sections into openings after rail or track installation. Remove or disassemble defective automatic mechanical door closers, using hand tools. Install door frames, rails, steel rolling curtains, electronic-eye mechanisms, and electric door openers and closers, using power tools, hand tools, and electronic test equipment. Apply hardware to door sections, such as drilling holes to install locks. Assemble and fasten tracks to structures or bucks, using impact wrenches or welding equipment. Run low-voltage wiring on ceiling surfaces, using insulated staples. Cut door stops and angle irons to fit openings. Study blueprints and schematic diagrams to determine appropriate methods of installing and repairing automated door openers. Operate lifts, winches, or chain falls to move heavy curtain doors. Order replacement springs, sections, and slats. Bore and cut holes in flooring as required for installation, using hand tools and power tools. Set in and secure floor treadles for door-activating mechanisms; then connect power packs and electrical panelboards to treadles. Lubricate door closer oil chambers and pack spindles with leather washers. Install dock seals, bumpers, and shelters. Fabricate replacements for worn or broken parts, using welders, lathes, drill presses, and shaping and milling machines. Clean door closer parts, using caustic soda, rotary brushes, and grinding wheels.

Personality Type: Realistic. Realistic occupations frequently involve work activities that include practical, hands-on problems and solutions. They often deal with plants; animals; and real-world materials such as wood, tools, and machinery. Many of the occupations require working outside and do not involve a lot of paperwork or working closely with others.

GOE—Interest Area: 13. Manufacturing. **Work Group:** 13.13. Machinery Repair. **Other Jobs in This Work Group:** Bicycle Repairers; Control and Valve Installers and Repairers, Except Mechanical Door; Home Appliance Repairers; Industrial Machinery Mechanics; Locksmiths and Safe Repairers; Maintenance Workers, Machinery; Millwrights; Signal and Track Switch Repairers.

Skills—Installation: Installing equipment, machines, wiring, or programs to meet specifications. **Repairing:** Repairing machines or systems by using the needed tools. **Troubleshooting:** Determining causes of operating errors and deciding what to do about them. **Equipment Maintenance:** Performing routine maintenance on equipment and determining when and what kind of maintenance is needed. **Equipment Selection:** Determining the kind of tools and equipment needed to do a job. **Time Management:** Managing one's own time and the time of others.

Education and Training Program: Industrial Mechanics and Maintenance Technology. **Related Knowledge/Courses: Building and Construction:** The materials, methods, and tools involved in the construction or repair of houses, buildings, or other structures such as highways and roads. **Mechanical Devices:** Machines and tools, including their designs, uses, repair, and maintenance. **Engineering and Technology:** The practical application of engineering science and technology. This includes applying principles, techniques, procedures, and equipment to the design and production of various goods and services. **Sales and Marketing:** Principles and methods for showing, promoting, and selling products or services. This includes marketing strategy and tactics, product demonstration, sales techniques, and sales control systems. **Design:** Design techniques, tools, and principles involved in production of precision technical plans, blueprints, drawings, and models.

Work Environment: Outdoors; very hot or cold; hazardous equipment; standing; climbing ladders, scaffolds, or poles; using hands on objects, tools, or controls.

Mechanical Drafters

- Education/Training Required:
  Postsecondary vocational training
- Annual Earnings: $43,350
- Growth: 5.5%
- Annual Job Openings: 7,000
- Self-Employed: 5.5%
- Part-Time: 8.4%

Level of Solitary Work: 56.3 (out of 100)

Level of Contact with Others: 83.7 (out of 100)

Prepare detailed working diagrams of machinery and mechanical devices, including dimensions, fastening methods, and other engineering information. Develop detailed design drawings and specifications for mechanical equipment, dies, tools, and controls, using computer-assisted drafting (CAD) equipment. Coordinate with and consult other workers to design, lay out, or detail components and systems and to resolve design or other problems. Review and analyze specifications, sketches, drawings, ideas, and related data to assess factors affecting component designs and the procedures and instructions to be followed. Position instructions and comments onto drawings. Compute mathematical formulas to develop and design detailed specifications for components or machinery, using computer-assisted equipment. Modify and revise designs to correct operating deficiencies or to reduce production problems. Design scale or full-size blueprints of specialty items such as furniture and automobile body or

chassis components. Check dimensions of materials to be used and assign numbers to the materials. Lay out and draw schematic, orthographic, or angle views to depict functional relationships of components, assemblies, systems, and machines. Confer with customer representatives to review schematics and answer questions pertaining to installation of systems. Draw freehand sketches of designs, trace finished drawings onto designated paper for the reproduction of blueprints, and reproduce working drawings on copy machines. Supervise and train other drafters, technologists, and technicians. Lay out, draw, and reproduce illustrations for reference manuals and technical publications to describe operation and maintenance of mechanical systems. Shade or color drawings to clarify and emphasize details and dimensions or eliminate background, using ink, crayon, airbrush, and overlays.

Personality Type: Realistic. Realistic occupations frequently involve work activities that include practical, hands-on problems and solutions. They often deal with plants; animals; and real-world materials such as wood, tools, and machinery. Many of the occupations require working outside and do not involve a lot of paperwork or working closely with others.

GOE—Interest Area: 15. Scientific Research, Engineering, and Mathematics. **Work Group:** 15.09. Engineering Technology. **Other Jobs in This Work Group:** Aerospace Engineering and Operations Technicians; Cartographers and Photogrammetrists; Civil Engineering Technicians; Electrical and Electronic Engineering Technicians; Electrical and Electronics Drafters; Electrical Drafters; Electrical Engineering Technicians; Electro-Mechanical Technicians; Electronic Drafters; Electronics Engineering Technicians; Environmental Engineering Technicians; Mapping Technicians; Mechanical Engineering Technicians; Surveying and Mapping Technicians; Surveying Technicians.

Skills—Technology Design: Generating or adapting equipment and technology to serve user needs. **Installation:** Installing equipment, machines, wiring, or programs to meet specifications. **Quality Control**

Analysis: Conducting tests and inspections of products, services, or processes to evaluate quality or performance. **Equipment Selection:** Determining the kind of tools and equipment needed to do a job. **Operations Analysis:** Analyzing needs and product requirements to create a design. **Mathematics:** Using mathematics to solve problems.

Education and Training Program: Mechanical Drafting and Mechanical Drafting CAD/CADD. **Related Knowledge/Courses: Design:** Design techniques, tools, and principles involved in production of precision technical plans, blueprints, drawings, and models. **Engineering and Technology:** The practical application of engineering science and technology. This includes applying principles, techniques, procedures, and equipment to the design and production of various goods and services. **Building and Construction:** The materials, methods, and tools involved in the construction or repair of houses, buildings, or other structures such as highways and roads. **Physics:** Physical principles and laws and their interrelationships and applications to understanding fluid, material, and atmospheric dynamics and mechanical, electrical, atomic, and subatomic structures and processes. **Mathematics:** Arithmetic, algebra, geometry, calculus, and statistics and their applications. **English Language:** The structure and content of the English language, including the meaning and spelling of words, rules of composition, and grammar.

Work Environment: Indoors; noisy; sitting; using hands on objects, tools, or controls; repetitive motions.

Mechanical Engineering Technicians

- Education/Training Required: Associate degree
- Annual Earnings: $44,830
- Growth: 12.3%
- Annual Job Openings: 5,000
- Self-Employed: 0.4%
- Part-Time: 6.7%

Level of Solitary Work: 50.0 (out of 100)

Level of Contact with Others: 70.7 (out of 100)

Apply theory and principles of mechanical engineering to modify, develop, and test machinery and equipment under direction of engineering staff or physical scientists. Prepare parts sketches and write work orders and purchase requests to be furnished by outside contractors. Draft detail drawing or sketch for drafting room completion or to request parts fabrication by machine, sheet, or wood shops. Review project instructions and blueprints to ascertain test specifications, procedures, and objectives and test nature of technical problems such as redesign. Review project instructions and specifications to identify, modify, and plan requirements fabrication, assembly, and testing. Devise, fabricate, and assemble new or modified mechanical components for products such as industrial machinery or equipment and measuring instruments. Discuss changes in design, method of manufacture and assembly, and drafting techniques and procedures with staff and coordinate corrections. Set up and conduct tests of complete units and components under operational conditions to investigate proposals for improving equipment performance. Inspect lines and figures for clarity and return erroneous drawings to designer for correction. Analyze test results in relation to design or rated specifications and test objectives and modify or adjust equipment to meet specifications. Evaluate tool drawing designs by measuring drawing dimensions and comparing with original specifications for form and function, using engineering skills. Confer with technicians and submit reports of test results to engineering department and recommend design or material changes. Calculate required capacities for equipment of proposed system to obtain specified performance and submit data to engineering personnel for approval. Record test procedures and results, numerical and graphical data, and recommendations for changes in product or test methods. Read dials and meters to determine amperage, voltage, and electrical output and input at specific operating temperature to analyze parts performance. Estimate cost factors, including labor and material, for purchased and fabricated parts and costs for assembly, testing, or installing. Set up prototype and test apparatus and operate test-controlling equipment to observe and record prototype test results.

Personality Type: Realistic. Realistic occupations frequently involve work activities that include practical, hands-on problems and solutions. They often deal with plants; animals; and real-world materials such as wood, tools, and machinery. Many of the occupations require working outside and do not involve a lot of paperwork or working closely with others.

GOE—Interest Area: 15. Scientific Research, Engineering, and Mathematics. **Work Group:** 15.09. Engineering Technology. **Other Jobs in This Work Group:** Aerospace Engineering and Operations Technicians; Cartographers and Photogrammetrists; Civil Engineering Technicians; Electrical and Electronic Engineering Technicians; Electrical and Electronics Drafters; Electrical Drafters; Electrical Engineering Technicians; Electro-Mechanical Technicians; Electronic Drafters; Electronics Engineering Technicians; Environmental Engineering Technicians; Mapping Technicians; Mechanical Drafters; Surveying and Mapping Technicians; Surveying Technicians.

Skills—Installation: Installing equipment, machines, wiring, or programs to meet specifications. **Troubleshooting:** Determining causes of operating errors and deciding what to do about them. **Technology Design:** Generating or adapting equipment and technology to serve user needs. **Operations Analysis:** Analyzing needs and product requirements to create a design. **Equipment Selection:** Determining the kind of tools and equipment needed to do a job. **Systems Evaluation:** Identifying measures or indicators of system performance and the actions needed to improve or correct performance relative to the goals of the system.

Education and Training Programs: Mechanical Engineering Related Technologies/Technician Training, Other; Mechanical Engineering/Mechanical Technology/Technician Training. **Related Knowledge/Courses: Engineering and Technology:** The practical application of engineering science and technology. This includes applying principles, techniques, procedures, and equipment to the design and production of various goods and services. **Design:** Design techniques, tools, and principles involved in production of precision technical plans, blueprints, drawings, and models. **Mechanical Devices:** Machines and tools, including their designs, uses, repair, and maintenance. **Physics:** Physical principles and laws and their interrelationships and applications to understanding fluid, material, and atmospheric dynamics and mechanical, electrical, atomic, and subatomic structures and processes. **Production and Processing:** Raw materials, production processes, quality control, costs, and other techniques for maximizing the effective manufacture and distribution of goods. **Chemistry:** The chemical composition, structure, and properties of substances and of the chemical processes and transformations that they undergo. This includes uses of chemicals and their danger signs, production techniques, and disposal methods.

Work Environment: Indoors; noisy; contaminants; hazardous equipment; sitting.

Medical Appliance Technicians

◎ Education/Training Required: Long-term on-the-job training

◎ Annual Earnings: $29,080

◎ Growth: 13.3%

◎ Annual Job Openings: 1,000

◎ Self-Employed: 9.7%

◎ Part-Time: 11.2%

Level of Solitary Work: 75.0 (out of 100)

Level of Contact with Others: 77.3 (out of 100)

Construct, fit, maintain, or repair medical supportive devices, such as braces, artificial limbs, joints, arch supports, and other surgical and medical appliances. Fit appliances onto patients and make any necessary adjustments. Make orthotic/prosthetic devices using materials such as thermoplastic and thermosetting materials, metal alloys and leather, and hand and power tools. Read prescriptions or specifications to determine the type of product or device to be fabricated and the materials and tools that will be required. Repair, modify, and maintain medical supportive devices, such as artificial limbs, braces, and surgical supports, according to specifications. Instruct patients in use of prosthetic or orthotic devices. Take patients' body or limb measurements for use in device construction. Construct or receive casts or impressions of patients' torsos or limbs for use as cutting and fabrication patterns. Bend, form, and shape fabric or material so that it conforms to prescribed contours needed to fabricate structural components. Drill and tap holes for rivets and glue, weld, bolt, and rivet parts together to form prosthetic or orthotic devices. Lay out and mark dimensions of parts, using templates and precision measuring instruments. Test medical supportive devices for proper alignment, movement, and biomechanical stability, using meters and alignment fixtures. Cover or pad metal or plastic structures and devices, using coverings such as rubber, leather, felt, plastic, or fiberglass. Polish artificial limbs, braces, and supports, using grinding and buffing wheels. Service and repair machinery used in the fabrication of appliances. Mix pigments to match patients' skin coloring, according to formulas, and apply mixtures to orthotic or prosthetic devices.

Personality Type: Realistic. Realistic occupations frequently involve work activities that include practical, hands-on problems and solutions. They often deal with plants; animals; and real-world materials such as wood, tools, and machinery. Many of the occupations require working outside and do not involve a lot of paperwork or working closely with others.

GOE—Interest Area: 13. Manufacturing. **Work Group:** 13.06. Production Precision Work. **Other Jobs in This Work Group:** Bookbinders; Dental Laboratory Technicians; Electrical and Electronic Equipment Assemblers; Electromechanical Equipment Assemblers; Engine and Other Machine Assemblers; Gem and Diamond Workers; Jewelers; Jewelers and Precious Stone and Metal Workers; Molding, Coremaking, and Casting Machine Setters, Operators, and Tenders, Metal and Plastic; Ophthalmic Laboratory Technicians; Precious Metal Workers; Semiconductor Processors; Timing Device Assemblers, Adjusters, and Calibrators.

Skills—Technology Design: Generating or adapting equipment and technology to serve user needs. **Repairing:** Repairing machines or systems by using the needed tools. **Installation:** Installing equipment, machines, wiring, or programs to meet specifications. **Quality Control Analysis:** Conducting tests and inspections of products, services, or processes to evaluate quality or performance. **Active Learning:** Understanding the implications of new information for both current and future problem solving and decision making. **Science:** Using scientific rules and methods to solve problems.

Education and Training Programs: Assistive/Augmentative Technology and Rehabiliation Engineering; Orthotist/Prosthetist Training. **Related**

Knowledge/Courses: Production and Processing: Raw materials, production processes, quality control, costs, and other techniques for maximizing the effective manufacture and distribution of goods. **Design:** Design techniques, tools, and principles involved in production of precision technical plans, blueprints, drawings, and models. **Mechanical Devices:** Machines and tools, including their designs, uses, repair, and maintenance. **Medicine and Dentistry:** The information and techniques needed to diagnose and treat human injuries, diseases, and deformities. This includes symptoms, treatment alternatives, drug properties and interactions, and preventive health-care measures. **Customer and Personal Service:** Principles and processes for providing customer and personal services. This includes customer needs assessment, meeting quality standards for services, and evaluation of customer satisfaction. **Engineering and Technology:** The practical application of engineering science and technology. This includes applying principles, techniques, procedures, and equipment to the design and production of various goods and services.

Work Environment: Indoors; noisy; contaminants; disease or infections; hazardous equipment; using hands on objects, tools, or controls.

Medical Equipment Preparers

- ◎ Education/Training Required: Short-term on-the-job training
- ◎ Annual Earnings: $24,880
- ◎ Growth: 20.0%
- ◎ Annual Job Openings: 8,000
- ◎ Self-Employed: 2.7%
- ◎ Part-Time: 27.5%

Level of Solitary Work: 71.7 (out of 100)

Level of Contact with Others: 87.0 (out of 100)

Prepare, sterilize, install, or clean laboratory or health-care equipment. May perform routine laboratory tasks and operate or inspect equipment. Organize and assemble routine and specialty surgical instrument trays and other sterilized supplies, filling special requests as needed. Clean instruments to prepare them for sterilization. Operate and maintain steam autoclaves, keeping records of loads completed, items in loads, and maintenance procedures performed. Record sterilizer test results. Disinfect and sterilize equipment such as respirators, hospital beds, and oxygen and dialysis equipment, using sterilizers, aerators, and washers. Start equipment and observe gauges and equipment operation to detect malfunctions and to ensure equipment is operating to prescribed standards. Examine equipment to detect leaks, worn or loose parts, or other indications of disrepair. Report defective equipment to appropriate supervisors or staff. Check sterile supplies to ensure that they are not outdated. Maintain records of inventory and equipment usage. Attend hospital in-service programs related to areas of work specialization. Purge wastes from equipment by connecting equipment to water sources and flushing water through systems. Deliver equipment to specified hospital locations or to patients' residences. Assist hospital staff with patient care duties such as providing transportation or setting up traction. Install and set up medical equipment, using hand tools.

Personality Type: Realistic. Realistic occupations frequently involve work activities that include practical, hands-on problems and solutions. They often deal with plants; animals; and real-world materials such as wood, tools, and machinery. Many of the occupations require working outside and do not involve a lot of paperwork or working closely with others.

GOE—Interest Area: 08. Health Science. **Work Group:** 08.06. Medical Technology. **Other Jobs in This Work Group:** Biological Technicians; Cardiovascular Technologists and Technicians; Diagnostic Medical Sonographers; Medical and Clinical Laboratory Technicians; Medical and Clinical Laboratory Technologists; Medical Records and Health Information Technicians; Nuclear

Medicine Technologists; Opticians, Dispensing; Orthotists and Prosthetists; Radiologic Technicians; Radiologic Technologists; Radiologic Technologists and Technicians.

Skills—Operation Monitoring: Watching gauges, dials, or other indicators to make sure a machine is working properly. **Management of Material Resources:** Obtaining and seeing to the appropriate use of equipment, facilities, and materials needed to do certain work. **Equipment Maintenance:** Performing routine maintenance on equipment and determining when and what kind of maintenance is needed. **Quality Control Analysis:** Conducting tests and inspections of products, services, or processes to evaluate quality or performance. **Service Orientation:** Actively looking for ways to help people. **Operation and Control:** Controlling operations of equipment or systems.

Education and Training Programs: Allied Health and Medical Assisting Services, Other; Medical/Clinical Assistant Training. **Related Knowledge/Courses: Chemistry:** The chemical composition, structure, and properties of substances and of the chemical processes and transformations that they undergo. This includes uses of chemicals and their danger signs, production techniques, and disposal methods. **Biology:** Plant and animal organisms and their tissues, cells, functions, interdependencies, and interactions with each other and the environment. **Medicine and Dentistry:** The information and techniques needed to diagnose and treat human injuries, diseases, and deformities. This includes symptoms, treatment alternatives, drug properties and interactions, and preventive health-care measures. **Production and Processing:** Raw materials, production processes, quality control, costs, and other techniques for maximizing the effective manufacture and distribution of goods. **Education and Training:** Principles and methods for curriculum and training design, teaching and instruction for individuals and groups, and the measurement of training effects. **Customer and Personal Service:** Principles and processes for providing customer and personal services. This includes customer needs assessment, meeting quality standards for services, and evaluation of customer satisfaction.

Work Environment: Indoors; contaminants; disease or infections; standing; using hands on objects, tools, or controls; repetitive motions.

Medical Equipment Repairers

- Education/Training Required: Associate degree
- Annual Earnings: $39,570
- Growth: 14.8%
- Annual Job Openings: 4,000
- Self-Employed: 16.2%
- Part-Time: 12.1%

Level of Solitary Work: 56.3 (out of 100)

Level of Contact with Others: 76.8 (out of 100)

Test, adjust, or repair biomedical or electromedical equipment. Inspect and test malfunctioning medical and related equipment following manufacturers' specifications, using test and analysis instruments. Examine medical equipment and facility's structural environment and check for proper use of equipment to protect patients and staff from electrical or mechanical hazards and to ensure compliance with safety regulations. Disassemble malfunctioning equipment and remove, repair, and replace defective parts such as motors, clutches, or transformers. Keep records of maintenance, repair, and required updates of equipment. Perform preventive maintenance or service such as cleaning, lubricating, and adjusting equipment. Test and calibrate components and equipment, following manufacturers' manuals and troubleshooting techniques and using hand tools, power tools, and measuring devices. Explain and demonstrate correct operation and preventive maintenance of medical equipment to personnel. Study technical manuals and attend training sessions provided by equipment manufacturers to maintain current knowledge. Plan and carry out work assignments, using blueprints, schematic drawings, technical manuals, wiring diagrams, and liquid and air flow sheets, following prescribed regulations, directives, and other instructions as required. Solder loose connections, using soldering iron. Test, evaluate, and classify excess or in-use medical equipment and determine serviceability, condition, and disposition in accordance with regulations. Research catalogs and repair part lists to locate sources for repair parts, requisitioning parts and recording their receipt. Evaluate technical specifications to identify equipment and systems best suited for intended use and possible purchase based on specifications, user needs, and technical requirements. Contribute expertise to develop medical maintenance standard operating procedures. Compute power and space requirements for installing medical, dental, or related equipment and install units to manufacturers' specifications. Supervise and advise subordinate personnel. Repair shop equipment, metal furniture, and hospital equipment, including welding broken parts and replacing missing parts, or bring item into local shop for major repairs.

Personality Type: Realistic. Realistic occupations frequently involve work activities that include practical, hands-on problems and solutions. They often deal with plants; animals; and real-world materials such as wood, tools, and machinery. Many of the occupations require working outside and do not involve a lot of paperwork or working closely with others.

GOE—Interest Area: 13. Manufacturing. **Work Group:** 13.15. Medical and Technical Equipment Repair. **Other Jobs in This Work Group:** Camera and Photographic Equipment Repairers; Watch Repairers.

Skills—Repairing: Repairing machines or systems by using the needed tools. **Installation:** Installing equipment, machines, wiring, or programs to meet specifications. **Equipment Maintenance:** Performing routine maintenance on equipment and determining when and what kind of maintenance is needed. **Troubleshooting:** Determining causes of operating errors and deciding what to do about them. **Systems Analysis:** Determining how a system should work and how changes in conditions, operations, and the environment will affect outcomes. **Operation Monitoring:** Watching gauges, dials, or other indicators to make sure a machine is working properly.

Education and Training Program: Biomedical Technology/Technician Training. **Related Knowledge/Courses: Mechanical Devices:** Machines and tools, including their designs, uses, repair, and maintenance. **Computers and Electronics:** Circuit boards, processors, chips, electronic equipment, and computer hardware and software, including applications and programming. **Engineering and Technology:** The practical application of engineering science and technology. This includes applying principles, techniques, procedures, and equipment to the design and production of various goods and services. **Physics:** Physical principles and laws and their interrelationships and applications to understanding fluid, material, and atmospheric dynamics and mechanical, electrical, atomic, and subatomic structures and processes. **Telecommunications:** Transmission, broadcasting, switching, control, and operation of telecommunications systems. **Medicine and Dentistry:** The information and techniques needed to diagnose and treat human injuries, diseases, and deformities. This includes symptoms, treatment alternatives, drug properties and interactions, and preventive health-care measures.

Work Environment: Indoors; contaminants; disease or infections; standing; using hands on objects, tools, or controls.

Medical Scientists, Except Epidemiologists

◎ Education/Training Required: Doctoral degree

◎ Annual Earnings: $61,730

◎ Growth: 34.1%

◎ Annual Job Openings: 15,000

◎ Self-Employed: 0.4%

◎ Part-Time: 5.5%

Level of Solitary Work: 62.5 (out of 100)

Level of Contact with Others: 79.5 (out of 100)

Conduct research dealing with the understanding of human diseases and the improvement of human health. Engage in clinical investigation or other research, production, technical writing, or related activities. Conduct research to develop methodologies, instrumentation, and procedures for medical application, analyzing data and presenting findings. Plan and direct studies to investigate human or animal disease, preventive methods, and treatments for disease. Follow strict safety procedures when handling toxic materials to avoid contamination. Evaluate effects of drugs, gases, pesticides, parasites, and microorganisms at various levels. Teach principles of medicine and medical and laboratory procedures to physicians, residents, students, and technicians. Prepare and analyze organ, tissue, and cell samples to identify toxicity, bacteria, or microorganisms or to study cell structure. Standardize drug dosages, methods of immunization, and procedures for manufacture of drugs and medicinal compounds. Investigate cause, progress, life cycle, or mode of transmission of diseases or parasites. Confer with health department, industry personnel, physicians, and others to develop health safety standards and public health improvement programs. Study animal and human health and physiological processes. Consult with and advise physicians, educators, researchers, and others regarding medical applica-

tions of physics, biology, and chemistry. Use equipment such as atomic absorption spectrometers, electron microscopes, flow cytometers, and chromatography systems.

Personality Type: Investigative. Investigative occupations frequently involve working with ideas and require an extensive amount of thinking. These occupations can involve searching for facts and figuring out problems mentally.

GOE—Interest Area: 15. Scientific Research, Engineering, and Mathematics. **Work Group:** 15.03. Life Sciences. **Other Jobs in This Work Group:** Biochemists and Biophysicists; Biologists; Environmental Scientists and Specialists, Including Health; Epidemiologists; Microbiologists.

Skills—Science: Using scientific rules and methods to solve problems. **Management of Financial Resources:** Determining how money will be spent to get the work done and accounting for these expenditures. **Judgment and Decision Making:** Considering the relative costs and benefits of potential actions to choose the most appropriate one. **Reading Comprehension:** Understanding written sentences and paragraphs in work-related documents. **Writing:** Communicating effectively in writing as appropriate for the needs of the audience. **Time Management:** Managing one's own time and the time of others.

Education and Training Programs: Anatomy; Biochemistry; Biomedical Sciences, General; Biophysics; Biostatistics; Cardiovascular Science; Cell Physiology; Endocrinology; Epidemiology; Human/Medical Genetics; Immunology; Medical Microbiology and Bacteriology; Molecular Biology; Molecular Pharmacology; Neurobiology and Neurophysiology; Oncology and Cancer Biology; Pathology; Pharmacology; Pharmacology and Toxicology; Physiology, General; Reproductive Biology; Toxicology; Vision Science/Physiological Optics; others. **Related Knowledge/Courses: Biology:** Plant and animal organisms and their tissues, cells, functions, interdependencies, and interactions with each other and the environment. **Medicine and Dentistry:** The information and techniques needed to diagnose and treat human injuries, diseases, and deformities. This includes symptoms, treatment alternatives, drug properties and interactions, and preventive health-care measures. **Chemistry:** The chemical composition, structure, and properties of substances and of the chemical processes and transformations that they undergo. This includes uses of chemicals and their danger signs, production techniques, and disposal methods. **Communications and Media:** Media production, communication, and dissemination techniques and methods. This includes alternative ways to inform and entertain via written, oral, and visual media. **Personnel and Human Resources:** Principles and procedures for personnel recruitment, selection, training, compensation and benefits, labor relations and negotiation, and personnel information systems. **Mathematics:** Arithmetic, algebra, geometry, calculus, and statistics and their applications.

Work Environment: Indoors; sitting; using hands on objects, tools, or controls.

Merchandise Displayers and Window Trimmers

- ◎ Education/Training Required: Moderate-term on-the-job training
- ◎ Annual Earnings: $22,590
- ◎ Growth: 10.3%
- ◎ Annual Job Openings: 13,000
- ◎ Self-Employed: 25.9%
- ◎ Part-Time: 21.3%

Level of Solitary Work: 68.8 (out of 100)

Level of Contact with Others: 89.8 (out of 100)

Plan and erect commercial displays, such as those in windows and interiors of retail stores and at trade exhibitions. Take photographs of displays and signage. Plan and erect commercial displays to entice and appeal to customers. Place prices and descriptive signs on backdrops, fixtures, merchandise, or floor. Change or rotate window displays, interior display areas, and signage to reflect changes in inventory or promotion. Obtain plans from display designers or display managers and discuss their implementation with clients or supervisors. Develop ideas or plans for merchandise displays or window decorations. Consult with advertising and sales staff to determine type of merchandise to be featured and time and place for each display. Arrange properties, furniture, merchandise, backdrops, and other accessories as shown in prepared sketches. Construct or assemble displays and display components from fabric, glass, paper, and plastic according to specifications, using hand tools and woodworking power tools. Collaborate with others to obtain products and other display items. Use computers to produce signage. Dress mannequins for displays. Maintain props and mannequins, inspecting them for imperfections and applying preservative coatings as necessary. Select themes, lighting, colors, and props to be used. Attend training sessions and corporate planning meetings to obtain new ideas for product launches. Instruct sales staff in color-coordination of clothing racks and counter displays. Store, pack, and maintain records of props and display items. Prepare sketches, floor plans, or models of proposed displays. Cut out designs on cardboard, hardboard, and plywood according to motif of event. Install booths, exhibits, displays, carpets, and drapes as guided by floor plan of building and specifications. Install decorations such as flags, banners, festive lights, and bunting on or in building, street, exhibit hall, or booth. Create and enhance mannequin faces by mixing and applying paint and attaching measured eyelash strips, using artist's brush, airbrush, pins, ruler, and scissors.

Personality Type: Artistic. Artistic occupations frequently involve working with forms, designs, and patterns. They often require self-expression, and the work can be done without following a clear set of rules.

GOE—Interest Area: 03. Arts and Communication. **Work Group:** 03.05. Design. **Other Jobs in This**

Work Group: Commercial and Industrial Designers; Fashion Designers; Floral Designers; Graphic Designers; Interior Designers; Set and Exhibit Designers.

Skills—Persuasion: Persuading others to change their minds or behavior. **Negotiation:** Bringing others together and trying to reconcile differences. **Management of Personnel Resources:** Motivating, developing, and directing people as they work; identifying the best people for the job. **Coordination:** Adjusting actions in relation to others' actions. **Management of Financial Resources:** Determining how money will be spent to get the work done and accounting for these expenditures.

Education and Training Program: Commercial and Advertising Art. **Related Knowledge/Courses: Sales and Marketing:** Principles and methods for showing, promoting, and selling products or services. This includes marketing strategy and tactics, product demonstration, sales techniques, and sales control systems. **Design:** Design techniques, tools, and principles involved in production of precision technical plans, blueprints, drawings, and models. **Administration and Management:** Business and management principles involved in strategic planning, resource allocation, human resources modeling, leadership technique, production methods, and coordination of people and resources. **Computers and Electronics:** Circuit boards, processors, chips, electronic equipment, and computer hardware and software, including applications and programming. **Customer and Personal Service:** Principles and processes for providing customer and personal services. This includes customer needs assessment, meeting quality standards for services, and evaluation of customer satisfaction.

Work Environment: Indoors; contaminants; walking and running; using hands on objects, tools, or controls; bending or twisting the body; repetitive motions.

Microbiologists

- Education/Training Required: Doctoral degree
- Annual Earnings: $56,870
- Growth: 17.2%
- Annual Job Openings: 1,000
- Self-Employed: 2.9%
- Part-Time: 8.2%

Level of Solitary Work: 75.0 (out of 100)

Level of Contact with Others: 70.0 (out of 100)

Investigate the growth, structure, development, and other characteristics of microscopic organisms, such as bacteria, algae, or fungi. Includes medical microbiologists who study the relationship between organisms and disease or the effects of antibiotics on microorganisms. Isolate and make cultures of bacteria or other microorganisms in prescribed media, controlling moisture, aeration, temperature, and nutrition. Perform tests on water, food, and the environment to detect harmful microorganisms and to obtain information about sources of pollution and contamination. Examine physiological, morphological, and cultural characteristics, using microscope, to identify and classify microorganisms in human, water, and food specimens. Provide laboratory services for health departments, for community environmental health programs, and for physicians needing information for diagnosis and treatment. Observe action of microorganisms upon living tissues of plants, higher animals, and other microorganisms and on dead organic matter. Investigate the relationship between organisms and disease, including the control of epidemics and the effects of antibiotics on microorganisms. Supervise biological technologists and technicians and other scientists. Study growth, structure, development, and general characteristics of bacteria and other microorganisms to understand their relationship to human, plant, and animal health. Prepare technical reports and recommendations based upon research outcomes. Study the structure and function of human, animal, and plant tissues, cells, pathogens, and toxins. Use a variety of specialized equipment such as electron microscopes, gas chromatographs and high-pressure liquid chromatographs, electrophoresis units, thermocyclers, fluorescence-activated cell sorters, and phosphoimagers. Conduct chemical analyses of substances such as acids, alcohols, and enzymes. Research use of bacteria and microorganisms to develop vitamins, antibiotics, amino acids, grain alcohol, sugars, and polymers.

Personality Type: Investigative. Investigative occupations frequently involve working with ideas and require an extensive amount of thinking. These occupations can involve searching for facts and figuring out problems mentally.

GOE—Interest Area: 15. Scientific Research, Engineering, and Mathematics. **Work Group:** 15.03. Life Sciences. **Other Jobs in This Work Group:** Biochemists and Biophysicists; Biologists; Environmental Scientists and Specialists, Including Health; Epidemiologists; Medical Scientists, Except Epidemiologists.

Skills—Science: Using scientific rules and methods to solve problems. **Operation Monitoring:** Watching gauges, dials, or other indicators to make sure a machine is working properly. **Repairing:** Repairing machines or systems by using the needed tools. **Equipment Maintenance:** Performing routine maintenance on equipment and determining when and what kind of maintenance is needed. **Quality Control Analysis:** Conducting tests and inspections of products, services, or processes to evaluate quality or performance. **Technology Design:** Generating or adapting equipment and technology to serve user needs.

Education and Training Programs: Biochemistry/Biophysics and Molecular Biology; Cell/Cellular Biology and Anatomical Sciences, Other; Microbiology, General; Neuroanatomy; Soil Microbiology; Structural Biology. **Related Knowledge/**

Courses: Biology: Plant and animal organisms and their tissues, cells, functions, interdependencies, and interactions with each other and the environment. **Chemistry:** The chemical composition, structure, and properties of substances and of the chemical processes and transformations that they undergo. This includes uses of chemicals and their danger signs, production techniques, and disposal methods. **Clerical Practices:** Administrative and clerical procedures and systems such as word processing, managing files and records, stenography and transcription, designing forms, and other office procedures and terminology. **English Language:** The structure and content of the English language, including the meaning and spelling of words, rules of composition, and grammar. **Computers and Electronics:** Circuit boards, processors, chips, electronic equipment, and computer hardware and software, including applications and programming. **Administration and Management:** Business and management principles involved in strategic planning, resource allocation, human resources modeling, leadership technique, production methods, and coordination of people and resources.

Work Environment: Indoors; contaminants; disease or infections; hazardous conditions; using hands on objects, tools, or controls; repetitive motions.

Millwrights

- Education/Training Required: Long-term on-the-job training
- Annual Earnings: $44,780
- Growth: 5.9%
- Annual Job Openings: 5,000
- Self-Employed: 1.1%
- Part-Time: 1.1%

Level of Solitary Work: 56.3 (out of 100)

Level of Contact with Others: 71.7 (out of 100)

Install, dismantle, or move machinery and heavy equipment according to layout plans, blueprints, or other drawings. Replace defective parts of machine or adjust clearances and alignment of moving parts. Align machines and equipment, using hoists, jacks, hand tools, squares, rules, micrometers, and plumb bobs. Connect power unit to machines or steam piping to equipment and test unit to evaluate its mechanical operation. Repair and lubricate machines and equipment. Assemble and install equipment, using hand tools and power tools. Position steel beams to support bedplates of machines and equipment, using blueprints and schematic drawings to determine work procedures. Signal crane operator to lower basic assembly units to bedplate and align unit to centerline. Insert shims, adjust tension on nuts and bolts, or position parts, using hand tools and measuring instruments to set specified clearances between moving and stationary parts. Move machinery and equipment, using hoists, dollies, rollers, and trucks. Attach moving parts and subassemblies to basic assembly unit, using hand tools and power tools. Assemble machines and bolt, weld, rivet, or otherwise fasten them to foundation or other structures, using hand tools and power tools. Lay out mounting holes, using measuring instruments, and drill holes with power drill. Bolt parts, such as side and deck plates, jaw plates, and journals, to basic assembly unit. Dismantle machines, using hammers, wrenches, crowbars, and other hand tools. Level bedplate and establish centerline, using straightedge, levels, and transit. Shrink-fit bushings, sleeves, rings, liners, gears, and wheels to specified items, using portable gas heating equipment. Dismantle machinery and equipment for shipment to installation site, usually performing installation and maintenance work as part of team. Construct foundation for machines, using hand tools and building materials such as wood, cement, and steel. Install robot and modify its program, using teach pendant. Operate engine lathe to grind, file, and turn machine parts to dimensional specifications.

Personality Type: Realistic. Realistic occupations frequently involve work activities that include practical, hands-on problems and solutions. They often deal with plants; animals; and real-world materials such as wood, tools, and machinery. Many of the occupations require working outside and do not involve a lot of paperwork or working closely with others.

GOE—Interest Area: 13. Manufacturing. **Work Group:** 13.13. Machinery Repair. **Other Jobs in This Work Group:** Bicycle Repairers; Control and Valve Installers and Repairers, Except Mechanical Door; Home Appliance Repairers; Industrial Machinery Mechanics; Locksmiths and Safe Repairers; Maintenance Workers, Machinery; Mechanical Door Repairers; Signal and Track Switch Repairers.

Skills—Installation: Installing equipment, machines, wiring, or programs to meet specifications. **Repairing:** Repairing machines or systems by using the needed tools. **Troubleshooting:** Determining causes of operating errors and deciding what to do about them. **Equipment Maintenance:** Performing routine maintenance on equipment and determining when and what kind of maintenance is needed. **Mathematics:** Using mathematics to solve problems. **Equipment Selection:** Determining the kind of tools and equipment needed to do a job.

Education and Training Programs: Heavy/Industrial Equipment Maintenance Technologies, Other; Industrial Mechanics and Maintenance Technology. **Related Knowledge/Courses: Mechanical Devices:** Machines and tools, including their designs, uses, repair, and maintenance. **Building and Construction:** The materials, methods, and tools involved in the construction or repair of houses, buildings, or other structures such as highways and roads. **Engineering and Technology:** The practical application of engineering science and technology. This includes applying principles, techniques, procedures, and equipment to the design and production of various goods and services. **Physics:** Physical principles and laws and their interrelationships and applications to understanding fluid, material, and atmospheric dynamics and mechanical, electrical, atomic, and subatomic structures and processes. **Design:** Design techniques, tools, and principles involved in production of precision technical plans, blueprints, drawings, and models. **Public Safety and Security:** Relevant equipment, policies, procedures, and strategies to promote effective local, state, or national security operations for the protection of people, data, property, and institutions.

Work Environment: Noisy; very hot or cold; very bright or dim lighting; contaminants; hazardous equipment; using hands on objects, tools, or controls.

Mixing and Blending Machine Setters, Operators, and Tenders

- Education/Training Required: Moderate-term on-the-job training
- Annual Earnings: $28,890
- Growth: 2.0%
- Annual Job Openings: 16,000
- Self-Employed: 0.8%
- Part-Time: 3.7%

Level of Solitary Work: 65.5 (out of 100)

Level of Contact with Others: 76.5 (out of 100)

Set up, operate, or tend machines to mix or blend materials such as chemicals, tobacco, liquids, color pigments, or explosive ingredients. Weigh or measure materials, ingredients, and products to ensure conformance to requirements. Test samples of materials or products to ensure compliance with specifications, using test equipment. Start machines to mix or blend ingredients; then allow them to mix for specified times. Dump or pour specified amounts of materials into machinery and equipment. Operate or tend machines to mix or blend any of a wide variety of materials such as spices, dough batter, tobacco, fruit

juices, chemicals, livestock feed, food products, color pigments, or explosive ingredients. Observe production and monitor equipment to ensure safe and efficient operation. Stop mixing or blending machines when specified product qualities are obtained and open valves and start pumps to transfer mixtures. Collect samples of materials or products for laboratory testing. Add or mix chemicals and ingredients for processing, using hand tools or other devices. Examine materials, ingredients, or products visually or with hands to ensure conformance to established standards. Record operational and production data on specified forms. Transfer materials, supplies, and products between work areas, using moving equipment and hand tools. Tend accessory equipment such as pumps and conveyors to move materials or ingredients through production processes. Read work orders to determine production specifications and information. Compound and process ingredients or dyes according to formulas. Unload mixtures into containers or onto conveyors for further processing. Clean and maintain equipment, using hand tools. Dislodge and clear jammed materials or other items from machinery and equipment, using hand tools. Open valves to drain slurry from mixers into storage tanks.

Personality Type: Realistic. Realistic occupations frequently involve work activities that include practical, hands-on problems and solutions. They often deal with plants; animals; and real-world materials such as wood, tools, and machinery. Many of the occupations require working outside and do not involve a lot of paperwork or working closely with others.

GOE—Interest Area: 13. Manufacturing. **Work Group:** 13.03. Production Work, Assorted Materials Processing. **Other Jobs in This Work Group:** Bakers; Cementing and Gluing Machine Operators and Tenders; Chemical Equipment Operators and Tenders; Cleaning, Washing, and Metal Pickling Equipment Operators and Tenders; Coating, Painting, and Spraying Machine Setters, Operators, and Tenders; Cooling and Freezing Equipment Operators and Tenders; Cutting and Slicing Machine

Setters, Operators, and Tenders; Extruding and Forming Machine Setters, Operators, and Tenders, Synthetic and Glass Fibers; Extruding, Forming, Pressing, and Compacting Machine Setters, Operators, and Tenders; Food and Tobacco Roasting, Baking, and Drying Machine Operators and Tenders; Food Batchmakers; Food Cooking Machine Operators and Tenders; Furnace, Kiln, Oven, Drier, and Kettle Operators and Tenders; Heat Treating Equipment Setters, Operators, and Tenders, Metal and Plastic; Helpers—Production Workers; Meat, Poultry, and Fish Cutters and Trimmers; Metal-Refining Furnace Operators and Tenders; Packaging and Filling Machine Operators and Tenders; Plating and Coating Machine Setters, Operators, and Tenders, Metal and Plastic; Pourers and Casters, Metal; Sawing Machine Setters, Operators, and Tenders, Wood; Separating, Filtering, Clarifying, Precipitating, and Still Machine Setters, Operators, and Tenders; Sewing Machine Operators; Shoe Machine Operators and Tenders; Slaughterers and Meat Packers; Team Assemblers; Textile Bleaching and Dyeing Machine Operators and Tenders; Tire Builders; Woodworking Machine Setters, Operators, and Tenders, Except Sawing.

Skills—Operation Monitoring: Watching gauges, dials, or other indicators to make sure a machine is working properly. **Operation and Control:** Controlling operations of equipment or systems. **Equipment Maintenance:** Performing routine maintenance on equipment and determining when and what kind of maintenance is needed. **Repairing:** Repairing machines or systems by using the needed tools. **Troubleshooting:** Determining causes of operating errors and deciding what to do about them. **Technology Design:** Generating or adapting equipment and technology to serve user needs.

Education and Training Program: Agricultural and Food Products Processing. **Related Knowledge/ Courses: Production and Processing:** Raw materials, production processes, quality control, costs, and other techniques for maximizing the effective manufacture and distribution of goods. **Chemistry:** The chemical composition, structure, and properties of

substances and of the chemical processes and transformations that they undergo. This includes uses of chemicals and their danger signs, production techniques, and disposal methods. **Mechanical Devices:** Machines and tools, including their designs, uses, repair, and maintenance. **Physics:** Physical principles and laws and their interrelationships and applications to understanding fluid, material, and atmospheric dynamics and mechanical, electrical, atomic, and subatomic structures and processes. **Education and Training:** Principles and methods for curriculum and training design, teaching and instruction for individuals and groups, and the measurement of training effects. **Mathematics:** Arithmetic, algebra, geometry, calculus, and statistics and their applications.

Work Environment: Noisy; contaminants; hazardous conditions; standing; walking and running; using hands on objects, tools, or controls.

Mobile Heavy Equipment Mechanics, Except Engines

- ◎ Education/Training Required: Postsecondary vocational training
- ◎ Annual Earnings: $39,410
- ◎ Growth: 8.8%
- ◎ Annual Job Openings: 14,000
- ◎ Self-Employed: 2.9%
- ◎ Part-Time: 3.0%

Level of Solitary Work: 46.7 (out of 100)

Level of Contact with Others: 74.0 (out of 100)

Diagnose, adjust, repair, or overhaul mobile mechanical, hydraulic, and pneumatic equipment, such as cranes, bulldozers, graders, and conveyors, used in construction, logging, and surface mining. Test mechanical products and equipment after repair or assembly to ensure proper performance and compliance with manufacturers' specifications. Repair and replace damaged or worn parts. Diagnose faults or malfunctions to determine required repairs, using engine diagnostic equipment such as computerized test equipment and calibration devices. Operate and inspect machines or heavy equipment to diagnose defects. Dismantle and reassemble heavy equipment, using hoists and hand tools. Clean, lubricate, and perform other routine maintenance work on equipment and vehicles. Examine parts for damage or excessive wear, using micrometers and gauges. Read and understand operating manuals, blueprints, and technical drawings. Schedule maintenance for industrial machines and equipment and keep equipment service records. Overhaul and test machines or equipment to ensure operating efficiency. Assemble gear systems and align frames and gears. Fit bearings to adjust, repair, or overhaul mobile mechanical, hydraulic, and pneumatic equipment. Weld or solder broken parts and structural members, using electric or gas welders and soldering tools. Clean parts by spraying them with grease solvent or immersing them in tanks of solvent. Adjust, maintain, and repair or replace subassemblies, such as transmissions and crawler heads, using hand tools, jacks, and cranes. Adjust and maintain industrial machinery, using control and regulating devices. Fabricate needed parts or items from sheet metal. Direct workers who are assembling or disassembling equipment or cleaning parts.

Personality Type: Realistic. Realistic occupations frequently involve work activities that include practical, hands-on problems and solutions. They often deal with plants; animals; and real-world materials such as wood, tools, and machinery. Many of the occupations require working outside and do not involve a lot of paperwork or working closely with others.

GOE—Interest Area: 13. Manufacturing. **Work Group:** 13.14. Vehicle and Facility Mechanical Work. **Other Jobs in This Work Group:** Aircraft Mechanics and Service Technicians; Aircraft Structure, Surfaces, Rigging, and Systems Assemblers; Automotive Body and Related Repairers; Automotive Glass Installers and Repairers; Automotive Master Mechanics; Automotive Service Technicians and Mechanics; Automotive Specialty Technicians; Bus and Truck Mechanics and Diesel Engine Specialists; Farm Equipment Mechanics; Fiberglass Laminators and Fabricators; Motorboat Mechanics; Motorcycle Mechanics; Outdoor Power Equipment and Other Small Engine Mechanics; Rail Car Repairers; Recreational Vehicle Service Technicians; Tire Repairers and Changers.

Skills—Installation: Installing equipment, machines, wiring, or programs to meet specifications. **Repairing:** Repairing machines or systems by using the needed tools. **Equipment Maintenance:** Performing routine maintenance on equipment and determining when and what kind of maintenance is needed. **Operation Monitoring:** Watching gauges, dials, or other indicators to make sure a machine is working properly. **Troubleshooting:** Determining causes of operating errors and deciding what to do about them. **Operation and Control:** Controlling operations of equipment or systems.

Education and Training Programs: Agricultural Mech-anics and Equipment/Machine Technology; Heavy Equipment Maintenance Technology/Technician Training. **Related Knowledge/Courses: Mechanical Devices:** Machines and tools, including their designs, uses, repair, and maintenance. **Engineering and Technology:** The practical application of engineering science and technology. This includes applying principles, techniques, procedures, and equipment to the design and production of various goods and services. **Physics:** Physical principles and laws and their interrelationships and applications to understanding fluid, material, and atmospheric dynamics and mechanical, electrical, atomic, and subatomic structures and processes. **Production and Processing:** Raw materials, production processes, quality control, costs, and other techniques for maximizing the effective manufacture and distribution of goods.

Work Environment: Noisy; contaminants; hazardous equipment; minor burns, cuts, bites, or stings; standing; using hands on objects, tools, or controls.

Motorboat Mechanics

- ☺ Education/Training Required: Long-term on-the-job training
- ☺ Annual Earnings: $32,780
- ☺ Growth: 15.1%
- ☺ Annual Job Openings: 7,000
- ☺ Self-Employed: 18.9%
- ☺ Part-Time: 13.2%

Level of Solitary Work: 56.3 (out of 100)

Level of Contact with Others: 11.8 (out of 100)

Repairs and adjusts electrical and mechanical equipment of gasoline or diesel-powered inboard or inboard-outboard boat engines. Replace parts such as gears, magneto points, piston rings, and spark plugs and reassemble engines. Adjust generators and replace faulty wiring, using hand tools and soldering irons. Mount motors to boats and operate boats at various speeds on waterways to conduct operational tests. Document inspection and test results and work performed or to be performed. Start motors and monitor performance for signs of malfunctioning such as smoke, excessive vibration, and misfiring. Set starter locks and align and repair steering or throttle controls, using gauges, screwdrivers, and wrenches. Repair engine mechanical equipment such as power tilts, bilge pumps, or power take-offs. Inspect and repair or adjust propellers and propeller shafts. Disassemble and inspect motors to locate defective parts, using mechanic's hand tools and gauges. Adjust carburetor mixtures, electrical point settings, and timing while motors are running in water-filled test tanks. Repair or rework parts, using machine tools such as lathes, mills, drills, and grinders. Idle motors and observe thermometers to determine the effectiveness of cooling systems.

Personality Type: Realistic. Realistic occupations frequently involve work activities that include practical, hands-on problems and solutions. They often deal with plants; animals; and real-world materials such as wood, tools, and machinery. Many of the occupations require working outside and do not involve a lot of paperwork or working closely with others.

GOE—Interest Area: 13. Manufacturing. **Work Group:** 13.14. Vehicle and Facility Mechanical Work. **Other Jobs in This Work Group:** Aircraft Mechanics and Service Technicians; Aircraft Structure, Surfaces, Rigging, and Systems Assemblers; Automotive Body and Related Repairers; Automotive Glass Installers and Repairers; Automotive Master Mechanics; Automotive Service Technicians and Mechanics; Automotive Specialty Technicians; Bus and Truck Mechanics and Diesel Engine Specialists; Farm Equipment Mechanics; Fiberglass Laminators and Fabricators; Mobile Heavy Equipment Mechanics, Except Engines; Motorcycle Mechanics; Outdoor Power Equipment and Other Small Engine Mechanics; Rail Car Repairers; Recreational Vehicle Service Technicians; Tire Repairers and Changers.

Skills—Repairing: Repairing machines or systems by using the needed tools. **Quality Control Analysis:** Conducting tests and inspections of products, services, or processes to evaluate quality or performance. **Installation:** Installing equipment, machines, wiring, or programs to meet specifications. **Equipment Maintenance:** Performing routine maintenance on equipment and determining when and what kind of maintenance is needed. **Troubleshooting:** Determining causes of operating errors and deciding what to do about them. **Operation Monitoring:** Watching gauges, dials, or other indicators to make sure a machine is working properly.

Education and Training Programs: Marine Maintenance/Fitter and Ship Repair Technology/Technician Training; Small Engine Mechanics and Repair Technology/Technician Training. **Related Knowledge/Courses: Mechanical Devices:** Machines and tools, including their designs, uses, repair, and maintenance. **Engineering and Technology:** The practical application of engineering science and technology. This includes applying principles, techniques, procedures, and equipment to the design and production of various goods and services.

Work Environment: More often indoors than outdoors; standing; using hands on objects, tools, or controls.

Motorcycle Mechanics

- ◎ Education/Training Required: Long-term on-the-job training
- ◎ Annual Earnings: $29,450
- ◎ Growth: 13.7%
- ◎ Annual Job Openings: 6,000
- ◎ Self-Employed: 15.7%
- ◎ Part-Time: 13.2%

Level of Solitary Work: 59.2 (out of 100)

Level of Contact with Others: 68.0 (out of 100)

Diagnose, adjust, repair, or overhaul motorcycles, scooters, mopeds, dirt bikes, or similar motorized vehicles. Repair and adjust motorcycle subassemblies such as forks, transmissions, brakes, and drive chains according to specifications. Replace defective parts, using hand tools, arbor presses, flexible power presses, or power tools. Connect test panels to engines and measure generator output, ignition timing, and other engine performance indicators. Listen to engines, examine vehicle frames, and confer with customers to determine nature and extent of malfunction or damage. Reassemble and test subassembly units. Dismantle engines and repair or replace defective parts, such as magnetos, carburetors, and generators. Remove cylinder heads; grind valves; scrape off carbon; and replace defective valves, pistons, cylinders, and rings, using hand tools and power tools. Repair or replace other parts, such as headlights, horns, handlebar controls, gasoline and oil tanks, starters, and mufflers. Disassemble subassembly units and examine condition, movement, or alignment of parts visually or by using gauges. Hammer out dents and bends in frames, weld tears and breaks, and reassemble frames and reinstall engines.

Personality Type: Realistic. Realistic occupations frequently involve work activities that include practical, hands-on problems and solutions. They often deal with plants; animals; and real-world materials such as wood, tools, and machinery. Many of the occupations require working outside and do not involve a lot of paperwork or working closely with others.

GOE—Interest Area: 13. Manufacturing. **Work Group:** 13.14. Vehicle and Facility Mechanical Work. **Other Jobs in This Work Group:** Aircraft Mechanics and Service Technicians; Aircraft Structure, Surfaces, Rigging, and Systems Assemblers; Automotive Body and Related Repairers; Automotive Glass Installers and Repairers; Automotive Master Mechanics; Automotive Service Technicians and Mechanics; Automotive Specialty Technicians; Bus and Truck Mechanics and Diesel Engine Specialists; Farm Equipment Mechanics; Fiberglass Laminators and Fabricators; Mobile Heavy Equipment Mechanics, Except Engines; Motorboat Mechanics; Outdoor Power Equipment and Other Small Engine Mechanics; Rail Car Repairers; Recreational Vehicle Service Technicians; Tire Repairers and Changers.

Skills—Repairing: Repairing machines or systems by using the needed tools. **Installation:** Installing equipment, machines, wiring, or programs to meet specifications. **Troubleshooting:** Determining causes of operating errors and deciding what to do about them. **Equipment Maintenance:** Performing routine maintenance on equipment and determining when and what kind of maintenance is needed. **Technology Design:** Generating or adapting equipment and technology to serve user needs. **Science:** Using scientific rules and methods to solve problems.

Education and Training Program: Motorcycle Maintenance and Repair Technology/Technician Training. **Related Knowledge/Courses: Mechanical Devices:** Machines and tools, including their designs, uses, repair, and maintenance. **Design:** Design techniques, tools, and principles involved in production of precision technical plans, blueprints, drawings, and models. **Engineering and Technology:** The practical application of engineering science and technology. This includes applying principles, techniques, procedures, and equipment to the design and production of various goods and services. **Physics:** Physical principles and laws and their interrelationships and applications to understanding fluid, material, and atmospheric dynamics and mechanical, electrical, atomic, and subatomic structures and processes. **Transportation:** Principles and methods for moving people or goods by air, rail, sea, or road, including the relative costs and benefits. **Sales and Marketing:** Principles and methods for showing, promoting, and selling products or services. This includes marketing strategy and tactics, product demonstration, sales techniques, and sales control systems.

Work Environment: Indoors; noisy; contaminants; standing; using hands on objects, tools, or controls; bending or twisting the body.

Multiple Machine Tool Setters, Operators, and Tenders, Metal and Plastic

- Education/Training Required: Moderate-term on-the-job training
- Annual Earnings: $29,780
- Growth: 0.3%
- Annual Job Openings: 6,000
- Self-Employed: 0.0%
- Part-Time: 18.6%

Level of Solitary Work: 62.5 (out of 100)

Level of Contact with Others: 72.5 (out of 100)

Set up, operate, or tend more than one type of cutting or forming machine tool or robot. Inspect workpieces for defects and measure workpieces to determine accuracy of machine operation, using rules, templates, or other measuring instruments.

Observe machine operation to detect workpiece defects or machine malfunctions; adjust machines as necessary. Read blueprints or job orders to determine product specifications and tooling instructions and to plan operational sequences. Set up and operate machines such as lathes, cutters, shears, borers, millers, grinders, presses, drills, and auxiliary machines to make metallic and plastic workpieces. Position, adjust, and secure stock material or workpieces against stops; on arbors; or in chucks, fixtures, or automatic feeding mechanisms manually or by using hoists. Select, install, and adjust alignment of drills, cutters, dies, guides, and holding devices, using templates, measuring instruments, and hand tools. Change worn machine accessories such as cutting tools and brushes, using hand tools. Make minor electrical and mechanical repairs and adjustments to machines and notify supervisors when major service is required. Start machines and turn handwheels or valves to engage feeding, cooling, and lubricating mechanisms. Perform minor machine maintenance, such as oiling or cleaning machines, dies, or workpieces or adding coolant to machine reservoirs. Select the proper coolants and lubricants and start their flow. Remove burrs, sharp edges, rust, or scale from workpieces, using files, hand grinders, wire brushes, or power tools. Instruct other workers in machine setup and operation. Record operational data such as pressure readings, lengths of strokes, feed rates, and speeds. Extract or lift jammed pieces from machines, using fingers, wire hooks, or lift bars. Set machine stops or guides to specified lengths as indicated by scales, rules, or templates. Move controls or mount gears, cams, or templates in machines to set feed rates and cutting speeds, depths, and angles. Compute data such as gear dimensions and machine settings, applying knowledge of shop mathematics. Align layout marks with dies or blades. Measure and mark reference points and cutting lines on workpieces, using traced templates, compasses, and rules.

Personality Type: Realistic. Realistic occupations frequently involve work activities that include practical, hands-on problems and solutions. They often deal with plants; animals; and real-world materials such as

M

wood, tools, and machinery. Many of the occupations require working outside and do not involve a lot of paperwork or working closely with others.

GOE—Interest Area: 13. Manufacturing. **Work Group:** 13.02. Machine Setup and Operation. **Other Jobs in This Work Group:** Crushing, Grinding, and Polishing Machine Setters, Operators, and Tenders; Cutting, Punching, and Press Machine Setters, Operators, and Tenders, Metal and Plastic; Drilling and Boring Machine Tool Setters, Operators, and Tenders, Metal and Plastic; Extruding and Drawing Machine Setters, Operators, and Tenders, Metal and Plastic; Forging Machine Setters, Operators, and Tenders, Metal and Plastic; Grinding, Lapping, Polishing, and Buffing Machine Tool Setters, Operators, and Tenders, Metal and Plastic; Lathe and Turning Machine Tool Setters, Operators, and Tenders, Metal and Plastic; Milling and Planing Machine Setters, Operators, and Tenders, Metal and Plastic; Paper Goods Machine Setters, Operators, and Tenders; Rolling Machine Setters, Operators, and Tenders, Metal and Plastic; Textile Cutting Machine Setters, Operators, and Tenders; Textile Knitting and Weaving Machine Setters, Operators, and Tenders; Textile Winding, Twisting, and Drawing Out Machine Setters, Operators, and Tenders.

Skills—Operation Monitoring: Watching gauges, dials, or other indicators to make sure a machine is working properly. **Repairing:** Repairing machines or systems by using the needed tools. **Equipment Maintenance:** Performing routine maintenance on equipment and determining when and what kind of maintenance is needed. **Quality Control Analysis:** Conducting tests and inspections of products, services, or processes to evaluate quality or performance. **Troubleshooting:** Determining causes of operating errors and deciding what to do about them. **Operation and Control:** Controlling operations of equipment or systems.

Education and Training Programs: Machine Shop Technology/Assistant; Machine Tool Technology/ Machinist. **Related Knowledge/Courses: Mechanical Devices:** Machines and tools, including their

designs, uses, repair, and maintenance. **Production and Processing:** Raw materials, production processes, quality control, costs, and other techniques for maximizing the effective manufacture and distribution of goods. **Design:** Design techniques, tools, and principles involved in production of precision technical plans, blueprints, drawings, and models. **Engineering and Technology:** The practical application of engineering science and technology. This includes applying principles, techniques, procedures, and equipment to the design and production of various goods and services. **Mathematics:** Arithmetic, algebra, geometry, calculus, and statistics and their applications.

Work Environment: Noisy; contaminants; hazardous equipment; minor burns, cuts, bites, or stings; standing; using hands on objects, tools, or controls.

Museum Technicians and Conservators

- Education/Training Required: Bachelor's degree
- Annual Earnings: $34,090
- Growth: 14.1%
- Annual Job Openings: 2,000
- Self-Employed: 9.4%
- Part-Time: 23.4%

Level of Solitary Work: 50.0 (out of 100)

Level of Contact with Others: 61.8 (out of 100)

Prepare specimens, such as fossils, skeletal parts, lace, and textiles, for museum collection and exhibits. May restore documents or install, arrange, and exhibit materials. Install, arrange, assemble, and prepare artifacts for exhibition, ensuring the artifacts' safety, reporting their status and condition, and identifying and correcting any problems with the setup. Coordinate exhibit installations, assisting with design; constructing displays, dioramas, display cases, and models; and ensuring the availability of necessary materials. Determine whether objects need repair and choose the safest and most effective method of repair. Clean objects, such as paper, textiles, wood, metal, glass, rock, pottery, and furniture, using cleansers, solvents, soap solutions, and polishes. Prepare artifacts for storage and shipping. Supervise and work with volunteers. Present public programs and tours. Specialize in particular materials or types of object, such as documents and books, paintings, decorative arts, textiles, metals, or architectural materials. Recommend preservation procedures, such as control of temperature and humidity, to curatorial and building staff. Classify and assign registration numbers to artifacts and supervise inventory control. Direct and supervise curatorial and technical staff in the handling, mounting, care, and storage of art objects. Perform on-site fieldwork, which may involve interviewing people, inspecting and identifying artifacts, note-taking, viewing sites and collections, and repainting exhibition spaces. Repair, restore, and reassemble artifacts, designing and fabricating missing or broken parts, to restore them to their original appearance and prevent deterioration. Prepare reports on the operation of conservation laboratories, documenting the condition of artifacts, treatment options, and the methods of preservation and repair used. Study object documentation or conduct standard chemical and physical tests to ascertain the object's age, composition, original appearance, need for treatment or restoration, and appropriate preservation method. Cut and weld metal sections in reconstruction or renovation of exterior structural sections and accessories of exhibits. Perform tests and examinations to establish storage and conservation requirements, policies, and procedures.

Personality Type: Artistic. Artistic occupations frequently involve working with forms, designs, and patterns. They often require self-expression, and the work can be done without following a clear set of rules.

GOE—Interest Area: 05. Education and Training. **Work Group:** 05.05. Archival and Museum Services. **Other Jobs in This Work Group:** Archivists; Audio-Visual Collections Specialists; Curators.

Skills—Management of Material Resources: Obtaining and seeing to the appropriate use of equipment, facilities, and materials needed to do certain work. **Repairing:** Repairing machines or systems by using the needed tools. **Installation:** Installing equipment, machines, wiring, or programs to meet specifications. **Technology Design:** Generating or adapting equipment and technology to serve user needs. **Equipment Maintenance:** Performing routine maintenance on equipment and determining when and what kind of maintenance is needed. **Time Management:** Managing one's own time and the time of others.

Education and Training Programs: Art History, Criticism, and Conservation; Museology/Museum Studies; Public/Applied History and Archival Administration. **Related Knowledge/Courses: History and Archeology:** Historical events and their causes, indicators, and effects on civilizations and cultures. **Fine Arts:** The theory and techniques required to compose, produce, and perform works of music, dance, visual arts, drama, and sculpture. **Sociology and Anthropology:** Group behavior and dynamics, societal trends and influences, human migrations, ethnicity, and cultures and their history and origins. **Design:** Design techniques, tools, and principles involved in production of precision technical plans, blueprints, drawings, and models. **Clerical Practices:** Administrative and clerical procedures and systems such as word processing, managing files and records, stenography and transcription, designing forms, and other office procedures and terminology. **Education and Training:** Principles and methods for curriculum and training design, teaching and instruction for individuals and groups, and the measurement of training effects.

Work Environment: Indoors; standing; using hands on objects, tools, or controls.

Music Composers and Arrangers

This job can be found in the Part II lists under the title Music Directors and Composers.

- ☺ Education/Training Required: Work experience plus degree
- ☺ Annual Earnings: $34,810
- ☺ Growth: 10.4%
- ☺ Annual Job Openings: 11,000
- ☺ Self-Employed: 44.8%
- ☺ Part-Time: 46.1%

The job openings listed here are shared with Music Directors.

Level of Solitary Work: 60.1 (out of 100)

Level of Contact with Others: 40.0 (out of 100)

Write and transcribe musical scores. Determine voices, instruments, harmonic structures, rhythms, tempos, and tone balances required to achieve the effects desired in a musical composition. Experiment with different sounds and types and pieces of music, using synthesizers and computers as necessary to test and evaluate ideas. Explore and develop musical ideas based on sources such as imagination or sounds in the environment. Fill in details of orchestral sketches, such as adding vocal parts to scores. Rewrite original musical scores in different musical styles by changing rhythms, harmonies, or tempos. Create original musical forms or write within circumscribed musical forms such as sonatas, symphonies, or operas. Use computers and synthesizers to compose, orchestrate, and arrange music. Score compositions so that they are consistent with instrumental and vocal capabilities such as ranges and keys, using knowledge of music theory. Write changes directly into compositions or use computer software to make changes. Transcribe ideas for musical compositions into musical notation, using instruments, pen and paper, or computers. Write music for commercial media, including advertising jingles or film soundtracks. Transpose music from one voice or instrument to another to accommodate particular musicians. Collaborate with other colleagues, such as copyists, to complete final scores. Study films or scripts to determine how musical scores can be used to create desired effects or moods. Accept commissions to create music for special occasions. Write musical scores for orchestras, bands, choral groups, or individual instrumentalists or vocalists, using knowledge of music theory and of instrumental and vocal capabilities. Study original pieces of music to become familiar with them prior to making any changes. Guide musicians during rehearsals, performances, or recording sessions. Copy parts from scores for individual performers. Confer with producers and directors to define the nature and placement of film or television music. Apply elements of music theory to create musical and tonal structures, including harmonies and melodies.

Personality Type: Artistic. Artistic occupations frequently involve working with forms, designs, and patterns. They often require self-expression, and the work can be done without following a clear set of rules.

GOE—Interest Area: 03. Arts and Communication. **Work Group:** 03.07. Music. **Other Jobs in This Work Group:** Music Directors; Music Directors and Composers; Musicians and Singers; Musicians, Instrumental; Singers; Talent Directors.

Skills—None met the criteria.

Education and Training Programs: Conducting; Music Management and Merchandising; Music Performance, General; Music Theory and Composition; Music, Other; Musicology and Ethnomusicology; Religious/Sacred Music; Voice and Opera. **Related Knowledge/Courses: Fine Arts:** The theory and techniques required to compose, produce, and perform works of music, dance, visual arts, drama, and sculpture.

Work Environment: Indoors; sitting.

Music Directors

This job can be found in the Part II lists under the title Music Directors and Composers.

- Education/Training Required: Master's degree
- Annual Earnings: $34,810
- Growth: 10.4%
- Annual Job Openings: 11,000
- Self-Employed: 44.8%
- Part-Time: 46.1%

The job openings listed here are shared with Music Composers and Arrangers.

Level of Solitary Work: 60.1 (out of 100)

Level of Contact with Others: 40.0 (out of 100)

Direct and conduct instrumental or vocal performances by musical groups such as orchestras or choirs. Coordinate and organize tours or hire touring companies to arrange concert dates, venues, accommodations, and transportation for longer tours. Position members within groups to obtain balance among instrumental or vocal sections. Study scores to learn the music in detail and to develop interpretations. Use gestures to shape the music being played, communicating desired tempo, phrasing, tone, color, pitch, volume, and other performance aspects. Collaborate with music librarians to ensure availability of scores. Meet with composers to discuss interpretations of their work. Perform administrative tasks such as applying for grants, developing budgets, negotiating contracts, and designing and printing programs and other promotional materials. Confer with clergy to select music for church services. Plan and implement fundraising and promotional activities. Assign and review staff work in such areas as scoring, arranging, and copying music and vocal coaching. Plan and schedule rehearsals and performances and arrange details such as locations, accompanists, and instrumentalists. Transcribe musical compositions and melodic lines to adapt them to a particular group or to create a particular musical style. Engage services of composers to write scores. Direct groups at rehearsals and live or recorded performances to achieve desired effects such as tonal and harmonic balance dynamics, rhythm, and tempo. Consider such factors as ensemble size and abilities, availability of scores, and the need for musical variety to select music to be performed. Conduct guest soloists in addition to ensemble members. Audition and select performers for musical presentations. Meet with soloists and concertmasters to discuss and prepare for performances.

Personality Type: Artistic. Artistic occupations frequently involve working with forms, designs, and patterns. They often require self-expression, and the work can be done without following a clear set of rules.

GOE—Interest Area: 03. Arts and Communication. **Work Group:** 03.07. Music. **Other Jobs in This Work Group:** Music Composers and Arrangers; Music Directors and Composers; Musicians and Singers; Musicians, Instrumental; Singers; Talent Directors.

Skills—Management of Personnel Resources: Motivating, developing, and directing people as they work; identifying the best people for the job. **Coordination:** Adjusting actions in relation to others' actions. **Time Management:** Managing one's own time and the time of others. **Systems Analysis:** Determining how a system should work and how changes in conditions, operations, and the environment will affect outcomes. **Operations Analysis:** Analyzing needs and product requirements to create a design. **Instructing:** Teaching others how to do something.

Education and Training Programs: Conducting; Music Management and Merchandising; Music Performance, General; Music Theory and Composition; Music, Other; Musicology and Ethnomusicology; Religious/Sacred Music; Voice and Opera. **Related Knowledge/Courses: Fine Arts:** The theory and techniques required to compose, produce, and perform works of music, dance, visual arts, drama, and sculpture. **Personnel and Human Resources:** Principles and procedures for personnel recruitment, selection, training, compensation and benefits, labor relations and negotiation, and personnel information systems. **Administration and Management:** Business and management principles involved in strategic planning, resource allocation, human resources modeling, leadership technique, production methods, and coordination of people and resources.

Work Environment: Indoors; more often standing than sitting.

Music Directors and Composers

See the descriptions of these jobs:

- Music Composers and Arrangers
- Music Directors

Network Systems and Data Communications Analysts

- Education/Training Required: Bachelor's degree
- Annual Earnings: $61,750
- Growth: 54.6%
- Annual Job Openings: 43,000
- Self-Employed: 19.9%
- Part-Time: 10.0%

Level of Solitary Work: 59.2 (out of 100)

Level of Contact with Others: 75.5 (out of 100)

Analyze, design, test, and evaluate network systems, such as local area networks (LAN); wide area networks (WAN); and Internet, intranet, and other data communications systems. Perform network modeling, analysis, and planning. Research and recommend network and data communications hardware and software. Includes telecommunications specialists who deal with the interfacing of computer and communications equipment. May supervise computer programmers. Maintain needed files by adding and deleting files on the network server and backing up files to guarantee their safety in the event of problems with the network. Monitor system performance and provide security measures, troubleshooting, and maintenance as needed. Assist users to diagnose and solve data communication problems. Set up user accounts, regulating and monitoring file access to ensure confidentiality and proper use. Design and implement systems, network configurations, and network architecture, including hardware and software technology, site locations, and integration of technologies. Maintain the peripherals, such as printers, that are connected to the network. Identify areas of operation that need upgraded equipment such as modems, fiber-optic cables, and telephone wires. Train users in use of equipment. Develop and write procedures for installation, use, and troubleshooting of communications hardware and software. Adapt and modify existing software to meet specific needs. Work with other engineers, systems analysts, programmers, technicians, scientists, and top-level managers in the design, testing, and evaluation of systems. Test and evaluate hardware and software to determine efficiency, reliability, and compatibility with existing system and make purchase recommendations. Read technical manuals and brochures to determine which equipment meets establishment requirements. Consult customers, visit workplaces, or conduct surveys to determine present and future user needs. Visit vendors, attend conferences or training, and study technical journals to keep up with changes in technology.

Personality Type: Investigative. Investigative occupations frequently involve working with ideas and require an extensive amount of thinking. These occupations can involve searching for facts and figuring out problems mentally.

GOE—**Interest Area:** 11. Information Technology. **Work Group:** 11.02. Information Technology Specialties. **Other Jobs in This Work Group:** Computer and Information Scientists, Research; Computer Operators; Computer Programmers; Computer Security Specialists; Computer Software Engineers, Applications; Computer Software Engineers, Systems Software; Computer Support Specialists; Computer Systems Analysts; Computer Systems Engineers/Architects; Database Administrators; Network Designers; Software Quality Assurance Engineers and Testers; Web Administrators; Web Developers.

Skills—Installation: Installing equipment, machines, wiring, or programs to meet specifications. **Systems Analysis:** Determining how a system should work and how changes in conditions, operations, and the environment will affect outcomes. **Technology Design:** Generating or adapting equipment and technology to serve user needs. **Troubleshooting:** Determining causes of operating errors and deciding what to do about them. **Programming:** Writing computer programs for various purposes. **Systems Evaluation:** Identifying measures or indicators of system performance and the actions needed to improve or correct performance relative to the goals of the system.

Education and Training Programs: Computer and Information Sciences, General; Computer and Information Systems Security; Computer Systems Analysis/Analyst Training; Computer Systems Networking and Telecommunications; Information Technology; System, Networking, and LAN/WAN Management/Manager Training. **Related Knowledge/Courses: Telecommunications:** Transmission, broadcasting, switching, control, and operation of telecommunications systems. **Computers and Electronics:** Circuit boards, processors, chips, electronic equipment, and computer hardware and software, including applications and programming. **Customer and Personal Service:** Principles and processes for providing customer and personal services. This includes customer needs assessment, meeting quality standards for services, and evaluation of cus-

tomer satisfaction. **Engineering and Technology:** The practical application of engineering science and technology. This includes applying principles, techniques, procedures, and equipment to the design and production of various goods and services. **Education and Training:** Principles and methods for curriculum and training design, teaching and instruction for individuals and groups, and the measurement of training effects. **Design:** Design techniques, tools, and principles involved in production of precision technical plans, blueprints, drawings, and models.

Work Environment: Indoors; sitting.

Nuclear Equipment Operation Technicians

This job can be found in the Part II lists under the title Nuclear Technicians.

- ◎ Education/Training Required: Associate degree
- ◎ Annual Earnings: $61,120
- ◎ Growth: 13.7%
- ◎ Annual Job Openings: 1,000
- ◎ Self-Employed: 0.0%
- ◎ Part-Time: 22.7%

The job openings listed here are shared with Nuclear Monitoring Technicians.

Level of Solitary Work: 59.2 (out of 100)

Level of Contact with Others: 82.9 (out of 100)

Operate equipment used for the release, control, and utilization of nuclear energy to assist scientists in laboratory and production activities. Follow policies and procedures for radiation workers to ensure personnel safety. Modify, devise, and maintain equipment used in operations. Set control panel switches, according to standard procedures, to route electric power from sources and direct particle beams through injector units. Submit computations to supervisors for review. Calculate equipment operating factors, such as radiation times, dosages, temperatures, gamma intensities, and pressures, using standard formulas and conversion tables. Perform testing, maintenance, repair, and upgrading of accelerator systems. Warn maintenance workers of radiation hazards and direct workers to vacate hazardous areas. Monitor instruments, gauges, and recording devices in control rooms during operation of equipment under direction of nuclear experimenters. Write summaries of activities and record experimental data, such as accelerator performance, systems status, particle beam specification, and beam conditions obtained.

Personality Type: Realistic. Realistic occupations frequently involve work activities that include practical, hands-on problems and solutions. They often deal with plants; animals; and real-world materials such as wood, tools, and machinery. Many of the occupations require working outside and do not involve a lot of paperwork or working closely with others.

GOE—Interest Area: 15. Scientific Research, Engineering, and Mathematics. **Work Group:** 15.05. Physical Science Laboratory Technology. **Other Jobs in This Work Group:** Chemical Technicians; Nuclear Technicians.

Skills—Operation Monitoring: Watching gauges, dials, or other indicators to make sure a machine is working properly. **Operation and Control:** Controlling operations of equipment or systems. **Science:** Using scientific rules and methods to solve problems. **Mathematics:** Using mathematics to solve problems. **Equipment Maintenance:** Performing routine maintenance on equipment and determining when and what kind of maintenance is needed. **Quality Control Analysis:** Conducting tests and inspections of products, services, or processes to evaluate quality or performance.

Education and Training Programs: Industrial Radiologic Technology/Technician Training; Nuclear and Industrial Radiologic Technologies/Technician Training, Other; Nuclear Engineering Technology/Technician Training; Nuclear/Nuclear Power Technology/Technician Training; Radiation Protection/Health Physics Technician Training. **Related Knowledge/Courses: Physics:** Physical principles and laws and their interrelationships and applications to understanding fluid, material, and atmospheric dynamics and mechanical, electrical, atomic, and subatomic structures and processes. **Chemistry:** The chemical composition, structure, and properties of substances and of the chemical processes and transformations that they undergo. This includes uses of chemicals and their danger signs, production techniques, and disposal methods. **Engineering and Technology:** The practical application of engineering science and technology. This includes applying principles, techniques, procedures, and equipment to the design and production of various goods and services. **Public Safety and Security:** Relevant equipment, policies, procedures, and strategies to promote effective local, state, or national security operations for the protection of people, data, property, and institutions. **Mechanical Devices:** Machines and tools, including their designs, uses, repair, and maintenance. **Telecommunications:** Transmission, broadcasting, switching, control, and operation of telecommunications systems.

Work Environment: Indoors; noisy; very hot or cold; radiation; hazardous conditions; hazardous equipment.

Nuclear Monitoring Technicians

This job can be found in the Part II lists under the title Nuclear Technicians.

- Education/Training Required: Associate degree
- Annual Earnings: $61,120
- Growth: 13.7%
- Annual Job Openings: 1,000
- Self-Employed: 0.0%
- Part-Time: 22.7%

The job openings listed here are shared with Nuclear Equipment Operation Technicians.

Level of Solitary Work: 59.2 (out of 100)

Level of Contact with Others: 82.9 (out of 100)

Collect and test samples to monitor results of nuclear experiments and contamination of humans, facilities, and environment. Calculate safe radiation exposure times for personnel, using plant contamination readings and prescribed safe levels of radiation. Provide initial response to abnormal events and to alarms from radiation monitoring equipment. Monitor personnel in order to determine the amounts and intensities of radiation exposure. Inform supervisors when individual exposures or area radiation levels approach maximum permissible limits. Instruct personnel in radiation safety procedures and demonstrate use of protective clothing and equipment. Determine intensities and types of radiation in work areas, equipment, and materials, using radiation detectors and other instruments. Collect samples of air, water, gases, and solids to determine radioactivity levels of contamination. Set up equipment that automatically detects area radiation deviations and test detection equipment to ensure its accuracy. Determine or recommend radioactive decontamination procedures according to the size and nature of equipment and the degree of contamination. Decontaminate objects by cleaning with soap or solvents or by abrading with wire brushes, buffing wheels, or sandblasting machines. Place radioactive waste, such as sweepings and broken sample bottles, into containers for disposal. Calibrate and maintain chemical instrumentation sensing elements and sampling system equipment, using calibration instruments and hand tools. Place irradiated nuclear fuel materials in environmental chambers for testing and observe reactions through cell windows. Enter data into computers in order to record characteristics of nuclear events and locating coordinates of particles. Operate manipulators from outside cells to move specimens into and out of shielded containers, to remove specimens from cells, or to place specimens on benches or equipment workstations. Prepare reports describing contamination tests, material and equipment decontaminated, and methods used in decontamination processes. Confer with scientists directing projects to determine significant events to monitor during tests. Immerse samples in chemical compounds to prepare them for testing.

Personality Type: Realistic. Realistic occupations frequently involve work activities that include practical, hands-on problems and solutions. They often deal with plants; animals; and real-world materials such as wood, tools, and machinery. Many of the occupations require working outside and do not involve a lot of paperwork or working closely with others.

GOE—Interest Area: 07. Government and Public Administration. **Work Group:** 07.03. Regulations Enforcement. **Other Jobs in This Work Group:** Agricultural Inspectors; Aviation Inspectors; Compliance Officers, Except Agriculture, Construction, Health and Safety, and Transportation; Construction and Building Inspectors; Environmental Compliance Inspectors; Equal Opportunity Representatives and Officers; Financial Examiners; Fire Inspectors; Fish and Game Wardens; Forest Fire Inspectors and Prevention Specialists; Freight and Cargo Inspectors; Government Property Inspectors and Investigators; Immigration and Customs Inspectors; Licensing Examiners and Inspectors; Occupational Health and

Safety Specialists; Occupational Health and Safety Technicians; Tax Examiners, Collectors, and Revenue Agents; Transportation Vehicle, Equipment, and Systems Inspectors, Except Aviation.

Skills—Science: Using scientific rules and methods to solve problems. **Operation Monitoring:** Watching gauges, dials, or other indicators to make sure a machine is working properly. **Equipment Maintenance:** Performing routine maintenance on equipment and determining when and what kind of maintenance is needed. **Mathematics:** Using mathematics to solve problems. **Systems Analysis:** Determining how a system should work and how changes in conditions, operations, and the environment will affect outcomes. **Operation and Control:** Controlling operations of equipment or systems.

Education and Training Programs: Industrial Radiologic Technology/Technician Training; Nuclear and Industrial Radiologic Technologies/Technician Training, Other; Nuclear Engineering Technology/Technician Training; Nuclear/Nuclear Power Technology/Technician Training; Radiation Protection/Health Physics Technician Training. **Related Knowledge/Courses: Physics:** Physical principles and laws and their interrelationships and applications to understanding fluid, material, and atmospheric dynamics and mechanical, electrical, atomic, and subatomic structures and processes. **Chemistry:** The chemical composition, structure, and properties of substances and of the chemical processes and transformations that they undergo. This includes uses of chemicals and their danger signs, production techniques, and disposal methods. **Public Safety and Security:** Relevant equipment, policies, procedures, and strategies to promote effective local, state, or national security operations for the protection of people, data, property, and institutions. **Engineering and Technology:** The practical application of engineering science and technology. This includes applying principles, techniques, procedures, and equipment to the design and production of various goods and services. **Design:** Design techniques, tools, and principles involved in production of precision technical plans, blueprints, drawings, and mod-

els. **Biology:** Plant and animal organisms and their tissues, cells, functions, interdependencies, and interactions with each other and the environment.

Work Environment: Indoors; noisy; very hot or cold; contaminants; radiation; hazardous conditions.

Nuclear Technicians

See the descriptions of these jobs:

◎ Nuclear Equipment Operation Technicians

◎ Nuclear Monitoring Technicians

Numerical Tool and Process Control Programmers

◎ Education/Training Required: Long-term on-the-job training

◎ Annual Earnings: $41,830

◎ Growth: –1.1%

◎ Annual Job Openings: 2,000

◎ Self-Employed: 0.0%

◎ Part-Time: 0.3%

Level of Solitary Work: 71.7 (out of 100)

Level of Contact with Others: 66.8 (out of 100)

Develop programs to control machining or processing of parts by automatic machine tools, equipment, or systems. Determine the sequence of machine operations and select the proper cutting tools needed to machine workpieces into the desired shapes. Revise programs or tapes to eliminate errors and retest programs to check that problems have been solved. Analyze job orders, drawings, blueprints, specifications, printed circuit board pattern films, and design data to calculate dimensions, tool selection, machine speeds, and feed rates. Determine reference points, machine cutting paths, or hole locations and compute angular and linear dimensions, radii, and curvatures. Observe machines on trial runs or conduct computer simulations to ensure that programs and machinery will function properly and produce items that meet specifications. Compare encoded tapes or computer printouts with original part specifications and blueprints to verify accuracy of instructions. Enter coordinates of hole locations into program memories by depressing pedals or buttons of programmers. Write programs in the language of a machine's controller and store programs on media such as punch tapes, magnetic tapes, or disks. Modify existing programs to enhance efficiency. Enter computer commands to store or retrieve parts patterns, graphic displays, or programs that transfer data to other media. Prepare geometric layouts from graphic displays, using computer-assisted drafting software or drafting instruments and graph paper. Write instruction sheets and cutter lists for a machine's controller to guide setup and encode numerical control tapes. Sort shop orders into groups to maximize materials utilization and minimize machine setup time. Draw machine tool paths on pattern film, using colored markers and following guidelines for tool speed and efficiency. Align and secure pattern film on reference tables of optical programmers and observe enlarger scope views of printed circuit boards.

Personality Type: Realistic. Realistic occupations frequently involve work activities that include practical, hands-on problems and solutions. They often deal with plants; animals; and real-world materials such as wood, tools, and machinery. Many of the occupations require working outside and do not involve a lot of paperwork or working closely with others.

GOE—Interest Area: 13. Manufacturing. **Work Group:** 13.05. Production Machining Technology. **Other Jobs in This Work Group:** Computer-Controlled Machine Tool Operators, Metal and Plastic; Foundry Mold and Coremakers; Lay-Out Workers, Metal and Plastic; Machinists; Model Makers, Metal and Plastic; Patternmakers, Metal and Plastic; Tool and Die Makers; Tool Grinders, Filers, and Sharpeners.

Skills—Programming: Writing computer programs for various purposes. **Installation:** Installing equipment, machines, wiring, or programs to meet specifications. **Mathematics:** Using mathematics to solve problems. **Operation Monitoring:** Watching gauges, dials, or other indicators to make sure a machine is working properly. **Repairing:** Repairing machines or systems by using the needed tools. **Equipment Selection:** Determining the kind of tools and equipment needed to do a job.

Education and Training Programs: Computer Programming/Programmer, General; Data Processing and Data Processing Technology/Technician Training. **Related Knowledge/Courses: Design:** Design techniques, tools, and principles involved in production of precision technical plans, blueprints, drawings, and models. **Mechanical Devices:** Machines and tools, including their designs, uses, repair, and maintenance. **Engineering and Technology:** The practical application of engineering science and technology. This includes applying principles, techniques, procedures, and equipment to the design and production of various goods and services. **Mathematics:** Arithmetic, algebra, geometry, calculus, and statistics and their applications. **Physics:** Physical principles and laws and their interrelationships and applications to understanding fluid, material, and atmospheric dynamics and mechanical, electrical, atomic, and subatomic structures and processes. **Production and Processing:** Raw materials, production processes, quality control, costs, and other techniques for maximizing the effective manufacture and distribution of goods.

Work Environment: Indoors; noisy; contaminants; hazardous equipment; standing; using hands on objects, tools, or controls.

Operating Engineers and Other Construction Equipment Operators

- ◎ Education/Training Required: Moderate-term on-the-job training
- ◎ Annual Earnings: $35,830
- ◎ Growth: 11.6%
- ◎ Annual Job Openings: 37,000
- ◎ Self-Employed: 5.4%
- ◎ Part-Time: 2.9%

Level of Solitary Work: 57.7 (out of 100)

Level of Contact with Others: 72.0 (out of 100)

Operate one or several types of power construction equipment, such as motor graders, bulldozers, scrapers, compressors, pumps, derricks, shovels, tractors, or front-end loaders, to excavate, move, and grade earth; erect structures; or pour concrete or other hard-surface pavement. May repair and maintain equipment in addition to other duties. Learn and follow safety regulations. Take actions to avoid potential hazards and obstructions such as utility lines, other equipment, other workers, and falling objects. Adjust handwheels and depress pedals to control attachments such as blades, buckets, scrapers, and swing booms. Start engines; move throttles, switches, and levers; and depress pedals to operate machines such as bulldozers, trench excavators, road graders, and backhoes. Locate underground services, such as pipes and wires, prior to beginning work. Monitor operations to ensure that health and safety standards are met. Align machines, cutterheads, or depth gauge makers with reference stakes and guidelines or ground or position equipment by following hand signals of other workers. Load and move dirt, rocks, equipment, and materials, using trucks, crawler tractors, power cranes, shovels, graders, and related equipment. Drive and maneuver equipment equipped with blades in successive passes over working areas to remove topsoil, vegetation, and rocks and to distribute and level earth or terrain. Coordinate machine actions with other activities, positioning or moving loads in response to hand or audio signals from crew members. Operate tractors and bulldozers to perform such tasks as clearing land, mixing sludge, trimming backfills, and building roadways and parking lots. Repair and maintain equipment, making emergency adjustments or assisting with major repairs as necessary. Check fuel supplies at sites to ensure adequate availability. Connect hydraulic hoses, belts, mechanical linkages, or power takeoff shafts to tractors. Operate loaders to pull out stumps, rip asphalt or concrete, rough-grade properties, bury refuse, or perform general cleanup. Select and fasten bulldozer blades or other attachments to tractors, using hitches. Test atmosphere for adequate oxygen and explosive conditions when working in confined spaces. Operate compactors, scrapers, and rollers to level, compact, and cover refuse at disposal grounds. Talk to clients and study instructions, plans, and diagrams to establish work requirements.

Personality Type: Realistic. Realistic occupations frequently involve work activities that include practical, hands-on problems and solutions. They often deal with plants; animals; and real-world materials such as wood, tools, and machinery. Many of the occupations require working outside and do not involve a lot of paperwork or working closely with others.

GOE—Interest Area: 02. Architecture and Construction. **Work Group:** 02.04. Construction Crafts. **Other Jobs in This Work Group:** Boilermakers; Brickmasons and Blockmasons; Carpet Installers; Cement Masons and Concrete Finishers; Commercial Divers; Construction Carpenters; Crane and Tower Operators; Drywall and Ceiling Tile Installers; Electricians; Fence Erectors; Floor Layers, Except Carpet, Wood, and Hard Tiles; Floor Sanders and Finishers; Glaziers; Hazardous Materials Removal Workers; Insulation Workers, Floor, Ceiling, and Wall; Insulation Workers, Mechanical; Manufactured Building and Mobile Home Installers; Painters, Construction and Maintenance; Paperhangers; Paving, Surfacing, and Tamping

Equipment Operators; Pile-Driver Operators; Pipe Fitters and Steamfitters; Pipelayers; Plasterers and Stucco Masons; Plumbers; Plumbers, Pipefitters, and Steamfitters; Rail-Track Laying and Maintenance Equipment Operators; Refractory Materials Repairers, Except Brickmasons; Reinforcing Iron and Rebar Workers; Riggers; Roofers; Rough Carpenters; Security and Fire Alarm Systems Installers; Segmental Pavers; Sheet Metal Workers; Stone Cutters and Carvers, Manufacturing; Stonemasons; Structural Iron and Steel Workers; Tapers; Terrazzo Workers and Finishers; Tile and Marble Setters.

Skills—Equipment Maintenance: Performing routine maintenance on equipment and determining when and what kind of maintenance is needed. **Installation:** Installing equipment, machines, wiring, or programs to meet specifications. **Operation Monitoring:** Watching gauges, dials, or other indicators to make sure a machine is working properly. **Operation and Control:** Controlling operations of equipment or systems. **Repairing:** Repairing machines or systems by using the needed tools. **Management of Financial Resources:** Determining how money will be spent to get the work done and accounting for these expenditures.

Education and Training Programs: Construction/Heavy Equipment/Earthmoving Equipment Operation; Mobile Crane Operation/Operator Training. **Related Knowledge/Courses: Building and Construction:** The materials, methods, and tools involved in the construction or repair of houses, buildings, or other structures such as highways and roads. **Mechanical Devices:** Machines and tools, including their designs, uses, repair, and maintenance. **Engineering and Technology:** The practical application of engineering science and technology. This includes applying principles, techniques, procedures, and equipment to the design and production of various goods and services. **Design:** Design techniques, tools, and principles involved in production of precision technical plans, blueprints, drawings, and models. **Production and Processing:** Raw materials, production processes, quality control, costs, and other techniques for maximizing the effective manufacture and distribution of goods. **Public Safety and Security:** Relevant equipment, policies, procedures, and strategies to promote effective local, state, or national security operations for the protection of people, data, property, and institutions.

Work Environment: Outdoors; noisy; very hot or cold; contaminants; whole-body vibration; using hands on objects, tools, or controls.

Operations Research Analysts

- Education/Training Required: Master's degree
- Annual Earnings: $62,180
- Growth: 8.4%
- Annual Job Openings: 7,000
- Self-Employed: 1.2%
- Part-Time: 5.4%

Level of Solitary Work: 62.5 (out of 100)

Level of Contact with Others: 57.2 (out of 100)

Formulate and apply mathematical modeling and other optimizing methods, using a computer to develop and interpret information that assists management with decision making, policy formulation, or other managerial functions. May develop related software, service, or products. Frequently concentrates on collecting and analyzing data and developing decision support software. May develop and supply optimal time, cost, or logistics networks for program evaluation, review, or implementation. Formulate mathematical or simulation models of problems, relating constants and variables, restrictions, alternatives, and conflicting objectives and their numerical parameters. Collaborate with others in the organization to ensure successful implementation of chosen problem solutions. Analyze information obtained from management in order to conceptualize and define operational problems.

Perform validation and testing of models to ensure adequacy; reformulate models as necessary. Collaborate with senior managers and decision-makers to identify and solve a variety of problems and to clarify management objectives. Define data requirements; then gather and validate information, applying judgment and statistical tests. Study and analyze information about alternative courses of action in order to determine which plan will offer the best outcomes. Prepare management reports defining and evaluating problems and recommending solutions. Break systems into their component parts, assign numerical values to each component, and examine the mathematical relationships between them. Specify manipulative or computational methods to be applied to models. Observe the current system in operation and gather and analyze information about each of the parts of component problems, using a variety of sources. Design, conduct, and evaluate experimental operational models in cases where models cannot be developed from existing data. Develop and apply time and cost networks in order to plan, control, and review large projects. Develop business methods and procedures, including accounting systems, file systems, office systems, logistics systems, and production schedules.

Personality Type: Investigative. Investigative occupations frequently involve working with ideas and require an extensive amount of thinking. These occupations can involve searching for facts and figuring out problems mentally.

GOE—Interest Area: 04. Business and Administration. **Work Group:** 04.05. Accounting, Auditing, and Analytical Support. **Other Jobs in This Work Group:** Accountants; Accountants and Auditors; Auditors; Budget Analysts; Industrial Engineering Technicians; Logisticians; Management Analysts.

Skills—Programming: Writing computer programs for various purposes. **Systems Analysis:** Determining how a system should work and how changes in conditions, operations, and the environment will affect outcomes. **Operations Analysis:** Analyzing needs and product requirements to create a design. **Mathematics:** Using mathematics to solve problems. **Systems Evaluation:** Identifying measures or indicators of system performance and the actions needed to improve or correct performance relative to the goals of the system. **Science:** Using scientific rules and methods to solve problems.

Education and Training Programs: Educational Evaluation and Research; Educational Statistics and Research Methods; Management Science, General; Management Sciences and Quantitative Methods, Other; Operations Research. **Related Knowledge/Courses: Mathematics:** Arithmetic, algebra, geometry, calculus, and statistics and their applications. **Engineering and Technology:** The practical application of engineering science and technology. This includes applying principles, techniques, procedures, and equipment to the design and production of various goods and services. **Computers and Electronics:** Circuit boards, processors, chips, electronic equipment, and computer hardware and software, including applications and programming. **Production and Processing:** Raw materials, production processes, quality control, costs, and other techniques for maximizing the effective manufacture and distribution of goods. **Economics and Accounting:** Economic and accounting principles and practices, the financial markets, banking, and the analysis and reporting of financial data. **Administration and Management:** Business and management principles involved in strategic planning, resource allocation, human resources modeling, leadership technique, production methods, and coordination of people and resources.

Work Environment: Indoors; sitting.

Outdoor Power Equipment and Other Small Engine Mechanics

- ◎ Education/Training Required: Moderate-term on-the-job training
- ◎ Annual Earnings: $25,810
- ◎ Growth: 14.0%
- ◎ Annual Job Openings: 10,000
- ◎ Self-Employed: 19.2%
- ◎ Part-Time: 13.2%

Level of Solitary Work: 56.3 (out of 100)

Level of Contact with Others: 11.8 (out of 100)

Diagnose, adjust, repair, or overhaul small engines used to power lawn mowers, chain saws, and related equipment. Sell parts and equipment. Show customers how to maintain equipment. Record repairs made, time spent, and parts used. Grind, ream, rebore, and retap parts to obtain specified clearances, using grinders, lathes, taps, reamers, boring machines, and micrometers. Test and inspect engines to determine malfunctions, to locate missing and broken parts, and to verify repairs, using diagnostic instruments. Replace motors. Repair or replace defective parts such as magnetos, water pumps, gears, pistons, and carburetors, using hand tools. Remove engines from equipment and position and bolt engines to repair stands. Perform routine maintenance such as cleaning and oiling parts, honing cylinders, and tuning ignition systems. Obtain problem descriptions from customers and prepare cost estimates for repairs. Dismantle engines, using hand tools, and examine parts for defects. Adjust points, valves, carburetors, distributors, and spark plug gaps, using feeler gauges. Repair and maintain gasoline engines used to power equipment such as portable saws, lawn mowers, generators, and compressors. Reassemble engines after repair or maintenance work is complete.

Personality Type: Realistic. Realistic occupations frequently involve work activities that include practical, hands-on problems and solutions. They often deal with plants; animals; and real-world materials such as wood, tools, and machinery. Many of the occupations require working outside and do not involve a lot of paperwork or working closely with others.

GOE—Interest Area: 13. Manufacturing. **Work Group:** 13.14. Vehicle and Facility Mechanical Work. **Other Jobs in This Work Group:** Aircraft Mechanics and Service Technicians; Aircraft Structure, Surfaces, Rigging, and Systems Assemblers; Automotive Body and Related Repairers; Automotive Glass Installers and Repairers; Automotive Master Mechanics; Automotive Service Technicians and Mechanics; Automotive Specialty Technicians; Bus and Truck Mechanics and Diesel Engine Specialists; Farm Equipment Mechanics; Fiberglass Laminators and Fabricators; Mobile Heavy Equipment Mechanics, Except Engines; Motorboat Mechanics; Motorcycle Mechanics; Rail Car Repairers; Recreational Vehicle Service Technicians; Tire Repairers and Changers.

Skills—Repairing: Repairing machines or systems by using the needed tools. **Equipment Maintenance:** Performing routine maintenance on equipment and determining when and what kind of maintenance is needed. **Troubleshooting:** Determining causes of operating errors and deciding what to do about them. **Installation:** Installing equipment, machines, wiring, or programs to meet specifications. **Quality Control Analysis:** Conducting tests and inspections of products, services, or processes to evaluate quality or performance. **Operation and Control:** Controlling operations of equipment or systems.

Education and Training Program: Small Engine Mechanics and Repair Technology/Technician Training. **Related Knowledge/Courses: Mechanical Devices:** Machines and tools, including their designs, uses, repair, and maintenance. **Engineering and Technology:** The practical application of engineering science and technology. This includes applying principles, techniques, procedures, and equipment to the design and production of various goods and services.

Work Environment: Indoors; contaminants; hazardous equipment; standing; kneeling, crouching, stooping, or crawling; using hands on objects, tools, or controls.

Packaging and Filling Machine Operators and Tenders

- Education/Training Required: Short-term on-the-job training
- Annual Earnings: $22,930
- Growth: 2.3%
- Annual Job Openings: 80,000
- Self-Employed: 0.1%
- Part-Time: 6.7%

Level of Solitary Work: 68.8 (out of 100)

Level of Contact with Others: 67.8 (out of 100)

Operate or tend machines to prepare industrial or consumer products for storage or shipment. Includes cannery workers who pack food products. Observe machine operations to ensure quality and conformity of filled or packaged products to standards. Adjust machine components and machine tension and pressure according to size or processing angle of product. Tend or operate machine that packages product. Remove finished packaged items from machine and separate rejected items. Regulate machine flow, speed, or temperature. Stop or reset machines when malfunctions occur, clear machine jams, and report malfunctions to a supervisor. Secure finished packaged items by hand-tying, sewing, gluing, stapling, or attaching fastener. Stock and sort product for packaging or filling machine operation and replenish packaging supplies, such as wrapping paper, plastic sheet, boxes, cartons, glue, ink, or labels. Inspect and remove defective products and packaging material. Clean and remove damaged or otherwise inferior materials to prepare raw products for processing. Sort, grade, weigh, and inspect products, verifying and adjusting product weight or measurement to meet specifications. Clean, oil, and make minor adjustments or repairs to machinery and equipment, such as opening valves or setting guides. Monitor the production line, watching for problems such as pile-ups, jams, or glue that isn't sticking properly. Stack finished packaged items or wrap protective material around each item and pack the items in cartons or containers. Start machine by engaging controls. Count and record finished and rejected packaged items. Package the product in the form in which it will be sent out, for example, filling bags with flour from a chute or spout. Supply materials to spindles, conveyors, hoppers, or other feeding devices and unload packaged product. Attach identification labels to finished packaged items or cut stencils and stencil information on containers, such as lot numbers or shipping destinations. Clean packaging containers, line and pad crates, or assemble cartons to prepare for product packing.

Personality Type: Realistic. Realistic occupations frequently involve work activities that include practical, hands-on problems and solutions. They often deal with plants; animals; and real-world materials such as wood, tools, and machinery. Many of the occupations require working outside and do not involve a lot of paperwork or working closely with others.

GOE—Interest Area: 13. Manufacturing. **Work Group:** 13.03. Production Work, Assorted Materials Processing. **Other Jobs in This Work Group:** Bakers; Cementing and Gluing Machine Operators and Tenders; Chemical Equipment Operators and Tenders; Cleaning, Washing, and Metal Pickling Equipment Operators and Tenders; Coating, Painting, and Spraying Machine Setters, Operators, and Tenders; Cooling and Freezing Equipment Operators and Tenders; Cutting and Slicing Machine Setters, Operators, and Tenders; Extruding and Forming Machine Setters, Operators, and Tenders, Synthetic and Glass Fibers; Extruding, Forming, Pressing, and Compacting Machine Setters, Operators, and Tenders; Food and Tobacco Roasting,

Baking, and Drying Machine Operators and Tenders; Food Batchmakers; Food Cooking Machine Operators and Tenders; Furnace, Kiln, Oven, Drier, and Kettle Operators and Tenders; Heat Treating Equipment Setters, Operators, and Tenders, Metal and Plastic; Helpers—Production Workers; Meat, Poultry, and Fish Cutters and Trimmers; Metal-Refining Furnace Operators and Tenders; Mixing and Blending Machine Setters, Operators, and Tenders; Plating and Coating Machine Setters, Operators, and Tenders, Metal and Plastic; Pourers and Casters, Metal; Sawing Machine Setters, Operators, and Tenders, Wood; Separating, Filtering, Clarifying, Precipitating, and Still Machine Setters, Operators, and Tenders; Sewing Machine Operators; Shoe Machine Operators and Tenders; Slaughterers and Meat Packers; Team Assemblers; Textile Bleaching and Dyeing Machine Operators and Tenders; Tire Builders; Woodworking Machine Setters, Operators, and Tenders, Except Sawing.

Skills—Equipment Maintenance: Performing routine maintenance on equipment and determining when and what kind of maintenance is needed. **Operation and Control:** Controlling operations of equipment or systems. **Operation Monitoring:** Watching gauges, dials, or other indicators to make sure a machine is working properly. **Quality Control Analysis:** Conducting tests and inspections of products, services, or processes to evaluate quality or performance. **Repairing:** Repairing machines or systems by using the needed tools. **Troubleshooting:** Determining causes of operating errors and deciding what to do about them.

Education and Training Program: No related CIP programs; this job is learned through informal short-term on-the-job training. **Related Knowledge/ Courses: Production and Processing:** Raw materials, production processes, quality control, costs, and other techniques for maximizing the effective manufacture and distribution of goods. **Mechanical Devices:** Machines and tools, including their designs, uses, repair, and maintenance. **Sociology and Anthropology:** Group behavior and dynamics, societal trends and influences, human migrations, ethnicity, and cultures and their history and origins. **Psychology:** Human behavior and performance; individual differences in ability, personality, and interests; learning and motivation; psychological research methods; and the assessment and treatment of behavioral and affective disorders. **Public Safety and Security:** Relevant equipment, policies, procedures, and strategies to promote effective local, state, or national security operations for the protection of people, data, property, and institutions. **Education and Training:** Principles and methods for curriculum and training design, teaching and instruction for individuals and groups, and the measurement of training effects.

Work Environment: Noisy; contaminants; hazardous equipment; standing; using hands on objects, tools, or controls; repetitive motions.

Painters, Construction and Maintenance

- Education/Training Required: Moderate-term on-the-job training
- Annual Earnings: $30,800
- Growth: 12.6%
- Annual Job Openings: 102,000
- Self-Employed: 44.6%
- Part-Time: 15.0%

Level of Solitary Work: 56.3 (out of 100)

Level of Contact with Others: 68.3 (out of 100)

Paint walls, equipment, buildings, bridges, and other structural surfaces, using brushes, rollers, and spray guns. May remove old paint to prepare surface prior to painting. May mix colors or oils to obtain desired color or consistency. Cover surfaces with dropcloths or masking tape and paper to protect surfaces during painting. Fill cracks, holes, and joints with caulk, putty, plaster, or other fillers, using caulking guns or putty knives. Apply primers or sealers to

prepare new surfaces, such as bare wood or metal, for finish coats. Apply paint, stain, varnish, enamel, and other finishes to equipment, buildings, bridges, and other structures, using brushes, spray guns, or rollers. Calculate amounts of required materials and estimate costs, based on surface measurements and work orders. Read work orders or receive instructions from supervisors or homeowners to determine work requirements. Erect scaffolding and swing gates or set up ladders to work above ground level. Remove fixtures such as pictures, door knobs, lamps, and electric switch covers prior to painting. Wash and treat surfaces with oil, turpentine, mildew remover, or other preparations and sand rough spots to ensure that finishes will adhere properly. Mix and match colors of paint, stain, or varnish with oil and thinning and drying additives to obtain desired colors and consistencies. Remove old finishes by stripping, sanding, wire-brushing, burning, or using water or abrasive blasting. Select and purchase tools and finishes for surfaces to be covered, considering durability, ease of handling, methods of application, and customers' wishes. Smooth surfaces, using sandpaper, scrapers, brushes, steel wool, or sanding machines. Polish final coats to specified finishes. Use special finishing techniques such as sponging, ragging, layering, or faux finishing. Waterproof buildings, using waterproofers and caulking. Spray or brush hot plastics or pitch onto surfaces. Cut stencils and brush and spray lettering and decorations on surfaces. Bake finishes on painted and enameled articles, using baking ovens.

Personality Type: Realistic. Realistic occupations frequently involve work activities that include practical, hands-on problems and solutions. They often deal with plants; animals; and real-world materials such as wood, tools, and machinery. Many of the occupations require working outside and do not involve a lot of paperwork or working closely with others.

GOE—Interest Area: 02. Architecture and Construction. **Work Group:** 02.04. Construction Crafts. **Other Jobs in This Work Group:** Boilermakers; Brickmasons and Blockmasons; Carpet Installers; Cement Masons and Concrete Finishers; Commercial Divers; Construction Carpenters; Crane and Tower Operators; Drywall and Ceiling Tile Installers; Electricians; Fence Erectors; Floor Layers, Except Carpet, Wood, and Hard Tiles; Floor Sanders and Finishers; Glaziers; Hazardous Materials Removal Workers; Insulation Workers, Floor, Ceiling, and Wall; Insulation Workers, Mechanical; Manufactured Building and Mobile Home Installers; Operating Engineers and Other Construction Equipment Operators; Paperhangers; Paving, Surfacing, and Tamping Equipment Operators; Pile-Driver Operators; Pipe Fitters and Steamfitters; Pipelayers; Plasterers and Stucco Masons; Plumbers; Plumbers, Pipefitters, and Steamfitters; Rail-Track Laying and Maintenance Equipment Operators; Refractory Materials Repairers, Except Brickmasons; Reinforcing Iron and Rebar Workers; Riggers; Roofers; Rough Carpenters; Security and Fire Alarm Systems Installers; Segmental Pavers; Sheet Metal Workers; Stone Cutters and Carvers, Manufacturing; Stonemasons; Structural Iron and Steel Workers; Tapers; Terrazzo Workers and Finishers; Tile and Marble Setters.

Skills—Equipment Maintenance: Performing routine maintenance on equipment and determining when and what kind of maintenance is needed. **Management of Material Resources:** Obtaining and seeing to the appropriate use of equipment, facilities, and materials needed to do certain work. **Management of Personnel Resources:** Motivating, developing, and directing people as they work; identifying the best people for the job. **Repairing:** Repairing machines or systems by using the needed tools. **Equipment Selection:** Determining the kind of tools and equipment needed to do a job. **Monitoring:** Monitoring or assessing your own performance or that of other individuals or organizations to make improvements or take corrective action.

Education and Training Program: Painting/Painter and Wall Coverer Training. **Related Knowledge/ Courses: Design:** Design techniques, tools, and principles involved in production of precision technical plans, blueprints, drawings, and models. **Transportation:** Principles and methods for moving people or goods by air, rail, sea, or road, including the relative costs and benefits. **Building and Construction:** The materials, methods, and tools involved in the construction or repair of houses, buildings, or other structures such as highways and roads. **Customer and Personal Service:** Principles and processes for providing customer and personal services. This includes customer needs assessment, meeting quality standards for services, and evaluation of customer satisfaction. **Production and Processing:** Raw materials, production processes, quality control, costs, and other techniques for maximizing the effective manufacture and distribution of goods. **Administration and Management:** Business and management principles involved in strategic planning, resource allocation, human resources modeling, leadership technique, production methods, and coordination of people and resources.

Work Environment: Contaminants; standing; climbing ladders, scaffolds, or poles; using hands on objects, tools, or controls; bending or twisting the body; repetitive motions.

Painters, Transportation Equipment

- ◉ Education/Training Required: Long-term on-the-job training
- ◉ Annual Earnings: $34,840
- ◉ Growth: 14.1%
- ◉ Annual Job Openings: 10,000
- ◉ Self-Employed: 5.4%
- ◉ Part-Time: 5.7%

Level of Solitary Work: 65.5 (out of 100)

Level of Contact with Others: 70.0 (out of 100)

Operate or tend painting machines to paint surfaces of transportation equipment, such as automobiles, buses, trucks, trains, boats, and airplanes. Dispose of hazardous waste in an appropriate manner. Select paint according to company requirements and match colors of paint following specified color charts. Mix paints to match color specifications or vehicles' original colors; then stir and thin the paints, using spatulas or power mixing equipment. Remove grease, dirt, paint, and rust from vehicle surfaces in preparation for paint application, using abrasives, solvents, brushes, blowtorches, washing tanks, or sandblasters. Pour paint into spray guns and adjust nozzles and paint mixes to get the proper paint flow and coating thickness. Monitor painting operations to identify flaws such as blisters and streaks so that their causes can be corrected. Sand vehicle surfaces between coats of paint or primer to remove flaws and enhance adhesion for subsequent coats. Disassemble, clean, and reassemble sprayers and power equipment, using solvents, wire brushes, and cloths for cleaning duties. Remove accessories from vehicles, such as chrome or mirrors, and mask other surfaces with tape or paper to protect them from paint. Spray prepared surfaces with specified amounts of primers and decorative or finish coatings. Allow the sprayed product to dry and then touch up any spots that may have been missed. Apply rust-resistant undercoats and caulk and seal seams. Select the correct spray gun system for the material being applied. Apply primer over any repairs made to vehicle surfaces. Adjust controls on infrared ovens, heat lamps, portable ventilators, and exhaust units to speed the drying of vehicles between coats. Fill small dents and scratches with body fillers and smooth surfaces to prepare vehicles for painting. Apply designs, lettering, or other identifying or decorative items to finished products, using paint brushes or paint sprayers. Paint by hand areas that cannot be reached with a spray gun or those that need retouching, using brushes. Sand the final finish and apply sealer once a vehicle has dried properly. Buff and wax the finished paintwork. Lay out logos, symbols, or designs on painted surfaces according to blueprint specifications, using measuring instruments, stencils, and patterns.

Personality Type: Realistic. Realistic occupations frequently involve work activities that include practical, hands-on problems and solutions. They often deal with plants; animals; and real-world materials such as wood, tools, and machinery. Many of the occupations require working outside and do not involve a lot of paperwork or working closely with others.

GOE—Interest Area: 13. Manufacturing. **Work Group:** 13.09. Hands-On Work, Assorted Materials. **Other Jobs in This Work Group:** Coil Winders, Tapers, and Finishers; Cutters and Trimmers, Hand; Fabric and Apparel Patternmakers; Glass Blowers, Molders, Benders, and Finishers; Grinding and Polishing Workers, Hand; Molding and Casting Workers; Painting, Coating, and Decorating Workers; Sewers, Hand.

Skills—Repairing: Repairing machines or systems by using the needed tools. **Equipment Maintenance:** Performing routine maintenance on equipment and determining when and what kind of maintenance is needed. **Monitoring:** Monitoring or assessing your own performance or that of other individuals or organizations to make improvements or take corrective action. **Technology Design:** Generating or adapting equipment and technology to serve user needs. **Operation and Control:** Controlling operations of equipment or systems. **Coordination:** Adjusting actions in relation to others' actions.

Education and Training Program: Autobody/Collision and Repair Technology/Technician Training. **Related Knowledge/Courses: Chemistry:** The chemical composition, structure, and properties of substances and of the chemical processes and transformations that they undergo. This includes uses of chemicals and their danger signs, production techniques, and disposal methods. **Production and Processing:** Raw materials, production processes, quality control, costs, and other techniques for maximizing the effective manufacture and distribution of goods. **Mechanical Devices:** Machines and tools, including their designs, uses, repair, and maintenance.

Work Environment: Noisy; contaminants; hazardous conditions; standing; using hands on objects, tools, or controls; repetitive motions.

Paper Goods Machine Setters, Operators, and Tenders

- Education/Training Required: Moderate-term on-the-job training
- Annual Earnings: $31,160
- Growth: 2.4%
- Annual Job Openings: 15,000
- Self-Employed: 0.7%
- Part-Time: 4.1%

Level of Solitary Work: 65.5 (out of 100)

Level of Contact with Others: 58.2 (out of 100)

Set up, operate, or tend paper goods machines that perform a variety of functions, such as converting, sawing, corrugating, banding, wrapping, boxing, stitching, forming, or sealing paper or paperboard sheets into products. Examine completed work to detect defects and verify conformance to work orders and adjust machinery as necessary to correct production problems. Start machines and move controls to regulate tension on pressure rolls, to synchronize speed of machine components, and to adjust temperatures of glue or paraffin. Adjust guide assemblies, forming bars, and folding mechanisms according to specifications, using hand tools. Install attachments to machines for gluing, folding, printing, or cutting. Measure, space, and set saw blades, cutters, and perforators according to product specifications. Observe operation of various machines to detect and correct machine malfunctions such as improper forming, glue flow, or pasteboard tension. Place rolls of paper or cardboard on machine feedtracks and thread paper through gluing, coating, and slitting rollers. Stamp products with information such as dates, using hand stamps or automatic stamping devices. Fill glue and paraffin reservoirs and position rollers to dispense glue onto paperboard. Cut products to specified dimensions, using hand or power cutters. Monitor finished cartons as they drop from forming machines into rotating hoppers and then into gravity feed chutes to prevent jamming. Disassemble machines to maintain, repair, or replace broken or worn parts, using hand or power tools. Remove finished cores and stack or place them on conveyors for transfer to other work areas. Lift tote boxes of finished cartons and dump cartons into feed hoppers. Load automatic stapling mechanisms.

Personality Type: Realistic. Realistic occupations frequently involve work activities that include practical, hands-on problems and solutions. They often deal with plants; animals; and real-world materials such as wood, tools, and machinery. Many of the occupations require working outside and do not involve a lot of paperwork or working closely with others.

GOE—Interest Area: 13. Manufacturing. **Work Group:** 13.02. Machine Setup and Operation. **Other Jobs in This Work Group:** Crushing, Grinding, and Polishing Machine Setters, Operators, and Tenders; Cutting, Punching, and Press Machine Setters, Operators, and Tenders, Metal and Plastic; Drilling and Boring Machine Tool Setters, Operators, and Tenders, Metal and Plastic; Extruding and Drawing Machine Setters, Operators, and Tenders, Metal and Plastic; Forging Machine Setters, Operators, and Tenders, Metal and Plastic; Grinding, Lapping, Polishing, and Buffing Machine Tool Setters, Operators, and Tenders, Metal and Plastic; Lathe and Turning Machine Tool Setters, Operators, and Tenders, Metal and Plastic; Milling and Planing Machine Setters, Operators, and Tenders, Metal and Plastic; Multiple Machine Tool Setters, Operators, and Tenders, Metal and Plastic; Rolling Machine Setters, Operators, and Tenders, Metal and Plastic; Textile Cutting Machine Setters, Operators, and Tenders; Textile Knitting and Weaving Machine Setters, Operators, and Tenders; Textile Winding, Twisting, and Drawing Out Machine Setters, Operators, and Tenders.

Skills—Operation Monitoring: Watching gauges, dials, or other indicators to make sure a machine is working properly. **Operation and Control:**

Controlling operations of equipment or systems. **Equipment Maintenance:** Performing routine maintenance on equipment and determining when and what kind of maintenance is needed. **Repairing:** Repairing machines or systems by using the needed tools. **Troubleshooting:** Determining causes of operating errors and deciding what to do about them. **Quality Control Analysis:** Conducting tests and inspections of products, services, or processes to evaluate quality or performance.

Education and Training Programs: No related CIP programs; this job is learned through informal moderate-term on-the-job training. **Related Knowledge/Courses: Production and Processing:** Raw materials, production processes, quality control, costs, and other techniques for maximizing the effective manufacture and distribution of goods. **Mechanical Devices:** Machines and tools, including their designs, uses, repair, and maintenance. **Engineering and Technology:** The practical application of engineering science and technology. This includes applying principles, techniques, procedures, and equipment to the design and production of various goods and services.

Work Environment: Noisy; contaminants; standing; walking and running; using hands on objects, tools, or controls; repetitive motions.

Paperhangers

- Education/Training Required: Moderate-term on-the-job training
- Annual Earnings: $33,450
- Growth: 3.2%
- Annual Job Openings: 3,000
- Self-Employed: 43.9%
- Part-Time: 4.2%

Level of Solitary Work: 53.0 (out of 100)

Level of Contact with Others: 11.8 (out of 100)

Cover interior walls and ceilings of rooms with decorative wallpaper or fabric or attach advertising posters on surfaces such as walls and billboards. Duties include removing old materials from surface to be papered. Smooth rough spots on walls and ceilings, using sandpaper. Place strips or sections of paper on surfaces, aligning section edges and patterns. Staple or tack advertising posters onto fences, walls, billboards, or poles. Apply acetic acid to damp plaster to prevent lime from bleeding through paper. Trim excess material at ceilings or baseboards, using knives. Smooth strips or sections of paper with brushes or rollers to remove wrinkles and bubbles and to smooth joints. Set up equipment such as pasteboards and scaffolds. Remove paint, varnish, dirt, and grease from surfaces, using paint remover and water-soda solutions. Remove old paper, using water, steam machines, or solvents and scrapers. Trim rough edges from strips, using straightedges and trimming knives. Mix paste, using paste powder and water, and brush paste onto surfaces. Apply thinned glue to waterproof porous surfaces, using brushes, rollers, or pasting machines. Check finished wallcoverings for proper alignment, pattern matching, and neatness of seams. Apply adhesives to the backs of paper strips, using brushes, or dunk strips of prepasted wallcovering in water, wiping off any excess adhesive. Cover interior walls and ceilings of rooms with decorative wallpaper or fabric, using hand tools. Fill holes, cracks, and other surface imperfections preparatory to covering surfaces. Mark vertical guidelines on walls to align strips, using plumb bobs and chalk lines. Measure and cut strips from rolls of wallpaper or fabric, using shears or razors. Measure surfaces and review work orders to estimate the quantities of materials needed. Apply sizing to seal surfaces and maximize adhesion of coverings to surfaces.

Personality Type: Realistic. Realistic occupations frequently involve work activities that include practical, hands-on problems and solutions. They often deal with plants; animals; and real-world materials such as wood, tools, and machinery. Many of the occupations require working outside and do not involve a lot of paperwork or working closely with others.

GOE—Interest Area: 02. Architecture and Construction. **Work Group:** 02.04. Construction Crafts. **Other Jobs in This Work Group:** Boilermakers; Brickmasons and Blockmasons; Carpet Installers; Cement Masons and Concrete Finishers; Commercial Divers; Construction Carpenters; Crane and Tower Operators; Drywall and Ceiling Tile Installers; Electricians; Fence Erectors; Floor Layers, Except Carpet, Wood, and Hard Tiles; Floor Sanders and Finishers; Glaziers; Hazardous Materials Removal Workers; Insulation Workers, Floor, Ceiling, and Wall; Insulation Workers, Mechanical; Manufactured Building and Mobile Home Installers; Operating Engineers and Other Construction Equipment Operators; Painters, Construction and Maintenance; Paving, Surfacing, and Tamping Equipment Operators; Pile-Driver Operators; Pipe Fitters and Steamfitters; Pipelayers; Plasterers and Stucco Masons; Plumbers; Plumbers, Pipefitters, and Steamfitters; Rail-Track Laying and Maintenance Equipment Operators; Refractory Materials Repairers, Except Brickmasons; Reinforcing Iron and Rebar Workers; Riggers; Roofers; Rough Carpenters; Security and Fire Alarm Systems Installers; Segmental Pavers; Sheet Metal Workers; Stone Cutters and Carvers, Manufacturing; Stonemasons; Structural Iron and Steel Workers; Tapers; Terrazzo Workers and Finishers; Tile and Marble Setters.

Skills—None met the criteria.

Education and Training Program: Painting/Painter and Wall Coverer Training. **Related Knowledge/Courses: Building and Construction:** The materials, methods, and tools involved in the construction or repair of houses, buildings, or other structures such as highways and roads. **Design:** Design techniques, tools, and principles involved in production of precision technical plans, blueprints, drawings, and models.

Work Environment: Indoors; standing; climbing ladders, scaffolds, or poles; using hands on objects, tools, or controls; repetitive motions.

Park Naturalists

This job can be found in the Part II lists under the title Conservation Scientists.

- Education/Training Required: Bachelor's degree
- Annual Earnings: $53,350
- Growth: 6.3%
- Annual Job Openings: 2,000
- Self-Employed: 9.0%
- Part-Time: 6.7%

The job openings listed here are shared with Range Managers and with Soil and Water Conservationists.

Level of Solitary Work: 65.6 (out of 100)

Level of Contact with Others: 87.3 (out of 100)

Plan, develop, and conduct programs to inform public of historical, natural, and scientific features of national, state, or local park. Provide visitor services by explaining regulations; answering visitor requests, needs, and complaints; and providing information about the park and surrounding areas. Conduct field trips to point out scientific, historic, and natural features of parks, forests, historic sites, or other attractions. Prepare and present illustrated lectures and interpretive talks about park features. Perform emergency duties to protect human life, government property, and natural features of park. Confer with park staff to determine subjects and schedules for park programs. Assist with operations of general facilities, such as visitor centers. Plan, organize, and direct activities of seasonal staff members. Perform routine maintenance on park structures. Prepare brochures and write newspaper articles. Construct historical, scientific, and nature visitor-center displays. Research stories regarding the area's natural history or environment. Interview specialists in desired fields to obtain and develop data for park information programs. Compile and maintain official park photographic and information files. Take photographs and motion pictures for use in lectures and publications and to develop displays. Survey park to determine forest conditions and distribution and abundance of fauna and flora. Plan and develop audiovisual devices for public programs.

Personality Type: Social. Social occupations frequently involve working with, communicating with, and teaching people. These occupations often involve helping or providing service to others.

GOE—Interest Area: 01. Agriculture and Natural Resources. **Work Group:** 01.01. Managerial Work in Agriculture and Natural Resources. **Other Jobs in This Work Group:** Aquacultural Managers; Crop and Livestock Managers; Farm Labor Contractors; Farm, Ranch, and Other Agricultural Managers; Farmers and Ranchers; First-Line Supervisors/Managers of Agricultural Crop and Horticultural Workers; First-Line Supervisors/Managers of Animal Husbandry and Animal Care Workers; First-Line Supervisors/Managers of Aquacultural Workers; First-Line Supervisors/Managers of Construction Trades and Extraction Workers; First-Line Supervisors/Managers of Farming, Fishing, and Forestry Workers; First-Line Supervisors/Managers of Landscaping, Lawn Service, and Groundskeeping Workers; First-Line Supervisors/Managers of Logging Workers; Nursery and Greenhouse Managers; Purchasing Agents and Buyers, Farm Products.

Skills—Management of Personnel Resources: Motivating, developing, and directing people as they work; identifying the best people for the job. **Management of Financial Resources:** Determining how money will be spent to get the work done and accounting for these expenditures. **Service Orientation:** Actively looking for ways to help people. **Writing:** Communicating effectively in writing as appropriate for the needs of the audience. **Science:** Using scientific rules and methods to solve problems. **Management of Material Resources:** Obtaining and seeing to the appropriate use of equipment, facilities, and materials needed to do certain work.

P

Education and Training Programs: Forest Management/Forest Resources Management; Forest Sciences and Biology; Forestry, General; Forestry, Other; Land Use Planning and Management/Development; Natural Resources and Conservation, Other; Natural Resources Management and Policy, Other; Natural Resources/Conservation, General; Water, Wetlands, and Marine Resources Management; Wildlife and Wildlands Science and Management. **Related Knowledge/Courses: Biology:** Plant and animal organisms and their tissues, cells, functions, interdependencies, and interactions with each other and the environment. **History and Archeology:** Historical events and their causes, indicators, and effects on civilizations and cultures. **Geography:** Principles and methods for describing the features of land, sea, and air masses, including their physical characteristics; locations; interrelationships; and distribution of plant, animal, and human life. **Customer and Personal Service:** Principles and processes for providing customer and personal services. This includes customer needs assessment, meeting quality standards for services, and evaluation of customer satisfaction. **Sociology and Anthropology:** Group behavior and dynamics, societal trends and influences, human migrations, ethnicity, and cultures and their history and origins. **Communications and Media:** Media production, communication, and dissemination techniques and methods. This includes alternative ways to inform and entertain via written, oral, and visual media.

Work Environment: More often indoors than outdoors; very hot or cold; minor burns, cuts, bites, or stings; sitting; using hands on objects, tools, or controls.

Parking Enforcement Workers

- Education/Training Required: Short-term on-the-job training
- Annual Earnings: $29,070
- Growth: 15.1%
- Annual Job Openings: 1,000
- Self-Employed: 1.5%
- Part-Time: 27.6%

Level of Solitary Work: 75.0 (out of 100)

Level of Contact with Others: 79.3 (out of 100)

Patrol assigned area, such as public parking lot or section of city, to issue tickets to overtime parking violators and illegally parked vehicles. Patrol an assigned area by vehicle or on foot to ensure public compliance with existing parking ordinance. Maintain close communications with dispatching personnel, using two-way radios or cell phones. Write warnings and citations for illegally parked vehicles. Mark tires of parked vehicles with chalk, record time of marking, and return at regular intervals to ensure that parking time limits are not exceeded. Respond to and make radio dispatch calls regarding parking violations and complaints. Train new or temporary staff. Identify vehicles in violation of parking codes, checking with dispatchers when necessary to confirm identities or to determine whether vehicles need to be booted or towed. Perform simple vehicle maintenance procedures such as checking oil and gas; report mechanical problems to supervisors. Observe and report hazardous conditions such as missing traffic signals or signs and street markings that need to be repainted. Investigate and answer complaints regarding contested parking citations, determining their validity and routing them appropriately. Maintain assigned equipment and supplies such as handheld citation computers, citation books, rain gear, tire-marking chalk, and street cones. Provide information to the public regarding parking regulations and facilities and the location of streets, buildings, and points of interest. Appear in court at hearings regarding contested traffic citations. Make arrangements for illegally parked or abandoned vehicles to be towed and direct tow-truck drivers to the correct vehicles. Perform traffic control duties such as setting up barricades and temporary signs, placing bags on parking meters to limit their use, or directing traffic. Provide assistance to motorists needing help with problems such as flat tires, keys locked in cars, or dead batteries. Enter and retrieve information pertaining to vehicle registration, identification, and status, using handheld computers. Collect coins deposited in meters. Prepare and maintain required records, including logs of parking enforcement activities and records of contested citations.

Personality Type: Conventional. Conventional occupations frequently involve following set procedures and routines. These occupations can include working with data and details more than with ideas. Usually there is a clear line of authority to follow.

GOE—Interest Area: 12. Law and Public Safety. **Work Group:** 12.04. Law Enforcement and Public Safety. **Other Jobs in This Work Group:** Bailiffs; Correctional Officers and Jailers; Criminal Investigators and Special Agents; Detectives and Criminal Investigators; Fire Investigators; Forensic Science Technicians; Police and Sheriff's Patrol Officers; Police Detectives; Police Identification and Records Officers; Police Patrol Officers; Sheriffs and Deputy Sheriffs; Transit and Railroad Police.

Skills—Writing: Communicating effectively in writing as appropriate for the needs of the audience. **Speaking:** Talking to others to convey information effectively. **Active Listening:** Giving full attention to what other people are saying, taking time to understand the points being made, asking questions as appropriate, and not interrupting at inappropriate times. **Equipment Maintenance:** Performing routine maintenance on equipment and determining when and what kind of maintenance is needed. **Service**

Orientation: Actively looking for ways to help people. **Negotiation:** Bringing others together and trying to reconcile differences.

Education and Training Program: Security and Protective Services, Other. **Related Knowledge/Courses: Law and Government:** Laws, legal codes, court procedures, precedents, government regulations, executive orders, agency rules, and the democratic political process. **Public Safety and Security:** Relevant equipment, policies, procedures, and strategies to promote effective local, state, or national security operations for the protection of people, data, property, and institutions. **Customer and Personal Service:** Principles and processes for providing customer and personal services. This includes customer needs assessment, meeting quality standards for services, and evaluation of customer satisfaction. **Geography:** Principles and methods for describing the features of land, sea, and air masses, including their physical characteristics; locations; interrelationships; and distribution of plant, animal, and human life. **Transportation:** Principles and methods for moving people or goods by air, rail, sea, or road, including the relative costs and benefits. **Psychology:** Human behavior and performance; individual differences in ability, personality, and interests; learning and motivation; psychological research methods; and the assessment and treatment of behavioral and affective disorders.

Work Environment: Outdoors; very hot or cold; more often sitting than standing; walking and running; repetitive motions.

Paving, Surfacing, and Tamping Equipment Operators

- ◉ Education/Training Required: Moderate-term on-the-job training
- ◉ Annual Earnings: $30,320
- ◉ Growth: 15.6%
- ◉ Annual Job Openings: 7,000
- ◉ Self-Employed: 1.2%
- ◉ Part-Time: 6.3%

Level of Solitary Work: 56.3 (out of 100)

Level of Contact with Others: 75.5 (out of 100)

Operate equipment used for applying concrete, asphalt, or other materials to roadbeds, parking lots, or airport runways and taxiways or equipment used for tamping gravel, dirt, or other materials. Includes concrete and asphalt paving machine operators, form tampers, tamping machine operators, and stone spreader operators. Start machine, engage clutch, and push and move levers to guide machine along forms or guidelines and to control the operation of machine attachments. Operate machines to spread, smooth, level, or steel-reinforce stone, concrete, or asphalt on road beds. Inspect, clean, maintain, and repair equipment, using mechanics' hand tools, or report malfunctions to supervisors. Operate oil distributors, loaders, chip spreaders, dump trucks, and snowplows. Coordinate truck dumping. Set up and tear down equipment. Operate tamping machines or manually roll surfaces to compact earth fills, foundation forms, and finished road materials according to grade specifications. Shovel blacktop. Drive machines onto truck trailers and drive trucks to transport machines and material to and from job sites. Observe distribution of paving material to adjust machine settings or material flow and indicate low spots for workers to add material. Light burners or start heating units of machines and regulate screed

temperatures and asphalt flow rates. Control paving machines to push dump trucks and to maintain a constant flow of asphalt or other material into hoppers or screeds. Set up forms and lay out guidelines for curbs according to written specifications, using string, spray paint, and concrete/water mixes. Fill tanks, hoppers, or machines with paving materials. Drive and operate curbing machines to extrude concrete or asphalt curbing. Cut or break up pavement and drive guardrail posts, using machines equipped with interchangeable hammers. Install dies, cutters, and extensions to screeds onto machines, using hand tools. Operate machines that clean or cut expansion joints in concrete or asphalt and that rout out cracks in pavement. Place strips of material such as cork, asphalt, or steel into joints or place rolls of expansion-joint material on machines that automatically insert material.

Personality Type: Realistic. Realistic occupations frequently involve work activities that include practical, hands-on problems and solutions. They often deal with plants; animals; and real-world materials such as wood, tools, and machinery. Many of the occupations require working outside and do not involve a lot of paperwork or working closely with others.

GOE—Interest Area: 02. Architecture and Construc-tion. **Work Group:** 02.04. Construction Crafts. **Other Jobs in This Work Group:** Boilermakers; Brickmasons and Blockmasons; Carpet Installers; Cement Masons and Concrete Finishers; Commercial Divers; Construction Carpenters; Crane and Tower Operators; Drywall and Ceiling Tile Installers; Electricians; Fence Erectors; Floor Layers, Except Carpet, Wood, and Hard Tiles; Floor Sanders and Finishers; Glaziers; Hazardous Materials Removal Workers; Insulation Workers, Floor, Ceiling, and Wall; Insulation Workers, Mechanical; Manufactured Building and Mobile Home Installers; Operating Engineers and Other Construction Equipment Operators; Painters, Construction and Maintenance; Paperhangers; Pile-Driver Operators; Pipe Fitters and Steamfitters; Pipelayers; Plasterers and Stucco Masons; Plumbers; Plumbers, Pipefitters, and Steamfitters; Rail-Track Laying and Maintenance

Equipment Operators; Refractory Materials Repairers, Except Brickmasons; Reinforcing Iron and Rebar Workers; Riggers; Roofers; Rough Carpenters; Security and Fire Alarm Systems Installers; Segmental Pavers; Sheet Metal Workers; Stone Cutters and Carvers, Manufacturing; Stonemasons; Structural Iron and Steel Workers; Tapers; Terrazzo Workers and Finishers; Tile and Marble Setters.

Skills—Operation Monitoring: Watching gauges, dials, or other indicators to make sure a machine is working properly. **Equipment Maintenance:** Performing routine maintenance on equipment and determining when and what kind of maintenance is needed. **Operation and Control:** Controlling operations of equipment or systems. **Repairing:** Repairing machines or systems by using the needed tools. **Installation:** Installing equipment, machines, wiring, or programs to meet specifications. **Equipment Selection:** Determining the kind of tools and equipment needed to do a job.

Education and Training Program: Construction/ Heavy Equipment/Earthmoving Equipment Operation. **Related Knowledge/Courses: Building and Construction:** The materials, methods, and tools involved in the construction or repair of houses, buildings, or other structures such as highways and roads. **Mechanical Devices:** Machines and tools, including their designs, uses, repair, and maintenance. **Transportation:** Principles and methods for moving people or goods by air, rail, sea, or road, including the relative costs and benefits. **Public Safety and Security:** Relevant equipment, policies, procedures, and strategies to promote effective local, state, or national security operations for the protection of people, data, property, and institutions. **Engineering and Technology:** The practical application of engineering science and technology. This includes applying principles, techniques, procedures, and equipment to the design and production of various goods and services. **Production and Processing:** Raw materials, production processes, quality control, costs, and other techniques for maximizing the effective manufacture and distribution of goods.

Work Environment: Outdoors; noisy; very hot or cold; contaminants; hazardous equipment; using hands on objects, tools, or controls.

Payroll and Timekeeping Clerks

- ◉ Education/Training Required: Moderate-term on-the-job training
- ◉ Annual Earnings: $31,360
- ◉ Growth: 17.3%
- ◉ Annual Job Openings: 36,000
- ◉ Self-Employed: 1.1%
- ◉ Part-Time: 14.7%

Level of Solitary Work: 68.8 (out of 100)

Level of Contact with Others: 80.5 (out of 100)

Compile and post employee time and payroll data. May compute employees' time worked, production, and commission. May compute and post wages and deductions. May prepare paychecks. Process and issue employee paychecks and statements of earnings and deductions. Compute wages and deductions and enter data into computers. Compile employee time, production, and payroll data from time sheets and other records. Review time sheets, work charts, wage computation, and other information to detect and reconcile payroll discrepancies. Verify attendance, hours worked, and pay adjustments and post information onto designated records. Record employee information, such as exemptions, transfers, and resignations, to maintain and update payroll records. Keep informed about changes in tax and deduction laws that apply to the payroll process. Issue and record adjustments to pay related to previous errors or retroactive increases. Provide information to employees and managers on payroll matters, tax issues, benefit plans, and collective agreement provisions. Complete time sheets showing employees' arrival and departure times. Post relevant work hours

P

to client files to bill clients properly. Distribute and collect timecards each pay period. Complete, verify, and process forms and documentation for administration of benefits such as pension plans and unemployment and medical insurance. Prepare and balance period-end reports and reconcile issued payrolls to bank statements. Compile statistical reports, statements, and summaries related to pay and benefits accounts and submit them to appropriate departments. Coordinate special programs, such as United Way campaigns, that involve payroll deductions.

Personality Type: Conventional. Conventional occupations frequently involve following set procedures and routines. These occupations can include working with data and details more than with ideas. Usually there is a clear line of authority to follow.

GOE—Interest Area: 04. Business and Administration. **Work Group:** 04.06. Mathematical Clerical Support. **Other Jobs in This Work Group:** Billing and Posting Clerks and Machine Operators; Billing, Cost, and Rate Clerks; Bookkeeping, Accounting, and Auditing Clerks; Brokerage Clerks; Statement Clerks; Tax Preparers.

Skills—Mathematics: Using mathematics to solve problems. **Time Management:** Managing one's own time and the time of others. **Active Listening:** Giving full attention to what other people are saying, taking time to understand the points being made, asking questions as appropriate, and not interrupting at inappropriate times. **Writing:** Communicating effectively in writing as appropriate for the needs of the audience. **Speaking:** Talking to others to convey information effectively. **Learning Strategies:** Selecting and using training or instructional methods and procedures appropriate for the situation when learning or teaching new things.

Education and Training Program: Accounting Technology/Technician Training and Bookkeeping. **Related Knowledge/Courses: Clerical Practices:** Administrative and clerical procedures and systems such as word processing, managing files and records, stenography and transcription, designing forms, and other office procedures and terminology. **Economics**

and Accounting: Economic and accounting principles and practices, the financial markets, banking, and the analysis and reporting of financial data. **Administration and Management:** Business and management principles involved in strategic planning, resource allocation, human resources modeling, leadership technique, production methods, and coordination of people and resources. **Personnel and Human Resources:** Principles and procedures for personnel recruitment, selection, training, compensation and benefits, labor relations and negotiation, and personnel information systems. **Mathematics:** Arithmetic, algebra, geometry, calculus, and statistics and their applications. **Customer and Personal Service:** Principles and processes for providing customer and personal services. This includes customer needs assessment, meeting quality standards for services, and evaluation of customer satisfaction.

Work Environment: Indoors; noisy; sitting; repetitive motions.

Personal Financial Advisors

- Education/Training Required: Bachelor's degree
- Annual Earnings: $63,500
- Growth: 25.9%
- Annual Job Openings: 17,000
- Self-Employed: 38.9%
- Part-Time: 8.5%

Level of Solitary Work: 46.7 (out of 100)

Level of Contact with Others: 73.3 (out of 100)

Advise clients on financial plans, utilizing knowledge of tax and investment strategies, securities, insurance, pension plans, and real estate. Duties include assessing clients' assets, liabilities, cash flow, insurance coverage, tax status, and financial objectives to establish investment strategies. Open accounts for clients and disburse funds from account to creditors as agents for clients. Research and investigate available investment opportunities to determine whether they fit into financial plans. Recommend strategies clients can use to achieve their financial goals and objectives, including specific recommendations in such areas as cash management, insurance coverage, and investment planning. Sell financial products such as stocks, bonds, mutual funds, and insurance if licensed to do so. Collect information from students to determine their eligibility for specific financial aid programs. Conduct seminars and workshops on financial planning topics such as retirement planning, estate planning, and the evaluation of severance packages. Contact clients' creditors to arrange for payment adjustments so that payments are feasible for clients and agreeable to creditors. Meet with clients' other advisors, including attorneys, accountants, trust officers, and investment bankers, to fully understand clients' financial goals and circumstances. Authorize release of financial aid funds to students. Participate in the selection of candidates for specific financial aid awards. Determine amounts of aid to be granted to students, considering such factors as funds available, extent of demand, and financial needs. Build and maintain client bases, keeping current client plans up to date and recruiting new clients on an ongoing basis. Review clients' accounts and plans regularly to determine whether life changes, economic changes, or financial performance indicate a need for plan reassessment. Prepare and interpret information for clients such as investment performance reports, financial document summaries, and income projections. Answer clients' questions about the purposes and details of financial plans and strategies. Contact clients periodically to determine if there have been changes in their financial status. Devise debt liquidation plans that include payoff priorities and timelines. Explain and document for clients the types of services that are to be provided and the responsibilities to be taken by the personal financial advisor.

Personality Type: Social. Social occupations frequently involve working with, communicating with, and teaching people. These occupations often involve helping or providing service to others.

GOE—Interest Area: 06. Finance and Insurance. **Work Group:** 06.05. Finance/Insurance Sales and Support. **Other Jobs in This Work Group:** Advertising Sales Agents; Insurance Sales Agents; Sales Agents, Financial Services; Sales Agents, Securities and Commodities; Securities, Commodities, and Financial Services Sales Agents.

Skills—Management of Financial Resources: Determining how money will be spent to get the work done and accounting for these expenditures. **Speaking:** Talking to others to convey information effectively. **Service Orientation:** Actively looking for ways to help people. **Mathematics:** Using mathematics to solve problems. **Active Listening:** Giving full attention to what other people are saying, taking time to understand the points being made, asking questions as appropriate, and not interrupting at inappropriate times. **Judgment and Decision Making:** Considering the relative costs and benefits of potential actions to choose the most appropriate one.

Education and Training Programs: Finance, General; Financial Planning and Services. **Related Knowledge/Courses: Economics and Accounting:** Economic and accounting principles and practices, the financial markets, banking, and the analysis and reporting of financial data. **Mathematics:** Arithmetic, algebra, geometry, calculus, and statistics and their applications.

Work Environment: Indoors; sitting.

Pest Control Workers

- Education/Training Required: Moderate-term on-the-job training
- Annual Earnings: $27,170
- Growth: 18.4%
- Annual Job Openings: 4,000
- Self-Employed: 9.7%
- Part-Time: 6.0%

Level of Solitary Work: 68.8 (out of 100)

Level of Contact with Others: 91.5 (out of 100)

Spray or release chemical solutions or toxic gases and set traps to kill pests and vermin, such as mice, termites, and roaches, that infest buildings and surrounding areas. Record work activities performed. Inspect premises to identify infestation source and extent of damage to property, wall and roof porosity, and access to infested locations. Spray or dust chemical solutions, powders, or gases into rooms; onto clothing, furnishings, or wood; and over marshlands, ditches, and catch-basins. Clean work site after completion of job. Direct or assist other workers in treatment and extermination processes to eliminate and control rodents, insects, and weeds. Drive truck equipped with power spraying equipment. Measure area dimensions requiring treatment, using rule; calculate fumigant requirements; and estimate cost for service. Post warning signs and lock building doors to secure area to be fumigated. Cut or bore openings in building or surrounding concrete, access infested areas, insert nozzle, and inject pesticide to impregnate ground. Study preliminary reports and diagrams of infested area and determine treatment type required to eliminate and prevent recurrence of infestation. Dig up and burn or spray weeds with herbicides. Set mechanical traps and place poisonous paste or bait in sewers, burrows, and ditches. Clean and remove blockages from infested areas to facilitate spraying procedure and provide drainage, using broom, mop, shovel, and rake. Position and fasten edges of tarpaulins over building and tape vents to ensure airtight environment and check for leaks.

Personality Type: Realistic. Realistic occupations frequently involve work activities that include practical, hands-on problems and solutions. They often deal with plants; animals; and real-world materials such as wood, tools, and machinery. Many of the occupations require working outside and do not involve a lot of paperwork or working closely with others.

GOE—Interest Area: 01. Agriculture and Natural Resources. **Work Group:** 01.05. Nursery, Groundskeeping, and Pest Control. **Other Jobs in This Work Group:** Landscaping and Groundskeeping Workers; Nursery Workers; Pesticide Handlers, Sprayers, and Applicators, Vegetation; Tree Trimmers and Pruners.

Skills—Persuasion: Persuading others to change their minds or behavior. **Service Orientation:** Actively looking for ways to help people. **Equipment Selection:** Determining the kind of tools and equipment needed to do a job. **Social Perceptiveness:** Being aware of others' reactions and understanding why they react as they do. **Active Learning:** Understanding the implications of new information for both current and future problem solving and decision making. **Management of Material Resources:** Obtaining and seeing to the appropriate use of equipment, facilities, and materials needed to do certain work.

Education and Training Program: Agricultural/Farm Supplies Retailing and Wholesaling. **Related Knowledge/Courses: Sales and Marketing:** Principles and methods for showing, promoting, and selling products or services. This includes marketing strategy and tactics, product demonstration, sales techniques, and sales control systems. **Chemistry:** The chemical composition, structure, and properties of substances and of the chemical processes and transformations that they undergo. This includes uses of chemicals and their danger signs, production techniques, and disposal methods. **Biology:** Plant and animal organisms and their tissues, cells, functions, interdependencies, and interactions with each other and the environment. **Customer and Personal Service:** Principles and processes for providing customer and personal services. This includes customer needs assessment, meeting quality standards for services, and evaluation of customer satisfaction. **Education and Training:** Principles and methods for curriculum and training design, teaching and instruction for individuals and groups, and the measurement of training effects. **Building and Construction:** The materials, methods, and tools involved in the construction or repair of houses, buildings, or other structures such as highways and roads.

Work Environment: More often outdoors than indoors; very hot or cold; contaminants; hazardous conditions; using hands on objects, tools, or controls.

Pesticide Handlers, Sprayers, and Applicators, Vegetation

- ◎ Education/Training Required: Moderate-term on-the-job training
- ◎ Annual Earnings: $26,120
- ◎ Growth: 16.6%
- ◎ Annual Job Openings: 6,000
- ◎ Self-Employed: 19.6%
- ◎ Part-Time: 24.4%

Level of Solitary Work: 59.2 (out of 100)

Level of Contact with Others: 83.7 (out of 100)

Mix or apply pesticides, herbicides, fungicides, or insecticides through sprays, dusts, vapors, soil incorporation, or chemical application on trees, shrubs, lawns, or botanical crops. Usually requires specific training and state or federal certification. Fill sprayer tanks with water and chemicals according to formulas. Mix pesticides, herbicides, and fungicides for application to trees, shrubs, lawns, or botan-

ical crops. Cover areas to specified depths with pesticides, applying knowledge of weather conditions, droplet sizes, elevation-to-distance ratios, and obstructions. Lift, push, and swing nozzles, hoses, and tubes to direct spray over designated areas. Start motors and engage machinery such as sprayer agitators and pumps or portable spray equipment. Connect hoses and nozzles selected according to terrain, distribution pattern requirements, types of infestations, and velocities. Clean and service machinery to ensure operating efficiency, using water, gasoline, lubricants, and hand tools. Provide driving instructions to truck drivers to ensure complete coverage of designated areas, using hand and horn signals. Plant grass with seed spreaders and operate straw blowers to cover seeded areas with mixtures of asphalt and straw.

Personality Type: Realistic. Realistic occupations frequently involve work activities that include practical, hands-on problems and solutions. They often deal with plants; animals; and real-world materials such as wood, tools, and machinery. Many of the occupations require working outside and do not involve a lot of paperwork or working closely with others.

GOE—Interest Area: 01. Agriculture and Natural Resources. **Work Group:** 01.05. Nursery, Groundskeeping, and Pest Control. **Other Jobs in This Work Group:** Landscaping and Groundskeeping Workers; Nursery Workers; Pest Control Workers; Tree Trimmers and Pruners.

Skills—Repairing: Repairing machines or systems by using the needed tools. **Equipment Maintenance:** Performing routine maintenance on equipment and determining when and what kind of maintenance is needed. **Operation Monitoring:** Watching gauges, dials, or other indicators to make sure a machine is working properly. **Management of Material Resources:** Obtaining and seeing to the appropriate use of equipment, facilities, and materials needed to do certain work. **Installation:** Installing equipment, machines, wiring, or programs to meet specifications. **Trouble-shooting:** Determining causes of operating errors and deciding what to do about them.

Education and Training Programs: Landscaping and Groundskeeping; Plant Nursery Operations and Management; Turf and Turfgrass Management. **Related Knowledge/Courses: Biology:** Plant and animal organisms and their tissues, cells, functions, interdependencies, and interactions with each other and the environment. **Chemistry:** The chemical composition, structure, and properties of substances and of the chemical processes and transformations that they undergo. This includes uses of chemicals and their danger signs, production techniques, and disposal methods. **Mechanical Devices:** Machines and tools, including their designs, uses, repair, and maintenance. **Customer and Personal Service:** Principles and processes for providing customer and personal services. This includes customer needs assessment, meeting quality standards for services, and evaluation of customer satisfaction. **Transportation:** Principles and methods for moving people or goods by air, rail, sea, or road, including the relative costs and benefits. **Public Safety and Security:** Relevant equipment, policies, procedures, and strategies to promote effective local, state, or national security operations for the protection of people, data, property, and institutions.

Work Environment: Outdoors; noisy; contaminants; hazardous conditions; using hands on objects, tools, or controls; repetitive motions.

Petroleum Pump System Operators, Refinery Operators, and Gaugers

- Education/Training Required: Long-term on-the-job training
- Annual Earnings: $51,060
- Growth: −8.6%
- Annual Job Openings: 6,000
- Self-Employed: 0.1%
- Part-Time: 0.8%

Level of Solitary Work: 57.2 (out of 100)

Level of Contact with Others: 19.0 (out of 100)

Control the operation of petroleum-refining or -processing units. May specialize in controlling manifold and pumping systems, gauging or testing oil in storage tanks, or regulating the flow of oil into pipelines. Calculate test result values, using standard formulas. Clamp seals around valves to secure tanks. Signal other workers by telephone or radio to operate pumps, open and close valves, and check temperatures. Start pumps and open valves or use automated equipment to regulate the flow of oil in pipelines and into and out of tanks. Synchronize activities with other pumphouses to ensure a continuous flow of products and a minimum of contamination between products. Verify that incoming and outgoing products are moving through the correct meters and that meters are working properly. Prepare calculations for receipts and deliveries of oil and oil products. Read automatic gauges at specified intervals to determine the flow rate of oil into or from tanks and the amount of oil in tanks. Record and compile operating data, instrument readings, documentation, and results of laboratory analyses. Control or operate manifold and pumping systems to circulate liquids through a petroleum refinery. Monitor process indicators, instruments, gauges, and meters to detect and report any possible problems. Clean interiors of processing units by circulating chemicals and solvents within units. Operate control panels to coordinate and regulate process variables such as temperature and pressure and to direct product flow rate according to process schedules. Read and analyze specifications, schedules, logs, test results, and laboratory recommendations to determine how to set equipment controls to produce the required qualities and quantities of products. Perform tests to check the qualities and grades of products, such as assessing levels of bottom sediment, water, and foreign materials in oil samples, using centrifugal testers. Collect product samples by turning bleeder valves or by lowering containers into tanks to obtain oil samples. Patrol units to monitor the amount of oil in storage tanks and to verify that activities and operations are safe, efficient, and in compliance with regulations. Operate auxiliary equipment and control multiple processing units during distilling or treating operations, moving controls that regulate valves, pumps, compressors, and auxiliary equipment.

Personality Type: Realistic. Realistic occupations frequently involve work activities that include practical, hands-on problems and solutions. They often deal with plants; animals; and real-world materials such as wood, tools, and machinery. Many of the occupations require working outside and do not involve a lot of paperwork or working closely with others.

GOE—Interest Area: 13. Manufacturing. **Work Group:** 13.16. Utility Operation and Energy Distribution. **Other Jobs in This Work Group:** Chemical Plant and System Operators; Gas Compressor and Gas Pumping Station Operators; Gas Plant Operators; Nuclear Power Reactor Operators; Power Distributors and Dispatchers; Power Plant Operators; Ship Engineers; Stationary Engineers and Boiler Operators; Water and Liquid Waste Treatment Plant and System Operators.

Skills—Operation Monitoring: Watching gauges, dials, or other indicators to make sure a machine is working properly. **Operation and Control:** Controlling operations of equipment or systems. **Repairing:** Repairing machines or systems by using the needed tools. **Equipment Maintenance:** Performing routine maintenance on equipment and determining when and what kind of maintenance is needed. **Troubleshooting:** Determining causes of operating errors and deciding what to do about them. **Science:** Using scientific rules and methods to solve problems.

Education and Training Program: Mechanic and Repair Technologies/Technician Training, Other. **Related Knowledge/Courses: Mechanical Devices:** Machines and tools, including their designs, uses, repair, and maintenance. **Chemistry:** The chemical composition, structure, and properties of substances and of the chemical processes and transformations that they undergo. This includes uses of chemicals and their danger signs, production techniques, and disposal methods. **Physics:** Physical principles and laws and their interrelationships and applications to understanding fluid, material, and atmospheric dynamics and mechanical, electrical, atomic, and subatomic structures and processes. **Production and Processing:** Raw materials, production processes, quality control, costs, and other techniques for maximizing the effective manufacture and distribution of goods. **Engineering and Technology:** The practical application of engineering science and technology. This includes applying principles, techniques, procedures, and equipment to the design and production of various goods and services.

Work Environment: Indoors; contaminants; hazardous conditions; standing; using hands on objects, tools, or controls.

Physicists

◉ Education/Training Required: Doctoral degree

◉ Annual Earnings: $89,810

◉ Growth: 7.0%

◉ Annual Job Openings: 1,000

◉ Self-Employed: 0.0%

◉ Part-Time: 8.0%

Level of Solitary Work: 68.8 (out of 100)

Level of Contact with Others: 77.0 (out of 100)

Conduct research into the phases of physical phenomena, develop theories and laws on the basis of observation and experiments, and devise methods to apply laws and theories to industry and other fields. Perform complex calculations as part of the analysis and evaluation of data, using computers. Describe and express observations and conclusions in mathematical terms. Analyze data from research conducted to detect and measure physical phenomena. Report experimental results by writing papers for scientific journals or by presenting information at scientific conferences. Design computer simulations

P

to model physical data so that it can be better understood. Collaborate with other scientists in the design, development, and testing of experimental, industrial, or medical equipment, instrumentation, and procedures. Direct testing and monitoring of contamination of radioactive equipment and recording of personnel and plant area radiation exposure data. Observe the structure and properties of matter and the transformation and propagation of energy, using equipment such as masers, lasers, and telescopes, to explore and identify the basic principles governing these phenomena. Develop theories and laws on the basis of observation and experiments and apply these theories and laws to problems in areas such as nuclear energy, optics, and aerospace technology. Teach physics to students. Develop manufacturing, assembly, and fabrication processes of lasers, masers, and infrared and other light-emitting and light-sensitive devices. Conduct application evaluations and analyze results to determine commercial, industrial, scientific, medical, military, or other uses for electro-optical devices. Develop standards of permissible concentrations of radioisotopes in liquids and gases. Conduct research pertaining to potential environmental impacts of atomic energy–related industrial development to determine licensing qualifications. Advise authorities of procedures to be followed in radiation incidents or hazards and assist in civil defense planning.

Personality Type: Investigative. Investigative occupations frequently involve working with ideas and require an extensive amount of thinking. These occupations can involve searching for facts and figuring out problems mentally.

GOE—Interest Area: 15. Scientific Research, Engineering, and Mathematics. **Work Group:** 15.02. Physical Sciences. **Other Jobs in This Work Group:** Astronomers; Atmospheric and Space Scientists; Chemists; Geographers; Geoscientists, Except Hydrologists and Geographers; Hydrologists; Materials Scientists.

Skills—Programming: Writing computer programs for various purposes. **Science:** Using scientific rules and methods to solve problems. **Mathematics:** Using mathematics to solve problems. **Complex Problem Solving:** Identifying complex problems and reviewing related information to develop and evaluate options and implement solutions. **Management of Financial Resources:** Determining how money will be spent to get the work done and accounting for these expenditures. **Systems Analysis:** Determining how a system should work and how changes in conditions, operations, and the environment will affect outcomes.

Education and Training Programs: Acoustics; Astrophysics; Atomic/Molecular Physics; Elementary Particle Physics; Health/Medical Physics; Nuclear Physics; Optics/Optical Sciences; Physics, General; Physics, Other; Plasma and High-Temperature Physics; Solid State and Low-Temperature Physics; Theoretical and Mathematical Physics. **Related Knowledge/Courses: Physics:** Physical principles and laws and their interrelationships and applications to understanding fluid, material, and atmospheric dynamics and mechanical, electrical, atomic, and subatomic structures and processes. **Mathematics:** Arithmetic, algebra, geometry, calculus, and statistics and their applications. **Engineering and Technology:** The practical application of engineering science and technology. This includes applying principles, techniques, procedures, and equipment to the design and production of various goods and services. **Computers and Electronics:** Circuit boards, processors, chips, electronic equipment, and computer hardware and software, including applications and programming. **English Language:** The structure and content of the English language, including the meaning and spelling of words, rules of composition, and grammar. **Telecommunications:** Transmission, broadcasting, switching, control, and operation of telecommunications systems.

Work Environment: Indoors; sitting.

Pile-Driver Operators

- Education/Training Required: Moderate-term on-the-job training
- Annual Earnings: $48,900
- Growth: 11.9%
- Annual Job Openings: Fewer than 500
- Self-Employed: 0.0%
- Part-Time: 18.2%

Level of Solitary Work: 59.2 (out of 100)

Level of Contact with Others: 10.5 (out of 100)

Operate pile drivers mounted on skids, barges, crawler treads, or locomotive cranes to drive pilings for retaining walls, bulkheads, and foundations of structures such as buildings, bridges, and piers. Move levers and turn valves to activate power hammers or to raise and lower drophammers that drive piles to required depths. Clean, lubricate, and refill equipment. Conduct pre-operational checks on equipment to ensure proper functioning. Drive pilings to provide support for buildings or other structures, using heavy equipment with a pile-driver head. Move hand and foot levers of hoisting equipment to position piling leads, hoist piling into leads, and position hammers over pilings.

Personality Type: Realistic. Realistic occupations frequently involve work activities that include practical, hands-on problems and solutions. They often deal with plants; animals; and real-world materials such as wood, tools, and machinery. Many of the occupations require working outside and do not involve a lot of paperwork or working closely with others.

GOE—Interest Area: 02. Architecture and Construction. **Work Group:** 02.04. Construction Crafts. **Other Jobs in This Work Group:** Boilermakers; Brickmasons and Blockmasons; Carpet Installers; Cement Masons and Concrete Finishers; Commercial Divers; Construction Carpenters; Crane and Tower Operators; Drywall and Ceiling Tile Installers; Electricians; Fence Erectors; Floor Layers, Except Carpet, Wood, and Hard Tiles; Floor Sanders and Finishers; Glaziers; Hazardous Materials Removal Workers; Insulation Workers, Floor, Ceiling, and Wall; Insulation Workers, Mechanical; Manufactured Building and Mobile Home Installers; Operating Engineers and Other Construction Equipment Operators; Painters, Construction and Maintenance; Paperhangers; Paving, Surfacing, and Tamping Equipment Operators; Pipe Fitters and Steamfitters; Pipelayers; Plasterers and Stucco Masons; Plumbers; Plumbers, Pipefitters, and Steamfitters; Rail-Track Laying and Maintenance Equipment Operators; Refractory Materials Repairers, Except Brickmasons; Reinforcing Iron and Rebar Workers; Riggers; Roofers; Rough Carpenters; Security and Fire Alarm Systems Installers; Segmental Pavers; Sheet Metal Workers; Stone Cutters and Carvers, Manufacturing; Stonemasons; Structural Iron and Steel Workers; Tapers; Terrazzo Workers and Finishers; Tile and Marble Setters.

Skills—Operation and Control: Controlling operations of equipment or systems. **Operation Monitoring:** Watching gauges, dials, or other indicators to make sure a machine is working properly.

Education and Training Program: Construction/Heavy Equipment/Earthmoving Equipment Operation. **Related Knowledge/Courses: Building and Construction:** The materials, methods, and tools involved in the construction or repair of houses, buildings, or other structures such as highways and roads. **Engineering and Technology:** The practical application of engineering science and technology. This includes applying principles, techniques, procedures, and equipment to the design and production of various goods and services. **Mechanical Devices:** Machines and tools, including their designs, uses, repair, and maintenance.

Work Environment: Outdoors; noisy; whole-body vibration; hazardous equipment; sitting; using hands on objects, tools, or controls.

Pilots, Ship

This job can be found in the Part II lists under the title Captains, Mates, and Pilots of Water Vessels.

- ◎ Education/Training Required: Work experience in a related occupation
- ◎ Annual Earnings: $50,940
- ◎ Growth: 4.8%
- ◎ Annual Job Openings: 2,000
- ◎ Self-Employed: 5.4%
- ◎ Part-Time: 8.7%

The job openings listed here are shared with Mates—Ship, Boat, and Barge and with Ship and Boat Captains.

Level of Solitary Work: 34.2 (out of 100)

Level of Contact with Others: 57.2 (out of 100)

Command ships to steer them into and out of harbors, estuaries, straits, and sounds and on rivers, lakes, and bays. Must be licensed by U.S. Coast Guard with limitations indicating class and tonnage of vessels for which license is valid and route and waters that may be piloted. Serve as a vessel's docking master upon arrival at a port and when at a berth. Prevent ships under their navigational control from engaging in unsafe operations. Provide assistance to vessels approaching or leaving seacoasts, navigating harbors, and docking and undocking. Steer ships into and out of berths or signal tugboat captains to berth and unberth ships. Advise ships' masters on harbor rules and customs procedures. Learn to operate new technology systems and procedures through the use of instruction, simulators, and models. Maintain and repair boats and equipment. Maintain ship logs. Oversee cargo storage on or below decks. Provide assistance in maritime rescue operations. Relieve crew members on tugs and launches. Report to appropriate authorities any violations of federal or state pilotage laws. Make nautical maps. Operate amphibious craft during troop landings. Operate ship-to-shore radios to exchange information needed for ship operations. Direct courses and speeds of ships based on specialized knowledge of local winds, weather, water depths, tides, currents, and hazards. Give directions to crew members who are steering ships. Set ships' courses that avoid reefs, outlying shoals, and other hazards, utilizing navigational aids such as lighthouses and buoys. Consult maps, charts, weather reports, and navigation equipment to determine and direct ship movements.

Personality Type: Realistic. Realistic occupations frequently involve work activities that include practical, hands-on problems and solutions. They often deal with plants; animals; and real-world materials such as wood, tools, and machinery. Many of the occupations require working outside and do not involve a lot of paperwork or working closely with others.

GOE—Interest Area: 16. Transportation, Distribution, and Logistics. **Work Group:** 16.05. Water Vehicle Operation. **Other Jobs in This Work Group:** Captains, Mates, and Pilots of Water Vessels; Dredge Operators; Mates—Ship, Boat, and Barge; Motorboat Operators; Sailors and Marine Oilers; Ship and Boat Captains.

Skills—Operation and Control: Controlling operations of equipment or systems. **Systems Analysis:** Determin-ing how a system should work and how changes in conditions, operations, and the environment will affect outcomes. **Operation Monitoring:** Watching gauges, dials, or other indicators to make sure a machine is working properly. **Systems Evaluation:** Identifying measures or indicators of system performance and the actions needed to improve or correct performance relative to the goals of the system. **Judgment and Decision Making:** Considering the relative costs and benefits of potential actions to choose the most appropriate one. **Management of Personnel Resources:** Motivating, developing, and directing people as they work; identifying the best people for the job.

Education and Training Programs: Commercial Fishing; Marine Science/Merchant Marine Officer Training; Marine Transportation, Other. **Related**

Knowledge/Courses: Transportation: Principles and methods for moving people or goods by air, rail, sea, or road, including the relative costs and benefits. **Geography:** Principles and methods for describing the features of land, sea, and air masses, including their physical characteristics; locations; interrelationships; and distribution of plant, animal, and human life. **Physics:** Physical principles and laws and their interrelationships and applications to understanding fluid, material, and atmospheric dynamics and mechanical, electrical, atomic, and subatomic structures and processes. **Law and Government:** Laws, legal codes, court procedures, precedents, government regulations, executive orders, agency rules, and the democratic political process. **Engineering and Technology:** The practical application of engineering science and technology. This includes applying principles, techniques, procedures, and equipment to the design and production of various goods and services. **Public Safety and Security:** Relevant equipment, policies, procedures, and strategies to promote effective local, state, or national security operations for the protection of people, data, property, and institutions.

Work Environment: More often indoors than outdoors; more often standing than sitting; keeping or regaining balance; using hands on objects, tools, or controls.

Pipe Fitters and Steamfitters

This job can be found in the Part II lists under the title Plumbers, Pipefitters, and Steamfitters.

- ◉ Education/Training Required: Long-term on-the-job training
- ◉ Annual Earnings: $42,160
- ◉ Growth: 15.7%
- ◉ Annual Job Openings: 61,000
- ◉ Self-Employed: 13.3%
- ◉ Part-Time: 3.6%

The job openings listed here are shared with Plumbers.

Level of Solitary Work: 56.1 (out of 100)

Level of Contact with Others: 82.6 (out of 100)

Lay out, assemble, install, and maintain pipe systems, pipe supports, and related hydraulic and pneumatic equipment for steam, hot water, heating, cooling, lubricating, sprinkling, and industrial production and processing systems. Cut, thread, and hammer pipe to specifications, using tools such as saws, cutting torches, and pipe threaders and benders. Assemble and secure pipes, tubes, fittings, and related equipment according to specifications by welding, brazing, cementing, soldering, and threading joints. Attach pipes to walls, structures, and fixtures, such as radiators or tanks, using brackets, clamps, tools, or welding equipment. Inspect, examine, and test installed systems and pipelines, using pressure gauge, hydrostatic testing, observation, or other methods. Measure and mark pipes for cutting and threading. Lay out full scale drawings of pipe systems, supports, and related equipment, following blueprints. Plan pipe system layout, installation, or repair according to specifications. Select pipe sizes and types and related materials, such as supports, hangers, and hydraulic cylinders, according to specifications. Cut and bore holes in structures such as bulkheads, decks, walls, and mains prior to pipe installation, using hand and power tools. Modify, clean, and maintain pipe systems, units, fittings, and related machines and equipment, following specifications and using hand and power tools. Install automatic controls used to regulate pipe systems. Turn valves to shut off steam, water, or other gases or liquids from pipe sections, using valve keys or wrenches. Remove and replace worn components. Prepare cost estimates for clients. Inspect work sites for obstructions and to ensure that holes will not cause structural weakness. Operate motorized pumps to remove water from flooded manholes, basements, or facility floors. Dip nonferrous piping materials in a mixture of molten tin and lead to obtain a coating that prevents erosion or galvanic and electrolytic action.

Personality Type: Realistic. Realistic occupations frequently involve work activities that include practical, hands-on problems and solutions. They often deal with plants; animals; and real-world materials such as wood, tools, and machinery. Many of the occupations require working outside and do not involve a lot of paperwork or working closely with others.

GOE—Interest Area: 02. Architecture and Construction. **Work Group:** 02.04. Construction Crafts. **Other Jobs in This Work Group:** Boilermakers; Brickmasons and Blockmasons; Carpet Installers; Cement Masons and Concrete Finishers; Commercial Divers; Construction Carpenters; Crane and Tower Operators; Drywall and Ceiling Tile Installers; Electricians; Fence Erectors; Floor Layers, Except Carpet, Wood, and Hard Tiles; Floor Sanders and Finishers; Glaziers; Hazardous Materials Removal Workers; Insulation Workers, Floor, Ceiling, and Wall; Insulation Workers, Mechanical; Manufactured Building and Mobile Home Installers; Operating Engineers and Other Construction Equipment Operators; Painters, Construction and Maintenance; Paperhangers; Paving, Surfacing, and Tamping Equipment Operators; Pile-Driver Operators; Pipelayers; Plasterers and Stucco Masons; Plumbers; Plumbers, Pipefitters, and Steamfitters; Rail-Track Laying and Maintenance Equipment Operators; Refractory Materials Repairers, Except Brickmasons; Reinforcing Iron and Rebar Workers; Riggers; Roofers; Rough Carpenters; Security and Fire Alarm Systems Installers; Segmental Pavers; Sheet Metal Workers; Stone Cutters and Carvers, Manufacturing; Stonemasons; Structural Iron and Steel Workers; Tapers; Terrazzo Workers and Finishers; Tile and Marble Setters.

Skills—Installation: Installing equipment, machines, wiring, or programs to meet specifications. **Repairing:** Repairing machines or systems by using the needed tools. **Management of Personnel Resources:** Motivating, developing, and directing people as they work; identifying the best people for

the job. **Systems Analysis:** Determining how a system should work and how changes in conditions, operations, and the environment will affect outcomes. **Equipment Maintenance:** Performing routine maintenance on equipment and determining when and what kind of maintenance is needed. **Operation Monitoring:** Watching gauges, dials, or other indicators to make sure a machine is working properly.

Education and Training Program: Pipefitting/Pipefitter and Sprinkler Fitter Training. **Related Knowledge/Courses: Building and Construction:** The materials, methods, and tools involved in the construction or repair of houses, buildings, or other structures such as highways and roads. **Design:** Design techniques, tools, and principles involved in production of precision technical plans, blueprints, drawings, and models. **Mechanical Devices:** Machines and tools, including their designs, uses, repair, and maintenance. **Engineering and Technology:** The practical application of engineering science and technology. This includes applying principles, techniques, procedures, and equipment to the design and production of various goods and services. **Economics and Accounting:** Economic and accounting principles and practices, the financial markets, banking, and the analysis and reporting of financial data. **Transportation:** Principles and methods for moving people or goods by air, rail, sea, or road, including the relative costs and benefits.

Work Environment: Outdoors; hazardous equipment; minor burns, cuts, bites, or stings; standing; using hands on objects, tools, or controls; repetitive motions.

Plumbers

This job can be found in the Part II lists under the title Plumbers, Pipefitters, and Steamfitters.

- ◎ Education/Training Required: Long-term on-the-job training
- ◎ Annual Earnings: $42,160
- ◎ Growth: 15.7%
- ◎ Annual Job Openings: 61,000
- ◎ Self-Employed: 13.3%
- ◎ Part-Time: 3.6%

The job openings listed here are shared with Pipe Fitters and Steamfitters.

Level of Solitary Work: 56.1 (out of 100)

Level of Contact with Others: 82.6 (out of 100)

Assemble, install, and repair pipes, fittings, and fixtures of heating, water, and drainage systems according to specifications and plumbing codes. Assemble pipe sections, tubing, and fittings, using couplings; clamps; screws; bolts; cement; plastic solvent; caulking; or soldering, brazing, and welding equipment. Fill pipes or plumbing fixtures with water or air and observe pressure gauges to detect and locate leaks. Review blueprints and building codes and specifications to determine work details and procedures. Prepare written work cost estimates and negotiate contracts. Study building plans and inspect structures to assess material and equipment needs, to establish the sequence of pipe installations, and to plan installation around obstructions such as electrical wiring. Keep records of assignments and produce detailed work reports. Perform complex calculations and planning for special or very large jobs. Locate and mark the position of pipe installations, connections, passage holes, and fixtures in structures, using measuring instruments such as rulers and levels. Measure, cut, thread, and bend pipe to required angle, using hand and power tools or machines such as pipe cutters, pipe-threading machines, and pipe-bending machines. Cut openings in structures to accommodate pipes and pipe fittings, using hand and power tools. Install pipe assemblies, fittings, valves, appliances such as dishwashers and water heaters, and fixtures such as sinks and toilets, using hand and power tools. Hang steel supports from ceiling joists to hold pipes in place. Repair and maintain plumbing, replacing defective washers, replacing or mending broken pipes, and opening clogged drains. Direct workers engaged in pipe cutting and preassembly and installation of plumbing systems and components. Install underground storm, sanitary, and water piping systems and extend piping to connect fixtures and plumbing to these systems. Clear away debris in a renovation. Install oxygen and medical gas in hospitals. Use specialized techniques, equipment, or materials, such as performing computer-assisted welding of small pipes or working with the special piping used in microchip fabrication.

Personality Type: Realistic. Realistic occupations frequently involve work activities that include practical, hands-on problems and solutions. They often deal with plants; animals; and real-world materials such as wood, tools, and machinery. Many of the occupations require working outside and do not involve a lot of paperwork or working closely with others.

GOE—Interest Area: 02. Architecture and Construction. **Work Group:** 02.04. Construction Crafts. **Other Jobs in This Work Group:** Boilermakers; Brickmasons and Blockmasons; Carpet Installers; Cement Masons and Concrete Finishers; Commercial Divers; Construction Carpenters; Crane and Tower Operators; Drywall and Ceiling Tile Installers; Electricians; Fence Erectors; Floor Layers, Except Carpet, Wood, and Hard Tiles; Floor Sanders and Finishers; Glaziers; Hazardous Materials Removal Workers; Insulation Workers, Floor, Ceiling, and Wall; Insulation Workers, Mechanical; Manufactured Building and Mobile Home Installers; Operating Engineers and Other Construction Equipment Operators; Painters, Construction and Maintenance; Paperhangers; Paving, Surfacing, and

Tamping Equipment Operators; Pile-Driver Operators; Pipe Fitters and Steamfitters; Pipelayers; Plasterers and Stucco Masons; Plumbers, Pipefitters, and Steamfitters; Rail-Track Laying and Maintenance Equipment Operators; Refractory Materials Repairers, Except Brickmasons; Reinforcing Iron and Rebar Workers; Riggers; Roofers; Rough Carpenters; Security and Fire Alarm Systems Installers; Segmental Pavers; Sheet Metal Workers; Stone Cutters and Carvers, Manufacturing; Stonemasons; Structural Iron and Steel Workers; Tapers; Terrazzo Workers and Finishers; Tile and Marble Setters.

Skills—Installation: Installing equipment, machines, wiring, or programs to meet specifications. **Repairing:** Repairing machines or systems by using the needed tools. **Systems Evaluation:** Identifying measures or indicators of system performance and the actions needed to improve or correct performance relative to the goals of the system. **Management of Material Resources:** Obtaining and seeing to the appropriate use of equipment, facilities, and materials needed to do certain work. **Science:** Using scientific rules and methods to solve problems. **Management of Financial Resources:** Determining how money will be spent to get the work done and accounting for these expenditures.

Education and Training Programs: Pipefitting/ Pipefitter and Sprinkler Fitter Training; Plumbing and Related Water Supply Services, Other; Plumbing Technology/Plumber Training. **Related Knowledge/ Courses: Building and Construction:** The materials, methods, and tools involved in the construction or repair of houses, buildings, or other structures such as highways and roads. **Physics:** Physical principles and laws and their interrelationships and applications to understanding fluid, material, and atmospheric dynamics and mechanical, electrical, atomic, and subatomic structures and processes. **Mechanical Devices:** Machines and tools, including their designs, uses, repair, and maintenance. **Chemistry:** The chemical composition, structure, and properties of substances and of the chemical processes and transformations that they undergo. This includes uses of chemicals and their danger signs, production tech-

niques, and disposal methods. **Design:** Design techniques, tools, and principles involved in production of precision technical plans, blueprints, drawings, and models. **Sales and Marketing:** Principles and methods for showing, promoting, and selling products or services. This includes marketing strategy and tactics, product demonstration, sales techniques, and sales control systems.

Work Environment: Outdoors; contaminants; cramped work space, awkward positions; hazardous equipment; minor burns, cuts, bites, or stings; using hands on objects, tools, or controls.

Plumbers, Pipefitters, and Steamfitters

See the descriptions of these jobs:

- Pipe Fitters and Steamfitters
- Plumbers

Poets, Lyricists, and Creative Writers

This job can be found in the Part II lists under the title Writers and Authors.

- Education/Training Required: Bachelor's degree
- Annual Earnings: $46,420
- Growth: 17.7%
- Annual Job Openings: 14,000
- Self-Employed: 67.7%
- Part-Time: 30.7%

The job openings listed here are shared with Copy Writers.

Level of Solitary Work: 72.6 (out of 100)

Level of Contact with Others: 67.4 (out of 100)

Create original written works, such as scripts, essays, prose, poetry, or song lyrics, for publication or performance. Revise written material to meet personal standards and to satisfy needs of clients, publishers, directors, or producers. Choose subject matter and suitable form to express personal feelings and experiences or ideas or to narrate stories or events. Plan project arrangements or outlines and organize material accordingly. Prepare works in appropriate format for publication and send them to publishers or producers. Follow appropriate procedures to get copyrights for completed work. Write fiction or nonfiction prose such as short stories, novels, biographies, articles, descriptive or critical analyses, and essays. Develop factors such as themes, plots, characterizations, psychological analyses, historical environments, action, and dialogue to create material. Confer with clients, editors, publishers, or producers to discuss changes or revisions to written material. Conduct research to obtain factual information and authentic detail, using sources such as newspaper accounts, diaries, and interviews. Write narrative, dramatic, lyric, or other types of poetry for publication. Attend book launches and publicity events or conduct public readings. Write words to fit musical compositions, including lyrics for operas, musical plays, and choral works. Adapt text to accommodate musical requirements of composers and singers. Teach writing classes. Write humorous material for publication or for performances such as comedy routines, gags, and comedy shows. Collaborate with other writers on specific projects.

Personality Type: Artistic. Artistic occupations frequently involve working with forms, designs, and patterns. They often require self-expression, and the work can be done without following a clear set of rules.

GOE—Interest Area: 03. Arts and Communication. **Work Group:** 03.02. Writing and Editing. **Other Jobs in This Work Group:** Copy Writers; Editors; Technical Writers; Writers and Authors.

Skills—Writing: Communicating effectively in writing as appropriate for the needs of the audience. **Social Perceptiveness:** Being aware of others' reactions and understanding why they react as they do. **Persuasion:** Persuading others to change their minds or behavior. **Management of Financial Resources:** Determining how money will be spent to get the work done and accounting for these expenditures. **Active Listening:** Giving full attention to what other people are saying, taking time to understand the points being made, asking questions as appropriate, and not interrupting at inappropriate times. **Reading Comprehension:** Understanding written sentences and paragraphs in work-related documents.

Education and Training Programs: Communication Studies/Speech Communication and Rhetoric; Creative Writing; English Composition; Family and Consumer Sciences/Human Sciences Communication; Mass Communication/Media Studies; Playwriting and Screenwriting. **Related Knowledge/ Courses: Fine Arts:** The theory and techniques required to compose, produce, and perform works of music, dance, visual arts, drama, and sculpture. **Communications and Media:** Media production, communication, and dissemination techniques and methods. This includes alternative ways to inform and entertain via written, oral, and visual media. **Philosophy and Theology:** Different philosophical systems and religions. This includes their basic principles, values, ethics, ways of thinking, customs, and practices and their impact on human culture. **Sociology and Anthropology:** Group behavior and dynamics, societal trends and influences, human migrations, ethnicity, and cultures and their history and origins. **Sales and Marketing:** Principles and methods for showing, promoting, and selling products or services. This includes marketing strategy and tactics, product demonstration, sales techniques, and sales control systems. **English Language:** The structure and content of the English language, including the meaning and spelling of words, rules of composition, and grammar.

Work Environment: Indoors; sitting; using hands on objects, tools, or controls; repetitive motions.

Political Scientists

- Education/Training Required: Master's degree
- Annual Earnings: $84,100
- Growth: 7.3%
- Annual Job Openings: Fewer than 500
- Self-Employed: 4.7%
- Part-Time: 14.8%

Level of Solitary Work: 59.2 (out of 100)

Level of Contact with Others: 78.3 (out of 100)

Study the origin, development, and operation of political systems. Research a wide range of subjects, such as relations between the United States and foreign countries, the beliefs and institutions of foreign nations, or the politics of small towns or a major metropolis. May study topics such as public opinion, political decision making, and ideology. May analyze the structure and operation of governments as well as various political entities. May conduct public opinion surveys, analyze election results, or analyze public documents. Teach political science. Disseminate research results through academic publications, written reports, or public presentations. Identify issues for research and analysis. Develop and test theories, using information from interviews, newspapers, periodicals, case law, historical papers, polls, and/or statistical sources. Maintain current knowledge of government policy decisions. Collect, analyze, and interpret data such as election results and public opinion surveys; report on findings, recommendations, and conclusions. Interpret and analyze policies; public issues; legislation; and the operations of governments, businesses, and organizations. Evaluate programs and policies and make related recommendations to institutions and organizations. Write drafts of legislative proposals and prepare speeches, correspondence, and policy papers for governmental use. Forecast political, economic, and social trends. Consult with and advise government officials, civic bodies, research agencies, the media, political parties, and others concerned with political issues. Provide media commentary and/or criticism related to public policy and political issues and events.

Personality Type: Investigative. Investigative occupations frequently involve working with ideas and require an extensive amount of thinking. These occupations can involve searching for facts and figuring out problems mentally.

GOE—Interest Area: 15. Scientific Research, Engineering, and Mathematics. **Work Group:** 15.04. Social Sciences. **Other Jobs in This Work Group:** Anthropologists; Anthropologists and Archeologists; Archeologists; Economists; Historians; Industrial-Organizational Psychologists; School Psychologists; Sociologists.

Skills—Writing: Communicating effectively in writing as appropriate for the needs of the audience. **Reading Comprehension:** Understanding written sentences and paragraphs in work-related documents. **Critical Thinking:** Using logic and reasoning to identify the strengths and weaknesses of alternative solutions, conclusions, or approaches to problems. **Speaking:** Talking to others to convey information effectively. **Active Learning:** Understanding the implications of new information for both current and future problem solving and decision making. **Instructing:** Teaching others how to do something.

Education and Training Programs: American Government and Politics (United States); Canadian Government and Politics; International/Global Studies; Political Science and Government, General; Political Science and Government, Other. **Related Knowledge/Courses: History and Archeology:** Historical events and their causes, indicators, and effects on civilizations and cultures. **Law and Government:** Laws, legal codes, court procedures, precedents, government regulations, executive orders, agency rules, and the democratic political process. **Philosophy and Theology:** Different philosophical systems and religions. This includes their basic principles, values, ethics, ways of thinking, customs, and practices and their impact on human culture. **Sociology and Anthropology:** Group behavior and dynamics, societal trends and influences, human migrations, ethnicity, and cultures and their history and origins. **Foreign Language:** The structure and content of a foreign (non-English) language, including the meaning and spelling of words, rules of composition and grammar, and pronunciation. **Geography:** Principles and methods for describing the features of land, sea, and air masses, including their physical characteristics; locations; interrelationships; and distribution of plant, animal, and human life.

Work Environment: Indoors; sitting.

Postal Service Mail Carriers

- ◎ Education/Training Required: Short-term on-the-job training
- ◎ Annual Earnings: $46,330
- ◎ Growth: 0.0%
- ◎ Annual Job Openings: 19,000
- ◎ Self-Employed: 0.0%
- ◎ Part-Time: 9.8%

Level of Solitary Work: 100.0 (out of 100)

Level of Contact with Others: 83.5 (out of 100)

Sort mail for delivery. Deliver mail on established route by vehicle or on foot. Obtain signed receipts for registered, certified, and insured mail; collect associated charges; and complete any necessary paperwork. Sort mail for delivery, arranging it in delivery sequence. Deliver mail to residences and business establishments along specified routes by walking or driving, using a combination of satchels, carts, cars, and small trucks. Return to the post office with mail collected from homes, businesses, and public mailboxes. Turn in money and receipts collected along mail routes. Sign for cash-on-delivery and reg-

istered mail before leaving the post office. Record address changes and redirect mail for those addresses. Hold mail for customers who are away from delivery locations. Bundle mail in preparation for delivery or transportation to relay boxes. Leave notices telling patrons where to collect mail that could not be delivered. Meet schedules for the collection and return of mail. Return incorrectly addressed mail to senders. Maintain accurate records of deliveries. Answer customers' questions about postal services and regulations. Provide customers with change of address cards and other forms. Report any unusual circumstances concerning mail delivery, including the condition of street letter boxes. Register, certify, and insure parcels and letters. Travel to post offices to pick up the mail for routes or pick up mail from postal relay boxes. Enter change of address orders into computers that process forwarding address stickers. Complete forms that notify publishers of address changes. Sell stamps and money orders.

Personality Type: Conventional. Conventional occupations frequently involve following set procedures and routines. These occupations can include working with data and details more than with ideas. Usually there is a clear line of authority to follow.

GOE—Interest Area: 16. Transportation, Distribution, and Logistics. **Work Group:** 16.06. Other Services Requiring Driving. **Other Jobs in This Work Group:** Ambulance Drivers and Attendants, Except Emergency Medical Technicians; Bus Drivers, School; Bus Drivers, Transit and Intercity; Couriers and Messengers; Driver/Sales Workers; Parking Lot Attendants; Taxi Drivers and Chauffeurs.

Skills—None met the criteria.

Education and Training Program: General Office Occupations and Clerical Services. **Related Knowledge/Courses: Transportation:** Principles and methods for moving people or goods by air, rail, sea, or road, including the relative costs and benefits. **Public Safety and Security:** Relevant equipment, policies, procedures, and strategies to promote effective local, state, or national security operations for the protection of people, data, property, and institutions. **Customer and Personal Service:** Principles and processes for providing customer and personal services. This includes customer needs assessment, meeting quality standards for services, and evaluation of customer satisfaction.

Work Environment: Outdoors; very hot or cold; contaminants; standing; using hands on objects, tools, or controls; repetitive motions.

Prepress Technicians and Workers

- ◎ Education/Training Required: Postsecondary vocational training
- ◎ Annual Earnings: $32,840
- ◎ Growth: –8.4%
- ◎ Annual Job Openings: 10,000
- ◎ Self-Employed: 2.1%
- ◎ Part-Time: 15.0%

Level of Solitary Work: 72.3 (out of 100)

Level of Contact with Others: 73.0 (out of 100)

Set up and prepare material for printing presses. Enter, store, and retrieve information on computer-aided equipment. Enter, position, and alter text size, using computers, to make up and arrange pages so that printed materials can be produced. Maintain, adjust, and clean equipment and perform minor repairs. Operate and maintain laser plate-making equipment that converts electronic data to plates without the use of film. Examine photographic images for obvious imperfections prior to platemaking. Operate presses to print proofs of plates, monitoring printing quality to ensure that it is adequate. Monitor contact between cover glass and masks inside vacuum frames to prevent flaws resulting from overexposure or light reflection. Transfer images from master plates to unexposed plates and immerse plates

in developing solutions to develop images. Examine unexposed photographic plates to detect flaws or foreign particles prior to printing. Lower vacuum frames onto plate-film assemblies, activate vacuums to establish contact between film and plates, and set timers to activate ultraviolet lights that expose plates. Examine finished plates to detect flaws, verify conformity with master plates, and measure dot sizes and centers, using light-boxes and microscopes. Perform close alignment or registration of double and single flats to sensitized plates prior to exposure to produce composite images. Remove plate-film assemblies from vacuum frames and place exposed plates in automatic processors to develop images and dry plates. Position and angle screens for proper exposure. Inspect developed film for specified results and quality, using magnifying glasses and scopes; forward acceptable negatives or positives to other workers or to customers. Punch holes in light-sensitive plates and insert pins in holes to prepare plates for contact with positive or negative film. Unload exposed film from scanners and place film in automatic processors to develop images. Place masking paper on areas of plates not covered by positives or negatives to prevent exposure. Mount negatives and plates in cameras, set exposure controls, and expose plates to light through negatives to transfer images onto plates.

Personality Type: Realistic. Realistic occupations frequently involve work activities that include practical, hands-on problems and solutions. They often deal with plants; animals; and real-world materials such as wood, tools, and machinery. Many of the occupations require working outside and do not involve a lot of paperwork or working closely with others.

GOE—Interest Area: 13. Manufacturing. **Work Group:** 13.08. Graphic Arts Production. **Other Jobs in This Work Group:** Bindery Workers; Desktop Publishers; Etchers and Engravers; Job Printers; Photographic Process Workers; Photographic Processing Machine Operators; Printing Machine Operators.

Skills—Troubleshooting: Determining causes of operating errors and deciding what to do about them.

Equipment Selection: Determining the kind of tools and equipment needed to do a job. Installation: Installing equipment, machines, wiring, or programs to meet specifications. Equipment Maintenance: Performing routine maintenance on equipment and determining when and what kind of maintenance is needed. Operation and Control: Controlling operations of equipment or systems. Operations Analysis: Analyzing needs and product requirements to create a design.

Education and Training Programs: Graphic and Printing Equipment Operator, General Production; Graphic Communications, General; Graphic Communications, Other; Graphic Design; Platemaker/ Imager; Precision Production Trades, Other. Related Knowledge/Courses: Computers and Electronics: Circuit boards, processors, chips, electronic equipment, and computer hardware and software, including applications and programming. Communications and Media: Media production, communication, and dissemination techniques and methods. This includes alternative ways to inform and entertain via written, oral, and visual media. English Language: The structure and content of the English language, including the meaning and spelling of words, rules of composition, and grammar. Design: Design techniques, tools, and principles involved in production of precision technical plans, blueprints, drawings, and models. Production and Processing: Raw materials, production processes, quality control, costs, and other techniques for maximizing the effective manufacture and distribution of goods. Clerical Practices: Administrative and clerical procedures and systems such as word processing, managing files and records, stenography and transcription, designing forms, and other office procedures and terminology.

Work Environment: Indoors; noisy; contaminants; sitting; using hands on objects, tools, or controls; repetitive motions.

Printing Machine Operators

- Education/Training Required: Moderate-term on-the-job training
- Annual Earnings: $30,730
- Growth: 2.9%
- Annual Job Openings: 26,000
- Self-Employed: 3.2%
- Part-Time: 8.1%

Level of Solitary Work: 71.0 (out of 100)

Level of Contact with Others: 65.0 (out of 100)

Set up or operate various types of printing machines, such as offset, letterset, intaglio, or gravure presses or screen printers, to produce print on paper or other materials. Inspect and examine printed products for print clarity, color accuracy, conformance to specifications, and external defects. Push buttons, turn handles, or move controls and levers to start and control printing machines. Reposition printing plates, adjust pressure rolls, or otherwise adjust machines to improve print quality, using knobs, handwheels, or hand tools. Set and adjust speed, temperature, ink flow, and positions and pressure tolerances of equipment. Examine job orders to determine details such as quantities to be printed, production times, stock specifications, colors, and color sequences. Select and install printing plates, rollers, feed guides, gauges, screens, stencils, type, dies, and cylinders in machines according to specifications, using hand tools. Monitor feeding, printing, and racking processes of presses to maintain specified operating levels and to detect malfunctions; make any necessary adjustments. Operate equipment at slow speed to ensure proper ink coverage, alignment, and registration. Load, position, and adjust unprinted materials on holding fixtures or in equipment loading and feeding mechanisms. Pour or spread paint, ink, color compounds, and other materials into reservoirs, troughs, hoppers, or color holders of printing units, making measurements and adjustments to control color and viscosity. Repair, maintain, or adjust equipment. Blend and test paint, inks, stains, and solvents according to types of material being printed and work order specifications. Clean and lubricate printing machines and components, using oil, solvents, brushes, rags, and hoses. Remove printed materials from presses, using handtrucks, electric lifts, or hoists, and transport them to drying, storage, or finishing areas. Input instructions to program automated machinery, using a computer keyboard. Place printed items in ovens to dry or set ink. Squeeze or spread ink on plates, pads, or rollers, using putty knives, brushes, or sponges. Measure screens and use measurements to center and align screens in proper positions and sequences on machines, using gauges and hand tools.

Personality Type: Realistic. Realistic occupations frequently involve work activities that include practical, hands-on problems and solutions. They often deal with plants; animals; and real-world materials such as wood, tools, and machinery. Many of the occupations require working outside and do not involve a lot of paperwork or working closely with others.

GOE—Interest Area: 13. Manufacturing. **Work Group:** 13.08. Graphic Arts Production. **Other Jobs in This Work Group:** Bindery Workers; Desktop Publishers; Etchers and Engravers; Job Printers; Photographic Process Workers; Photographic Processing Machine Operators; Prepress Technicians and Workers.

Skills—Operation Monitoring: Watching gauges, dials, or other indicators to make sure a machine is working properly. **Operation and Control:** Controlling operations of equipment or systems. **Equipment Maintenance:** Performing routine maintenance on equipment and determining when and what kind of maintenance is needed. **Repairing:** Repairing machines or systems by using the needed tools. **Quality Control Analysis:** Conducting tests and inspections of products, services, or processes to evaluate quality or performance. **Troubleshooting:** Determining causes of operating errors and deciding what to do about them.

Education and Training Programs: Graphic and Printing Equipment Operator, General Production; Graphic Communications, Other; Printing Management; Printing Press Operator Training. **Related Knowledge/Courses: Mechanical Devices:** Machines and tools, including their designs, uses, repair, and maintenance. **Production and Processing:** Raw materials, production processes, quality control, costs, and other techniques for maximizing the effective manufacture and distribution of goods. **Chemistry:** The chemical composition, structure, and properties of substances and of the chemical processes and transformations that they undergo. This includes uses of chemicals and their danger signs, production techniques, and disposal methods.

Work Environment: Noisy; contaminants; hazardous conditions; hazardous equipment; standing; using hands on objects, tools, or controls.

Private Detectives and Investigators

- Education/Training Required: Work experience in a related occupation
- Annual Earnings: $32,650
- Growth: 17.7%
- Annual Job Openings: 7,000
- Self-Employed: 23.7%
- Part-Time: 16.1%

Level of Solitary Work: 46.7 (out of 100)

Level of Contact with Others: 70.0 (out of 100)

Detect occurrences of unlawful acts or infractions of rules in private establishment or seek, examine, and compile information for client. Question persons to obtain evidence for cases of divorce, child custody, or missing persons or information about individuals' character or financial status. Conduct private investigations on a paid basis. Confer with establishment officials, security departments, police, or postal officials to identify problems, provide information, and receive instructions. Observe and document activities of individuals to detect unlawful acts or to obtain evidence for cases, using binoculars and still or video cameras. Investigate companies' financial standings or locate funds stolen by embezzlers, using accounting skills. Monitor industrial or commercial properties to enforce conformance to establishment rules and to protect people or property. Search computer databases, credit reports, public records, tax and legal filings, and other resources to locate persons or to compile information for investigations. Write reports and case summaries to document investigations. Count cash and review transactions, sales checks, and register tapes to verify amounts and to identify shortages. Perform undercover operations such as evaluating the performance and honesty of employees by posing as customers or employees. Expose fraudulent insurance claims or stolen funds. Alert appropriate personnel to suspects' locations. Conduct background investigations of individuals, such as pre-employment checks, to obtain information about an individual's character, financial status, or personal history. Testify at hearings and court trials to present evidence. Warn troublemakers causing problems on establishment premises and eject them from premises when necessary. Obtain and analyze information on suspects, crimes, and disturbances to solve cases, to identify criminal activity, and to gather information for court cases. Apprehend suspects and release them to law enforcement authorities or security personnel.

Personality Type: Enterprising. Enterprising occupations frequently involve starting up and carrying out projects. These occupations can involve leading people and making many decisions. They sometimes require risk taking and often deal with business.

GOE—Interest Area: 12. Law and Public Safety. **Work Group:** 12.05. Safety and Security. **Other Jobs in This Work Group:** Animal Control Workers; Crossing Guards; Gaming Surveillance Officers and Gaming Investigators; Lifeguards, Ski Patrol, and Other Recreational Protective Service Workers; Security Guards; Transportation Security Screeners.

Skills—Systems Evaluation: Identifying measures or indicators of system performance and the actions needed to improve or correct performance relative to the goals of the system. **Systems Analysis:** Determining how a system should work and how changes in conditions, operations, and the environment will affect outcomes. **Persuasion:** Persuading others to change their minds or behavior. **Writing:** Communicating effectively in writing as appropriate for the needs of the audience. **Active Listening:** Giving full attention to what other people are saying, taking time to understand the points being made, asking questions as appropriate, and not interrupting at inappropriate times. **Speaking:** Talking to others to convey information effectively.

Education and Training Program: Criminal Justice/Police Science. **Related Knowledge/Courses: Public Safety and Security:** Relevant equipment, policies, procedures, and strategies to promote effective local, state, or national security operations for the protection of people, data, property, and institutions. **Law and Government:** Laws, legal codes, court procedures, precedents, government regulations, executive orders, agency rules, and the democratic political process.

Work Environment: More often indoors than outdoors; standing; walking and running.

P

Product Safety Engineers

This job can be found in the Part II lists under the title Health and Safety Engineers, Except Mining Safety Engineers and Inspectors.

- Education/Training Required: Bachelor's degree
- Annual Earnings: $65,210
- Growth: 13.4%
- Annual Job Openings: 2,000
- Self-Employed: 0.5%
- Part-Time: 2.6%

The job openings listed here are shared with Fire-Prevention and Protection Engineers and with Industrial Safety and Health Engineers.

Level of Solitary Work: 47.8 (out of 100)

Level of Contact with Others: 66.7 (out of 100)

Develop and conduct tests to evaluate product safety levels and recommend measures to reduce or eliminate hazards. Report accident investigation findings. Conduct research to evaluate safety levels for products. Evaluate potential health hazards or damage that could occur from product misuse. Investigate causes of accidents, injuries, or illnesses related to product usage in order to develop solutions to minimize or prevent recurrence. Participate in preparation of product usage and precautionary label instructions. Recommend procedures for detection, prevention, and elimination of physical, chemical, or other product hazards.

Personality Type: Investigative. Investigative occupations frequently involve working with ideas and require an extensive amount of thinking. These occupations can involve searching for facts and figuring out problems mentally.

GOE—Interest Area: 15. Scientific Research, Engineering, and Mathematics. **Work Group:** 15.08. Industrial and Safety Engineering. **Other Jobs in This Work Group:** Fire-Prevention and Protection Engineers; Health and Safety Engineers, Except Mining Safety Engineers and Inspectors; Industrial Engineers; Industrial Safety and Health Engineers.

Skills—Quality Control Analysis: Conducting tests and inspections of products, services, or processes to evaluate quality or performance. **Science:** Using scientific rules and methods to solve problems. **Operations Analysis:** Analyzing needs and product requirements to create a design. **Mathematics:** Using mathematics to solve problems. **Technology Design:** Generating or adapting equipment and technology to serve user needs. **Systems Evaluation:** Identifying measures or indicators of system performance and the actions needed to improve or correct performance relative to the goals of the system.

Education and Training Program: Environmental/ Environmental Health Engineering. **Related Knowledge/Courses: Chemistry:** The chemical composition, structure, and properties of substances and of the chemical processes and transformations that they undergo. This includes uses of chemicals and their danger signs, production techniques, and disposal methods. **Engineering and Technology:** The practical application of engineering science and technology. This includes applying principles, techniques, procedures, and equipment to the design and production of various goods and services. **Physics:** Physical principles and laws and their interrelationships and applications to understanding fluid, material, and atmospheric dynamics and mechanical, electrical, atomic, and subatomic structures and processes. **Biology:** Plant and animal organisms and their tissues, cells, functions, interdependencies, and interactions with each other and the environment. **Public Safety and Security:** Relevant equipment, policies, procedures, and strategies to promote effective local, state, or national security operations for the protection of people, data, property, and institutions.

Production and Processing: Raw materials, production processes, quality control, costs, and other techniques for maximizing the effective manufacture and distribution of goods.

Work Environment: Indoors; sitting; using hands on objects, tools, or controls.

Purchasing Agents and Buyers, Farm Products

- ◎ Education/Training Required: Work experience in a related occupation
- ◎ Annual Earnings: $46,680
- ◎ Growth: 7.0%
- ◎ Annual Job Openings: 2,000
- ◎ Self-Employed: 8.5%
- ◎ Part-Time: 10.3%

Level of Solitary Work: 46.7 (out of 100)

Level of Contact with Others: 66.8 (out of 100)

Purchase farm products for further processing or resale. Advise farm groups and growers on land preparation and livestock care techniques that will maximize the quantity and quality of production. Arrange for processing or resale of purchased products. Arrange for transportation and/or storage of purchased products. Examine and test crops and products to estimate their value, determine their grade, and locate any evidence of disease or insect damage. Maintain records of business transactions and product inventories, reporting data to companies or government agencies as necessary. Negotiate contracts with farmers for the production or purchase of farm products. Review orders to determine product types and quantities required to meet demand. Estimate land production possibilities, surveying property and studying factors such as crop rotation history, soil fertility, and irrigation facilities. Sell supplies such as seed, feed, fertilizers, and insecticides,

arranging for loans or financing as necessary. Coordinate and direct activities of workers engaged in cutting, transporting, storing, or milling products and in maintaining records. Purchase for further processing or for resale farm products such as milk, grains, and Christmas trees. Calculate applicable government grain quotas.

Personality Type: Enterprising. Enterprising occupations frequently involve starting up and carrying out projects. These occupations can involve leading people and making many decisions. They sometimes require risk taking and often deal with business.

GOE—Interest Area: 01. Agriculture and Natural Resources. **Work Group:** 01.01. Managerial Work in Agriculture and Natural Resources. **Other Jobs in This Work Group:** Aquacultural Managers; Crop and Livestock Managers; Farm Labor Contractors; Farm, Ranch, and Other Agricultural Managers; Farmers and Ranchers; First-Line Supervisors/Managers of Agricultural Crop and Horticultural Workers; First-Line Supervisors/Managers of Animal Husbandry and Animal Care Workers; First-Line Supervisors/Managers of Aquacultural Workers; First-Line Supervisors/Managers of Construction Trades and Extraction Workers; First-Line Supervisors/Managers of Farming, Fishing, and Forestry Workers; First-Line Supervisors/Managers of Landscaping, Lawn Service, and Groundskeeping Workers; First-Line Supervisors/Managers of Logging Workers; Nursery and Greenhouse Managers; Park Naturalists.

Skills—Negotiation: Bringing others together and trying to reconcile differences. **Management of Financial Resources:** Determining how money will be spent to get the work done and accounting for these expenditures. **Writing:** Communicating effectively in writing as appropriate for the needs of the audience. **Mathematics:** Using mathematics to solve problems. **Management of Material Resources:** Obtaining and seeing to the appropriate use of equipment, facilities, and materials needed to do certain work. **Speaking:** Talking to others to convey information effectively.

P

Education and Training Program: Agricultural/Farm Supplies Retailing and Wholesaling. **Related Knowledge/Courses: Food Production:** Techniques and equipment for planting, growing, and harvesting food products (both plant and animal) for consumption, including storage/handling techniques. **Production and Processing:** Raw materials, production processes, quality control, costs, and other techniques for maximizing the effective manufacture and distribution of goods. **Biology:** Plant and animal organisms and their tissues, cells, functions, interdependencies, and interactions with each other and the environment. **Communications and Media:** Media production, communication, and dissemination techniques and methods. This includes alternative ways to inform and entertain via written, oral, and visual media. **Economics and Accounting:** Economic and accounting principles and practices, the financial markets, banking, and the analysis and reporting of financial data. **Sales and Marketing:** Principles and methods for showing, promoting, and selling products or services. This includes marketing strategy and tactics, product demonstration, sales techniques, and sales control systems.

Work Environment: Indoors; more often sitting than standing; walking and running; using hands on objects, tools, or controls.

Rail Car Repairers

- ◎ Education/Training Required: Long-term on-the-job training
- ◎ Annual Earnings: $42,530
- ◎ Growth: −1.2%
- ◎ Annual Job Openings: 2,000
- ◎ Self-Employed: 2.1%
- ◎ Part-Time: 3.0%

Level of Solitary Work: 62.5 (out of 100)

Level of Contact with Others: 69.5 (out of 100)

Diagnose, adjust, repair, or overhaul railroad rolling stock, mine cars, or mass-transit rail cars. Repair or replace defective or worn parts such as bearings, pistons, and gears, using hand tools, torque wrenches, power tools, and welding equipment. Test units for operability before and after repairs. Remove locomotives, car mechanical units, or other components, using pneumatic hoists and jacks, pinch bars, hand tools, and cutting torches. Record conditions of cars and repair and maintenance work performed or to be performed. Inspect components such as bearings, seals, gaskets, wheels, and coupler assemblies to determine if repairs are needed. Inspect the interior and exterior of rail cars coming into rail yards to identify defects and to determine the extent of wear and damage. Adjust repaired or replaced units as needed to ensure proper operation. Perform scheduled maintenance and clean units and components. Repair and maintain electrical and electronic controls for propulsion and braking systems. Repair, fabricate, and install steel or wood fittings, using blueprints, shop sketches, and instruction manuals. Disassemble units such as water pumps, control valves, and compressors so that repairs can be made. Align car sides for installation of car ends and crossties, using width gauges, turnbuckles, and wrenches. Measure diameters of axle wheel seats, using micrometers, and mark dimensions on axles so that wheels can be bored to specified dimensions. Replace defective wiring and insulation and tighten electrical connections, using hand tools. Test electrical systems of cars by operating systems and using testing equipment such as ammeters. Install and repair interior flooring, fixtures, walls, plumbing, steps, and platforms. Examine car roofs for wear and damage and repair defective sections, using roofing material, cement, nails, and waterproof paint. Paint car exteriors, interiors, and fixtures. Repair car upholstery. Repair window sash frames, attach weather stripping and channels to frames, and replace window glass, using hand tools.

Personality Type: Realistic. Realistic occupations frequently involve work activities that include practical, hands-on problems and solutions. They often deal with plants; animals; and real-world materials such as

wood, tools, and machinery. Many of the occupations require working outside and do not involve a lot of paperwork or working closely with others.

GOE—Interest Area: 13. Manufacturing. **Work Group:** 13.14. Vehicle and Facility Mechanical Work. **Other Jobs in This Work Group:** Aircraft Mechanics and Service Technicians; Aircraft Structure, Surfaces, Rigging, and Systems Assemblers; Automotive Body and Related Repairers; Automotive Glass Installers and Repairers; Automotive Master Mechanics; Automotive Service Technicians and Mechanics; Automotive Specialty Technicians; Bus and Truck Mechanics and Diesel Engine Specialists; Farm Equipment Mechanics; Fiberglass Laminators and Fabricators; Mobile Heavy Equipment Mechanics, Except Engines; Motorboat Mechanics; Motorcycle Mechanics; Outdoor Power Equipment and Other Small Engine Mechanics; Recreational Vehicle Service Technicians; Tire Repairers and Changers.

Skills—Repairing: Repairing machines or systems by using the needed tools. **Installation:** Installing equipment, machines, wiring, or programs to meet specifications. **Equipment Maintenance:** Performing routine maintenance on equipment and determining when and what kind of maintenance is needed. **Troubleshooting:** Determining causes of operating errors and deciding what to do about them. **Operation Monitoring:** Watching gauges, dials, or other indicators to make sure a machine is working properly. **Technology Design:** Generating or adapting equipment and technology to serve user needs.

Education and Training Program: Heavy Equipment Maintenance Technology/Technician Training. **Related Knowledge/Courses: Mechanical Devices:** Machines and tools, including their designs, uses, repair, and maintenance. **Public Safety and Security:** Relevant equipment, policies, procedures, and strategies to promote effective local, state, or national security operations for the protection of people, data, property, and institutions. **Production and Processing:** Raw materials, production processes, quality control, costs, and other techniques for max-

imizing the effective manufacture and distribution of goods.

Work Environment: Outdoors; noisy; very hot or cold; contaminants; standing; using hands on objects, tools, or controls.

Range Managers

This job can be found in the Part II lists under the title Conservation Scientists.

- ◎ Education/Training Required: Bachelor's degree
- ◎ Annual Earnings: $53,350
- ◎ Growth: 6.3%
- ◎ Annual Job Openings: 2,000
- ◎ Self-Employed: 9.0%
- ◎ Part-Time: 6.7%

The job openings listed here are shared with Park Naturalists and with Soil and Water Conservationists.

Level of Solitary Work: 65.6 (out of 100)

Level of Contact with Others: 87.3 (out of 100)

Research or study range land management practices to provide sustained production of forage, livestock, and wildlife. Regulate grazing and help ranchers plan and organize grazing systems to manage, improve, and protect rangelands and maximize their use. Measure and assess vegetation resources for biological assessment companies, environmental impact statements, and rangeland monitoring programs. Maintain soil stability and vegetation for non-grazing uses, such as wildlife habitats and outdoor recreation. Mediate agreements among rangeland users and preservationists as to appropriate land use and management. Study rangeland management practices and research range problems to provide sustained production of forage, livestock, and wildlife. Manage forage resources through fire, herbicide use, or revegetation to maintain a sustainable yield from the land. Offer advice to rangeland users on water management, forage production methods, and control of brush. Plan and direct construction and maintenance of range improvements such as fencing, corrals, stock-watering reservoirs, and soil-erosion control structures. Tailor conservation plans to landowners' goals, such as livestock support, wildlife, or recreation. Develop technical standards and specifications used to manage, protect, and improve the natural resources of rangelands and related grazing lands. Study grazing patterns to determine number and kind of livestock that can be most profitably grazed and to determine the best grazing seasons. Plan and implement revegetation of disturbed sites. Study forage plants and their growth requirements to determine varieties best suited to particular range. Develop methods for protecting range from fire and rodent damage and for controlling poisonous plants. Manage private livestock operations. Develop new and improved instruments and techniques for activities such as range reseeding.

Personality Type: Investigative. Investigative occupations frequently involve working with ideas and require an extensive amount of thinking. These occupations can involve searching for facts and figuring out problems mentally.

GOE—Interest Area: 01. Agriculture and Natural Resources. **Work Group:** 01.02. Resource Science/Engineering for Plants, Animals, and the Environment. **Other Jobs in This Work Group:** Agricultural Engineers; Animal Scientists; Conservation Scientists; Environmental Engineers; Foresters; Mining and Geological Engineers, Including Mining Safety Engineers; Petroleum Engineers; Soil and Plant Scientists; Soil and Water Conservationists; Zoologists and Wildlife Biologists.

Skills—Negotiation: Bringing others together and trying to reconcile differences. **Science:** Using scientific rules and methods to solve problems. **Management of Financial Resources:** Determining how money will be spent to get the work done and accounting for these expenditures. **Persuasion:**

Persuading others to change their minds or behavior. **Coordination:** Adjusting actions in relation to others' actions. **Systems Evaluation:** Identifying measures or indicators of system performance and the actions needed to improve or correct performance relative to the goals of the system.

Education and Training Programs: Forest Management/Forest Resources Management; Forest Sciences and Biology; Forestry, General; Forestry, Other; Land Use Planning and Management/Development; Natural Resources and Conservation, Other; Natural Resources Management and Policy; Natural Resources Management and Policy, Other; Natural Resources/Conservation, General; Water, Wetlands, and Marine Resources Management; Wildlife and Wildlands Science and Management. **Related Knowledge/Courses: Biology:** Plant and animal organisms and their tissues, cells, functions, interdependencies, and interactions with each other and the environment. **Geography:** Principles and methods for describing the features of land, sea, and air masses, including their physical characteristics; locations; interrelationships; and distribution of plant, animal, and human life. **Food Production:** Techniques and equipment for planting, growing, and harvesting food products (both plant and animal) for consumption, including storage/handling techniques. **History and Archeology:** Historical events and their causes, indicators, and effects on civilizations and cultures. **Law and Government:** Laws, legal codes, court procedures, precedents, government regulations, executive orders, agency rules, and the democratic political process. **Engineering and Technology:** The practical application of engineering science and technology. This includes applying principles, techniques, procedures, and equipment to the design and production of various goods and services.

Work Environment: More often outdoors than indoors; noisy; very hot or cold; minor burns, cuts, bites, or stings; sitting.

Recreational Vehicle Service Technicians

- ◎ Education/Training Required: Long-term on-the-job training
- ◎ Annual Earnings: $30,480
- ◎ Growth: 19.5%
- ◎ Annual Job Openings: 3,000
- ◎ Self-Employed: 3.6%
- ◎ Part-Time: 19.6%

Level of Solitary Work: 53.0 (out of 100)

Level of Contact with Others: 75.0 (out of 100)

Diagnose, inspect, adjust, repair, or overhaul recreational vehicles, including travel trailers. May specialize in maintaining gas, electrical, hydraulic, plumbing, or chassis/towing systems as well as repairing generators, appliances, and interior components. Examine or test operation of parts or systems that have been repaired to ensure completeness of repairs. Repair plumbing and propane gas lines, using caulking compounds and plastic or copper pipe. Inspect recreational vehicles to diagnose problems; then perform necessary adjustment, repair, or overhaul. Locate and repair frayed wiring, broken connections, or incorrect wiring, using ohmmeters, soldering irons, tape, and hand tools. Confer with customers, read work orders, and examine vehicles needing repair to determine the nature and extent of damage. List parts needed, estimate costs, and plan work procedures, using parts lists, technical manuals, and diagrams. Connect electrical systems to outside power sources and activate switches to test the operation of appliances and light fixtures. Connect water hoses to inlet pipes of plumbing systems and test operation of toilets and sinks. Remove damaged exterior panels and repair and replace structural frame members. Open and close doors, windows, and drawers to test their operation, trimming edges to fit as necessary. Repair leaks with caulking compound or replace pipes, using pipe wrenches. Refinish wood surfaces on cabinets, doors, moldings, and floors, using power sanders, putty, spray equipment, brushes, paints, or varnishes. Reset hardware, using chisels, mallets, and screwdrivers. Seal open sides of modular units to prepare them for shipment, using polyethylene sheets, nails, and hammers.

Personality Type: Realistic. Realistic occupations frequently involve work activities that include practical, hands-on problems and solutions. They often deal with plants; animals; and real-world materials such as wood, tools, and machinery. Many of the occupations require working outside and do not involve a lot of paperwork or working closely with others.

GOE—Interest Area: 13. Manufacturing. **Work Group:** 13.14. Vehicle and Facility Mechanical Work. **Other Jobs in This Work Group:** Aircraft Mechanics and Service Technicians; Aircraft Structure, Surfaces, Rigging, and Systems Assemblers; Automotive Body and Related Repairers; Automotive Glass Installers and Repairers; Automotive Master Mechanics; Automotive Service Technicians and Mechanics; Automotive Specialty Technicians; Bus and Truck Mechanics and Diesel Engine Specialists; Farm Equipment Mechanics; Fiberglass Laminators and Fabricators; Mobile Heavy Equipment Mechanics, Except Engines; Motorboat Mechanics; Motorcycle Mechanics; Outdoor Power Equipment and Other Small Engine Mechanics; Rail Car Repairers; Tire Repairers and Changers.

Skills—Repairing: Repairing machines or systems by using the needed tools. **Installation:** Installing equipment, machines, wiring, or programs to meet specifications. **Troubleshooting:** Determining causes of operating errors and deciding what to do about them. **Equipment Maintenance:** Performing routine maintenance on equipment and determining when and what kind of maintenance is needed. **Operation Monitoring:** Watching gauges, dials, or other indicators to make sure a machine is working properly. **Technology Design:** Generating or adapting equipment and technology to serve user needs.

Education and Training Program: Vehicle Maintenance and Repair Technologies, Other. **Related**

R

Knowledge/Courses: Mechanical Devices: Machines and tools, including their designs, uses, repair, and maintenance. **Building and Construction:** The materials, methods, and tools involved in the construction or repair of houses, buildings, or other structures such as highways and roads. **Chemistry:** The chemical composition, structure, and properties of substances and of the chemical processes and transformations that they undergo. This includes uses of chemicals and their danger signs, production techniques, and disposal methods. **Physics:** Physical principles and laws and their interrelationships and applications to understanding fluid, material, and atmospheric dynamics and mechanical, electrical, atomic, and subatomic structures and processes. **Design:** Design techniques, tools, and principles involved in production of precision technical plans, blueprints, drawings, and models. **Engineering and Technology:** The practical application of engineering science and technology. This includes applying principles, techniques, procedures, and equipment to the design and production of various goods and services.

Work Environment: Noisy; contaminants; cramped work space, awkward positions; hazardous equipment; standing; using hands on objects, tools, or controls.

Refrigeration Mechanics and Installers

This job can be found in the Part II lists under the title Heating, Air Conditioning, and Refrigeration Mechanics and Installers.

- Education/Training Required: Long-term on-the-job training
- Annual Earnings: $37,040
- Growth: 19.0%
- Annual Job Openings: 33,000
- Self-Employed: 13.1%
- Part-Time: 3.6%

The job openings listed here are shared with Heating and Air Conditioning Mechanics and Installers.

Level of Solitary Work: 68.8 (out of 100)

Level of Contact with Others: 83.0 (out of 100)

Install and repair industrial and commercial refrigerating systems. Braze or solder parts to repair defective joints and leaks. Observe and test system operation, using gauges and instruments. Test lines, components, and connections for leaks. Dismantle malfunctioning systems and test components, using electrical, mechanical, and pneumatic testing equipment. Adjust or replace worn or defective mechanisms and parts and reassemble repaired systems. Read blueprints to determine location, size, capacity, and type of components needed to build refrigeration system. Supervise and instruct assistants. Perform mechanical overhauls and refrigerant reclaiming. Install wiring to connect components to an electric power source. Cut, bend, thread, and connect pipe to functional components and water, power, or refrigeration system. Adjust valves according to specifications and charge system with proper type of refrigerant by pumping the specified gas or fluid into the system. Estimate, order, pick up, deliver, and install materials and supplies needed to maintain equipment in good working condition. Install expansion and control valves, using acetylene torches and wrenches. Mount compressor, condenser, and other components in specified locations on frames, using hand tools and acetylene welding equipment. Keep records of repairs and replacements made and causes of malfunctions. Schedule work with customers and initiate work orders, house requisitions, and orders from stock. Lay out reference points for installation of structural and functional components, using measuring instruments. Fabricate and assemble structural and functional components of refrigeration system, using hand tools, power tools, and welding equipment. Lift and align components into position, using hoist or block and tackle. Drill holes and install mounting brackets and hangers into floor and walls of building. Insulate shells and cabinets of systems.

Personality Type: Realistic. Realistic occupations frequently involve work activities that include practical, hands-on problems and solutions. They often deal with plants; animals; and real-world materials such as wood, tools, and machinery. Many of the occupations require working outside and do not involve a lot of paperwork or working closely with others.

GOE—Interest Area: 02. Architecture and Construction. **Work Group:** 02.05. Systems and Equipment Installation, Maintenance, and Repair. **Other Jobs in This Work Group:** Electrical and Electronics Repairers, Powerhouse, Substation, and Relay; Electrical Power-Line Installers and Repairers; Elevator Installers and Repairers; Heating and Air Conditioning Mechanics and Installers; Maintenance and Repair Workers, General; Telecommunications Equipment Installers and Repairers, Except Line Installers; Telecommunications Line Installers and Repairers.

Skills—Installation: Installing equipment, machines, wiring, or programs to meet specifications. **Repairing:** Repairing machines or systems by using the needed tools. **Equipment Maintenance:** Performing routine maintenance on equipment and determining when and what kind of maintenance is needed. **Operation Monitoring:** Watching gauges, dials, or other indicators to make sure a machine is working properly. **Systems Evaluation:** Identifying measures or indicators of system performance and the actions needed to improve or correct performance relative to the goals of the system. **Systems Analysis:** Determining how a system should work and how changes in conditions, operations, and the environment will affect outcomes.

Education and Training Programs: Heating, Air Conditioning, and Refrigeration Technology/Technician Training (ACH/ACR/ACHR/HRAC/HVAC); Heating, Air Conditioning, Ventilation, and Refrigeration Maintenance Technology/Technician Training; Solar Energy Technology/Technician Training. **Related Knowledge/Courses: Building and Construction:** The materials, methods, and tools involved in the construction or repair of houses, buildings, or other structures such as highways and roads. **Mechanical Devices:** Machines and tools, including their designs, uses, repair, and maintenance. **Engineering and Technology:** The practical application of engineering science and technology. This includes applying principles, techniques, procedures, and equipment to the design and production of various goods and services. **Physics:** Physical principles and laws and their interrelationships and applications to understanding fluid, material, and atmospheric dynamics and mechanical, electrical, atomic, and subatomic structures and processes. **Design:** Design techniques, tools, and principles involved in production of precision technical plans, blueprints, drawings, and models. **Chemistry:** The chemical composition, structure, and properties of substances and of the chemical processes and transformations that they undergo. This includes uses of chemicals and their danger signs, production techniques, and disposal methods.

Work Environment: Outdoors; very hot or cold; cramped work space, awkward positions; minor burns, cuts, bites, or stings; standing; using hands on objects, tools, or controls.

Reinforcing Iron and Rebar Workers

- Education/Training Required: Long-term on-the-job training
- Annual Earnings: $34,910
- Growth: 14.1%
- Annual Job Openings: 6,000
- Self-Employed: 2.3%
- Part-Time: 3.9%

Level of Solitary Work: 59.2 (out of 100)

Level of Contact with Others: 12.5 (out of 100)

Position and secure steel bars or mesh in concrete forms to reinforce concrete. Use a variety of fasteners, rod-bending machines, blowtorches, and hand

tools. Space and fasten together rods in forms according to blueprints, using wire and pliers. Cut and fit wire mesh or fabric, using hooked rods, and position fabric or mesh in concrete to reinforce concrete. Cut rods to required lengths, using metal shears, hacksaws, bar cutters, or acetylene torches. Bend steel rods with hand tools and rod-bending machines and weld them with arc-welding equipment. Position and secure steel bars, rods, cables, or mesh in concrete forms, using fasteners, rod-bending machines, blow-torches, and hand tools. Place blocks under rebar to hold the bars off the deck when reinforcing floors. Determine quantities, sizes, shapes, and locations of reinforcing rods from blueprints, sketches, or oral instructions.

Personality Type: Realistic. Realistic occupations frequently involve work activities that include practical, hands-on problems and solutions. They often deal with plants; animals; and real-world materials such as wood, tools, and machinery. Many of the occupations require working outside and do not involve a lot of paperwork or working closely with others.

GOE—Interest Area: 02. Architecture and Construction. **Work Group:** 02.04. Construction Crafts. **Other Jobs in This Work Group:** Boilermakers; Brickmasons and Blockmasons; Carpet Installers; Cement Masons and Concrete Finishers; Commercial Divers; Construction Carpenters; Crane and Tower Operators; Drywall and Ceiling Tile Installers; Electricians; Fence Erectors; Floor Layers, Except Carpet, Wood, and Hard Tiles; Floor Sanders and Finishers; Glaziers; Hazardous Materials Removal Workers; Insulation Workers, Floor, Ceiling, and Wall; Insulation Workers, Mechanical; Manufactured Building and Mobile Home Installers; Operating Engineers and Other Construction Equipment Operators; Painters, Construction and Maintenance; Paperhangers; Paving, Surfacing, and Tamping Equipment Operators; Pile-Driver Operators; Pipe Fitters and Steamfitters; Pipelayers; Plasterers and Stucco Masons; Plumbers; Plumbers, Pipefitters, and Steamfitters; Rail-Track Laying and Maintenance Equipment Operators; Refractory Materials Repairers, Except Brickmasons; Riggers;

Roofers; Rough Carpenters; Security and Fire Alarm Systems Installers; Segmental Pavers; Sheet Metal Workers; Stone Cutters and Carvers, Manufacturing; Stonemasons; Structural Iron and Steel Workers; Tapers; Terrazzo Workers and Finishers; Tile and Marble Setters.

Skills—None met the criteria.

Education and Training Program: Construction Trades, Other. **Related Knowledge/Courses: Building and Construction:** The materials, methods, and tools involved in the construction or repair of houses, buildings, or other structures such as highways and roads. **Physics:** Physical principles and laws and their interrelationships and applications to understanding fluid, material, and atmospheric dynamics and mechanical, electrical, atomic, and subatomic structures and processes. **Design:** Design techniques, tools, and principles involved in production of precision technical plans, blueprints, drawings, and models. **Engineering and Technology:** The practical application of engineering science and technology. This includes applying principles, techniques, procedures, and equipment to the design and production of various goods and services.

Work Environment: Outdoors; noisy; contaminants; minor burns, cuts, bites, or stings; standing; using hands on objects, tools, or controls.

Riggers

- Education/Training Required: Short-term on-the-job training
- Annual Earnings: $37,010
- Growth: 13.9%
- Annual Job Openings: 2,000
- Self-Employed: 0.0%
- Part-Time: 1.9%

Level of Solitary Work: 40.5 (out of 100)

Level of Contact with Others: 36.8 (out of 100)

Set up or repair rigging for construction projects, manufacturing plants, logging yards, ships and shipyards, or the entertainment industry. Manipulate rigging lines, hoists, and pulling gear to move or support materials such as heavy equipment, ships, or theatrical sets. Signal or verbally direct workers engaged in hoisting and moving loads to ensure safety of workers and materials. Dismantle and store rigging equipment after use. Control movement of heavy equipment through narrow openings or confined spaces, using chainfalls, gin poles, gallows frames, and other equipment. Attach pulleys and blocks to fixed overhead structures such as beams, ceilings, and gin pole booms, using bolts and clamps. Attach loads to rigging to provide support or prepare them for moving, using hand and power tools. Align, level, and anchor machinery. Select gear such as cables, pulleys, and winches according to load weights and sizes, facilities, and work schedules. Tilt, dip, and turn suspended loads to maneuver over, under, or around obstacles, using multi-point suspension techniques. Test rigging to ensure safety and reliability. Fabricate, set up, and repair rigging, supporting structures, hoists, and pulling gear, using hand and power tools. Install ground rigging for yarding lines, attaching chokers to logs and then to the lines. Clean and dress machine surfaces and component parts.

Personality Type: Realistic. Realistic occupations frequently involve work activities that include practical, hands-on problems and solutions. They often deal with plants; animals; and real-world materials such as wood, tools, and machinery. Many of the occupations require working outside and do not involve a lot of paperwork or working closely with others.

GOE—Interest Area: 02. Architecture and Construction. **Work Group:** 02.04. Construction Crafts. **Other Jobs in This Work Group:** Boilermakers; Brickmasons and Blockmasons; Carpet Installers; Cement Masons and Concrete Finishers; Commercial Divers; Construction Carpenters; Crane and Tower Operators; Drywall and Ceiling Tile Installers; Electricians; Fence Erectors; Floor Layers, Except Carpet, Wood, and Hard Tiles; Floor Sanders and Finishers; Glaziers; Hazardous Materials Removal Workers; Insulation Workers, Floor, Ceiling, and Wall; Insulation Workers, Mechanical; Manufactured Building and Mobile Home Installers; Operating Engineers and Other Construction Equipment Operators; Painters, Construction and Maintenance; Paperhangers; Paving, Surfacing, and Tamping Equipment Operators; Pile-Driver Operators; Pipe Fitters and Steamfitters; Pipelayers; Plasterers and Stucco Masons; Plumbers; Plumbers, Pipefitters, and Steamfitters; Rail-Track Laying and Maintenance Equipment Operators; Refractory Materials Repairers, Except Brickmasons; Reinforcing Iron and Rebar Workers; Roofers; Rough Carpenters; Security and Fire Alarm Systems Installers; Segmental Pavers; Sheet Metal Workers; Stone Cutters and Carvers, Manufacturing; Stonemasons; Structural Iron and Steel Workers; Tapers; Terrazzo Workers and Finishers; Tile and Marble Setters.

Skills—Repairing: Repairing machines or systems by using the needed tools. **Technology Design:** Generating or adapting equipment and technology to serve user needs. **Operation and Control:** Controlling operations of equipment or systems. **Science:** Using scientific rules and methods to solve problems. **Operation Monitoring:** Watching gauges, dials, or other indicators to make sure a machine is working properly. **Installation:** Installing equipment, machines, wiring, or programs to meet specifications.

Education and Training Program: Construction/ Heavy Equipment/Earthmoving Equipment Operation. **Related Knowledge/Courses: Mechanical Devices:** Machines and tools, including their designs, uses, repair, and maintenance. **Public Safety and Security:** Relevant equipment, policies, procedures, and strategies to promote effective local, state, or national security operations for the protection of people, data, property, and institutions. **Engineering and Technology:** The practical application of engineering science and technology. This includes applying principles, techniques, procedures, and equipment to the design and production of various goods and services. **Building and Construction:** The materials, methods,

R

and tools involved in the construction or repair of houses, buildings, or other structures such as highways and roads.

Work Environment: Outdoors; high places; standing; walking and running; climbing ladders, scaffolds, or poles; using hands on objects, tools, or controls.

Roofers

- ☺ Education/Training Required: Moderate-term on-the-job training
- ☺ Annual Earnings: $31,230
- ☺ Growth: 16.8%
- ☺ Annual Job Openings: 38,000
- ☺ Self-Employed: 23.8%
- ☺ Part-Time: 10.3%

Level of Solitary Work: 43.8 (out of 100)

Level of Contact with Others: 11.8 (out of 100)

Cover roofs of structures with shingles, slate, asphalt, aluminum, wood, and related materials. May spray roofs, sidings, and walls with material to bind, seal, insulate, or soundproof sections of structures. Install, repair, or replace single-ply roofing systems, using waterproof sheet materials such as modified plastics, elastomeric, or other asphaltic compositions. Apply alternate layers of hot asphalt or tar and roofing paper to roofs according to specification. Apply gravel or pebbles over top layers of roofs, using rakes or stiff-bristled brooms. Cement or nail flashing-strips of metal or shingle over joints to make them watertight. Cut roofing paper to size, using knives, and nail or staple roofing paper to roofs in overlapping strips to form bases for other materials. Punch holes in slate, tile, terra cotta, or wooden shingles, using punches and hammers. Hammer and chisel away rough spots or remove them with rubbing bricks to prepare surfaces for waterproofing. Spray roofs, sidings, and walls with material to bind, seal, insulate, or soundproof sections of structures, using spray guns, air compressors, and heaters. Cover exposed nailheads with roofing cement or caulking to prevent water leakage and rust. Clean and maintain equipment. Cut felt, shingles, and strips of flashing and fit them into angles formed by walls, vents, and intersecting roof surfaces. Glaze top layers to make a smooth finish or embed gravel in the bitumen for rough surfaces. Inspect problem roofs to determine the best procedures for repairing them. Align roofing materials with edges of roofs. Mop or pour hot asphalt or tar onto roof bases. Apply plastic coatings and membranes, fiberglass, or felt over sloped roofs before applying shingles. Install vapor barriers or layers of insulation on the roof decks of flat roofs and seal the seams. Install partially overlapping layers of material over roof insulation surfaces, determining distance of roofing material overlap by using chalk lines, gauges on shingling hatchets, or lines on shingles. Cover roofs and exterior walls of structures with slate, asphalt, aluminum, wood, gravel, gypsum, and/or related materials, using brushes, knives, punches, hammers, and other tools. Waterproof and damp-proof walls, floors, roofs, foundations, and basements by painting or spraying surfaces with waterproof coatings, or by attaching waterproofing membranes to surfaces. Estimate roofing materials and labor required to complete jobs and provide price quotes.

Personality Type: Realistic. Realistic occupations frequently involve work activities that include practical, hands-on problems and solutions. They often deal with plants; animals; and real-world materials such as wood, tools, and machinery. Many of the occupations require working outside and do not involve a lot of paperwork or working closely with others.

GOE—Interest Area: 02. Architecture and Construction. **Work Group:** 02.04. Construction Crafts. **Other Jobs in This Work Group:** Boilermakers; Brickmasons and Blockmasons; Carpet Installers; Cement Masons and Concrete Finishers; Commercial Divers; Construction Carpenters; Crane and Tower Operators; Drywall and Ceiling Tile Installers; Electricians; Fence Erectors; Floor Layers, Except Carpet, Wood, and Hard Tiles; Floor Sanders and Finishers; Glaziers; Hazardous Materials Removal Workers; Insulation Workers, Floor, Ceiling, and Wall; Insulation Workers, Mechanical; Manufactured Building and Mobile Home Installers; Operating Engineers and Other Construction Equipment Operators; Painters, Construction and Maintenance; Paperhangers; Paving, Surfacing, and Tamping Equipment Operators; Pile-Driver Operators; Pipe Fitters and Steamfitters; Pipelayers; Plasterers and Stucco Masons; Plumbers; Plumbers, Pipefitters, and Steamfitters; Rail-Track Laying and Maintenance Equipment Operators; Refractory Materials Repairers, Except Brickmasons; Reinforcing Iron and Rebar Workers; Riggers; Rough Carpenters; Security and Fire Alarm Systems Installers; Segmental Pavers; Sheet Metal Workers; Stone Cutters and Carvers, Manufacturing; Stonemasons; Structural Iron and Steel Workers; Tapers; Terrazzo Workers and Finishers; Tile and Marble Setters.

Skills—Repairing: Repairing machines or systems by using the needed tools. **Installation:** Installing equipment, machines, wiring, or programs to meet specifications.

Education and Training Program: Roofer Training. **Related Knowledge/Courses: Building and Construction:** The materials, methods, and tools involved in the construction or repair of houses, buildings, or other structures such as highways and roads. **Mechanical Devices:** Machines and tools, including their designs, uses, repair, and maintenance.

Work Environment: Outdoors; high places; minor burns, cuts, bites, or stings; kneeling, crouching, stooping, or crawling; keeping or regaining balance; using hands on objects, tools, or controls.

Sailors and Marine Oilers

- Education/Training Required: Short-term on-the-job training
- Annual Earnings: $29,360
- Growth: 5.2%
- Annual Job Openings: 4,000
- Self-Employed: 0.0%
- Part-Time: 9.2%

Level of Solitary Work: 42.3 (out of 100)

Level of Contact with Others: 42.8 (out of 100)

Stand watch to look for obstructions in path of vessel; measure water depth; turn wheel on bridge; or use emergency equipment as directed by captain, mate, or pilot. Break out, rig, overhaul, and store cargo-handling gear, stationary rigging, and running gear. Perform a variety of maintenance tasks to preserve the painted surface of the ship and to maintain line and ship equipment. Must hold government-issued certification and tankerman certification when working aboard liquid-carrying vessels. Steer ships under the direction of commanders or navigating officers or direct helmsmen to steer, following designated courses. Break out, rig, and stow cargo-handling gear, stationary rigging, and running gear. Chip and clean rust spots on decks, superstructures, and sides of ships, using wire brushes and hand or air chipping machines. Overhaul lifeboats and lifeboat gear and lower or raise lifeboats with winches or falls. Tie barges together into tow units for tugboats to handle, inspecting barges periodically during voyages and disconnecting them when destinations are reached. Paint or varnish decks, superstructures, lifeboats, or sides of ships. Stand gangway watches to prevent unauthorized persons from boarding ships while they are in port. Measure depth of water in shallow or unfamiliar waters, using leadlines, and telephone or shout depth information to vessel bridges. Maintain a ship's engines under the direction of the ship's engineering officers. Lubricate machinery, equipment, and engine parts such as gears, shafts, and bearings. Handle lines to moor vessels to wharfs, to tie up vessels to other vessels, or to rig towing lines. Examine machinery to verify specified pressures and lubricant flows. Maintain government-issued certifications as required. Give directions to crew members engaged in cleaning wheelhouses and quarterdecks. Record in ships' logs data such as weather conditions and distances traveled. Read pressure and temperature gauges or displays and record data in engineering logs. Participate in shore patrols. Lower and man lifeboats when emergencies occur. Operate, maintain, and repair ship equipment such as winches, cranes, derricks, and weapons system. Load or unload materials from vessels. Stand by wheels when ships are on automatic pilot and verify accuracy of courses, using magnetic compasses. Attach hoses and operate pumps to transfer substances to and from liquid cargo tanks. Sweep, mop, and wash down decks to remove oil, dirt, and debris, using brooms, mops, brushes, and hoses. Stand watch in ships' bows or bridge wings to look for obstructions in a ship's path or to locate navigational aids such as buoys and lighthouses.

Personality Type: Realistic. Realistic occupations frequently involve work activities that include practical, hands-on problems and solutions. They often deal with plants; animals; and real-world materials such as wood, tools, and machinery. Many of the occupations require working outside and do not involve a lot of paperwork or working closely with others.

GOE—Interest Area: 16. Transportation, Distribution, and Logistics. **Work Group:** 16.05. Water Vehicle Operation. **Other Jobs in This Work Group:** Captains, Mates, and Pilots of Water Vessels; Dredge Operators; Mates—Ship, Boat, and Barge; Motorboat Operators; Pilots, Ship; Ship and Boat Captains.

Skills—Equipment Maintenance: Performing routine maintenance on equipment and determining when and what kind of maintenance is needed. **Repairing:** Repairing machines or systems by using the needed tools. **Operation and Control:**

Controlling operations of equipment or systems. **Operation Monitoring:** Watching gauges, dials, or other indicators to make sure a machine is working properly.

Education and Training Program: Marine Transportation Services, Other. **Related Knowledge/Courses: Transportation:** Principles and methods for moving people or goods by air, rail, sea, or road, including the relative costs and benefits. **Geography:** Principles and methods for describing the features of land, sea, and air masses, including their physical characteristics; locations; interrelationships; and distribution of plant, animal, and human life. **Mechanical Devices:** Machines and tools, including their designs, uses, repair, and maintenance. **Engineering and Technology:** The practical application of engineering science and technology. This includes applying principles, techniques, procedures, and equipment to the design and production of various goods and services.

Work Environment: Outdoors; minor burns, cuts, bites, or stings; standing; keeping or regaining balance; using hands on objects, tools, or controls; bending or twisting the body.

Semiconductor Processors

- ◎ Education/Training Required: Associate degree
- ◎ Annual Earnings: $31,030
- ◎ Growth: –7.5%
- ◎ Annual Job Openings: 7,000
- ◎ Self-Employed: 0.0%
- ◎ Part-Time: 31.2%

Level of Solitary Work: 71.7 (out of 100)

Level of Contact with Others: 68.3 (out of 100)

Perform any or all of the following functions in the manufacture of electronic semiconductors: Load semiconductor material into furnace; saw formed ingots into segments; load individual segment into

S

crystal-growing chamber and monitor controls; locate crystal axis in ingot, using X-ray equipment, and saw ingots into wafers; and clean, polish, and load wafers into series of special-purpose furnaces, chemical baths, and equipment used to form circuitry and change conductive properties. Manipulate valves, switches, and buttons or key commands into control panels to start semiconductor processing cycles. Inspect materials, components, or products for surface defects and measure circuitry, using electronic test equipment, precision measuring instruments, microscope, and standard procedures. Maintain processing, production, and inspection information and reports. Clean semiconductor wafers, using cleaning equipment, such as chemical baths, automatic wafer cleaners, or blow-off wands. Study work orders, instructions, formulas, and processing charts to determine specifications and sequence of operations. Load and unload equipment chambers and transport finished product to storage or to area for further processing. Clean and maintain equipment, including replacing etching and rinsing solutions and cleaning bath containers and work area. Place semiconductor wafers in processing containers or equipment holders, using vacuum wand or tweezers. Set, adjust, and readjust computerized or mechanical equipment controls to regulate power level, temperature, vacuum, and rotation speed of furnace, according to crystal-growing specifications. Etch, lap, polish, or grind wafers or ingots to form circuitry and change conductive properties, using etching, lapping, polishing, or grinding equipment. Load semiconductor material into furnace. Monitor operation and adjust controls of processing machines and equipment to produce compositions with specific electronic properties, using computer terminals. Count, sort, and weigh processed items. Calculate etching time based on thickness of material to be removed from wafers or crystals. Inspect equipment for leaks, diagnose malfunctions, and request repairs. Align photo mask pattern on photoresist layer, expose pattern to ultraviolet light, and develop pattern, using specialized equipment. Stamp, etch, or scribe identifying information on finished component according to specifications. Operate saw to cut remelt into sections of specified size or to cut ingots into wafers. Scribe or separate wafers into dice. Connect reactor to computer, using hand tools and power tools.

Personality Type: Realistic. Realistic occupations frequently involve work activities that include practical, hands-on problems and solutions. They often deal with plants; animals; and real-world materials such as wood, tools, and machinery. Many of the occupations require working outside and do not involve a lot of paperwork or working closely with others.

GOE—Interest Area: 13. Manufacturing. **Work Group:** 13.06. Production Precision Work. **Other Jobs in This Work Group:** Bookbinders; Dental Laboratory Technicians; Electrical and Electronic Equipment Assemblers; Electromechanical Equipment Assemblers; Engine and Other Machine Assemblers; Gem and Diamond Workers; Jewelers; Jewelers and Precious Stone and Metal Workers; Medical Appliance Technicians; Molding, Coremaking, and Casting Machine Setters, Operators, and Tenders, Metal and Plastic; Ophthalmic Laboratory Technicians; Precious Metal Workers; Timing Device Assemblers, Adjusters, and Calibrators.

Skills—Operation Monitoring: Watching gauges, dials, or other indicators to make sure a machine is working properly. **Repairing:** Repairing machines or systems by using the needed tools. **Equipment Maintenance:** Performing routine maintenance on equipment and determining when and what kind of maintenance is needed. **Installation:** Installing equipment, machines, wiring, or programs to meet specifications. **Troubleshooting:** Determining causes of operating errors and deciding what to do about them. **Operation and Control:** Controlling operations of equipment or systems.

Education and Training Program: Industrial Electronics Technology/Technician Training. **Related Knowledge/Courses: Production and Processing:** Raw materials, production processes, quality control, costs, and other techniques for maximizing the effective manufacture and distribution of goods. **Chemistry:** The chemical composition, structure, and properties of substances and of the chemical processes and transformations that they undergo. This includes uses of chemicals and their danger signs, production techniques, and disposal methods. **Computers and Electronics:** Circuit boards, processors, chips, electronic equipment, and computer hardware and software, including applications and programming. **English Language:** The structure and content of the English language, including the meaning and spelling of words, rules of composition, and grammar. **Education and Training:** Principles and methods for curriculum and training design, teaching and instruction for individuals and groups, and the measurement of training effects. **Engineering and Technology:** The practical application of engineering science and technology. This includes applying principles, techniques, procedures, and equipment to the design and production of various goods and services.

Work Environment: Indoors; noisy; contaminants; hazardous conditions; standing; using hands on objects, tools, or controls.

Separating, Filtering, Clarifying, Precipitating, and Still Machine Setters, Operators, and Tenders

- Education/Training Required: Moderate-term on-the-job training
- Annual Earnings: $34,650
- Growth: 1.6%
- Annual Job Openings: 5,000
- Self-Employed: 0.6%
- Part-Time: 4.3%

Level of Solitary Work: 56.3 (out of 100)

Level of Contact with Others: 81.7 (out of 100)

Set up, operate, or tend continuous flow or vat-type equipment; filter presses; shaker screens; centrifuges; condenser tubes; precipitating, fermenting, or evaporating tanks; scrubbing towers; or batch stills. These machines extract, sort, or separate liquids, gases, or solids from other materials to recover a refined product. Includes dairy processing equipment operators. Set or adjust machine controls to regulate conditions such as material flow, temperature, and pressure. Monitor material flow and instruments such as temperature and pressure gauges, indicators, and meters to ensure optimal processing conditions. Start agitators, shakers, conveyors, pumps, or centrifuge machines; then turn valves or move controls to admit, drain, separate, filter, clarify, mix, or transfer materials. Examine samples visually or by hand to verify qualities such as clarity, cleanliness, consistency, dryness, and texture. Collect samples of materials or products for laboratory analysis. Maintain logs of instrument readings, test results, and shift production and send production information to computer databases. Test samples to determine viscosity, acidity, specific gravity, or degree of concentration, using test equipment such as viscometers, pH meters, and hydrometers. Measure or weigh materials to be refined, mixed, transferred, stored, or otherwise processed. Clean and sterilize tanks, screens, inflow pipes, production areas, and equipment, using hoses, brushes, scrapers, or chemical solutions. Inspect machines and equipment for hazards, operating efficiency, malfunctions, wear, and leaks. Dump, pour, or load specified amounts of refined or unrefined materials into equipment or containers for further processing or storage. Connect pipes between vats and processing equipment. Communicate processing instructions to other workers. Remove clogs, defects, and impurities from machines, tanks, conveyors, screens, or other processing equipment. Assemble fittings, valves, bowls, plates, disks, impeller shafts, and other parts to equipment to prepare equipment for operation. Install and maintain or repair hoses, pumps, filters, or screens to maintain processing equipment, using hand tools. Turn valves to pump sterilizing solutions and rinsewater through pipes and equipment and to spray vats with atomizers. Remove full bags or containers from discharge outlets and replace them with empty ones. Pack bottles into cartons or crates, using machines.

Personality Type: Realistic. Realistic occupations frequently involve work activities that include practical, hands-on problems and solutions. They often deal with plants; animals; and real-world materials such as wood, tools, and machinery. Many of the occupations require working outside and do not involve a lot of paperwork or working closely with others.

GOE—Interest Area: 13. Manufacturing. **Work Group:** 13.03. Production Work, Assorted Materials Processing. **Other Jobs in This Work Group:** Bakers; Cementing and Gluing Machine Operators and Tenders; Chemical Equipment Operators and Tenders; Cleaning, Washing, and Metal Pickling Equipment Operators and Tenders; Coating, Painting, and Spraying Machine Setters, Operators, and Tenders; Cooling and Freezing Equipment Operators and Tenders; Cutting and Slicing Machine Setters, Operators, and Tenders; Extruding and Forming Machine Setters, Operators, and Tenders, Synthetic and Glass Fibers; Extruding, Forming, Pressing, and Compacting Machine Setters, Operators, and Tenders; Food and Tobacco Roasting, Baking, and Drying Machine Operators and Tenders; Food Batchmakers; Food Cooking Machine Operators and Tenders; Furnace, Kiln, Oven, Drier, and Kettle Operators and Tenders; Heat Treating Equipment Setters, Operators, and Tenders, Metal and Plastic; Helpers—Production Workers; Meat, Poultry, and Fish Cutters and Trimmers; Metal-Refining Furnace Operators and Tenders; Mixing and Blending Machine Setters, Operators, and Tenders; Packaging and Filling Machine Operators and Tenders; Plating and Coating Machine Setters, Operators, and Tenders, Metal and Plastic; Pourers and Casters, Metal; Sawing Machine Setters, Operators, and Tenders, Wood; Sewing Machine Operators; Shoe Machine Operators and Tenders; Slaughterers and Meat Packers; Team Assemblers; Textile Bleaching and Dyeing Machine Operators

and Tenders; Tire Builders; Woodworking Machine Setters, Operators, and Tenders, Except Sawing.

Skills—Operation Monitoring: Watching gauges, dials, or other indicators to make sure a machine is working properly. **Repairing:** Repairing machines or systems by using the needed tools. **Equipment Maintenance:** Performing routine maintenance on equipment and determining when and what kind of maintenance is needed. **Operation and Control:** Controlling operations of equipment or systems. **Troubleshooting:** Determining causes of operating errors and deciding what to do about them. **Quality Control Analysis:** Conducting tests and inspections of products, services, or processes to evaluate quality or performance.

Education and Training Program: No related CIP programs; this job is learned through informal moderate-term on-the-job training. **Related Knowledge/Courses: Production and Processing:** Raw materials, production processes, quality control, costs, and other techniques for maximizing the effective manufacture and distribution of goods. **Chemistry:** The chemical composition, structure, and properties of substances and of the chemical processes and transformations that they undergo. This includes uses of chemicals and their danger signs, production techniques, and disposal methods. **Food Production:** Techniques and equipment for planting, growing, and harvesting food products (both plant and animal) for consumption, including storage/handling techniques. **Mechanical Devices:** Machines and tools, including their designs, uses, repair, and maintenance. **Public Safety and Security:** Relevant equipment, policies, procedures, and strategies to promote effective local, state, or national security operations for the protection of people, data, property, and institutions. **Education and Training:** Principles and methods for curriculum and training design, teaching and instruction for individuals and groups, and the measurement of training effects.

Work Environment: Noisy; very hot or cold; contaminants; high places; hazardous conditions; hazardous equipment.

Set and Exhibit Designers

- Education/Training Required: Bachelor's degree
- Annual Earnings: $37,390
- Growth: 9.3%
- Annual Job Openings: 2,000
- Self-Employed: 27.6%
- Part-Time: 21.3%

Level of Solitary Work: 59.2 (out of 100)

Level of Contact with Others: 77.5 (out of 100)

Design special exhibits and movie, television, and theater sets. May study scripts, confer with directors, and conduct research to determine appropriate architectural styles. Examine objects to be included in exhibits to plan where and how to display them. Acquire, or arrange for acquisition of, specimens or graphics required to complete exhibits. Prepare rough drafts and scale working drawings of sets, including floor plans, scenery, and properties to be constructed. Confer with clients and staff to gather information about exhibit space, proposed themes and content, timelines, budgets, materials, and promotion requirements. Estimate set- or exhibit-related costs, including materials, construction, and rental of props or locations. Develop set designs based on evaluation of scripts, budgets, research information, and available locations. Direct and coordinate construction, erection, or decoration activities to ensure that sets or exhibits meet design, budget, and schedule requirements. Inspect installed exhibits for conformance to specifications and satisfactory operation of special effects components. Plan for location-specific issues such as space limitations, traffic flow patterns, and safety concerns. Submit plans for approval and adapt plans to serve intended purposes or to conform to budget or fabrication restrictions. Prepare preliminary renderings of proposed exhibits, including detailed construction, layout, and material specifications and diagrams relating to aspects such as special effects and lighting. Select and purchase lumber and hardware necessary for set construction. Collaborate with those in charge of lighting and sound so that those production aspects can be coordinated with set designs or exhibit layouts. Research architectural and stylistic elements appropriate to the time period to be depicted, consulting experts for information as necessary. Design and produce displays and materials that can be used to decorate windows, interior displays, or event locations such as streets and fairgrounds. Coordinate the removal of sets, props, and exhibits after productions or events are complete. Select set props such as furniture, pictures, lamps, and rugs. Confer with conservators to determine how to handle an exhibit's environmental aspects, such as lighting, temperature, and humidity, so that objects will be protected and exhibits will be enhanced.

Personality Type: Artistic. Artistic occupations frequently involve working with forms, designs, and patterns. They often require self-expression, and the work can be done without following a clear set of rules.

GOE—Interest Area: 03. Arts and Communication. **Work Group:** 03.05. Design. **Other Jobs in This Work Group:** Commercial and Industrial Designers; Fashion Designers; Floral Designers; Graphic Designers; Interior Designers; Merchandise Displayers and Window Trimmers.

Skills—Persuasion: Persuading others to change their minds or behavior. **Installation:** Installing equipment, machines, wiring, or programs to meet specifications. **Management of Material Resources:** Obtaining and seeing to the appropriate use of equipment, facilities, and materials needed to do certain work. **Management of Personnel Resources:** Motivating, developing, and directing people as they work; identifying the best people for the job. **Operations Analysis:** Analyzing needs and product requirements to create a design. **Negotiation:** Bringing others together and trying to reconcile differences.

Education and Training Programs: Design and Applied Arts, Other; Design and Visual

Communications, General; Illustration; Technical Theatre/Theatre Design and Technology. **Related Knowledge/Courses: Fine Arts:** The theory and techniques required to compose, produce, and perform works of music, dance, visual arts, drama, and sculpture. **Design:** Design techniques, tools, and principles involved in production of precision technical plans, blueprints, drawings, and models. **History and Archeology:** Historical events and their causes, indicators, and effects on civilizations and cultures. **Communications and Media:** Media production, communication, and dissemination techniques and methods. This includes alternative ways to inform and entertain via written, oral, and visual media. **Sociology and Anthropology:** Group behavior and dynamics, societal trends and influences, human migrations, ethnicity, and cultures and their history and origins. **Computers and Electronics:** Circuit boards, processors, chips, electronic equipment, and computer hardware and software, including applications and programming.

Work Environment: Indoors; sitting; using hands on objects, tools, or controls.

Ship and Boat Captains

This job can be found in the Part II lists under the title Captains, Mates, and Pilots of Water Vessels.

- ◎ Education/Training Required: Work experience in a related occupation
- ◎ Annual Earnings: $50,940
- ◎ Growth: 4.8%
- ◎ Annual Job Openings: 2,000
- ◎ Self-Employed: 5.4%
- ◎ Part-Time: 8.7%

The job openings listed here are shared with Mates— Ship, Boat, and Barge and with Pilots, Ship.

Level of Solitary Work: 34.2 (out of 100)

Level of Contact with Others: 57.2 (out of 100)

Command vessels in oceans, bays, lakes, rivers, and coastal waters. Steer and operate vessels, using radios, depth finders, radars, lights, buoys, and lighthouses. Interview and hire crew members. Sort logs, form log booms, and salvage lost logs. Perform various marine duties such as checking for oil spills or other pollutants around ports and harbors and patrolling beaches. Contact buyers to sell cargo such as fish. Tow and maneuver barges or signal tugboats to tow barges to destinations. Signal passing vessels, using whistles, flashing lights, flags, and radios. Resolve questions or problems with customs officials. Read gauges to verify sufficient levels of hydraulic fluid, air pressure, and oxygen. Monitor the loading and discharging of cargo or passengers. Measure depths of water, using depth-measuring equipment. Calculate sightings of land, using electronic sounding devices and following contour lines on charts. Assign watches and living quarters to crew members. Arrange for ships to be fueled, restocked with supplies, or repaired. Collect fares from customers or signal ferryboat helpers to collect fares. Signal crew members or deckhands to rig tow lines, open or close gates and ramps, and pull guard chains across entries. Maintain records of daily activities, personnel reports, ship positions and movements, ports of call, weather and sea conditions, pollution control efforts, and cargo and passenger status. Inspect vessels to ensure efficient and safe operation of vessels and equipment and conformance to regulations. Direct and coordinate crew members or workers performing activities such as loading and unloading cargo; steering vessels; operating engines; and operating, maintaining, and repairing ship equipment. Compute positions, set courses, and determine speeds by using charts, area plotting sheets, compasses, sextants, and knowledge of local conditions. Purchase supplies and equipment. Maintain boats and equipment on board, such as engines, winches, navigational systems, fire extinguishers, and life preservers.

Personality Type: Enterprising. Enterprising occupations frequently involve starting up and carrying out projects. These occupations can involve leading people and making many decisions. They sometimes require risk taking and often deal with business.

GOE—Interest Area: 16. Transportation, Distribution, and Logistics. **Work Group:** 16.05. Water Vehicle Operation. **Other Jobs in This Work Group:** Captains, Mates, and Pilots of Water Vessels; Dredge Operators; Mates—Ship, Boat, and Barge; Motorboat Operators; Pilots, Ship; Sailors and Marine Oilers.

Skills—Management of Personnel Resources: Motivating, developing, and directing people as they work; identifying the best people for the job. **Operation Monitoring:** Watching gauges, dials, or other indicators to make sure a machine is working properly. **Operation and Control:** Controlling operations of equipment or systems. **Management of Material Resources:** Obtaining and seeing to the appropriate use of equipment, facilities, and materials needed to do certain work. **Systems Evaluation:** Identifying measures or indicators of system performance and the actions needed to improve or correct performance relative to the goals of the system. **Systems Analysis:** Determining how a system should work and how changes in conditions, operations, and the environment will affect outcomes.

Education and Training Programs: Commercial Fishing; Marine Science/Merchant Marine Officer Training; Marine Transportation, Other. **Related Knowledge/Courses: Transportation:** Principles and methods for moving people or goods by air, rail, sea, or road, including the relative costs and benefits. **Geography:** Principles and methods for describing the features of land, sea, and air masses, including their physical characteristics; locations; interrelationships; and distribution of plant, animal, and human life. **Physics:** Physical principles and laws and their interrelationships and applications to understanding fluid, material, and atmospheric dynamics and mechanical, electrical, atomic, and subatomic structures and processes. **Administration and Management:** Business and management principles involved in strategic planning, resource allocation,

human resources modeling, leadership technique, production methods, and coordination of people and resources. **Personnel and Human Resources:** Principles and procedures for personnel recruitment, selection, training, compensation and benefits, labor relations and negotiation, and personnel information systems. **Telecommunications:** Transmission, broadcasting, switching, control, and operation of telecommunications systems.

Work Environment: Outdoors; standing; using hands on objects, tools, or controls; repetitive motions.

Ship Engineers

- Education/Training Required: Postsecondary vocational training
- Annual Earnings: $52,780
- Growth: 12.7%
- Annual Job Openings: 1,000
- Self-Employed: 3.7%
- Part-Time: 17.4%

Level of Solitary Work: 50.0 (out of 100)

Level of Contact with Others: 35.0 (out of 100)

Supervise and coordinate activities of crew engaged in operating and maintaining engines; boilers; deck machinery; and electrical, sanitary, and refrigeration equipment aboard ship. Monitor engine, machinery, and equipment indicators when vessels are under way and report abnormalities to appropriate shipboard staff. Record orders for changes in ship speed and direction and note gauge readings and test data, such as revolutions per minute and voltage output, in engineering logs and bellbooks. Perform and participate in emergency drills as required. Fabricate engine replacement parts such as valves, stay rods, and bolts, using metalworking machinery. Install engine controls, propeller shafts, and propellers. Maintain and repair engines, electric motors, pumps, winches, and other mechanical and electrical equipment or assist other crew members with maintenance and repair duties. Monitor and test operations of engines and other equipment so that malfunctions and their causes can be identified. Operate and maintain off-loading liquid pumps and valves. Perform general marine vessel maintenance and repair work such as repairing leaks, finishing interiors, refueling, and maintaining decks. Start engines to propel ships and regulate engines and power transmissions to control speeds of ships according to directions from captains or bridge computers. Supervise the activities of marine engine technicians engaged in the maintenance and repair of mechanical and electrical marine vessels and inspect their work to ensure that it is performed properly. Act as a liaison between a ship's captain and shore personnel to ensure that schedules and budgets are maintained and that the ship is operated safely and efficiently. Order and receive engine room's stores such as oil and spare parts; maintain inventories and record usage of supplies. Maintain complete records of engineering department activities, including machine operations. Monitor the availability, use, and condition of lifesaving equipment and pollution preventatives to ensure that international regulations are followed. Maintain electrical power, heating, ventilation, refrigeration, water, and sewerage systems. Clean engine parts and keep engine rooms clean.

Personality Type: Realistic. Realistic occupations frequently involve work activities that include practical, hands-on problems and solutions. They often deal with plants; animals; and real-world materials such as wood, tools, and machinery. Many of the occupations require working outside and do not involve a lot of paperwork or working closely with others.

GOE—Interest Area: 13. Manufacturing. **Work Group:** 13.16. Utility Operation and Energy Distribution. **Other Jobs in This Work Group:** Chemical Plant and System Operators; Gas Compressor and Gas Pumping Station Operators; Gas Plant Operators; Nuclear Power Reactor Operators; Petroleum Pump System Operators,

Refinery Operators, and Gaugers; Power Distributors and Dispatchers; Power Plant Operators; Stationary Engineers and Boiler Operators; Water and Liquid Waste Treatment Plant and System Operators.

Skills—Operation and Control: Controlling operations of equipment or systems. **Operation Monitoring:** Watching gauges, dials, or other indicators to make sure a machine is working properly. **Repairing:** Repairing machines or systems by using the needed tools. **Equipment Maintenance:** Performing routine maintenance on equipment and determining when and what kind of maintenance is needed. **Management of Personnel Resources:** Motivating, developing, and directing people as they work; identifying the best people for the job. **Systems Evaluation:** Identifying measures or indicators of system performance and the actions needed to improve or correct performance relative to the goals of the system.

Education and Training Program: Marine Maintenance/Fitter and Ship Repair Technology/Technician Training. **Related Knowledge/Courses: Mechanical Devices:** Machines and tools, including their designs, uses, repair, and maintenance. **Transportation:** Principles and methods for moving people or goods by air, rail, sea, or road, including the relative costs and benefits. **Engineering and Technology:** The practical application of engineering science and technology. This includes applying principles, techniques, procedures, and equipment to the design and production of various goods and services. **Physics:** Physical principles and laws and their interrelationships and applications to understanding fluid, material, and atmospheric dynamics and mechanical, electrical, atomic, and subatomic structures and processes.

Work Environment: Indoors; standing; using hands on objects, tools, or controls.

Signal and Track Switch Repairers

- Education/Training Required: Moderate-term on-the-job training
- Annual Earnings: $49,200
- Growth: 2.3%
- Annual Job Openings: 1,000
- Self-Employed: 0.0%
- Part-Time: 11.3%

Level of Solitary Work: 53.0 (out of 100)

Level of Contact with Others: 10.5 (out of 100)

Install, inspect, test, maintain, or repair electric gate crossings, signals, signal equipment, track switches, section lines, or intercommunications systems within a railroad system. Inspect, maintain, and replace batteries as needed. Tighten loose bolts, using wrenches, and test circuits and connections by opening and closing gates. Inspect switch-controlling mechanisms on trolley wires and in track beds, using hand tools and test equipment. Inspect and test operation, mechanical parts, and circuitry of gate crossings, signals, and signal equipment such as interlocks and hotbox detectors. Lubricate moving parts on gate-crossing mechanisms and swinging signals. Test air lines and air cylinders on pneumatically operated gates. Maintain high tension lines, de-energizing lines for power companies when repairs are requested. Clean lenses of lamps with cloths and solvents. Inspect electrical units of railroad grade crossing gates and repair loose bolts and defective electrical connections and parts. Drive motor vehicles to job sites. Install, inspect, maintain, and repair various railroad service equipment on the road or in the shop, including railroad signal systems. Record and report information about mileage or track inspected, repairs performed, and equipment requiring replacement. Replace defective wiring, broken lenses, or burned-out light bulbs.

Personality Type: Realistic. Realistic occupations frequently involve work activities that include practical, hands-on problems and solutions. They often deal with plants; animals; and real-world materials such as wood, tools, and machinery. Many of the occupations require working outside and do not involve a lot of paperwork or working closely with others.

GOE—Interest Area: 13. Manufacturing. **Work Group:** 13.13. Machinery Repair. **Other Jobs in This Work Group:** Bicycle Repairers; Control and Valve Installers and Repairers, Except Mechanical Door; Home Appliance Repairers; Industrial Machinery Mechanics; Locksmiths and Safe Repairers; Maintenance Workers, Machinery; Mechanical Door Repairers; Millwrights.

Skills—Installation: Installing equipment, machines, wiring, or programs to meet specifications. **Repairing:** Repairing machines or systems by using the needed tools. **Equipment Maintenance:** Performing routine maintenance on equipment and determining when and what kind of maintenance is needed. **Troubleshooting:** Determining causes of operating errors and deciding what to do about them. **Operation Monitoring:** Watching gauges, dials, or other indicators to make sure a machine is working properly. **Quality Control Analysis:** Conducting tests and inspections of products, services, or processes to evaluate quality or performance.

Education and Training Program: Electrician Training. **Related Knowledge/Courses: Mechanical Devices:** Machines and tools, including their designs, uses, repair, and maintenance. **Transportation:** Principles and methods for moving people or goods by air, rail, sea, or road, including the relative costs and benefits. **Telecommunications:** Transmission, broadcasting, switching, control, and operation of telecommunications systems. **Engineering and Technology:** The practical application of engineering science and technology. This includes applying principles, techniques, procedures, and equipment to the design and production of various goods and services. **Physics:** Physical principles and laws and their interrelationships and applications to understanding fluid, material, and atmospheric dynamics and mechanical, electrical, atomic, and subatomic structures and processes. **Public Safety and Security:** Relevant equipment, policies, procedures, and strategies to promote effective local, state, or national security operations for the protection of people, data, property, and institutions.

Work Environment: Outdoors; hazardous conditions; hazardous equipment; minor burns, cuts, bites, or stings; standing; using hands on objects, tools, or controls.

Slaughterers and Meat Packers

- ◎ Education/Training Required: Moderate-term on-the-job training
- ◎ Annual Earnings: $21,220
- ◎ Growth: 13.8%
- ◎ Annual Job Openings: 22,000
- ◎ Self-Employed: 1.3%
- ◎ Part-Time: 10.5%

Level of Solitary Work: 62.5 (out of 100)

Level of Contact with Others: 11.0 (out of 100)

Work in slaughtering, meat packing, or wholesale establishments performing precision functions involving the preparation of meat. Work may include specialized slaughtering tasks, cutting standard or premium cuts of meat for marketing, making sausage, or wrapping meats. Remove bones and cut meat into standard cuts in preparation for marketing. Slaughter animals in accordance with religious law and determine that carcasses meet specified religious standards. Tend assembly lines, performing a few of the many cuts needed to process a carcass. Saw, split, or scribe carcasses into smaller portions to facilitate handling. Grind meat into hamburger and into trimmings used to prepare sausages, luncheon meats, and other meat products. Cut, trim, skin, sort, and wash viscera of slaughtered animals to separate edible portions from offal. Shave or singe and defeather carcasses and wash them in preparation for further processing or packaging. Slit open, eviscerate, and trim carcasses of slaughtered animals. Stun animals prior to slaughtering. Trim head meat and sever or remove parts of animals' heads or skulls. Trim, clean, and cure animal hides. Wrap dressed carcasses and meat cuts. Skin sections of animals or whole animals. Sever jugular veins to drain blood and facilitate slaughtering. Shackle hind legs of animals to raise them for slaughtering or skinning.

Personality Type: Realistic. Realistic occupations frequently involve work activities that include practical, hands-on problems and solutions. They often deal with plants; animals; and real-world materials such as wood, tools, and machinery. Many of the occupations require working outside and do not involve a lot of paperwork or working closely with others.

GOE—Interest Area: 13. Manufacturing. **Work Group:** 13.03. Production Work, Assorted Materials Processing. **Other Jobs in This Work Group:** Bakers; Cementing and Gluing Machine Operators and Tenders; Chemical Equipment Operators and Tenders; Cleaning, Washing, and Metal Pickling Equipment Operators and Tenders; Coating, Painting, and Spraying Machine Setters, Operators, and Tenders; Cooling and Freezing Equipment Operators and Tenders; Cutting and Slicing Machine Setters, Operators, and Tenders; Extruding and Forming Machine Setters, Operators, and Tenders, Synthetic and Glass Fibers; Extruding, Forming, Pressing, and Compacting Machine Setters, Operators, and Tenders; Food and Tobacco Roasting, Baking, and Drying Machine Operators and Tenders; Food Batchmakers; Food Cooking Machine Operators and Tenders; Furnace, Kiln, Oven, Drier, and Kettle Operators and Tenders; Heat Treating Equipment Setters, Operators, and Tenders, Metal and Plastic; Helpers—Production Workers; Meat, Poultry, and Fish Cutters and Trimmers; Metal-Refining Furnace Operators and Tenders; Mixing and Blending Machine Setters, Operators, and Tenders; Packaging and Filling Machine Operators and Tenders; Plating and Coating Machine Setters, Operators, and Tenders, Metal and Plastic; Pourers and Casters, Metal; Sawing Machine Setters, Operators, and Tenders, Wood; Separating, Filtering, Clarifying, Precipitating, and Still Machine Setters, Operators, and Tenders; Sewing Machine Operators; Shoe Machine Operators and Tenders; Team Assemblers; Textile Bleaching and Dyeing Machine Operators and Tenders; Tire Builders; Woodworking Machine Setters, Operators, and Tenders, Except Sawing.

Skills—None met the criteria.

Education and Training Program: Meat Cutting/Meat Cutter Training. **Related Knowledge/Courses: Food Production**: Techniques and equipment for planting, growing, and harvesting food products (both plant and animal) for consumption, including storage/handling techniques. **Biology**: Plant and animal organisms and their tissues, cells, functions, interdependencies, and interactions with each other and the environment. **Production and Processing**: Raw materials, production processes, quality control, costs, and other techniques for maximizing the effective manufacture and distribution of goods. **Public Safety and Security**: Relevant equipment, policies, procedures, and strategies to promote effective local, state, or national security operations for the protection of people, data, property, and institutions.

Work Environment: Indoors; contaminants; minor burns, cuts, bites, or stings; standing; using hands on objects, tools, or controls; repetitive motions.

Sociologists

- Education/Training Required: Master's degree
- Annual Earnings: $52,760
- Growth: 4.7%
- Annual Job Openings: Fewer than 500
- Self-Employed: 11.7%
- Part-Time: 14.8%

Level of Solitary Work: 53.0 (out of 100)

Level of Contact with Others: 72.5 (out of 100)

Study human society and social behavior by examining the groups and social institutions that people form, as well as various social, religious, political, and business organizations. May study the behavior and interaction of groups, trace their origin and growth, and analyze the influence of group activities on individual members. Analyze and interpret data in order to increase the understanding of human social behavior. Prepare publications and reports containing research findings. Plan and conduct research to develop and test theories about societal issues such as crime, group relations, poverty, and aging. Collect data about the attitudes, values, and behaviors of people in groups, using observation, interviews, and review of documents. Develop, implement, and evaluate methods of data collection, such as questionnaires or interviews. Teach sociology. Direct work of statistical clerks, statisticians, and others who compile and evaluate research data. Consult with and advise individuals such as administrators, social workers, and legislators regarding social issues and policies, as well as the implications of research findings. Collaborate with research workers in other disciplines. Develop approaches to the solution of groups' problems based on research findings in sociology and related disciplines. Observe group interactions and role affiliations to collect data, identify problems, evaluate progress, and determine the need for additional change. Develop problem intervention procedures, utilizing techniques such as interviews, consultations, role-playing, and participant observation of group interactions.

Personality Type: Investigative. Investigative occupations frequently involve working with ideas and require an extensive amount of thinking. These occupations can involve searching for facts and figuring out problems mentally.

GOE—Interest Area: 15. Scientific Research, Engineering, and Mathematics. **Work Group:** 15.04. Social Sciences. **Other Jobs in This Work Group:** Anthropologists; Anthropologists and Archeologists; Archeologists; Economists; Historians; Industrial-Organizational Psychologists; Political Scientists; School Psychologists.

Skills—Science: Using scientific rules and methods to solve problems. **Writing:** Communicating effectively in writing as appropriate for the needs of the audience. **Management of Financial Resources:** Determining how money will be spent to get the work done and accounting for these expenditures. **Reading Comprehension:** Understanding written sentences and paragraphs in work-related documents. **Critical Thinking:** Using logic and reasoning to identify the strengths and weaknesses of alternative solutions, conclusions, or approaches to problems. **Complex Problem Solving:** Identifying complex problems and reviewing related information to develop and evaluate options and implement solutions.

Education and Training Programs: Criminology; Demography and Population Studies; Sociology; Urban Studies/Affairs. **Related Knowledge/Courses: Sociology and Anthropology:** Group behavior and dynamics, societal trends and influences, human migrations, ethnicity, and cultures and their history and origins. **Philosophy and Theology:** Different philosophical systems and religions. This includes their basic principles, values, ethics, ways of thinking, customs, and practices and their impact on human culture. **History and Archeology:** Historical events and their causes, indicators, and effects on civilizations and cultures. **Psychology:** Human behavior and performance; individual differences in ability, person-

ality, and interests; learning and motivation; psychological research methods; and the assessment and treatment of behavioral and affective disorders. **English Language:** The structure and content of the English language, including the meaning and spelling of words, rules of composition, and grammar. **Mathematics:** Arithmetic, algebra, geometry, calculus, and statistics and their applications.

Work Environment: Indoors; sitting.

Soil and Plant Scientists

- Education/Training Required: Bachelor's degree
- Annual Earnings: $54,530
- Growth: 13.9%
- Annual Job Openings: 1,000
- Self-Employed: 35.9%
- Part-Time: No data available

Level of Solitary Work: 79.8 (out of 100)

Level of Contact with Others: 68.3 (out of 100)

Conduct research in breeding, physiology, production, yield, and management of crops and agricultural plants, their growth in soils, and control of pests or study the chemical, physical, biological, and mineralogical composition of soils as they relate to plant or crop growth. May classify and map soils and investigate effects of alternative practices on soil and crop productivity. Communicate research and project results to other professionals and the public or teach related courses, seminars or workshops. Provide information and recommendations to farmers and other landowners regarding ways in which they can best use land, promote plant growth, and avoid or correct problems such as erosion. Investigate responses of soils to specific management practices to determine the use capabilities of soils and the effects of alternative practices on soil productivity. Develop methods of conserving and managing soil that can be applied by farmers and forestry companies. Conduct experiments to develop new or improved varieties of field crops, focusing on characteristics such as yield, quality, disease resistance, nutritional value, or adaptation to specific soils or climates. Investigate soil problems and poor water quality to determine sources and effects. Study soil characteristics to classify soils on the basis of factors such as geographic location, landscape position, and soil properties. Develop improved measurement techniques, soil conservation methods, soil sampling devices, and related technology. Conduct experiments investigating how soil forms and changes and how it interacts with land-based ecosystems and living organisms. Identify degraded or contaminated soils and develop plans to improve their chemical, biological, and physical characteristics. Survey undisturbed and disturbed lands for classification, inventory, mapping, environmental impact assessments, environmental protection planning, and conservation and reclamation planning. Plan and supervise land conservation and reclamation programs for industrial development projects and waste management programs for composting and farming. Perform chemical analyses of the microorganism content of soils to determine microbial reactions and chemical mineralogical relationships to plant growth. Provide advice regarding the development of regulatory standards for land reclamation and soil conservation. Develop new or improved methods and products for controlling and eliminating weeds, crop diseases, and insect pests.

Personality Type: Investigative. Investigative occupations frequently involve working with ideas and require an extensive amount of thinking. These occupations can involve searching for facts and figuring out problems mentally.

GOE—Interest Area: 01. Agriculture and Natural Resources. **Work Group:** 01.02. Resource Science/Engineering for Plants, Animals, and the Environment. **Other Jobs in This Work Group:** Agricultural Engineers; Animal Scientists; Conservation Scientists; Environmental Engineers; Foresters; Mining and Geological Engineers, Including Mining Safety Engineers; Petroleum Engineers; Range Managers; Soil and Water Conservationists; Zoologists and Wildlife Biologists.

Skills—Science: Using scientific rules and methods to solve problems. **Management of Financial Resources:** Determining how money will be spent to get the work done and accounting for these expenditures. **Writing:** Communicating effectively in writing as appropriate for the needs of the audience. **Management of Personnel Resources:** Motivating, developing, and directing people as they work; identifying the best people for the job. **Management of Material Resources:** Obtaining and seeing to the appropriate use of equipment, facilities, and materials needed to do certain work. **Reading Comprehension:** Understanding written sentences and paragraphs in work-related documents.

Education and Training Programs: Soil Chemistry and Physics; Soil Microbiology; Soil Science and Agronomy, General. **Related Knowledge/Courses: Biology:** Plant and animal organisms and their tissues, cells, functions, interdependencies, and interactions with each other and the environment. **Food Production:** Techniques and equipment for planting, growing, and harvesting food products (both plant and animal) for consumption, including storage/handling techniques. **Geography:** Principles and methods for describing the features of land, sea, and air masses, including their physical characteristics; locations; interrelationships; and distribution of plant, animal, and human life. **Chemistry:** The chemical composition, structure, and properties of substances and of the chemical processes and transformations that they undergo. This includes uses of chemicals and their danger signs, production techniques, and disposal methods. **Physics:** Physical principles and laws and their interrelationships and applications to understanding fluid, material, and atmospheric dynamics and mechanical, electrical, atomic, and subatomic structures and processes. **Education and Training:** Principles and methods for curriculum and training design, teaching and instruction for individuals and groups, and the measurement of training effects.

Work Environment: More often indoors than outdoors; sitting.

Soil and Water Conservationists

This job can be found in the Part II lists under the title Conservation Scientists.

- ◎ Education/Training Required: Bachelor's degree
- ◎ Annual Earnings: $53,350
- ◎ Growth: 6.3%
- ◎ Annual Job Openings: 2,000
- ◎ Self-Employed: 9.0%
- ◎ Part-Time: 6.7%

The job openings listed here are shared with Park Naturalists and with Range Managers.

Level of Solitary Work: 65.6 (out of 100)

Level of Contact with Others: 87.3 (out of 100)

Plan and develop coordinated practices for soil erosion control, soil and water conservation, and sound land use. Develop and maintain working relationships with local government staff and board members. Advise land users such as farmers and ranchers on conservation plans, problems, and alternative solutions and provide technical and planning assistance. Apply principles of specialized fields of science, such as agronomy, soil science, forestry, or agriculture, to achieve conservation objectives. Plan soil management and conservation practices, such as crop rotation, reforestation, permanent vegetation, contour plowing, or terracing, to maintain soil and conserve water. Visit areas affected by erosion problems to seek sources and solutions. Monitor projects during and after construction to ensure projects conform to design specifications. Compute design specifications for implementation of conservation practices, using survey and field information technical guides, engineering manuals, and calculator. Revisit land users to view implemented land use practices and plans. Coordinate and implement technical, financial, and administrative assistance programs for local government units to ensure efficient program implementation and timely responses to requests for assistance. Analyze results of investigations to determine measures needed to maintain or restore proper soil management. Participate on work teams to plan, develop, and implement water and land management programs and policies. Develop, conduct, and/or participate in surveys, studies, and investigations of various land uses, gathering information for use in developing corrective action plans. Survey property to mark locations and measurements, using surveying instruments. Compute cost estimates of different conservation practices based on needs of land users, maintenance requirements, and life expectancy of practices. Provide information, knowledge, expertise, and training to government agencies at all levels to solve water and soil management problems and to assure coordination of resource protection activities. Respond to complaints and questions on wetland jurisdiction, providing information and clarification. Initiate, schedule, and conduct annual audits and compliance checks of program implementation by local government.

Personality Type: Investigative. Investigative occupations frequently involve working with ideas and require an extensive amount of thinking. These occupations can involve searching for facts and figuring out problems mentally.

GOE—Interest Area: 01. Agriculture and Natural Resources. **Work Group:** 01.02. Resource Science/Engineering for Plants, Animals, and the Environment. **Other Jobs in This Work Group:** Agricultural Engineers; Animal Scientists; Conservation Scientists; Environmental Engineers; Foresters; Mining and Geological Engineers, Including Mining Safety Engineers; Petroleum Engineers; Range Managers; Soil and Plant Scientists; Zoologists and Wildlife Biologists.

Skills—Persuasion: Persuading others to change their minds or behavior. **Operations Analysis:** Analyzing needs and product requirements to create a design. **Science:** Using scientific rules and methods to solve problems. **Quality Control Analysis:** Conducting tests and inspections of products, services, or processes to evaluate quality or performance. **Judgment and Decision Making:** Considering the relative costs and benefits of potential actions to choose the most appropriate one. **Installation:** Installing equipment, machines, wiring, or programs to meet specifications.

Education and Training Programs: Forest Management/Forest Resources Management; Forest Sciences and Biology; Forestry, General; Forestry, Other; Land Use Planning and Management/Development; Natural Resources and Conservation, Other; Natural Resources Management and Policy; Natural Resources Management and Policy, Other; Natural Resources/Conservation, General; Water, Wetlands, and Marine Resources Management; Wildlife and Wildlands Science and Management. **Related Knowledge/Courses: Geography:** Principles and methods for describing the features of land, sea, and air masses, including their physical characteristics; locations; interrelationships; and distribution of plant, animal, and human life. **Biology:** Plant and animal organisms and their tissues, cells, functions, interdependencies, and interactions with each other and the environment. **Engineering and Technology:** The practical application of engineering science and technology. This includes applying principles, techniques, procedures, and equipment to the design and production of various goods and services. **Design:** Design techniques, tools, and principles involved in production of precision technical plans, blueprints, drawings, and models. **History and Archeology:** Historical events and their causes, indicators, and effects on civilizations and cultures. **Physics:** Physical principles and laws and their interrelationships and applications to understanding fluid, material, and atmospheric dynamics and mechanical, electrical, atomic, and subatomic structures and processes.

Work Environment: More often outdoors than indoors; contaminants; sitting.

Solderers and Brazers

This job can be found in the Part II lists under the title Welders, Cutters, Solderers, and Brazers.

- Education/Training Required: Long-term on-the-job training
- Annual Earnings: $30,990
- Growth: 5.0%
- Annual Job Openings: 52,000
- Self-Employed: 6.3%
- Part-Time: 1.7%

The job openings listed here are shared with Welders, Cutters, and Welder Fitters.

Level of Solitary Work: 58.2 (out of 100)

Level of Contact with Others: 72.2 (out of 100)

Braze or solder together components to assemble fabricated metal parts, using soldering iron, torch, or welding machine and flux. Melt and apply solder along adjoining edges of workpieces to solder joints, using soldering irons, gas torches, or electric-ultrasonic equipment. Heat soldering irons or workpieces to specified temperatures for soldering, using gas flames or electric current. Examine seams for defects and rework defective joints or broken parts. Melt and separate brazed or soldered joints to remove and straighten damaged or misaligned components, using hand torches, irons, or furnaces. Melt and apply solder to fill holes, indentations, and seams of fabricated metal products, using soldering equipment. Clean workpieces to remove dirt and excess acid, using chemical solutions, files, wire brushes, or grinders. Guide torches and rods along joints of workpieces to heat them to brazing temperature, melt braze alloys, and bond workpieces together. Adjust electric current and timing cycles of resistance welding machines to heat metals to bonding temperature. Turn valves to start flow of gases and light flames and adjust valves to obtain desired colors and sizes of flames. Clean equipment parts, such as tips of soldering irons, using chemical solutions or cleaning compounds. Brush flux onto joints of workpieces or dip braze rods into flux to prevent oxidation of metal. Remove workpieces from fixtures, using tongs, and cool workpieces, using air or water. Align and clamp workpieces together, using rules, squares, or hand tools, or position items in fixtures, jigs, or vises. Sweat together workpieces coated with solder. Smooth soldered areas with alternate strokes of paddles and torches, leaving soldered sections slightly higher than surrounding areas for later filing. Remove workpieces from molten solder and hold parts together until color indicates that solder has set. Select torch tips, flux, and brazing alloys from data charts or work orders. Turn dials to set intensity and duration of ultrasonic impulses according to work order specifications. Dip workpieces into molten solder or place solder strips between seams and heat seams with irons to bond items together. Clean joints of workpieces with wire brushes or by dipping them into cleaning solutions.

Personality Type: Realistic. Realistic occupations frequently involve work activities that include practical, hands-on problems and solutions. They often deal with plants; animals; and real-world materials such as wood, tools, and machinery. Many of the occupations require working outside and do not involve a lot of paperwork or working closely with others.

GOE—Interest Area: 13. Manufacturing. **Work Group:** 13.04. Welding, Brazing, and Soldering. **Other Jobs in This Work Group:** Structural Metal Fabricators and Fitters; Welders, Cutters, and Welder Fitters; Welders, Cutters, Solderers, and Brazers; Welding, Soldering, and Brazing Machine Setters, Operators, and Tenders.

Skills—Quality Control Analysis: Conducting tests and inspections of products, services, or processes to evaluate quality or performance. **Installation:** Installing equipment, machines, wiring, or programs to meet specifications. **Operation and Control:** Controlling operations of equipment or systems. **Troubleshooting:** Determining causes of operating errors and deciding what to do about them. **Equipment Selection:** Determining the kind of tools and equipment needed to do a job. **Repairing:** Repairing machines or systems by using the needed tools.

Education and Training Program: Welding Technology/Welder Training. **Related Knowledge/Courses: Production and Processing:** Raw materials, production processes, quality control, costs, and other techniques for maximizing the effective manufacture and distribution of goods. **Mechanical Devices:** Machines and tools, including their designs, uses, repair, and maintenance. **Engineering and Technology:** The practical application of engineering science and technology. This includes applying principles, techniques, procedures, and equipment to the design and production of various goods and services.

Work Environment: Indoors; noisy; contaminants; minor burns, cuts, bites, or stings; using hands on objects, tools, or controls; repetitive motions.

Sound Engineering Technicians

- Education/Training Required: Postsecondary vocational training
- Annual Earnings: $38,390
- Growth: 18.4%
- Annual Job Openings: 2,000
- Self-Employed: 6.5%
- Part-Time: 18.3%

Level of Solitary Work: 56.3 (out of 100)

Level of Contact with Others: 77.3 (out of 100)

Operate machines and equipment to record, synchronize, mix, or reproduce music, voices, or sound

effects in sporting arenas, theater productions, recording studios, or movie and video productions. Confer with producers, performers, and others in order to determine and achieve the desired sound for a production such as a musical recording or a film. Set up, test, and adjust recording equipment for recording sessions and live performances; tear down equipment after event completion. Regulate volume level and sound quality during recording sessions, using control consoles. Prepare for recording sessions by performing activities such as selecting and setting up microphones. Report equipment problems and ensure that required repairs are made. Mix and edit voices, music, and taped sound effects for live performances and for prerecorded events, using sound mixing boards. Synchronize and equalize prerecorded dialogue, music, and sound effects with visual action of motion pictures or television productions, using control consoles. Record speech, music, and other sounds on recording media, using recording equipment. Reproduce and duplicate sound recordings from original recording media, using sound editing and duplication equipment. Separate instruments, vocals, and other sounds; then combine sounds later during the mixing or post-production stage. Keep logs of recordings. Create musical instrument digital interface programs for music projects, commercials, or film post-production.

Personality Type: Realistic. Realistic occupations frequently involve work activities that include practical, hands-on problems and solutions. They often deal with plants; animals; and real-world materials such as wood, tools, and machinery. Many of the occupations require working outside and do not involve a lot of paperwork or working closely with others.

GOE—Interest Area: 03. Arts and Communication. **Work Group:** 03.09. Media Technology. **Other Jobs in This Work Group:** Audio and Video Equipment Technicians; Broadcast Technicians; Camera Operators, Television, Video, and Motion Picture; Film and Video Editors; Multi-Media Artists and Animators; Photographers; Radio Operators.

Skills—Technology Design: Generating or adapting equipment and technology to serve user needs. **Operation Monitoring:** Watching gauges, dials, or other indicators to make sure a machine is working properly. **Operation and Control:** Controlling operations of equipment or systems. **Installation:** Installing equipment, machines, wiring, or programs to meet specifications. **Equipment Maintenance:** Performing routine maintenance on equipment and determining when and what kind of maintenance is needed. **Troubleshooting:** Determining causes of operating errors and deciding what to do about them.

Education and Training Programs: Communications Technology/Technician Training; Recording Arts Technology/Technician Training. **Related Knowledge/Courses: Fine Arts:** The theory and techniques required to compose, produce, and perform works of music, dance, visual arts, drama, and sculpture. **Communications and Media:** Media production, communication, and dissemination techniques and methods. This includes alternative ways to inform and entertain via written, oral, and visual media. **Telecommunications:** Transmission, broadcasting, switching, control, and operation of telecommunications systems. **Computers and Electronics:** Circuit boards, processors, chips, electronic equipment, and computer hardware and software, including applications and programming. **Customer and Personal Service:** Principles and processes for providing customer and personal services. This includes customer needs assessment, meeting quality standards for services, and evaluation of customer satisfaction. **Production and Processing:** Raw materials, production processes, quality control, costs, and other techniques for maximizing the effective manufacture and distribution of goods.

Work Environment: Indoors; noisy; sitting; using hands on objects, tools, or controls; repetitive motions.

Statement Clerks

This job can be found in the Part II lists under the title Billing and Posting Clerks and Machine Operators.

- Education/Training Required: Moderate-term on-the-job training
- Annual Earnings: $27,780
- Growth: 3.4%
- Annual Job Openings: 70,000
- Self-Employed: 2.6%
- Part-Time: 14.5%

The job openings listed here are shared with Billing, Cost, and Rate Clerks and with Billing, Posting, and Calculating Machine Operators.

Level of Solitary Work: 67.7 (out of 100)

Level of Contact with Others: 89.4 (out of 100)

Prepare and distribute bank statements to customers, answer inquiries, and reconcile discrepancies in records and accounts. Encode and cancel checks, using bank machines. Take orders for imprinted checks. Compare previously prepared bank statements with canceled checks and reconcile discrepancies. Verify signatures and required information on checks. Post stop-payment notices to prevent payment of protested checks. Maintain files of canceled checks and customers' signatures. Match statements with batches of canceled checks by account numbers. Weigh envelopes containing statements to determine correct postage and affix postage, using stamps or metering equipment. Load machines with statements, cancelled checks, and envelopes to prepare statements for distribution to customers or stuff envelopes by hand. Retrieve checks returned to customers in error, adjusting customer accounts and answering inquiries about errors as necessary. Route statements for mailing or over-the-counter delivery to customers. Monitor equipment to ensure proper operation. Fix minor problems, such as equipment jams, and notify repair personnel of major equipment problems.

Personality Type: Conventional. Conventional occupations frequently involve following set procedures and routines. These occupations can include working with data and details more than with ideas. Usually there is a clear line of authority to follow.

GOE—Interest Area: 04. Business and Administration. **Work Group:** 04.06. Mathematical Clerical Support. **Other Jobs in This Work Group:** Billing and Posting Clerks and Machine Operators; Billing, Cost, and Rate Clerks; Bookkeeping, Accounting, and Auditing Clerks; Brokerage Clerks; Payroll and Timekeeping Clerks; Tax Preparers.

Skills—Critical Thinking: Using logic and reasoning to identify the strengths and weaknesses of alternative solutions, conclusions, or approaches to problems.

Education and Training Program: Accounting Technology/Technician Training and Bookkeeping. **Related Knowledge/Courses: Economics and Accounting:** Economic and accounting principles and practices, the financial markets, banking, and the analysis and reporting of financial data. **Clerical Practices:** Administrative and clerical procedures and systems such as word processing, managing files and records, stenography and transcription, designing forms, and other office procedures and terminology. **Administration and Management:** Business and management principles involved in strategic planning, resource allocation, human resources modeling, leadership technique, production methods, and coordination of people and resources. **Mathematics:** Arithmetic, algebra, geometry, calculus, and statistics and their applications.

Work Environment: Indoors; sitting; repetitive motions.

Stationary Engineers and Boiler Operators

◎ Education/Training Required: Long-term on-the-job training

◎ Annual Earnings: $44,600

◎ Growth: 3.4%

◎ Annual Job Openings: 5,000

◎ Self-Employed: 1.0%

◎ Part-Time: 3.5%

Level of Solitary Work: 59.5 (out of 100)

Level of Contact with Others: 65.8 (out of 100)

Operate or maintain stationary engines, boilers, or other mechanical equipment to provide utilities for buildings or industrial processes. Operate equipment such as steam engines, generators, motors, turbines, and steam boilers. Operate or tend stationary engines; boilers; and auxiliary equipment such as pumps, compressors and air-conditioning equipment to supply and maintain steam or heat for buildings, marine vessels, or pneumatic tools. Observe and interpret readings on gauges, meters, and charts registering various aspects of boiler operation to ensure that boilers are operating properly. Test boiler water quality or arrange for testing and take any necessary corrective action, such as adding chemicals to prevent corrosion and harmful deposits. Activate valves to maintain required amounts of water in boilers, to adjust supplies of combustion air, and to control the flow of fuel into burners. Monitor boiler water, chemical, and fuel levels and make adjustments to maintain required levels. Fire coal furnaces by hand or with stokers and gas- or oil-fed boilers, using automatic gas feeds or oil pumps. Monitor and inspect equipment, computer terminals, switches, valves, gauges, alarms, safety devices, and meters to detect leaks or malfunctions and to ensure that equipment is operating efficiently and safely. Analyze problems and take appropriate action to ensure continuous and reliable operation of equipment and systems.

Maintain daily logs of operation, maintenance, and safety activities, including test results, instrument readings, and details of equipment malfunctions and maintenance work. Adjust controls or valves on equipment to provide power and to regulate and set operations of system or industrial processes. Switch from automatic controls to manual controls and isolate equipment mechanically and electrically to allow for safe inspection and repair work. Clean and lubricate boilers and auxiliary equipment and make minor adjustments as needed, using hand tools. Check the air quality of ventilation systems and make adjustments to ensure compliance with mandated safety codes. Perform or arrange for repairs, such as complete overhauls; replacement of defective valves, gaskets, or bearings; or fabrication of new parts. Weigh, measure, and record fuel used.

Personality Type: Realistic. Realistic occupations frequently involve work activities that include practical, hands-on problems and solutions. They often deal with plants; animals; and real-world materials such as wood, tools, and machinery. Many of the occupations require working outside and do not involve a lot of paperwork or working closely with others.

GOE—Interest Area: 13. Manufacturing. **Work Group:** 13.16. Utility Operation and Energy Distribution. **Other Jobs in This Work Group:** Chemical Plant and System Operators; Gas Compressor and Gas Pumping Station Operators; Gas Plant Operators; Nuclear Power Reactor Operators; Petroleum Pump System Operators, Refinery Operators, and Gaugers; Power Distributors and Dispatchers; Power Plant Operators; Ship Engineers; Water and Liquid Waste Treatment Plant and System Operators.

Skills—Repairing: Repairing machines or systems by using the needed tools. **Operation Monitoring:** Watching gauges, dials, or other indicators to make sure a machine is working properly. **Equipment Maintenance:** Performing routine maintenance on equipment and determining when and what kind of maintenance is needed. **Installation:** Installing equipment, machines, wiring, or programs to meet specifications. **Systems Analysis:** Determining how a system should work and how changes in conditions, operations, and the environment will affect outcomes. **Operation and Control:** Controlling operations of equipment or systems.

Education and Training Program: Building/Property Maintenance and Management. **Related Knowledge/Courses: Mechanical Devices:** Machines and tools, including their designs, uses, repair, and maintenance. **Building and Construction:** The materials, methods, and tools involved in the construction or repair of houses, buildings, or other structures such as highways and roads. **Chemistry:** The chemical composition, structure, and properties of substances and of the chemical processes and transformations that they undergo. This includes uses of chemicals and their danger signs, production techniques, and disposal methods. **Physics:** Physical principles and laws and their interrelationships and applications to understanding fluid, material, and atmospheric dynamics and mechanical, electrical, atomic, and subatomic structures and processes. **Design:** Design techniques, tools, and principles involved in production of precision technical plans, blueprints, drawings, and models. **Engineering and Technology:** The practical application of engineering science and technology. This includes applying principles, techniques, procedures, and equipment to the design and production of various goods and services.

Work Environment: Noisy; very hot or cold; very bright or dim lighting; contaminants; hazardous conditions; hazardous equipment.

Statisticians

- ◎ Education/Training Required: Master's degree
- ◎ Annual Earnings: $62,450
- ◎ Growth: 4.6%
- ◎ Annual Job Openings: 2,000
- ◎ Self-Employed: 3.6%
- ◎ Part-Time: 10.9%

Level of Solitary Work: 81.2 (out of 100)

Level of Contact with Others: 69.0 (out of 100)

Engage in the development of mathematical theory or apply statistical theory and methods to collect, organize, interpret, and summarize numerical data to provide usable information. May specialize in fields such as bio-statistics, agricultural statistics, business statistics, economic statistics, or other fields. Report results of statistical analyses, including information in the form of graphs, charts, and tables. Process large amounts of data for statistical modeling and graphic analysis, using computers. Identify relationships and trends in data, as well as any factors that could affect the results of research. Analyze and interpret statistical data in order to identify significant differences in relationships among sources of information. Prepare data for processing by organizing information, checking for any inaccuracies, and adjusting and weighting the raw data. Evaluate the statistical methods and procedures used to obtain data in order to ensure validity, applicability, efficiency, and accuracy. Evaluate sources of information in order to determine any limitations in terms of reliability or usability. Plan data collection methods for specific projects and determine the types and sizes of sample groups to be used. Design research projects that apply valid scientific techniques and utilize information obtained from baselines or historical data in order to structure uncompromised and efficient analyses. Develop an understanding of fields to which statistical methods are to be applied in order to determine whether methods and results are appropriate. Supervise and provide instructions for workers collecting and tabulating data. Apply sampling techniques or utilize complete enumeration bases in order to determine and define groups to be surveyed. Adapt statistical methods in order to solve specific problems in many fields, such as economics, biology, and engineering. Develop and test experimental designs, sampling techniques, and analytical methods. Examine theories, such as those of probability and inference, in order to discover mathematical bases for new or improved methods of obtaining and evaluating numerical data.

Personality Type: Investigative. Investigative occupations frequently involve working with ideas and require an extensive amount of thinking. These occupations can involve searching for facts and figuring out problems mentally.

GOE—Interest Area: 15. Scientific Research, Engineering, and Mathematics. **Work Group:** 15.06. Mathematics and Data Analysis. **Other Jobs in This Work Group:** Actuaries; Mathematical Technicians; Mathematicians; Social Science Research Assistants; Statistical Assistants.

Skills—Programming: Writing computer programs for various purposes. **Science:** Using scientific rules and methods to solve problems. **Mathematics:** Using mathematics to solve problems. **Active Learning:** Understanding the implications of new information for both current and future problem solving and decision making. **Writing:** Communicating effectively in writing as appropriate for the needs of the audience. **Negotiation:** Bringing others together and trying to reconcile differences.

Education and Training Programs: Applied Mathematics; Biostatistics; Business Statistics; Mathematical Statistics and Probability; Mathematics, General; Statistics, General; Statistics, Other. **Related Knowledge/Courses: Mathematics:** Arithmetic, algebra, geometry, calculus, and statistics and their applications. **Computers and Electronics:** Circuit boards, processors, chips, electronic equipment, and computer hardware and software, including applications and programming. **English Language:** The structure and content of the English language, including the meaning and spelling of words, rules of composition, and grammar. **Education and Training:** Principles and methods for curriculum and training design, teaching and instruction for individuals and groups, and the measurement of training effects. **Law and Government:** Laws, legal codes, court procedures, precedents, government regulations, executive orders, agency rules, and the democratic political process.

Work Environment: Indoors; sitting; using hands on objects, tools, or controls; repetitive motions.

Stonemasons

- Education/Training Required: Long-term on-the-job training
- Annual Earnings: $34,640
- Growth: 13.0%
- Annual Job Openings: 2,000
- Self-Employed: 23.1%
- Part-Time: No data available

Level of Solitary Work: 59.2 (out of 100)

Level of Contact with Others: 85.2 (out of 100)

Build stone structures, such as piers, walls, and abutments. Lay walks; curbstones; or special types of masonry for vats, tanks, and floors. Lay out wall patterns or foundations, using straight edge, rule, or staked lines. Shape, trim, face, and cut marble or stone preparatory to setting, using power saws, cutting equipment, and hand tools. Set vertical and horizontal alignment of structures, using plumb bob, gauge line, and level. Mix mortar or grout and pour or spread mortar or grout on marble slabs, stone, or foundation. Remove wedges; fill joints between stones; finish joints between stones, using a trowel; and smooth the mortar to an attractive finish, using a tuckpointer. Clean excess mortar or grout from surface of marble, stone, or monument, using sponge, brush, water, or acid. Set stone or marble in place according to layout or pattern. Lay brick to build shells of chimneys and smokestacks or to line or reline industrial furnaces, kilns, boilers, and similar installations. Replace broken or missing masonry units in walls or floors. Smooth, polish, and bevel surfaces, using hand tools and power tools. Drill holes in marble or ornamental stone and anchor brackets in holes. Repair cracked or chipped areas of stone or marble, using blowtorch and mastic, and remove rough or defective spots from concrete, using power grinder or chisel and hammer. Remove sections of monument from truck bed and guide stone onto foundation, using skids, hoist, or truck crane.

Construct and install prefabricated masonry units. Dig trench for foundation of monument, using pick and shovel. Position mold along guidelines of wall, press mold in place, and remove mold and paper from wall. Line interiors of molds with treated paper and fill molds with composition-stone mixture.

Personality Type: Realistic. Realistic occupations frequently involve work activities that include practical, hands-on problems and solutions. They often deal with plants; animals; and real-world materials such as wood, tools, and machinery. Many of the occupations require working outside and do not involve a lot of paperwork or working closely with others.

GOE—Interest Area: 02. Architecture and Construction. **Work Group:** 02.04. Construction Crafts. **Other Jobs in This Work Group:** Boilermakers; Brickmasons and Blockmasons; Carpet Installers; Cement Masons and Concrete Finishers; Commercial Divers; Construction Carpenters; Crane and Tower Operators; Drywall and Ceiling Tile Installers; Electricians; Fence Erectors; Floor Layers, Except Carpet, Wood, and Hard Tiles; Floor Sanders and Finishers; Glaziers; Hazardous Materials Removal Workers; Insulation Workers, Floor, Ceiling, and Wall; Insulation Workers, Mechanical; Manufactured Building and Mobile Home Installers; Operating Engineers and Other Construction Equipment Operators; Painters, Construction and Maintenance; Paperhangers; Paving, Surfacing, and Tamping Equipment Operators; Pile-Driver Operators; Pipe Fitters and Steamfitters; Pipelayers; Plasterers and Stucco Masons; Plumbers; Plumbers, Pipefitters, and Steamfitters; Rail-Track Laying and Maintenance Equipment Operators; Refractory Materials Repairers, Except Brickmasons; Reinforcing Iron and Rebar Workers; Riggers; Roofers; Rough Carpenters; Security and Fire Alarm Systems Installers; Segmental Pavers; Sheet Metal Workers; Stone Cutters and Carvers, Manufacturing; Structural Iron and Steel Workers; Tapers; Terrazzo Workers and Finishers; Tile and Marble Setters.

Skills—Installation: Installing equipment, machines, wiring, or programs to meet specifications. **Management of Personnel Resources:** Motivating, developing, and directing people as they work; identifying the best people for the job. **Repairing:** Repairing machines or systems by using the needed tools. **Equipment Maintenance:** Performing routine maintenance on equipment and determining when and what kind of maintenance is needed. **Equipment Selection:** Determining the kind of tools and equipment needed to do a job. **Mathematics:** Using mathematics to solve problems.

Education and Training Program: Mason Training/Masonry. **Related Knowledge/Courses: Building and Construction:** The materials, methods, and tools involved in the construction or repair of houses, buildings, or other structures such as highways and roads. **Design:** Design techniques, tools, and principles involved in production of precision technical plans, blueprints, drawings, and models. **Mechanical Devices:** Machines and tools, including their designs, uses, repair, and maintenance. **Mathematics:** Arithmetic, algebra, geometry, calculus, and statistics and their applications. **Education and Training:** Principles and methods for curriculum and training design, teaching and instruction for individuals and groups, and the measurement of training effects. **Public Safety and Security:** Relevant equipment, policies, procedures, and strategies to promote effective local, state, or national security operations for the protection of people, data, property, and institutions.

Work Environment: Outdoors; standing; walking and running; kneeling, crouching, stooping, or crawling; using hands on objects, tools, or controls; bending or twisting the body.

Structural Metal Fabricators and Fitters

◉ Education/Training Required: Moderate-term on-the-job training

◉ Annual Earnings: $30,290

◉ Growth: 2.9%

◉ Annual Job Openings: 18,000

◉ Self-Employed: 3.1%

◉ Part-Time: 6.0%

Level of Solitary Work: 65.8 (out of 100)

Level of Contact with Others: 50.7 (out of 100)

Fabricate, lay out, position, align, and fit parts of structural metal products. Position, align, fit, and weld parts to form complete units or subunits, following blueprints and layout specifications and using jigs, welding torches, and hand tools. Verify conformance of workpieces to specifications, using squares, rulers, and measuring tapes. Tack-weld fitted parts together. Lay out and examine metal stock or workpieces to be processed to ensure that specifications are met. Align and fit parts according to specifications, using jacks, turnbuckles, wedges, drift pins, pry bars, and hammers. Locate and mark workpiece bending and cutting lines, allowing for stock thickness, machine and welding shrinkage, and other component specifications. Position or tighten braces, jacks, clamps, ropes, or bolt straps or bolt parts in position for welding or riveting. Study engineering drawings and blueprints to determine materials requirements and task sequences. Move parts into position manually or by using hoists or cranes. Set up and operate fabricating machines such as brakes, rolls, shears, flame cutters, grinders, and drill presses to bend, cut, form, punch, drill, or otherwise form and assemble metal components. Hammer, chip, and grind workpieces to cut, bend, and straighten metal. Smooth workpiece edges and fix taps, tubes, and valves. Design and construct templates and fixtures, using hand tools. Straighten warped or bent parts, using sledges, hand torches, straightening presses, or bulldozers. Mark reference points onto floors or face blocks and transpose them to workpieces, using measuring devices, squares, chalk, and soapstone. Set up face blocks, jigs, and fixtures. Remove high spots and cut bevels, using hand files, portable grinders, and cutting torches. Direct welders to build up low spots or short pieces with weld. Lift or move materials and finished products, using large cranes. Heat-treat parts, using acetylene torches. Preheat workpieces to make them malleable, using hand torches or furnaces. Install boilers, containers, and other structures. Erect ladders and scaffolding to fit together large assemblies.

Personality Type: Realistic. Realistic occupations frequently involve work activities that include practical, hands-on problems and solutions. They often deal with plants; animals; and real-world materials such as wood, tools, and machinery. Many of the occupations require working outside and do not involve a lot of paperwork or working closely with others.

GOE—Interest Area: 13. Manufacturing. **Work Group:** 13.04. Welding, Brazing, and Soldering. **Other Jobs in This Work Group:** Solderers and Brazers; Welders, Cutters, and Welder Fitters; Welders, Cutters, Solderers, and Brazers; Welding, Soldering, and Brazing Machine Setters, Operators, and Tenders.

Skills—Quality Control Analysis: Conducting tests and inspections of products, services, or processes to evaluate quality or performance. **Operation Monitoring:** Watching gauges, dials, or other indicators to make sure a machine is working properly. **Equipment Maintenance:** Performing routine maintenance on equipment and determining when and what kind of maintenance is needed. **Installation:** Installing equipment, machines, wiring, or programs to meet specifications. **Repairing:** Repairing machines or systems by using the needed tools. **Operation and Control:** Controlling operations of equipment or systems.

Education and Training Program: Machine Shop Technology/Assistant Training. **Related Knowledge/**

S

Courses: Design: Design techniques, tools, and principles involved in production of precision technical plans, blueprints, drawings, and models. **Building and Construction:** The materials, methods, and tools involved in the construction or repair of houses, buildings, or other structures such as highways and roads. **Mechanical Devices:** Machines and tools, including their designs, uses, repair, and maintenance. **Production and Processing:** Raw materials, production processes, quality control, costs, and other techniques for maximizing the effective manufacture and distribution of goods.

Work Environment: Noisy; contaminants; hazardous equipment; minor burns, cuts, bites, or stings; standing; using hands on objects, tools, or controls.

Subway and Streetcar Operators

- Education/Training Required: Moderate-term on-the-job training
- Annual Earnings: $47,500
- Growth: 13.7%
- Annual Job Openings: 1,000
- Self-Employed: 0.0%
- Part-Time: No data available

Level of Solitary Work: 71.7 (out of 100)

Level of Contact with Others: 87.2 (out of 100)

Operate subway or elevated suburban train with no separate locomotive or electric-powered streetcar to transport passengers. May handle fares. Operate controls to open and close transit vehicle doors. Drive and control rail-guided public transportation, such as subways; elevated trains; and electric-powered streetcars, trams, or trolleys, to transport passengers. Monitor lights indicating obstructions or other trains ahead and watch for car and truck traffic at crossings to stay alert to potential hazards. Direct emergency evacuation procedures. Regulate vehicle speed and the time spent at each stop to maintain schedules. Report delays, mechanical problems, and emergencies to supervisors or dispatchers, using radios. Make announcements to passengers, such as notifications of upcoming stops or schedule delays. Complete reports, including shift summaries and incident or accident reports. Greet passengers; provide information; and answer questions concerning fares, schedules, transfers, and routings. Attend meetings on driver and passenger safety to learn ways in which job performance might be affected. Collect fares from passengers and issue change and transfers. Record transactions and coin receptor readings to verify the amount of money collected.

Personality Type: Realistic. Realistic occupations frequently involve work activities that include practical, hands-on problems and solutions. They often deal with plants; animals; and real-world materials such as wood, tools, and machinery. Many of the occupations require working outside and do not involve a lot of paperwork or working closely with others.

GOE—Interest Area: 16. Transportation, Distribution, and Logistics. **Work Group:** 16.04. Rail Vehicle Operation. **Other Jobs in This Work Group:** Locomotive Engineers; Locomotive Firers; Rail Yard Engineers, Dinkey Operators, and Hostlers.

Skills—Operation and Control: Controlling operations of equipment or systems. **Operation Monitoring:** Watching gauges, dials, or other indicators to make sure a machine is working properly. **Troubleshooting:** Determining causes of operating errors and deciding what to do about them. **Service Orientation:** Actively looking for ways to help people. **Active Listening:** Giving full attention to what other people are saying, taking time to understand the points being made, asking questions as appropriate, and not interrupting at inappropriate times.

Education and Training Program: Truck and Bus Driver Training/Commercial Vehicle Operation. **Related Knowledge/Courses: Transportation:** Principles and methods for moving people or goods by air, rail, sea, or road, including the relative costs and benefits. **Public Safety and Security:** Relevant equipment, policies, procedures, and strategies to promote effective local, state, or national security operations for the protection of people, data, property, and institutions. **Customer and Personal Service:** Principles and processes for providing customer and personal services. This includes customer needs assessment, meeting quality standards for services, and evaluation of customer satisfaction. **Telecommunications:** Transmission, broadcasting, switching, control, and operation of telecommunications systems. **Mechanical Devices:** Machines and tools, including their designs, uses, repair, and maintenance. **Psychology:** Human behavior and performance; individual differences in ability, personality, and interests; learning and motivation; psychological research methods; and the assessment and treatment of behavioral and affective disorders.

Work Environment: Outdoors; noisy; contaminants; sitting; using hands on objects, tools, or controls; repetitive motions.

Surveying and Mapping Technicians

See the descriptions of these jobs:

- Mapping Technicians
- Surveying Technicians

Surveying Technicians

This job can be found in the Part II lists under the title Surveying and Mapping Technicians.

- Education/Training Required: Moderate-term on-the-job training
- Annual Earnings: $31,290
- Growth: 9.6%
- Annual Job Openings: 9,000
- Self-Employed: 4.3%
- Part-Time: 4.3%

The job openings listed here are shared with Mapping Technicians.

Level of Solitary Work: 51.5 (out of 100)

Level of Contact with Others: 71.6 (out of 100)

Adjust and operate surveying instruments, such as theodolite and electronic distance-measuring equipment, and compile notes, make sketches, and enter data into computers. Adjust and operate surveying instruments such as prisms, theodolites, and electronic distance-measuring equipment. Compile information necessary to stake projects for construction, using engineering plans. Run rods for benches and cross-section elevations. Position and hold the vertical rods, or targets, that theodolite operators use for sighting to measure angles, distances, and elevations. Record survey measurements and descriptive data, using notes, drawings, sketches, and inked tracings. Perform calculations to determine earth curvature corrections, atmospheric impacts on measurements, traverse closures and adjustments, azimuths, level runs, and placement of markers. Conduct surveys to ascertain the locations of natural features and man-made structures on the Earth's surface, underground, and underwater, using electronic distance-measuring equipment and other surveying instruments. Search for section corners, property irons, and survey points. Operate and manage land-information computer systems, performing tasks such as storing data, making inquiries, and producing plots and reports. Direct and supervise work of subordinate members of surveying parties. Set out and recover stakes, marks, and other monumentation. Lay out grids and determine horizontal and vertical controls. Compare survey computations with applicable standards to determine adequacy of data. Collect information needed to carry out new surveys, using source maps, previous survey data, photographs, computer records, and other relevant information. Prepare topographic and contour maps of land surveyed, including site features and other relevant information such as charts, drawings, and survey notes. Maintain equipment and vehicles used by surveying crews. Place and hold measuring tapes when electronic distance-measuring equipment is not used. Provide assistance in the development of methods and procedures for conducting field surveys. Perform manual labor, such as cutting brush for lines; carrying stakes, rebar, and other heavy items; and stacking rods.

Personality Type: Realistic. Realistic occupations frequently involve work activities that include practical, hands-on problems and solutions. They often deal with plants; animals; and real-world materials such as wood, tools, and machinery. Many of the occupations require working outside and do not involve a lot of paperwork or working closely with others.

GOE—Interest Area: 15. Scientific Research, Engineering, and Mathematics. **Work Group:** 15.09. Engineering Technology. **Other Jobs in This Work Group:** Aerospace Engineering and Operations Technicians; Cartographers and Photogrammetrists; Civil Engineering Technicians; Electrical and Electronic Engineering Technicians; Electrical and Electronics Drafters; Electrical Drafters; Electrical Engineering Technicians; Electro-Mechanical Technicians; Electronic Drafters; Electronics Engineering Technicians; Environmental Engineering Technicians; Mapping Technicians; Mechanical Drafters; Mechanical Engineering Technicians; Surveying and Mapping Technicians.

Skills—Mathematics: Using mathematics to solve problems. **Troubleshooting:** Determining causes of operating errors and deciding what to do about them. **Equipment Maintenance:** Performing routine maintenance on equipment and determining when and what kind of maintenance is needed. **Coordination:** Adjusting actions in relation to others' actions. **Equipment Selection:** Determining the kind of tools and equipment needed to do a job. **Technology Design:** Generating or adapting equipment and technology to serve user needs.

Education and Training Programs: Cartography; Surveying Technology/Surveying. **Related Knowledge/Courses: Building and Construction:** The materials, methods, and tools involved in the construction or repair of houses, buildings, or other structures such as highways and roads. **Design:** Design techniques, tools, and principles involved in production of precision technical plans, blueprints, drawings, and models. **Geography:** Principles and methods for describing the features of land, sea, and air masses, including their physical characteristics; locations; interrelationships; and distribution of plant, animal, and human life. **Engineering and Technology:** The practical application of engineering science and technology. This includes applying principles, techniques, procedures, and equipment to the design and production of various goods and services. **Mathematics:** Arithmetic, algebra, geometry, calculus, and statistics and their applications. **Physics:** Physical principles and laws and their interrelationships and applications to understanding fluid, material, and atmospheric dynamics and mechanical, electrical, atomic, and subatomic structures and processes.

Work Environment: Outdoors; very hot or cold; very bright or dim lighting; hazardous equipment; minor burns, cuts, bites, or stings; using hands on objects, tools, or controls.

Tapers

- ◎ Education/Training Required: Moderate-term on-the-job training
- ◎ Annual Earnings: $39,870
- ◎ Growth: 5.9%
- ◎ Annual Job Openings: 5,000
- ◎ Self-Employed: 21.0%
- ◎ Part-Time: 8.0%

Level of Solitary Work: 59.2 (out of 100)

Level of Contact with Others: 10.5 (out of 100)

Seal joints between plasterboard or other wallboard to prepare wall surface for painting or papering. Mix sealing compounds by hand or with portable electric mixers. Sand rough spots of dried cement between applications of compounds. Select the correct sealing compound or tape. Apply additional coats to fill in holes and make surfaces smooth. Sand or patch nicks or cracks in plasterboard or wallboard. Spread sealing compound between boards or panels and over cracks, holes, and nail and screw heads, using trowels, broadknives, or spatulas. Spread and smooth cementing material over tape, using trowels or floating machines to blend joints with wall surfaces. Use mechanical applicators that spread compounds and embed tape in one operation. Press paper tape over joints to embed tape into sealing compound and to seal joints. Install metal molding at wall corners to secure wallboard. Countersink nails or screws below surfaces of walls before applying sealing compounds, using hammers or screwdrivers. Check adhesives to ensure that they will work and will remain durable. Apply texturizing compounds and primers to walls and ceilings before final finishing, using trowels, brushes, rollers, or spray guns. Remove extra compound after surfaces have been covered sufficiently.

Personality Type: Realistic. Realistic occupations frequently involve work activities that include practical, hands-on problems and solutions. They often deal with plants; animals; and real-world materials such as wood, tools, and machinery. Many of the occupations require working outside and do not involve a lot of paperwork or working closely with others.

GOE—Interest Area: 02. Architecture and Construction. **Work Group:** 02.04. Construction Crafts. **Other Jobs in This Work Group:** Boilermakers; Brickmasons and Blockmasons; Carpet Installers; Cement Masons and Concrete Finishers; Commercial Divers; Construction Carpenters; Crane and Tower Operators; Drywall and Ceiling Tile Installers; Electricians; Fence Erectors; Floor Layers, Except Carpet, Wood, and Hard Tiles; Floor Sanders and Finishers; Glaziers; Hazardous Materials Removal Workers; Insulation Workers, Floor, Ceiling, and Wall; Insulation Workers, Mechanical; Manufactured Building and Mobile Home Installers; Operating Engineers and Other Construction Equipment Operators; Painters, Construction and Maintenance; Paperhangers; Paving, Surfacing, and Tamping Equipment Operators; Pile-Driver Operators; Pipe Fitters and Steamfitters; Pipelayers; Plasterers and Stucco Masons; Plumbers; Plumbers, Pipefitters, and Steamfitters; Rail-Track Laying and Maintenance Equipment Operators; Refractory Materials Repairers, Except Brickmasons; Reinforcing Iron and Rebar Workers; Riggers; Roofers; Rough Carpenters; Security and Fire Alarm Systems Installers; Segmental Pavers; Sheet Metal Workers; Stone Cutters and Carvers, Manufacturing; Stonemasons; Structural Iron and Steel Workers; Terrazzo Workers and Finishers; Tile and Marble Setters.

Skills—None met the criteria.

Education and Training Program: Construction Trades, Other. **Related Knowledge/Courses: Building and Construction:** The materials, methods, and tools involved in the construction or repair of houses, buildings, or other structures such as highways and roads.

Work Environment: Indoors; contaminants; minor burns, cuts, bites, or stings; standing; using hands on objects, tools, or controls; bending or twisting the body.

Tax Preparers

- Education/Training Required: Moderate-term on-the-job training
- Annual Earnings: $25,700
- Growth: 10.6%
- Annual Job Openings: 11,000
- Self-Employed: 35.6%
- Part-Time: 31.2%

Level of Solitary Work: 65.5 (out of 100)

Level of Contact with Others: 92.8 (out of 100)

Prepare tax returns for individuals or small businesses, but do not have the background or responsibilities of an accredited or certified public accountant. Compute taxes owed or overpaid, using adding machines or personal computers, and complete entries on forms, following tax form instructions and tax tables. Prepare or assist in preparing simple to complex tax returns for individuals or small businesses. Use all appropriate adjustments, deductions, and credits to keep clients' taxes to a minimum. Interview clients to obtain additional information on taxable income and deductible expenses and allowances. Review financial records such as income statements and documentation of expenditures in order to determine forms needed to prepare tax returns. Furnish taxpayers with sufficient information and advice in order to ensure correct tax form completion. Consult tax law handbooks or bulletins in order to determine procedures for preparation of atypical returns. Calculate form preparation fees according to return complexity and processing time required. Check data input or verify totals on forms prepared by others to detect errors in arithmetic, data entry, or procedures.

Personality Type: Conventional. Conventional occupations frequently involve following set procedures and routines. These occupations can include working with data and details more than with ideas. Usually there is a clear line of authority to follow.

GOE—Interest Area: 04. Business and Administration. **Work Group:** 04.06. Mathematical Clerical Support. **Other Jobs in This Work Group:** Billing and Posting Clerks and Machine Operators; Billing, Cost, and Rate Clerks; Bookkeeping, Accounting, and Auditing Clerks; Brokerage Clerks; Payroll and Timekeeping Clerks; Statement Clerks.

Skills—Service Orientation: Actively looking for ways to help people. **Mathematics:** Using mathematics to solve problems. **Complex Problem Solving:** Identifying complex problems and reviewing related information to develop and evaluate options and implement solutions. **Active Learning:** Understanding the implications of new information for both current and future problem solving and decision making. **Learning Strategies:** Selecting and using training or instructional methods and procedures appropriate for the situation when learning or teaching new things. **Management of Financial Resources:** Determining how money will be spent to get the work done and accounting for these expenditures.

Education and Training Programs: Accounting Technology/Technician Training and Bookkeeping; Taxation. **Related Knowledge/Courses: Economics and Accounting:** Economic and accounting principles and practices, the financial markets, banking, and the analysis and reporting of financial data. **Clerical Practices:** Administrative and clerical procedures and systems such as word processing, managing files and records, stenography and transcription, designing forms, and other office procedures and terminology. **Mathematics:** Arithmetic, algebra, geometry, calculus, and statistics and their applications. **Computers and Electronics:** Circuit boards, processors, chips, electronic equipment, and computer hardware and software, including applications and programming. **Customer and Personal Service:**

Principles and processes for providing customer and personal services. This includes customer needs assessment, meeting quality standards for services, and evaluation of customer satisfaction. **Law and Government:** Laws, legal codes, court procedures, precedents, government regulations, executive orders, agency rules, and the democratic political process.

Work Environment: Indoors; sitting.

Technical Writers

- Education/Training Required: Bachelor's degree
- Annual Earnings: $55,160
- Growth: 23.2%
- Annual Job Openings: 5,000
- Self-Employed: 7.3%
- Part-Time: 7.3%

Level of Solitary Work: 56.3 (out of 100)

Level of Contact with Others: 81.7 (out of 100)

Write technical materials, such as equipment manuals, appendices, or operating and maintenance instructions. May assist in layout work. Organize material and complete writing assignment according to set standards regarding order, clarity, conciseness, style, and terminology. Maintain records and files of work and revisions. Edit, standardize, or make changes to material prepared by other writers or establishment personnel. Confer with customer representatives, vendors, plant executives, or publisher to establish technical specifications and to determine subject material to be developed for publication. Review published materials and recommend revisions or changes in scope, format, content, and methods of reproduction and binding. Select photographs, drawings, sketches, diagrams, and charts to illustrate material. Study drawings, specifications, mockups, and product samples to integrate and delineate technology, operating procedure, and production sequence and detail. Interview production and engineering personnel and read journals and other material to become familiar with product technologies and production methods. Observe production, developmental, and experimental activities to determine operating procedure and detail. Arrange for typing, duplication, and distribution of material. Assist in laying out material for publication. Analyze developments in specific field to determine need for revisions in previously published materials and development of new material. Review manufacturer's and trade catalogs, drawings, and other data relative to operation, maintenance, and service of equipment. Draw sketches to illustrate specified materials or assembly sequence.

Personality Type: Artistic. Artistic occupations frequently involve working with forms, designs, and patterns. They often require self-expression, and the work can be done without following a clear set of rules.

GOE—Interest Area: 03. Arts and Communication. **Work Group:** 03.02. Writing and Editing. **Other Jobs in This Work Group:** Copy Writers; Editors; Poets, Lyricists, and Creative Writers; Writers and Authors.

Skills—Writing: Communicating effectively in writing as appropriate for the needs of the audience. **Technology Design:** Generating or adapting equipment and technology to serve user needs. **Active Listening:** Giving full attention to what other people are saying, taking time to understand the points being made, asking questions as appropriate, and not interrupting at inappropriate times. **Quality Control Analysis:** Conducting tests and inspections of products, services, or processes to evaluate quality or performance. **Coordination:** Adjusting actions in relation to others' actions. **Reading Comprehension:** Understanding written sentences and paragraphs in work-related documents.

Education and Training Programs: Business/Corporate Communications; Communication Studies/Speech Communication and Rhetoric; Technical and Business Writing. **Related Knowledge/**

Courses: Communications and Media: Media production, communication, and dissemination techniques and methods. This includes alternative ways to inform and entertain via written, oral, and visual media. **Clerical Practices:** Administrative and clerical procedures and systems such as word processing, managing files and records, stenography and transcription, designing forms, and other office procedures and terminology. **English Language:** The structure and content of the English language, including the meaning and spelling of words, rules of composition, and grammar. **Computers and Electronics:** Circuit boards, processors, chips, electronic equipment, and computer hardware and software, including applications and programming. **Education and Training:** Principles and methods for curriculum and training design, teaching and instruction for individuals and groups, and the measurement of training effects. **Engineering and Technology:** The practical application of engineering science and technology. This includes applying principles, techniques, procedures, and equipment to the design and production of various goods and services.

Work Environment: Indoors; sitting; using hands on objects, tools, or controls; repetitive motions.

Telecommunications Equipment Installers and Repairers, Except Line Installers

- Education/Training Required: Long-term on-the-job training
- Annual Earnings: $50,620
- Growth: –4.9%
- Annual Job Openings: 21,000
- Self-Employed: 6.6%
- Part-Time: 4.9%

Level of Solitary Work: 58.7 (out of 100)

Level of Contact with Others: 85.0 (out of 100)

Set up, rearrange, or remove switching and dialing equipment used in central offices. Service or repair telephones and other communication equipment on customers' property. May install equipment in new locations or install wiring and telephone jacks in buildings under construction. Note differences in wire and cable colors so that work can be performed correctly. Test circuits and components of malfunctioning telecommunications equipment to isolate sources of malfunctions, using test meters, circuit diagrams, polarity probes, and other hand tools. Test repaired, newly installed, or updated equipment to ensure that it functions properly and conforms to specifications, using test equipment and observation. Drive crew trucks to and from work areas. Inspect equipment on a regular basis to ensure proper functioning. Repair or replace faulty equipment such as defective and damaged telephones, wires, switching system components, and associated equipment. Remove and remake connections to change circuit layouts, following work orders or diagrams. Demonstrate equipment to customers, explain how it is to be used, and respond to any inquiries or complaints. Analyze test readings, computer printouts, and trouble reports to determine equipment repair needs and required repair methods. Adjust or modify equipment to enhance equipment performance or to respond to customer requests. Remove loose wires and other debris after work is completed. Request support from technical service centers when on-site procedures fail to solve installation or maintenance problems. Assemble and install communication equipment such as data and telephone communication lines, wiring, switching equipment, wiring frames, power apparatus, computer systems, and networks. Communicate with bases, using telephones or two-way radios to receive instructions or technical advice or to report equipment status. Collaborate with other workers to locate and correct malfunctions. Review manufacturer's instructions, manuals, technical specifications, building permits, and ordinances to determine communication equipment requirements and procedures. Test connections to ensure that power supplies are adequate and that communications links function. Refer to manufacturers' manuals to obtain maintenance instructions pertaining to specific malfunctions. Climb poles and ladders, use truck-mounted booms, and enter areas such as manholes and cable vaults to install, maintain, or inspect equipment.

Personality Type: Realistic. Realistic occupations frequently involve work activities that include practical, hands-on problems and solutions. They often deal with plants; animals; and real-world materials such as wood, tools, and machinery. Many of the occupations require working outside and do not involve a lot of paperwork or working closely with others.

GOE—Interest Area: 02. Architecture and Construction. **Work Group:** 02.05. Systems and Equipment Installation, Maintenance, and Repair. **Other Jobs in This Work Group:** Electrical and Electronics Repairers, Powerhouse, Substation, and Relay; Electrical Power-Line Installers and Repairers; Elevator Installers and Repairers; Heating and Air Conditioning Mechanics and Installers; Maintenance and Repair Workers, General; Refrigeration Mechanics and Installers; Telecommunications Line Installers and Repairers.

Skills—Installation: Installing equipment, machines, wiring, or programs to meet specifications. **Repairing:** Repairing machines or systems by using the needed tools. **Troubleshooting:** Determining causes of operating errors and deciding what to do about them. **Technology Design:** Generating or adapting equipment and technology to serve user needs. **Systems Analysis:** Determining how a system should work and how changes in conditions, operations, and the environment will affect outcomes. **Equipment Selection:** Determining the kind of tools and equipment needed to do a job.

Education and Training Program: Communications Systems Installation and Repair Technology. **Related Knowledge/Courses: Telecommunications:** Transmission, broadcasting, switching, control, and opera-

tion of telecommunications systems. **Mechanical Devices:** Machines and tools, including their designs, uses, repair, and maintenance. **Computers and Electronics:** Circuit boards, processors, chips, electronic equipment, and computer hardware and software, including applications and programming. **Engineering and Technology:** The practical application of engineering science and technology. This includes applying principles, techniques, procedures, and equipment to the design and production of various goods and services. **Design:** Design techniques, tools, and principles involved in production of precision technical plans, blueprints, drawings, and models. **Customer and Personal Service:** Principles and processes for providing customer and personal services. This includes customer needs assessment, meeting quality standards for services, and evaluation of customer satisfaction.

Work Environment: Outdoors; noisy; very hot or cold; contaminants; cramped work space, awkward positions; using hands on objects, tools, or controls.

Telecommunications Line Installers and Repairers

- ◉ Education/Training Required: Long-term on-the-job training
- ◉ Annual Earnings: $42,410
- ◉ Growth: 10.8%
- ◉ Annual Job Openings: 23,000
- ◉ Self-Employed: 1.5%
- ◉ Part-Time: 2.5%

Level of Solitary Work: 68.8 (out of 100)

Level of Contact with Others: 83.7 (out of 100)

String and repair telephone and television cable, including fiber optics and other equipment for transmitting messages or television programming. Travel to customers' premises to install, maintain, and repair audio and visual electronic reception equipment and accessories. Inspect and test lines and cables, recording and analyzing test results, to assess transmission characteristics and locate faults and malfunctions. Splice cables, using hand tools, epoxy, or mechanical equipment. Measure signal strength at utility poles, using electronic test equipment. Set up service for customers, installing, connecting, testing, and adjusting equipment. Place insulation over conductors and seal splices with moisture-proof covering. Access specific areas to string lines and install terminal boxes, auxiliary equipment, and appliances, using bucket trucks or by climbing poles and ladders or entering tunnels, trenches, or crawl spaces. String cables between structures and lines from poles, towers, or trenches and pull lines to proper tension. Install equipment such as amplifiers and repeaters to maintain the strength of communications transmissions. Lay underground cable directly in trenches or string it through conduits running through trenches. Pull up cable by hand from large reels mounted on trucks; then pull lines through ducts by hand or with winches. Clean and maintain tools and test equipment. Explain cable service to subscribers after installation and collect any installation fees that are due. Compute impedance of wires from poles to houses to determine additional resistance needed for reducing signals to desired levels. Use a variety of construction equipment to complete installations, including digger derricks, trenchers, and cable plows. Dig trenches for underground wires and cables. Dig holes for power poles, using power augers or shovels; set poles in place with cranes; and hoist poles upright, using winches. Fill and tamp holes, using cement, earth, and tamping devices. Participate in the construction and removal of telecommunication towers and associated support structures.

Personality Type: Realistic. Realistic occupations frequently involve work activities that include practical, hands-on problems and solutions. They often deal with plants; animals; and real-world materials such as wood, tools, and machinery. Many of the occupations require working outside and do not involve a lot of paperwork or working closely with others.

GOE—Interest Area: 02. Architecture and Construction. **Work Group:** 02.05. Systems and Equipment Installation, Maintenance, and Repair. **Other Jobs in This Work Group:** Electrical and Electronics Repairers, Powerhouse, Substation, and Relay; Electrical Power-Line Installers and Repairers; Elevator Installers and Repairers; Heating and Air Conditioning Mechanics and Installers; Maintenance and Repair Workers, General; Refrigeration Mechanics and Installers; Telecommunications Equipment Installers and Repairers, Except Line Installers.

Skills—Installation: Installing equipment, machines, wiring, or programs to meet specifications. **Troubleshooting:** Determining causes of operating errors and deciding what to do about them. **Repairing:** Repairing machines or systems by using the needed tools. **Programming:** Writing computer programs for various purposes. **Equipment Maintenance:** Performing routine maintenance on equipment and determining when and what kind of maintenance is needed. **Technology Design:** Generating or adapting equipment and technology to serve user needs.

Education and Training Program: Communications Systems Installation and Repair Technology. **Related Knowledge/Courses: Telecommunications:** Transmission, broadcasting, switching, control, and operation of telecommunications systems. **Customer and Personal Service:** Principles and processes for providing customer and personal services. This includes customer needs assessment, meeting quality standards for services, and evaluation of customer satisfaction. **Engineering and Technology:** The practical application of engineering science and technology. This includes applying principles, techniques, procedures, and equipment to the design and production of various goods and services. **Building and Construction:** The materials, methods, and tools involved in the construction or repair of houses, buildings, or other structures such as highways and roads. **Design:** Design techniques, tools, and principles involved in production of precision technical plans, blueprints, drawings, and models.

Transportation: Principles and methods for moving people or goods by air, rail, sea, or road, including the relative costs and benefits.

Work Environment: Outdoors; very hot or cold; contaminants; cramped work space, awkward positions; hazardous equipment; using hands on objects, tools, or controls.

Terrazzo Workers and Finishers

- Education/Training Required: Long-term on-the-job training
- Annual Earnings: $32,030
- Growth: 15.2%
- Annual Job Openings: 1,000
- Self-Employed: 3.4%
- Part-Time: 8.5%

Level of Solitary Work: 50.0 (out of 100)

Level of Contact with Others: 76.5 (out of 100)

Apply a mixture of cement, sand, pigment, or marble chips to floors, stairways, and cabinet fixtures to fashion durable and decorative surfaces. Blend marble chip mixtures and place into panels; then push a roller over the surface to embed the chips. Cut metal division strips and press them into the terrazzo base wherever there is to be a joint or change of color, to form desired designs or patterns, and to help prevent cracks. Measure designated amounts of ingredients for terrazzo or grout according to standard formulas and specifications, using graduated containers and scale, and load ingredients into portable mixer. Mold expansion joints and edges, using edging tools, jointers, and straightedges. Spread, level, and smooth concrete and terrazzo mixtures to form bases and finished surfaces, using rakes, shovels, hand or power trowels, hand or power screeds, and floats. Grind curved surfaces and areas inaccessible to surfacing machine, such as stairways and cabinet tops, with portable hand grinder. Grind surfaces with a power grinder and polish surfaces with polishing or surfacing machines. Position and secure moisture membrane and wire mesh prior to pouring base materials for terrazzo installation. Modify mixing, grouting, grinding, and cleaning procedures according to type of installation or material used. Wash polished terrazzo surface, using cleaner and water, and apply sealer and curing agent according to manufacturer's specifications, using brush or sprayer. Mix cement, sand, and water to produce concrete, grout, or slurry, using hoe, trowel, tamper, scraper, or concrete-mixing machine. Sprinkle colored marble or stone chips, powdered steel, or coloring powder over surface to produce prescribed finish. Wet surface to prepare for bonding, fill holes and cracks with grout or slurry, and smooth, using trowel. Cut out damaged areas, drill holes for reinforcing rods, and position reinforcing rods to repair concrete, using power saw and drill. Clean installation site, mixing and storage areas, tools, machines, and equipment and store materials and equipment. Fill slight depressions left by grinding with a matching grout material and then hand-trowel for a smooth, uniform surface. Chip, scrape, and grind high spots, ridges, and rough projections to finish concrete, using pneumatic chisel, hand chisel, or other hand tools.

Personality Type: Realistic. Realistic occupations frequently involve work activities that include practical, hands-on problems and solutions. They often deal with plants; animals; and real-world materials such as wood, tools, and machinery. Many of the occupations require working outside and do not involve a lot of paperwork or working closely with others.

GOE—Interest Area: 02. Architecture and Construction. **Work Group:** 02.04. Construction Crafts. **Other Jobs in This Work Group:** Boilermakers; Brickmasons and Blockmasons; Carpet Installers; Cement Masons and Concrete Finishers; Commercial Divers; Construction Carpenters; Crane and Tower Operators; Drywall and Ceiling Tile Installers; Electricians; Fence Erectors; Floor Layers, Except Carpet, Wood, and Hard Tiles; Floor Sanders and Finishers; Glaziers; Hazardous Materials Removal Workers; Insulation Workers, Floor, Ceiling, and Wall; Insulation Workers, Mechanical; Manufactured Building and Mobile Home Installers; Operating Engineers and Other Construction Equipment Operators; Painters, Construction and Maintenance; Paperhangers; Paving, Surfacing, and Tamping Equipment Operators; Pile-Driver Operators; Pipe Fitters and Steamfitters; Pipelayers; Plasterers and Stucco Masons; Plumbers; Plumbers, Pipefitters, and Steamfitters; Rail-Track Laying and Maintenance Equipment Operators; Refractory Materials Repairers, Except Brickmasons; Reinforcing Iron and Rebar Workers; Riggers; Roofers; Rough Carpenters; Security and Fire Alarm Systems Installers; Segmental Pavers; Sheet Metal Workers; Stone Cutters and Carvers, Manufacturing; Stonemasons; Structural Iron and Steel Workers; Tapers; Tile and Marble Setters.

Skills—Installation: Installing equipment, machines, wiring, or programs to meet specifications. **Repairing:** Repairing machines or systems by using the needed tools. **Equipment Maintenance:** Performing routine maintenance on equipment and determining when and what kind of maintenance is needed. **Coordination:** Adjusting actions in relation to others' actions. **Equipment Selection:** Determining the kind of tools and equipment needed to do a job. **Management of Material Resources:** Obtaining and seeing to the appropriate use of equipment, facilities, and materials needed to do certain work.

Education and Training Program: Building/ Construction Finishing, Management, and Inspection, Other. **Related Knowledge/Courses: Building and Construction:** The materials, methods, and tools involved in the construction or repair of houses, buildings, or other structures such as highways and roads. **Production and Processing:** Raw materials, production processes, quality control, costs, and other techniques for maximizing the effective manufacture and distribution of goods. **Mechanical Devices:** Machines and tools, including their designs, uses, repair, and maintenance. **Administration and Management:** Business and

management principles involved in strategic planning, resource allocation, human resources modeling, leadership technique, production methods, and coordination of people and resources. **Sales and Marketing:** Principles and methods for showing, promoting, and selling products or services. This includes marketing strategy and tactics, product demonstration, sales techniques, and sales control systems. **Design:** Design techniques, tools, and principles involved in production of precision technical plans, blueprints, drawings, and models.

Work Environment: Noisy; contaminants; standing; walking and running; using hands on objects, tools, or controls; repetitive motions.

Tile and Marble Setters

- Education/Training Required: Long-term on-the-job training
- Annual Earnings: $36,530
- Growth: 22.9%
- Annual Job Openings: 9,000
- Self-Employed: 24.4%
- Part-Time: 12.3%

Level of Solitary Work: 59.2 (out of 100)

Level of Contact with Others: 81.7 (out of 100)

Apply hard tile, marble, and wood tile to walls, floors, ceilings, and roof decks. Align and straighten tile, using levels, squares, and straightedges. Determine and implement the best layout to achieve a desired pattern. Cut and shape tile to fit around obstacles and into odd spaces and corners, using hand- and power-cutting tools. Finish and dress the joints and wipe excess grout from between tiles, using damp sponge. Apply mortar to tile back, position the tile, and press or tap with trowel handle to affix tile to base. Mix, apply, and spread plaster, concrete, mortar, cement, mastic, glue, or other adhesives to form a bed for the tiles, using brush, trowel, and screed. Prepare cost and labor estimates based on calculations of time and materials needed for project. Measure and mark surfaces to be tiled, following blueprints. Level concrete and allow to dry. Build underbeds and install anchor bolts, wires, and brackets. Prepare surfaces for tiling by attaching lath or waterproof paper or by applying a cement mortar coat onto a metal screen. Study blueprints and examine surface to be covered to determine amount of material needed. Cut, surface, polish, and install marble and granite or install pre-cast terrazzo, granite, or marble units. Install and anchor fixtures in designated positions, using hand tools. Cut tile backing to required size, using shears. Remove any old tile, grout, and adhesive, using chisels and scrapers, and clean the surface carefully. Lay and set mosaic tiles to create decorative wall, mural, and floor designs. Assist customers in selection of tile and grout. Remove and replace cracked or damaged tile. Measure and cut metal lath to size for walls and ceilings, using tin snips. Select and order tile and other items to be installed, such as bathroom accessories, walls, panels, and cabinets, according to specifications. Mix and apply mortar or cement to edges and ends of drain tiles to seal halves and joints. Spread mastic or other adhesive base on roof deck to form base for promenade tile, using serrated spreader. Apply a sealer to make grout stain- and water-resistant. Brush glue onto manila paper on which design has been drawn and position tiles, finished side down, onto paper.

Personality Type: Realistic. Realistic occupations frequently involve work activities that include practical, hands-on problems and solutions. They often deal with plants; animals; and real-world materials such as wood, tools, and machinery. Many of the occupations require working outside and do not involve a lot of paperwork or working closely with others.

GOE—Interest Area: 02. Architecture and Construction. **Work Group:** 02.04. Construction Crafts. **Other Jobs in This Work Group:** Boilermakers; Brickmasons and Blockmasons; Carpet Installers; Cement Masons and Concrete Finishers; Commercial Divers; Construction Carpenters; Crane and Tower Operators; Drywall and Ceiling Tile Installers; Electricians; Fence Erectors; Floor Layers, Except Carpet, Wood, and Hard Tiles; Floor Sanders and Finishers; Glaziers; Hazardous Materials Removal Workers; Insulation Workers, Floor, Ceiling, and Wall; Insulation Workers, Mechanical; Manufactured Building and Mobile Home Installers; Operating Engineers and Other Construction Equipment Operators; Painters, Construction and Maintenance; Paperhangers; Paving, Surfacing, and Tamping Equipment Operators; Pile-Driver Operators; Pipe Fitters and Steamfitters; Pipelayers; Plasterers and Stucco Masons; Plumbers; Plumbers, Pipefitters, and Steamfitters; Rail-Track Laying and Maintenance Equipment Operators; Refractory Materials Repairers, Except Brickmasons; Reinforcing Iron and Rebar Workers; Riggers; Roofers; Rough Carpenters; Security and Fire Alarm Systems Installers; Segmental Pavers; Sheet Metal Workers; Stone Cutters and Carvers, Manufacturing; Stonemasons; Structural Iron and Steel Workers; Tapers; Terrazzo Workers and Finishers.

Skills—Installation: Installing equipment, machines, wiring, or programs to meet specifications. **Management of Financial Resources:** Determining how money will be spent to get the work done and accounting for these expenditures. **Mathematics:** Using mathematics to solve problems. **Management of Material Resources:** Obtaining and seeing to the appropriate use of equipment, facilities, and materials needed to do certain work. **Social Perceptiveness:** Being aware of others' reactions and understanding why they react as they do. **Equipment Selection:** Determining the kind of tools and equipment needed to do a job.

Education and Training Program: Mason Training/ Masonry. **Related Knowledge/Courses: Building and Construction:** The materials, methods, and tools involved in the construction or repair of houses, buildings, or other structures such as highways and roads. **Design:** Design techniques, tools, and principles involved in production of precision technical plans, blueprints, drawings, and models. **Production and Processing:** Raw materials, production processes, quality control, costs, and other techniques for maximizing the effective manufacture and distribution of goods. **Economics and Accounting:** Economic and accounting principles and practices, the financial markets, banking, and the analysis and reporting of financial data. **Administration and Management:** Business and management principles involved in strategic planning, resource allocation, human resources modeling, leadership technique, production methods, and coordination of people and resources. **Transportation:** Principles and methods for moving people or goods by air, rail, sea, or road, including the relative costs and benefits.

Work Environment: Noisy; contaminants; cramped work space, awkward positions; standing; using hands on objects, tools, or controls; bending or twisting the body.

Tire Repairers and Changers

- Education/Training Required: Short-term on-the-job training
- Annual Earnings: $20,960
- Growth: 4.5%
- Annual Job Openings: 17,000
- Self-Employed: 3.4%
- Part-Time: 19.6%

Level of Solitary Work: 62.5 (out of 100)

Level of Contact with Others: 75.8 (out of 100)

Repair and replace tires. Identify and inflate tires correctly for the size and ply. Place wheels on balancing machines to determine counterweights required to balance wheels. Raise vehicles, using hydraulic jacks. Remount wheels onto vehicles. Locate punctures in tubeless tires by visual inspection or by immersing inflated tires in water baths and observing air bubbles. Unbolt wheels from vehicles and remove them, using lug wrenches and other hand and power

tools. Reassemble tires onto wheels. Replace valve stems and remove puncturing objects. Hammer required counterweights onto rims of wheels. Rotate tires to different positions on vehicles, using hand tools. Inspect tire casings for defects, such as holes and tears. Seal punctures in tubeless tires by inserting adhesive material and expanding rubber plugs into punctures, using hand tools. Glue boots (tire patches) over ruptures in tire casings, using rubber cement. Assist mechanics and perform other duties as directed. Separate tubed tires from wheels, using rubber mallets and metal bars or mechanical tire changers. Patch tubes with adhesive rubber patches or seal rubber patches to tubes by using hot vulcanizing plates. Inflate innertubes and immerse them in water to locate leaks. Clean sides of whitewall tires. Apply rubber cement to buffed tire casings prior to vulcanization process. Drive automobile or service trucks to industrial sites to provide services and respond to emergency calls. Prepare rims and wheel drums for reassembly by scraping, grinding, or sandblasting. Order replacements for tires and tubes. Roll new rubber treads, known as camelbacks, over tire casings and mold the semi-raw rubber treads onto the buffed casings. Buff defective areas of innertubes, using scrapers. Place casing-camelback assemblies in tire molds for the vulcanization process and exert pressure on the camelbacks to ensure good adhesion.

Personality Type: Realistic. Realistic occupations frequently involve work activities that include practical, hands-on problems and solutions. They often deal with plants; animals; and real-world materials such as wood, tools, and machinery. Many of the occupations require working outside and do not involve a lot of paperwork or working closely with others.

GOE—Interest Area: 13. Manufacturing. **Work Group:** 13.14. Vehicle and Facility Mechanical Work. **Other Jobs in This Work Group:** Aircraft Mechanics and Service Technicians; Aircraft Structure, Surfaces, Rigging, and Systems Assemblers; Automotive Body and Related Repairers; Automotive Glass Installers and Repairers; Automotive Master Mechanics; Automotive Service Technicians and Mechanics; Automotive Specialty

Technicians; Bus and Truck Mechanics and Diesel Engine Specialists; Farm Equipment Mechanics; Fiberglass Laminators and Fabricators; Mobile Heavy Equipment Mechanics, Except Engines; Motorboat Mechanics; Motorcycle Mechanics; Outdoor Power Equipment and Other Small Engine Mechanics; Rail Car Repairers; Recreational Vehicle Service Technicians.

Skills—Repairing: Repairing machines or systems by using the needed tools. **Installation:** Installing equipment, machines, wiring, or programs to meet specifications. **Equipment Maintenance:** Performing routine maintenance on equipment and determining when and what kind of maintenance is needed. **Troubleshooting:** Determining causes of operating errors and deciding what to do about them. **Management of Material Resources:** Obtaining and seeing to the appropriate use of equipment, facilities, and materials needed to do certain work. **Management of Personnel Resources:** Motivating, developing, and directing people as they work; identifying the best people for the job.

Education and Training Program: No related CIP programs; this job is learned through informal short-term on-the-job training. **Related Knowledge/Courses: Mechanical Devices:** Machines and tools, including their designs, uses, repair, and maintenance. **Transportation:** Principles and methods for moving people or goods by air, rail, sea, or road, including the relative costs and benefits. **Sales and Marketing:** Principles and methods for showing, promoting, and selling products or services. This includes marketing strategy and tactics, product demonstration, sales techniques, and sales control systems. **Engineering and Technology:** The practical application of engineering science and technology. This includes applying principles, techniques, procedures, and equipment to the design and production of various goods and services.

Work Environment: Noisy; contaminants; standing; walking and running; using hands on objects, tools, or controls; repetitive motions.

Title Examiners, Abstractors, and Searchers

- ◎ Education/Training Required: Moderate-term on-the-job training
- ◎ Annual Earnings: $35,120
- ◎ Growth: 0.9%
- ◎ Annual Job Openings: 8,000
- ◎ Self-Employed: 10.7%
- ◎ Part-Time: 12.0%

Level of Solitary Work: 68.8 (out of 100)

Level of Contact with Others: 94.7 (out of 100)

Search real estate records, examine titles, or summarize pertinent legal or insurance details for a variety of purposes. May compile lists of mortgages, contracts, and other instruments pertaining to titles by searching public and private records for law firms, real estate agencies, or title insurance companies. Prepare lists of all legal instruments applying to a specific piece of land and the buildings on it. Read search requests in order to ascertain types of title evidence required and to obtain descriptions of properties and names of involved parties. Examine documentation such as mortgages, liens, judgments, easements, plat books, maps, contracts, and agreements in order to verify factors such as properties' legal descriptions, ownership, or restrictions. Copy or summarize recorded documents, such as mortgages, trust deeds, and contracts, that affect property titles. Examine individual titles to determine if restrictions, such as delinquent taxes, will affect titles and limit property use. Prepare reports describing any title encumbrances encountered during searching activities and outlining actions needed to clear titles. Verify accuracy and completeness of land-related documents accepted for registration; prepare rejection notices when documents are not acceptable. Confer with real estate agents, lending institution personnel, buyers, sellers, contractors, surveyors, and courthouse personnel to exchange title-related information or to resolve problems. Enter into recordkeeping systems appropriate data needed to create new title records or update existing ones. Direct activities of workers who search records and examine titles, assigning, scheduling, and evaluating work and providing technical guidance as necessary. Obtain maps or drawings delineating properties from company title plants, county surveyors, and/or assessors' offices. Prepare and issue title commitments and title insurance policies based on information compiled from title searches. Summarize pertinent legal or insurance details or sections of statutes or case law from reference books so that they can be used in examinations or as proofs or ready reference. Retrieve and examine real estate closing files for accuracy and to ensure that information included is recorded and executed according to regulations. Prepare real estate closing statements, utilizing knowledge and expertise in real estate procedures.

Personality Type: Conventional. Conventional occupations frequently involve following set procedures and routines. These occupations can include working with data and details more than with ideas. Usually there is a clear line of authority to follow.

GOE—Interest Area: 12. Law and Public Safety. **Work Group:** 12.03. Legal Support. **Other Jobs in This Work Group:** Law Clerks; Paralegals and Legal Assistants.

Skills—Writing: Communicating effectively in writing as appropriate for the needs of the audience. **Critical Thinking:** Using logic and reasoning to identify the strengths and weaknesses of alternative solutions, conclusions, or approaches to problems. **Management of Financial Resources:** Determining how money will be spent to get the work done and accounting for these expenditures. **Reading Comprehension:** Understanding written sentences and paragraphs in work-related documents. **Technology Design:** Generating or adapting equipment and technology to serve user needs. **Management of Material Resources:** Obtaining and seeing to the appropriate use of equipment, facilities, and materials needed to do certain work.

Education and Training Program: Legal Assistant/Paralegal. **Related Knowledge/Courses: Clerical Practices:** Administrative and clerical procedures and systems such as word processing, managing files and records, stenography and transcription, designing forms, and other office procedures and terminology. **Law and Government:** Laws, legal codes, court procedures, precedents, government regulations, executive orders, agency rules, and the democratic political process. **Geography:** Principles and methods for describing the features of land, sea, and air masses, including their physical characteristics; locations; interrelationships; and distribution of plant, animal, and human life. **Customer and Personal Service:** Principles and processes for providing customer and personal services. This includes customer needs assessment, meeting quality standards for services, and evaluation of customer satisfaction. **Computers and Electronics:** Circuit boards, processors, chips, electronic equipment, and computer hardware and software, including applications and programming. **English Language:** The structure and content of the English language, including the meaning and spelling of words, rules of composition, and grammar.

Work Environment: Indoors; sitting; repetitive motions.

Tool and Die Makers

- Education/Training Required: Long-term on-the-job training
- Annual Earnings: $43,580
- Growth: –2.6%
- Annual Job Openings: 7,000
- Self-Employed: 2.7%
- Part-Time: 4.8%

Level of Solitary Work: 56.3 (out of 100)

Level of Contact with Others: 74.8 (out of 100)

Analyze specifications; lay out metal stock; set up and operate machine tools; and fit and assemble parts to make and repair dies, cutting tools, jigs, fixtures, gauges, and machinists' hand tools. Study blueprints, sketches, models, or specifications to plan sequences of operations for fabricating tools, dies, or assemblies. Verify dimensions, alignments, and clearances of finished parts for conformance to specifications, using measuring instruments such as calipers, gauge blocks, micrometers, and dial indicators. Visualize and compute dimensions, sizes, shapes, and tolerances of assemblies, based on specifications. Set up and operate conventional or computer numerically controlled machine tools such as lathes, milling machines, and grinders to cut, bore, grind, or otherwise shape parts to prescribed dimensions and finishes. File, grind, shim, and adjust different parts to properly fit them together. Fit and assemble parts to make, repair, or modify dies, jigs, gauges, and tools, using machine tools and hand tools. Conduct test runs with completed tools or dies to ensure that parts meet specifications; make adjustments as necessary. Inspect finished dies for smoothness, contour conformity, and defects. Smooth and polish flat and contoured surfaces of parts or tools, using scrapers, abrasive stones, files, emery cloths, or power grinders. Lift, position, and secure machined parts on surface plates or worktables, using hoists, vises, v-blocks, or angle plates. Measure, mark, and scribe metal or plastic stock to lay out machining, using instruments such as protractors, micrometers, scribes, and rulers. Cut, shape, and trim blanks or blocks to specified lengths or shapes, using power saws, power shears, rules, and hand tools. Select metals to be used from a range of metals and alloys, based on properties such as hardness and heat tolerance. Design jigs, fixtures, and templates for use as work aids in the fabrication of parts or products. Set up and operate drill presses to drill and tap holes in parts for assembly. Develop and design new tools and dies, using computer-aided design software. Set pyrometer controls of heat-treating furnaces and feed or place parts, tools, or assemblies into furnaces to harden.

Personality Type: Realistic. Realistic occupations frequently involve work activities that include practical, hands-on problems and solutions. They often deal with plants; animals; and real-world materials such as wood, tools, and machinery. Many of the occupations require working outside and do not involve a lot of paperwork or working closely with others.

GOE—Interest Area: 13. Manufacturing. **Work Group:** 13.05. Production Machining Technology. **Other Jobs in This Work Group:** Computer-Controlled Machine Tool Operators, Metal and Plastic; Foundry Mold and Coremakers; Lay-Out Workers, Metal and Plastic; Machinists; Model Makers, Metal and Plastic; Numerical Tool and Process Control Programmers; Patternmakers, Metal and Plastic; Tool Grinders, Filers, and Sharpeners.

Skills—Repairing: Repairing machines or systems by using the needed tools. **Mathematics:** Using mathematics to solve problems. **Troubleshooting:** Determining causes of operating errors and deciding what to do about them. **Technology Design:** Generating or adapting equipment and technology to serve user needs. **Equipment Selection:** Determining the kind of tools and equipment needed to do a job. **Installation:** Installing equipment, machines, wiring, or programs to meet specifications.

Education and Training Program: Tool and Die Technology/Technician Training. **Related Knowledge/Courses: Design:** Design techniques, tools, and principles involved in production of precision technical plans, blueprints, drawings, and models. **Mechanical Devices:** Machines and tools, including their designs, uses, repair, and maintenance. **Engineering and Technology:** The practical application of engineering science and technology. This includes applying principles, techniques, procedures, and equipment to the design and production of various goods and services. **Production and Processing:** Raw materials, production processes, quality control, costs, and other techniques for maximizing the effective manufacture and distribution of goods. **Mathematics:** Arithmetic, algebra, geometry, calculus, and statistics and their applications. **Public Safety and Security:** Relevant equipment, policies, procedures, and strategies to promote effective local, state, or national security operations for the protection of people, data, property, and institutions.

Work Environment: Noisy; contaminants; hazardous equipment; minor burns, cuts, bites, or stings; standing; using hands on objects, tools, or controls.

Traffic Technicians

- ◎ Education/Training Required: Short-term on-the-job training
- ◎ Annual Earnings: $37,070
- ◎ Growth: 14.1%
- ◎ Annual Job Openings: 1,000
- ◎ Self-Employed: 0.0%
- ◎ Part-Time: No data available

Level of Solitary Work: 65.5 (out of 100)

Level of Contact with Others: 84.7 (out of 100)

Conduct field studies to determine traffic volume, speed, effectiveness of signals, adequacy of lighting, and other factors influencing traffic conditions under direction of traffic engineer. Interact with the public to answer traffic-related questions; respond to complaints and requests; or discuss traffic control ordinances, plans, policies, and procedures. Prepare drawings of proposed signal installations or other control devices, using drafting instruments or computer automated drafting equipment. Plan, design, and improve components of traffic control systems to accommodate current and projected traffic and to increase usability and efficiency. Analyze data related to traffic flow, accident rate data, and proposed development to determine the most efficient methods to expedite traffic flow. Prepare work orders for repair, maintenance, and changes in traffic systems. Study factors affecting traffic conditions, such as lighting and sign and marking visibility, to assess their effectiveness. Visit development and worksites to determine projects' effect on traffic and the adequacy of plans to control traffic and maintain safety and to suggest traffic control measures. Lay out pavement markings for striping crews. Operate counters and record data to assess the volume, type, and movement of vehicular and pedestrian traffic at specified times. Provide technical supervision regarding traffic control devices to other traffic technicians and laborers. Gather and compile data from hand-count sheets, machine-count tapes, and radar speed checks and code data for computer input. Place and secure automatic counters, using power tools, and retrieve counters after counting periods end. Measure and record the speed of vehicular traffic, using electrical timing devices or radar equipment. Study traffic delays by noting times of delays, the numbers of vehicles affected, and vehicle speed through the delay area. Review traffic control/barricade plans to issue permits for parades and other special events and for construction work that affects rights-of-way, providing assistance with plan preparation or revision as necessary. Prepare graphs, charts, diagrams, and other aids to illustrate observations and conclusions.

Personality Type: Realistic. Realistic occupations frequently involve work activities that include practical, hands-on problems and solutions. They often deal with plants; animals; and real-world materials such as wood, tools, and machinery. Many of the occupations require working outside and do not involve a lot of paperwork or working closely with others.

GOE—Interest Area: 16. Transportation, Distribution, and Logistics. **Work Group:** 16.07. Transportation Support Work. **Other Jobs in This Work Group:** Bridge and Lock Tenders; Cargo and Freight Agents; Cleaners of Vehicles and Equipment; Laborers and Freight, Stock, and Material Movers, Hand; Railroad Brake, Signal, and Switch Operators.

Skills—Operation Monitoring: Watching gauges, dials, or other indicators to make sure a machine is working properly. **Coordination:** Adjusting actions in relation to others' actions. **Technology Design:** Generating or adapting equipment and technology to serve user needs. **Systems Evaluation:** Identifying measures or indicators of system performance and the actions needed to improve or correct performance relative to the goals of the system. **Systems Analysis:**

Determining how a system should work and how changes in conditions, operations, and the environment will affect outcomes. **Writing:** Communicating effectively in writing as appropriate for the needs of the audience.

Education and Training Program: Traffic, Customs, and Transportation Clerk/Technician Training. **Related Knowledge/Courses: Design:** Design techniques, tools, and principles involved in production of precision technical plans, blueprints, drawings, and models. **Building and Construction:** The materials, methods, and tools involved in the construction or repair of houses, buildings, or other structures such as highways and roads. **Engineering and Technology:** The practical application of engineering science and technology. This includes applying principles, techniques, procedures, and equipment to the design and production of various goods and services. **Customer and Personal Service:** Principles and processes for providing customer and personal services. This includes customer needs assessment, meeting quality standards for services, and evaluation of customer satisfaction. **Law and Government:** Laws, legal codes, court procedures, precedents, government regulations, executive orders, agency rules, and the democratic political process. **Public Safety and Security:** Relevant equipment, policies, procedures, and strategies to promote effective local, state, or national security operations for the protection of people, data, property, and institutions.

Work Environment: More often indoors than outdoors; noisy; very hot or cold; hazardous equipment; sitting.

Transportation Inspectors

See the descriptions of these jobs:

- Aviation Inspectors
- Freight and Cargo Inspectors
- Transportation Vehicle, Equipment, and Systems Inspectors, Except Aviation

Transportation Vehicle, Equipment, and Systems Inspectors, Except Aviation

This job can be found in the Part II lists under the title Transportation Inspectors.

- Education/Training Required: Work experience in a related occupation
- Annual Earnings: $49,490
- Growth: 11.4%
- Annual Job Openings: 2,000
- Self-Employed: 1.9%
- Part-Time: 2.3%

The job openings listed here are shared with Aviation Inspectors and with Freight and Cargo Inspectors.

Level of Solitary Work: 58.9 (out of 100)

Level of Contact with Others: 57.6 (out of 100)

Inspect and monitor transportation equipment, vehicles, or systems to ensure compliance with regulations and safety standards. Investigate and make recommendations on carrier requests for waiver of federal standards. Prepare reports on investigations or inspections and actions taken. Examine carrier operating rules, employee qualification guidelines, and carrier training and testing programs for compliance with regulations or safety standards. Examine transportation vehicles, equipment, or systems to detect damage, wear, or malfunction. Inspect repairs to transportation vehicles and equipment to ensure that repair work was performed properly. Inspect vehicles or equipment to ensure compliance with rules, standards, or regulations. Investigate complaints regarding safety violations. Investigate incidents or violations, such as delays, accidents, and equipment failures. Issue notices and recommend corrective actions when infractions or problems are found.

Inspect vehicles and other equipment for evidence of abuse, damage, or mechanical malfunction. Conduct vehicle or transportation equipment tests, using diagnostic equipment.

Personality Type: Realistic. Realistic occupations frequently involve work activities that include practical, hands-on problems and solutions. They often deal with plants; animals; and real-world materials such as wood, tools, and machinery. Many of the occupations require working outside and do not involve a lot of paperwork or working closely with others.

GOE—Interest Area: 07. Government and Public Administration. **Work Group:** 07.03. Regulations Enforcement. **Other Jobs in This Work Group:** Agricultural Inspectors; Aviation Inspectors; Compliance Officers, Except Agriculture, Construction, Health and Safety, and Transportation; Construction and Building Inspectors; Environmental Compliance Inspectors; Equal Opportunity Representatives and Officers; Financial Examiners; Fire Inspectors; Fish and Game Wardens; Forest Fire Inspectors and Prevention Specialists; Freight and Cargo Inspectors; Government Property Inspectors and Investigators; Immigration and Customs Inspectors; Licensing Examiners and Inspectors; Nuclear Monitoring Technicians; Occupational Health and Safety Specialists; Occupational Health and Safety Technicians; Tax Examiners, Collectors, and Revenue Agents.

Skills—Operation Monitoring: Watching gauges, dials, or other indicators to make sure a machine is working properly. **Quality Control Analysis:** Conducting tests and inspections of products, services, or processes to evaluate quality or performance. **Systems Evaluation:** Identifying measures or indicators of system performance and the actions needed to improve or correct performance relative to the goals of the system. **Troubleshooting:** Determining causes of operating errors and deciding what to do about them.

Education and Training Programs: No related CIP programs; this job is learned through work experience in a related occupation. **Related Knowledge/**

Courses: Transportation: Principles and methods for moving people or goods by air, rail, sea, or road, including the relative costs and benefits. **Public Safety and Security:** Relevant equipment, policies, procedures, and strategies to promote effective local, state, or national security operations for the protection of people, data, property, and institutions. **Mechanical Devices:** Machines and tools, including their designs, uses, repair, and maintenance.

Work Environment: Outdoors; standing; using hands on objects, tools, or controls.

Tree Trimmers and Pruners

- Education/Training Required: Short-term on-the-job training
- Annual Earnings: $27,920
- Growth: 16.5%
- Annual Job Openings: 11,000
- Self-Employed: 22.2%
- Part-Time: 24.4%

Level of Solitary Work: 62.5 (out of 100)

Level of Contact with Others: 10.5 (out of 100)

Cut away dead or excess branches from trees or shrubs to maintain right-of-way for roads, sidewalks, or utilities or to improve appearance, health, and value of tree. Prune or treat trees or shrubs, using handsaws, pruning hooks, shears, and clippers. May use truck-mounted lifts and power pruners. May fill cavities in trees to promote healing and prevent deterioration. Supervise others engaged in tree-trimming work and train lower-level employees. Transplant and remove trees and shrubs and prepare trees for moving. Climb trees, using climbing hooks and belts, or climb ladders to gain access to work areas. Operate boom trucks, loaders, stump chippers, brush chippers, tractors, power saws, trucks, sprayers, and other equipment and tools. Operate shredding and chipping equipment and feed limbs and brush into the machines. Remove broken limbs from wires, using hooked extension poles. Prune, cut down, fertilize, and spray trees as directed by tree surgeons. Spray trees to treat diseased or unhealthy trees, including mixing chemicals and calibrating spray equipment. Clean, sharpen, and lubricate tools and equipment. Trim, top, and reshape trees to achieve attractive shapes or to remove low-hanging branches. Cable, brace, tie, bolt, stake, and guy trees and branches to provide support. Clear sites, streets, and grounds of woody and herbaceous materials, such as tree stumps and fallen trees and limbs. Collect debris and refuse from tree trimming and removal operations into piles, using shovels, rakes, or other tools. Load debris and refuse onto trucks and haul it away for disposal. Inspect trees to determine if they have diseases or pest problems. Cut away dead and excess branches from trees or clear branches around power lines, using climbing equipment or buckets of extended truck booms and/or chain saws, hooks, hand saws, shears, and clippers. Apply tar or other protective substances to cut surfaces to seal surfaces and to protect them from fungi and insects. Split logs or wooden blocks into bolts, pickets, posts, or stakes, using hand tools such as ax wedges, sledgehammers, and mallets. Trim jagged stumps, using saws or pruning shears. Water, root-feed, and fertilize trees. Harvest tanbark by cutting rings and slits in bark and stripping bark from trees, using spuds or axes. Install lightning protection on trees. Plan and develop budgets for tree work and estimate the monetary value of trees. Provide information to the public regarding trees, such as advice on tree care.

Personality Type: Realistic. Realistic occupations frequently involve work activities that include practical, hands-on problems and solutions. They often deal with plants; animals; and real-world materials such as wood, tools, and machinery. Many of the occupations require working outside and do not involve a lot of paperwork or working closely with others.

GOE—Interest Area: 01. Agriculture and Natural Resources. **Work Group:** 01.05. Nursery, Grounds-keeping, and Pest Control. **Other Jobs in This Work Group:** Landscaping and Groundskeeping Workers; Nursery Workers; Pest Control Workers; Pesticide Handlers, Sprayers, and Applicators, Vegetation.

Skills—Operation and Control: Controlling operations of equipment or systems.

Education and Training Program: Applied Horticulture/Horticultural Business Services, Other. **Related Knowledge/Courses: Biology:** Plant and animal organisms and their tissues, cells, functions, interdependencies, and interactions with each other and the environment. **Chemistry:** The chemical composition, structure, and properties of substances and of the chemical processes and transformations that they undergo. This includes uses of chemicals and their danger signs, production techniques, and disposal methods. **Mechanical Devices:** Machines and tools, including their designs, uses, repair, and maintenance.

Work Environment: Outdoors; high places; minor burns, cuts, bites, or stings; standing; climbing ladders, scaffolds, or poles; using hands on objects, tools, or controls.

Truck Drivers, Heavy and Tractor-Trailer

- Education/Training Required: Moderate-term on-the-job training
- Annual Earnings: $34,280
- Growth: 12.9%
- Annual Job Openings: 274,000
- Self-Employed: 9.3%
- Part-Time: 9.1%

Level of Solitary Work: 71.7 (out of 100)

Level of Contact with Others: 84.7 (out of 100)

Drive a tractor-trailer combination or a truck with a capacity of at least 26,000 GVW to transport and deliver goods, livestock, or materials in liquid, loose,

or packaged form. **May be required to unload truck. May require use of automated routing equipment. Requires commercial drivers' license.** Follow appropriate safety procedures when transporting dangerous goods. Check vehicles before driving them to ensure that mechanical, safety, and emergency equipment is in good working order. Maintain logs of working hours and of vehicle service and repair status, following applicable state and federal regulations. Obtain receipts or signatures when loads are delivered and collect payment for services when required. Check all load-related documentation to ensure that it is complete and accurate. Maneuver trucks into loading or unloading positions, following signals from loading crew as needed; check that vehicle position is correct and any special loading equipment is properly positioned. Drive trucks with capacities greater than 3 tons, including tractor-trailer combinations, to transport and deliver products, livestock, or other materials. Secure cargo for transport, using ropes, blocks, chain, binders, or covers. Read bills of lading to determine assignment details. Report vehicle defects, accidents, traffic violations, or damage to the vehicles. Read and interpret maps to determine vehicle routes. Couple and uncouple trailers by changing trailer jack positions, connecting or disconnecting air and electrical lines, and manipulating fifth-wheel locks. Collect delivery instructions from appropriate sources, verifying instructions and routes. Drive trucks to weigh stations before and after loading and along routes to document weights and to comply with state regulations. Operate equipment such as truck cab computers, CB radios, and telephones to exchange necessary information with bases, supervisors, or other drivers. Check conditions of trailers after contents have been unloaded to ensure that there has been no damage. Crank trailer landing gear up and down to safely secure vehicles. Wrap goods, using pads, packing paper, and containers, and secure loads to trailer walls, using straps. Perform basic vehicle maintenance tasks such as adding oil, fuel, and radiator fluid or performing minor repairs. Load and unload trucks or help others with loading and unloading, operating any special loading-related equipment on vehicles and using other equipment as necessary.

Personality Type: Realistic. Realistic occupations frequently involve work activities that include practical, hands-on problems and solutions. They often deal with plants; animals; and real-world materials such as wood, tools, and machinery. Many of the occupations require working outside and do not involve a lot of paperwork or working closely with others.

GOE—Interest Area: 16. Transportation, Distribution, and Logistics. **Work Group:** 16.03. Truck Driving. **Other Jobs in This Work Group:** Truck Drivers, Light or Delivery Services.

Skills—Equipment Maintenance: Performing routine maintenance on equipment and determining when and what kind of maintenance is needed. **Repairing:** Repairing machines or systems by using the needed tools. **Operation Monitoring:** Watching gauges, dials, or other indicators to make sure a machine is working properly. **Troubleshooting:** Determining causes of operating errors and deciding what to do about them. **Operation and Control:** Controlling operations of equipment or systems.

Education and Training Program: Truck and Bus Driver Training/Commercial Vehicle Operation. **Related Knowledge/Courses: Transportation:** Principles and methods for moving people or goods by air, rail, sea, or road, including the relative costs and benefits. **Geography:** Principles and methods for describing the features of land, sea, and air masses, including their physical characteristics; locations; interrelationships; and distribution of plant, animal, and human life. **Public Safety and Security:** Relevant equipment, policies, procedures, and strategies to promote effective local, state, or national security operations for the protection of people, data, property, and institutions. **Law and Government:** Laws, legal codes, court procedures, precedents, government regulations, executive orders, agency rules, and the democratic political process. **Mechanical Devices:** Machines and tools, including their designs, uses, repair, and maintenance.

Work Environment: Outdoors; very hot or cold; contaminants; sitting; using hands on objects, tools, or controls; repetitive motions.

Truck Drivers, Light or Delivery Services

- Education/Training Required: Short-term on-the-job training
- Annual Earnings: $24,790
- Growth: 15.7%
- Annual Job Openings: 169,000
- Self-Employed: 8.9%
- Part-Time: 9.1%

Level of Solitary Work: 81.2 (out of 100)

Level of Contact with Others: 98.5 (out of 100)

Drive a truck or van with a capacity of under 26,000 GVW primarily to deliver or pick up merchandise or to deliver packages within a specified area. May require use of automatic routing or location software. May load and unload truck. Obey traffic laws and follow established traffic and transportation procedures. Inspect and maintain vehicle supplies and equipment such as gas, oil, water, tires, lights, and brakes to ensure that vehicles are in proper working condition. Report any mechanical problems encountered with vehicles. Present bills and receipts and collect payments for goods delivered or loaded. Load and unload trucks, vans, or automobiles. Turn in receipts and money received from deliveries. Verify the contents of inventory loads against shipping papers. Maintain records such as vehicle logs, records of cargo, or billing statements in accordance with regulations. Read maps and follow written and verbal geographic directions. Report delays, accidents, or other traffic and transportation situations to bases or other vehicles, using telephones or mobile two-way radios. Sell and keep records of sales for products from truck inventory. Drive vehicles with capacities

under three tons to transport materials to and from specified destinations such as railroad stations, plants, residences, and offices or within industrial yards. Drive trucks equipped with public address systems through city streets to broadcast announcements for advertising or publicity purposes. Use and maintain the tools and equipment found on commercial vehicles, such as weighing and measuring devices. Perform emergency repairs such as changing tires or installing light bulbs, fuses, tire chains, and spark plugs.

Personality Type: Realistic. Realistic occupations frequently involve work activities that include practical, hands-on problems and solutions. They often deal with plants; animals; and real-world materials such as wood, tools, and machinery. Many of the occupations require working outside and do not involve a lot of paperwork or working closely with others.

GOE—Interest Area: 16. Transportation, Distribution, and Logistics. **Work Group:** 16.03. Truck Driving. **Other Jobs in This Work Group:** Truck Drivers, Heavy and Tractor-Trailer.

Skills—Equipment Maintenance: Performing routine maintenance on equipment and determining when and what kind of maintenance is needed. **Operation Monitoring:** Watching gauges, dials, or other indicators to make sure a machine is working properly. **Operation and Control:** Controlling operations of equipment or systems. **Social Perceptiveness:** Being aware of others' reactions and understanding why they react as they do. **Service Orientation:** Actively looking for ways to help people.

Education and Training Program: Truck and Bus Driver Training/Commercial Vehicle Operation. **Related Knowledge/Courses: Transportation:** Principles and methods for moving people or goods by air, rail, sea, or road, including the relative costs and benefits. **Production and Processing:** Raw materials, production processes, quality control, costs, and other techniques for maximizing the effective manufacture and distribution of goods.

Work Environment: Outdoors; very hot or cold; contaminants; cramped work space, awkward positions; minor burns, cuts, bites, or stings; using hands on objects, tools, or controls.

Water and Liquid Waste Treatment Plant and System Operators

◉ Education/Training Required: Long-term on-the-job training

◉ Annual Earnings: $34,930

◉ Growth: 16.2%

◉ Annual Job Openings: 6,000

◉ Self-Employed: 0.0%

◉ Part-Time: 5.2%

Level of Solitary Work: 50.0 (out of 100)

Level of Contact with Others: 58.5 (out of 100)

Operate or control an entire process or system of machines, often through the use of control boards, to transfer or treat water or liquid waste. Add chemicals such as ammonia, chlorine, or lime to disinfect and deodorize water and other liquids. Operate and adjust controls on equipment to purify and clarify water, process or dispose of sewage, and generate power. Inspect equipment or monitor operating conditions, meters, and gauges to determine load requirements and detect malfunctions. Collect and test water and sewage samples, using test equipment and color analysis standards. Record operational data, personnel attendance, or meter and gauge readings on specified forms. Maintain, repair, and lubricate equipment, using hand tools and power tools. Clean and maintain tanks and filter beds, using hand tools and power tools. Direct and coordinate plant workers engaged in routine operations and maintenance activities.

Personality Type: Realistic. Realistic occupations frequently involve work activities that include practical, hands-on problems and solutions. They often deal with plants; animals; and real-world materials such as wood, tools, and machinery. Many of the occupations require working outside and do not involve a lot of paperwork or working closely with others.

GOE—Interest Area: 13. Manufacturing. **Work Group:** 13.16. Utility Operation and Energy Distribution. **Other Jobs in This Work Group:** Chemical Plant and System Operators; Gas Compressor and Gas Pumping Station Operators; Gas Plant Operators; Nuclear Power Reactor Operators; Petroleum Pump System Operators, Refinery Operators, and Gaugers; Power Distributors and Dispatchers; Power Plant Operators; Ship Engineers; Stationary Engineers and Boiler Operators.

Skills—Operation Monitoring: Watching gauges, dials, or other indicators to make sure a machine is working properly. **Installation:** Installing equipment, machines, wiring, or programs to meet specifications. **Operation and Control:** Controlling operations of equipment or systems. **Troubleshooting:** Determining causes of operating errors and deciding what to do about them. **Management of Material Resources:** Obtaining and seeing to the appropriate use of equipment, facilities, and materials needed to do certain work. **Operations Analysis:** Analyzing needs and product requirements to create a design.

Education and Training Program: Water Quality and Wastewater Treatment Management and Recycling Technology/Technician Training. **Related Knowledge/Courses: Biology:** Plant and animal organisms and their tissues, cells, functions, interdependencies, and interactions with each other and the environment. **Chemistry:** The chemical composition, structure, and properties of substances and of the chemical processes and transformations that they undergo. This includes uses of chemicals and their danger signs, production techniques, and disposal methods. **Physics:** Physical principles and laws and their interrelationships and applications to understanding fluid, material, and atmospheric dynamics

W

and mechanical, electrical, atomic, and subatomic structures and processes. **Public Safety and Security:** Relevant equipment, policies, procedures, and strategies to promote effective local, state, or national security operations for the protection of people, data, property, and institutions. **Mechanical Devices:** Machines and tools, including their designs, uses, repair, and maintenance. **Law and Government:** Laws, legal codes, court procedures, precedents, government regulations, executive orders, agency rules, and the democratic political process.

Work Environment: More often outdoors than indoors; noisy; very hot or cold; contaminants; minor burns, cuts, bites, or stings.

Welders, Cutters, and Welder Fitters

This job can be found in the Part II lists under the title Welders, Cutters, Solderers, and Brazers.

- Education/Training Required: Long-term on-the-job training
- Annual Earnings: $30,990
- Growth: 5.0%
- Annual Job Openings: 52,000
- Self-Employed: 6.3%
- Part-Time: 1.7%

The job openings listed here are shared with Solderers and Brazers.

Level of Solitary Work: 58.2 (out of 100)

Level of Contact with Others: 72.2 (out of 100)

Use hand-welding or flame-cutting equipment to weld or join metal components or to fill holes, indentations, or seams of fabricated metal products. Operate safety equipment and use safe work habits.

Weld components in flat, vertical, or overhead positions. Ignite torches or start power supplies and strike arcs by touching electrodes to metals being welded, completing electrical circuits. Clamp, hold, tack-weld, heat-bend, grind, or bolt component parts to obtain required configurations and positions for welding. Detect faulty operation of equipment or defective materials and notify supervisors. Operate manual or semi-automatic welding equipment to fuse metal segments, using processes such as gas tungsten arc, gas metal arc, flux-cored arc, plasma arc, shielded metal arc, resistance welding, and submerged arc welding. Monitor the fitting, burning, and welding processes to avoid overheating of parts or warping, shrinking, distortion, or expansion of material. Examine workpieces for defects and measure workpieces with straightedges or templates to ensure conformance with specifications. Recognize, set up, and operate hand and power tools common to the welding trade, such as shielded metal arc and gas metal arc welding equipment. Lay out, position, align, and secure parts and assemblies prior to assembly, using straightedges, combination squares, calipers, and rulers. Chip or grind off excess weld, slag, or spatter, using hand scrapers or power chippers, portable grinders, or arc-cutting equipment. Analyze engineering drawings, blueprints, specifications, sketches, work orders, and material safety data sheets to plan layout, assembly, and welding operations. Connect and turn regulator valves to activate and adjust gas flow and pressure so that desired flames are obtained. Weld separately or in combination, using aluminum, stainless steel, cast iron, and other alloys. Determine required equipment and welding methods, applying knowledge of metallurgy, geometry, and welding techniques. Mark or tag material with proper job number, piece marks, and other identifying marks as required. Prepare all material surfaces to be welded, ensuring that there is no loose or thick scale, slag, rust, moisture, grease, or other foreign matter.

Personality Type: Realistic. Realistic occupations frequently involve work activities that include practical, hands-on problems and solutions. They often deal with plants; animals; and real-world materials such as wood, tools, and machinery. Many of the occupations require working outside and do not involve a lot of paperwork or working closely with others.

GOE—Interest Area: 13. Manufacturing. **Work Group:** 13.04. Welding, Brazing, and Soldering. **Other Jobs in This Work Group:** Solderers and Brazers; Structural Metal Fabricators and Fitters; Welders, Cutters, Solderers, and Brazers; Welding, Soldering, and Brazing Machine Setters, Operators, and Tenders.

Skills—Repairing: Repairing machines or systems by using the needed tools. **Equipment Maintenance:** Performing routine maintenance on equipment and determining when and what kind of maintenance is needed. **Installation:** Installing equipment, machines, wiring, or programs to meet specifications. **Quality Control Analysis:** Conducting tests and inspections of products, services, or processes to evaluate quality or performance. **Operation and Control:** Controlling operations of equipment or systems. **Equipment Selection:** Determining the kind of tools and equipment needed to do a job.

Education and Training Program: Welding Technology/Welder Training. **Related Knowledge/Courses: Building and Construction:** The materials, methods, and tools involved in the construction or repair of houses, buildings, or other structures such as highways and roads. **Mechanical Devices:** Machines and tools, including their designs, uses, repair, and maintenance. **Design:** Design techniques, tools, and principles involved in production of precision technical plans, blueprints, drawings, and models. **Engineering and Technology:** The practical application of engineering science and technology. This includes applying principles, techniques, procedures, and equipment to the design and production of various goods and services.

Work Environment: Noisy; contaminants; minor burns, cuts, bites, or stings; standing; using hands on objects, tools, or controls; repetitive motions.

Welders, Cutters, Solderers, and Brazers

See the descriptions of these jobs:

- Solderers and Brazers
- Welders, Cutters, and Welder Fitters

Welding, Soldering, and Brazing Machine Setters, Operators, and Tenders

- Education/Training Required: Moderate-term on-the-job training
- Annual Earnings: $30,430
- Growth: 0.4%
- Annual Job Openings: 7,000
- Self-Employed: 7.4%
- Part-Time: 1.7%

Level of Solitary Work: 69.5 (out of 100)

Level of Contact with Others: 76.0 (out of 100)

Set up, operate, or tend welding, soldering, or brazing machines or robots that weld, braze, solder, or heat-treat metal products, components, or assemblies. Turn and press knobs and buttons or enter operating instructions into computers to adjust and start welding machines. Set up, operate, and tend welding machines that join or bond components to fabricate metal products or assemblies. Load or feed workpieces into welding machines to join or bond components. Correct problems by adjusting controls or by stopping machines and opening holding devices. Give directions to other workers regarding machine setup and use. Inspect, measure, or test completed metal workpieces to ensure conformance to specifications, using measuring and testing devices. Record operational information on specified production reports. Start, monitor, and adjust robotic welding production lines. Read blueprints, work orders, and production schedules to determine product or job instructions and specifications. Assemble, align, and clamp workpieces into holding fixtures to bond, heat-treat, or solder fabricated metal components. Lay out, fit, or connect parts to be bonded, calculating production measurements as necessary. Conduct trial runs before welding, soldering or brazing; make necessary adjustments to equipment. Dress electrodes, using tip dressers, files, emery cloths, or dressing wheels. Remove workpieces and parts from machinery after work is complete, using hand tools. Observe meters, gauges, and machine operations to ensure that soldering or brazing processes meet specifications. Select, position, align, and bolt jigs, holding fixtures, guides, and stops onto machines, using measuring instruments and hand tools. Compute and record settings for new work, applying knowledge of metal properties, principles of welding, and shop mathematics. Select torch tips, alloys, flux, coil, tubing, and wire according to metal types and thicknesses, data charts, and records. Clean, lubricate, maintain, and adjust equipment to maintain efficient operation, using air hoses, cleaning fluids, and hand tools. Prepare metal surfaces and workpieces, using hand-operated equipment such as grinders, cutters, or drills. Set dials and timing controls to regulate electrical current, gas flow pressure, heating and cooling cycles, and shutoff.

Personality Type: Realistic. Realistic occupations frequently involve work activities that include practical, hands-on problems and solutions. They often deal with plants; animals; and real-world materials such as wood, tools, and machinery. Many of the occupations require working outside and do not involve a lot of paperwork or working closely with others.

GOE—Interest Area: 13. Manufacturing. **Work Group:** 13.04. Welding, Brazing, and Soldering. **Other Jobs in This Work Group:** Solderers and Brazers; Structural Metal Fabricators and Fitters; Welders, Cutters, and Welder Fitters; Welders, Cutters, Solderers, and Brazers.

Skills—Equipment Maintenance: Performing routine maintenance on equipment and determining when and what kind of maintenance is needed. **Operation Monitoring:** Watching gauges, dials, or other indicators to make sure a machine is working properly. **Operation and Control:** Controlling operations of equipment or systems. **Repairing:** Repairing machines or systems by using the needed tools. **Installation:** Installing equipment, machines, wiring, or programs to meet specifications. **Troubleshooting:** Determining causes of operating errors and deciding what to do about them.

Education and Training Program: Welding Technology/Welder. **Related Knowledge/Courses: Production and Processing:** Raw materials, production processes, quality control, costs, and other techniques for maximizing the effective manufacture and distribution of goods. **Mechanical Devices:** Machines and tools, including their designs, uses, repair, and maintenance. **Engineering and Technology:** The practical application of engineering science and technology. This includes applying principles, techniques, procedures, and equipment to the design and production of various goods and services. **Design:** Design techniques, tools, and principles involved in production of precision technical plans, blueprints, drawings, and models. **Personnel and Human Resources:** Principles and procedures for personnel recruitment, selection, training, compensation and benefits, labor relations and negotiation, and personnel information systems. **Public Safety and Security:** Relevant equipment, policies, procedures, and strategies to promote effective local, state, or national security operations for the protection of people, data, property, and institutions.

Work Environment: Noisy; contaminants; standing; using hands on objects, tools, or controls; bending or twisting the body; repetitive motions.

Word Processors and Typists

- ◎ Education/Training Required: Moderate-term on-the-job training
- ◎ Annual Earnings: $29,020
- ◎ Growth: –15.3%
- ◎ Annual Job Openings: 30,000
- ◎ Self-Employed: 7.5%
- ◎ Part-Time: 26.0%

Level of Solitary Work: 62.5 (out of 100)

Level of Contact with Others: 73.0 (out of 100)

Use word processor/computer or typewriter to type letters, reports, forms, or other material from rough draft, corrected copy, or voice recording. May perform other clerical duties as assigned. Check completed work for spelling, grammar, punctuation, and format. Perform other clerical duties such as answering telephone, sorting and distributing mail, running errands, or sending faxes. Gather, register, and arrange the material to be typed, following instructions. File and store completed documents on computer hard drive or disk and maintain a computer filing system to store, retrieve, update, and delete documents. Type correspondence, reports, text, and other written material from rough drafts, corrected copies, voice recordings, dictation, or previous versions, using a computer, word processor, or typewriter. Print and make copies of work. Keep records of work performed. Compute and verify totals on report forms, requisitions, or bills, using adding machine or calculator. Collate pages of reports and other documents prepared. Electronically sort and compile text and numerical data, retrieving, updating, and merging documents as required. Reformat documents, moving paragraphs or columns. Search for specific sets of stored, typed characters in order to make changes. Adjust settings for format, page layout, line spacing, and other style requirements.

Address envelopes or prepare envelope labels, using typewriter or computer. Operate and resupply printers and computers, changing print wheels or fluid cartridges; adding paper; and loading blank tapes, cards, or disks into equipment. Transmit work electronically to other locations. Work with technical material, preparing statistical reports, planning and typing statistical tables, and combining and rearranging material from different sources. Use data entry devices, such as optical scanners, to input data into computers for revision or editing. Transcribe stenotyped notes of court proceedings.

Personality Type: Conventional. Conventional occupations frequently involve following set procedures and routines. These occupations can include working with data and details more than with ideas. Usually there is a clear line of authority to follow.

GOE—Interest Area: 04. Business and Administration. **Work Group:** 04.08. Clerical Machine Operation. **Other Jobs in This Work Group:** Billing, Posting, and Calculating Machine Operators; Data Entry Keyers; Mail Clerks and Mail Machine Operators, Except Postal Service; Office Machine Operators, Except Computer; Switchboard Operators, Including Answering Service.

Skills—Installation: Installing equipment, machines, wiring, or programs to meet specifications. **Social Perceptiveness:** Being aware of others' reactions and understanding why they react as they do. **Equipment Selection:** Determining the kind of tools and equipment needed to do a job. **Writing:** Communicating effectively in writing as appropriate for the needs of the audience. **Learning Strategies:** Selecting and using training or instructional methods and procedures appropriate for the situation when learning or teaching new things. **Speaking:** Talking to others to convey information effectively.

Education and Training Programs: General Office Occupations and Clerical Services; Word Processing. **Related Knowledge/Courses: Clerical Practices:** Administrative and clerical procedures and systems such as word processing, managing files and records, stenography and transcription, designing forms, and other office procedures and terminology. **Computers and Electronics:** Circuit boards, processors, chips, electronic equipment, and computer hardware and software, including applications and programming. **Customer and Personal Service:** Principles and processes for providing customer and personal services. This includes customer needs assessment, meeting quality standards for services, and evaluation of customer satisfaction. **English Language:** The structure and content of the English language, including the meaning and spelling of words, rules of composition, and grammar.

Work Environment: Indoors; sitting.

Writers and Authors

See the descriptions of these jobs:

- ◎ Copy Writers
- ◎ Poets, Lyricists, and Creative Writers

Zoologists and Wildlife Biologists

- ◎ Education/Training Required: Bachelor's degree
- ◎ Annual Earnings: $52,050
- ◎ Growth: 13.0%
- ◎ Annual Job Openings: 1,000
- ◎ Self-Employed: 2.5%
- ◎ Part-Time: 8.2%

Level of Solitary Work: 59.2 (out of 100)

Level of Contact with Others: 79.0 (out of 100)

Study the origins, behavior, diseases, genetics, and life processes of animals and wildlife. May specialize in wildlife research and management, including the collection and analysis of biological data to deter-

mine the environmental effects of present and potential use of land and water areas. Study animals in their natural habitats, assessing effects of environment and industry on animals, interpreting findings, and recommending alternative operating conditions for industry. Inventory or estimate plant and wildlife populations. Analyze characteristics of animals to identify and classify them. Make recommendations on management systems and planning for wildlife populations and habitat, consulting with stakeholders and the public at large to explore options. Disseminate information by writing reports and scientific papers or journal articles and by making presentations and giving talks for schools, clubs, interest groups, and park interpretive programs. Study characteristics of animals such as origin, interrelationships, classification, life histories and diseases, development, genetics, and distribution. Perform administrative duties such as fundraising, public relations, budgeting, and supervision of zoo staff. Organize and conduct experimental studies with live animals in controlled or natural surroundings. Oversee the care and distribution of zoo animals, working with curators and zoo directors to determine the best way to contain animals, maintain their habitats, and manage facilities. Coordinate preventive programs to control the outbreak of wildlife diseases. Prepare collections of preserved specimens or microscopic slides for species identification and study of development or disease. Raise specimens for study and observation or for use in experiments. Collect and dissect animal specimens and examine specimens under microscope.

Personality Type: Investigative. Investigative occupations frequently involve working with ideas and require an extensive amount of thinking. These occupations can involve searching for facts and figuring out problems mentally.

GOE—Interest Area: 01. Agriculture and Natural Resources. **Work Group:** 01.02. Resource Science/Engineering for Plants, Animals, and the Environment. **Other Jobs in This Work Group:** Agricultural Engineers; Animal Scientists; Conservation Scientists; Environmental Engineers;

Foresters; Mining and Geological Engineers, Including Mining Safety Engineers; Petroleum Engineers; Range Managers; Soil and Plant Scientists; Soil and Water Conservationists.

Skills—Science: Using scientific rules and methods to solve problems. **Management of Financial Resources:** Determining how money will be spent to get the work done and accounting for these expenditures. **Writing:** Communicating effectively in writing as appropriate for the needs of the audience. **Coordination:** Adjusting actions in relation to others' actions. **Persuasion:** Persuading others to change their minds or behavior. **Management of Personnel Resources:** Motivating, developing, and directing people as they work; identifying the best people for the job.

Education and Training Programs: Animal Behavior and Ethology; Animal Physiology; Cell/Cellular Biology and Anatomical Sciences, Other; Ecology; Entomology; Wildlife and Wildlands Science and Management; Wildlife Biology; Zoology/Animal Biology; Zoology/Animal Biology, Other. **Related Knowledge/Courses: Biology:** Plant and animal organisms and their tissues, cells, functions, interdependencies, and interactions with each other and the environment. **Geography:** Principles and methods for describing the features of land, sea, and air masses, including their physical characteristics; locations; interrelationships; and distribution of plant, animal, and human life. **Law and Government:** Laws, legal codes, court procedures, precedents, government regulations, executive orders, agency rules, and the democratic political process. **English Language:** The structure and content of the English language, including the meaning and spelling of words, rules of composition, and grammar. **Administration and Management:** Business and management principles involved in strategic planning, resource allocation, human resources modeling, leadership technique, production methods, and coordination of people and resources. **Computers and Electronics:** Circuit boards, processors, chips, electronic equipment, and computer hardware and software, including applications and programming.

Work Environment: More often indoors than outdoors; sitting.

N

APPENDIX A

Resources for Further Exploration

The facts and pointers in this book provide a good beginning to the subject of jobs that have appeal for introverts. If you want additional details, we suggest you consult some of the resources listed here.

Facts About Careers

The *Occupational Outlook Handbook* (or the *OOH*) (JIST): Updated every two years by the U.S. Department of Labor, this book provides descriptions for almost 270 major jobs covering more than 85 percent of the workforce.

The *Enhanced Occupational Outlook Handbook* (JIST): Includes all descriptions in the *OOH* plus descriptions of more than 6,300 more-specialized jobs related to them.

The *O*NET Dictionary of Occupational Titles* (JIST): The only printed source of the more than 900 jobs described in the U.S. Department of Labor's Occupational Information Network database. It covers all the jobs in the book you're now reading, but it offers more topics than we were able to fit here.

The *New Guide for Occupational Exploration* (JIST): An important career reference that allows you to explore all major O*NET jobs based on your interests. (You can find an outline of the Interest Areas and Work Groups in Appendix B.)

Career Decision Making and Planning

Overnight Career Choice, by Michael Farr (JIST): This book can help you choose a career goal based on a variety of criteria, including skills, interests, and values. It is part of the *Help in a Hurry* series, so it is designed to produce quick results.

50 Best Jobs for Your Personality, by Michael Farr and Laurence Shatkin, Ph.D. (JIST): Built around the six Holland personality types, this book includes an assessment to help you identify your dominant and secondary personality types, plus lists and descriptions of high-paying and high-growth jobs linked to those personality types.

Job Hunting

Same-Day Resume, by Michael Farr (JIST): Learn how to write an effective resume in an hour. This book includes dozens of sample resumes from professional writers and even offers advice on cover letters, online resumes, and more.

Seven-Step Job Search, by Michael Farr (JIST): In seven easy steps, learn what it takes to land the right job fast. Quick worksheets will help you identify your skills, define your ideal job, use the most effective job search methods, write a superior resume, organize your time to get two interviews a day, dramatically improve your interviewing skills, and follow up on all job leads effectively.

The Career Coward's Guide to Interviewing, by Katy Piotrowski, M.Ed. (JIST): Some introverts have fears about the interviewing process, such as a reluctance to talk about themselves lest they seem to be "bragging." This book analyzes each aspect of a successful job search and provides easy steps for facing job search challenges in a unique and easy-to-tackle format. Other books in the series discuss creating resumes and changing careers.

Job Banks by Occupation. This is a set of links offered by America's Career InfoNet. At www.acinet.org, find the Career Tools box. Click Career Resource Library and then click Job & Resume Banks. The Job Banks by Occupation link leads you to groups of jobs such as "Healthcare Practitioners and Technical Occupations" and "Legal Occupations," which in turn lead you to more-specific job titles and occupation-specific job-listing sites maintained by various organizations.

Career Development for Introverts. Visit Introvert Insights at www.introvertinsights.com for a blog and other information designed to help introverts in their careers. Founded by Peter Vogt and Pamela Braun.

APPENDIX B

GOE Interest Areas and Work Groups

As Part III explains, the GOE is a way of organizing the world of work into large Interest Areas and more specific Work Groups containing jobs that have a lot in common. Part II defines the 16 GOE Interest Areas, and Part III also identifies the Work Groups for each job described. We thought you would want to see the complete GOE taxonomy so you would understand how any job that interests you fits into this structure.

Interest Areas have two-digit code numbers; Work Groups have four-digit code numbers beginning with the code number for the Interest Area in which they are classified. These are the 16 GOE Interest Areas and 117 Work Groups:

01 Agriculture and Natural Resources

    01.01 Managerial Work in Agriculture and Natural Resources

    01.02 Resource Science/Engineering for Plants, Animals, and the Environment

    01.03 Resource Technologies for Plants, Animals, and the Environment

    01.04 General Farming

    01.05 Nursery, Groundskeeping, and Pest Control

    01.06 Forestry and Logging

    01.07 Hunting and Fishing

    01.08 Mining and Drilling

02 Architecture and Construction

    02.01 Managerial Work in Architecture and Construction

    02.02 Architectural Design

    02.03 Architecture/Construction Engineering Technologies

    02.04 Construction Crafts

    02.05 Systems and Equipment Installation, Maintenance, and Repair

    02.06 Construction Support/Labor

03 Arts and Communication

        03.01 Managerial Work in Arts and Communication

        03.02 Writing and Editing

        03.03 News, Broadcasting, and Public Relations

        03.04 Studio Art

        03.05 Design

        03.06 Drama

        03.07 Music

        03.08 Dance

        03.09 Media Technology

        03.10 Communications Technology

        03.11 Musical Instrument Repair

04 Business and Administration

        04.01 Managerial Work in General Business

        04.02 Managerial Work in Business Detail

        04.03 Human Resources Support

        04.04 Secretarial Support

        04.05 Accounting, Auditing, and Analytical Support

        04.06 Mathematical Clerical Support

        04.07 Records and Materials Processing

        04.08 Clerical Machine Operation

05 Education and Training

        05.01 Managerial Work in Education

        05.02 Preschool, Elementary, and Secondary Teaching and Instructing

        05.03 Postsecondary and Adult Teaching and Instructing

        05.04 Library Services

        05.05 Archival and Museum Services

        05.06 Counseling, Health, and Fitness Education

06 Finance and Insurance

        06.01 Managerial Work in Finance and Insurance

        06.02 Finance/Insurance Investigation and Analysis

        06.03 Finance/Insurance Records Processing

        06.04 Finance/Insurance Customer Service

        06.05 Finance/Insurance Sales and Support

07 Government and Public Administration

>07.01 Managerial Work in Government and Public Administration

>07.02 Public Planning

>07.03 Regulations Enforcement

>07.04 Public Administration Clerical Support

08 Health Science

>08.01 Managerial Work in Medical and Health Services

>08.02 Medicine and Surgery

>08.03 Dentistry

>08.04 Health Specialties

>08.05 Animal Care

>08.06 Medical Technology

>08.07 Medical Therapy

>08.08 Patient Care and Assistance

>08.09 Health Protection and Promotion

09 Hospitality, Tourism, and Recreation

>09.01 Managerial Work in Hospitality and Tourism

>09.02 Recreational Services

>09.03 Hospitality and Travel Services

>09.04 Food and Beverage Preparation

>09.05 Food and Beverage Service

>09.06 Sports

>09.07 Barber and Beauty Services

10 Human Service

>10.01 Counseling and Social Work

>10.02 Religious Work

>10.03 Child/Personal Care and Services

>10.04 Client Interviewing

11 Information Technology

>11.01 Managerial Work in Information Technology

>11.02 Information Technology Specialties

>11.03 Digital Equipment Repair

12 Law and Public Safety

>12.01 Managerial Work in Law and Public Safety

>12.02 Legal Practice and Justice Administration

>12.03 Legal Support

12.04 Law Enforcement and Public Safety

12.05 Safety and Security

12.06 Emergency Responding

12.07 Military

13 Manufacturing

13.01 Managerial Work in Manufacturing

13.02 Machine Setup and Operation

13.03 Production Work, Assorted Materials Processing

13.04 Welding, Brazing, and Soldering

13.05 Production Machining Technology

13.06 Production Precision Work

13.07 Production Quality Control

13.08 Graphic Arts Production

13.09 Hands-On Work, Assorted Materials

13.10 Woodworking Technology

13.11 Apparel, Shoes, Leather, and Fabric Care

13.12 Electrical and Electronic Repair

13.13 Machinery Repair

13.14 Vehicle and Facility Mechanical Work

13.15 Medical and Technical Equipment Repair

13.16 Utility Operation and Energy Distribution

13.17 Loading, Moving, Hoisting, and Conveying

14 Retail and Wholesale Sales and Service

14.01 Managerial Work in Retail/Wholesale Sales and Service

14.02 Technical Sales

14.03 General Sales

14.04 Personal Soliciting

14.05 Purchasing

14.06 Customer Service

15 Scientific Research, Engineering, and Mathematics

15.01 Managerial Work in Scientific Research, Engineering, and Mathematics

15.02 Physical Sciences

15.03 Life Sciences

15.04 Social Sciences

15.05 Physical Science Laboratory Technology

15.06 Mathematics and Data Analysis

15.07 Research and Design Engineering

15.08 Industrial and Safety Engineering

15.09 Engineering Technology

16 Transportation, Distribution, and Logistics

16.01 Managerial Work in Transportation

16.02 Air Vehicle Operation

16.03 Truck Driving

16.04 Rail Vehicle Operation

16.05 Water Vehicle Operation

16.06 Other Services Requiring Driving

16.07 Transportation Support Work

Index

A

B

C

L

M

N

T–V

W–Z